A GENERAL HISTORY OF EUROPE

EDITED BY DENYS HAY

SEVENTEENTH-CENTURY EUROPE

D. H. PENNINGTON

LONGMAN

LONGMAN GROUP LIMITED
LONDON

*Associated companies, branches and representatives throughout
the world*

© Longman Group Limited 1970

First published 1970

SBN 582 48209 7

To
Gail and Piers

Printed in Great Britain
by Butler & Tanner Ltd, Frome and London

Contents

CONTENTS

CONTENTS

MAPS

Acknowledgements

In the inexcusably long period this volume has taken to produce, many people have helped, encouraged, and advised. The editor of the series, Professor Denys Hay, has given me most valuable guidance, and applied only the gentlest of pressure to get the book finished. Others who have read and commented on the drafts at various stages are Professor Gerald Aylmer, Professor Ivan Roots, and Dr Dennis Witcombe. I am grateful also to Mrs Mary Stableford for her expert work on the maps and genealogies; to Miss Pat Lloyd who did most of the typing; to Mr Michael Katz who corrected many blunders in East European names and transliterations without having the chance to scrutinise them all; and to Mr Christopher Grayson who read the proofs and took on a large part of the burden of indexing. My son and daughter have contributed in innumerable ways; and the deepest thanks of all must go to my wife, who has helped immensely both with the substance of the book and with the mechanical tasks of producing it, and has borne with endless patience the spells of depression and fury associated with Seventeenth-Century Europe. The errors, omissions, and confusions are all my own work.

D. H. P.

Oxford
January 1970

We are grateful to the copyright owners, B. Arthaud, Grenoble, for permission to base maps 1, 2 and 3(*b*) on maps appearing in *La Civilisation de l'Europe Classique* by P. Chaunu.

DATES

Dates of birth and death, and of the reigns of monarchs, are generally given in the index and not in the text. Years are reckoned in the 'new style' which most countries except Britain, Russia, and the Ottoman Empire had adopted in the sixteenth century, with the year beginning on 1 January.

Introduction

1600 was an ordinary enough year in Europe. There was a shortage of rain, but not a major famine; there were moderate local outbreaks of plague; in the west there were isolated rebellions while in Russia the new tsar was in danger of losing his throne. In Rome Giordano Bruno was burnt at the stake. He was described as an impenitent heretic, an upholder of Arian opinions on the Trinity, a magician. He was also—though the Inquisition was less interested in this—well disposed towards the ideas of Copernicus. Behind the elaborate accusations his unpardonable offence was to show too publicly his disbelief in the Church's ability to satisfy his quest for an understanding of mankind and the universe. Most of the other people who met the same fate as Bruno were guilty merely of witchcraft.

In Sweden four members of the royal council were executed for supporting King Sigismund III, the Catholic monarch who had just been deposed in favour of the Protestant Charles IX. In Madrid Philip III was hopefully organising a new army to restore the rebellious Protestants of the northern Netherlands to their allegiance, though they were winning new victories in Flanders. Negotiations had begun for ending the state of war between Spain and England. Henry IV of France, now almost safe on his throne after the decades of religious civil war, settled a minor territorial argument with the Duke of Savoy by invading his territory. At home Henry was proving that it was possible for Catholics and Protestants to live in the same state with much the same civil rights and protection. But this was achieved by separation, not by mutual acceptance. Nearly everywhere it was assumed that religious minorities were a threat to internal security, and religion a major reason for international alliances, rivalries, and wars. The Emperor Rudolf II was facing irreconcilable conflict between the Catholic and Protestant states under his ineffective suzerainty. Meanwhile El Greco was completing some of his last paintings; Shakespeare was writing *Twelfth Night* and *Julius Caesar*; the building of St Peter's in Rome continued.

A hundred years later, in 1700, King Charles II of Spain died. Over the succession to his enfeebled empire the great powers were ready to fight another of the now familar wars in whose origins diplomatic, dynastic, and strategic manœuvres left little room for religious alignments, or even for material interests. Louis XIV in France and William III in England and the Netherlands were securely at the head of states whose authority was beyond challenge. Peter the Great, back from his journey through western Europe, had overcome the latest revolt of the *Streltsi*, the guards of Moscow, and was badly beaten by the Swedes in the war for supremacy among Baltic countries. It was one of Sweden's last military triumphs. It was in 1700 too that the Emperor Leopold II signed the compact by which Prussia became a kingdom. In the same year the new king had founded the Berlin Academy of Sciences, with Leibnitz as its president. In England Isaac Newton was at the height of his career. Everywhere men of leisure and culture were avid for news of scientific curiosities, of travel in remote countries, of economic progress. The churches had lost some of their zeal for persecution and most of their hopes for new conquests in Europe. Opera was the fashionable entertainment. Nobles and princes demanded such imitations of Versailles as were within their means. Swift and Defoe were perfecting their satirical techniques.

To most Europeans famine was as great a danger in 1700 as in 1600. Some landlords, 'new' in possession or in outlook, made more productive use of their estates. The scale of industry and commerce had grown; the accumulation of capital was easier and more secure. But improvements in methods of production and increases in the amount of food and goods available had rarely been spectacular. In many places, such as Spain, Italy, and the worst damaged parts of central Europe, the general level of prosperity, like the population, was probably lower in 1700 than in 1600. Even France showed very little sign of improvement. The idea that this was a century of marked—even of 'revolutionary'—progress in economic affairs has given place to the well-measured evidence that it was in many ways one of depression or stagnation. Power and wealth remained in the hands of a minority hardly less small, even if it was not quite the same minority. The great territorial lords had become both less able and less eager to challenge or ignore the control of the state. Though in many countries their authority was as extensive as ever, it was usually exercised through and not against that of the monarch. Their private armies of tenants and dependants had largely disappeared. Where they still dominated central politics, they did so because the monarch had brought about or deliberately accepted such a situation. Though cities, some of them greatly enlarged, offered better and more varied prospects of enrichment than before, the mark of having arrived at the top was still, for most aspiring town-dwellers, to acquire land. Nevertheless, there had been, at least in the west, some movement towards the separation of landed property from power in the community. This had been the great age of the buying of 'office', and the age when kings had some success in imposing the principle that status should be linked with service to the Crown. For those not born into the highest circles, the quickest way to get there might well be to acquire a position in government, local or central. It was often a better means than land ownership of extracting wealth for oneself from one's fellow men. The rewards of enterprise, the penalties for inaction and miscalculation, and the hazards in the path of the propertied family were great enough to make society comparatively 'mobile'. Even so, the governing class had changed far less than seemed likely during the great conflicts of the century. Inherited wealth, family connection, and patronage were still the essential means to success.

As at other times, many tremendous events failed to occur. The forces of the Counter-Reformation did not reconquer Europe; but the Holy Roman Empire was not destroyed by its Protestant enemies. The Turks did not overrun central Europe; but their empire too survived. The English monarchy was not permanently overthrown: despite the victory of men outside the normal ruling circle, the 'revolution' had not established a decisive and permanent change in the distribution of political or of economic power. James II did not take England back to Catholicism. Of the many other rebellions only the one that made Portugal a kingdom independent of Spain had any lasting success. Sweden did not extend her territory round the whole Baltic coastline; France gained only minor improvements in her eastern frontier. Russia, in face of repeated massive threats from inside and out, did not disintegrate.

Is there, in this span of time defined by the accident of the calendar, any shape or coherence that is not artificially imposed? It is often suggested that it is divided into sharply contrasted halves by a mid-century crisis that marked the boundary between one historical era and another. For some the 1640s and 1650s were a decisive moment in the transition from a feudal to a capitalist economy; for others they were the dividing-line between the Renaissance and the Enlightenment; others see them as ushering in the age of absolutism. There is no doubt that in much of Europe those decades were, and were felt to be, a time of even greater turmoil and instability than was normal. But 'crisis' has become the most overworked term in historical writing. When we find it applied equally to the economic, social, political, diplomatic, cultural, moral, and scientific aspects of more or less the whole century,[1] it is hard to see what meaning it can have. There was a crisis 'of European, even worldwide proportions, centring on the year 1620'.[2] There was a *crise de la conscience européenne* from 1680 to 1715.[3] The great problem for the historian is to delineate the major features of a landscape seen from one angle and at the same time recognise that they will change or disappear when it is seen from another. There is an element of deception in any picture worth painting. Nevertheless, the landscape of the seventeenth century exists; and what makes the central feature in it different from others is that whether we choose the viewpoint labelled 'society' or 'government' or 'economy' or almost any other, a mountain is still there, even if its height and shape appear to vary disturbingly. The chapters that follow treat with a moderate amount of scepticism accounts of the mid-century upheaval that push all other events into symmetrical subordination. It does not mean that the division of the century had no reality—only that the changes were less decisive and uniform than it is satisfying to believe.[4]

To impose an internal pattern on the century is one temptation; another is to give it an undeserved uniformity of character. The notion that every period is 'the age of' something or other is not always merely a harmless response to the fact that books must have a title. In one field of human activity—the visual arts—a distinctive style came into prominence in many western countries around the beginning of the century and was superseded or greatly modified somewhere about 1700. The name 'baroque' was only bestowed on it much later. With the gradual extension of the meaning of the term, the idea has developed that 'the baroque' was a whole *Weltanschauung*, an outlook on the world, in terms of which all behaviour in the period can be explained. It is a claim that can easily take us out of the realm of evidence into that of rhetoric. To some extent it has drawn attention away from the much more obvious fact that though in the first part of the century the influence of Italy was still predominant in many cultural matters, by the end France had become the unchallenged leader. And here there is a danger that has been revived in a completely new form—the danger of seeing the history of Europe as the history of France and its neighbours. The rise of

[1] See the contents-list in *Histoire générale des civilisations*, vol. 4 (Paris, 1956).
[2] H. Kamen in *Past and Present*, no. 39 (1968), p. 45.
[3] The book with this title by P. Hazard appears in English as *The European Mind, 1680–1715* (London, 1953). [4] See pp. 217–21.

France to its prominence in art, letters, and fashion coincided—by no means necessarily, as the rôle of Italy in the Renaissance shows—with the period when diplomacy and warfare were centred on the activities of Louis XIV and when a good many rulers regarded French methods of government as the ideal. Now that diplomatic and constitutional affairs tend to be less pre-eminent in history than social and economic ones there is a different reason for the prominence of France: it is there that the most intensive and methodical study of the newer types of historical problem has been undertaken. In this the seventeenth century has had a large share of attention. At the moment therefore the supply of information encourages an unspoken assumption that what was French was typical.

There is one corrective that can be applied to many of the distortions that enter into our impression of the century. Material is becoming increasingly available in western languages for the study of countries that were once of interest only through their wars in the west. The internal affairs of Sweden, and even—though still inadequately—of Turkey can now provide some instructive comparisons. But it is Russia above all that puts the trivial frontier wars and internal disorders of the west into proportion. There are no rational standards by which the huge territorial changes, the disastrous famines, rebellions, invasions, the brutalities of rulers and collapses of government in the east can be regarded as minor episodes in the history of the continent as a whole. It is equally absurd to leave England out of Europe. But a price has to be paid for attempts to give weight to a larger number of countries. Words, whether written or spoken, have a single dimension. History requires at least three—those of time and place and subject-matter. Chroniclers who narrated the deeds of kings had an easy life. To attempt to survey the manifold affairs of the government and peoples of even a dozen states and empires over a period of a hundred years involves a constant fight against confusion, repetition, and illogical selection. It is a war that ends in compromise rather than victory.

The first half of this book is devoted to some of what seem the most important historical themes of the period, the second half to a chronological account of separate areas or groups of states. Only France (despite the strictures above on its undue prominence in seventeenth-century history) is accorded two chapters of its own. Other topics could well have been chosen for special treatment—diplomacy, for instance, or colonisation, or the life and appearance of towns. Inevitably some events have been used as material for the topical chapters while others of a similar kind have found their way into the chronological ones. A more conventional separation of the latter into individual states would have avoided some awkward leaps backward and forward at the cost of missing what seem important connections and parallels. Frequent cross-references in footnotes and the table of political events will it is hoped mitigate the difficulty. Bibliographies at the beginning of each chapter are intended more as suggestions for further reading than as a list of sources. They are biased in favour of works first in English and secondly in French, and they try to include recent writing wherever possible. Articles in reasonably accessible periodicals, especially those that indicate the lines of current research and controversy, have often been mentioned in preference to detailed books. Compiling such lists shows all too clearly how unevenly our knowledge is spread.

No-one can get far in understanding the history of any period without some knowledge of the sources from which its history is written. The first chapter will try to show a little of their character, their opportunities, and their dangers, and to indicate where original materials can be found. Those who find its details oppressive may well prefer to begin with chapter two and turn back to consider the significance of the sources later.

I

Sources

Historians like to think that their work is shaped by some consistent idea of what is important. In practice it has to be admitted that their choice of topics and the methods of dealing with them depend heavily on what sources are available. The nature of the evidence that existed and has survived is itself part of the history of a period. But survival is not the only thing that matters. Even the most assiduous writer of scholarly monographs is unlikely to be able to make use of everything that would help. For all but the narrowest topics what is 'available' is mainly that part of the relevant material that has been assembled, classified, and indexed. There are taking place at the moment changes— greater than any since the invention of printing—in methods by which we can make use of historical sources. Microphotography and electrical devices for recording, sorting and extracting information may some day make the researcher who ploughs through inadequate indexes and travels with pencil and notebook round collections of archives look as inefficient as the monk copying out a chronicle. But so far we still rely mainly on what the individual worker can find and read. Sources that are printed, in full or in summarised 'calendars', are bound to have more influence than others of their kind that are not. Countries and towns where a large proportion of manuscripts can be seen in libraries and record offices get better historical treatment than those with fewer facilities.

For the seventeenth century, a period in which the vernacular was used more and more, another major problem is whether material is accessible, directly or indirectly, in a language the individual historian can understand. Despite what has been done in translating documents and secondary works there is no escaping the fact that, even within Europe, language barriers remain one of the greatest obstacles to a rationally balanced and comparative account of political and still more of economic and social history. The knowledge of Turkey, Poland, and even of Russia which westerners ignorant of East European languages can acquire is still deplorably small in comparison with what they know of France, England, or Spain. Historical scholarship is far slower than the sciences in becoming international.

Our period is richer in records than any earlier one. More documents were left behind by the processes of government, by economic activity, and by the conflict of ideas. Contemporaries wrote more narratives, memoirs, and diaries. In the sixteenth century the amount of administration, and hence of its paper, had grown more rapidly in western than in eastern countries. The growth continued at every level; and by 1700 Russia, Sweden, and Brandenburg were—in central government at least—as bureaucratised as western monarchies. Archives were copied, sorted, and preserved not only for their immediate usefulness: men educated in the western Renaissance tradition were strongly aware of history, both as something they looked back to and as something they were themselves creating for the future. It was no longer the concern mainly of the churches and their chroniclers. 'That posterity may not be deceived . . .'—with these words the Earl of Clarendon opened his massive history of the English Civil War in which he had been the King's chief adviser. Among his enemies Sir Simonds D'Ewes was as zealous in writing his own account of the Long Parliament he sat in as he was in compiling the records of Elizabethan ones, and its clerk John Rushworth used the opportunities his position gave him to amass his *Historical Collections* of state papers. His selection and comments discreetly favoured the Parliamentary cause. On the other side his rival John Nalson began, but never completed, a much larger *Impartial Collection*. Though no other country produced a statesman-historian of Clarendon's calibre, kings and ministers everywhere were concerned to write the memoirs and commentaries which were designed partly for the benefit of their immediate successors in office, partly for posterity in general. Often they reach us uncertainly through the work of secretaries or the amendments, additions, and forgeries of editors. But they give us closer contact with large numbers of the rulers of nations than is possible for any previous age.

The records of government

The decisions and public enactments of most seventeenth-century governments are readily accessible. How much of the process by which they were produced and of the organisation that enabled them to be put into effect can be reconstructed is more variable. The sphere of government that preserved its formal records most assiduously was probably diplomacy.[1] Increasingly collections of treaties became a popular addition to gentlemanly bookshelves. Such works as the *Acta Publica* of the Holy Roman Empire by Michael Caspar Lundorp (or Londorpius), which first appeared at Frankfurt in 1640, gave texts and commentaries starting with remoter periods but concentrating on what was still topical: Lundorp devoted a heavy volume to the years from 1608 to 1620. *Theatrum Europaeum*, a work begun by J. P. Abelin in the 1630s, gave the public version of international relations in narrative form. Continued by several other writers, it had reached 21 volumes by 1738. William III appointed his own historiographer, Thomas Rymer, to edit a complete collection of the treaties made by English monarchs, with their related documents. His *Foedera* took nine volumes to reach the 1650s. Two and a half were devoted to the seventeenth century. In the next century such publications were able to draw on documents previously kept secret: the negotiations that led to the Treaties of Westphalia appeared at Leipzig in the 1730s. A popular compilation published in French at Amsterdam, the *Corps universel diplomatique du droit des gens* (ed. J. Dumont, 1726–31) began with Charlemagne but devoted four of its eight volumes to the period since 1559. The market for such compilations continued to flourish. But it was only after the French Revolution that the archives of the great powers were generally thrown open and editing and printing became more exact. Then there came the great nineteenth-century boom in the official publication of state papers, whose products now provide the basic raw material of political histories. The most lavish undertakings were those of Britain and France, where the Public Records and the *Archives Nationales* have accumulated large if sometimes frustrating indexes. The series of *Documents inédits sur l'histoire de France* includes among its diplomatic material the *Negotiations relatives à la succession d'Espagne* (ed. F. A. M. Mignet, 4 vols., 1835–42). The collection of *Instructions données aux ambassadeurs et ministres de France depuis les traités de Westphalie* began in 1884 and still continues. The fate of the English *Calendar of State Papers Foreign* has shown how even before 1600 the sheer quantity of the surviving documents is a major problem: though publication began in 1863 with the papers for 1547, the Calendar had only reached 1589 in 1950, when it was abandoned in favour of a more abridged form. The material for the seventeenth century remains in manuscript. A collection that has

[1] See the *Guide to the Diplomatic Archives of Western Europe*, ed. D. H. Thomas and C. M. Case (Philadelphia, 1959).

been calendared down to 1673 is the *Venetian State Papers*—the letters of the Venetian ambassadors to London. Like their colleagues in other capitals they have provided one of the sources most quoted—and sometimes too readily believed—for internal as well as foreign affairs. The papers of the Venetian ambassadors to the Emperor were printed in another great series of state archives, the *Fontes Rerum Austriacarum* (vols. 26 and 27). Formal reports to the Senate from ambassadors in Spain, France, Turkey and other states (*Relazioni . . . degli ambasciatori veneti nel secolo XVII*) were published in Italy between 1856 and 1871.

Seventeenth-century statesmen were prolific writers of letters and memoranda. Most of them employed secretaries who copied outgoing mail and methodically preserved it. At its best it can give an insight into their manœuvres that can never be obtained in the same way for the age of more laconic and ephemeral communications. Again, much of the outstandingly important material has been printed. The *Documents inédits* include the letters of Henry IV (9 vols., ed. B. de Xivrey and others, 1843–76), the *Lettres, instructions, et papiers du Cardinal de Richelieu* (ed. L. Avernel, 7 vols., 1853–74), the *Lettres du Cardinal de Mazarin* (10 vols., ed. M. A. Cheruel, 1872–1906), and the *Lettres, Instructions, et Mémoires* of Colbert (8 vols., ed. P. Clément, 1861–82). Ten volumes of Peter the Great's letters and papers have been published in Russia, the first in 1887, the last in 1956. There are several collections of those of De Witt, beginning with the six volumes of his diplomatic correspondence that appeared in the 1720s. Three volumes of Oldenbarnevelt's letters are among the great variety of correspondence included in the Dutch archives series, *Rijks Geschiedkundige Publicatien*. William Knowler's selection of Strafford's letters was published in 1739; but it is only in our own time that the whole body of manuscripts from which they were drawn has become accessible.

It was a natural assumption of those who held office that their documents, like their job, were private property. Most of Richelieu's papers went, after his death, to his niece the Duchesse d'Aiguillon. Mazarin bequeathed his to Colbert who set in motion the formidable task of classifying them. (They were eventually bound into more than 400 volumes.) By this time the French central government was beginning to accept the idea that official papers should remain in its care. When Lionne died in 1671, Louis XIV ordered that the government should retain possession of all state documents. By the end of his reign an official repository for papers thought to be worth preserving for their historic interest had been established.[1] In England archives were still scattered among a number of collections. The Chancery records were in the Tower and at the 'Rolls' in Chancery Lane; the Exchequer had four separate repositories in Westminster; various private houses and cellars were used, with grievous effects on the documents.

State papers have constantly to be supplemented from the collections, great and small, of archives that either remained with the families of those originally in charge of them or passed into the hands of private collectors and often from them to the big libraries. Students of English history are more fortunate than any others in the quantity of private collections that have been calendared by the Historical Manuscripts Commission, though the quality of its work in its earlier years varied greatly. Even with central political questions, the loss of documents can have a decisive effect on the scope of historical writing. Evidence about Spanish government policies in this period is poor, partly because Olivares, having put the main decisions into the hands of his special juntas, kept their papers himself. Most of them were destroyed in the eighteenth century.[2] The collection of state papers in the *Archivo General de Simanacas* was seized by Napoleon, and many concerned with French affairs remain in Paris.

When we move from the level of monarchs and great ministers to that of detailed and local administration, the proportion of material that has survived and has been sorted—let alone printed—is naturally less representative; but there is still a vast amount of it. Among the various series in the *Documents inédits* are the *Mémoires militaires relatives à la succession d'Espagne* (11 vols., 1835–62), and the *Comtes des bâtiments du roi* (5 vols., 1881–91) for the period of Louis XIV. A well-known recent example of how historical study is influenced by the fate of documents is provided by the controversies on the local rebellions in France in the period before the Fronde. The Chancellor Séguier demanded from intendants and other local officials the most detailed reports of every episode. These remained in France until the Revolution, when an enthusiastic collector of archives attached to the Russian embassy, Peter Dubrovsky, acquired many, but not all, of Séguier's papers and took them home. It was consequently to Russian historians that they first became available, in the Saltykov Shchedrin library at Leningrad, and they formed the main source for the large-scale study of the

---

[1] L. Delisle, 'L'origine des archives du ministère des affaires étrangères' in *École des Chartes*, vol. 35 (1874).
[2] J. H. Elliott, *The Revolt of the Catalans* (Cambridge, 1963), p. 579.

rebellions by Boris Porchnev, who printed a small number of the reports. A larger, but still incomplete, selection has since been edited by Mme A. D. Lublinskaya. In the meantime Roland Mousnier in France had attacked Porchnev's interpretation of the revolts and edited a selection of the Séguier papers that were still in Paris. The argument continues.[1]

One of the main modern developments in historical writing on the seventeenth century has been the recognition that to understand its conflicts and political changes we have to look at local and regional no less than at central affairs. Such work has been helped a great deal by the earlier activities of local historical societies in preserving and publishing records. Many French provinces and English counties have their record societies, though their output is often a good deal smaller now than it was at the end of the nineteenth century. As interest has shifted to more complex economic and demographic problems, the work of assiduous local antiquaries is proving immensely useful in methods of research that were quite unknown to them. Urban records are among those most often lost or destroyed; but they can provide a corrective to the impression of the effectiveness of central authority that comes only from its own reports. For the Thirty Years War the many collections of the archives of German towns are an essential source. Nevertheless, centralisation itself created records of local affairs that would not otherwise have existed. The dossiers of the French Intendants, in the well-used 'series C' of the *Archives nationales*, provide a magnificent range of evidence on every aspect of urban and rural life.

Among the political records most thoroughly explored today are the proceedings of representative assemblies. In their struggle for survival most of them were strongly aware of the importance of precedent and of constitutional formality, and at the same time of protecting their members against criminal charges arising from their speeches. They were anxious therefore to keep full accounts of their decisions and formal actions, but not of the arguments that led to them. The *Journals* of the House of Commons and the House of Lords, in slightly different forms, are fuller than for any earlier period but rigorously exclude reports of debates. Many of the Commons records we should most like to have—such as those of its committees—have largely disappeared. The proceedings of the States-General of the Netherlands, which on foreign and military affairs held more detailed discussion than other national assemblies, also show how limited was its range of effective authority. Summarised versions of the *Resolutien der Staten-General*, which are

[1] See pp. 217, 222–3

12

being published at intervals in the series *Rijks Geschiedkundige Publi-catien*, so far cover only the early years of the seventeenth century. Another piece of modern editing is making the *Svenska Riksdagsakter* available, though this too has only reached the beginning of our period. Proceedings of the various German assemblies have not been brought together in any comprehensive form; but volumes such as the *Würtem-bergische Landtagsakten*, 1608–20 (1919) and the *Landtagsakten von Jülich und Berg* (1925) are to be found for a good many states. Unofficial records of proceedings are often much more informative. None of the continental assemblies can produce accounts of debates as copious as those of the English parliamentary diarists. The task of piecing together the many fragmentary accounts is now occupying scholars in England and America, and is showing how much can still be added to knowledge even of so familiar a subject. After the Restoration the development of party in English politics was accompanied by more zealous circulation of parliamentary news and gossip. Unofficial lists of voting and alle-giances, letters giving details of political alliances, and—despite the laws against them—accounts of debates became abundant.

Reporting and comment

Mention of parliamentary diarists takes us outside the field of docu-ments left behind from the process of political and administrative action into that of the reporting by individuals of events they had seen or taken part in. There were many occasions besides national assemblies of Estates where speeches were made that seemed worth writing down. The debates in the New Model Army in 1647 provided one of the first occasions when shorthand was used to make possible something like a verbatim record of impromptu speeches. Various accounts of the de-bates in the Paris Parlement in the period of the Fronde were produced for immediate publication. The makers of speeches, the preachers of sermons, even the victims of trials were beginning to realise the value of having their words preserved in print. Much more than before, printed material that was designed to inform and influence the contemporary public can—with suitable caution—be used by the historian.

It was in the seventeenth century that newspapers began. The earliest of them are naturally not of much value as sources of informa-tion on the events they report, though they are themselves a significant part of the history of the time. Augsburg had its *Relation oder Zeitung* in 1609, and other German printing centres brought out occasional publications of the same kind. In the Netherlands the 'coranto' was familiar in the 1620s—usually no more than a single sheet containing news or rumour of foreign affairs and war. Richelieu's *Gazette de France* in the 1630s, which may well have been the first weekly, was an instrument of government propaganda, significant because the Cardinal himself supplied or controlled its diplomatic news. But it was the Civil War in England, the Fronde in France, and the Thirty Years War in Germany that made the printing of news, exhortation, and scurrility a thriving industry. The brilliantly vituperative Royalist paper *Mercurius Aulicus* and its many Parliamentarian rivals are sometimes, despite their capacity for invention, a help in piecing together details of the fighting. They are far more valuable in showing how the war and the political manœuvres appeared to their readers.

There was no clear difference of purpose between the newspaper and the pamphlet. The *Mazarinades*—the broadsheets, pamphlets and verses that poured from Paris presses during the Fronde—offer some vivid examples of popular wit and malice and of more serious political thought. In the Netherlands the writing of political verses became a well-developed skill—used among other things for spreading Dutch ideas in the south.

From Germany in the early years of the Thirty Years War there came some of the best seventeenth-century specimens of another form of popular satire, the cartoon and caricature. Usually printed on a single sheet, with verses or dialogue to expound their point further, they offer crude but detailed pictures of the life of soldiers and civilians as well as indications of the black-and-white versions of the conflict that were thought to make good propaganda.

By 1660 the distribution of solid news was a well-established business, which governments had usually brought under fairly successful control. For the educated and leisured Parisians the *Mercure Galant* and the *Journal des Sçavants* gave news not only of politics but of all the fashionable forms of cultural activity. Those who aspired to inside knowledge preferred the 'letters of intelligence', copied by hand and circulated at a high price. But no public source was yet felt to supply anything like the range of comment, gossip, and information of which the cultured gentleman felt in need. He—and his wife—continued to rely heavily on correspondents of their own, preferably in the capital or at court. Not every country or social circle could find the equivalent of Mme de Sévigné, whose witty and perceptive letters are the most quoted of all sources for the life of the court and of the provincial *noblesse*. But letter-writing was everywhere a form of art well developed among educated men and women. Collections of family correspondence like that of the Verneys in England, which covers the whole century; the strange correspondence between Philip IV of Spain and the nun Sor Maria de Agreda; the sorrowful outpourings of Elizabeth of Bohemia; the exhortations of St François de Sales and St Vincent de Paul; the voluminous comments on politics and literature from Jean Louis de Balzac—examples could be multiplied indefinitely.

Most important of all the correspondence is that between scholars. In the early part of the century, more perhaps than at any other time, it was through the interchange of letters that scientists, philosophers and mathematicians made known their ideas and fought their intellectual battles. Marin Mersenne in Paris acted as something of a clearing-house for scientific discussion, handing on in particular the ideas of his most assiduous correspondent Descartes. Nor was it only to other scholars that letters containing major ideas and news of experiments were written. Governor John Winthrop of Connecticut was one of the more unexpected recipients of letters from Boyle, Hooke, Hartlib, and other leading scientists. Galileo sent his account of sunspots and their astronomical implications to an Augsburg merchant, Mark Welser—though these, like his celebrated Letter to the Grand Duchess Christina, were clearly meant for publication. The growth of bodies like the *Académie des Sciences* and the Royal Society, whose proceedings are major sources for the impact of scientific developments on the wider intellectual community, did not make correspondence unnecessary. *The Correspondence of Isaac Newton* (ed. H. W. Turnbull, (Vol. 1, 1959) and the various collections of the letters of Leibnitz contain many of their ideas not found anywhere else.

Memoirs and travel

The writing of memoirs was an occupation almost as widespread among cultured men and women, in the later part of the century at least, as correspondence. The French seemed especially addicted to it. *Les Sources de l'histoire de France*, 1610–1715 describes more than 250 such works, many of them printed in the great collections—*Nouvelle Collection des mémoires pour servir à l'histoire de France* (ed. F. Michaud and J-J. F. Poujoulat, Paris, 1836–9) and *Collection des Mémoires relatifs à l'histoire de France* (ed. M. Petitot and others, Paris, 1815–29). Not all the writers are statesmen, generals, or cultured ladies. Oudard Coquault was an ordinary merchant in Rheims who described vividly the effects of warfare on life in his town; Louis de Pontis was a minor army officer who in old age retired to Port Royal and wrote his imaginative recollections. Memoirs can be more of a temptation than a help to the historian. The much-quoted St Simon wrote up his account of Louis XIV's later years from his own unreliable notes and recollections and from the journal of Philippe de Dangeau which he mercilessly attacked. He has certainly been taken too seriously. The literary ladies round the court, such as Anne of Austria's devoted admirer Mme de Motteville, or Mlle de Montpensier, daughter of Gaston of Orleans, have usually a narrow range of observation even when they were closely involved in great events. But men like de Retz, Omer Talon, and Molé give an insight into the Fronde that can be matched in the same way for later periods. The 'memoirs' of Louis XIV himself, even though they are a compilation from his writings and dictated notes, are among the most valuable of all.

If France was the most productive source of polished memoirs, it had no equal of the two great English diarists. Pepys and Evelyn were both well placed to give in their sustained daily recollections a picture of English society a little below the court and ministerial level. The only misfortune is that they were so close together in time and in activities. But while Pepys was a busy civil servant, Evelyn had leisure for the occupation that in every country encouraged men to write of their experiences—travel. The numerous editions and translations of the 'itineraries' that appeared all over Europe show that there was a good market for such works. Martin Zeiller, whose accounts of most of the western countries appeared originally in Latin and later in several other languages, was one of many popular writers. The quaint story and the glib generalisation were as much a part of travel literature then as now. Endless curiosity about remote parts of the world was rewarded by a spate of lurid accounts more relevant for the insight they give into the minds of the writer and his audience than for factual information. But scholars, merchants, and statesmen tried hard to collect more reliable evidence. Charles X of Sweden commissioned the *Account of Muscovy* by Grigory Kotoshikin which proved to be one of the most exact factual surveys. Sir William Petty's survey of Ireland brought a new standard of accuracy to topographical measuring and counting.

Social and economic history

Even for historians not primarily interested in politics or administration, the expansion of government activity in the seventeenth century provides a large part of the raw material. What has come to be called 'quantitative history'—the study of large-scale changes in economic

activity and in the social structure by statistical rather than impressionistic methods—is for this period less hampered than might be imagined
by lack of information. The demographer is not short of sources, even
though much of his work consists of detecting and correcting their deficiencies. Most of his material comes either from the churches or from
the tax-collectors. The Council of Trent had already made the recording
of baptisms and marriages a well-defined part of the duty of parish
clergy. In 1614 Pope Paul V announced that they must also record
deaths and confirmations—the latter a valuable indication of the numbers surviving through childhood. Later in the century some registers
—in France at least—become much more detailed. Parish registers are
never infallible; but they survive in sufficient numbers to provide the
essential starting-point for demographic studies. Taxation, with its
obvious incentives for inaccurate recording, nevertheless provides a
mass of usable material, much of it still only roughly sorted. (It was
mainly for this purpose that countries as unlike as Russia and the
Netherlands held occasional and incomplete censuses.) Tax-collectors
were also responsible for many of the figures that make it possible to
build up more exact and detailed estimates on commerce than can be
achieved for earlier centuries. Most ports and many inland towns kept
records of taxable trade which often survive in a form that makes comparison between different periods feasible. The long series of statistics
set out and analysed by H. and P. Chaunu in the eleven volumes of
Séville et l'Atlantique (Paris, 1955–9) show what can be made of them.

The history of prices and wages has long been recognised as the starting-point for many lines of economic enquiry. With the spread of
arabic numerals, account-keeping was a less laborious process used further down the social scale than was usual earlier. Compilations like those
of Lord Beveridge for England, N. W. Posthumus for the Netherlands,
and M. J. Elsas for Germany as well as innumerable local and specialised
studies of prices show both the opportunities and the difficulties.[1] From
every part of western and central Europe detailed series of price-move-
ments have now been collected. The analysis of prices is naturally
inseparable from that of wages, and here too the problem is to use the
great abundance of sources with adequate technical skill. If historians
in the past have sometimes been too ready to accept contemporary
impressions because of their literary merit, the modern danger may well

---

[1] The bibliography to chapter 7 of the *Cambridge Economic History of Europe*,
vol. 4, lists a large number of these. See also the map on p. 486 of the same
volume.

be the spurious authority of a column of figures. There is still a large gap between the general deductions that have to be relied on for most purposes and the elaborate methods of analysis used by French historians especially. Despite their difficulties, demographic and monetary statistics are more easily collected and used than those for agricultural or for industrial production. Long-term changes as well as sudden catastrophes in the yield of corn are one of the fundamental pieces of quantitative information. An obvious snag is that it is the exceptionally enterprising rather than the normal cultivator who is most likely to keep detailed records. In Protestant countries the lack of those meticulous monastic accounts of agriculture and housekeeping that are the basis of so much medieval economic history is a serious handicap. On the other hand landowners and tenants at every level were now acquiring, as a necessary part of property agreements, much more detailed and accurate surveys.

No-one was more assiduous than lawyers in making and keeping documents—even if their object was not always to convey the whole truth. The seventeenth century was notoriously an age of expansion for the legal profession. What in France are called *minutes notoriales* record in such forms as wills, inventories, contracts of service, agreements on tenures and loans a great variety of information about ordinary life and small-scale economic activity much of which has yet to be effectively used. The abundant records of the French *parlements* have yielded material for many different lines of enquiry. The depositions in innumerable tedious disputes that found their way into the Chancery records in London can give far better insight into the outlook of the members of a village community than most descriptions of it by detached observers. The rolls and order-books of Quarter Sessions that survive in nearly every English county for some if not all the century, monotonous though they may appear, are among the foundations for the study of local and regional conflicts that are proving one of the most rewarding fields of research. Types of crime, and the relative severity of punishments, can reveal a great deal about the underlying assumptions of any society; and here at least there is no lack of information. The processes by which authority harassed the poor but also kept them alive left a mass of documentation in the orders on settlement, bastardy, and recruiting. Lawyers were also involved in another essential part of social activity, the giving and receiving of charity. The extent and nature of bequests, and their unpredictable fate, can give insight into a wide assortment of social and economic changes.

Charity is one of the fields in which the records of the church are used alongside those of the state. Besides their demographic value, ecclesiastical records ranging from those in the parish chest to the massive archives of the Vatican can contribute to nearly every broad study of social and economic topics. The various kinds of 'visitation' by which church authorities gathered information were often more searching than any organised by the state. Religious sects, even the persecuted ones, often kept extensive records which their successors have been zealous in publishing. The registers of schools and universities are a major source for any social investigation that involves analysis of biographical information. Nor was it only institutions whose record-keeping improved. The chances are a good deal better for this than for earlier centuries of finding, from families down to the yeoman and artisan level, the collections of legal and financial papers that must be the basis of answers to many of the most formidable general questions.

II

People and States

'Europe' is an awkward term. The wildly indented peninsula has no natural or political eastern limit: its boundary is vaguely assumed to extend from the Dardanelles and the Bosphorus across the Black Sea, the Caucasus Mountains, and the Steppes to the Urals, a line of hills

BIBLIOGRAPHY. No general survey of seventeenth-century Europe or any large part of it is comparable to F. Braudel, *La Méditerranée et le Monde méditerranéen à l'Époque de Philippe II* (Paris, 1949), which has a great deal of material relevant to the early seventeenth century. W. Gordon East, *An Historical Geography of Europe* (4th ed., London, 1950) is an introduction to many assorted aspects of the subject. E. G. R. Taylor, *Late Tudor and Early Stuart Geography* (London, 1934), shows how the world appeared in 1600.

Despite its age, W. Z. Ripley, *The Races of Europe* (New York and London, 1900) is still a sound authority. Julian Huxley and A. C. Haddon *We Europeans* (London, 1935) is an entertaining short account. A very brief introduction to historical demography is Carlo Cipolla, *The Economic History of World Population* (London, 1962). The chapter on the Population of Europe by K. F. Helleiner in *The Cambridge Economic History of Europe*, vol. 4 (Cambridge, 1967) shows the modern approach to the subject—though it was written twelve years before its publication. *Population in History*, ed. D. V. Glass and D. E. C. Eversley (London, 1965) is a miscellaneous collection with several articles bearing on this period. There is a general account of the problems by R. Mousnier, 'La Démographie européenne au XVIIᵉ et XVIIIᵉ siècles' in *Problèmes de Population* published by the *Centre Universitaire des Hautes Études européennes* (Strasburg, 1951). Another article by R. Mousnier, 'Études sur la population de la France' in *XVIIᵉ Siècle*, no. 16 (Paris, 1952) gives some indication of the intensive study of the subject there. Many others have appeared in the periodical *Population*, such as J. Meuvret, 'Les crises de subsistances et la démographie de la France d'Ancien Régime' (in vol. I, 1946) and M. Reinhard, 'La population française au XVIIᵉ Siècle' (in vol. XIII, 1958). Studies of epidemics include L. F. Hirst, *The Conquest of Plague* (Oxford, 1953); R. Pollitzer, *Plague* (Geneva, 1954); A. Costa 'La Peste in Genova negli anni 1656–7' in *Atti del Congresso Internazionale per gli Studi sulla Popolazione, 1931*, vol. I (Rome, 1933); and—for those not put off by its 'uniquely personal' style—H. Zinsser, *Rats, Lice, and History* (New York, 1934).

running conveniently from north to south but too low to form a significant barrier. In 1600 'Christendom' was a commoner and more meaningful word. During the century several slow developments made Europe politically and even emotionally a better-defined unit. Russia, which had seemed almost as remote as China from the diplomatic and economic affairs of the west, was by the time of Peter the Great's death in 1725 firmly committed to the conflicts and much of the outlook of the continent as a whole. (Siberia as a colonial area gave it few links with Asiatic states). The Ottoman Empire, though it still held in some form of subjection much the same territory at the end of the century as at the beginning, had made what proved its last attempt at westward expansion. While Russia was drawn further into the European system, the sultan was now of less concern to any but the masses he exploited. In place of the occasional calls for Christendom to unite against the Turk, the enemies of Louis XIV, especially the Dutch, began to speak of the interest of Europe in curtailing the excessive power of one of its own states.[1] It was already apparent that the virtues of a balanced and stable European system were most readily upheld by those governments immediately threatened by any move to upset it.

Groups and languages

In many ways the peoples of Europe now had less in common than in the centuries when Roman law, Roman Christianity, and the Latin language produced some cultural unity. Racially the differences between them did not mean much. There was a little more separation than there is today between the tall, Teutonic peoples of the north, the shorter, round-headed Celtic or Alpine peoples of the west, and the dark, long-headed Mediterranean peoples. The most distinctive major group was the Slavs—a word of disputed meaning with a mythology of its own. Originally they were the westward-moving tribes that Charlemagne had checked on a fairly well-defined boundary. The people regarded as their descendants were those who spoke Slavonic languages. The 'western'

General works on the major countries dealt with here are mentioned in the bibliographies to chapters 12 to 18. On cities and towns, modern works include R. Cessi, *Storia della Repubblica de Venezia* (2 vols., Milan, 1944–6); P. Burckhardt, *Geschichte der Stadt Basel* (Basel, 1942); and P. Lavedan, *Les Villes françaises* (Paris, 1960). The various writings of Lewis Mumford, such as *The City in History* (London, 1961), have a great range of periods and places.

[1] H. D. Schmidt, 'The Establishment of "Europe" as a political expression' in *Historical Journal*, vol. 9, 1966.

Slavs were becoming less identifiable as German speech spread into the Slav regions of the Holy Roman Empire; but Slavonic dialects were still the popular tongue well to the west of the Polish frontier. In Russia, the 'eastern' Slavs were absorbing their invaders of more recent Asiatic origin, whose countless languages were dying out. The 'southern' Slavs of the Balkans and parts of the Danube plain were largely cut off from the rest by the Germans and Magyars, but were by no means losing their identity under Ottoman or Austrian rule. One of the demonstrations that the Turks remained an alien power was that even after so many generations their language made little progress in the Balkans outside the bureaucracy.

The establishment of national languages was one of the achievements of the period by which Europeans were becoming more separate from each other.[1] Luther's German, though the Catholic states long resisted it, came to be accepted as the language of literature and government over most of the Habsburg Empire. Parisian French was understood by the whole country, and then, in the wake of Louis XIV's diplomatic prestige, became a substitute for Latin as an international language of government and fashionable culture. Spain was ruled in Spanish; Galileo wrote not only in Latin but in an Italian that would be familiar in most of the peninsula. The languages used by central governments were driving out Latin on one hand and popular local speech on the other. Since the latter often survived as the tongue of the uneducated, there was growing linguistic distinction between classes and sometimes between dominant and subject peoples. The Habsburg government had the greatest problem, and fear, of national languages. It organised, after the Bohemian revolt, a determined attack on Czech speech and literature; it banned the dictionary and grammars of the Slovene language that had appeared at the end of the previous century; later it tried to replace Magyar by German. In Poland, with a feebler government, minority languages survived, and Latin was still used for legal and cultural purposes. In Britain English became the only language of townsmen and landlords in regions where the poor of the countryside spoke Welsh or Gaelic. Cornish died out almost completely. Henry IV of France was reported[2] to have asserted the principle that those who spoke the same language ought to belong to the same state. He was one of the few rulers whose territories would not have been divided by this: the others could only hope to force their language on those subjects who did not use it.

[1] See the Appendix on 'Races and Languages' in G. N. Clark, *The Seventeenth Century* (Oxford, 1960). [2] See also p. 157.

There were a few groups that constituted minorities in more than a linguistic sense. In southern Spain the Moriscoes, Christians of Moorish descent, formed until Philip III's ruthless expulsion a prosperous and even envied part of the community. At the other extreme, culturally as well as geographically, the Lapps of northern Scandinavia, a people of Mongolian origin who had mixed comparatively little with others, remained all but independent of the Danish or Swedish kings, and were only just being converted to Christianity. Almost everywhere there were the gypsies. As true nomads, avoiding as far as possible all contact with the state and its systems of law and property, they left little record of their existence. Inevitably they tended to become less identifiable as a racial group and to merge with the growing throng of vagabonds. Governments and propertied individuals were generally agreed that the number of vagrants was increasing. Victims of one form or another of economic misfortune, of war, and of persecution, they were a constant reminder that the state was not yet an all-inclusive institution.

The most firmly excluded minority was of course the Jews. Even they were not a 'race' in any scientific sense. Their own tradition emphasised the difference between the southern 'Sephardim', many of whom had fled from Spain to other parts of Europe, and the more numerous and generally less prosperous 'Ashkenazim' of the north and east. Nevertheless they were a group readily identifiable and seemingly made for persecution. Papists, witches, or Turks might be blamed in different places and periods for almost every evil; but the Jew was denounced unanimously. He was an enemy of Christianity, guilty, by some irrational hereditary principle, of the crucifixion and responsible for all kinds of desecration. For many believers in the millennium, the unconverted Jews were an obstacle to its arrival; and extermination was claimed, oddly, as a way of fulfilling the prophecies of their conversion and propitiating an angry god. If morality depended on religion, it followed that the Jews were totally immoral. As their exclusion from most other forms of economic activity led some of them to commerce and money-lending, the picture of Shylock was firmly established. But gradually during the century their hopes improved a little. Many found refuge in the Netherlands. The Great Elector of Brandenburg readmitted them, with restrictions and additional taxes. Cromwell, against widespread objections, allowed them into England; Olivares made a vain attempt to relax their exclusion from Spain. In the towns of Poland, where their proportion was probably highest, they remained a segregated and hated but not completely rightless minority.

Population

We do not know how many people there were in seventeenth-century Europe. Nor would totals for the continent or the various political units tell us much in themselves, even if they were more accurate than in most cases now possible. To make any real assessment of the effects of population changes on economic and political affairs, it is necessary to see year by year the numerical rise and fall of different age-groups, different localities, and different social strata, and to distinguish the long-term trends from the sudden ups and downs that were one of the outstanding characteristics of the period. Such questions are now being investigated with possibly more thoroughness and refinement of technique than any other branch of historical study; and firm answers are beginning to emerge. It was in the seventeenth century itself that the study of demography started. A few writers and a few organisers of taxation and recruiting tried to work out methodically the population of whole countries. The genealogist Gregory King in England, the Italian Jesuit Riccioli, and Marshal Vauban in France were three very different characters who in the later part of the century compiled figures that are still useful. Despite the formidable difficulties, there was a large-scale census in Russia in 1678. Peter the Great's 'registration of souls' in 1718 came nearer than anything attempted earlier to achieving a comprehensive count. But all such sources have to be seen in the light of the motives and shortcomings of the compiler and of his human material.

At the beginning of the century the main regions of comparatively dense rural population appear to be concentrated in a broad belt running from north to south.[1] There were 40 to 50 people per square kilometre (about 100 to 130 per square mile), in south-east Ireland and south-east England, in the Netherlands and much of lowland France, in the regions of the Rhine and the upper Danube, in all the northern part of Italy and in much of Sicily and the kingdom of Naples. Few regions showed any marked long-term increase during the century. England, the Netherlands, and some parts of Scandinavia probably became more populous, though at nothing like the rate that began three or four generations later. England and Wales may have had about four and a half million people at the beginning of the century and more than five million at the end. In some areas the evidence of decline is strong. In Spain, especially

---

[1] See map on pp. 26–7. A summary of current demographic work is in P. Chaunu, *La civilisation de l'Europe classique*, chapter 5.

Castile, it was generally thought at the time that the population was falling. Though migration certainly accounted for some of the empty fields and villages, it now seems certain that there was a drop of a quarter or more by 1650 followed by a slight recovery at the end of the century. Poland in the same period suffered a drastic decline which by restricting the surplus of wheat may have had widespread repercussions outside. In Germany the question of the effects of the Thirty Years War compared with other factors is still unsettled; but the evidence is overwhelming that in many areas the fall in population was very large and in some the recovery slow.[1] In Italy too there was a sharp fall between 1600 and 1660, but here most of the loss seems to have been made good by 1700. France, with sixteen or seventeen millions in 1600, was if anything slightly less densely populated a hundred years later. For Russia, where not only the political frontiers but the areas of cultivation surrounded by marsh and forest varied rapidly, comparative totals became almost meaningless. All that is certain is the widespread depopulation and migration.

The sixteenth century had seen some great increases in the population of cities, through influx and expansion rather than any steady excess of births over deaths. Paris had probably over 200,000 inhabitants by 1600; London may have had about the same; Amsterdam was nearer to 100,000. All these continued to grow. But Naples, possibly the biggest sixteenth-century city, declined—as did many of the towns of northern Italy. Urban life had its own dangers—notably fire which both in war and in peace was responsible for innumerable disasters. But for town and country alike hunger and epidemic disease were the two great factors that restricted population growth. The land available to the ordinary countryman did not consistently yield, for his own use, enough to feed his children adequately. Most parts of Europe were constantly on the edge of a 'crisis of subsistence' that from time to time turned into widespread starvation. Trade in grain, essential for many areas, was not easily adaptable to meet sudden shortages. Most towns were fed largely by their immediately surrounding countryside. When bad weather reduced supplies, hunger reduced population.[2] Infant mortality rose sharply, and famine may well have been an encouragement to the various attempts at contraception that were commonly practised. Two or three years of outstandingly bad harvests were enough to produce one of the *classes creuses* in the population, when the shortage of young

---

[1] See pp. 298–300.   [2] See pp. 50–2.

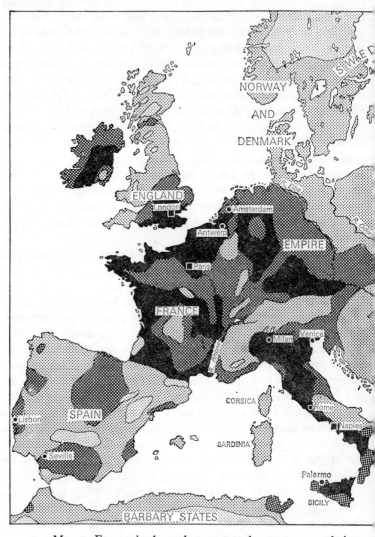

Map 1. Europe in the early seventeenth century: population

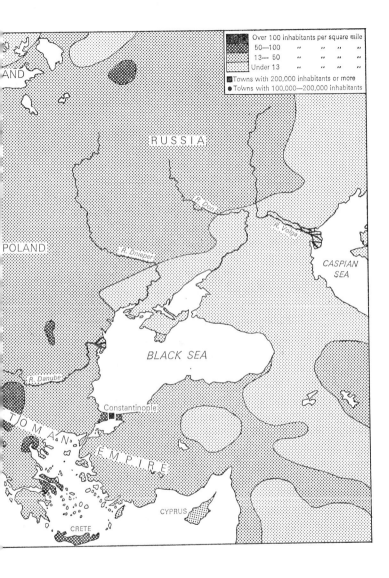

adults twenty to thirty years later led to another, less sharp, drop in the birth-rate.

The worst calamity was when famine coincided with epidemic, as happened in Spain between 1597 and 1602. Disease was more erratic, but more devastating in its worst attacks, than famine. Bubonic plague, the Black Death of the fourteenth century, had existed ever since in comparatively mild and localised form. Throughout the seventeenth century the crowded, rat-infested cities and the armies were everywhere liable to be hit. There were major epidemics in Spain in 1599, Switzerland in 1610 and 1615, in Germany and the Netherlands in 1623–4 and in 1634–5. Two of the most lethal were those of 1630 and 1656–7 in northern Italy. In 1661 there was a severe outbreak in Turkey which spread during the next ten years over almost all Europe. It hit the Netherlands in 1663–4, London in 1665, Austria in 1668. Thereafter the scale of plague diminished. Improvements in urban housing conditions no doubt deserve some of the credit. The reduction has also been ascribed to a great war of an unusual kind—the one in which the brown rat, an Asiatic invader, fought and conquered the black rat. For *Xenopsylla cheopia*, the parasite mainly responsible for the spread of plague, preferred the black rat. But black rats appear to have been common until the eighteenth century, and it may be that a reduction in the potency of the virus was the principal cause. Plague was not of course the only dangerous epidemic. Typhus, spread by rat-fleas and human lice, was a more constant threat, prevalent wherever armies marched and more deadly than any of their weapons. The Thirty Years War took it everywhere in central Europe; the Civil War spread it in England. Syphilis had become less lethal than in its first appearance in the 1490s; smallpox was just beginning to be widely known.

Both hunger and disease were often the direct or indirect result of war, the greatest destroyer and waster of resources. Spectacular disasters like the burning of Magdeburg in 1631 and the devastation of the Palatinate in 1688, were in the long run less important than the steady misuse of human labour, the break-up of families, the seizure of money and materials. The worst damage was not done in fighting, or in deliberate destruction, but by armies living on the countryside, ruining or consuming someone else's harvest while they left their own ungathered. Where land was scarce, devastated areas were usually quickly repopulated. But every loss of production had diminished the already low level of prosperity. Since we have little idea of the numbers killed in actual warfare, it tends to be dismissed as unimportant. Scraps of evidence—

such as the existence in parts of northern Europe, after the wars at the end of the century, of a great excess of females over males in the adult population—suggest that this may be a mistake.[1] It is another unanswered question.

Sovereigns and frontiers

An elementary source of error in early estimates of population change is that the area covered by one calculation was different from that of the next. Every unit, from a city to an empire, had limits that changed and could be defined in different ways. The modern map of Europe can nearly everywhere have firm black boundary-lines separating self-contained political units. All the territory of Switzerland is within its clear frontier, and all territory within it is Swiss. Within the black lines are others of varying thickness that separate smaller units of government, whose power is well defined. It all fulfils the ideal that seventeenth-century political theorists sought when they wrote of 'sovereignty'; and it is only just becoming accepted that a thinning of some black lines may be desirable and even possible. Most seventeenth-century boundaries, though rulers increasingly deplored the fact, had to be seen not in confident and continuous black, but as varying shades of grey, often broken and uncertain. Parts of the Russian frontier were until Peter the Great's reign a barrier that could be moved a hundred miles backwards or forwards in a minor campaign. Other parts were not demarcated at all. Even in the west, the Peace of Westphalia settled some local boundaries that had not been established before. Almost every ruler of any importance had islands of territory outside his borders and islands of someone else's within them. A monarch was unlikely to have the same relationship, in theory or in practice, with every piece of land over which he reigned. Though this was still true at the end of the century, there had been an unmistakable trend towards the nation-state and the sovereign ruler.

Sully, in his speculations about a logical rearrangement of European states, started from the common supposition that monarchies could be divided into the elective and the hereditary. 'Election' had often become a formality behind which the power of a single ruling family was built up; but electing the ruler involved the recognition of a firm distinction between political rule and proprietorship. It was still normal for the two to be intermingled. A monarch was for many purposes the first —or even the second—in a hierarchy that extended downward to the

[1] Glass and Eversley, eds., *Population in History* (London, 1965), p. 80.

Map 2. Europe in the early seventeenth century: frontiers

Stable frontiers

Uncertain frontiers and regions of conflict

Boundaries within larger political units

Regions of broken frontiers and 'Islands' of territory

Spanish possessions

ESTONIA

INGRIA

LIVONIA

Moscow

R U S S I A

KALMUKS

LITHUANIA

POLAND

DON COSSACKS

CASPIAN SEA

ZAPAROZHIAN COSSACKS

JEDISAN

MOLDAVIA

KHANATE OF THE CRIMEA

TRANSYLVANIA

WALLACHIA

BLACK SEA

ARMENIA

SERBIA

BULGARIA

TREBIZOND

O T T O M A N

Constantinople

μisa

ALBANIA

E M P I R E

KURDISTAN

ANATOLIA

MOREA

CYPRUS

CRETE

manorial lord. The same ruler could in one part of his territory be primarily a sovereign, while in another part he was primarily a great landowner.[1] It was sometimes convenient to assume that the accepted laws concerning landed property applied to sovereignty—the notion which Louis XIV elaborated with more than usual chicanery in his claims to territory by 'devolution'.[2] It was not easy to reconcile the fact that states were transferred from one monarch to another—by marriage, sale, barter, and bequest—with the supposed duty of subjects to give emotional and almost religious allegiance to their rulers. In a great many parts of the continent there were two monarchs, one of them the overlord in a real or nominal sense of the other. Sometimes the sovereign was too remote for his authority to be effective except through delegation. By the end of the century it seemed clear that the consolidated, centralised states were thriving and the huge empires declining. Pufendorf, writing in 1684, contrasted the weakness of Spain, whose provinces were 'mightily disjoined' and controlled by 'governors remote from the sight of the prince' with the strength of the unified French kingdom, 'swarming with people and sowed thick with cities and towns'. Germany had the disadvantage of being 'neither an entire kingdom nor properly a confederacy, but participating of both kinds'. On the other hand some unified and prosperous states, such as England and Holland, were suffering from the decline of their zeal for war and the presumptuousness of the 'rabble'.[3]

The Ottoman Empire

The largest units in Europe were the two vast empires of the tsar and the sultan and the three kinds of 'Habsburg' territory—the Holy Roman Empire, the hereditary domains of the German Habsburgs, and the possessions of the Spanish Crown. The Turkish possessions in Europe were the only lands whose sovereign openly regarded them as a mere source of men and money for his further plans of aggression. It was the sacred duty of the sultan to conquer the world. As part of the 'Domain of War' the lands peopled by Christians could, for the time being, retain their religion and pay their tribute. They were to be ruled by military commanders for military purposes. But the theory was now, except on the rare occasions of a major campaign, remote from the facts.

[1] See for instance pp. 289 and 343 for the Duchy of Holstein and pp. 40 and 307 for Prussia.
[2] See p. 433.
[3] Pufendorf, *Introduction to the History of Europe* (English trans., 1697), pp. 138, 229, 261, 304.

The great estates with which provincial rulers were rewarded did not encourage them to maintain their zeal as warriors. Unintentionally, the Turkish system was changing from one based on permanent warfare to one of stable frontiers and landed property. It was a change which, even after the Turks were driven back from Vienna in 1683, was far from complete. The Tartar Khans of the Crimea, themselves members of the Moslem ruling house, repaid the sultan for accepting their virtual independence by recognising, in their devastating raids, some slight difference between his lands and those of his enemies. Two thousand miles from the Crimea, the three Barbary States of north Africa were governed, in theory, by pashas whom the sultan appointed and dismissed. In practice their pirate corporations gave or refused co-operation to the sultan as they chose. The Grand Admiral in Constantinople who was supposed to control all the Mediterranean coastal lands of the Ottoman Empire could never be sure of the co-operation of the rulers of the states and they in their turn could not determine what the corsairs would do. 'If', wrote the *divan*, the sultan's principal council, to Louis XIV, 'we had the good fortune to enjoy such obedience as Your Majesty has from his subjects, we would not withhold anything that could afford him pleasure.'[1] Frenchmen under the most secure of monarchies, and Algerian pirates dimly aware of a remote sultan, were at the two extremes. Most Europeans, in their relationship with the state, came somewhere between them. Most rulers had reason to share the envy aroused by Louis, and to know that in the behaviour of their generals and provincial governors something of the Corsair and the Tartar could be found.

Throughout the century there were three regions of conflict between the Ottoman Empire and the Christian powers. In the Mediterranean, while every maritime nation grumbled about the corsairs, Venice was usually left to fight a lone struggle against Turkish expansion. In the Ukraine both Russians and Poles were involved in the slow consolidation of frontiers. In the Danube plains the demarcation between the Habsburg Emperor and the sultan remained unstable. It was only in 1606 that the emperor ceased to pay tribute to the sultan for his Hungarian territories. Transylvania continued to recognise Turkish suzerainty, even when Gabriel Bethlen became another independent military ruler remotely connected with Ottoman power. While Wallachia, north of the Danube, and Moldavia, between the Carpathians and

[1] G. N. Clark, *War and Society in the Seventeenth Century* (Cambridge, 1958), p. 111.

the Black Sea, were Christian provinces where greater stability accompanied local autonomy, the condition of Hungary depended on the amount of military pressure the emperor and sultan were able from time to time to put on each other. There was comparative stability in the Balkans too. Until the fall of Belgrade to the Austrian armies in 1688 the Orthodox Serbs found Turkish rule as tolerable as any, while in Bosnia a Mohammedan aristocracy of Slav origin had a strong interest in defending their lands against Habsburg attack. Turkish power in the Balkans seemed as secure at the end as at the beginning of the century. The Treaty of Karlowitz in 1699 had deprived the sultan of far less territory than at one time seemed likely.[1] Only the establishment of Habsburg power in Hungary and Transylvania marked a decisive retreat.

The Russian Empire

The empire of the tsar had only one defined frontier—in the west; and much of this was, at the beginning of the century, a negligible line in the path of successive invaders. Away from the central regions of Muscovy, land was there for the taking. 'A great many parts', Pufendorf still believed at the end of the century, 'are mere wildernesses scarce inhabited at all.'[2] Political control was a matter more of lines of communication from which taxing and recruiting authority could spread out than of permanently defended boundaries. The tsar held power over peoples rather than territories. Not all those who were regarded as Russian were his subjects. In the west, many White Russians were under Polish rule; in the south, Little Russians east of the Dnieper sometimes fled from Turkish or Polish lands into those of the tsar. But Muscovy had achieved greater expansion than any other European state. By the end of the fifteenth century it had absorbed most of the rival states of Russia. Ivan the Terrible had conquered the kingdoms of Kazan and Astrakhan on the Volga. Beyond the Urals he achieved an uncertain recognition of the tsar's supremacy by more or less nomadic tribes. In collecting up the fragments of the shattered empire of the Golden Horde, Russia became a colonial power, developing like the others as much by the private enterprise of traders and fighters as by the efforts of the monarchy, but with no oceans to define the differences between colony and homeland. Between the tsar's sovereignty over Crown peasants, and the nominal allegiance of a Siberian tribe, lay endless degrees and var-

[1] See p. 374.
[2] *Introduction to the History of Europe* (1697 trans.), p. 354.

34

ieties of subordination to Moscow. In the south of the tsar's empire were the people furthest of all in Europe from the centralised frontier-enclosed state. The Cossacks were not a race, or nation, or tribe—they were a gang, or association of gangs, a defiance on a magnificent scale to the ordered society of the territorial sovereign. *Kazak*, said to mean a 'free warrior', was a word borrowed from the Tartars of the Golden Horde, and applied first to men who fought with them, or against them, in the steppe, and then to almost any landless inhabitant. As Tartar organisation broke up, the whole region north of the Caspian and Black Seas was occupied, though not exclusively, by men who lived as warriors, hunters, herdsmen and even traders, and for whom the tsar was at most a half-deified figurehead. The Cossacks were free—of land, property, taxes and all the growing apparatus of the state. Men of all classes were reported to have abandoned their families and possessions to join the Cossacks, as others did to enter monasteries. Cossack organisation was often a democratic one, but liable to be seized upon by a successful leader.

By the seventeenth century there were various groups of the Cossacks. Those of the lower Dnieper, the Zaporozhian Cossacks, were nominally in Polish territory. A few thousand were 'registered Cossacks', supposedly full subjects of the Polish state, but this did not effectively separate them from the mass of those with no such allegiance. It was common to lead a Cossack existence in the summer and return to a Polish town for the winter. Nevertheless, there were signs of a trend towards stability. Round the fortified camps, agrarian villages were appearing. The Cossack arsenal of Tretchnikov, a necessary base for military campaigns, was not far from being the capital city of a republic.

The Don Cossacks were less corrupted by civilisation. The unlimited land of the steppe and the intermixture with the Tartars helped them to keep the character of a 'host'. Yet both Russia and Poland were able sometimes to get the Cossacks to do their fighting on behalf of the state instead of against it, and the armies they could muster were perhaps the biggest in Europe. Much of the expansion of Russian territory was their work. They remained in general men for whom the state meant oppression rather than security.

In the seventeenth century the Don Cossacks began to regard themselves as a part of something that was new in popular imagination and hope—'Holy Russia'. There had been in the sixteenth century two great cohesive forces in Russia. One was the tsar himself. The rulers who had once been venerated as the 'saintly princes', Christ-like manifestations of God on earth, had by the time of Ivan the Terrible added another rôle in the eyes of their subjects: they were the successors of Caesar and Byzantium, and under them Russia was to be the everlasting empire of the third Rome. The other force was the Orthodox Church, identified with Russia no less closely than was the Moslem institution with the lands of the sultan. But in the 'troubles' after Ivan's death there developed the cult of the Nation itself, a nation that existed irrespective of frontiers, conquests, or revolutions, and needed nothing from outside. It was not a view that made much impact on the tsars. Throughout the century they were concerned more with the threats of disintegration that their empire seemed constantly to face, both from within and from without. Yet even before the advent of Peter the Great, Russia had made territorial gains on a scale that in the west would have been astonishing. Poland had surrendered in 1667 a slice of territory east of the Dnieper as large as England, and Sweden had left most of the eastern shore of the Baltic in Russian control. There was far less to fear than before from any aggression by the Turks. Almost alone among European monarchs, the tsar could claim gains from a century of war that were comparable with the price his subjects had paid.

The Habsburg Empires

Both tsar and sultan had, in their quest for power, the immense asset of a supernatural aura bestowed on them by their peoples and in no way related to their usually lamentable personal qualities and behaviour. No western rulers had anything to compare with this. Nevertheless the one great ruling family, the Habsburgs, had achieved the status of a 'dynasty' whose power and policy were associated more with its name than with its territory. Even after the partition of Charles V's vast possessions between the Austrian and Spanish branches it was still normal to speak of 'Habsburg power'. It was a term that meant more to politicians than to ordinary men. In the conflicts among rulers, the firmest division of western Europe was still, in 1600, into Habsburg and anti-Habsburg.

The Austrian Habsburgs held two overlapping empires. One of these had no existence without them: in their hereditary lands they were as much proprietors as sovereigns, and these possessions, at the beginning of the century, were ruled by different members of the house. Rudolf II had Upper and Lower Austria, and to the north Bohemia and the other lands of the Crown of St Wenceslas which were now claimed as an inheritance of the Habsburgs. He held the Hungarian Crown too, though it gave him in effect only about a quarter of the former Magyar territories, together with the precarious Adriatic kingdom of Croatia. To the south Styria, Carinthia and Carniola were under Rudolf's cousin the Archduke Ferdinand. To the west the Tyrol had come to his brother and successor Matthias through marriage to another cousin.

It was never certain that the head, or any other member of the Austrian Habsburgs, would be elected Holy Roman Emperor. In the seventeenth century, however, he always was, though sometimes after tough manœuvring; but his position as emperor remained an institutional one depending on the verdict of the seven electors. The title meant nothing outside the wrangles of ministers and archdukes: its prestige was political. To many of the lands that constituted it, the Empire had no significance at all; in some, hardly anyone knew or cared whether they were inside or out. Its nominal frontiers could be drawn, though even these left some important queries. It was tacitly assumed that the Swiss Confederation, after successfully fighting against the emperor, no longer belonged. In the Netherlands struggle it had scarcely mattered that the frontier of the Empire ran through the disputed territory. Some Habsburg possessions were inside it; some were not. Yet even in 1648 the Netherlands, with Franche-Comté and Luxemburg, were supposed to constitute the Burgundian Circle, one of ten such groupings created by Maximilian I and now remembered as a possibly useful weapon in the conflicts. The most ludicrous doubt was whether Bohemia was in the Empire or not, though its throne, held by the Habsburgs themselves, certainly carried a vote in the imperial election.

Relations between the Empire and its constituent parts were inevitably an illogical mixture of legal theory and political practice. The emperor was the overlord of his vassals. Among them the 'Imperial Free Knights', though they could not claim to rule even the smallest political units, still boasted independence of everyone except the emperor. He alone bestowed imperial titles. Until the Peace of Westphalia, no other ruler was supposed to make treaties with foreign powers. The 'Free Cities', which could include considerable rural areas, guarded the independent status upheld by the emperor's charters. Bishops, whose appointments often depended more on princely families than on the Church, owed homage to the emperor for the lands they ruled. Principalities and duchies were divided between brothers and cousins as casually as the fields of a yeoman, and sometimes retained ties with each other that were perpetuated in the familiar hyphenated names. The possessions of most rulers had grown and crumbled over generations of marriage, inheri-

37

tance, purchase, and robbery. Nevertheless, the major states in the Empire, such as Bavaria, Brandenburg, and Saxony, were well able to hold their own in conflicts with the emperor.

The Habsburgs did not seriously expect from all this a general loyalty to their dynasty. What ties they had were naturally with the Catholic states: but the notion of the Emperor as a political leader of European Catholicism was accepted more by his enemies than by his co-religionaries. Within his possessions the line between Catholic and Protestant was neither continuous nor, it seemed, permanent. Attempts to form alliances of German states on a religious basis did not achieve much solidarity.[1] Such popular recognition as the Empire received had little to do with the Habsburgs. Occasionally in sixteenth-century and seventeenth-century writings there appeared the term 'Holy Roman Empire of the German Nation'. The notion was closely parallel to that found in Russia: there was deemed to be continuity with the Roman Empire, through Charlemagne instead of Byzantium, and a sacredness linked to what seemed to be dimly its own church. Like Russia too the Empire could, from time to time, appear as defender of Christianity against the Infidel. But in Germany, especially in the Protestant north, there had arisen more strongly a national emotion opposed to the dynastic Empire. Luther himself had appealed to the 'German nation' to throw off the domination of the Roman Church and the Roman Law. Though the Empire had its institution, the diet, which could in theory have been the centre of a non-dynastic unity, there were few political attractions in this. Pressure against the Habsburgs remained 'particularist'. One of the decisive changes during the century in the map of Europe was to be the almost total fading of the frontier of the Empire, and the intensifying of those of the states, including Austria itself.

If religious unity brought strength to a monarch, not even the tsar had more to gain from it than the second Habsburg ruler, the King of Spain. The revolt of the northern provinces of the Netherlands left him with an empire in which Catholicism was almost unchallenged. Nowhere else were heretics so successfully eliminated; but there was little holy mystique attached to the Spanish monarchy. A more substantial asset was its progress towards the national unity of the peninsula. Though the sea and the Pyrenees provided perfect 'natural frontiers', within them other frontiers could still be heavily drawn. Castile, with its rich capital of Madrid, and its deceptively affluent ruling class, claimed supremacy over the other states. Portugal, differing in language and

[1] See pp. 285-6.

joined unwillingly to Madrid by the union of the crowns in 1580, was a separate political unit. Aragon, Valencia, and Catalonia, which had formed the lands of the medieval 'Crown of Aragon', were attached more firmly to each other than to Castile. Their financial, legal, and military organisations were largely independent. Of the three Catalonia had been much the most prosperous, with a strong merchant class and a tradition of political liberty. The American conquests and the shift of economic power away from the Mediterranean had been a blow to Catalonia, but also a further incentive to resist 'Castilianisation' and even to strengthen associations with France. Certainly none of the Aragonese kingdoms had any intention of accepting a status like that of the conquered Arab province of Granada.

Beyond the peninsula lay something no other crown possessed—remote dependencies in Europe itself. The Netherlands, or those southern provinces that remained under Spanish control, had been ceded on Philip II's death to his son-in-law the Archduke Albert in full sovereignty. He was so firmly devoted to Spain and to the Church that it made little difference when in 1621 his possessions reverted to the Spanish Crown. No-one could regard the Spanish Netherlands as a rational unit. The frontiers were a military accident, sometimes following the established boundaries of provinces, sometimes wholly new. The language division did not coincide with any political or geographical one. Flanders had a predominantly Dutch-speaking and a predominantly French-speaking area; but the first language of an individual could be determined by class, or simply family habit. Nowhere illustrates the confusion of the political frontiers better than the other Spanish possessions in the north. The ironically named Franche-Comté—the Free County of the Burgundian circle of the Holy Roman Empire—was held by the Spanish Crown until it was seized by Louis XIV; but its chief town, Besançon, was until 1654 an Imperial Free City.

The Italian possessions of the Spanish Crown suffered a more thoroughly colonial government than the Netherlands. Milan, though notoriously a region of declining wealth and population, had well-established Estates able to resist a little the efforts of the viceroys to insert Spaniards into every effective office. In Naples, Sicily and Sardinia increasing poverty helped the viceroys, with Spanish naval and military power rather uncertainly behind them, to maintain an incompetent absolutism in face of endless sporadic rebellion. Spain's losses between 1598 and 1713 seemed disastrous. The northern provinces of the Netherlands were abandoned after more than half a century of exhausting war. Portugal broke away with comparatively little resistance. The European war that centred on the disputed Spanish throne ended with the handing over to the Austrian Habsburgs of the Italian possessions and the southern Netherlands.[1] But the great American empire remained. Despite all the economic and military decline, Spain was still a major factor in European quarrels.

The Polish Kingdom

The empires of Europe could hardly be expected to have the characteristics of unified states. In 1600 the kingdoms were for the most part hardly less complex in their territories and constitutions. By far the largest of them was Poland. Since the formal merging in 1569 of the crowns of Poland and Lithuania, which had been personally united since 1386, their lands stretched for nearly a thousand miles from far beyond the Dnieper almost to the Oder, and from the Baltic almost to the Black Sea. They had come together partly because the Polish kings had seemed to offer to ordinary landowners some protection against foreign conquest and against the power of territorial magnates without imposing too much authority or taxation. In the 'royal republic' relations between the monarch and his subjects depended more on their revocable agreement than on national loyalties. The Jagiello dynasty which had brought about the union, had been a family of magnates like many others, with the same type of great estates carrying almost limitless power over the tenants. When it came to an end in 1572 there began the practice of electing as kings outsiders who might be expected to bring useful alliances as well as being dependent on the nobles who had supported them. Despite the scorn that has been poured on it, the practice did something to avoid the civil wars that few other monarchies escaped. It was a typical process of bargaining that had given the throne in 1587 to Sigismund, son and heir of the King of Sweden. Only his deposition in Stockholm prevented the formation of what would have been a fantastically large and disunited kingdom.

Even without Sweden, Sigismund's lands were assorted enough. He offered to hand over to the Polish state his personal possession of Estonia—for which the Polish nobility showed no enthusiasm, since the Swedes remained in military occupation. In Eastern ('Ducal') Prussia, he was a nominal overlord. The Western ('Royal') part was attached more firmly to the Polish state and contributed money and men. Danzig was a free city recognising only the most shadowy allegiance to the

[1] See pp. 454–5.

40

Crown. In the south there was the great Cossack problem. Religion was a worse source of disunity to Poland than to the German Empire. Though both Lutheran and Calvinist Protestantism had been highly successful in the sixteenth century, neither had built up anything like a national Church. They were regarded by many of the gentry as German and urban religions. The one decisive victory of the Counter-Reformation had been the re-establishment—largely through the Jesuits—of Polish Catholicism. The University of Cracow, and Jesuit schools and colleges everywhere, gave Catholicism almost a monopoly of education. But over much of the eastern regions the Orthodox Church kept its hold on the peasants and townsmen. The 'Uniate Church' which the papacy had approved in 1595 was supposed to offer to the Orthodox a compromise with Catholicism that would strengthen their loyalty to the state. In practice the attempts to impose what Catholics regarded as an inferior substitute for their own religion and Orthodox Christians as heresy led to bitter conflicts, persecution, and for a good many to flight across the Russian frontier. The tsars, when it suited them, could appear as protectors of their fellow-worshippers. For a kingdom whose whole enormous frontier was devoid of natural defences everything that increased the links between its subjects and outside powers was a source of alarm. In 1657, when the insignificant claim to East Prussia was abandoned, there began the long succession of territorial losses that was to end with the eighteenth-century partitions.

Denmark and Sweden

The Polish King, for all his troubles, came very near to ruling over a consolidated block of territory. In the Baltic region, which seemed to offer some magnificent natural frontiers, political divisions were erratic. The two Scandinavian kingdoms, solidly Lutheran and hitherto not much involved in the conflicts of the rest of Europe, were bitter rivals in expansion. The possessions of the Kings of Denmark comprised the Jutland peninsula, extending southward to include, as a personal estate of the Oldenburg family, the German Duchy of Holstein which was also a part of the Holy Roman Empire. There were the islands of Fynen and Zeeland, and across the Sound the provinces of Halland and Scania. The remoter islands, Bornholm, Gotland, and Osel, gave the Danes a line leading to the eastern shore of the Baltic. Norway was theirs too, one of the poorest and least populous areas of the continent but developing a little its trade in timber. Its most easterly province, Jämtland, extended far to the Swedish side of the mountains. The Danish King and nobility had never recognised as permanent the rebellion by which in 1523 the first Gustav Vasa had made himself king of an independent Sweden. It was extremely fortunate for the Danes that they had been able to keep their hold on Scania, which gave them complete control of the entrance to the Baltic—a sound too narrow for ships to escape the levy of the lucrative dues—and a base for any future reconquest of Sweden. On the other hand the Swedes had retained a precarious outlet to the North Sea at Älvsborg, where they were able to build the port of Göteborg. (There were even schemes for a canal to link it with the Baltic.) Swedish kings had already established a firm hold on the much-contested east shore: Finland was occupied; and in 1595 the tsar had accepted their conquest of Estonia and Narva, almost cutting off the Russians from the Baltic. In the far north frontiers were vague. Sweden, Denmark, and Russia had since the 1580s thought it worth while to contest territories there, and the Swedes held firmly to their access to the Arctic Ocean. Charles IX's claim to the poetic title of 'King of the Lapps of the Northland' meant that he hoped Swedish agents could occasionally collect taxes from them. Clearly conflict between the two kingdoms would continue, though it would have been hard to foresee that of the two Sweden would become the great European power and Denmark suffer repeated defeat.

Britain

The most fortunate of early seventeenth-century monarchs was James VI of Scotland, who in 1603 acquired through the accidents of royal marriage and non-marriage the crown of England, Wales, and Ireland. With an absence of opposition that a decade earlier would have seemed too much to hope for, he inherited a kingdom more stable and more uniform in its machinery of government than any of comparable size in Europe. Yet taken as a whole his dominions presented many of the familiar anomalies. All moves towards a political and administrative union of the two kingdoms were rejected by the alarmingly powerful parliament in England. Though Scots born after 1603 were grudgingly accepted as subjects of the English Crown, they remained for many legal purposes, as in the popular opinion of Englishmen, foreigners. The union imposed by Cromwell's army did not, in spite of the appearance of Scottish M.Ps at Westminster, become much more than a military conquest; and when in 1660 Charles II, King of Scotland, recovered his English kingdom there was no question of a closer connection. In 1707 the ruling political circle of a Scotland poor and supposedly full of

Jacobite plots accepted with little enthusiastic support the English scheme for union. In Ireland royal government was a precarious business, extended with difficulty from the fortified 'Pale of Dublin' to the remoter areas. Like many frontier zones, it had become a region of landgrabbing for successive generations of lords, gentry, and soldiers. Nowhere was there a sharper division between the religion of the alien ruling minority and that of the mass of the people and their native lords. It was a great asset to English kings that this area of conflict was cut off by the sea both from Europe and from Britain.

France

Henry IV of France had behind him not a Tudor monarchy but a long civil war in which the royal house had almost completely reverted to its status as one of many rival families. The struggle had revealed how close the French state still was to being a federation of provinces. In 1598 Henry had devoted all his military resources to the reconquest of Brittany, and its submission had been the subject of a formal treaty with its military ruler, the Duc de Mercœur. It was this expedition that made Nantes, where the king had come to terms with the provincial Estates, the place from which the celebrated Edict was issued. In it he sacrificed some of the newly acquired unity by giving to his scattered Protestant subjects political guarantees more extensive than any other religious minority in Europe could claim. But they were compared by the Huguenot leaders not with the positions of Protestants in Spain or Catholics in England but with their demands announced four years earlier at Sainte-Foy. By these the whole kingdom would have been divided into Protestant 'circles' each with its council sending deputies to an annual assembly. A complete Huguenot state would have existed on the same territory as the monarchy—in which the Protestants would still have had equal rights with Catholics. For Henry the Edict of Nantes was the best he could do, for the time being, to avoid such a fantastic situation.

He had still to complete the settlement of the eastern frontier, where the Peace of Vervins had given him almost a consolidated line but had left unsettled the demands of the Duke of Savoy. There was one faint international authority to which Catholic powers unwilling either to fight or to agree could occasionally resort: the Pope, it was resolved, should settle the disputed claims to the future of the tiny Marquisate of Saluzzo. When Clement VIII failed to produce an agreement, Henry decided on the invasion of Savoy. Its duke eventually kept Saluzzo and lost all his western territory between the Saône and the Rhone. It marked the beginning of a century of frontier wars in which the men, money, and administrative activity of France were devoted lavishly to acquiring territory in what would have seemed in eastern Europe trivial amounts. Monotonously, military occupation of a substantial area was followed by diplomatic compromise in which the acquisitions were reduced. The French frontier became the unhappy field of a western European power-game devoid of rational motive. By 1713 the boundary with the Netherlands left by Henry IV had been pushed back by a distance ranging from twenty to fifty miles. North of the Swiss border the whole province of Franche-Comté had been taken. But between these two substantial acquisitions was the patchwork of lands in Lorraine, where conquest and proprietorship had between them produced a tangle of claims that made nonsense of any national allegiances. Further east Alsace, formerly an area of even more intricate varieties of legal and political overlordship, had now become an almost unified block of French territory with the Rhine as a stategic frontier. In due course the game was resumed.

Savoy

Henry IV's enemy Charles-Emanuel of Savoy ruled the state whose history in the seventeenth century reproduced in miniature some of the worst characteristics of the great powers. Savoy itself, extending from the French to the Italian side of the Alps, was a completely irrational unit. Proportionately to its size, its frontiers underwent possibly greater changes than those of any other state. It maintained its political existence solely by war and diplomacy. Savoyard soldiers were among the most valued in Europe; and the Dukes, by selling and withdrawing their support at the right moments, could profit by the rise and fall of French fortunes especially. As a loyal but expendable ally of Richelieu Savoy did reasonably well in exchanges of territory. Then it suffered the disaster of a regency and a civil war that left it at the Peace of Westphalia powerless and diminished. In the wars of Louis XIV Victor-Amadeus II played his cards so well that by 1713 he had made gains in northern Italy and became, briefly, King of Sicily. Those who found themselves, from time to time, Savoyard citizens had to share the risks.

The Federal Republics

There were a few territorial units in Europe over which no individual could claim either effective or nominal supremacy. Switzerland was hardly even a confederation of states. It was an alliance of thirteen cantons, with other associates that included the Bishopric of Basel in the north and the 'Grey Leagues' in the south-east. An assortment of subject or vaguely allied lands and towns had become attached to one or more of the cantons. Four of the cantons were Protestant; two tolerated both religions; the rest were Catholic. Six were large rural areas, seven were towns with their dependent countryside. Though the three 'forest cantons' of Schwyz, Uri, and Unterwalden that had originated the confederation successfully resisted any attack on their independence, it was the towns that now dominated such joint activities as there were. The only federal institution was a Diet called at irregular intervals on the initiative of the Canton of Zurich. Consequently it was almost impossible for Switzerland to be involved collectively in European politics. The advantages were great. The development of Swiss towns as international financial centres began during the century; and the occasional wars between cantons never brought in the allies that would have enabled them to be prolonged. But the Swiss from time to time tried to establish what seemed the first essential of a state—an army. In 1647, when there was a threat of invasion by the French and Swedes in search of new lands to devastate, it was agreed to set up a permanent defensive force, with an elaborate system of shared command. Since the agreements were abandoned when each successive danger was over, they did not produce a formidable army. Swiss soldiers much preferred—as they had since the fifteenth century—to serve in forces that offered a prospect of plunder. Swiss frontiers remained virtually unchanged.

The history of the 'free lands, provinces, and towns' of the Netherlands—as they described themselves in the truce with their former Spanish sovereign—showed that a federation could become a great power and a republic turn by gradual and harassed stages into a monarchy. In 1600 the United Provinces were rebels still fighting for their liberation. In 1700 there were the first signs that the military and economic glories of the Netherlands might be coming to an end. Nearly everywhere else success in the power-game had little connection with national prosperity. Here the two were inseparable. The Union of Utrecht in 1579 had been a temporary device for getting the northern provinces to fight more effectively against Spain. The notion of a Greater Netherlands, reuniting north and south, never ceased to be a political force on both sides of the arbitrary frontier. The terms of the Union acquired almost the status of a written constitution—not because they created a unified state but because they were a guarantee against it. The one effective institution created by the Union—the States General—was a meeting at The Hague of mandated delegates from the seven provincial assemblies.[1] Only through the States General could the Union control its armies and navies, raise money, and establish relations with other powers. But it was far from being a representative body for the whole country. The part of Brabant that was held by the Union, and the province of Drente in the north-east, had no voice in it at all.

The states of the Union had little in common; nor had the line that divided them from the south any significance in language, religion, or economic interest. The inland provinces of Guelderland, Utrecht, and Overyssel, German in speech and culture, were dominated by land-holders, mostly small, against whom the towns could do no more than defend their privileges. Groningen's one fortified city was in perpetual conflict with an impoverished countryside. In Friesland the eleven towns, meeting in one section of the exceptionally democratic provincial Estates, shared power with the three country sections. Zeeland, where landholders had only as much representation in the Estates as each of six towns, reproduced on a small scale the extraordinary political conditions of its great neighbour and ally Holland. The English could scarcely be blamed for applying the name of this one province to the whole Union, not only because it was the naval and commercial power of Holland that chiefly concerned them, but because the ruling class of Holland itself regarded the other provinces, with some justification, as its dependencies. Holland provided more revenue than all the rest together. It provided the ships, the capital, and the enterprise that turned the provinces into a great power. All this was the achievement of the closed bourgeois oligarchy of the 'Regents'. While in every other state of any size effective authority was in one way or another bound up with the ownership of land, it was the great urban families in the eighteen towns of Holland who determined the policies of the province and for long periods dominated the whole Union. They controlled the delegations from the eighteen towns, each of which had as much power in the Estates as the single delegation of the nobility. The only effective challenge to them came not from the rural provinces as such but from the military leadership that gave to the House of Orange a unique position from which to build up opposition to the Regents. In the long internal struggle that followed the final defeat of the Spaniards, the dynasty was eventually victorious—but not to the extent of destroying urban power.

[1] See p. 212.

The centralisation that did take place left the Netherlands in 1700 still an outstanding exception in the political uniformity of Europe.

The little states

One of the least spectacular but most important changes in sixteenth-century Europe had been the decline of the medieval city-state.[1] Novgorod had already lost its independence before 1500; Lübeck in 1536 made the peace with Denmark that ended its days as the leading city in the Hanseatic League and the greatest commercial power of the Baltic. Florence, after a gradual transfer of power from the town to the Medici family, became in 1569 the Grand Duchy of Tuscany. Nevertheless, urban independence, in one degree or another, was still, in 1600, one of the essential features of European government. Every town, however small, guarded jealously its control over its own tolls and regulations. Seville and Antwerp largely ran their own affairs within the Spanish monarchy. There were still, in name, about fifty Imperial Free Cities of which a few, such as Nüremberg and Frankfurt, remained as strong as ever. Others, both during and after the Thirty Years War, were absorbed by the surrounding states.

Two of the cities of northern Italy were still important states controlling large rural and coastal dependencies. Genoa had already lost its Mediterranean possessions, and become, despite sporadic opposition, an ally of Spain. Venice, a century earlier one of the most formidable of all European states not only in commerce but in armed strength too, was by now an anomaly. Despite the diminution of its trading activity, its agents and ambassadors were still active in most of the courts and capitals of the continent. Though its government was not noticeably less oligarchic than that of other cities, there had developed an almost inescapable convention among writers on politics to praise the Venetian constitution as the ideal combination of liberty and order. Its commercial prosperity was grievously diminished during the prolonged struggle against the Turks, yet even so it was among the states that gained territory during the century. Crete had eventually to be abandoned to the Turk; but Venice recovered control of almost the whole eastern shore of the Adriatic.[2] Only the lesser city-state of Ragusa broke the line of Venetian coast and showed that, given a little care in maintaining good relations with the stronger nations, a minor trading community could still preserve its independence. (The final collapse of Ragusa's

---

[1] See H. G. Koenigsberger and G. L. Mosse, *Europe in the Sixteenth Century* (London, 1968), chap. 4.   [2] See p. 252.

prosperity was determined not by war or even plague but by the disastrous earthquake of 1667.) A less serious but highly annoying enemy of Venice was the Uskoks. A small stretch of northern Adriatic coast was in the possession of the Habsburgs; and there they tolerated, and indeed encouraged, the activities of these equivalents of the Barbary Corsairs. The piracy of the Uskoks continued even after the Emperor had agreed, in return for a small addition to his land in the region of Trieste, to repudiate them.

A third enemy of Venice was the Papacy, much the largest of the independent Italian states. For many years at the beginning of the century there was dispute and intermittent war between papal and Venetian governments, both about frontiers and about the unique asset of the pope as a temporal power—his ability to use the privileges and immunities of the clergy and the legal authority claimed by the Church as a political weapon. The popes were now almost without question Italians. Rome was one of the thriving city-states, with its highly profitable industry of religion doing something—but not enough—to balance the large expenses of the popes and their office-holders. The great estates of the papal aristocracy and the splendours of the court existed amid deep agrarian poverty.

Rome was far from being the only ecclesiastical state. Throughout Catholic Europe, bishoprics retained their temporal independence and their sometimes extensive lands. Something like a third of the western half of the Holy Roman Empire was church land of one sort or another. As Electors, the Archbishops of Mainz, Cologne, and Trier were powers the emperor could not afford to ignore. The Bishopric of Liège formed a major piece of territory dividing the Spanish Netherlands and subjected to repeated invasions by the great armies. Münster was another sizeable state. Of the lesser ecclesiastical possessions some were towns, or parts of towns, others widely scattered scraps of rural land. Even before the Edict of Restitution of 1629, ecclesiastical land had been a source of endless local disputes. A glimpse of the relationship between the lands of the Church and the men of property and power was offered by the provisions of the Peace of Westphalia concerning the See of Osnabrück. The Catholic Bishop was to be succeeded by Duke Ernst Augustus of Brunswick-Lüneburg who had hoped to acquire the lands outright. After him a Catholic and a Protestant Bishop were to hold the See alternately, the ducal house having first claim on the choice of Protestant bishops. But out of the revenues a large payment of compensation had to be made to another claimant, a bastard of Gustav Adolf.

In conditions like this, many ecclesiastical states survived through the century. The fate of kingdoms was settled in much the same way.

In 1600 the notion of a Europe of sovereign states claiming the uniform allegiance of their subjects and affording them protection and justice was a myth further from reality in some places than others. By 1700 it had become, here and there, rather nearer to the truth. But the frontiers, the wars, and the bargains of the rulers remained for the great majority of Europeans more a meaningless burden and a threat of disaster than a source of emotional or material benefit. The situation has not entirely changed.

III

Economic Life

The land

Most people in seventeenth-century Europe, like most people in twentieth-century Asia, were uncertain whether they would starve next year. The most important thing in their material lives was the weather; and it seems possible that the weather had been, and still was, getting

BIBLIOGRAPHY. No other aspect of the period is producing so much modern work at every level—though even here most of what is available in western languages concentrates heavily on the more highly developed countries. All earlier general books in English will be superseded by the *Cambridge Economic History of Europe*, vol. 4 (1967) and vol. 5 (planned for publication in 1969), ed. E. E. Rich and C. H. Wilson. Both cover the sixteenth and seventeenth centuries, and the division between them is not chronological. A selection of the specialised material that has appeared in the *Economic History Review* appears in *Essays in Economic History*, ed. E. M. Carus-Wilson (London, vol. 1 1954, vol. 2 1962). Much of the work of the French school that applies modern quantitative methods to the broad problems of economic history is to be found in the periodical *Annales: Économies, Sociétés, Civilisations.* One major study of the European economy as a whole has had outstanding influence on later discussions—Werner Sombart, *Der moderne Kapitalismus* (six parts, Munich, 1916–27). Its main ideas are examined in F. L. Nussbaum, *A History of the Economic Institutions of Modern Europe* (New York, 1933). On a much smaller scale, Maurice Dobb, *Studies in the Development of Capitalism* (London, 1946) gives an undogmatically Marxist interpretation. E. Heckscher, *Mercantilism*, revised ed., 2 vols., trans. M. Shapiro (London, 1955) has become a standard, though much-criticised, work. B. H. Schlicher van Bath, *Agrarian History of Western Europe*, trans. O. Ordish (London, 1963) treats this period briefly. A great deal of information on industrial developments can be found in *A History of Technology* (ed. C. Singer and others, vol. III, Oxford, 1957). Two good recent additions to the numerous works on overseas enterprises are C. R. Boxer, *The Dutch Seaborne Empire* (London, 1965) and J. H. Parry, *The Spanish Seaborne Empire* (London, 1966). The authoritative work on climate is E. Le Roy Ladurie, *Histoire du climat depuis l'an 1000* (Paris, 1967).

On England the classic textbook E. Lipson, *Economic History of England*, vols. II and III (6th ed., London, 1956) is still useful. Charles Wilson, *England's* worse.[1] One piece of evidence for this is the position of alpine glaciers, which were further advanced than now and appear to have had three periods of maximum extent—in the first few years of the century, the early 1640s, and the mid 1670s. Another is the frequent freezing of the Thames and the Baltic Sound. But we cannot be sure how it affected agriculture. All that is certain is that disastrous crop-failures hit large parts of the continent more or less simultaneously: there was one around 1649, another in 1660 and 1661, and the worst of all in the 1690s. For Russia 1601–3 was a famine period. In many other years there were

Apprenticeship (London, 1965) is a good modern survey. B. E. Supple, *Commercial Crisis and Change in England, 1600–42* (Cambridge, 1959) is one of the most important newer works. Among studies of state economic action are R. Ashton, *The Crown and the Money Market, 1603–1640* (Oxford, 1960) and L. A. Harper, *The Navigation Laws* (New York, 1939).

The period is included in two books on France by Henri Sée—*Histoire économique de la France* (Paris, 1939) and *L'évolution commerciale et industrielle de la France sous l'Ancien Régime* (Paris, 1948). On commerce there are the large-scale works in English by C. W. Cole—*Colbert and a Century of French Mercantilism* (2 vols., New York, 1939) and *French Mercantilism 1683–1700* (New York, 1943). Much of the work of the leading French economic historians such as Pierre Goubert, Pierre Chaunu, Jean Meuvret, and Emmanuel Le Roy Ladurie is in periodicals: R. Mandrou, *La France au XVIIe et XVIIIe siècles* (Paris, 1967) has a select list.

The central feature of Dutch economic success is treated in a good monograph in English—Violet Barbour, *Capitalism in Amsterdam in the Seventeenth Century* (Baltimore, 1950). On Spain the well-known article by E. J. Hamilton reprinted in *Essays in Economic History* (see above) is reassessed but not demolished by J. H Elliott in *Past and Present*, no. 20 (1961). Most of the extensive writing by E. F. Heckscher on Swedish economic history is untranslated; but his *Economic History of Sweden* (Cambridge, Mass., 1954) contains essential material. For Russia J. Mavor, *An Economic History of Russia* (2nd ed., 2 vols., London, 1925) and P. Lyashchenko, *A History of the National Economy of Russia* (English trans., New York, 1949) are rather thin on the period before Peter.

Some of the huge quantity of work on the history of prices is listed in the bibliography to the difficult chapter on this subject, by F. P. Braudel and F. Spooner, in the *Cambridge Economic History*, vol. 4. The statistical compilations include Lord Beveridge, *Prices and Wages in England from the twelfth to the nineteenth century* (London, 1939) and N. W. Postumus, *Inquiry into the History of Prices in Holland* (2 vols., Leiden, 1946 and 1965). E. J. Hamilton contributed a short account of recent work, 'The History of Prices before 1750' in *XIth International Congress of Historical Sciences, Rapports*, vol. 1 (Stockholm, 1960). *Annales* has had many controversial articles on the subject, such as those by R. Baehrel, J. Meuvret, and C. M. Cipolla in 1954 and 1955.

---

[1] For a critical survey of the evidence, see E. Le Roy Ladurie in *Annales*, vol. 14 (1959), p. 3, and vol. 15 (1960), p. 434.

more localised failures, such as those in France in 1629 and 1630. Such calamities were possible only because at the best of times European agriculture wasted the resources of the land. At the furthest extreme of 'extensive' cropping were the areas of central and northern Russia and parts of Sweden, where land on which forest had been cut and burned yielded a single crop and was then abandoned for an indefinite period. Normally some form of rotation enabled soil to give a continuous supply of cereals. The commonest of these in 1600 was rye. The surplus of rye grown in central Europe directly or indirectly enabled many of the industrial workers of other countries to live. During the century the proportion of wheat increased, though even in France it remained something of a luxury. Maize was becoming common in a few southern regions. But there was not much incentive to break away from traditional crops: by 1650 prices of grain had everywhere ceased to rise, except in famines. Though this brought benefits, to townsmen especially, it seems very likely that on an average the people of Europe were getting less to eat.[1]

In 1600 it was the eastern half of Europe that had a surplus of food and sought to increase it. The Mediterranean, once the main grain-exporting area, was less productive and poorer than before. Italian towns were buying grain from the Levant. In Spain, the amount of arable land, already restricted by the activities of the Mesta—the now moribund organisation of graziers—shrank still more; grain was imported from Baltic ports and sometimes from France. But France itself is estimated to have left half its possible arable land unused, while most of its peasants had hardly enough for subsistence. The vine was becoming a more profitable crop. On the other hand many Bohemian nobles before 1618 were rapidly improving the yield of their estates; and the Polish gentry were often trying hard to increase the amount of grain they could send to western markets.[2] Much depended on the effects of war, but also on the relative importance in the eyes of landlords of farming and of parkland or hunting. By 1700 grain from the east was scarcer. France and England usually produced all they consumed and in the good years had a surplus for export. The south and east of Europe had become the hungriest places.

Compared with the many areas of stagnant or decaying farming,

[1] J. Jacquard, 'La production agricole dans la France' in *XVIIᵉ Siècle*, no. 70 (1966), p. 21.
[2] M. Malowist, 'The Economic and Social Development of Baltic Countries' in *Economic History Review*, 2nd ser., vol. 12 (1959), pp. 177–89.

improvements in agriculture were small.[1] The one clear instance of a new crop that changed the normal diet of the people was the potato. In 1600 it was an exotic vegetable grown by gardeners; by 1700 it had become in Ireland—but nowhere else—a major source of food.[2] Nevertheless, there were developments great enough to modify any idea of a sudden 'agrarian revolution' in the next century. Most countries had a few districts, usually around the big towns, where land was used more intensively. Kent was becoming orchard and hop territory; and in such villages as Chelsea, Fulham, and Kensington, turnips and parsnips were introduced into the crop rotation by the 1630s. But it was in the populous and urbanised Netherlands that innovation went furthest. Corn yields rose astonishingly. There were new systems of rotation; peat and lime were used; winter feeding of cattle produced more manure. By carefully placed sowing and a variety of secondary crops, far better use was made of every acre of land. Market-gardening offered profitable exports. There were industrial crops too—oil seed, madder, and flax. The 1630s saw the great boom in tulips which collapsed in one of the first speculative 'bubbles'. Netherlands engineers such as Jan Leeghwater and Cornelius Vermuyden used advanced techniques of drainage which added six or seven square miles every year to the area available for cultivation. It was an important gain to the Netherlands, but in European terms ludicrous in comparison with the amount that was being neglected or devastated.

If the Netherlands carried out the most improvements, it was the English who wrote and read about them. 'Farming-books' were among the best-selling literature of the day. The classic sixteenth-century writers like Tusser were superseded by Gervase Markham on horse and cattle breeding and Sir Richard Weston whose *Discourse of the Husbandry used in Brabant and Flanders* was the best-known of many eulogies on Netherlands farming. It owed its success largely to its editor, Samuel Hartlib.[3] Like John Dury and their master Commenius himself, Hartlib regarded reform of agriculture as one of the greatest practical forms of enlightenment, and the zeal of these writers was communicated to some of their puritan associates. To some landlords new ideas in agriculture were largely a gentlemanly hobby. There was

---

[1] See the articles by W. G. Hoskins and others in *Tenth International Congress of Historical Sciences, Relazioni* (Florence, 1955), vol. 4.

[2] A lot of doubt has recently been thrown on the importance of the potato in Irish history. See the article by L. M. Cullen in *Past and Present* no. 40 (1968).

[3] See p. 143.

often an immense difference between the cattle and horses that were bred by landowners ranging from English gentry to the Tsar Alexis, and the animals of the ordinary tenant. But it was from the landlord that improvement was bound to come. It was made possible partly by extending the demesne at the expense of peasant holdings, a process which had been common in the sixteenth century and which in many places was now quickened. To the ordinary countryman ideas that looked so salutary to readers of Hartlib were an added threat to his livelihood. 'Better' use of land could mean the loss of the extra food and fuel provided by woodland or waste. The men who lived a savage existence in Italian swamps or English fens did not welcome drainage engineers. The Breton peasant, lacking barns, stables, and heavy ploughs, had no prospect of benefiting from better cattle-farming. Worse still, improvement for the landlord could depend on extracting far more labour from the tenant.

Shortage of labour was a barrier to successful demesne farming, but one that in the east could be overcome by serfdom, and in many other places by increased restrictions that came near to it.[1] The state, with its judicial powers firmly in the hands of landlords and its central authority weak, offered little resistance to the tightening of bondage. But it was also necessary to have capital that could be invested in improvement. In this the west was in a stronger position than either eastern Europe or the Mediterranean. In much of Germany and the Habsburg territories, the merchant was hindered from acquiring land by the rigid distinction between noble and non-noble estates. Conflicts between town and countryside were embittered by the financial and administrative systems. Social convention made it essential for the landlord to make provision for sons and daughters whose status was preserved from the contamination of commerce. But the success of the Prussian *Junker* showed that such obstacles could be overcome. *Gutsherrschaft*,[2] the tenurial system that gave the landlord the benefits of feudal authority with few of its obligations, helped to establish their prosperity. So did the tax-exemption that extended to the estate as well as to the individual. Even the losses in war and the fall in grain prices did not diminish the contrast between these thriving estates of the north and the deserted villages of Castile or Sicily.

[1] See pp. 83–5.

[2] *Gutsherrschaft* and *Grundherrschaft* are explained briefly in H. Holborn, *A History of Modern Germany* (London, 1965), vol. 1, pp. 64–5, and vol. 2, pp. 25–6. For a full account see F. Lütge, *Die Mitteldeutche Grundherrschaft* (Jena, 1934).

Industry

At least nine-tenths of the people of Europe worked on the land. Manufacture was, in that sense, a minor activity. There was probably less difference between one part of Europe and another in industry than there was in agriculture. For industry meant, nearly everywhere, the villager with his forge, mill, or loom and the small urban master helped by his few journeymen and apprentices. A large part of it was conducted by men who provided their own capital, in the form of equipment unchanged for centuries, and who sold their output directly to the consumer. If economic historians say little about the blacksmith and the miller it is because they were independent workers whose production made no impact on wider markets and whose prosperity or poverty went largely unrecorded. But they were not insignificant. Such men whose work was indispensable had better opportunities to thrive than the ordinary villager. The English midland blacksmith was among the founders of the Black Country iron industry; the Russian miller was the villager most able to become a moneylender and a 'rich' peasant. They were a good deal higher in the industrial scale than the countrymen who got part of their living through specialising in the kind of work their neighbours could at a pinch do for themselves—the coopers, wheelwrights, and sawyers with neither means nor incentive to change their traditional methods.

In Europe as a whole the output of manufactured goods probably rose a good deal during the century. Certainly in the west more metal goods, more leather, glass, and pottery were being produced in 1700 than in 1600. There were some, though by later standards very small, improvements in the processes by which many of these were made. But the most widespread change was the movement of industry away from the towns and into the countryside. It was a process that had in many places already begun. The town, with its restrictive guild system, its higher taxation, and its greater hazards of plague, fire, and enemy action, was not a place where the enterprising organiser of industry could thrive. Small-scale production naturally remained for the most part where its market was to be found; but even such universal activities as brewing and distilling found benefits in moving outside the walls of the towns.[1]

[1] See the articles by A. Kellenbenz in *Annales*, vol. 18 (1963), and by Joan Thirsk in *Essays in the Economic and Social History of Tudor and Stuart England*, ed. F. J. Fisher (Cambridge, 1961).

Textiles

There was a vast difference between the activities that could be run entirely by the craftsman and his assistants and the one great industry that dominated the whole of European commerce. The making of cloth involved so many processes and so much variety that large organisations and international markets had existed for many centuries. It had never been stagnant: some centres had declined and others risen; there had been booms and depressions; new methods had evolved, such as the use of the water-powered fulling-mill. The early seventeenth century was the climax of slow but drastic changes in both the product and its distribution. The international market for 'woollens'—the blanket-like material made from short-staple wool—had declined in the last quarter of the sixteenth century. Germany and northern Europe still used a lot of the older types of cloth but produced more of it locally; in the West, the Mediterranean, and the growing markets of the Near East it was the 'new draperies', especially the cheaper varieties, that formed the main stocks of the successful merchants. Each successive depression, local or general, hit the older textiles harder: the places that produced them had either to adapt themselves or fall into permanent industrial decay.

It was the textile industry more than any lesser ones that changed its location. The decline of some of the old textile centres had begun in the later Middle Ages. Now the industry prospered in new countries, and in new areas; above all it became an activity of the countryside. An industry adopting new materials and new markets, struggling to survive in periods of slump and to make the best of booms, was even less ready than more stable ones to tolerate urban conservatism. A further reason in some areas was that as the countryman became poorer he was glad to undertake spinning and weaving for the market—work which, since it had little seasonal change, could easily be fitted into the periods when agricultural labour was least needed. Country wages were therefore often much lower than those artificially fixed in towns. This was the great age of the 'putting-out system', which depended on widely scattered domestic labour. Where the industry had already developed this system, or now began to do so, it expanded. The regions that decayed were largely those of small-scale urban manufacture.

The most spectacular collapse of a textile industry was in northern Italy. What had been down to the end of the sixteenth century a group of flourishing industrial towns and cities, whose wealth was evident in their buildings, became in the next fifty years an impoverished region dependent almost entirely on its agriculture. The cloth produced in Venice was reduced during the seventeenth century to a tenth of its former amount. Milan, Florence, and Genoa suffered almost as badly. Some of this was due to the movement into the countryside; but the industry there never found adequate markets. Its luxury textiles were driven out by the French and Dutch whose costs were lower, and it lacked the capital to develop the newer products.[1] The industry of Castile was almost as badly hit: the general economic troubles of Spain helped to make imported cloth, even when made with Spanish wool, cheaper than their own, and the captive market of South America was lost as local industries grew up. The wealth of the Mesta steadily declined while it kept in theory its enormous powers to exploit the land for grazing. But Spanish wool was still the best material in Europe for high-quality cloth and was an essential ingredient of many of the new draperies: sheep-farming was the most profitable activity for the wretched Spanish peasant who was seldom given the opportunity to produce cloth for the market.

Further north there were many areas where a new rural textile industry flourished. In Switzerland at the beginning of the century the valleys round Zurich began to prosper through the weaving previously monopolised by the city. In Picardy, Normandy, and Brittany the production of cheap textiles for export became in some of the villages the main source of income, again to the distress of the towns. There was specialisation both in the type of material and in the work done. Some villages devoted themselves entirely to the various finishing processes. Elsewhere in France the old *métiers* of the towns made little effort to adapt their high-quality products to the wider markets, and by the middle of the century the industry was at a low ebb. One of Colbert's successful acts of economic intervention was to call in Flemish and Dutch merchants to help in its revival. Van Robais established at Abbeville one of the few large textile factories of its day, while in Languedoc there was an attempt to specialise in exports to the Near East. In Germany the wars completed the collapse of many urban centres of industry, and the impoverishment of the countryside was often mitigated a little by the extension of the familiar putting-out of textile work; but foreign cloth was soon able to dominate most of the market.

In the Netherlands the shift of industry took a different form. The medieval clothing towns of Flanders suffered badly in the Revolt.

[1] C. M. Cipolla, 'The Decline of Italy' in *Economic History Review*, 2nd ser., vol. v, pp. 178–87.

Many of their weavers fled to the north and re-established their industry in Leiden and the surrounding area. Technically they were in advance of the rest of Europe: despite opposition by owners of old single looms, machines with twelve shuttles worked by one weaver were well established by the 1620s. But spinning and weaving were the least profitable part of the textile trade. With little sheep-farming of their own, Dutch clothiers had to rely on imported wool, mainly high-quality varieties from Spain. The business was dominated not by clothiers but by the merchants who dealt in finished cloth, and it was in the finishing processes—dressing, bleaching, and above all dyeing—that Netherlands superiority was most evident. Even this industry, much of it in large urban units, was a poor relation of commerce. The wealth of the trading community contrasted sharply with the poverty of the men, women, and children who were employed in the clothing industry but kept alive partly by charity. There were many complaints that cloth made abroad was dyed and re-exported as a Dutch product. England and Holland especially were rivals who nevertheless needed each other's activities, though as the disastrous project of Alderman Cockayne in 1614 demonstrated,[1] the Dutch were not dependent on a single source of cloth. It was only when Colbert's tariffs added to the slowly growing difficulties of the Leiden cloth industry that it suffered a depression as severe as those England had known half a century earlier. It was then the turn of the Dutch merchants to discover the virtues of scattered rural industry: the villagers of Brabant worked for even lower wages than the townsmen.

Mining

The one field in which there were big changes in technique and organisation was mining and metal-working. As forests in many parts of the west shrank, a new source of fuel was needed; armies and navies kept the demand high. Mining more than any other activity needed a big investment in equipment and a skilled full-time labour force. It involved risks both that supply of ore would fail and that markets would be satiated. It was therefore an industry in which the large-scale organiser had the best prospect of success; and since mines—especially the new deep coal-mines—often proved an unexpected addition to the property of a landowner, they were an obvious means by which enterprising landed gentry could be involved in industrial activity. Not that large-scale organisation was universal in mining: in many places from the Cornish stannaries to the Urals it was a co-operative business of men

[1] See p. 394.

who held a traditional right to exploit shallow or opencast workings. But they had not much chance to resist the power of big and technically progressive concerns to control the widening markets.

The problems of a rapidly growing mineral industry were shown very clearly in Sweden.[1] The great copper mine of Falun was a source of wealth which, though not comparable with the silver of Peru, expanded rapidly enough in the first half of the century to transform the fortunes of the Swedish Crown. It would have been more important still if the economic aspects had been as well managed as the technical ones. The methods of extraction were designed by German experts. The actual working was run by a closed democratic body of some five hundred miners. The Crown controlled them partly by legislation, partly by organising the processing and marketing of the ore either directly or through a monopoly company. The company repeatedly got into difficulties. The Crown demanded more for its war expenditure than the mine, properly worked, could afford; and though Sweden was practically the only source of copper in Europe the price tended to fall rapidly as supplies increased. In 1628 the Dutch financier Louis de Geer, already a shareholder in the company, was given what soon amounted to complete control. But efforts to rig the market and to consume large amounts of copper by minting it were constantly unsuccessful. Behind the immediate incompetence lay the inescapable fact that one piece of industrial progress could not get far unless demand for its product was kept up by others. Swedish iron-mining, much less spectacular in its expansion than copper, proved by 1700 a better source of wealth for the country as a whole. It had the advantages of widespread supplies of high-grade ore and of still abundant forests. At the beginning of the century the industry was at every stage on a small scale, dependent on French and German immigrant workers for such technical advance as there was. By the end the great ironmasters and exporters were controlling undertakings that supplied nearly half the iron used in England, and prospered on the demands of continental armies. The greatest single contribution to the change had again come from Louis de Geer.

Louis de Geer

De Geer, exceptional in the size of his economic empire, was neverthless typical of the financiers who, in close association with governments,

[1] E. F. Hecksher, *Economic History of Sweden* (Cambridge, 1954); M. Roberts, *Gustavus Adolphus* vol. 1 (London, 1953), p. 89. See also p. 347 below.

were now beginning to put capital into large-scale industry. The truce in the Netherlands enabled him to move from his home in Liège to Amsterdam, which remained his headquarters throughout his life. Profits from warfare began with the sale of guns and bullets to France, Venice, and the States General. Then, from his control of the copper industry, he came to dominate the whole economic life of Sweden. His concern with iron ranged from the mines, where he introduced from Liège, new methods and the men who applied them, to the export of cannon and the retail sale of knives. He ran textile and paper manufactures; he produced salt, sulphur, rope; he built and owned merchant ships; he established a bank and, without much success, an African trading company. He financed Gustav Adolf's expedition to Germany, and most of its equipment came from one or another of De Geer's concerns. But this was only one of the many armies in the Thirty Years War that he supplied: Mansfield was one of his first customers and debtors; Denmark, France, and Holland itself depended on him too. One of his later achievements was to assemble, equip, and man in Holland the Swedish navy that in 1645 defeated a Danish one, also supplied from Holland. De Geer was in fact the first great international armament magnate; but he was by no means the only one of his kind. His nephews of the Trip family in Amsterdam, and his partner De Besche in Sweden operated on almost the same scale. When De Geer died, as a member of the Swedish landed nobility and perhaps the richest subject Europe had yet seen, he had plenty of successors to profit from the wars of Louis XIV. He was in fact only one representative of the greatest single force in European economic life—the wealth of Amsterdam.[1]

Amsterdam

Amsterdam's dominant position in the whole merchant activity of the century has never been equalled. Once its pre-eminence had been accepted after the division of the Netherlands, not even the incessant rivalry of England and then of France could do more than slowly erode it. It is easy to find the reasons for this, less easy to show convincingly that no other city could have done the same. Amsterdam was, in the first place, the successor to Antwerp which had become the first northern centre of finance and had been ruined by the rule of Spain and the revolt against

[1]Raymond Carr, 'Two Swedish Financiers' in *Historical Essays 1600–1750, presented to David Ogg*, ed. H. E. Bell and R. L. Ollard, pp. 18–34; M. Roberts, *Gustavus Adolphus* vol. 2, (London, 1958), c. 2.

it. The Dutch welcomed refugees, with little regard to their religion. Amsterdam was almost unassailable by armies. It profited from war. It profited from famine, switching its grain trade and—so it was generally believed—hoarding supplies in the huge warehouses that were the biggest outward sign of its wealth. The Netherlands offered less temptation than most countries to put wealth accumulated in the city into landed estates. It was the great men of the city who held political power and used it for the benefit of commerce.

The twelve-year truce with Spain provided the opportunity for Amsterdam to establish itself completely as the new centre round which the international economic life of Europe revolved. The exchange and deposit bank opened in 1609 was closely linked with the state. For the first time it became normal for bullion and coin to stay in the bank's vaults while payments were made by paper. More and more of Europe's silver came to Amsterdam, and it was largely through transactions there that rates of exchange among the chaotic currencies of Europe were settled.[1] In the political upheavals of one country after another, merchants and politicians alike used it as a refuge for capital. Though the bank itself did not lend money except to the government, its facilities made borrowing easy and helped to preserve one of the city's great commercial assets: rates of interest, at 4 per cent or less, were the lowest in Europe. In 1611 came a second institution, the new Exchange. Originally a market for commodities, whose prices often determined those for much of the world, it became the scene of purely speculative dealing. By the middle of the century there developed the traffic in 'futures' and in options to buy or sell which meant that fortunes could be made and lost by speculation in goods that never existed at all. Efforts by the States General to prevent these aspects of capitalist activity had not much success.

Amsterdam's position in European finance was secure partly because, far more than Antwerp had ever been, it was also the centre of shipping. Within Europe the most important trade route at the beginning of the century was that from the ports of the southern Baltic to the west and south. It was by the rivers leading to Stettin, Riga, and Danzig that grain was exported from Poland and northern Germany. After 1620 the grain trade very slowly diminished; but there was an ever-growing

---

[1] There is a brief explanation of 'money of account' and its relation to exchange rates in *Cambridge Economic History*, vol. 4, p. 378. See also B. E. Supple, 'Currency and Commerce in the early seventeenth century' in *Economic History Review*, 2nd ser., vol. x, pp. 239–54.

demand for timber. German oaks found their way to Stettin. Russian firs came to Memel, though a good deal of the Scandinavian timber and timber products escaped the dues levied by the Danes on traffic through the Sound by using Göteborg and the smaller Norwegian ports. Return cargoes included textiles from England and France, wine from the Mediterranean, and a growing proportion of luxuries from overseas. But the Baltic and eastern Europe also absorbed in this way a good deal of silver and gold. By far the greatest part of Baltic trade was carried in Dutch ships. The *fluit* was a merchant vessel cheap to build and to man. Unlike English and Spanish ships designed for the more hazardous life of the Mediterranean, it was not armed for defence against pirates or enemies; and it was readily adaptable to new types of cargo. Often its owners were a small, co-operative group able to switch quickly from one enterprise to another. Dutch shipbuilding was probably the most technically advanced of all the industries of Europe. With cranes and wind-powered sawmills it was possible, in spite of the lack of home supplies of timber, to produce ships at half the cost of foreign rivals. Even when France and England in the later part of the century made great efforts to increase their merchant shipping, the Dutch remained by far the biggest carriers of the world's commerce, and many of the ships owned in other countries were built in Holland.

Fish

Part of the Dutch success in shipping came from the fishing industry. Fish, mostly preserved by drying and salting, formed a major part of the food supply of almost every part of Europe. Much of it was of course caught and sold locally by small-scale fishermen; but for centuries fishing in the southern Baltic, where herrings gathered to spawn, had been a big commercial enterprise. One of the principal activities of the Hanse had been the transport of salt from Lüneburg—and later from the French coast—to the Baltic fishing ports, and the sale of the salted herring. During the sixteenth century herrings began to prefer the North Sea as a place for spawning. (A change in the amount of salt in the water is a possible explanation.) The Dutch, who had already captured a good deal of the Baltic fishing, were obviously better placed to dominate the North Sea industry. The *buiz* was a ship equipped to salt and pack the fish on board and to remain at sea for months at a time, transferring its load to faster vessels to be landed. The catch was sold in the Baltic ports that the fish had deserted, and to the English and Scots from whose home waters much of it had come. The fishermen aroused in fact more hostility than the traders. Privateering, and more organised attacks in wartime, were a constant hazard that often made it necessary to provide fishing fleets with armed escort. The expansion of the herring industry caused a demand for salt that could only be met, when the Dutch were excluded—officially—from Spanish and Portuguese sources, by bringing it from the West Indies.

The compulsory fish diet of the Catholic Mediterranean was provided partly by such local supplies as tunny but also by cod, now coming mainly from the coasts of Iceland and North America. England, with the great advantage of controlling much of the Newfoundland coast where the fish was processed, did better in this than the Dutch. It was also the English who by the end of the century dominated the most difficult and profitable of all forms of sea hunting, the pursuit of whales. When the Dutch industry based in Spitzbergen declined through the excessive catching which destroyed the whale population, the market for their oil had to be supplied by spectacular voyages to the most remote parts of the ocean.

Overseas trade and colonies

Most of the commerce of Europe was still, in 1700, within the continent itself, and there may be a danger of exaggerating the importance of overseas trade. The two countries most involved, the Netherlands and England,[1] were sending perhaps a tenth of their tonnage across the Atlantic and a little more to the east. Nevertheless it was in this that the greatest changes of the century took place. In western Europe at least, overseas goods became for the first time an essential part of the consumption of families as far down as the artisan level. Sugar, mainly West Indian, was in demand everywhere, though both war and the exhaustion of the first plantations caused some big fluctuations in supply. Coffee, still a rarity in 1660, was by the end of the century a notorious feature of urban life and a major part of Asian trade. Tea was still an upper-class drink, but imports from China were beginning to grow. More alarming both to economic theorists and to the workers who thought themselves threatened was the sudden boom in Asiatic textiles. Printed calicoes, the merchants discovered to their surprise, could be imported cheaply enough to be sold in large quantities to the 'poor people'. The French government in 1686 tried, with only partial success,

[1] But see. J. Delumeau in *Dix-Septième Siècle*, nos. 70–71 (1966) for evidence that in spite of the wars, French overseas trade increased more than is usually recognised.

to impose a complete ban. In England the use of imported textiles was denounced year after year until in 1696 a bill to restrict them was supported by riots of weavers at Westminster. The East Indian interests in the House of Lords were strong enough to defeat it.

In 1600 Spain and Portugal were still the most active countries in overseas trade, and the only ones with colonial possessions of any size. In the east the Portuguese base at Goa was the centre of a trading system that extended from East Africa to China and Japan. The Cape route had formidable difficulties for the big ships that the Portuguese, short of timber and of sailors, found most economical: something like a fifth of the vessels that set out from Lisbon failed to return. There was little support at home in either supplies of exportable goods or new capital. Nevertheless for more than a century the Portuguese had no effective rivals. Their eventual decline was due partly to the misfortune of being involved first in Spain's war against the Dutch and then, after 1640, in war with Spain. Not that peace or war in Europe made much difference to such activities as the Dutch blockade of Goa that began in 1637. It was the superiority of Dutch and English organisations and the support of their states that proved decisive. In the west too Portuguese commerce was slowly eroded by the pressure of Dutch and English rivals. The distinctions between peace and war, trade and robbery, hardly existed in the contest for American wealth. Spain's commercial position deteriorated more rapidly. The output of the silver mines began to decline; the dead hand of the Castilian aristocracy and the poverty of the Crown prevented the expansion of a merchant community; the constant wars in Europe made it impossible to protect the Atlantic traders or attack the pirates and smugglers. In the 1640s the annual sailing of the fleet from Seville and arrival of the silver supplies came to an end. Even so, in terms of territory controlled the South American empires of Spain and Portugal made them still the greatest colonial powers. Portuguese Brazil enjoyed a new boom in gold and diamond mining at the end of the century.

The Dutch, in contrast to their easy mastery of the sea-borne trade within Europe, had to fight a constant and in the end a losing battle in Asian and Near Eastern commerce. At the beginning of the century they seemed capable of driving out their rivals rapidly. The Dutch East India Company was founded in 1602 when the States General as part of the war against Spain demanded the merging of the separate enterprises that were attacking Portugal's trading empire. From its beginning it had the strikingly modern characteristic of being run by a few highly rewarded directors while most of its capital came from a much larger body of investors. Yet like the Netherlands state itself, the company was an awkward compromise between centralised power and federal equality. The Amsterdam members, who controlled most of the capital, increasingly imposed their schemes on the other five towns involved. The seventeen directors, mainly men of the Regent class who could ensure political support for almost anything the company did, were nominally elected but in fact a closed oligarchy. It was therefore not difficult for the company to become virtually the government of Dutch overseas territories. It could wage war and make treaties, establish military as well as trading bases, and set up Calvinist missions which —no doubt incidentally—helped to undermine the authority of the Catholic Portuguese. There was no clear intention that the company should become a territorial power; but in Ceylon and Java, the process of excluding the Portuguese and asserting enough power over local rulers to get the trading conditions they wanted led rapidly to political control. Dutch rule involved a good deal of brutality that the respectable assemblies at home were happy to accept without being involved. The most determined 'colonist' in the early years of the company, Jan Pieterszoon Coen, told the directors that it was impossible 'to carry on trade without war or war without trade'. In 1619 he seized the port of Jakarta and established himself as virtual ruler of a new state. In South Africa it was mainly the incentive to supply ships rounding the Cape with stores produced on the spot that led to the slow growth of a Dutch colony. Van Riebeeck, who made the first territorial claim in 1652, tried in vain to use Chinese labourers or African slaves to make farming possible; but by the end of the century an assortment of immigrants began to occupy territory inland.

For the theorists who measured the wealth of a state entirely in terms of bullion, trade with Asia was highly undesirable: it drained bullion away from Europe, in contrast to the American trade which brought it in. This did not prevent East India companies from appearing at one time or another not only in the established commercial countries but in Sweden, Denmark, and Prussia. The English East India Company tried from its foundation in 1601 to justify its activities by sending goods rather than money and by showing that the bullion it did export was balanced by payments for the Indian produce it re-exported to European markets. A common complaint was that it attracted capital that had formerly gone into the older and less dangerous undertakings. Its leading members came mainly from the Levant Company and the

Russia Company, and the purpose of their charter was largely to establish a monopoly excluding other Englishmen from the trade of the Far
East. At first it collected a separate 'stock' for each voyage. The first two
of these eventually yielded a profit of nearly 100 per cent; some of the
others did even better, and some on which ships were lost produced
nothing. On average it must have compared well with the 30 per cent
paid by the Dutch company in its first ten years. In 1613 the first 'joint
stock' for a longer period was raised, and thereafter there was frequent
argument about the merits of the two forms of organisation. It was only
when Cromwell revised the charter in 1657 that the company finally
established a big permanent capital, to which it added money borrowed
at a fixed rate of interest. Despite the backing of the state in its early
years, the loosely organised English company was not ideally fitted to
compete with the Dutch. It was not until the post-Restoration period
that the company abandoned its policy of reliance on agreements with
local rulers rather than on military strength. By then its fortunes were
deeply involved with political disputes at home. Puritan, and later
Whig, groups among the merchants and politicians regarded the company as a creature of the Stuart court and resisted the continuation of
its monopoly. For some years after 1698 the existence of two rival
English companies made eastern trade unprofitable, at a time when it
had almost overtaken that of the Dutch.

The French companies in the east were significant only as demonstrations of the weakness of commerce that sprang from political rather
than economic initiative. Henry IV had set up an East India Company
that hardly got as far as any serious trading activity at all. Richelieu's
two companies for eastern trade also died at birth. Colbert's so-called
East India Company, launched in 1664 with the glory of royal subscrip-
tion to its shares and full monopolistic powers, was originally concerned
mainly with Madagascar. It failed to get the capital it needed, and only
by shedding its exclusive privileges and allowing independent merchants to use its ships and bases was it able to survive. In North
America France had the prospect of much greater success. In spite of
manifest lack of support from the merchant community for such
ventures, the French conquest of a huge if ill-defined area of Canada
was the biggest piece of true colonisation since the achievements of
Spain a century earlier. In 1663 a grand scheme for French America
was adopted. Canada became Crown property, administered like a
French province. A new West India Company was to organise an
economic system in which the northern colony and the tropical posses-

sions in the Antilles would supply each other as well as conducting a balanced trade with the home country. All this was to make possible territorial conquests that would extend westward to the Pacific and southward to Mexico. But the ambitions of the 'expansionist' rulers such as Jean Talon and Frontenac did not coincide with those of the fur traders or of the Jesuits, neither of whom regarded political organisation as much of a help to their activities. Canada could rely on neither men nor money from home. Though Colbert gave cautious promises of support, it was soon apparent that wars for scraps of territory in Europe were regarded as vastly more important than the acquisition of a continent. The limits to French expansion in Canada were set not by the successes and failures of the few thousand colonists but by the Treaty of Utrecht. In the West Indies the French buccaneers were able to fight their sporadic warfare against both English and Spanish rivals with less regard to Louis' diplomacy. The sugar plantations of Guadeloupe and the slave trade that supplied them made fortunes for the independent merchants of Nantes and the other Atlantic ports. But the problem of political control was unsolved. The companies that began the settlements in the 1620s sold them piecemeal to small groups of merchants, from whom Colbert recovered them for the benefit of his new West India Company. In the seventies the company, its bankruptcy completed by the wars with the Dutch, was replaced by the system of rule by colonial governors, varying in their power and their relations with the planters.

Both English and Dutch activities in North America showed the limits that were imposed on economic enterprise by home politics. For Holland, America seemed in the middle of the century to have provided the single exception to their triumphs. The West India Company, set up in 1621 on much the same lines as the eastern one, never produced comparable profits. It assumed from the outset that success would come easily from plundering and eventually capturing the trade and possessions of Spain and Portugal. But episodes like the capture of the silver fleet in 1628 could not compensate for the slow and costly effort to drive the Portuguese out of Brazil. In 1654 the Dutch had to abandon the colonising effort which the Amsterdam merchants had decided was no longer worth supporting. It was only after this failure that they began to build up a purely economic predominance in the West Indies. From the small base at Curaçao they were able to sell to the Spaniards slaves from African ports they had seized from Portugal. Religious objections to slavery were quickly overcome as profits rose: after all, the slaves might be taught the virtues of Christianity. The English were slower to establish themselves in the Caribbean. Peace with Spain, established under James I, and the example made of Raleigh, discouraged piracy: much of the English trade with Spanish possessions was now conducted legally through Cadiz. London merchants were staking out claims in the 1620s, when Charles I made the Earl of Carlisle 'Lord Proprietor of the Carribees'. But it was only after the Cromwellian conquest of Jamaica that the West Indies became a major enterprise, supplied with slaves by the Royal African Company. Relations between the company and the planters were always bad, the company complaining that their fellow-countrymen did not pay as well as the Spaniards and the planters denouncing it as an inefficient court-sponsored monopoly. In spite of the efforts, towards the end of the century, to establish the rule of law in the area, none of the companies seems to have done as well as the international pirates.

The North American colonies were still in 1700 of very minor economic interest to European powers. In 1674 the States General were happy, in return for acceptance of their claim to Surinam, to hand over New Amsterdam to English possession. (Charles II had granted the task of occupying the area to his brother James, Duke of York, whose later misfortunes made the name New York an unhappy choice.) English colonies on the Atlantic coast had come through their first difficulties. The failure of the Virginia Company had shown that the colonising of northern lands was not a source of the quick profits that investors demanded. But the 'Pilgrim Fathers' found that the mixture of economic enterprise with flight from religious oppression was a good formula for survival in unpromising conditions. Two English ventures, the Providence Island Company and the Massachusetts Bay Company, had a strong connection with opponents of the Stuart régime. The Massachusetts charter was granted in 1629 at a moment when the incentive for puritan emigration was at its greatest. The colony claimed something like 4,000 settlers in its first five years and 40,000 by 1660. They were naturally not the most eager of men to agree on a political organisation; but between them the small English companies had established their control over most of the eastern seaboard by the time the stream of assorted European refugees began to arrive in the eighties and nineties. They had also become involved in the first of the disputes that were to explode in the next century over the relations between colonial assemblies and the English Crown and Parliament.

The state and the economy

There was a world of difference between the attitude of western governments to their tropical colonies and traders, who were expected to be a source of wealth for the home country, and that towards the North American settlements most of which were at best a reluctant and impoverished market for home produce. Behind the quarrels that developed lay the whole question of the rôle of the state in economic activity. It was generally agreed that one of the functions of central government was to encourage trade and industry. How this should be done was another matter. The simplest process was collaboration between a government and a few of its favoured subjects to produce an industrial or commercial monopoly. It could be a means of using the power of the state to encourage investment and enterprise while taking its share of the profits; but it also became—as the English opposition insisted— a device of the courtiers and the office-holders to extract money for themselves and the Treasury.[1] Everywhere monarchs and ministers included among the achievements for which they took credit a rather monotonous list of services to the cause of economic superiority. From Henry IV, and his theorist of state enterprise Barthelmy Laffemas, to Peter the Great, the process of using the power of the Crown to establish manufactures, improve transport and agriculture, capture markets, and bring bullion into the country has much the same character.[2] Prosperity was sought for its own sake, and as a direct demonstration of national greatness; but it was sought also as a means of strengthening the state for war. With dismal regularity war became the main purpose, and its cost and destruction absorbed the material gains.

Two of the rulers whose sponsoring of economic expansion had the greatest difficulties to overcome and the most emphatic results were in the east. In Brandenburg after the worst of the Thirty Years War was over, the Great Elector became the first German ruler to use the power of the state on a large scale for economic development. He did not so much help his subjects to achieve prosperity as impose it on them. The agricultural and industrial reforms, the trading companies, the canals and roads, the immigration of skilled foreigners were schemes devised by the state with little positive support either from the aristocracy in general or from the towns. They were inseparable from his struggle for heavier and more widespread taxation, and from his interference, for the benefit of his military power, with the old order of landholding and

[1] See p. 393. [2] See pp. 256, 381.

privilege. There was no serious attempt to plan the use of land or find means of applying to it an economic system that would make the most of its potentialities. The mulberry trees flourished and the African trading company did not; but the state continued to assume—not unreasonably—that any economic development was better than stagnation. The main test of success was whether the land would eventually support more men.[1]

Even the Great Elector's experiments were more realistic than much of the state-created economic progress that Peter the Great imposed on Russia. The tsar's celebrated imitation of western methods was largely a matter of technical detail: his real assumption was that the free capital and enterprise of Holland or England could be dispensed with in a state that could supply conscript labour, own materials and equipment, and coerce merchants into undertaking the tasks it required. The aim generally was to transfer state-established factories to private possession—and punish the owners if they were not successful. The endless regulations governing economic life were often made without much regard to what was feasible. When foreign cloth was believed to be preferred because it was wider, the state decreed that Russian weavers must make it wider too, without suggesting how they would acquire and house new looms. The foreign traders and technicians Peter attracted in his early years were to be replaced by Russians, competent or not. (The fact that many foreigners evaded such decrees at least indicated that Russian economy had something to offer them.) In making Russia more a part of the western commercial system and less an area for foreign exploitation, Peter's intervention was certainly effective. His internal measures proved on the whole a small and temporary part of the growth of the war-making service-state.[2]

Colbert

Jean-Baptiste Colbert perhaps appears outstanding in the history of state-sponsored economy more through the status his country achieved than through any unique success of his own. The notion that all Europe imitated a new French economic system known as 'Colbertism' has long been discredited, and with it the picture of Colbert as a benefactor whose good work was destroyed by a quest for 'glory' of which he disapproved. More money, he said 'would increase the power, the greatness, and the affluence of the state'. It was in that order that most statesmen would have put the aims of their governments in increasing

[1] See pp. 304–7.   [2] See p. 381.

the initiative and control they applied to economic affairs. How far the state's intervention succeeded is another matter. Colbert himself was distressed by the stagnation of France compared with the Netherlands. To combat it he was prepared to use every possible variety of state assistance to industry. The establishments formed of local groups of small craftsmen, like the hosiers of Troyes, were given the status of *manufactures royales* with protection from home and foreign competition. State capital was put into large-scale enterprises: van Robais at Abbeville got subsidies for his great textile factory in return for close state supervision. In some industries—especially those involved in army and naval supplies—outright nationalisation was the favoured method. The successful entrepreneur was as much the state's servant as was the intendant or the captain of horse; and though it was seldom easy to persuade the nobility to involve themselves in industry, it was made clear that one way to royal favour was to invest in state enterprises. Ambitious industrialists were from time to time ennobled.

There were many forms of state intervention. One was simply to make the worker work harder. Colbert's ideal workshop was a place of quasi-military discipline, where idleness and inefficiency were punished. It was not only Protestantism that could bring religion into the service of productivity: the workers of Paris and Lyons found their festival days reduced, and religious observances introduced into the workshop itself as an antidote to idleness. An occasional royal visit to great new industries was held to be a valuable encouragement. It was part of the state's concern to raise the quality of French produce—not simply by taking over the traditional guild regulation of standards in craftsmanship, but by emulating the most sought-after specialities of other countries. Every technician or craftsman won from abroad was a minor victory. The Academy was expected to apply scientific skill to the invention of new industrial processes. The improvement of inland communications —with the Languedoc Canal as the great showpiece—was a form of assistance for which provincial governments had to pay their share. Colbert managed it all like any other process of government. Lists of industries and their products were assembled, scrutinised, compared. Regulations and edicts poured steadily through the machinery of royal government. In 1670 two outstanding merchants, Savary and Bellinzani, were put at the head of a new campaign to bring every individual town and village under the care of a *commis* who would supervise existing organisations or impose new ones. To those involved it meant the constant presence of the malevolent but usually corruptible inspector.

Every stage of manufacture and marketing was supposed to be controlled. Inferior articles would be destroyed, and those responsible could find themselves in the pillory. It seems to have surprised Colbert that his orders were evaded. Masters continued to make the goods that brought them the best profits rather than those they were told should be exported; workers monotonously earned one of his most damning terms of reproof—'idle'.

There was no doubt that by his own practical tests Colbert's activities seemed to have some success. Output did increase; French products acquired a reputation for the highest quality and most fashionable style; real wages of the skilled worker were, by comparison with other western countries, high. Some of the success could be attributed to a decade of good harvests that kept food prices low; some to the fact he refused to recognise—that world demand was increasing. Colbert's theories of foreign trade, familiar enough in themselves but asserted with new dogmatic confidence, were, on the surface, nonsense. After a century and a half in which new overseas markets were being constantly developed, he could claim that the total amount of trade was fixed. After the immense changes produced by South American silver, he could say the same about the amount of bullion. But these were truths in a religious rather then a scientific sense: they showed the way to salvation. French commerce could expand only at the expense of the Dutch and to a lesser extent of the English. There was, in spite of the growth of devices like the Bill of Exchange, an apparent shortage of bullion in France and no means of acquiring it except by trade. Asia was absorbing more than before, Spain supplying less. Bullion was the only form of wealth the government could use for most of its purposes, and Colbert was well aware that everything depended on its circulation. Only money that found its way into the hands of tax-paying classes would return to the Treasury. That some of it was also invested in commercial and industrial enterprise was more important, even for his own purposes, than Colbert saw. His object was, more and more, to defeat the national enemies—which to him meant the Dutch above all. Tariffs directed against them, which began in 1664 as a comparatively small part of his industrial policy, quickly turned into commercial war. In 1667 duties on textiles were doubled, and on some other manufactures increased still more.

Colbert's tariffs did not in their extreme form last long: the Dutch after their success in the war made reduced tariffs one of the first conditions of peace. But they had brought France into the struggle for world trade which England had long been fighting. The damage inflicted on the Netherlands at this stage by their two rivals seems to have been much less severe than used to be supposed.[1] European trade was still, in 1700, overwhelmingly a Dutch affair. The English Navigation Act of 1651 was nevertheless outstandingly important in the state's relations with economic activity. A group of the City merchants most hostile to Dutch control of overseas commerce was able to manoeuvre the Rump Parliament, unsure of its own survival, into passing the law that prohibited imports in foreign ships or through a foreign country other than the one where they originated. It was too sudden and sweeping a measure to be fully enforceable in the conditions of the time; and it was only one of the sources of the quarrels that led to the outbreak of war between the two republics. In the successive renewals of the act after the Restoration there was better enforcement but more exceptions. Yet to England it marked a new attitude to trade. In place of the 'bullionist' idea that all export of precious metals, and therefore all avoidable imports, must be minimised—if necessary by state action—the emphasis shifted to the use of colonies as a cheap and unharmful source of raw materials and as a growing market. As the name of the acts suggested, their immediate object was to increase the number and activity of English merchant ships; and in this they appeared to have great success. The quantity and prestige of shipping was one of the most visible ways in which state power and private wealth went hand in hand. It was one of the clearest applications of 'mercantilism'.

Mercantilism

Ever since the term was applied by Adam Smith to what he regarded as the evil seventeenth-century system, it has been commonly accepted that the economy of western states was 'mercantilist'. But the meaning of the word is elusive. The most celebrated contemporary account of such ideas came from the English merchant Thomas Mun, whose 'discourse' *England's Treasure by Foreign Trade* was written when he was a member of the commission set up by James I in 1622 to investigate the trade depression, but only published after the Restoration. It was already a commonplace that the loss of coin and bullion was the root of the state's economic troubles. Mun's objection was that remedies which concentrated on reducing the amount of coin paid out obscured the simple first necessity: 'we must ever observe this rule; to sell more to strangers yearly than we consume of theirs in value'. Bullion was only a

[1] C. H. Wilson, 'The Economic Decline of the Netherlands' in *Essays in Economic History*, ed. Carus-Wilson, vol. 1, pp. 254–69.

means whereby the economic activity of the country could be increased. Though Mun did not stress the idea of a fixed amount of world trade that had to be fought for, he certainly assumed that 'strangers' were rivals and that to increase English wealth at their expense entailed the intervention of the state. One source of confusion is that mercantilism has sometimes been regarded as a system that put the profit of merchants before the good of the state, and sometimes as the reverse of this. The usual assumption was that the two were inseparable. The merchant needed state support—in the privileges granted and upheld by the sovereign, in the treaties, the threats, the convoys with which foreign interference was restricted, and from time to time in war itself. Mercantilists, though they expected monarchs to behave frugally and find their own sources of treasure, seldom condemned expenditure on war as such. It was the willingness of Colbert and the other statesmen who devoted themselves to economic expansion to see their schemes used and destroyed in war that led to the description of mercantilism as 'a system for forcing economic policy into the service of power as an end in itself'.[1] But it might reasonably be claimed that only the powerful state could give security to the prosperous and work to the poor. The great failure was that while the balance of trade was carefully calculated no-one measured the cost of war against the benefits it was believed to bring.

In the later part of the century the 'bullionist' element in mercantilist theory was giving way to what looked on the surface a more enlightened view of economic policy. The Austrian manufacturer Johan Becher, whose *Politiche Discurs* was published in 1668, was one of the first writers to regard employment, and the maintenance of the level of population, as more significant tests of success than the accumulation of gold. But it was not the humanitarian aspects of the argument that interested Becher. He was one of the originators of the economic aspect of 'cameralism'.[2] The power of the state would be best enhanced by a prosperous, and a thoroughly organised, people. One of his immediate themes was the contrast between the backwardness of Habsburg territories and the success of the Netherlands. He did not emphasise the fact that the Dutch believed in a state that supported economic activity but did not interfere with it. Though Dutch wars were fought for commercial benefits as much as for territorial defence, the normal course of trade was expected to continue as far as possible without regard to

[1] E. F. Hecksher, *Mercantilism*, vol. 2, p. 17. For the controversies on the whole subject, see *Revisions in Mercantilism*, ed. D. C. Coleman (London, 1969).
[2] See p. 195.

diplomatic or military hostilities. In the Netherlands at least, the strong state was the means and prosperity the end.

Depression and recovery

Mercantilist ideas owed much of their success to the belief that one country could only expand its trade, and hence its general prosperity, at the expense of others. All the evidence seemed to show that left to itself trade stagnated or declined. Complaints of economic decay, often supported by memories of more land under the plough, more looms, more ships a generation or two earlier, came from almost every part of Europe. The impressions of contemporaries can now be tested by measurements that are improving rapidly both in the amount of raw statistical material that has been compiled and in the techniques of using it. But at present the more sophisticated our quantitive studies become the harder it seems to be to arrive at any general conclusions. Nevertheless, some agreed points have emerged. The seventeenth century and the first part of the eighteenth can be seen as a period of fluctuation— and on the whole of slow decline—between the phases of expansion in the sixteenth century and in the industrial revolution. The clearest indication of this comes from the many graphs of price-changes that can now be drawn for a great variety of commodities and places. It has to be remembered that prices can only be measured in terms of some other variable, such as gold, silver, or the local money of account. But despite the complications there is no doubt that the general rise ceased and that there were then some violent ups and downs within a slowly falling average. It is agreed too that, whatever the reason, 'trade and prices move in broad unison'.[1] This is not the same as saying that prices are a safe guide to the level of economic activity as a whole; but in their general character the graphs that can be drawn for local output of commodities such as grain, cloth, and metals give the same impression of sharp fluctuations— some for evident special reasons—but seldom of lasting improvement.

Great efforts have been made to detect within the 'secular' trend a variety of shorter cycles. Trade figures sometimes seem to show cycles of between six and eight years; an old-established theory that is still debated is the existence of an agricultural cycle related to sunspot activity; a fifty-year rise and fall is another that has been studied in elaborate detail. Some of the calculations that try to correlate a number of such claims in explaining an apparently irregular set of figures may

[1] F. P. Brandel and F. Spooner in *Cambridge Economic History of Europe*, vol. 4, p. 454.

seem to the unconvinced to have a suspicious resemblance to football-pool predictions, and their nomenclature can come close to the ludicrous. Even so, it is possible to arrive at some tentative conclusions on the sequence of seventeenth-century changes. The varied signs of depression appeared at different times during the first quarter of the century. Spain, with plague in 1599 and 1600 followed by the expulsion of the Moriscoes and the decline in imports of silver, was one of the first places to suffer.[1] In England the general rise in prices was halted by 1614. Then Cockayne's Project[2] proved a sudden blow to the textile trade, and the early twenties were still years of stagnation and uncertainty. But English trade thereafter recovered a good deal of its prosperity and the rise in prices was resumed. For France, where the early depression had been less sudden, the 1630s produced a mixture of further decline, such as that of the eastern trade, with some signs of recovery. Here, as in many other places, there was a great difference between the fate of the merchant and that of the peasant or the poor townsman. Shortage of good currency combined with fluctuating prices and high taxation to produce a feeling of growing poverty. In Germany debasement of currency in the early stages of the Thirty Years War—the *Kipper- und Wipperzeit*—helped to make the twenties a time of depression. Italy had its critical years between 1619 and 1622, in the north especially. For Poland it was not until well into the thirties that the collapse of agricultural prosperity became decisive.

Even in the places that had in one way or another experienced some improvement, the middle decades of the century were a time of economic as well as political troubles. For this period it is possible to show evidence that does suggest in many different parts of Europe a regular short-term cycle, with high prices around 1643, 1649 (a year of famine and of revolt), and 1653. The 1660s seem, in the west at least, to have been another period of recovery. But by about 1670 there were again signs of a severe shortage of currency—a situation that continued to the end of the century. In the nineties, though some states had been highly successful in building up commerce, for the mass of the population scarcity of food, unemployment, and high taxation were the main facts of economic life. Neither statistics nor contemporary evidence make it possible to generalise confidently about the human impact of the fluctuations. There were times no doubt when a fall in the prices of food brought some relief to the urban worker. In England real wages probably showed a slight average rise. But for most Europeans erratic price-

[1] See p. 335.   [2] See p. 394.

movements were no better than general inflation. With the state, the landlord, and the employer all tending to increase their demands for money, the ordinary man had good reason to feel that he bore the brunt of the losses without sharing in the gains.

The modern view of the seventeenth century as a period of economic misfortune and uncertainty is not totally incompatible with the claim that this was the time when feudal society was giving way to an expanding capitalism. But on this too the more our information becomes exact, the less convincing any simple pattern appears to be. For western Europe the whole period has often been labelled, in Marx's phrase, as that of 'primary accumulation', when the capital that was to make possible the industrial revolution of the next century was acquired by an enterprising bourgeoisie. This was 'the adolescence of capitalist industry'[1]—an adolescence that had its most disturbed moment in the mid-century revolutions. Exactly how a change of purpose and outlook was related to the measurable facts of production, exchange, and consumption is not easily demonstrated. 'Capital accumulation' is a notion that puts together a number of different and imponderable processes— the acquisition of land by men who used it to produce a surplus of real wealth, the lending of money to governments who were expected to repay it out of revenue, the development of banking and credit systems, and so on. One specific claim is that the price-rise of the sixteenth century, by keeping real wages low, helped to provide the surplus that was now put into mining, industry, and trade.[2] But too many other factors are involved for any simple connection between wage and price movements and long-term economic developments to be proved. In the present state of economic history the general seventeenth-century picture has to be one of contradictions and doubts. Trends were no surer at the end than at the beginning. Holland was slowly losing its lead—and its failure to become a great industrial state has been blamed on the effect of the commercial boom in preventing investment in new developments. It is as hard to balance the successes of French commerce against the wartime impoverishment as it is to say what importance could in the long run be attached to the artificial stimulus provided in Russia or Prussia. Yet amid all the waste and destruction of resources, all the hunger and failure and brutality, conditions were developing in which the new age of industrial expansion could emerge.

[1] M. Dobb, *Studies in the Development of Capitalism* (London, 1946), p. 209.
[2] For a critical discussion of this see the essay by J. U. Nef in E. M. Carus-Wilson (ed.), *Essays in Economic History*, vol. I, p. 88.

IV

Society

Social history can claim to be developing at present more rapidly than any other aspect of the subject. Recent work on it is naturally more prolific for some countries—notably France—than for others; and the advances certainly do not cover every part of the field. The questions that are being answered most successfully are those that lend themselves to quantitative methods. It is possible, for the seventeenth century, to

BIBLIOGRAPHY. A comprehensive introduction to the social history of Europe in the early modern period is one of the unwritten and much-needed works. The short but wide-ranging chapter by Sir George Clark, 'The Social Foundations of States' in the *New Cambridge Modern History*, vol. 5 (Cambridge, 1961) is an indication of what could be done. At the other extreme are the large-scale regional studies of demographic and social history in France. P. Goubert, *Beauvais et les Beauvaisais, 1600–1730* (Paris, 1960) is established as the leading example. Some of its conclusions are summarised in his article, 'The French Peasantry of the Seventeenth Century: a regional example' in *Past and Present*, no. 10 (1960). The outstanding study of the peasants is E. Le Roy Ladurie, *Les paysans de Languedoc* (2 vols., Paris, 1966). Other works on French society include R. Mandrou, *Classes et luttes de classes en France au début du XVIIe siècle* (Florence, 1965); P. Sagnac, *La formation de la société française moderne*, vol. 1 (Paris, 1945); G. Montgrédien, *La vie quotidienne sous Louis XIV* (Paris, 1948). *XVIIe Siècle*, nos. 25–26 (1955) has a group of articles by R. Mousnier and others under the title *Comment les français voyaient la France au XVIIe siècle*.

The most successful recent work on English society, despite the doubts raised by some of its statistics, is L. Stone, *The Crisis of the Aristocracy* (Oxford, 1965). His article on 'Social Mobility in England' in *Past and Present*, no. 33 (1966), and the accompanying one by A. Everitt, make use of a variety of detailed studies to produce 'a model that might be applicable to any European society' in the period. Everitt's book *The Community of Kent and the Great Rebellion* (Leicester, 1966) is one of the best products of the new approach to local history. W. T. MacCaffrey, *Exeter 1540–1640* (Cambridge, Mass., 1958) is among the recent work on urban communities. Mildred Campbell, *The English Yeoman* (New Haven, 1942) and G. E. Fussell, *The English Rural Labourer* (London, 1949) have a good deal of seventeenth-century material.

arrive at detailed estimates of the numbers—in any manageable geographical area—of clergy, or lawyers, or titled nobility. We can study arithmetically the changes in their incomes, in the size of their families, in their expectation of life, and a dozen similarly definable topics. We can discuss, on a solid if incomplete numerical basis, the economic 'rise' or 'decline' of particular groups and the mobility of individuals between them, or migration between town and country, or the consequences of differing laws and customs of inheritance. Progress is far less easy in understanding collective attitudes—to governments, or to churches, or to wars—and the origins of changes in accepted behaviour. The terminology and methods of the sociologist are still distrusted by the historian. Obviously some kinds of material for social history are likely to come mainly from the literate and the leisured. It is not, for this period, an insuperable obstacle. Legal depositions, sermons, the massive reports of official enquiries, the complaints of petitioners and pamphleteers can all, when their motives and circumstances are taken into account, provide abundant information.

For the social historian one advantage of the seventeenth century is that the main categories into which the population was divided were still comparatively few and simple. It was often easier and more relevant to define a man's social group than to define his nationality. The English gentleman travelling in Italy or the French *seigneur* in western Germany might make the alleged national characteristics of his hosts the subject of a stock joke or a neat turn of phrase; but little in his way of life was essentially different from that of his equals abroad. Costume, retinue, and manner made apparent a man's 'degree' and assured him of the respect that was his due. At home they would indicate his relationship to the state and to the community. The individual was part of a triangle of service and protection. One side of this was the link between master and man, landlord and tenant; the other two sides were formed by the state's connection with each of these. The notion that all subjects should be equal in their relationship with the state seemed an odd philosophical concept remote from reality. Everyone had his duty to the state; everyone received benefits from it; but they were entirely different according to his place in the social order. For those most heavily

On serfdom, J. Blum, *Lord and Peasant in Russia* (Princeton, 1961) is the main work in western languages. Articles include G. Vernadsky, 'Serfdom in Russia' in Tenth International Congress of Historical Sciences Relazione, vol. 3 (Florence, 1955) and D. Odinetz, 'Les origines du servage en Russie' in *Revue historique de droit français et étranger*, 4th ser., vol. 10 (1931).

dependent on their superiors, the direct bond with state authority could almost cease to exist, since their duties and—such as they were—rights were held to be exercised through the man they served. The extreme instance of this was the serf.

Peasant and serf in Russia

The extension of serfdom is the most conspicuous social change of the century. It is a change that can be made to appear far too simple and dramatic. Sometimes it is suggested that a line can be drawn dividing Europe into an eastern part where, by the second half of the century, the peasants had been reduced to serfdom and abysmal poverty, and a western part where they were free and comparatively prosperous. The differences were a good deal more complex than that. Serfdom meant the lack of freedom to move—but without the total subjection to a master that constituted slavery. It was normally accompanied by a mass of other burdens. Labour dues might be increased almost without limit; the jurisdiction of the lord could become more or less complete; every aspect of the peasant's life—marriage, children, inheritance, death—could be used by the lord as an opportunity for new exactions. But all these misfortunes could exist without serfdom. The serf who had a fair prospect of illegally running away and eluding recapture was often in a less hopeless plight than the free peasant who was in practice bound to his lord by debt or by the sheer lack of any alternative short of vagabondage. In Spain and Italy many villagers were materially no better off than in Russia. Even in Denmark and Switzerland life for the peasant became worse no less decisively than in the east. Life was hard for those who found themselves tied to the land; it was hard too for those who, like some Swedish and Irish peasants, found that after generations of security they could be evicted without warning.

The fate of the Russian peasant showed more clearly than any other how the different interests of the state and the lord produced a condition for their victim that suited them both. The state required, more and more, taxes and service. Ivan IV, in his effort to cut through the tangle of land tenure and obligation and to break the power of the Boyars and the church, had created his fantastic institution of the *Oprichnina*. This was the tsar's personal domain, distinct from the *Zemshchina* where the power of the landlords remained unchallenged. The *Oprichniki* were the civil and military servants of the tsar, a privileged section of the community dependent for their status and livelihood entirely on their devotion to him. Whole villages and districts became part of the *Oprichnina* until the country was divided almost equally into a favoured and an unfavoured section, deemed to be allies respectively of the central government and of the independent land-owners. The *oprichnik* was usually able to exploit his peasants more ruthlessly than did his predecessors. But so, increasingly, did all land-lords, especially those of the smaller estates granted by service tenure —the *pomiestia* that had long been growing more common.

The distinction between the *pomiestie*, which in theory was not here-ditary, and the *votchina*, which was, involves formidable confusions between legal terminology and practice. What naturally mattered to the holder was that he should be able to hand on his estate to his heirs, and this in general seems to have become easier for successful families, whatever their theoretical position. What mattered to the state was that the land should be used to provide in the first place soldiers—especially soldiers already bound to the men who commanded them—and secondly civilian servants of the tsar who could maintain his authority, and organise the regular supply of his revenue in money and goods. Not much of the *Oprichnina* idea survived for long after Ivan's death; but in its place there emerged a defined and closed caste of state servants— the *dvoriane*. This is another of the words that confuses through its multiplicity of meanings; but it was applied by the middle of the century to the holders of land by military tenure whose status came not from ancient lineage but from their privileged relationship to the state.[1] The next stage would naturally be the decline of those sections of propertied society, mainly the older nobility and the high clergy, who were not so firmly attached to the service system.

To the peasant these technicalities were irrelevant. His aim was to escape some of the ever-growing burdens; and there were ways in which this could be done. It was possible to sell oneself into slavery, a condi-tion that could compare favourably with that of the ordinary villager. The voluntary slave might be in a strong bargaining position. As a man without property he could not be taxed; nor could the army seize him without violating the rights of his owner. The status of a slave varied enormously. Permanent bonded slaves were usually household servants; but the voluntary *kabala* slaves might be in bondage only for a year as a way of repaying a debt, or might thrive as craftsmen or even traders.

---

[1] The *dvorianie* of Moscow had a markedly higher status and a larger allocation of land than the rest. For short definitions of many of these terms, see *Readings in Russian Civilisation*, vol. I, ed. T. Riha (Chicago and London, 1964), pp. 174–5.

A succession of laws put obstacles in the way of slavery, and with unnoticed paradox compelled the unfree to return to freedom—or quarterfreedom. A much commoner way for the peasant to escape his troubles was simply to run away. The movement of peasants—to the north, to the newly colonised areas in the east, and most of all to the Ukraine (a word meaning 'borderland')—had been growing in the sixteenth century. By the early seventeenth the depopulation of the central area of Muscovy became disastrous. It was a process that developed its own momentum. When peasants left an estate, the *barshchina*—the labour service on the lord's land—was increased for those who remained. Two or three days' work a week became common. Taxation, and the erratic burden of conscription, were shared among the community and became heavier for those who remained. The lord's own standard of living was reduced when he had to use his household slaves in the fields, and often let land go out of cultivation altogether. From Ivan IV's time particular years—more and more of them—were proclaimed as 'forbidden years' in which no such departures were allowed. After about 1610 hardly any years were not 'forbidden'. The peasants still disappeared.

In the first three years of the seventeenth century the harvest over most of European Russia was bad. Hoarding by landlords and speculators, and the spread of disease, completed the ruin. Village communities broke down completely. Men left their homes no longer always in the hope of finding new ones but to join the nomadic groups that plundered and killed to survive. Whether the disasters of this period or the slowly growing pressure on the peasants contributed more to the depopulation can be disputed.[1] It can even be argued that 'nomadism' had always been common and that the losses of population were exaggerated to avoid taxation. What is certain is that even when economic prosperity and political stability returned in the 1620s to a level no worse than usual, and deserted lands began to be repopulated, the problem of labour shortage remained. The wealth of a landowner was reckoned by the number of 'souls' on his estates rather than by their money value. It was more important that control of men should be secure and hereditary than that all the land should remain in the family. With or without legal sanction, every effort was made to deprive the peasant of all his mobility and of all restriction on the burdens he had to bear. The chaotic legal code of 1649,[2] a convenient point from which to date the full imposition of serfdom, contained no new principle. But it brought

[1] J. Blum, *Lord and Peasant in Russia* (Princeton, 1964 ed.), pp. 153–65.
[2] See pp. 376–7.

together and extended the provisions for dealing with the runaway peasant. There was no longer to be any time limit after which it was illegal to recapture him. A lord who employed fugitives therefore took the risk of losing them if someone else could claim them back, and as a sort of interest on his capital the claimant could have them with their children and the families of their children. Serfs could be transferred without restriction from one estate to another, except that the state protected its own interests by forbidding their removal from land held on one type of tenure to land held on another. To these demonstrations of the serf's status as movable property were added several colourful touches, such as the rule that if he murdered the serf of another lord he was not to be hanged but, after the routine flogging, handed over to replace his victim—unless he was no longer in good condition. In that case a better substitute could be claimed.

There naturally remained a good many gaps between legislation and practice. But in the decades after 1649 serfdom as an almost universal system was gradually established, until under Peter the Great perhaps nine-tenths of the working population were serfs, or in one of the enormous variety of categories on the fringes of serfdom. So far as documents made any difference, the peasant might be affected less by the law than by the contract he or his forebears made with his lord. This no longer laid down any limit to the amount of work he was to do on the lord's land, or to the size of his own holding; but it might promise a plot of land of some sort. Often it would appear to bind the serf to the lord personally even if legally he was bound to the land. One consequence of the combination of servitude, insecurity, and new forms of tenure was the decline of the *mir*, the village community, and its organised form, the *volost*. To many peasants the village had been as much a part of their individual existence as the family. Their misfortunes, the land allotted for their own livelihood, their burdens of tax and service were shared with the rest of the village. Its customs were not to be broken; its leaders and its collective decisions were accepted readily. Now, slowly, the power of the *mir* receded. Even so, devotion to village traditions still offered a shred of protection. If no natural disaster or outside enemy upset completely the routine of the estate, the lord who tried to make sudden and drastic changes for the worse in the life of his peasants was quite likely to face the risk of local rebellion. He could not count on much effective help from the state in suppressing it.

Peasant and serf in central Europe

The empty lands of Russia were not the only origin of the 'second serfdom': it was almost as widespread in many parts of the Habsburg Empire and of Poland. In northern and eastern Germany the tightening of the landlords' powers had been going on since the fifteenth century. What now looked like new developments were often the legal ratification of earlier piecemeal changes. The demand in the west for imported corn[1] made demesne farming profitable at a time when here too there were not enough peasants to supply all the labour that could be used. By turning some tenants off the land to increase the demesne and imposing new labour services on those who remained, landowners in the great corn-producing areas started the same process as in Russia of more migrations and greater measures to stop them. In Brandenburg there was legislation against the runaway peasant as early as 1518. A century later the Estates of Pomerania resolved that all peasants were bound to the land but liable to be evicted from it at the will of their lord. They could be made to do unlimited labour on his lands, and they had no rights of inheritance. It proved a matter of bitter political dispute.[2] Towns not involved in the export trade suffered from the impoverishment of peasants and the loss of rural markets. At least one great city—Königsberg—resisted serfdom and refused to allow runaway peasants within its jurisdiction to be recaptured. In Saxony peasant obligations remained for the most part limited by law. Generally a free and prosperous peasantry was in the interests of German rulers, who (since landowners were exempt from most forms of taxation) relied on the tenant for their revenue. During and after the Thirty Years War the movement of peasants increased. Many went into the devastated regions where the demand for labour was highest and land abundant. Others fled from persecution: Austrian and Bohemian Protestants were found in Saxony and even in East Prussia. But the Catholic south was on the whole an area more free from serfdom. With a smaller market for their produce, the landlords had little of the enthusiasm shown by the Junkers for profitable exploitation.

Even in the countries where serfdom was most rigidly and widely enforced, the 'free peasant' was a fairly familiar figure. The Russian 'Black Lands', though grants by tsars and robbery by magnates had reduced their size, still maintained peasants whose only allegiance was

[1] See p. 52.
[2] F. L. Carsten, *The Origins of Prussia* (Oxford, 1964), chap. 11.

to the Crown or the state and who had few of the agrarian burdens of the landlords' serfs. Since they were drawn on heavily for military service they were often in practice no less restricted than those on seignorial lands. Peter the Great's efforts to increase the number of 'state' or 'treasury' peasants was certainly not a move towards the alleviation of misery. Nevertheless there were the few among them who found it possible to increase their holdings, to bring others into their subjection through keeping them in their debt, and to buy their way out of most of their obligations. Prussia had a far more flourishing class of free peasants, the *Cölmer*, who not only remained exempt from compulsory labour but often became large farmers not far removed in the size of their holdings and their way of life from the smallest of the nobility. Even in the most firmly ordered rural society, there was always some possibility of rising a little above the economic level of the majority; and once money began to accumulate it could usually be the means of an advance in social status.

The western peasant

Great though the differences in the east were, the vast majority of peasants there experienced the same tightening of obligations and reduction of the prospects of material improvement. In the west not even such hazy generalisations as these can be made. There was little in common between the thriving yeoman of the English midlands and the half-starved Neapolitan or Castilian struggling to live on what landlord and tax-collector left him from the produce of a patch of stony earth. Differences within the same country and the same region were often almost as great. The more intensively the French peasantry in particular have been examined, the more meaningless any broad categories, whether legal or economic, have proved. In times of general famine or man-made disaster it was generally easier in western than in eastern Europe for some families to prosper at the expense of the rest: possibly the most important of all lines of division was between those with enough reserves to enable them to profit by general scarcity and the majority who faced the threat of hunger, debt, eviction, and vagabondage. In times of abundance a little capital and the accidents of temperament and family circumstance could be decisive in distinguishing those able to profit by their surplus from those who found low market prices ruinous. Both upward and downward movements were on the whole greater in the more advanced economies.

The French peasant was intensely aware of his social status. The *laboureur*—a term dangerously easy to mistranslate into English and originally meaning 'ploughman'—was as conscious of his superiority as any inheritor or purchaser of title or office. His status depended a good deal on local usage. In the Beauvais region he was 'almost by definition a man who owned a plough and a pair of horses';[1] in Poitou he could be poorer; in Burgundy the term covered a wide range of prosperity. In the course of the century the number of *laboureurs* fell: their disappearance was one of the signs of depression repeatedly noted by the officials of Louis XIV. The fortunate few might build up their holdings at the expense of the rest and join the exalted circle of the *fermiers*, owning land or holding it on long leases, employing wage-labourers (*journaliers*), lending out money, and sometimes terrorising the villagers more ruthlessly than did the *seigneur*. The usual fate of the *laboureur* was to sink to the level of the *manœuvrier*. This was the ordinary term for the majority who held by *métayage*—the system in which the landlord owned land, stock, seed, and farm implements and took a fixed share, usually half, of the produce—or by one of the many other varieties of heavily burdened tenure. Usually the holding was barely adequate to feed their families, even in years of plenty and even on the poorest diet of rye-bread and pease. The *seigneur*, besides his claim to a third or a half of their corn-crop, commonly exercised an assortment of rights such as his monopoly of mills or wine-presses. Taxes and tithes seemed to remove nearly everything that was left. In practice their standard of life varied greatly. The comparatively fortunate were those living in a district of the *pays d'état* that escaped the heaviest forms of taxation; or those in areas of thriving rural industry whose families could pick up a fairly regular money wage; or even those for whom a pig, a cow, or the cultivation of vines provided a source of money income. It was always the poorest who were hardest hit by unpredictable calamities. Not only famine and the depredation of armies, but a lordly hunting-party, a sudden increase in the demands of the landlord, or simply accumulated debt could bring the moment when they were turned off the land and found such possessions as they had seized by the bailiff. Able-bodied men might resort to the army; for the rest there was nothing left but to drift on to the roads, beg, steal, and die.

It is not obvious that the French peasant in general was more free or prosperous than the eastern serf. The authority of the *seigneur*, to whom even the richest tenants still took solemn oaths of subjection, was in

[1] P. Goubert in *Past and Present*, no. 10 (1956), p. 13.

most areas enormous. Manorial powers of justice could be more limited in theory than in practice. The *corvée seigneuriale* amounting to a few days' unpaid labour in the year was not comparable to the weekly work of the serf; but the difference between devoting half the time to growing the lord's crop and surrendering to him half what was produced on the tenant's holding was not much more than a technicality. In a land that had reached the limit of the population it could support in existing agrarian conditions, the French peasant might often be tied to his soil more effectively than was the Russian who could flee to the frontier areas. A great many were like the *censitaires* in Burgundy, whose condition in 1672 was described simply as 'servitude'. The situation in western Germany was much the same. The free peasant in the north, the *Meier*, sometimes had a heritable tenancy with abundant opportunity to compete with his neighbours for the extension of his lands; sometimes he held only on a year-to-year basis. Since he provided most of the state's revenue from taxation, it was in the interest of governments to support him and to prevent any threat of large-scale evictions. In Bavaria life tenure was common, but the burdens of recruiting and quartering of troops helped the long deterioration of the peasant's economic standards. In Spain, and especially in Castile, conditions had been getting worse ever since the beginning of Philip II's reign; there were accounts of deserted villages, of the few rich peasants exploiting the indebtedness of the majority, of an unceasing drift from the country into the cities.

Most European peasants had reason to envy the English yeoman— a term that could now apply to a wide range of society between gentry and husbandmen. The ordinary leaseholder, secure for three lives or ninety-nine years, was often paying in his entry fine and his rent a good deal less than the current value of the land. He could easily aspire, with energy and luck, to become a substantial freeholder with the not too closely guarded status of 'gentleman'. The number of lords of manors whose ancestors had been on the yeoman level a few generations back was everywhere high. Not much was left of the rough equality between medieval holders of the yardland or virgate in the common fields. But even the copyholder, whose tenure was secured by manorial custom rather than contract, was unlikely to lose it unless a succession of misfortunes brought him to the point where rents went unpaid and debts accumulated. With a burden of taxation that would have seemed negligible to his continental equivalents, he had less cause for complaint than he believed. Nevertheless, for the younger son, for the family dependent on a decaying part of the textile industry, or for the victim of unrelenting increase in rent the outlook could still be grim.

Social mobility

Even in discussing the peasantry, the huge stable mass on which the slender structure of the remainder of society rested, we have repeatedly encountered the question of 'mobility'. (The term has both a geographical sense and an economic one; but since hardly anyone moved from one place to another unless forced by poverty or attracted by prosperity 'social mobility' is often a combination of both.) The problem of comparing mobility in different classes, countries, and periods has in recent decades produced abundant controversy and confusion. It involves both the movement of individuals and families from one group to another and the change in character of the groups themselves. The old clichés about a 'rising middle class' have sometimes been meaningless through lack of definition and because they confused the enrichment of the 'middle class' as a whole with the upward movement of families into and out of it. The questions would be complex enough if they could be answered in measurable economic terms. But social groups are created by opinion. The members of any group above the level of the masses have an interest in concealing the existence of mobility: the newcomer puts up a pretence of antiquity and the old aristocrat insists that the holder of new wealth and title should remain inferior. Three generations, the time deemed necessary to remove the stigma of manual labour, also became the period which the old French aristocracy tried—with little success—to insist that the official and legal families of the robe must wait before they could attain the status of noblesse. The mania for titles was one product of the demand of those who had moved upwards for a demonstration that their position was secure and accepted. When men insisted on the importance of degree, and on the divinely ordained social hierarchy, they appeared to be denying the manifest changes in it. But, however illogically, both the newly-risen and the old-established seem to have been reassured by the pretence that society was immutable.

Mobility was not simply a question of rise or fall within landed society. Certainly no source of prestige could compare with the possession of land: even the mighty Dutch townsmen tended increasingly to acquire country estates when they reached the peak of success. But the way to advance in the hierarchy of the land was often by moving outside it and back again. For a great many, movement was made inescapable by the one problem that affected every landed family from the greatest noble to the poorest peasant: even in a stable or declining population, most of them had more than one son who reached maturity. Where, as in England and Castile, primogeniture was the accepted practice the younger son was often left with no land at all to support him. Where holdings were commonly divided it was obviously necessary that some means of restricting the process should exist. Unless there were unoccupied lands to acquire, the city was the easiest refuge for those who did not inherit. The younger son of the noble or gentleman who became a merchant was not as common a figure as is sometimes supposed; nor did the enterprising peasant son find it easy to make his fortune as a townsman—though the legendary Dick Whittington, unlike the real one, was a seventeenth-century figure.[1] The movement was certainly in two directions: at the lower levels there was the constant drift into the towns by the poor, liable to increase suddenly in times of bad harvests. An outward movement came only when some exceptional situation, such as the desertion of lands in the worst areas of the Thirty Years War, made opportunities in the country greater. Higher up the scale the balance was better, with successful townsmen, new or old, acquiring land for the sake of prestige, of freedom from the many perils of urban life, sometimes of its secure profitability.

For many younger sons it was the occupations on the fringe of landed society that gave a temporary or permanent answer. The church, at any rate in Catholic and Orthodox countries, still in a limited way offered even to the poor the chance of education and admission into its ranks. Its higher posts were naturally the preserve of those whose birth demonstrated their merits. The law had some of the same characteristics: its lower levels, though more sparse than those of the church, gave some opportunities to the literate but unprivileged; its great offices carried impressive rewards. Between them it had what the church lacked—a large middle section comparable in status to the minor gentry and merchants and giving access to a variety of administrative positions that could be the way to riches and authority. Neither of these professions carried the stigma that in most countries was attached by the landowning classes to trade. The notorious attitude of the Spaniards was only a more extravagant and unconcealed version of a contempt stimulated by envy that was not unknown even in England.

Most of the means of survival or advancement outside landed society depended on the patronage of superiors. The apprentice and the great

[1] L. Stone in *Past and Present*, no. 33 (1966), p. 22.

minister were alike in having a master whose favour they had to win and retain—even though of the two the apprentice was more secure. The one virtue in the devotion of great men to ostentatious households and retinues was that they provided at every level the chance of getting into a highly competitive way of life in which the pageboy might some-day become the Duke of Buckingham. The expansion both of government service and of royal courts added to the number of openings for advancement. Crown office was no longer mainly a prize for the few at the top: one of the greatest sources of opportunity was the multiplication of minor local offices, with patronage often in practice divided between the great men of the region and the central government.[1] The expansion of armies gave another opening. Military service could be a ruinous burden for some: for others it provided a livelihood in which, though the barriers between upper and lower ranks were almost insurmountable, there were many ways of achieving prosperity. Yet when all the methods of earning and advancement are put together, there must have been many, high and low, for whom mobility was decisively downward. What in general became of the younger sons who lacked all the escape-routes, and of the families who were the victims of the more successful? Men of title or good connection could often live in debt for a great many years; but the tenant or labourer who bore a distinguished name and could claim a distant relationship with its prosperous holders was a common witness to the misfortunes that were justly feared.

In England the early part of the seventeenth century has become firmly linked with the later sixteenth as an age of change in landed society. There is little doubt about the comparatively frequent transfers of land ownership. The sale of monastic lands had been followed by repeated alienations of Crown property. Rising prices had helped to ruin the improvident or unlucky and to give others the capital to buy up their estates. The merchant, who was as ready as in most other countries to put his gains into land, had seldom much difficulty in finding it. Tawney's phrase the 'rise of the gentry' has produced a controversy so widely reported and so much over-simplified in its later stages as to bring the whole subject into undeserved disrepute.[2] There is nothing surprising

---

[1] See pp. 201–3.

[2] One of the best discussions of it is the correspondence in *Encounter*, vol. 10 (1958) which followed the publication in no. 5 of the article 'Storm over the Gentry' by J. H. Hexter, since reprinted in his *Reappraisals in History* (London, 1960).

in the fact that the rise of some families was accompanied by the decline of others of much the same kind. An important question is whether there were distinctively new forms of the exploitation of land that were characteristic of new owners and that could, with ordinary skill and luck, bring them appreciably greater wealth. Certainly there were many ways in which the yield of the land for its owners was being raised—enclosing commons and woods, charging economic rents when the opportunity arose, encouraging technical improvements, and so on. It remains difficult to show that these were adopted by any identifiable group of landowners and neglected by another. Nor is it apparent that the income from land alone normally left the provident member of the gentry richer at the end of his career than at the beginning. The hazards and opportunities of inheritance, marriage, litigation, and the quest for prestige were too great and variable for statistical conclusions about economic trends among the gentry collectively to be helpful. What is beyond doubt is that men in the fairly wide range from the great county families to the lord of a single manor were now extremely important figures in both local and central affairs. Within the group there was a high rate of upward and downward movement; as a whole it remained one of the most stable sections of European society. Its success was a demonstration of the benefits that could come from avoiding social isolation. Hardly anywhere else was so little stigma attached to marriage-links between landed and commercial families; hardly anywhere was the legal profession so closely involved with a landed class. The gentry who were directly concerned with overseas commerce were no doubt a small minority; so were those who had the chance to take part in such enterprises as coal-mining. But while the *hidalgo* would rather starve than demean himself in such ways, the English gentleman was secure in the knowledge that the highest families in the land were often glad to be involved in trade and industry. Lord Paget's ironworks, the Earl of Newcastle's coal-mines, and the Earl of Warwick's shipping interests were only a few of the instances of profitable activities by the peers.

Land and title

The wealth and power of the owners of land seldom came only from the profits of their estates and the control they exercised over their tenants. Countless sources of superiority were open to them which law or habit denied to others. Almost everywhere it went without saying that this was also the ruling class. To use such a term is to assume that it had reasonably definite boundaries, and that whatever the differences within it between country and country, greater and lesser, its members behaved in basically the same way. It is arguable that this is not so because—increasingly—the 'capitalist' landowner who treated his property primarily as an investment in a means of production was quite different from the 'feudal' lord more concerned with his social position and more bound by tradition. But to divide landowners into two such groups involves some very arbitrary conduct on the historian's part. It is remarkable how much, despite all the geographic, economic, and institutional differences, the *dvorianin* on the Volga continued to have in common with the English squire, the Austrian *Freiherr* or the Swedish *knapar*. The same is true of their superiors.

It was a life in which estate management could well play a large part. The smaller the lands the less the chance that they would be run by a steward instead of by the owner. Nevertheless landlords of every kind found time for a great deal more. The exercise of judicial power was a regular interlude, in England at the sessions, in Russia perhaps with the personal wielding of the knout. Nearly everywhere landowners devoted themselves zealously to mimicking, in one way or another, their almost lost function of fighting wars. The one seemingly indispensable occupation of the nobility was hunting. The hunt was a game that offered the pleasures of commanding in war with fewer dangers or discomforts. There was a mixture of discipline and freedom, an aggression in which the victim might not lose but could not win, a satisfaction of the primitive blood-lust. No assertion of superiority over the tenant was quite as satisfying as riding over his crops. There were other war-games nearer to reality. The privilege of fighting duels against each other was guarded by the French nobility against all Richelieu's efforts to stop it. Private armies had sometimes been reduced to ceremonial liveried retainers; but there were few countries in which fighting between noble houses was inconceivable. Even where it was, the nobility was deeply conscious of the family as a unit for loyalty and assertion. For them almost as much as for royalty, marriage remained a diplomatic and economic rather than an emotional matter, with elaborate systems of precedence and prestige. The betrothal could well be the mark of victory in a ruthless campaign and accompanied by elaborate treaties designed, usually with little success, to shape the future.

Within landed society the gradations were widely felt to be less clear and stable than they had been, or ought to be. The point on the scale of wealth and social standing at which a line was drawn between 'noble' and 'commoner' varied enormously in different countries and different parts of the century. The significance of a title was not easily assessed, not only because of linguistic confusion such as that between the narrow and exactly defined English nobility and the much more numerous French *noblesse*, but also because of the sale of titles. The 'inflation of honours' was a widespread phenomenon. The only limit to it was the fall in cash value that would result if any particular title became too common; and the demand proved remarkably elastic. The new order of baronets introduced by James I of England, hereditary but not involving the political rights of peerages, was intended to supply a market in which knighthood had become so debased in value that Charles I later resorted to the ill-fated attempt to make it compulsory for those with the prescribed amount of property. In Spain Philip III increased the higher ranks of the peerage by about half, and sales of titles continued under his successors. The French *officier* normally expected at the appropriate stage in his career to pay a substantial extra sum for his letters of nobility—or, since he hated to admit that the title was a new one—of 'rehabilitation'. It was a nice illustration of the general problems of title-holding: the state wanted to make rank dependent on service and yet to sell it to whoever would buy; the seeker of a title wanted it to be easily acquired at reasonable price, but when he had it he demanded that others should be excluded. Both were prepared, to the disgust of the old landed classes, to separate title-holding from territorial possessions.

Considering the many ways in which titles were acquired, they corresponded surprisingly well to current gradations of wealth. Only occasionally did venality reduce them to complete absurdity: Venice at the beginning of the century had 25 princes, 41 dukes, 147 marquises and counts, and 600 barons.[1] It was usually only at a level of nobility clearly marked off as inferior that 'inflation' got out of bounds. In Spain the barrier between commoners and *hidalgos*, the lowest grade of nobility, was of the utmost practical importance. In theory only the Crown could confer the status and privileges of *hidalguia*. In practice wild claims to forgotten hereditary nobility were made until in many places almost every head of a household who was not a manual worker proclaimed himself a *hidalgo*. In Poland there was a lower nobility so extensive that it included men on much the same level as the English yeoman or the French *fermier*. The *szlachta* was not the product of a recent sale of titles but of the efforts of medieval kings to buy military support. More successfully than most lesser nobilities they had built

[1] F. Braudel, *La Méditerranée et le monde méditerranéen*, p. 628.

up a strong constitutional position, with the insecure monarchy finding more support from them than from the magnates.

There was in many countries one perfectly rational motive for buying a title. Though nobility had long since ceased to carry the obligation of military service, it was often in effect a certificate of exemption from direct taxes. But in England, where no such exemption in practice existed, there was little sign that titles sold any less well. As in so many other matters, power and prestige were driving forces at least as important as money. In the countryside even those who did not seek authority needed an adequate label of status to escape the presumption of those who did. At the centre there was usually a strong probability that the politically eminent would not for long lack a title appropriate to their authority. For many monarchs the age-old problem of the over-mighty subject was taking a new and complex form. Landed nobilities still claimed, when it suited them, a right to power in the state. New office-holders asserted their equality in rank, esteem, and way of life with the ancient aristocrats. Almost every system of representative Estates,[1] so long as they kept any effective function, gave to each member of the nobility, or at least of its higher orders, a chance to participate in government from time to time. But there was no more natural identity of interests between aristocracies and state governments than there had been in the days of medieval baronial warfare against kings.

The nobility and the state

One of the most carefully planned attacks on the problem of the state's relationship with the nobles was in Sweden.[2] Gustav Adolf owed his throne to their support: his aim was to make them its active and almost its sole servants. Some of their privileges, including exemption from taxation, were curtailed, but the pride and solidarity of the caste were to be strengthened by excluding from it anyone whose conduct or economic position made him unworthy. At the same time it was made clear that the Crown would if it chose employ a complete outsider, ennoble him, and expect him to be received as an equal. The notion of a service-nobility with easy access to its ranks did not work smoothly. The ancient aristocracy grew more resentful of the intruders, built up their own provincial power, and became the political opponents of both Crown and commoners. Grants of new peerages went not only to Crown servants but to the professions and the townsmen. In the 1650s there

[1] See pp. 207–14. [2] See pp. 347–8.

94

began the long struggle between the monarchy and the old nobility that made possible the 'popular absolutism' of Charles XI and Charles XII.[1]

In Russia, inevitably, the rôle of the higher nobility in the state was settled not by political bargaining but in wars, mass executions, and vast confiscations of property. The only title recognised everywhere was that of prince—*kniaz*—and the 'sovereign princes' regarded themselves as little less than allies of the tsar. The rest of the high nobility, the boyars, claimed to be hereditary counsellors on whose goodwill the power if not the life of the monarch depended. They behaved to each other with all the jealousy and unscrupulous anarchism of rulers of nations. Precedence among them, in theory settled by the elaborate points system of the *mestnichestvo*[2] according to their genealogy and the offices they held, was a matter for bloodthirsty disputes. Ivan IV's massive attack on the princes and the boyars in the 1560s had destroyed many of the greatest estates and some of their owners; but it had left the angry survivors who fought each other and the Crown in the Time of Troubles at the beginning of the new century.[3] The Romanovs, boyars themselves, were able to create their own inner circle of twenty or thirty great families, some from the ancient nobility, others made rich by grants of crown land. The Council of Boyars became a meeting of the chosen favourites and office-holders rather than an assembly of magnates as a class. By Peter the Great's time the notion of nobility as a reward for service was becoming accepted. Peter's 'Table of Ranks' expressed in precise terms what was happening in one way or another throughout Europe. Ancient families retained their dignities: indeed it was Peter who introduced for them a variety of titles in the western style. But only meritorious service could give their members a place in the complex arrangement of ranks. He had perhaps more success than any other ruler in making those who attained nobility through service the equals and even the superiors of the holders of ancient titles.

There was much to be said for a division, in the words of the sociologist Pareto, between a 'governing élite' and a 'non-governing élite'. This is what Louis XIV to some extent achieved. Certainly in the great days of Versailles the nobility were more sharply divided than before into those who were attached to the court and the *noblesse campagnarde* who remained on their estates and took little part in the affairs of the monarchy. It did not mean that a rigid line could be drawn separating courtiers who devoted themselves entirely to the splendour and ceremony surrounding the king from the men who got on with the job of

[1] See pp. 355–7. [2] See pp. 375–6. [3] See pp. 363–7.

running the state. The old landed nobility could no longer assume that political power and office were theirs for the taking. But few of those who had risen to high positions in central government were content to leave the titles and privileges of nobility to others. The status and security of the family was as important to them as it was at nearly every other level of French society. Louis was generally willing enough to ensure that the statesmen and administrators were respected and rewarded. The distinction that was still clearly recognised between the *noblesse d'épée* and the *noblesse de robe* did not mean that those involved in the running of the state were inferior. The *noblesse d'épée* had long since ceased to be the preserve of ancient families. Sales of honours, and evasion of the rules that were supposed to govern admission to its ranks, made it easier to enter this than the well-guarded select circle of the *'grande robe'*. Those who belonged, or pretended to belong, to the old-established nobility did not accept without protest either the infiltration of outsiders or the diminution of power. The commissions set up by Colbert to investigate titles to nobility and preserve some of the exclusiveness of the class showed that the state recognised the need to win the support even of the provincial nobles. Even in the worst moments of financial distress, the French government could move only very cautiously in encroaching on their exemption from taxation.[1]

The townsmen

In many ways the distinction between town and country was becoming, for the rich, less important. Not only was land being constantly acquired with money made in the city, but—in the west at least—the landed nobility, great and small, was becoming more urbanised. If buying land remained a mark of success for the townsman, income derived from the town often seemed a necessary supplement to landlords' revenues that were barely adequate to preserve the estate and the standard of life associated with it. For any family with high political or social aspirations a house in the capital was increasingly necessary. The city might be evil-smelling, plague-ridden, and disorderly; but it was acquiring ornate buildings, new avenues and squares, even—by the end of the century—street lighting. It was the one centre of cultured life. It was often the necessary resort of the younger son who had to find a living in the professions: the law, at every level, was largely an urban occupation. An office in government, even a local one, could well involve regular visits to the provincial or national capital. In one way

[1] See pp. 445, 451.

or another the city-dwelling landowner who spent only part of the year on his estates was becoming more common. He was not always, in his way of life, as distinct as he liked to think from the successful bourgeois. The habits and accomplishments of the landowner remained the standard to which the social climber of the towns aspired. If Molière's *bourgeois gentilhomme* was a successful figure of fun, the Paris audiences that rejoiced in his blunders must have included many with a foot on each side of the barrier. There was little to distinguish the Parisian whose capital was invested mainly in the *rentes*—the loans to the government which were backed by the Paris municipality—from his neighbour who drew rents from a landed estate.

Both in the city and in the lesser town power was likely to be in the hands of a narrow ruling group no longer closely controlled by the nominally democratic institutions. Its character varied a good deal. In many places it was composed of men who took no active part in commerce or industry. They were successful lawyers, financiers, or purchasers of office, sometimes closely connected by marriage or cousinhood with the court and the landed nobility. It was still possible for a merchant oligarchy to remain comparatively self-contained; but the temptations and opportunities for the townsman who had achieved power and wealth to break away from his commercial background were strong. Though some of the Amsterdam regents continued to divide their time between government and commerce, many became purely office-holders and investors. In French towns the *parlementaires* were often a group of families who fought hard to prevent outsiders from joining them. The leading *marchands-fabricants* of Paris, the men involved in an assortment of industrial and commercial enterprises who belonged to the exclusive *Six-Corps*, had many relations in the high offices of state. By looking at the careers of individuals prominent in the urban community it is easy to get the impression that they were firmly separated in their status and way of life from the landowners. It is only when they are seen as part of their families that the links become apparent.

For those lower down the scale, opportunities of advancement, and even of security, in the towns seemed to be diminishing. It was not only the ruling oligarchy that kept entry to its circle almost impossible for those outside the privileged families. The status of master, once the realistic aim of every member of a guild, was now more easily acquired by heredity than by excellence. Prospects for the urban journeyman were seldom brighter than for the rural tenant; and the discontent of men who felt themselves to be oppressed wage-labourers was a notorious source of unrest. Their complaints all over western Europe and the Empire seemed to be much the same: masters used guild regulations as a means of keeping down wages, extracting an assortment of dues and fines, and restricting the numbers employed. From time to time there arose the secret *compagnonnages* which very occasionally managed to organise something approaching a strike. Fears of their sinister activities were seldom well-founded, though the Dutch thought it worth while to legislate against them.

Journeymen and apprentices, and casual labourers for whom what was left of the guild system meant nothing, provided the core of one of the important and little-understood phenomena of the time, the urban crowd. It was among the skilled artisans that resentment at their exclusion from privilege and opportunity could develop into rebellions with both specific local grievances and broader political ideas. Periods of unemployment, a feature of urban life closely connected with famine and depression in the countryside, could bring their discontent to a head. But the crowd also drew together men and women from the urban underworld. While industries were moving out of the towns,[1] the poor of the countryside were constantly moving in, and adding to the un-counted throngs who picked up a living as best they could in streets or harbours or market-places. A frequent complaint was that towns great and small were losing the old-style working population and gaining both the very rich and the very poor. London and Paris tried, with no great success, to restrict the building of new houses. Londoners were already worried about the traffic problem in the streets,[2] and this too was the subject of occasional legislation. In Russia the concern was more about a general loss of population. It was not only the peasants who were forbidden to move by the Code of 1649: townsmen too were ordered to remain where they were—though for the rest of the century the law had to be repeated and penalties strengthened. The aim of the Russian burgher in moving was often to escape both taxation and restrictions on industry. Another section of the Code tried to destroy the *sloboda*, the settlements—often controlled by landlords or monasteries—that had grown up outside the walls. It was symptomatic of a *malaise* in urban life that was to be found everywhere. Less inde-pendent, taxed by the state, plundered by its armies, dominated by its great men, the town had cause to be a centre of opposition.

[1] See pp. 55–8.

[2] J. Stow, *Survey of London* (1603), Everyman edition, p. 77.

A picture of European society divided neatly into town-dwellers and country-dwellers each in their strata from the great men to the hopelessly poor is far from complete. It leaves out the church: though the life of the bishop was likely to be much the same as that of the noble family from which he probably came, and the life of the parish priest not far removed from that of the peasant, the monasteries still provided at every social level a way of escape into an entirely different existence. Less agreeably, the mercenary soldier led a different life too. For the officer army service was a career which he could usually interrupt or abandon if he chose. For others it meant unpredictable wandering, danger, and opportunity. But the soldier was one of many for whom a home and a settled community were things unattainable or irrevocably lost. To humanity in general, seventeenth-century Europe must have been on balance a fairly unpleasant place.

V

Religion and the Churches

Europeans in the early seventeenth century believed in God. The effect of this on their lives is very difficult for the twentieth century to understand; for belief was, to normal men, active, unquestioning, and—it seemed—almost unshakable. Few practising Christians now act on the assumption that a supernatural being habitually intervenes in the

BIBLIOGRAPHY. On almost any aspect of religious history there is a formidable quantity of writing; but the topics in this period treated in modern books of high quality are unevenly distributed. An article by P. Chaunu, 'Le XVIIe siècle réligieux: réflexions préalables' in *Annales*, vol. 22 (1967) discusses the need to approach the study of religion from outside the churches and suggests that a new attitude to it is beginning to appear. No general survey of religious thought in earlier decades of the century has the same breadth of approach as parts one and two of P. Hazard, *The European Mind 1680–1715* (English trans. London, 1953). E. Troeltsch. *The Social Teaching of the Christian Churches* (English trans., New York, 1931) shows one aspect of the ideas of an author whose works in German are especially important for Protestant thought. The celebrated controversy begun by Max Weber, *The Protestant Ethic and the Spirit of Capitalism* (English trans., New York, 1930) and R. H. Tawney, *Religion and the Rise of Capitalism* (London, 1926) is relevant to this as well as to the previous century.

For factual detail there are numerous multi-volumed authorities. On the Catholic countries are L. von Pastor, *The History of the Popes*, vols. 25–32, trans. and ed. E. Graf (London, 1938–40) and the volumes by E. Préclin and E. Jarry in *Histoire de l'Énglise depuis les origines jusqu'à nos jours*, ed. A. Fliche and V. Martin, vols. 18 and 19 (Paris, 1955–60). General books on Protestantism include E. G. Léonard, *Histoire générale du Protestantisme*, vol. 2 (Paris, 1961) and vol. 5 of P. Fargues, *Histoire du Christianisme* (Paris, 1939). K. S. Latourette *A History of the Expansion of Christianity*, vol. 3 (London, 1939) deals dispassionately with missionary activities. At the other extreme of size, G. R. Cragg, *The Church and the Age of Reason, 1648–1789* (London, 1960) is a compact survey touching on east as well as west. Of the accounts of the Russian Orthodox Church P. N. Miliukov, *Outlines of Russian Culture*, vol. 1: *Religion and the Church*, trans. V. Ughet and E. Davis (Philadelphia, 1942) deals with the spiritual and W. K. Medlin, *Moscow and East Rome* (Geneva, 1952) with the political normal functioning of the universe; or that the world, created a few thousand years ago, is likely—as part of a prophetically revealed divine plan—to come to an end in a matter of decades if not years; or that a malign force, the Devil or Antichrist, takes possession of the bodies and 'souls' of men and women, manifests itself in bogus Christian churches, and is responsible for countless general and individual disasters. All these things seemed in 1600 an essential part of ordinary life. So did the assumption that those who did not conform to the locally accepted forms of worship were evil-doers who must be punished and rejected by society. Even in the regions where the grip of modern Christianity is strongest, it has not much in common with that of an age when to most Protestants the Bible was the only important book, to most members of the Orthodox and the Roman Catholic Churches the clergy

aspects. Pierre Pascal, *Avvakum et les débuts du Raskol* (Paris, 1938) is very sympathetic.

Among works on particular movements and organisations are: N. Abercrombie, *The Origins of Jansenism* (Oxford, 1936), which is more critical than A. Gazier, *Histoire générale du mouvement janséniste* (2 vols., Paris, 1922); R. A. Knox, *Enthusiasm* (Oxford, 1950); P. Dudon, *Le quiétisme espagnol* (Paris, 1921). Differing opinions of the Jesuits can be found in J. Broderick, S.J., *The economic morals of the Jesuits* (Oxford, 1934) and F. A. Ridley, *The Jesuits: a study in Counter-Revolution* (London, 1938). Their activities in Paraguay are described in M. Mörner, *The Political and Economic Activities of the Jesuits in the La Plata Region* (Stockholm, 1953). A selection of views on Puritanism could be derived from W. Haller, *The Rise of Puritanism* (New York, 1938), Michael Waltzer, *The Revolution of the Saints* (London, 1966), and Christopher Hill, *Society and Puritanism* (London, 1964). Perry Miller, *The New England Mind* (New York, 1939) includes a wide survey of the religious background of the emigrants. Other aspects of English religion are dealt with in H. R. Trevor-Roper, *William Laud* (London, 1940); W. K. Jordan, *The Development of Religious Toleration in England*, 4 vols. (London, 1932–40); Christopher Hill, *Economic Problems of the Church from Archbishop Whitgift to the Long Parliament* (Oxford, 1956).

V. Giraud, *Bossuet* (Paris, 1930) and P. Souday, *Bossuet* (Paris, 1931) are two of many studies. The standard work on Simon is still H. Margival, *Richard Simon et la critique biblique au XVII*e *siècle* (Paris, 1900). Bérulle's importance is shown in J. Dagens, *Bérulle et les origines de la restauration catholique* (Bruges, 1952). J. Orcibal, *Louis XIV et les protestants* (Paris, 1951) shows something of popular attitudes as well as political motives.

Some illusions about witchcraft are dispelled by H. R. Trevor-Roper's essay in his *Religion, the Reformation, and Social Change* (London, 1967), which has no mercy on the claims about surviving pre-Christian beliefs made familiar by Margaret Murray in *The Witch Cult in Western Europe* (London, 1921). One of the best national studies of the subject is W. Notestein, *A History of Witchcraft in England* (Washington, 1911).

were the one immediate source of education and authoritative guidance, and to nearly everyone the next world was a vivid reality.

By the end of the century there had been a change. In many ways it was deeper and more important in its ultimate effects than the Reformation of the sixteenth century; but it is far less apparent and definable. For scholars, by 1700, the intellectual certainty of religion had gone for ever. However they solved the problem, they were aware that reason and observation led to conclusions not easily reconciled with those of accepted 'faith'. The religions that attracted many of them were those that minimised revelation, institutions, and dogma. Some clergy were afraid of the rapid erosion of belief; others were content to accept it. Ordinary men, it is true, attended church much as before. They could still be stirred by comets or Popish plots or new miracles. But they no longer believed in witches; they were beginning to forget that they were surrounded by agents of the devil, and to accept a mechanically ordered universe in which life was an end in itself. Very slowly, religion was moving into a mental compartment of its own.

The political power of religion also mattered less. After the great counter-attack of the Catholic powers, the territorial extent of the main churches in Europe was fairly stable. The Puritan revolution in England had ended in Anglican moderation and the rejection of a Catholic king. Protestantism was eliminated from France as a political force. Wars were no longer alleged to be in defence of one Christian church against its enemy. It is impossible to fix the Peace of Westphalia or any other event as the decisive moment of change in this: it was one manifestation of that slow narrowing of the section of life controlled by religion. The diminution of clerical power in politics was another. Even in the period of piety at the end of his reign, Louis XIV did not give political power to the Church. England did not have another Laud, nor Russia another Patriarch Nikon.

The Orthodox Church

In 1600 there were something like 42 million Europeans in Catholic areas and 28 million under one form or another of Protestantism. Perhaps another 28 million belonged to the Orthodox Church.[1] About two-thirds of them were Russian; the rest were subjects of the Ottoman Empire, in whose European territories Islam was in general the religion of the rulers, Greek Orthodox Christianity that of the ruled. Christians

[1] Figures are based on those given in P. Chaunu, *La civilisation de l'Europe classique*, pp. 474, 484, 502.

as such were by no means oppressed: the Greek patriarchs and bishops were encouraged to exercise some of the judicial authority that was an essential part of the functions of the Moslem Institution. But theirs was not the only subject religion: in the towns especially, Jews and Armenians formed strong communities. The Greek Church had not much effective unity. The Patriarchs of Ipek (Pec) in Serbia and Ohrid in Macedonia were ecclesiastical magnates largely independent of Constantinople. The Bishops of Cetinje were virtual sovereigns of Montenegro, which never came completely under Turkish authority. In Bosnia, once the centre of the Bogomil heresy, native landowners had accepted Islam and Christianity was a religion of the poor; in Albania Christians had been reduced to a small minority. Greek Orthodoxy, among the most inflexible and authoritarian of creeds, became during the century a little more 'westernised'. The retreat of the Turks after their attack on Vienna in 1683 enabled Catholics to penetrate into areas from which they had been firmly excluded, and it even seemed possible that the papacy might achieve some sort of reunion with the Greek Church. But when Turkish frontiers were stabilised again the Orthodox confession remained firmly established and isolated.

In religion as in many other topics, Russia provided a grim exaggeration of the conflicts of the west. The Russian Church had broken its connection with the Greek Church in the fifteenth century, and now claimed to be the only guardian of the true Christian religion. It demonstrated this largely by passionate adherence to its garbled and often nonsensical texts and to its forms of ritual. There were it is true some matters for learned dispute: the question whether 'Alleluia' should be said three times or only twice had been debated for a hundred years or so. But the service as a whole had remained in theory untouchable, even if its inordinate length was sometimes made tolerable by performing three different parts of it simultaneously. In practice the sacred words gradually moved further from their Greek origins, through being learnt parrot-wise by generations of illiterate clergy who knew no Greek at all. It was a magical religion, in which neither moral teaching nor biblical history played much part. Redemption, the curing of disease, the growth of crops were alike secured through the exact repetition by the priest of formulae meaningless to his flock and usually to himself. Equally necessary was the worship of ikons, which at due times provided miraculous demonstrations of their power.

The village priests, living on much the same level of poverty and ignorance as the peasants, were only the lowest stratum of a clerical society comparable in wealth and authority with the state itself. The proportion of land held by the church in the country as a whole was nothing like as great as in some central areas where it owned more than a third of all the arable.[1] But its estates had increased enormously during the sixteenth century, partly through acquisitions in the newly conquered areas, partly by growing pressure on landowners to save their souls by bequests to the church. Since church property escaped taxation, the landowner often found it profitable to hand over his estate and retain the benefit of it during his life. Over its own lands the church exercised practically complete judicial power, as it did over clergy everywhere. Most of this land was monastic. It was only through the monasteries, which could attain the size and independence of fortified towns, that it was possible to escape from the brutalities of the state and to rise in the church hierarchy. The Trinity Sergius Monastery became, in the years of the 'Troubles', a capital of the religious and intellectual community more effective than was Moscow for the laity. Not that the church regarded itself publicly as an authority in conflict with the state. For a century or more, Moscow had been seen as the 'Third Rome', the empire chosen to guard the true faith until the millennium. The tsar was the 'Holy Father', a figure who, whatever the church's quarrels with his real manifestation in the palace, could be presented as a god-like, even an immortal, being. Any serious attack on the ways of the church could only be the work of an Antichrist or usurper who would infallibly be overthrown.[2]

Nevertheless, the seventeenth century saw such attacks succeed. There was an enormous gulf between the unchanging church of the priests and lesser monasteries and that of the higher clergy at the centre, among whom doctrinal quarrels were familiar enough. Only they, at the beginning of the century, were aware of the pressure on the Orthodox Church, both from the Greek hierarchy which was reasserting its own theological superiority, and from the west. In 1595 the Polish Orthodox Church had announced its reunion with Rome—though many of its members refused to accept this and became a persecuted minority. Jesuits saw the new 'Uniate Church' as a means of extending their work into Russia. When Polish armies invaded an almost helpless Russia, bringing militant Catholicism with them, it seemed possible that Orthodoxy might begin to disintegrate at the centre. But church

[1] J. Blum, *Lord and Peasant in Russia* (1964 ed.), pp. 188–9.
[2] Filaret's aims in Church and state are discussed by J. H. L. Keep in *Slavonic and Eastern European Review*, vol. 38 (1940).

and state survived the Troubles together. The church was rescued in the course of the century by the ruthless work of its two mighty Patriarchs. Filaret, appointed in 1619, was a Wolsey magnified to the Russian scale.[1] His experiences in Poland had made him a ferocious opponent of everything tainted with Latinising. After removing all potential rivals and enemies he used his authority to introduce a stronger clerical discipline, encouraged the monasteries to do something towards producing a rather more educated clergy. But he had no intention of giving the church any institutional independence. The strengthening of the state in the 30s and 40s brought the church more closely into the civil machine. The legal code of 1649[2] established a new department to control its temporal affairs and encroached a good deal on its judicial functions. At the moment when a real secularisation of the state seemed possible there appeared the second of the great Patriarchs, Nikon. On the face of it, Nikon's position was the same as that of Filaret. But their aims had not much in common. Nikon was a peasant, who had risen in the church by his own ambition and unscrupulous skill. He did not merely seek for the church an equal partnership in the landlord-dominated, isolated Holy Russia: he dreamed of the Universal Church, with the Russian Patriarch as its greatest potentate. To achieve this it was necessary to restore first the unity of the Greek and Russian forms of Orthodoxy—which meant accepting reform of the debased Russian texts and rituals. The corrected text, and the Greek view on such passionately argued matters as how many fingers should be used in making the sign of the cross, were imposed by Nikon almost without warning. From churches and houses images that did not fit the new rules were thrown out by Nikon's inquisitorial teams; and there was never a shortage of disasters for which this could be blamed. It could only be done haphazardly: clergy who resisted never knew whether they would be left to continue the old practices in peace or sent to Siberia. Many did their best to cope with the incomprehensible demands; but year by year resistance grew, by every means from martyrdom to armed revolt. Russia soon experienced a phenomenon that most western countries knew only too well, a militant religious minority.

Nikon's optimistic view was that the *staroveri*,[3] the Old Believers, would prove to be a mass of helpless peasants and a few nobles and court intriguers exploiting the situation for their own ends. In fact they became a movement so widespread and diverse that almost any oppo-

[1] See p. 375.   [2] See pp. 376–7.
[3] The other term *Raskolniky*—schismatics—was used mainly by their opponents.

sition could be attached to it. Its core came to be the 'easterners' who resisted Peter the Great's activities and the centralised state in general. In 1666 Nikon, having quarrelled with the tsar and misjudged the extent of his support, was tried by a Church Council, with the tsar as prosecutor, and banished; but the church had firmly accepted his reforms. In the priest Avvakum—Habakkuk—the Old Believers found a hero-figure who was eventually burnt at the stake. Successive waves of mass suicides by burning swept across the north. Old Believers fled from the state to set up primitive free communities in the forest. Some, paradoxically, arrived at the very new belief that the clergy had betrayed the true church, and must be dispensed with entirely. The Cossacks happily retained the Old Belief. In the far north the Solovetsky monastery withstood a siege of eight years before it surrendered. Only very slowly could mass persecution on one side and mass hysteria on the other turn into the stolid conservatism of the outcast group.

The clergy and the state in western Europe

However spectacular and tragic the schism in the Russian Church was for those concerned, it has to be remembered that the peasant and his priest were not on the whole profoundly affected. In the west too, the conflicts and the recession have to be seen against the huge background of unquestioning continuity. In both Catholic and Protestant areas, the parish survived—a natural unit in rural society, an increasingly irrelevant one in towns. Even Calvinism, from its need to take over both the buildings and often the clergy who officiated in them, had usually fitted itself into the old pattern. The baroque churches of the south, or Wren's rebuilding in London, did not suggest shortage of money or energy to keep the parochial system going. But the parish clergy remained poor, and often incompetent. From Sweden to Naples, from Ireland to Poland, every village had its clergyman, whose standard of living was seldom much above that of his flock. Often he was a peasant himself, cultivating his own land for much of his sustenance. Tithe was more a source of resentment to the payer than of wealth to the parochial clergy. In England it was likely to be impropriated by a lay patron; in Sweden two-thirds of it went to the Crown or the landlord; in most Catholic countries the monasteries absorbed a large part. Over much of the west, as of the east, the church still meant not only the parishes but the parasitic community of the 'regular' clergy. The poorer the country the greater the incentive to find material as well as spiritual salvation in the church. Spain and Muscovy had in common the fact that much of their best land belonged, in 1600, to monasteries: Olivares and Alexis I could do only a little to restrict them. The monastic orders were perhaps the greatest gap in the state's omnipotence, and were correspondingly unpopular with absolutist politicians. Church and state were in fact as ardent as ever in loving and hating each other simultaneously. The church relied on the state to defend its privileges, the state on the church to preach conformity and obedience. Yet the state was becoming less ready to share any part of its authority.

Struggles for power concerned mainly a third section of the church —the ecclesiastical aristocracy. There are few countries where we cannot find some high church dignitary playing a leading part in lay politics, for a variety of reasons. It was their royal connections that made Archduke Albert of the Spanish Netherlands an archbishop and a cardinal and Filaret a patriarch. Richelieu's bishopric showed how the French aristocracy had learnt to acquire the wealth of the church not by attacking it but by joining it—at the top; both he and Mazarin became cardinals because they were statesmen, not the other way round. Rich bishoprics were among the normal possessions of the aristocracy; cardinals' hats were a matter for political pressure. Laud, on the other hand, was a bishop first, a statesmen and courtier second. Either way the highest level of the Church was hardly distinguishable from the highest level of lay society. In Sweden, one of the most priest-ridden of all countries, the Lutheran bishoprics were confined more rigidly than before to the heads of great landed families. The archbishopric of Upsala became the monopoly of a very small noble circle.

Seen from below, the distinction between church and state was still by no means clear. Every established church was in one way or another a law-giving authority. Nearly all Europeans came within ecclesiastical jurisdiction, if only at their baptism, marriage, and death. On the whole, the poorer men were, the more it was for them the church rather than the state that represented the organised community. It was the church that educated them, the church that laid down codes of moral and social behaviour, the church that would relieve them in destitution. Men might quarrel about the kind of religious organizations they wanted; very few of them could conceive of a society with no such organisation in it at all.

The Papacy

With the end of the religious wars in France, it was clear that the Catholic Church would remain, both spiritually and politically, a dominant force over the whole of southern Europe. The Papacy, run as much as other monarchies by venality, corruption, and faction, was still a great power in the world of diplomacy. As sovereign of an Italian state, the pope was represented by 'nuncios' not only in capitals and other cities of Catholic countries but in, for instance, Moscow and Stockholm. But he could never be an ordinary member of the community of rulers. Popes, once elected, were virtually irremovable monarchs with the manifold powers and inducements they could use as vicars of Christ to back their diplomacy. On the other hand they were chosen by the College of Cardinals which was formed and influenced by a great diversity of pressures, among which those of Catholic sovereigns were prominent. Henry IV had found that military success convinced the College of Cardinals of the depth of his penitence, and that divorce from his first wife became possible when he chose a Habsburg as his second. He then spent, it was alleged, 300,000 ducats to secure — against the wishes of Philip III — a Medici as the next pope. It proved a poor investment, since Leo XI died after three weeks in office. Useful as the power of the Papacy was to rulers who could exploit it skilfully, it could never fit happily into the Europe of absolutist states. Though religion was still a great unifying force in the Habsburg Empire, the pope could no longer dispute with the emperor as an equal, and was not prepared to be the Habsburg Minister of Propaganda.

In Italy at least, while Spain had so much else to defend, the Papacy seemed to have a chance to become a great political power. In the 1560s and 1570s it had been dominated by a nobility as anarchic and destructive as any in Europe. Sixtus V had improved its administration a little. In 1605 there appeared in Paul V the first modern absolutist among the popes, who by the familiar process of handing out titles and estates to his family, created something of a 'Tudor aristocracy'. It was his mission, he proclaimed, to free the church from 'usurpation and violence'. In spite of a few gestures, such as his order that English Catholics should refuse the Oath of Allegiance, he did not seriously plan a campaign against Protestantism. Much more important to him were his visions of Rome becoming once more the capital of the peninsula. The result was to demonstrate that the pope's standing in power politics was a lowly one. Paul's conflict with Venice, where the state had just tightened its already strong control over the clergy, ended in failure. The Venetian clergy, led by the friar Paolo Sarpi, supported the Republic; and the assassins sent by the pope's nephew to deal with Sarpi bungled their job. In the Valtelline, papal troops who were supposed to be the guardians of the valley did not risk a clash with Spain or France.[1] But in 1626 Urban VIII was able to spite both France and Venice with the smart diplomacy that encouraged France in the Treaty of Monzon to desert her ally. As the European struggle developed, Urban faced the difficulty that his diplomatic interests were in supporting not the loyally Catholic Spaniards but the Gallican French, and worse still the heretical Swedes. The Papacy did not maintain an army worth having by the new standards; and at the Treaty of Westphalia its pronouncements were treated with contempt. Innocent X, refusing to recognise the religious division of Europe and the seizure of church lands, pronounced the settlement null and void. No-one took much notice.

The Jesuits

In spite of the political weakness of the Papacy, the settlement in 1648 was far from being a disaster for Catholicism. On the contrary it marked the end of Protestant progress in Europe and the acceptance of Catholic reconquests. Poland, Bohemia, and royal Hungary were now firmly Catholic. The Huguenots were no longer a threat to the French church or state. Catholics had reason to hope for further progress in Germany, and even conceivably in Scandinavia. An eastward drive into the territory of the Orthodox Church was not impossible. The Pope had to co-exist with both Protestantism and Gallicanism; but he could not altogether desert the 'lost sheep' of Europe or repudiate outright the efforts of those exponents of the true faith who tried to recapture them. The expansion of Catholicism was still the great task of the Society of Jesus. Indeed the Jesuits and their general seemed to have taken over from the pope a good many of his functions in the effective leadership of the church. In politics they found it expedient to remain on the side of Spain and the great armies. In religion they were their own masters; and they did not intend to allow dogmatic niceties to stand in the way of the growth of the church's power. They demanded of their followers unquestioning and active allegiance rather than personal morality or doctrinal rigidity. Moral problems were solved by the system of 'casuistry' whereby the confessor could justify almost anything if its 'intent' was good—that is in the interests of the faith and in particular of the Order. According to the theory of 'probabilism' an opinion not manifestly absurd or explicitly condemned by the church could be accepted—especially if some clerical scholar could be found

[1] See p. 270.

to have mentioned it—even in preference to one that was better supported. How far this could go was a matter of technical dispute between the Probabilists who required a reasonable degree of plausibility and the 'Laxists' who would accept anything not held to be positively disproved. No-one on the right side of the rigid barrier that excluded heresy and the few mortal sins needed to worry about his salvation provided he remained loyal to the church and to his confessor. By bringing the consolations of this attitude to the rich and the powerful, Jesuit confessors were naturally welcomed into the most influential circles; and the confessional became one of the chief means of propaganda.

The Jesuit attitude was an extraordinary mixture. On the one hand they were using sinister methods of securing a hold on the minds and actions of their followers; on the other they were taking a tolerant and almost humanist standpoint. Man, they claimed, could work for the greater glory of God through art, literature, even science rather than merely through piety. The first step in saving one's neighbour was to educate him. By providing tutors and seminaries acceptable to the courts and aristocracies, Jesuits could see that the seats of power were occupied by men whose underlying assumptions were theirs. The general pattern instilled by the teacher could be filled in by the day-to-day advice of the confessor. Ferdinand II was the outstanding royal product of Jesuit control. Louis XIV's confessors, La Chaise and his successor Le Tellier, were among the strongest influences, at least on his religious policies. In Spain Nithard, the Austrian confessor of the queen mother, became the greatest political power at the court of Charles II. Sigismund III, 'King of the Jesuits', had owed them much of the credit for his reconquest of Poland and enabled them to establish a complete control over the religion and education of the country.[1]

Jesuits did not accept as permanent any division of the world into Catholic and Protestant territories. The English view of them as a sinister underground conspiracy against the state was exaggerated but not totally unfounded. Overseas they were both the allies and the rivals of the trading companies, eager to extend European power but often defending their converts against the unscrupulous behaviour of merchants and colonists. There too the Jesuit technique was to start at the top and to adapt their teaching to the audience. Roberto de Nobili in southern India, ignoring the conversions made among the poor by the Portuguese, appealed entirely to the Brahmin caste, adopting their costume, learning their language, and preaching not the contrast between

[1] See pp. 283, 349, 426.

Christianity and evil paganism but how, with a little stretching, the two religions could be shown to have much in common. Indians enrolled into the Jesuit order gave up neither their caste nor much of their ritual. In China Jesuits suggested that the emperor might help to merge Christian and Confucian religions. In Japan they met with their one reverse when the Samurai became disillusioned with a religion that no longer seemed to hold the only key to trade with the west.

In South America the Jesuits achieved something like their ultimate ideal, the theocracy of Paraguay. Philip III conceded to them full control, subject only to his own sovereignty over the Guaranis in the River Plate region. By a mixture of force, propaganda, and material benefits they created the villages where the natives were 'reduced' to Catholic, monogamous, authoritarian life. Spanish colonists and slave-traders were kept out by well-equipped native forces; mines, foundries, and weaving-sheds were added to the resources of collective agriculture. Clothes and tea replaced feathers and alcohol; the whip was used, but not the death-penalty, since the vows of the Jesuits prevented them from carrying it out and no-one else could be trusted to do so. It was a society that paid for its sudden security and prosperity by submission to the minute and rigid control of the European priesthood. Here the divine summons to the religious life came only to white men. Services were conducted in local languages; but the Bible, apt to be misunderstood, remained—as it had formerly been for so many laymen in Europe —in the secrecy of a foreign tongue. The native was taught to be content with two days' work on his own land and four on the property of God, of which the Jesuits were custodians. The idealism was soon whittled away. New generations of missionaries became more closely connected with the ruling aristocrats of the Spanish colonies. A good deal of energy went into keeping out the rival Paulist missionaries. It all became a revealing parody of the churches' relations with state and society in seventeenth-century Europe.

The Jesuits could reasonably claim to be a progressive element in the church, adapting it to the realities of political and economic change. Other orders too were involved in the mixture of temporal and spiritual activity and in the tendency towards a centralised and 'aristocratic' form of organisation. The Capucins, founded in 1525 as a further Franciscan order, did not confine themselves to helping the victims of poverty, plague, and war. They came to specialise in diplomacy. Father Joseph was a Capucin; so was Father Hyacinth whom Maximilian of Bavaria employed as an agent to win Catholic support in Germany against the Habsburgs. Indeed the Capucins were generally identified with anti-Habsburg movements among Catholic powers and Jesuits with the pro-Habsburg ones. Overseas, Franciscans, Dominicans, and Augustinians quarrelled with each other and with the Jesuits over spoils that were not solely religious ones.

Religion in France

In France opposition to the Jesuits came both from the rival orders and from the various movements of a mystical and individualist character that arose within the church at the beginning of the century. Against the Jesuit concentration on free will was set the theocratic outlook of Pierre de Bérulle, a Jesuit pupil who was made a cardinal not long before his death. His ideal man was expected to merge himself into Christ and God by prayer and contemplation. Bérulle's followers were by no means cut off from political or social activity. His ideas were popular with the exclusive groups at court, and later in the literary salons. In 1611 he founded the Oratory, an association of Catholic clergy devoted to improving the status and morals of the parish priests and to ending the Jesuit domination of education. Bérulle himself and many of the leading figures in Paris were involved in the kind of mysticism that led them to the circle of visionary women like Mme Acarie and Marie de Valence. Two of Bérulle's associates were in due course canonised. François de Sales, the Catholic Bishop of Geneva, claimed massive conversions among Swiss and French Protestants. Vincent de Paul had a genius for leadership and organisation that produced the Lazarists, the *filles de la charité*, and the schemes for bringing help and the consolations of religion to galley-slaves and the starving poor of Paris. His devotion did something to make life tolerable for victims of war and hunger; but it did not lead him to question or break away from the high political and social circles of the capital.

From different theological starting-points, both the Jesuit and the Bérullien religions could comfort their followers with the assurance that the world and its customs were not altogether evil and that religious duty was compatible with a pleasant and privileged life. The price of it was to accept clerical domination in a wide range of activities. The *cabale des dévots* made great efforts to use state authority in stamping out heresy and indifference. They were alarmed to see the growth of tolerant cultural and literary groups in which Catholics and Huguenots met in each other's houses. But militant Catholics had always to face the problems that arose from France's relations with the Papacy.

In the year of Henry's death, 1610, literate Frenchmen were excited by the reappearance of *De Regis et Rege Institutione*, a pamphlet by the Jesuit Mariana arguing that the subject might be absolved through his faith from obedience to the sovereign, and justifying the assassination of kings who failed to further the interests of the faith. An opposite view was put in Edmond Richer's *De Ecclesiastica et Politica Potestate* (1611) which claimed apostolic succession for all priests independently of the Pope. Divine power would be exercised primarily by bishops, who could of course be good Frenchmen. This was a form of Gallicanism directed as much against the king as against the pope. To those who believed that the success of French Catholicism depended on a firm alliance with the Papacy it was a help that Louis XIII's legitimacy depended on the Pope's recognition of the right of his father to remarry: the nobles hostile to the King had more reason to challenge papal supremacy. Under Louis XIV Gallican theories became, as they had been in the sixteenth century and earlier, involved with royal claims to revenue and authority, as well as with diplomatic alignments.[1] Catholicism by then was safe; but its character remained uncertain. While some were seeking a religion in which they could feel intellectually satisfied, the devotion which Louis in his later years supported meant increasingly the cult of the Virgin Mary and the Sacred Heart, visions and miracles.

Henry IV's conversion and the Edict of Nantes did not mark an obvious end to the possibility of new attempts by the Huguenots to conquer the country. It was not until the Peace of Alais in 1629 that their internal dispute on the merits of armed resistance was settled in favour of loyalty to the state. Politically and socially there seemed good reason for France to become a Protestant state. French Jesuits were making little headway against Huguenots. There was no apparent weakening of the discipline imposed by the national synods or of their conviction that Catholicism was the essence of evil. Yet once the revolts of the 1620s were defeated, the French Protestant Church became the first to accept the rôle of pacific dissent.[2] The Huguenots had lost the factious nobility who led them into the sixteenth-century wars; the townsmen and men of the *robe* who now made their policy were not disposed to risk their lives and property in a losing battle against the state.

[1] See pp. 439–42.   [2] See p. 266.

The Protestant Churches

Whatever religious or material factors may have determined the original spread of the Reformation, the boundaries between Catholic and Protestant Europe were eventually drawn by political power. So, very largely, were those between the various Protestant churches, which now had little in common beyond their rejection of the pope and their faith in the Bible as the ultimate spiritual authority. Lutheranism was by the mid-seventeenth century an orthodoxy at least as rigid in theory as Catholicism. Theologians devoted themselves to expounding the arid minutiae of such doctrines as the 'ubiquity' of Christ and attacking the errors of Calvinism. The Lutheran Church demanded the support of the state. Great ecclesiastical families, who held bishoprics and prebends almost as hereditary titles and church lands as private estates, relied on orthodoxy to preserve what was now the established order. In Germany especially,[1] Lutheranism was conservative in outlook and ready to accept a good deal of secular authority in religious affairs in return for defence against its enemies. It did not draw much distinction between Calvinism and Catholicism as threats. The Lutheran Berliners stoned Calvinist troops from Saxony who came to their aid in the Thirty Years War. In Gustav Adolf's Sweden the church imposed its moral code almost as fiercely as in Calvin's Geneva. It also became a local administrative machine of the state, assessing and collecting taxes, and even helping to organise conscription. In spite of this the Clerical Estate often acted, in Gustav's phrase, as 'Tribunes of the People', resisting more effectively than the fourth Estate could, the burdens imposed both by the state and by the landowners.

If Lutheranism now tended to be a religion of conformity and of collaboration with the state, Calvinism could not be regarded as simply the opposite: it could be adapted to submission as well as to challenge. Once they had succeeded in winning power, Calvinists could use the state as a means of imposing the most tyrannical orthodoxy. Their founder had shown what could be achieved in this; and Geneva was still an absolutism in which power was shared by clerical and civil authorities. Scottish Presbyterianism fought a fluctuating battle for power against the Stuart kings before the clumsy efforts of the English government to destroy it made it the centre of the national resistance that produced the Bishops' Wars. It had not always been a united movement: after Knox's death there had been incessant conflicts about

[1] See the map on p. 299.

its organisation. Edinburgh militancy was still resisted by Aberdeen conservatism. But in the General Assembly and the mixed lay and clerical hierarchy the Kirk had a set of institutions well adapted to the exercise of political power and to winning support from a wide range of the community. The Covenant of 1638 was a magnificent example of how religious zeal could be organised for political ends: momentarily it achieved something approaching national unity in the most unlikely conditions. On the other hand, Calvinism had characteristics that were bound to lead to fragmentation. In religion as in politics, the more radical the beliefs the harder it was to hold them together. Predestination was above all the faith of sects, each believing itself to be the 'elect' minority. Its appeal was strongest to men striving to assert a status they had made for themselves; for whoever the elect were, they would not be known by inherited wealth or power.

Arminianism

England and the Netherlands showed these conflicting traits well; though while in England it was the Puritan opposition to established doctrine that was derived from Calvinism, in the Netherlands it was the official Church. In both the resistance to rigid Calvinism made use of the doctrines that had been expounded, with caution and ambiguity, by Jacob Harmensz—'Arminius'—a Professor of Theology at Leiden.[1] Out of the turgid 'supralapsarian' versus 'infralapsarian' controversy, he developed ideas that left little of predestination in any recognisable form. All who had faith retained a chance of salvation; only those who rejected 'grace' were damned. Moreover he was prepared to introduce a certain amount of decoration and ceremony into the austere Dutch churches. In 1610 his ideas were incorporated into the 'Remonstrance' presented to the Estates of Holland and Friesland, which asked merely that men should not be bound to doctrines they found incredible. To the Calvinist clergy and their followers all this seemed a move towards popery, and hence towards subjection to Spain. Anything stressing doubt rather than certainty was bad for clerical power. The orthodox faith was defended by Francis Gomar, a colleague of Arminius at Leiden and an unrelenting preacher of damnation. The Remonstrants, generally speaking, were the party of the prosperous merchants against the countryside, of Holland and the maritime provinces against the less advanced areas, of Republicanism against the House of Orange. The Synod of Dort, which met in 1618 at the height of the political crisis

[1] See pp. 389–90.

that absorbed the religious quarrel, was a 'counter-Remonstrant' assembly that listened to Remonstrant ministers only to condemn them. It produced a set of canons defining doctrine on strict Gomarist lines; Remonstrant ministers were ejected; dissenters were in theory to be excluded from office and from many of the benefits of citizenship. In practice not many of the civil authorities were prepared, except against Catholics, to impose the full claims of the church. In 1627 power in Amsterdam went to the 'libertine' party of Andries Bicker which had some success in maintaining religious tolerance. Protestant sectaries and even Catholics found that discretion, and perhaps money, could cause laws to be forgotten. Amsterdam, against the protests of the clergy, became the scene of flourishing intellectual and cultural activity.

What was now in Holland the heresy of a sect became in England the religion imposed by the monarchy and resisted by an opposition that found in its own version of Calvinism abundant support for its political and commercial interests. Arminianism, it is true, was a label more or less accidentally attached to the Laudian Church. In England it meant not a liberalising of Calvinism but a form of worship that demonstrated in the repetitive ceremonies, the priestly vestments, and the railed-off altar the notion of salvation through obedience to those in power. English clergy, secure in the ambiguities of the thirty-nine articles, were not much concerned about supralapsarianism or irresistible grace. 'People', Charles I remarked, 'are more governed by the pulpit than the sword in peace'; and when Laud became Archbishop of Canterbury in 1633 the King expected him to maintain the church as 'the chiefest support of royal authority'. The virtues of submission and passive acceptance of the existing order of society were instilled through careful central control of both the organisation and the services of the church. Doctrine and political purpose apart, it was certainly in need of reform. The 'visitations' reporting on every diocese revealed not only the opposition of Puritan clergy but in many areas a dismal state of poverty and incompetence. There were some signs of improvement, such as the marked increase since the sixteenth century in the number of graduate clergy. How far reform could have been extended by Laud's system can only be guessed: all it achieved in the end was to contribute to the revolution that brought the Archbishop to his death.

Puritanism

Against the Laudian Church was an alliance of religious beliefs known, mainly to their enemies, as Puritan. The term had such wide application that Puritanism is more easily defined by what it opposed than by what it upheld. Inevitably when it triumphed in the Civil War it broke into fragments, ranging from supporters of an established Presbyterian Church to the multitude of radical sects. But in the 1630s it was united in the conviction that Arminianism was half-way to Popery and that the bishops and the whole Church organisation were making religion the instrument of tyranny instead of the faith of individuals. Nearly all Puritans accepted in some form the Calvinist division of mankind into the elect and the damned. In theory the damned included the unfortunate passive majority. In practice the struggle was against all who participated, however unwittingly, in the great campaign of evil led by the Popish Antichrist. Among the elect all were equal in the eyes of the Lord, though not in earthly status and possessions. Their election might be made manifest in their godly life and the success with which their just endeavours to improve their lot on earth would in due course be blessed. Having undergone the great inner experience of conversion, they must constantly receive the word of God through the scriptures and through preaching.

The scriptures—though Puritans would have been horrified at such a suggestion—were not important mainly for what they said. It would have been difficult for the unguided reader to derive much moral or spiritual message from such a mass of apparent inconsistencies. The primary function of the Bible was to be for every individual a talisman that gave him the assurance of direct contact with God irrespective of the mediation of a superior clerical caste. Of course the Puritan convinced himself and others, with massive quotation and summary, that he derived directly from the Bible the whole of his faith and his habits of thought and behaviour. But to do this he needed other parts of the Puritan system. One was the 'godly preaching ministry' whose sermons were for most of the flock the principal means of contact with the great conflict in the rest of the world. But the minister was not the voice of priestly authority: he differed from the congregation only in his professional skill and knowledge. Puritans learned their creed as much from their fellow laymen as from the experts.

In the successes and failure of Puritanism under Elizabeth there had emerged a difference of emphasis between those who tried to meet these needs within the established church and the sectarians who repudiated all existing organisations and claimed a monopoly of salvation for their own saintly minority. For most, the ideal was the 'gathered church' in which all believers joined to build from below whatever organisation was needed. It could take many different forms. Individual congregations, like the celebrated Coleman Street church of the City Puritans, could achieve a spontaneous unity of their own within the old establishment. During the Interregnum the English Presbyterian Church imposed its new system, with lay participation, uneasily on the old parish structure. It never seemed to have much popular zeal behind it. The more active Puritans tended to be 'Independents' who rejected Presbyterianism as a compromise with evil and envisaged a loose alliance of congregations with a minimum of imposed uniformity. The Parliamentary army, with its regimental preachers, provided a form of 'gathering' that was hardly spontaneous but could give to its captive audience the rare satisfaction that came from proof of the Lord's blessing on their cause: they had already, by their own efforts, destroyed the power of Antichrist in its Royalist guise. How easily leadership of the cause of individualism in religion could turn into a new authoritarianism was soon apparent.

The moment when the state seemed to have disintegrated was also the great opportunity for the sects. To the true sectary the smaller his group and the further removed from temporal power, the stronger his assurance. The 'Saints' were in his view a tiny minority, unrecognised except by each other, but about to come—in some not too closely defined way—into their own. Some of the sects had sixteenth-century origins and widespread connections. Each of them in theory should, as the sole elect, have been intolerant of all its rivals; but their common struggle against persecution made them, pending their triumph, advocate toleration for other forms of Christianity. To the vast majority the term naturally excluded popery.

Anabaptism, with its convenient insistence that infant baptism could not compel anyone to belong to a church he had not freely chosen, survived incessant attacks, particularly in England and the Netherlands. In Holland it became the creed of the urban poor, whose interests neither Remonstrants nor Counter-Remonstrants represented. It was from an alliance between Dutch and English Anabaptists that the Pilgrim Fathers sprang. Several of the Civil War sects originated in Anabaptism. One of the most effective sectarian beliefs was an emphasis on the prophecies of the millennium. To the most successful of the millennarian groups, the Fifth Monarchists, the reign of Christ on earth was an immediate practical prospect, for which they could work by rebellion against the existing political order. Most of the sects were less concerned with actual revolt than with survival as an unrecognised elect. Messianic characters like Lodowick Muggleton or James Naylor could collect for a time a passionate following. Groups like the Ranters and the Family of Love sometimes attracted support and horror by meetings that turned into orgies. But the crime of most was simply to take the moral and social teaching of the New Testament seriously.

The whole period of the Civil War and Interregnum was for the sects a struggle in which the moment of triumph seemed always at hand but always postponed as one authority after another rejected the light of sainthood and imposed the tyranny of the state. Determination to resist was part of their common creed. Often they refused to pay tithe to the church they had rejected; for tithe was part not only of the hated clerical system but of the distinction between property-owner and poor. When the Presbyterian Thomas Edwards denounced sectarian principles as 'destructive to human society, to all kinds of government, political, ecclesiastical, and economical'[1] he was only exaggerating what was at that stage certainly true. Religious radicalism was inseparable from political and social radicalism. It seemed possible at last for the levelling ideas of Christianity to take on a practical meaning. Extreme Puritanism flourished most in the towns and in the army. It drew support from the artisans, the apprentices, the ordinary soldiers who were also the mainstay of democratic political movements. Puritanism was a religion of revolt. But successful revolt, in this as in everything else, could only be achieved by accepting some form of authority. To many sectaries successive new authorities seemed as bad as the old.

Some sects seemed to thrive on defeat and contraction; but for many the Protectorate and the Restoration were disappointments difficult to explain away. They tended to move away from militancy towards faith in a more remote millennium or towards renunciation of worldy activity. Partial toleration, as was intended, removed some of their appeal. The most assertive group of English dissenters after the Restoration was the Quakers. In the days of George Fox they were anything but pacific; but their energy was directed more to denouncing the sins of the church than to advertising a positive creed of their own. Dogma was the great evil; non-conformity a virtue in itself. An organised sect or systematised worship would have been seen as barriers to the direct experience of the 'inner light' that was their great source of reassurance. Under the leadership of William Penn they made toleration a major principle rather than a matter of expediency. Conversion ceased to be

[1] *Gangraena* (2nd ed. 1646), quoted in C. Hill and E. Dell, *The Good Old Cause* (London, 1949), p. 320.

an important aim. Within their society there was room for a range of beliefs from visionary mysticism to an emphasis on the moral aspect of Christianity that left little of the supernatural in it. It was the Quakers who made notorious the self-conscious idiosyncrasies of dress and speech often attributed to Puritans in general. Where the law was wrong, as it usually was, it had to be rejected at whatever cost. They thrived on martyrdom, which the Stuart government provided rather half-heartedly. But they did not seek revenge. The combination of Christ-like morality with the repudiation of the state led them eventually to denounce the most universally accepted of the state's activities, war. Other Christians continued to find it compatible with their devotion to New Testament texts.

Mystics, Pietists, and Quietists

In their asceticism, introspection, and determination to save religion from the clergy, the Quakers had a good deal in common with the various forms of mystical religion that were managing to survive in both Protestant and Catholic Europe. Popular movements that asserted the power of the 'inner light' against the wealth and wordly authority of the church had existed in every age. Early in the century one of the most successful preachers and writers in this tradition was Jakob Boehme, the shoe-maker who despite Lutheran persecution spread the news of his visions of the conflict between good and evil, and the 're-birth' that would bring salvation. Half a century later Philip Spener popularised a doctrine of individual piety attractive to those who resented Calvinist or Lutheran discipline but were not consciously affected by rational doubts. If knowledge increasingly eroded the old sources of religious certainty, it was still possible to claim others that were incommunicable in words. The 'Pietists' were repelled by scholastic argument, and by what they saw as the growing worldliness and indifference of the clergy. They wanted a religion neither frightening nor complex in its creed, but giving a sense of zeal and virtue. Some found it in meeting to sing emotional hymns like those of Paul Gerhardt. Others devoted themselves to religious teaching and organised charity. In Brandenburg at the end of the century, Halle became a great centre of Pietist activity, with its new university, a model orphanage, schools, and religious presses. Amorphous though Pietism was, a variety of later dissenting groups, including the Moravian Brethren and the Methodists, claimed it as one of their origins.

'Quietism' was a cult different from Pietism less in its mood than in the people to whom it appealed. This too was an anti-clerical, individualist form of religion with strongly mystical tendencies. It began in the followers of the Spanish priest Miguel Molinos who acquired a fashionable reputation in both Rome and Paris—though he was eventually imprisoned by the Inquisition. In the 1680s French high society was full of the reputation of Madame Guyon, whose claims to direct divine guidance closely resembled those of modern spiritualist mediums, and who won devotees in much the same way. The Quietists sought only the annihilation of all individual activity in the love of God. Nevertheless, Madame Guyon became a centre less of tranquillity than of intrigue and faction. Not only the dilettante philosophers of the court were involved, but also the two outstanding French theologians, François Fénelon and Jacques-Bénigne Bossuet. Fénelon, the passionate intellectual, the believer in educational reform and cautious critic of the monarchy, came completely under her spell. Bossuet, the bishop, historian, and rigid upholder of authority, was one of the principal destroyers of the cult.

Jansenism

The most effective independent religious movement in Louis XIV's France, Jansenism, managed to combine an element of mysticism with an almost Calvinist view of redemption. Cornelius Jansen was an old-style theologian at Louvain, who in his *Augustinus* set out, like countless other writers, the views of St Augustine in a manner slanted for his own purpose—to attack the Jesuits. Obedience, and the power of the confessor, on which Jesuit influence was based, depended on free will. To extol the rôle in salvation of Grace at the expense of free will was therefore to diminish Jesuit authority. Jansen's two associates, Duvergier de Hauranne, Abbé de St Cyran, and Antoine Arnauld, were largely responsible for reforming the two Convents of Port Royal, one in Paris and one in the country, which became the headquarters of an aristocratic and intellectual clique devoted to propaganda and to educational work. Arnauld's daughter was made Abbess at the age of seven. His son, the younger Antoine, who became its effective master, was the author of the tract, *De la Fréquente Communion*, which provided the popular source of Jansenist arguments. With its associated semi-monastic male group, Port Royal was a fashionable centre of hostility to the court. Its reputation was enhanced by the miraculous powers of its fragment of the Crown of Thorns. But Jansenism was not simply an affair of a rich intellectual clique. It managed to fulfil in a small way the rôle of an opposition creed which Puritanism played in England. De Retz and many of the Frondeurs held Jansenist views. Against it the Jesuits had the support of the Sorbonne, and of Pope Innocent X. His Bull of 1653 condemning five 'Propositions' which it said were in the *Augustinus* led to an intricate argument that involved the vital question of the relationship between faith defined authoritatively and observed fact. If the pope said the Propositions were heretical, the Jansenists would accept his ruling. But on the factual question of whether they were in Jansen's book, they insisted that he was wrong. The style of the law-courts was mixed with that of theologians in the quarrel, and in the intermittent attempts at compromise. In 1661 the nuns of Port Royal were expelled and their schools closed. In 1667, after approaches from the French diplomat Lionne, Clement IX produced a formula in which the crucial phrase 'purely and simply' was replaced by 'sincerely'. Since this, for reasons clear to theologians, made all the difference, Port Royal was restored, and was more readily tolerated in Rome because of its continued disagreements with Gallicanism. Only in Louis' fanatical last years was it eventually destroyed.

The greatest figure in the controversy was not regarded as a thoroughgoing Jansenist. Blaise Pascal, whose *Lettres Provinciales*, written at Port Royal des Champs between 1655 and 1657, are a masterpiece of ironical denunciation, did not find in Jansenism a complete answer to his quest for certainty. His attack on Jesuit casuistry was so merciless and enjoyable that he came to fear the popularity it achieved among people who might apply it more widely than he intended. Jansenism, in attacking the Jesuit version of Catholic dogma, sometimes seemed close to rejecting the church, or even churches in general. Its later leaders Pierre Nicole and his successor the fiery Pasquier Quesnel, were eager to provoke a further conflict with the Jesuits in the hope of getting them expelled from the country entirely. But the new Jansenist writings were condemned uncompromisingly in two Papal Bulls, *Vineam Domini* in 1705 and *Unigenitus* in 1713. By then the movement was more deeply involved in a struggle of quite different origins—for the 'liberties' of the Gallican Church. Jansenist bishops were the first to oppose the extension of the *régale*,[1] while Jesuits, on bad terms with Innocent X, found themselves supporting the Crown. Neither now appeared to find their theological views relevant to any serious criticism of the society or state they lived in.

[1] See pp. 439–40.

Doubt

To look at the disputes over free will and the Gallican articles that penetrated into the French salons, or at the mysticism and miracle-working, does not give the impression that there was a decline in religious belief. In Lutheran Germany the picture of petty theological feuds within a state-imposed orthodoxy was much the same. The grip of monasticism and the Inquisition on Spain was as strong as ever. Nevertheless, many different strands of thought and behaviour were leading away from religious domination. Some originated within the theological circles. In Germany 'Syncretism', the intellectual approach to a merging of the doctrines of Calvinism and Lutheranism, and even of Catholicism too, had been preached by George Calixt and taken up mildly by the Great Elector, who saw it as a useful solution to the troubles brought about by clerical controversy. In the 1690s Bossuet, who became increasingly convinced of the dangers in any such schemes, was involved in a long controversy with the most eminent living philosopher, Gottfried Leibnitz. Leibnitz, despite his own ideas of the relation between God and the universe, was a Protestant willing to defend orthodox Christianity, miracles included, as a rational possibility. Union of the Catholic and Protestant Churches was a cause he took up with great energy, but with arguments that led him into a questioning of scriptural authority intolerable to Bossuet.

In England there had survived through all the bitter religious conflicts a quiet Christian humanism that deplored both Laudian authority and Puritan fanaticism. Before the Civil War the little circle of scholarly gentry at Great Tew discussed the virtues of tolerance and Christian unity. After the war the Cambridge Platonists, aware of the implications of scientific discovery, argued that if complex religious dogma could be escaped reason and revelation would somehow lead to the same conclusions. The Latitudinarian movement within the church offered to scientists the assurance that all their discoveries were demonstrating the power and goodness of the Creator and thereby strengthening religious belief. But behind the effort of all these schools of thought there was anxiety: to say that reason and new knowledge were compatible with the existence of a God did not mean they supported faith in the biblical story of the creation, the fall, and the redemption or in the God who upset the course of nature in response to persuasion by prayer. A different solution to the contradictions was put forward by the Deists, who by stressing the perfection of God's works, including the rational faculty in man, were able to leave Christian revelation as either a supplement to reason or, for the more daring, a contradiction to be rejected. The most soothing version of it was that of John Toland who asserted that once the absurd accretions of theologians had been removed there was nothing mysterious or irrational in the essentials of Christianity. It was a view that left many obvious difficulties unanswered.

A few writers were able to face the conflict between faith and reason openly. France produced—and drove out—one figure who was always sure of an audience for the most unconventional religious views. Pierre Bayle has a good claim to be the first popular journalist of literary and intellectual criticism. In his monthly *Nouvelles de la République des Lettres*, published in the Netherlands, he poured forth, from 1684 to 1687, a spate of brilliant invective against Catholic tyranny and intolerance. He flatly denounced belief in miracles an as insult to a God who had no cause to break his own laws. Then, in the *Dictionnaire historique et critique*, he adopted a new technique. In the guise of factual information he was able to present to those prepared to search for it a massive demonstration of the inconsistencies, distortions, and pretentious nonsense that filled the work of the most respected writers. His own conviction that nothing was certain grew as the work went on. This was not the doubt of Descartes[1] that had merely led to a selective re-establishing of beliefs. It was doubt that remained universal. The scriptures were not exempt from the process of questioning. Between the religious and the rational outlooks, no compromise was defensible. This did not mean that reason could offer definitive answers to fundamental questions; but at least it could admit its inability to do so.

Bayle never claimed to have formulated a coherent system of thought. He did not admit to being an atheist, though he had come to attack the Protestantism in which he had once believed as bitterly as all other religions. Some of his pronouncements make him appear to be a Deist, accepting a God unrelated to revelation, salvation, or morality. But the term his innumerable enemies commonly applied to him was 'Socinian'. The sect that derived its name and original form from the ideas of the Italians Laelius Socinus and his nephew Faustus had a different character from most of its kind. Faustus, who had travelled through Europe on his heretical missions, had his first successes in Poland and Transylvania. After popular demonstrations were organised against them by the church, their followers migrated to Germany, France and Holland, from which the creed soon spread to England. Their shocking belief was

[1] See pp. 135–7.

in unitarianism. To deny the Trinity, and hence the divintiy of Christ, was regarded as tantamount to atheism. In many Western countries, Socinianism in a more questioning form became a creed of those intellectuals who sought to reconcile rationalism with some kind of religious belief. From Grotius at the beginning of the century to Newton at the end, a good many of the outstanding minds found themselves nearer to Socinianism than to any other religion. Its emphasis now was less on a single set of heretical opinions than on the application of rational tests to every element of religious dogma, and the rejection of whatever failed. The moral element of Christianity could be completely separated from the miraculous.

It was another Frenchman, Richard Simon, who made critical study of the Bible a matter for public dispute. One demonstration of the power religion had held is that through so many centuries the text of the scriptures had been minutely studied and debated by the greatest intellects with hardly a thought being given to the obvious human explanation of the contradictions and impossibilities. The question of textual corruption was of course familiar. The notion of biblical narratives as allegories had appeared from time to time as a daring aberration. Spinoza[1] in 1670 had set out firmly the principles on which scientific method should be applied to an investigation of the Bible. But Spinoza was a Jew whose blasphemies Christians could ignore. Simon was a priest, a member of the Oratory. Moreover, despite the immense learning in his work, its conclusions were only too comprehensible. His *Historie critique du Vieux Testament* of 1678 was followed by a series of studies of the New Testament on the same lines. All the powers of suppression that church and state could muster were used to prevent him from becoming widely known. His enemies may well have seen more clearly than he did where his ideas would lead: for Simon himself claimed to remain a good Catholic.

Witchcraft

Repeatedly in the history of the growing doubts of the scholars one problem reappears. Belief in supernatural events—in the portents of comets, the cures of sorcerers, the misdeeds of evil spirits—was being pushed back by scientific knowledge. If some of the supernatural was rejected, where was the line drawn? Were the powers of holy relics, or the miracles of early saints, or only biblical miracles, or only such basic ones as the Resurrection acceptable? One great change in popular

[1] See also pp. 187–8.

belief that came about during the century was in many ways more important to the churches than the scholarly arguments. Down to the middle decades, men of every religious allegiance and social class believed in witches. They did not merely suppose that a few old women could cast spells, or that some of their neighbours attended secret rituals. They knew that they were surrounded and menaced by agents of the devil, who must be extirpated by the most ruthless and unrelenting persecution. It is one of the hardest phenomena to assess and explain. The evidence about it naturally comes almost entirely from its enemies, and there is no reason to assume that the varying extent of actual participation in witchcraft had much relation to the amount of persecution. Often the details of the practices were obtained under torture or the threat of it—though torture was not used in England. Many confessions were no doubt put into the mouths of the victims or derived from popular gossip. But it is disturbing for the historian who has to compare the value of his sources to realise that the habits of the devil when he appeared in human or animal shape are recorded more voluminously and with greater precision and consistency from every part of Europe than many of the social and economic facts we rely on. Behind the lurid fabrications of the trials there may well have existed a remnant of pagan religion attractive to people at every level who felt the need to belong to a group other than the accepted society. In the secrecy, in the defiance of the most deep-rooted conventions and beliefs, in the sexual orgies and the frenzies, in the illusion of power, all the instinctive desires of the deprived and dissatisfied were met. How many villages really had their covens, how many people really assembled on the Brocken or the local hill-top on the High Days we shall never know. What we do know abundantly is that the persecution of witches was an innovation that revealed some of the blackest aspects of the state and the churches. We know too that by the turn of the century the massive persecutions and fears had in most places come to an end.

In the Middle Ages the Church had on the whole regarded witchcraft as a fairly harmless aberration of the ignorant or an incidental manifestation of heresy. There were 'evil spirits', as the New Testament made clear; and there were witches who, the Book of Exodus commanded, were not to be suffered to live. But the Inquisition in the fifteenth century was the first body to make the destruction of witches a large-scale activity. Throughout the sixteenth century the fear of witches had grown. The Reformation may well have helped to spread it—not because there was much difference between Catholic and Protestant attitudes, but because both stressed the existence of different, evil, religions and the duty to attack them without mercy. By the 1590s the panic and the attack were well established. The inflation of witchcraft is like that of prices in having sharp rises and falls within the general trend. The periods of greatest intensity vary from country to country, for reasons sometimes obvious and sometimes obscure. The Civil War in England was a time of furious witch-hunting; but the area where Matthew Hopkins, the 'witch-finder-general', carried out most of his monotonous trials was Essex and East Anglia, prosperous and comparatively little affected by the fighting. Distress and disorder could not explain the other peak period in England, the reign of James I. The king's own early work on Demonology, derived from trials in Scotland, may have done something to encourage the activity. For a time he seems to have suffered a paranoiac conviction that witches were behind all his political troubles. Later he became cautiously sceptical and enjoyed himself in revealing fraudulent and hysterical cases of 'possession'. In England witches were hanged. Nearly everywhere else, including Scotland, burning was the only death that suited their crime or destroyed their power. The Thirty Years War provided conditions that favoured both popular belief and persecution uninhibited by legal technicalities. But again extreme distress and disorder seem to have been less effective in producing panics than the presence of a few enthusiastic and powerful witch-hunters. In the 1620s the Prince-Bishops of Bamberg and Würzburg each averaged something like a hundred burnings a year. The Rhineland bishoprics were almost as bad. Many of the areas of witch-burning were also areas of famine and devastation; but these seem at the most to have strengthened a process already begun. Moreover the western side of the Rhine, Franche-Comté and Lorraine, claimed as many witches as the eastern. Catholic Germany was if anything more witch-ridden than was Protestant.

Persecution, once started, was all too easy to continue. As in other inquisitorial processes, the great aim of the torturer was to extract the names of other guilty persons. No further evidence was required, though the familiar stories incessantly reappeared from eye-witnesses. There could be no better way for one group in a village to damage another, or for the victim to have his posthumous revenge on old enemies. It could be useful to those seeking to impose religious conformity: Calvinists and Jesuits alike were the most zealous of witch-hunters. Most of the intellectual leaders of every kind joined in the outcry, or at least kept silent. Bacon, Descartes, and Kepler all accepted witchcraft as an obvious part of life. Bodin had been one of the most insistent persecutors. The opponents of witch-burning did not deny that the practice existed: they merely claimed that the confessions and denunciations extracted under torture were not adequate proof of guilt, and that some professed witches were fraudulent or deluded. Only a few eccentrics like the Dutchman Balthasar Bekker in the 1690s went so far as to deny that the Devil interfered in human affairs at all.

Witchcraft did not disappear easily. In Spain it even achieved, in the darkest years of Charles II, something of a revival. Nor could the decline of persecution be acclaimed as a triumph of reason over superstition. Most people believed in the less diabolical forms of magic. To the peasant its laws remained as much a part of life as the laws of the landlord and the state. There were still many statesmen, generals, and scientists who thought astrology worth taking into account. Throughout literate society it was necessary for all but the most defiant to adopt a double, or rather a multiple, standard of belief. For most practical purposes the universe had become a mechanistic one. The supernatural could occupy a larger or a smaller segment of the mind according to circumstances; and this applied to Christian as well as to non-Christian beliefs. The connection was proclaimed, for his own ends, by Joseph Glanvill, the most popular of the English defenders of witch-beliefs at the time when they were receding into the background:

> Those that dare not bluntly say, 'There is no God' content themselves (for a fair step and introduction) to deny that there are spirits and witches.[1]

It was a smear with some logical sense behind it. Most of those who believed in sporadic divine interference with the workings of nature, and who accepted the Christian doctrine of a personal Devil as well as a personal God, now denounced the hysteria and injustice of witch persecution. They could not easily claim that the supposed supernatural happenings were either impossible or unimportant. Total rejection of the discredited notion of witchcraft could only come as part of a separation of religious ways of thought from those on which daily life was based. All who were aware of the general field of human knowledge and thought could see that within it the area of the scientific and the material was expanding at the expense of that of the divine and the magical. In the first, certainty was steadily increasing, in the second, doubt. If between the two there was a vast no-man's-land of ambiguity and hypocrisy, we are in no position to sneer today.

[1] *Philosophical Considerations touching Witches and Witchcraft* (1667).

VI

Science

In most kinds of human activity the seventeenth century was, in the end, a period of failure. Hopeful revolutions were crushed; political and social ideals faded; intolerance and oppression flourished; hardly anything was done to mitigate disease and famine; where material

BIBLIOGRAPHY. There is now an abundance of works, comprehensible to the non-scientist, dealing with the movement in general. E. J. Dijksterhuis, *The Mechanisation of the World Picture* (English trans., Oxford, 1961), covering the period from Plato to Newton, combines a brilliantly argued interpretation with arrangement that makes it an easy work of reference. A. C. Crombie, *Augustine to Galileo* (2nd ed., London, 1961, 2 vols.) is another authoritative account that stresses the continuity of development. More specifically on this period are Marie Boas, *The Scientific Renaissance 1450–1630* (London, 1962) and A. R. Hall, *From Galileo to Newton, 1630–1720* (London, 1963), both in the 'Rise of Modern Science' series. The earlier work by A. R. Hall, *The Scientific Revolution, 1500–1800* (London, 1954) is slightly more technical. All these include good bibliographies. Hugh Kearney, *Origins of the Scientific Revolution* (London, 1964) is a survey of modern writing on the subject with short selections from seventeenth-century works.

For the connection of science with social and economic change, see the controversy between Christopher Hill, Hugh Kearney, T. K. Rabb, and others in *Past and Present*, nos. 27–32 (1964–5). R. K. Merton, 'Science, Technology, and Society in Seventeenth-century England' in *Osiris*, no. 4 (1938) is one of the clearest statements of the view that causal connections existed. G. N. Clark, *Science and Social Welfare in the Age of Newton* (Oxford, 1937) argues against the Marxist claims.

On astronomy S. Drake, *Discoveries and Opinions of Galileo* (New York, 1957) is one of the few selections that make the original writing of the scientists readily and cheaply available. D. C. Allen, *The Star-crossed Renaissance* (Durham, N. Carolina, 1941) and T. S. Kuhn, *The Copernican Revolution* (Cambridge, Mass., 1957) are two reputable works. A. Koestler, *The Sleepwalkers* (London, 1959) is a very readable non-academic commentary, largely on Kepler. One of the most important current writers is A. Koyré, whose books include *From the Closed World to the Infinite Universe* (Baltimore, 1957); *La révolution astronomique* (Paris, 1961); *Études galiléennes*, (new ed., Paris, 1965); and *Newtonian Studies* (London, 1965).

resources increased, they were squandered in war. No other century until the twentieth produced so much unnecessary destruction. But in one achievement these years are outstanding. The great barriers in human thought that held back the advance in understanding the material universe were decisively breached. The 'Scientific[1] Revolution', a term that would have meant nothing to historians of the period a couple of generations ago, is now recognised by many as one of its most significant aspects.

There are two ways in which knowledge can be accepted: a thing can be believed because it has always been believed, because 'everyone' believes it, because it is written in an unchallenged authority; or it can be believed because observation and reasoning make it seem more likely than any alternative, and because it is compatible with other beliefs established in this way. Few individuals have exclusively one kind of outlook or the other; and none of the seventeenth-century scientists crossed the barriers of tradition and authority completely. Everyone knows the legend of Galileo recanting his errors before the Inquisition and murmuring 'All the same, it does move.' The story itself is as unscientific a piece of history as anyone could find: it seems to have been invented in the eighteenth century. But Galileo and most such men did behave in the way the remark suggests. They were neither martyrs nor rebels by nature: they insisted that new knowledge was compatible with old belief. From Kepler at the beginning of the century to Newton at the end, the most eminent scientists were fascinated by such pursuits as alchemy, astrology, or numerology that now seem wholly irrational.

Galileo made his explanation of the Bible's misstatements about the material universe perfectly clear: they were there because it was intended for the common people who would be confused by more unfamiliar versions. He did not claim any originality for such a view. St. Augustine had insisted that the scriptures should not be taken as a literal explanation of physical phenomena: for 'why should the Bible

Among the biographical studies are L. Chauvois, *William Harvey* (London, 1957); R. Lenoble, *Mersenne, ou la naissance du mécanisme* (Paris, 1943); A. Kenny, *Descartes* (New York, 1968); S. Brodetsky, *Sir Isaac Newton* (London, 1927); M.' Éspinasse, *Robert Hooke* (London, 1956).

---

[1] The terms 'science' and 'scientist' are used here in their modern sense. In 1600 'science' usually meant something wider—almost 'knowledge'—and the study of the material universe was called 'natural philosophy'. By 1700 in both French and English, the more limited sense in which Descartes had begun to use the word was common.

be believed concerning the resurrection of the dead . . . when it is considered to be erroneously written as to points which admit of direct demonstration or unquestionable reasoning?'[1] Even the later enthusiasm for the study of geology and of fossils led men to ask not whether but how their evidence could be reconciled with the story of the creation and the flood. But religion was not the only kind of dogma. If the authority of the Bible could not be attacked, the authority of the 'ancients', and in particular of Aristotle, undoubtedly could. A century earlier the concern of Renaissance philosophy with Plato had deprived Aristotle of some of his pre-eminence. To denounce him—or at least his devotees—as the personification of an anti-scientific attitude now became a typical mark of the new scholarship.

Bacon

One of the most forthright enemies of all authority that restricted the quest for knowledge was Francis Bacon. Whatever his merits as a lawyer and writer, he has never had unqualified admiration from scientists. He rejected Copernicus, saw no useful connection between science and mathematics, believed in indiscriminate rather than planned experiments, distrusted deduction from general principles. He also had a great capacity for proclaiming other people's ideas as his own. Nevertheless, even though he did not always stress the infinite amount that was yet to be discovered, he did more than anyone to destroy the idea of the Aristotelians that little of importance remained to be added to human knowledge. He had no patience with those who 'almost incorporated the contentious philosophy of Aristotle into the Christian religion', and who thought that 'the secrets of nature were secrets of God' into which men should not probe.[2] Baconian science, whatever its intellectual shortcomings, was full of optimism and of practical purpose. His scheme for the 'advancement of learning' blended—some would say confused—its utilitarian aspect with a vision of knowledge expanding for its own sake. In England at least, his prestige and the popularity of his writings did much to make scientific activity reputable.

Astronomy

The most controversial of the early seventeenth-century scientific activities was clearly that of the astronomers. They could claim practical reasons for their studies: predictions about the moon and tides, charts

---

[1] Quoted by Galileo in his Letter to the Grand Duchess (Drake, *Galileo*, p. 208).   [2] *Filum Labyrinthi*, Section 7.

of the stars for navigation, and even the calendar itself were notoriously inaccurate; and any mistakes in astrological prediction of human affairs were likewise attributed to mistakes in observation. By 1600 the work of Copernicus, written seventy years before, was fairly well known to scholars. It had been designed partly to remove the observational inconsistencies and unnecessary complexities in Ptolemy's system of spheres, partly perhaps to uphold a mystical belief in the sun as the source of life. The idea of the sun as the centre of the universe was not entirely novel, and though Protestants attacked it as contrary to biblical texts, the Catholic Church was not at first much worried. The strong religious objections only came when followers of Copernicus suggested that a universe that appears unchanged from different positions of a moving earth must be infinitely large and presumably contained other inhabited planets. One of the offences of Giordano Bruno was that he had supported this notion of the 'Plurality of worlds'. A multiplicity of redeeming Christs was an intolerable heresy. This was an objection of theologians. The greater danger to religion came when observation of the universe seemed to suggest that it could keep going without a divine power to drive it. When the churches found that astronomers, whatever they said, were making a personal God less necessary, they began to attack them with the familiar weapon of biblical texts. It was this attack that first showed the Catholic Church as more hostile than Protestantism to the 'new philosophy'.

Galileo

In 1609 Galileo Galilei heard how 'a certain Fleming' had devised a glass by which distant objects were made to appear nearer. Here, he realised, was an invention that might help to settle through observation the conflict between the Ptolemaic and the Copernican systems. But Galileo was not primarily an observer or experimenter. He had become a distinguished Professor of Mathematics at Padua, already a centre of scientific ideas and of comparative freedom from authoritarian interference with scholarship. It was through mathematics rather than through the unreliable evidence of the senses that Galileo sought to discover laws of motion. But though his theories were those of Plato's idealism, he could never resist the pleasure of experiment—and not always the temptation to be too readily convinced that it had given the right result. Aristotle's view that the heavier a body the more rapidly it fell could be questioned simply by imagining what happens if two stones of unequal weight are tied together and dropped. Mathematics alone could show what the rate of acceleration must be. Galileo still spent enormous energy on the famous experiments with pendulums and with balls rolled down an inclined plane. In his first sophisticated formulae relating weight, acceleration, and motion, he accepted the idea that motion must arise either from 'impetus' or from the 'tendency' of bodies to return to their original place. Gradually his emphasis turned from the cause of motion to the calculation of its changes. The idea of an 'inertia' of motion as well as of rest replaced the Aristotelian assumption that only continued force could maintain movement. No experiment on earth could show this directly. But the orbits of the planets could be an instance of motion without resistance; this mathematical aspect of astronomy was naturally not grasped by those who saw his teachings simply as an attack on established belief. Nor was it the only thing that mattered to Galileo himself.

Within a few months of his first experiment with lenses, he had a telescope that revealed the moons revolving round Jupiter and the innumerable stars of the Milky Way. A year later, in 1610, his pamphlet *Siderius Nuncius* (meaning, he said, news of the stars—not that he was claiming to be a messenger of heaven) set down some of the revelations of the telescope. Its success among scholars made the Jesuits and the Inquisition take up Copernican astronomy as a major topic of theological arguments—some highly abstruse, some on the level of 'How did Joshua stop the sun if it was not moving?' At this stage the new ideas were regarded not as damnable heresy but as matter for argument, sometimes bitter, sometimes good-humoured. 'Ye Galileans, why stand ye gazing up into heaven?'[1] Father Cacchini, who was reported to have taken this as the text of a sermon that became celebrated for its violence, was so sweeping and irresponsible in his denunciation of every intelligent idea that Galileo could make good use of him. The replies, written in Italian and full of gently ironical concessions, avoided outright heresy. But they established his success, unique among the leaders of the new thought, as a popular writer, and it was popularity that made him a menace to the authority of the Church. He could no longer be taken lightly. Hence in 1615 came Galileo's first trial by the Holy Office, in which he recanted his errors and was let off with the penalty of reciting seven psalms a week. If it was hoped that this would cure him, the optimism was mutual. For Galileo did not question that the Catholic Church was a desirable institution: so great was its wisdom

[1] Acts of the Apostles c. 1 v. 11—but the pun may be one of the many apocryphal stories about Galileo.

that eventually it would see it was mistaken in persecuting him. Meanwhile it was better to accept its mistakes than let it make a worse one in killing him.

In 1632 Galileo produced his *Dialogue, on the two chief systems of the world,* ostensibly an impartial debate between Copernican ideas and those of the Ptolemaics and Aristotelians who 'make an oracle of a log'. It was enjoyed everywhere as a triumph for heliocentric theory over the church. The church returned to the attack and, despite further abjurations, he spent his last years in fairly lenient imprisonment. By then he had produced arguments that, imperfect and sometimes self-contradictory though they were, destroyed all rational belief in Aristotle's tightly knit system. He had no equally comprehensive or unified system to put in its place: his answers were not complete, and usually not quite right. He did not use the telescope for accurate observation. His own preconceptions in favour of simplicity—especially his belief that all orbits are circular—were almost as unscientific as those he scoffed at. He was by no means averse from constructing a theory first, making observations second, and if they disagreed concluding that the observations must be wrong. His mathematical knowledge was applied more in formulae than in measurement. His conclusions are qualitative rather than quantitative, and very many of them destructive rather than constructive. But ignorance has never, since his attack, been quite as easy to preserve.

Kepler

The astronomer who went furthest towards our own notions of the universe, Johann Kepler, was completely different in outlook, achievement, and mistakes. Kepler was a German and a Protestant. His interest in mathematics was a more abstract one: his work on astronomy arose from a study of conic sections rather than weights and cannon-balls. Driven from the University of Graz by religious persecution, he joined and afterwards succeeded Tycho Brahe as 'court mathematician' to Rudolph II, an indiscriminate patron of scholars and pseudo-scholars. But like most of the emperor's financial affairs, this patronage of learning was heavily in arrears, and Kepler lived largely on the proceeds of freelance astrology, in which he appears to have had a convenient half belief. Indeed, no-one typified better the outlook of the new scientists: his idea that the divine harmony of the universe was expressed in some hidden magic of numbers led him to fantastic efforts to find a pattern in the stars that would fit the shapes of regular solids or the spacing of notes in musical scales. But his work was more fruitful than that of any contemporary astronomer. His indefatigable labour on charts and calculations, and his rejection of failure after failure in the belief that a true solution would turn up eventually, were sometimes in the spirit of the medieval alchemist rather than the modern researcher. Yet where Galileo wrote popular controversial works, Kepler wrote for mathematicians. His three 'laws' were arrived at largely by checking, with the help of the observation tower designed by Tycho and of some laborious and skilful mathematics, a whole series of imagined explanations of planetary motions. The first, that planets move round the sun in elliptical orbits, was apparently what Copernicus and others had accepted, but Kepler's ellipses were established by exact measurement. The second law showed that as a planet moves further from the sun, its speed decreases, so that a line from planet to sun always sweeps across the same area in any given time. He established it by first trying a variety of theories that would give some mathematical law to fit the apparently irregular speed; then hitting on a calculation that confirmed the theory of the equal areas; and finally discovering the mistakes that had cancelled each other out. These discoveries were announced in 1609. It was not until ten years later that the third law appeared as a mere afterthought. It found that the square of the time taken by a planet to complete its orbit bears a constant ratio to the cube of its mean distance from the sun. Kepler's descriptions of what happened in the heavens reached a level of mathematical understanding far in advance of anything achieved before. When he asked how it happened he came to the verge of a more fundamental change. Movements as closely integrated as those he had described could not be the result of independent spirits moving each planet separately. 'If the word "soul" (*anima*) is replaced by "force" (*vis*),' he said, we have the principle on which his physics rests.[1] It was a principle that remained unexplained even by Newton.

Descartes

In 1637, when Galileo's work was almost at an end, there appeared from the freer printing-presses of Leiden an anonymous book, in French, that attracted little attention—the *Discourse on Method*. René Descartes was the son of a minor office-holder in Brittany with aspirations towards

[1] Dijkserthuis, who quotes this (*Mechanization of the World Picture*, p. 310), gives Kepler more credit than do many writers for moving from an animistic to a mechanistic outlook.

the *noblesse*. He had suffered what he regarded as the misfortune of a Jesuit education, fought as a gentleman volunteer in the Thirty Years War, and—for reasons which he insisted had nothing to do with persecution—settled in Holland. Throughout his youth, as he explained in the *Discourse*, his scepticism about the contradictory and ill-founded teachings of scholastics had grown. He devoted himself not to reading but to thinking; and thinking had led to his three 'principles'—to accept as certain nothing of which the least doubt was possible, to divide the problems he studied into the smallest possible 'packets'; and to reason always from the simpler to the more complex questions. His aim was nothing less than to construct a new universal system of knowledge. Seeking for a starting-point for the deductive process that would make this possible, he arrived at the statement—much less clear in its meaning than he imagined—'I think, therefore I am'. From this he went on (by a process very like the familiar arguments of the schoolmen he purported to reject) to discover that 'God' also exists. So, for reasons that were moving rapidly away from the proclaimed principle of certainty, did a material universe entirely distinct from the human mind. To the study of this he was now ready to devote himself.

In his later writings, and in his vast correspondence, he put forward ideas—his 'subtle matter' that filled the universe, the 'vortices' in it that produced motion, the 'soul' situated in the pineal gland and controlling the body through the 'nervous fluid'—which mingled scientific precision with brilliant but often bizarre imaginings. It is not for any practical discoveries, or even for his highly important work in geometry, that he won his pre-eminent place in the scientific movement as well as in the history of philosophy. Perhaps unjustly, he became the figurehead of the trend towards a separation of the material from the religious spheres of thought. Descartes' God was, so far as the natural universe was concerned, the watchmaker who no longer interfered with his machine. To Cartesians questions about everything from the stars to microscopic creatures must be answered with as little reference to spirits, humours, mystical or magical principles as to biblical or classical texts. If the answers were wrong this did not matter so much as the recognition that they could be replaced by others. Descartes was in fact regarded by both disciples and enemies as the principal author of the 'bargain' by which the study of the material universe could continue unimpeded by faith in an immaterial one—a bargain which intelligent divines came to recognise as being to their advantage, but which the churches in general never accepted. He was even less eager than

Galileo to involve himself in open conflict with religious authority. However certain his conclusions appeared to him, he would not, he claimed, 'for anything in the world uphold them against the authority of the church'.[1] The church refrained from persecuting him; but his works remained on the Index of forbidden books. The more popular 'Cartesianism' became among educated Frenchmen, the greater the church's hostility. It was one thing to reconcile a mechanical universe with 'God', another to reconcile it with transubstantiation.

Measurement

Galileo, Kepler, and Descartes all in their different ways recognised that the basis of any new understanding of the universe must be a mathematical one. Already a fashionable part of the interest of educated gentlemen, mathematics in the seventeenth century made progress that took it far beyond the understanding of all who lack the special talents it demands. But many of the most necessary advances of the mathematicians concerned simply the equipment and terminology they used, and far from being the most abstruse part of science had immediate practical application. Arabic numerals, already familiar to scholars, came into general use around the middle of the century. Simon Stevin, the military engineer, introduced the decimal point. The table of logarithms worked out by John Napier and the slide-rule became common aids to calculation. A more fundamental change in the working of mathematics came with the application to classical geometry of the new algebra. From the work of mathematicians all over Europe there developed the whole new system of analytic geometry and the measurement of change. Kepler and many others saw the possibilities of measuring a curve by imagining it to consist of a very large number of very small straight lines. From this the stage was reached where Newton and Leibnitz produced at the same time[2] and in slightly different forms the differential and the integral calculus. Without it astronomical measurements, however good, could not make complete sense.

Side by side with higher mathematics, the simple apparatus of measurement was improving all the time. The links between craftsman and scientist were closer in the seventeenth century than in the generations before and after; and it was in measurement that they were most apparent. Realisation of the need for agreed quantitative standards in everything came very slowly. For a few purposes anyone can devise his own ways of measuring. Galileo made a thermometer, as did several

[1] Descartes' letter to Mersenne, April 1634.   [2] See p. 146.

of his contemporaries, each using his own arbitrary scale. It was not until 1724 that Gabriel Fahrenheit calibrated his mercury thermometer with the now accepted system. In the same way the principle of the barometer was known long before it was used to give precise measurements of atmospheric pressure. Even with weight, vital to trade and finance as well as manufactures and science, the balance was in the seventeenth century more accurate than the units it compared. The distance of the moon, or the focal length of a lens, were still worked out in units derived from the plough or the thumb. Only angular measurement, as fractions of the circle, could be indefinitely narrowed in accuracy just by more precisely made instruments.

But one measuring device, whose production was an industry in itself, was everywhere the same and was steadily improved by practical skill and scientific knowledge. The accuracy of clocks could be tested fairly well by the sun; in them the astronomer and the navigator seeking to measure longitude at sea both demanded precision and reliability. The Dutch physicist Christian Huygens constructed in the 1650s clocks specifically for use in navigation. He had already seen that the simple pendulum is not quite 'isochronous'; to discover the curve that it needs to follow to be really accurate involved a major mathematical achievement that occupied him for twenty years and contributed directly to the work of Newton. The difficulties were not only in suspension: they came from the differences in the earth's gravity and axial motion, and from heat expansion. While Huygens was working on the problems, the *Académie des Sciences* organised the expedition to Cayenne in French Guiana which found that a one-second pendulum is one-tenth of an inch shorter near the equator than in Paris. It was comparatively easy to calculate, and demonstrate, that taking a pendulum clock up a mountain would make it lose time. Both Huygens and Hooke had examined the alternative to the pendulum, the balance wheel and hair spring; but these too demand temperature compensation. The clock is only the most obvious instance of the links between mathematics, experimental science, craftsmanship, and demand. The development of lens-making is a similar story. But it cannot be claimed that the scientist and the craftsman always worked in happy collaboration. If anything by the end of the century the social barriers between them seemed more rigid than before, and scientific interest shifted away from the topics of immediate practical value.

The human body

Besides the universe, the thing most mysterious and important for men to observe was their own bodies. Here too new knowledge had to struggle against entrenched belief. Hippocrates, and still more the works ascribed to the Hellenic physician Galen, were for the student of anatomy and medicine authorities as exalted as Aristotle for the physicist. To most people the body was as directly governed by its soul as the universe by its maker; but, like the universe, the body was also the site of an endless conflict between good and evil. There was no rigid distinction between a possessing 'spirit' and a material fluid. The four 'humours' of the body, vaguely linking visible substances with mental and physical states, were accepted with just the pseudo-scientific credulity doctors and patients always find helpful. Remedies were derived partly from the principles of magic, partly from more or less successful trial and error. As in other ages, there was not much connection between their popularity and their efficacy. In understanding the chemistry of the body the seventeenth century made little headway, and the understanding of it as a machine brought few practical benefits. Men suffered and died with about the same balance of benefit and harm from their physicians and surgeons in 1700 as in 1600. But ways to improvement previously closed were now wide open.

There was no obvious reason to dispute Galen's anatomical system: indeed, it seemed to show admirably the perfect wisdom of God. From the liver, the source of the vital spirit, or 'pneuma', the nourishing blood of the veins was sent outward through the body. Some of it was drawn in by the heart, where, as it passed from the right ventricle to the left, the life-giving spirit was infused into it. Then it went outward as the different blood of the arteries. The lungs were primarily a cooling system supplying the heart with air. Several anatomists, notably Vesalius and Cesalpino in the sixteenth century, had come near to recognising the circulation of the blood without achieving the rejection of Galen that would have led to the simplest explanation of what they saw. Hironimus Fabricius, professor of anatomy at Padua, had described the valves that prevent blood in the veins from going outwards, without drawing the obvious conclusion. William Harvey was a pupil of Fabricius at Padua in Galileo's time, but his career was spent mainly at St. Bartholomew's Hospital and at the court of James I and Charles I. (One of his jobs was the physical examination of witches.) He was at first a faithful follower of Aristotle and Galen, anxious to reconcile their statements with his own observation. But on the heart this was impossible: even the crudest measurement showed that it pumped out blood much faster than the body could conceivably manufacture and absorb it. Circulation was the only possible solution. How it was achieved Harvey did not know: the microscope involved more difficult problems of accurate lens grinding than the telescope, and the capillaries that link veins with arteries were not seen until half a century later. What is now regarded as Harvey's great discovery was not proclaimed, and probably not seen, by him as a challenging new revelation. His book *On the Motion of the Heart*, published (in Latin) in Frankfurt in 1628, flattered Charles I with the conventional analogies between the heart, the sun, and the king, and identified the blood with the 'spirit'. Later he seemed to regard the blood as the real source of life. Whether a social and political significance can be attached to his 'dethroning of the heart' has been hotly argued.[1] What in practice mattered more was his increasing escape from analogies and from 'spirits' into a purely material view of the body. Like Descartes, he reduced the soul almost to the status of a chemical component of the body. The danger in the enthusiasm for studying the body as a machine was that nearly all those who did so convinced themselves that a complete explanation of its working was within their grasp and when they were defeated resorted to specious theories and undefined terms which they confused with observed facts.

Reproduction

Men, animals, and plants had one characteristic in common which contained disturbing scientific and religious implications. They reproduced themselves, and in doing so handed on recognisable characteristics to their descendants. With animals reproduction was not the only way. One of the most firmly held of the scientific teachings of Aristotle, expanded by many medieval writers, was spontaneous generation. To question this, Sir Thomas Browne had said, 'is to question reason, sense, and experience'. Johann van Helmont, the discoverer of carbon dioxide, produced a recipe for making mice out of cheese and dirty linen. Everyone knew that putrefied meat generated maggots; but some accounts of the spontaneous appearance of bees and frogs reached almost the same level of mythology as the phoenix. Harvey was uncertain about it. It was not until 1688 that Francesco Redi after experiments

[1] See the article by Christopher Hill in *Past and Present*, no. 27 (1964), pp. 54–72, and the discussion of it in nos. 30 and 31.

and observations—such as the not very difficult one of protecting the meat from flies—claimed that all life arises from reproduction.

Some of the most absurd theories arose from the most successful observations. Marcello Malpighi in Italy, and Jan Swammerdam in Holland, after studying the foetus in eggs, and discovering that minute insects had organs not unlike those of larger animals, popularised the theory of 'preformation'—that a tiny but complete animal existed in the ovum. The apparently logical extension of this idea was the doctrine of 'encapsulation'—that every female would contain all her descendants, inside each other in ever-diminishing scale. Eve had therefore contained the entire human species which at some predetermined time would come to an end. The rôle of the male was merely to stimulate the development of the next generation. This seemed to threaten one of the fundamental assumptions of European society—that the noble qualities inherent in the upper classes descended, like property, in the male line. The greatest of the Dutch microscopists of his generation, Antoni van Leeuwenhoek, who in the 1670s discovered the existence of male spermatozoa, modified these distressingly feminist notions in favour of what came to be called animalculism. It was after all the male, as Aristotle had said, who mattered. He provided the tiny animal: the female was merely a convenient place for it to develop. Neither view of course was remotely compatible with the then familiar facts about heredity. Yet fantasy of this kind was combined with an insatiable zeal in observing forms of life as small as the single cell. Leeuwenhoek's microscope was not improved on for well over a century. The capacity to observe was at this point far ahead of the developments in chemistry that were necessary to make sense of what was seen.

Classification

Observation—patient, unprejudiced, and on a large scale—was in many fields of science the greatest advance that could be made. Many writers, both classical and medieval, had named and classified plants and animals. Interest in this had received a new impetus from the unheard-of specimens brought back from America and the tropics. Bestiaries and catalogues of herbs abounded. The fascination of mere lists of names was delightfully exploited by Shakespeare and Milton. But naturalists were seeking more meaningful nomenclature and grouping. A great variety of publications attempted this. The Swiss Konrad Gesner had produced in the sixteenth century encyclopaedic works on all the known plants and animals. New methods of classification appeared constantly in the next hundred years, and new plants were identified by the thousand. Perhaps the greatest name in this field is that of the Englishman John Ray, who had the best kind of collector's mind—full of zeal for additions to his catalogues, meticulous in his knowledge and accuracy. Many of his methods of grouping and naming were taken over by Linnaeus and others in the next generation to form the basis of modern classification. But like the men in so many fields who achieved the breakthrough to the scientific method, Ray was original mainly in his rejection of irrational assumptions and his readiness to admit imperfection.

Biology was almost as deeply involved as astronomy in awkward religious questions. How were ovist and animalculist theories reconciled with the miraculous birth of Christ? Was the last judgment timed for the moment when the stock of human beings was exhausted? Could all the newly discovered species have fitted into the ark? Arguments of this kind, though a great deal of print was devoted to them, did not produce in England and Holland anything like the organised repression that had almost killed scientific studies in Italy after Galileo. English Puritanism and the more tolerant Dutch Calvinism not merely refrained from persecuting science: they were, within limits, favourable to it. The Puritan believed in utility and in knowledge, and he hated obscurantist theology. He was prepared both to applaud the practical application of studies of nature and to see them as a tribute to the glory of God. Whether this undoubted shift of the main centres of scientific activity from Catholic to Protestant countries can be extended to the claim that individuals who held strongly Protestant views were more likely than others to become scientists is another matter. The numbers involved are so small that arguments about it tend to turn into the inconclusive listing of names. What is certain is that there existed everywhere, in greater or less degree, conservative forces in the churches and in the universities that were hostile to every manifestation of the 'new philosophy'. Victory over these would come less through the persuasive powers of a few men of genius, than through the acceptance of science that spread through a large part of politically and economically powerful society. Merchant communities were interested in the practical value of scientific discovery in such fields as navigation, and prepared to some extent to patronise them. But it was among men of leisure as well as education that there appeared the enthusiastic amateurs who formed the link between the scholars and the community at large.

Scientific societies

Organised assemblies for the exchange of scholarly information were by no means new. The literary 'academy' had been fashionable in Renaissance Italy. One of Bacon's schemes had been for large-scale corporate activity in which he believed anyone with leisure could contribute to knowledge. Galileo belonged to the *Accademia dei Lincei*; but this was no more than an association of men who corresponded without attempting any collective enterprise. The first of the active societies—and for a long time the last notable Italian contribution to science—was the *Accademia del Cimento*, founded in 1657 by the Grand Duke of Tuscany. If the Medici could no longer afford splendid palaces, they could pay for the best laboratories and instruments available, and though they allowed the project to die after ten years, it had shown the attractions of co-operative work and publication of results. Societies of this character arose in Germany, but they lacked the opportunity to develop beyond a local scale; and despite the example of the *Académie française*, which Richelieu established as an official institution in 1635, the French societies before Louis XIV were small groups of friends and correspondents.

Elizabethan England had produced the unique institution of Gresham College, endowed by the great financier and supported by merchants of the city as a centre for a form of education more practical than any the universities provided. It was also a meeting-place of scientists; and from it derived the informal groups of mathematicians, astronomers, physicians, and others who began during the Civil War to hold weekly meetings. One of them was Cromwell's brother-in-law John Wilkins, who asked why his age had not the same means as the ancient Romans to attempt 'mechanical discoveries'. Another was the German refugee Theodore Haak, a correspondent of most of the chief European scholars. A second group with a more technological bias, that gathered round the versatile Polish refugee Samuel Hartlib, a merchant with a wide interest in science but no claim to academic learning, was associated with what Boyle occasionally called the 'Invisible College'. Under the Commonwealth members of these informal associations who moved to Oxford established the discussion group that was later regarded as a precursor of the Royal Society.[1] When Charles II sponsored the formation of

[1] The various groups have often been made to appear more distinct and organised than the evidence justifies. See Christopher Hill, *Intellectual Origins of the English Revolution* (London, 1965), c. 3, part 4, and M. Purver, *The Royal Society, Concept and Creation* (London, 1967).

the Royal Society, many of its fellows were as amateur as the King himself, who was proudly reported to spend long hours in his laboratory. Lacking substantial resources and genuine state encouragement, it never approached the ideals of collective discovery expounded by Bacon or Comenius. Many of its members never got beyond the zeal for reporting curious natural phenomena; others were closely concerned with the collecting of information with an immediate economic value; a few were among the great original experimenters. To all of them the Society gave a reliable means of communication. The *Philosophical Transactions*, to which scholars in many other countries subscribed and contributed, established the modern means of circulating news of scientific and academic activities through the 'learned journal' rather than prolific individual correspondence.

In France one of the most assiduous of correspondents, the friar Marin Mersenne, helped to create the group of Paris scientists which after his death developed into a circle perhaps too fashionable for high scholarly standards. But from it arose in 1666, with Colbert's backing, the *Académie royale des Sciences*. Unlike the Royal Society it had abundant state support. To its observatory—better than Greenwich— came Cassini from Italy, Roemer from Denmark, Huygens from Holland. Astronomy here was a matter not for half-theological theory but for accurate measurement. The shape of the solar system was already recognised: the *Académie* and its outstanding native member Jean Picard began the assessment of its size. The expedition to Cayenne made possible a fairly accurate measurement of the distances of Mars and of the sun. Louis' government was the first to invest generously in discoveries that combined the prestige of spectacular achievement with information of direct value to the state. Colbert, to whom the *Académie des Sciences* was only a part of the centralisation of learning under the state, occasionally reminded it of the relationship of science to industry. It was this aspect of the learned society that appealed strongly to the German princes and municipal governments who encouraged small-scale learned societies of their own. The Scientific Academy created by the Elector of Brandenburg in 1700 was, as even Leibnitz wanted it to be, wholly devoted to the prestige and well-being of the state. By this time the days when the gentlemanly dilettante and the scientist could work happily together were coming to an end. As higher mathematics became an essential part of most of the arguments, the squires and rich townsmen were less and less able to understand what it was all about.

Boyle

The most distinguished of the Royal Society's members was a man whose life and outlook were typical of many aspects of European science in the second half of the century. Robert Boyle, son of the Earl of Cork and educated in the normal manner of his class, combined his scientific work with the study of ancient languages, a directorship of the East India Company, and a zeal for the propagation of the gospel. To try to understand the phenomena of nature was a Christian duty. They should be studied both for the sake of knowledge itself and as a means to economic progress. He showed no contempt for the Baconian type of random experiment and observation. His work with air pumps was at first concerned only with the quality of 'elasticity'. It was only in response to criticism of it that he began the quantitative measurements leading to the 'law'—'that pressures and expansions be in reciprocal proportions'—which immortalised his name. The experiments were also intended to uphold a theory of the nature of matter.

None of the 'ancient' beliefs had shown more staying-power than the Aristotelian theory of the four elements and the rival doctrine of Paracelsus that matter consisted of the three 'principles' of salt, sulphur, and mercury. Descartes' explanation of matter, though claiming to reject all the magical or metaphysical trappings of earlier ideas, had reduced it to three elements whose character depended on the fineness of the particles of which they were composed. It had therefore something in common with another idea of classical origins, now refurbished by the French mathematician Pierre Gassend—Gassendi—that matter consisted of atoms with nothing between them. Boyle in his *Sceptical Chymist* (1661) denounced the lack of proof for any of these, but at the same time put forward as a hypothesis a variant of the atomist theories stressing the idea that atoms form, according to their size and arrangement, elements of differing characteristics which can be blended into compounds. The notion of 'forms' and 'qualities' distinguishable from the material structure of substances was thrown out completely. It sounds like the basis of modern chemistry. But he never found how to identify specific substances as elements or compounds or how a chemical reaction could be explained. Even so, his chemical experiments were so well organised and so accurately recorded that it is hard to realise that while he was publishing these to the Royal Society he was also working secretly as an alchemist, seeking the Philosophers' Stone and the universal remedy for disease. To some extent his scientific activities were divided into compartments where different criteria applied. A similar separation provided his answer to the problem of divine revelation. It did not lead him to diminish his religious faith, nor to move from orthodox Anglican Christianity towards deism. He insisted that God continued to direct the machine he had created: things only worked in accordance with fixed laws because God saw to it that they did.

Newton

The seventeenth century never arrived at the terminology and method necessary for decisive progress in chemistry. Its greatest scientific achievement was the mathematical system that turned its idea of cosmology from coherent observation into measured and apparently irrefutable fact. Isaac Newton was not in his lifetime regarded, at any rate outside England, as a genius standing above all his contemporaries. His reputation was certainly not helped by the paranoiac tendencies that led to his disputes with Hooke and Leibnitz about who thought of what first. Coming from a family of minor gentry or higher yeomanry, he belonged first to a Cambridge purged of its Puritanism, later to the Royal Society and the highest London circles. His Socinian religious beliefs were hidden behind a nominal Anglicanism. Like Boyle, he accepted Holy Writ, and indeed was fascinated by its details. Gradually he seems to have come to regard some of it as allegory rather than fact.[1] Alchemy, and biblical chronology interpreted through astronomy were for long periods among his greatest enthusiasms. Science as a contribution to human welfare made no appeal to him at all: he did a good deal to destroy the links between the Royal Society and manufacturers. Much of his greatest work was done in short bursts of activity, and he was in no hurry to publish it. By the time he became a national figure in the 1690s he was no longer much of a working scientist. It was when Newton was a refugee from the plague in the mid sixties that he first worked on the binomial theorem and began to circulate among his friends the system of 'fluxions'. No full account of it had been published when in 1675 Gottfried Leibnitz, the philosopher to whom mathematics was also a sporadic interest, worked out the infinitesimal calculus which solved the same problems of the measurement of rates of change with a simpler notation. When Leibnitz published his account of the calculus in 1684 there developed the bitter controversy that almost broke off the connections of England with European mathematics. No substantial

[1] See his *General Scholium* in *Works* (2nd ed.), p. 546.

evidence for Newton's charges of plagiarism seems to have existed, and it was certainly Leibnitz whose reputation was enhanced.

Long before the quarrel with Leibnitz's supporters had developed its further implications, Newton was involved in another dispute arising from the optical experiments described in the *Philosophical Transactions*. The subject of light appeared to produce more stubbornness than any other among the scientists of the seventeenth century. For those who believed that everything consisted of matter, light was not easy to explain. There was a familiar dispute between the idea of 'corpuscles' and that of the movement of some kind of 'medium' through which light was transmitted. Descartes had compromised on corpuscles moving, and producing pressure, in his *matière subtile*. Robert Hooke, Newton's greatest English rival, and Christian Huygens independently developed 'wave' theories of transmission. A central problem in optics was that of the colours produced by a prism and— annoyingly—by a lens. If a beam of light fell obliquely on a transparent surface, Hooke argued that one 'edge' of it would hit the surface before the other, and if the new medium transmitted light less (or more) easily than the air, the beam would not only be bent, but 'confused', producing red lights at one 'edge' and blue at the other. Colours were therefore the confused version of pure white light. Working especially with thin layers of mica that produce 'Newton's rings', Hooke achieved some elaborate measurement and mathematical analysis: the rest was speculation with no solid experimental basis and as Newton pointed out was uncomfortably vague when it shifted from the 'waves' to the 'beam'.

Newton's experiments with prisms did not explain the fundamental nature of light: but he showed that colour was not an aberration but white light a 'heterogeneous mixture of rays'. Once separated by one prism, they were not changed further by a second, but could be recombined into white light. Hooke and Huygens bitterly attacked the idea without offering comparable evidence against it. On both sides the argument had something in it of the old philosophy as well as the new. Newton claimed that light must be a substance since only a substance could have the 'quality' of colour. His opponents resented the idea that the light of the sun was not the 'pure' form; coloured light *ought* to be the deviation from it. Nevertheless the controversy led both Hooke and Newton to modify their views; Newton adopted the idea of an 'ether' in which the corpuscles whose existence he still insisted on produced vibrations; Hooke considered the relation of colour to changes in the force of the vibrations. Ironically the man who came closest to the idea that light has a measurable wavelength, shortest for violet and longest for red, was Descartes' disciple Malebranche, who arrived at it from an analogy with sound and with comparatively little mathematical or experimental knowledge. He first put forward his theory in 1699, long after those of Newton and Hooke, but apparently without having heard of them.

When Newton at last brought together and published his work on light, in the *Optiks* of 1704, he referred to differences in the 'bigness' of the vibrations as a possible explanation of colour. This was in the 'Queries' which he appended to the book because as he said, in words that sound like a claim to divinity, 'I have not finished this part of my Design.' He was admittedly modifying his claim not to 'deal in conjectures' and he never answered the question, even though he had long ago performed an experiment that demonstrated the wavelength solution very clearly. (It showed that a ray of light of a single colour had regular short intervals—'fits' as he called them—of easy penetration alternating with easy reflection.) Not only did Newton's reluctance to abandon corpuscles block his own acceptance of the best answer: when his towering reputation was established the wavelength idea came into thorough disrepute merely because he had not asserted it. A Newtonian orthodoxy became as rigid as once the Aristotelian one had been.

In the work that gave him this unique status, written in Latin and having the austere title *Mathematical Principles of Natural Philosophy*, Newton completed as certainties, calculated precisely and in vast detail, what Galileo, Kepler, Hooke, and many others had seen in part. The problem of gravitation seemed very like that of light: in each case something was transmitted that could not be accounted for in obvious mechanical terms. Borelli had suggested that the sun's rays could be acting like levers pushing the planets round. Even those who accepted the idea of an inertia of motion felt that there ought to be a material link between bodies that were attracted to each other—otherwise the mechanical universe was being spoilt by letting in occult qualities producing action at a distance. Descartes and his followers had talked of vortices in the subtle matter, diverting the moon and planets from the straight course they would otherwise have followed for ever. Newton showed that these did not make mathematical sense, and that universal gravitation did. There was nothing new in the idea that all heavenly bodies attracted each other. It could be found in Kepler's discussion of mutual attraction between earth and moon; Hooke had discussed it at the Royal Society, and in correspondence with Newton. The essential equation—that the force of gravity between two bodies varies in inverse proportion to the square of the distance between them—emerged in a way typical of Newton's mathematical mind. He had arrived at it, from work on Kepler's laws and his own measurements of centrifugal force, by 1666, and finding great mathematical difficulties in completing the proof had given it up. Only when Hooke put it to him in 1679 did he take up the idea again. With the help of Picard's accurate measurement of the size of the earth, and of some corrections from Hooke, Newton produced an exact explanation on this basis of the orbits of the planets. Five years later, when the manuscript of the *Principia* was presented to the Royal Society, Hooke and Newton began mutual accusations of plagiarism. In the final version of the *Principia*, Newton announced that Wren, Hooke, and Halley as well as himself had all independently deduced the inverse square law from Kepler's statement.

Newton had no particular yearning for immortality as the discoverer of the 'law of gravity', still less of 'nature's laws' as a whole. He was well aware that gravity was only one of the many phenomena of nature that might be understood in the same way. His real achievement was to establish a scientific outlook more fruitful and consistent than those of Bacon or Descartes. Neither observation nor deduction were enough in themselves: they must yield answers capable of exact measurement and mathematical verification. There should be no confusion between facts that had been proved in this way and theories that had not.[1] The fact of universal gravitation was demonstrable. How it worked was still to be solved. It was this difficulty that the Cartesians seized on in their attack on Newton, who had dismissed their vortices and subtle matter with some contempt. Gravitation, they argued, was not a brilliant advance but a return to the idea of occult forces. Moreover Leibnitz was now their hero; and Newton's God who had to keep his universe going seemed inferior to Leibnitz's 'most perfect being'.

The differences between Newtonian and Cartesian universes were the subject of long and sterile argument. It was a difference altogether smaller than that between the agreed supremacy of observation and deduction and measurement over the ancient reliance on authority and magic. There was of course no total victory. The last years of the

---

[1] 'Hypotheses non fingo'—though repeated in various forms—is not an assertion that can be taken too literally. Among the many discussions of his method are A. Koyré, 'L'hypothèse et l'expérience chez Newton' in *Bulletin de la société française de Philosophie*, no. 1 (1956) and A. C. Crombie, 'Newton's Conception of Scientific Method' in *Bulletin of the Institute of Physics* (1957).

century in England saw the 'Battle of the Books' in which Sir William Temple and his friends came stoutly to the defence of ancient learning against the moderns.[1] In France Bernard de Fontenelle, the most successful populariser of Cartesianism and of the new astronomy, was an early exponent of the idea of progress. Ancients and moderns would in the future, he asserted, be seen alike as contributors to the unlimited expansion of knowledge, which must now be made available to the masses as well as to the intelligentsia. Obstacles to such progress were still formidable. Catholic control over thought seemed stronger than ever over much of southern Europe; and Protestant Churches were seldom ready to assimilate scientific ideas. But, usually without much inkling of the change, men whose grandfathers had lived in a world made of spirits as well as matter pushed these assumptions into a compartment of their thought where they did not interfere with a universe that worked in accordance with laws capable of mechanical explanation. The 'Scientific Revolution' had succeeded.

[1] Swift's *Battle of the Books*, written while he was in Temple's service, made it a celebrated dispute. See R. F. Jones, *Ancients and Moderns* (St Louis, 1936).

VII

Education and the Arts

One of the hardest tasks in the study of human activities is to explain convincingly developments in art, music, and literature. Up to a point, the influence of material conditions on cultural fashion is obvious enough. However brave and unselfish the artist may be, the production and survival of his works do depend on the demand for them, and

BIBLIOGRAPHY. Most cultural aspects of the period are discussed briefly in F. B. Artz, *From the Renaissance to Romanticism* (Chicago, 1962). Preserved Smith, *The Origins of Modern Culture 1543–1667* and *The Enlightenment, 1687–1776* (New York, 1934) make an attempt, often condemned for old-fashioned liberal and materialist ideas, to correlate developments in politics, science, religion, education, and the arts. C. J. Friedrich, *The Age of the Baroque* (New York, 1952), the volume on the early seventeenth century in the 'Rise of Modern Europe' series, makes the 'baroque outlook' the key to every aspect of history.

On education, W. Boyd, *The History of Western Education* (8th ed., revised, London, 1966) is still a standard authority. S. D'Irsay, *Histoire des universités* (2 vols., Paris, 1935) covers the period briefly. C. Jourdain, *L'Université de Paris aux XVIIe et XVIIIe siècles* (2 vols., Paris, 1862–6) and M. H. Curtis, *Oxford and Cambridge in Transition* (Oxford, 1959) are an old and a newer example of the specialised studies. F. Paulsen, *The German Universities* (English trans., London, 1906) is one of the few books on education in central Europe available in English. Among accounts of reform proposals is J. E. Sadler, *Comenius and the Concept of Universal Education* (London, 1966).

National histories of literature are abundant but seldom inspiring. The more recent include J. G. Robertson, *A History of German Literature* (3rd ed. Edinburgh, 1962) and E. H. Wilkins, *A History of Italian Literature* (London, 1954). Those confined to the period range in size from A. Adam, *Histoire de la littérature française au XVIIe siècle* (5 vols., Paris, 1956) to *The Pelican History of English Literature*, ed. Boris Ford, vol. 3, *From Donne to Marvell* (London, 1956). Examples of the varied approaches to the history of drama are L. C. Knights, *Drama and Society in the Age of Jonson* (London, 1937), M. Turnell, *The Classical Moment* (London, 1946)—on Molière, Corneille, and Racine—H. Kindermann, *Das Theater der Barockzeit* (Salzburg, 1959) and H. A. Rennert, *The Spanish stage in the time of Lope de Vega* (New York, 1909). *XVIIe Siécle*, no. 39 (1958) has a group of articles on 'La vie théâtrale au XVIIe siécle'.

therefore on the whole condition of the society he lives in. Every class produces and patronises, in however small a degree, its own forms of art and they can all to some extent be used for propaganda and for prestige. But when all the causal interpretations of this kind have been exhausted, they seldom amount to a satisfying explanation of why, for instance, England should not have produced a school of painting comparable to that of the United Netherlands. The links between styles in the arts and the periods in which they flourish are even more elusive. Efforts to show the seventeenth century as an 'age of the baroque', in which the characteristics of politics, religion, and commerce were all related to the ornate and swirling shapes, the sense of movement and striving, that were fashionable in painting sometimes seem to owe more to imagination than to evidence.[1] Analysis and explanation of cultural history are a necessary part of the understanding of any period—but they have to be approached with as cautious a regard for the facts as are the other parts.

Education

The activities of schools and universities might reasonably be expected to have a major effect on the arts. In fact their positive influence on taste and creativity was lamentably small. The newness and vigour of seventeenth-century arts came largely from men whose education must have done more to crush initiative than to encourage it. The day-to-day work of most educational institutions in the period forms a dismal contrast with the ideas and energy of those who sought to reform and expand them. It contrasts too with the achievements in science and

On the visual arts the supply of commentaries, most of the modern ones lavishly illustrated, is even wider. One that goes beyond the routine accounts of leading artists and architects is V-L. Tapié, *The Age of Grandeur* (English trans., London, 1960). Among books on the main countries are R. Wittkower, *Art and Architecture in Italy 1600–1710* (London, 1958); F. Haskell, *Patrons and Painters: relations between Italian Art and Society in the age of the Baroque* (London, 1963); A. Blunt, *Art and Architecture in France 1500–1700* (London, 1953); S. Sitwell, *German Baroque Art* (London, 1928); and J. Lees-Milne, *Baroque in Spain and Portugal* (London, 1960).

The period is covered in vol. 2 of *The Pelican History of Music*, ed. A. Robertson and D. Stevens (London, 1963) and in M. F. Bukofzer, *Music in the Baroque Era* (New York, 1947).

[1] 'La sensibilité baroque . . . est fonction des crises économiques, sociales, politiques, intellectuelles . . .' Mousnier, *Histoire générale des civilisations*, vol. 4, p. 176.

culture outside them. The sixteenth century had been in many countries a period of rapid expansion in the amount of schooling available, and in some the process still went on. It has been suggested that perhaps 'early seventeenth-century England was at all levels the most literate society the world had ever known' but that the level then declined sharply.[1] The Netherlands may well have maintained an equally high rate of elementary schooling. With Puritans and Jesuits having active, though very different, interests in education, and with the endowment of schools a widely accepted form of charitable virtue, the demand for literate workers and that for highly educated administrators was being met. But the distribution of schools was patchy and accidental: one village, town, or province could often be far better provided for than its neighbour. Against the instances of expansion must be set the grim decline of education in Germany during the Thirty Years War and in many similarly afflicted regions. Moreover, the character of teaching changed far less easily than the amount. Many enthusiasts for educating the lower orders still assumed that writing, simple religion, and useful trades were the limit of their ability. Prospects for the aspiring poor scholar were often worse than in earlier centuries. Even for those whose social position fitted them for more prolonged studies, Renaissance humanism had not left much mark on the process or content of teaching. The revival of classical learning could easily take the form of Latin grammar instilled with the help of the birch.

There was no lack of official concern with education. Kings, from Gustav Adolf to Peter the Great, took a personal interest in schemes to reform it; states and cities, as well as private benefactors, felt that they won prestige by financing it. But none of the activities of laymen did much to disturb the dominance of the churches over teaching at every level. There is not much doubt that in this part of the struggle Catholicism was on the whole doing better than any form of Protestantism. Lutherans, despite their theoretical belief that the scriptures should be available to everyone, did little to enable the poor to read. Their system of teaching for the minority who did receive a substantial education put the emphasis heavily on Latin grammar and verbal memorising. Calvin's educational ideas had survived rather better than Luther's, at least in extending the use of the vernacular in schools. But no-one brought to Protestant education anything like the zeal and systematic skill of the Jesuits. Their *Ratio Studiorum*, issued in its final form in 1599, established a system of primary and secondary

[1] Lawrence Stone in *Past and Present*, no. 28 (1964), p. 68.

schooling wider in its subject-matter and far more enlightened in its methods than any other in use. Though its ultimate purpose was the victory of Catholicism, religious conformity was instilled into pupils unobtrusively—or insidiously—rather than by the rigid discipline imposed within the Order itself. Aristotle and Aquinas remained the essential sources of knowledge and wisdom; some dangerous ideas were firmly banned; but within the rules there was room for a range of teaching wide enough to make the schools attractive to Protestants as well as to Catholics. Bacon remarked how much they had 'quickened and strengthened the state of learning',[1] and suggested that to 'consult the schools of the Jesuits' was the quickest way to see how education should be reformed. In France the number of great men in literature and scholarship who had been educated in Jesuit schools was very large, though Descartes was not alone in doubting the benefits of it. Their pupils were not drawn from any one social class. Investigation of their origins in various regions and years[2] shows that sons of merchants and office-holders had the largest share of places; but those of artisans and *laboureurs* were something like a quarter or a third of the total.

Jesuit schools, open to literate pupils whatever their origin and aim, were not likely to appeal strongly to the nobility; and the demand for a type of education suited to the exclusive requirements of the court and the landed classes found its own response. In France the Bérulle's Oratory began to offer to the sons of aristocrats as well as to future priests teaching rivalling that of the Jesuits; and from the middle of the century the schools of Port Royal became a centre of enlightened teaching for the courtly intelligentsia. In Germany after the Thirty Years War the 'knightly academies' (*Ritterakademien*), which soon came strongly under French influence, met the same need for an almost vocational training in the accomplishments of a gentleman. French became at least the equal of Latin as a language of the élite; useful subjects such as law, heraldry, and military science were included in the curriculum; and pupils were even encouraged to know enough about art and music for conversational purposes. Sweden's new *Gymnasia*, established mainly in the 1630s and 1640s, were controlled by the bishops and extended their scope only cautiously beyond the old religious and classical subjects; but they helped to produce a ruling class that was culturally equal to those of the other powers. Not that ambitious nobles and gentlemen necessarily regarded schools of any kind

[1] *Works*, ed. Spedding and Ellis, vol. 3, p. 300; vol. 4, p. 494.
[2] F. Dainville in *Population*, no. 3 (1957).   [3] See p. 112.

as suitable for their heirs. The best form of education was often felt—in England perhaps most of all—to be provided by the private tutor at home or during foreign travel. It was a job that offered a comfortable and reasonably leisured existence to scholars: Bossuet, Leibnitz, and Hobbes were among those who lived in this way.

The century was not a glorious one for universities. Between their functions as centres of ecclesiastical training and propaganda and as finishing-schools for gentlemen, up-to-date scholarship usually took a lesser place. There were exceptions. After the foundation of Leiden in 1574 several of the Netherlands cities and provinces created their own universities where new scientific and literary ideas held their own against traditional Aristotelian formulae. Strassburg, both under Imperial and under French control, had flourishing schools of mathematics and history. The opening of the University of Halle in 1694, intended by the Elector Frederick III as a mark of national prestige, came to be regarded as the beginning of a new era of enlightenment and freedom in German education. But few of the great intellectual achievements of the century owed much to the universities. In Galileo's day both Pisa and Padua still had a good deal of their Renaissance initiative and freedom. Their teaching of mathematics, medicine, and 'natural philosophy' brought them students from all over Europe. By the middle of the century their reputation had almost disappeared. Oxford under the Commonwealth enjoyed a brief period as a centre of the new science. There however, as at Cambridge, teaching was slow to respond to the demands of an enterprising minority for a less narrowly scholastic outlook. Geometry, Astronomy, and Natural Philosophy were added to the Oxford professorships; but they were handled on cautiously traditional lines. The establishment of the Royal Society was part of a general tendency for both leading scholars and intelligent amateurs to come together in societies and academies unconnected with the universities.[1] The Inns of Court offered for lawyers a seven-year professional training and for the sons of gentlemen the opportunity in one year to pick up pleasantly a smattering of law.

Nearly everyone in a position to control education shared the same basic assumptions. Boys (and in a very limited way girls) must learn a definite and unquestioned body of factual information and acquire an appropriate degree of skill in written and spoken language. A few might move on from fact to understanding, but with the range of permissible investigation and dispute limited by authority. Throughout the century

[1] See pp. 143–4.

155

these assumptions were challenged by some of the most powerful writers, and revolutionary ideas on education were even, here and there, put into practice; but their achievement by 1700 did not amount to much. Richard Mulcaster, high master of St Paul's School until 1608, had advocated universal primary education and denounced the excessive importance attached to Latin with arguments some of which have been renewed, and rejected, in twentieth-century Oxford. Bacon's *Advancement of Learning* was followed by a stream of English writings on educational reform, many of them from Puritans, among which Milton's *Treatise on Education* (1644) was the best-known but by no means the most radical.

The distinction between knowledge, understanding, and judgment was the basis of the elaborate schemes devised by Comenius—Jan Amos Komensky—who in his native Poland, in Sweden, the Netherlands, and briefly in England, campaigned for the reform of education on lines that owed a good deal to Bacon. 'The entire youth of both sexes, none being excepted' would be taught in a way that would make them 'learned in the sciences, pure in morals, trained in piety'[1]—a shocking order of priority. This was to be in local schools provided by lay authorities. For the few who could advance beyond mere knowledge there were to be gymnasia in every city and universities in every province. The aim of it all was not merely the improvement of the individual, but the achievement of a new civilisation with universal peace. He was widely read, and ignored. The one philosopher who had a clear practical influence on education was Descartes. From him there came not theories on the method of teaching but the attitude to knowledge that firmly rejected the authoritarian scholastic tradition. If the way to achieve certainty was first to doubt everything that could be doubted, there was no room for the professor who thought it his main job to elucidate received texts. The test of truth was not whether a statement rested on ancient authority, but whether it was conceived clearly and demonstrably. Cartesian education aimed therefore not to impart ready-made beliefs, but to instil the habit of questioning and the method of distinguishing as far as may be truth from falsehood. There was usually a wide gap between the aim and the achievement.

Literature and language

Despite all the obstacles and setbacks in education, the market for the printed word was large, and appeared to be growing. Censorship, im-

[1] From the full title of *The Great Didactic* (1642).

posed in most countries by both church and state, was a major obstacle, but one that could—at the risk of brutal punishments—be avoided. The comparatively free presses of the Netherlands offered one solution. Paper was produced more cheaply and in greater quantities than before. The printing industry expanded and its technical standards improved. In nearly every western country the number and variety of books appearing rose decisively. One reason was the steady extension of the use of vernacular languages. 'Linguistic nationalism' took various forms. In 1569 Johannes Becanus (though he Latinised his own name of Jan van Hilvarenbeek) had announced his discovery that Dutch, which was spoken by Adam, had been exempted from the unfortunate affair of the Tower of Babel. There was great enthusiasm during the Netherlands Revolt for making the greatest possible use of the language. In Sweden Skogekär Bergbo wrote in the 1630s a poem deploring the neglect of Swedish for literary and administrative purposes and its corruption by German and Latin infiltrations. Similar complaints were made about German itself by Martin Opitz, who thought that a rigid set of grammatical and stylistic rules was necessary to raise the level of native literature. Efforts to purify and define the French language had continued since the days of Ronsard and the *Pléiade*. In 1647 Claude Vaugelas published his *Remarques sur la langue française*, which laid down the rules for a pure and unambiguous literary French. The *Académie* had the same object. Its official dictionary, completed in the 1690s, was compiled on the principle that words and phrases had differences of status as clear and important as those between men. The language of the peasant and the bourgeois was not to be confused with that of the court and the *salon*; and it was only the purest literary French that was worthy to succeed Latin as the international language of diplomacy and culture.

Vernacular prose

Throughout the century most prose writings were meant to inform and convince rather than to entertain. But such works as the scientific arguments of Galileo, the political and religious pronouncements of Bossuet, the sermons of Donne or even such revolutionary pamphleteering as the best of the Mazarinades and Leveller tracts must be ranked as literature in their own right. With Pascal the '*pensée*' that might be a few words or a few sentences was a form that lent itself to his aim of revealing unresolved conflicts. Less introspective writers like La Bruyère and La Rochefoucauld showed what the French language could make of the aphorism and the epigrammatic sketch. In England the miniature portrait of a type or an individual was a favourite amusement. John Earle's *Microcosmography* and John Aubrey's *Brief Lives* combined a gently satirical touch with satisfied observation of their society. More expansive writing could still too readily become ponderous and contrived. The scholarly belief that Latin, even though it was no longer exclusively Ciceronian Latin, was the perfect model for English died hard. But often sheer joy in the power of words and a readiness to experiment broke through the conventions. Sir Thomas Browne, even when he is manifestly striving for effect, gives the reader the feeling that he is being asked to take part in an exciting and not too strenuous diversion. On the whole the tendency as the century went on was for English prose to become less artificial, simpler, and more relaxed.

Vernacular prose was surprisingly slow to develop as a vehicle for purely imaginative writing. The *novella*, which had been a popular form of amusement in the sixteenth century, survived without growing into serious fiction. The one great work that has something in common with the modern novel is *Don Quixote*, the first part of which was finished in 1604. In using a tale in a familiar mould to attack the out-dated assumptions of Spanish noble society, and in making out of the stereotyped figure of the *picaro*—the rootless, wandering rogue—a character so vivid and significant, Cervantes achieved a triumph that proved completely isolated. Perhaps its nearest successor was Grimmelshausen's *Simplicius Simplicissimus*, published anonymously in 1668; and this owes its modern reputation more to its realistic portrayal of Germany in the depths of wartime misfortune than to literary skill. Prolonged reading was still the activity of the scholar, the lawyer, and the seeker for religious truth rather than a pastime. In the later part of the century the popularity of Bunyan's *Pilgrim's Progress* suggested that at the lower levels of literate society the religious allegory that also made a good story was now more attractive than the printed sermon. The *Arabian Nights* appeared in French in twelve successive volumes during the Spanish Succession War. But it was only when Defoe produced his best works of fiction that this form of art took on anything like its modern importance.

Poetry

Every kind of artistic creation was involved to some extent in a conflict between the quest for new freedom of thought and expression and the desire to conform to well-defined rules. Energy and movement had somehow to be reconciled with symmetry and harmony. In poetry such a conflict seems almost essential. Seventeenth-century verse was often rhymed and nearly always obeyed rigid metrical rules; yet it was generally felt to be the one form in which language could attain as high a level as painting. Poets were willing to accept the conventions and to rejoice in the astonishing variety of emotions, ideas, and sounds that could be created within them. At its best the combination of harmonious and predictable forms with adventurous imagery and vocabulary could make a more powerful impact than was possible in any other medium. But there was no doubt about the risks involved. The phrases, the allusions, and the themes could become as stereotyped as the arrangement of rhyme and rhythm. Artificiality and too self-conscious skill were seldom far away. The gap between the exalted and the ludicrous could be a very narrow one.

The ability to turn out a well-contrived sonnet was almost as much a part of the cultured western gentleman's accomplishments as fencing. Writers of indifferent verse were often patrons and avid readers of good: in England, France, and Italy poetry had a wide circulation in cultured society. But it was no less popular among the townsmen of the Netherlands. Though Dutch verse could not, for the obvious reason, achieve the international repute of Dutch painting, it was as important a part of the national culture. Constantin Huygens, the father of the scientist, was one highly popular poet, who despite his courtly and intellectual background took many of his themes from ordinary urban and rural life. Jacob Cats, Pensionary of Holland in the 1640s, 'whose works could be found alongside the Bible in every Dutch home for two centuries' had a reputation as a poet which Huizinga describes as 'somewhat of a blot on our national character'.[1] But the greatest of the Dutch poets, Joost van den Vondel, has been ranked with Milton as an outstanding writer of the century. He had, it is claimed, a majestic command of language which rose above the limitations of his scriptural subjects and his strict observance of classical rules.

In England religious themes in poetry had to compete more openly with courtly ones. The religious element was seldom specifically Puritan. Its typical products were the devotional poetry of George Herbert, who renounced the worldly pleasures that were open to him and brooded on his own unworthiness; of Henry Vaughan, who found his manifestations of God in nature as well as in immortality; and of

---

[1] J. H. Huizinga, *Dutch Civilisation in the Seventeenth Century* (London, 1968), pp. 65–6, 70.

Richard Crashaw, Laudian and eventually Catholic, whose imagery came as close as any English writing to the baroque atmosphere. The contrast between these and the 'Cavalier' poets is by no means complete. Thomas Carew, Robert Herrick, Richard Lovelace, and the rest were as ready to apply their deliberately far-fetched imagery to the fate of their souls as to the inconstancy of their mistresses. The incongruity between and within their poems was not accidental: behind it was the pervading suspicion that the universe as they had been taught to see it and the social conventions of their time did not altogether make sense. Both the devout and the courtly owed much to the most original of the early seventeenth-century poets, John Donne, who had more success than anyone else in combining intellectual argument and verbal ingenuity with lyrical beauty. The wit, the extravagant analogies, the sureness of touch with which he can switch from the colloquial to the classical seemed as apt in his early love-poems as in his later religious ones. Some of the same qualities appeared a generation later in Andrew Marvell, but with a more relaxed lyricism and a more light-hearted approach even to his most deeply felt arguments. He is the complete answer to the notion that a Cromwellian Puritan must be a mealy-mouthed prig.

Inevitably the dominant figure of the century in English poetry is Milton. Few poets have ever aroused so much angry controversy so long after their deaths: whether they are good poems or bad, it can scarcely be denied that some of the immense reputation of *Paradise Lost* and *Paradise Regained* has come less from their real qualities than from the firmly inculcated belief that they are mighty works of Christian faith. His decision to reject such topics as the legend of Arthur and to combine his ambition to write a great epic of conflict with the duty to teach Christian doctrine created, as he well knew, great literary difficulties. The unrelieved solemnity, the allusions that have now become formidably unfamiliar, and the ponderous evenness of the blank verse need not prevent us from recognising the command of language and the vividly human qualities given to the superhuman characters. But they do make it difficult to enjoy them. The great works of the defeated post-Restoration Milton tend to obscure the Milton who was a passionate exponent of the Parliamentary cause, an enemy of censorship, and a poet with a wide range of style and subject-matter. By the end of the century the literary world of Donne and Milton seemed utterly remote. Doubt and incongruity had almost disappeared. English poetry was now the rational and usually restrained classicism of Dryden, ranging from political satire to the few emotional odes. The neatly rounded heroic couplet was more appropriate to self-satisfied wit than to lyrical beauty or tortured doubt. Dryden was a writer of prose no less than of poetry, and consciously minimised the difference between them. Analysis and criticism could be applied almost as much to religion as to politics. Pope and the 'Augustan age' were not far away.

The theatre

Even in the areas where education was most widespread, the theatre was at least as important as the printing press in enabling creative literature to reach large numbers of people. It was only in the 1580s and 1590s that the permanent theatre had become a part of the life of cities. There were two theatres in London when Shakespeare arrived there in 1586, and five in 1600. By then a large number of Spanish towns had theatres, and they were appearing in Italy and in some German states. Paris was slow to follow. The *Théâtre du Marais*, equipped for elaborate stage spectacles, was founded in 1624. Its first rival was the *Hôtel de Bourgogne*, headquarters of the *Comédiens du Roi*, where most of Corneille's plays were produced. Molière first established himself in Paris in 1658 at the *Salle du Petit-Bourbon*, which he had to share with an Italian company. When this was demolished to make room for the extensions to the Louvre, the king handed over the *Salle du Palais Royal*, which later became the centre for the *Opéra*.

Nearly everywhere the company of players rather than the building was the centre of organisation. It was likely to depend heavily on royal or noble patronage. Many French plays were performed first at Versailles and afterwards in the city: court approval was naturally an important step towards popular success. It was Louis XIV's personal support that brought Molière to prominence. Shakespeare began his career in a company maintained by the Earl of Leicester, and he had a succession of court patrons before his players were taken under James's official protection in 1603. Court fashion and taste were responsible for the comedies of Restoration England as much as for the classical tradition and stringent rules of French tragedy. But the theatre was nowhere the exclusive preserve of the aristocratic or educated minority. The majority of early seventeenth-century plays, from *Hamlet* down to the hastily botched-up routine comedies, managed to include something for everybody. Noble theatregoers did not of course mingle excessively with the multitude: they occupied the *loges* of the Paris theatres, arranged in appropriate grades; they watched open-air performances in Spain from windows or balconies; everywhere they were liable to invade the stage and interfere with the performance. The approval of the 'groundlings', standing and—it was hoped—tightly packed together, was hardly less necessary for commercial success. Actors were often paid on the spot out of takings to which the cheaper parts of the theatre contributed substantially. It was a profession that could be close both to court luxury and to poverty. The view that players were much the same as other vagabonds was not confined to English Puritans.

The writer who provided the actors with their necessary material seldom had an easy or secure existence. Scripts were demanded in enormous quantities, and payment for them was usually very small. The manufacture of plays was an industry in which collaboration, open or anonymous, was common. Plots and characters were borrowed as freely as jokes. Alexandre Hardy, the first popular French playwright of the century, was said to have written six hundred plays, few of which were printed; Lope de Vega in Spain was credited with even more. Both for economic reasons and to acquire such status and protection as were possible, the writer of plays was more in need than the poet of patrons who were highly placed, or even merely rich. Corneille at the height of his success had to produce a ludicrously fulsome dedication to the tax-farmer who had subsidised his publication.[1] Calderon and Lope de Vega eventually found security in the church. Ben Jonson, despite his turbulent career, won both steady patronage and a wide circle of friends at the Jacobean court. But it was significant that Shakespeare achieved only the fringe of provincial gentility and that there was some difficulty in arranging a respectable Christian burial for Molière.

In this situation the choice of topics and attitudes was inevitably restricted in many ways. Fear of government or ecclesiastical censorship, powerful though these could be, was only one reason for the conservatism that was a common characteristic of drama everywhere. It was obviously believed that both the popular and the courtly audience preferred conformity to innovation. Spanish drama was perhaps the most heavily committed to patriotism, monarchy, and the old ideas of chivalry and virtue. Though in every country the lower orders could be treated sympathetically as well as humorously, rebellion was always evil. The sins and follies of the nobility could be denounced; but the hierarchical structure of society was as sacred as the institution of monarchy. The highest thoughts and deepest emotions were expected to be depicted in royal or at least in aristocratic personages. Marriage was

[1] It is quoted in Lough, *Introduction to Seventeenth-Century France*, p. 187.

sought almost exclusively on the appropriate social level. There was little indication that drama was widening its scope as the century went on. French classical tragedy, which became one of the dominant influences, was the most restricted of all forms. Its insistence on an unvarying verse form and on the 'dramatic unities' of time, place, and action was appropriate to an equally narrow range of themes.

Despite all the obstacles, seventeenth-century plays are among the greatest achievements of the age. Shakespeare is of course unmatched in the variety and power of his work. There is little point in arguing about the century, or the style, to which he should be attached. As it happens the patriotic histories and the lighter comedies are nearly all Elizabethan in date; all the great tragedies, *Cymbeline* and *Coriolanus*, *The Winter's Tale* and *The Tempest* belong to the seventeenth century. The emphasis has moved from success and ebullience to inward doubts and tensions and to struggles with a mysterious and generally malign fate. The Italian court, the London tavern, and the Warwickshire countryside become less prominent than the storm, the witch-haunted heath, the dark castle, and the magic island. He remained as much an entrepreneur of the theatrical industry in writing *Hamlet* as he was in the popular comedies and the serialised historical epic. But awareness of the demands of his various audiences did not bring him to introduce the political, social, or religious conflicts of the day directly into the plays. His kings, his mobs, his statesmen, and his soldiers are on the whole as timeless as his mental conflicts. Not all his contemporaries and immediate successors shared this attitude. Ben Jonson was a master of topical satire: projectors, monopolists, acquisitive and hypocritical Puritans were some of his victims. Philip Massinger's *New Way to Pay Old Debts* is a caricature of the troubles of landowners in their search for new sources of wealth in which Overreach is blatantly modelled on Sir Giles Mompesson who had just been impeached for his monopolistic abuses.

The Interregnum, despite the pressures of Puritanism and the removal of most sources of patronage, was not a total disaster for English drama. (One thing it ended was the exclusion of women from the stage.) But after it Restoration comedy, with its uninhibited commentary on the contrast between marriage for the sake of property or status and sexual competition outside it, was rarely more than highly skilled light entertainment. It was in France that Shakespeare found his real successors—sharply divided between the comic and the tragic and shunning variety of mood or scene. Molière—the merchant's son Jean-

Baptiste Poquelin—was a magnificent counterpoise to court solemnity. The royal visit to *Les Précieuses Ridicules* in 1660 had no perceptible effect on the cultural pretensions of the court or the salons; but the play established Molière securely. Though the *Compagnie du Saint-Sacrament* succeeded in banning *Tartuffe*, the daring attack on religious hypocrisy and casuistry, *le Bourgeois Gentilhomme*, *le Medicin malgré lui*, *les Femmes Savantes*, and the other satires on familiar types and attitudes survived unscathed. The two great tragedians, Pierre Corneille and—more than thirty years younger—Jean Racine were less remote from contemporary conflicts than their classical subjects and their firm concentration on the inward struggles of the idealized hero or heroine would suggest. The glories of military conquest were a theme sure of official welcome. When Corneille repeatedly showed the power of the free will faced by a moral dilemma, he was not only using a dramatic device familiar to the Greeks but upholding one aspect of Jesuit theology. Racine the Jansenist was more concerned with the 'Hidden God' of Pascal,[1] the mysterious fate that it was pointless to resist. Romantic love is, both for men and for the women to whom he devoted his greatest poetry and characterisation, sufficient in itself. He was never sure of a favourable reception, and when *Phèdre* was attacked by his enemies at court he abandoned the theatre altogether, returning only to write the two biblical plays, *Esther* and *Athalie*, for schoolgirls patronised by Madame de Maintenon. It was no doubt a tremendous achievement to convey such passion through his monotonously balanced verse, his small stock of words and phrases, and his rigid exclusion of all irrelevance or ornamentation. Even the most enthusiastic devotees of the idea of an all-pervading baroque would find it hard to apply the term to Racine.

The baroque in Italy

It is generally agreed that the centre from which baroque art spread through Europe was the Italy of the Counter-Reformation. Here at least there was a clear connection between artistic style and ideas prevalent in other spheres. The demand by the church for the services of architects and painters was now more important than that of individuals or lay authorities; and the church insisted that art must be adapted to the glorifying of religion in its Catholic form. Rome was the headquarters of the most expensive and spectacular advertising campaign

[1] For the links between Pascal and Racine see L. Goldmann, *The Hidden God* (English trans., 1964).

ever devised. Everything was to be the opposite of the austerity and individualism of the Protestants. Light and colour and aspiring movement beautified the churches. The heavens opening, hosts of angels glorifying God, biblical scenes with throngs of the faithful adoring Christ, splendour surrounding the Virgin and the Saints—all these were treated in a manner supposed to draw the spectator in rather than to overawe him. There was no separation between the functions of architect, sculptor, and painter. A sideline of the baroque was the 'Illusionism' that could disguise the boundary between three-dimensional structure and flat painting. It did not mean that artists were deliberately rejecting older habits: the painters most influential around 1600 such as Annibale Carracci and Polidoro da Caravaggio, had grown up in the Renaissance tradition much of which survived behind their strong individual traits. (Caravaggio was denounced by churchmen for the realistic poverty of some of his figures.) But it was the boldness and splendour of the new works that impressed visitors to the city. Sixtus V in 1585 had initiated a scheme for new streets in Rome; and a succession of seventeenth-century popes, Urban VIII, Innocent X, and Alexander VII, were anxious that the whole city as well as its churches should be a worthy attraction for the faithful.

Some of the most startling productions of mid-century Rome were the churches of Francesco Borromini with his insistence on using a curve rather than a straight line wherever it could be contrived. The greatest creator of Italian baroque, Gian Lorenzo Bernini, became a major European celebrity. Though it is for sculpture and architecture that he is remembered, he was at least as enthusiastic as a painter: the idea that the three could be different skills and their products unrelated would not have seemed tolerable to him. In 1629 he was appointed architect of the half-finished St Peter's, where he made the splendid colonnades of the piazza and the huge canopy, or *baldacchino*, on twisted pillars over the altar. (Bronze was torn from the roof of the Pantheon to provide material for it.) His sculpture and building, his fountains and altars, appeared everywhere in the city and in the other Italian towns. From the palaces of the cardinals downwards, baroque domestic architecture and decoration became the accepted mark of prestige. In gardens, squares, and the new broad avenues of planned city development, baroque ideas were proclaimed. The courts and towns of the rest of Europe adopted and modified the fashion with an enthusiasm that tended to diminish in proportion to their distance—physical and spiritual—from Rome. In Italy itself the stimulus given to art by the church's patronage may well have been outweighed by the narrow range of subjects and manner it now approved.

Rubens

At the turn of the century the Duke of Mantua appointed as court painter Peter-Paul Rubens, son of a prominent Antwerp magistrate. He visited Rome, Venice, and Genoa, and spent a year in Spain. In 1608 he returned to Antwerp, with a well-established reputation and style, and was received into the establishment of the Archduke Albert. The city that had lost its commercial pre-eminence became the centre of what turned into a minor industry of art. Though Rubens completed his greatest works and many of his courtly portraits himself, his output —like that of masters in other crafts—was expanded with the help of numerous apprentices and assistants, and he kept a careful eye on the market-price. The styles of his great range of subjects were imitated in, and far beyond, the Spanish Netherlands. Much of his work seemed as passionately religious as anything in Rome. Before too much is made of the spiritual inspiration behind his scenes of apotheosis it is worth remembering that the figure borne heavenwards by cherubim is James I in one of them and Henry IV of France in another. Formal portraits, allegorical scenes of royal triumph like the series on the life of Marie de Medici, and episodes from pagan mythology were no less welcome as topics than the religious ones. It is undeniable that to most twentieth-century eyes the fat women with chinless insipid faces are not for their own sake attractive, and they have become—unjustly— the best-known characteristic feature of his work and even of baroque painting in general. He was capable of the most perceptive and sympathetic portraiture—as in the *Four Negro Heads* or the *Old Woman warming herself*—and of such realistic scenes as *The Prodigal Son* and *The Boar Hunt*. In his later years, when he claimed to have 'conceived a horror of Courts'[1] and had acquired a lavish country house, he produced more landscapes, peaceful and even subdued. But he never ceased to accept commissions for an immense variety of work. One of the orders for which he assembled a distinguished team of collaborators was the state entry of the Prince-Cardinal Ferdinand into Antwerp in 1635. The triumphal arches, the sculptures and paintings arranged in great open-air displays, the processions and ceremonies were coordinated into one huge theatrical display. The fact that it was temporary did not make it seem any less important.

[1] P. Cabanne, *Rubens* (London, 1967), p. 233.

There was nothing unheard-of in the 'entry of Ferdinand'. Seventeenth-century painters did not assume that their main task was to produce on an easel works that would hang in an art gallery or glorify the home of whatever rich purchaser could be found. They were part of a single continuing process of providing visual beauty. The chief beneficiaries were necessarily those who paid for it; but it was not only in churches or on the exteriors of buildings that the people as a whole saw the products of art. The *festa* that was a regular part of the life of every Italian town, with its fireworks, its processions and decorations, its mixture of comic and religious performances had many counterparts elsewhere. At the top of the scale of extravagance and quality were the festivities of Louis XIV who could spend unlimited money on his water-displays, his cavalcades and ballets, his dwarfs and monsters. At the bottom of the scale were the tawdry village saints' days and the little travelling shows. Punch and Judy can claim baroque qualities as confidently as any painted ceiling or sculptured fountain, and it was in this period that their popularity became established.

The baroque in central Europe and Spain

It was probably in the Catholic part of central Europe that the baroque was, by 1700, most prominently visible. The Thirty Years War did not altogether put a stop to lavish building: the palace that Wallenstein built for himself in Prague between 1625 and 1629, and filled with looted treasure, originated the popularity of the style in a city which in the next generation became full of it. After the Peace of Westphalia, both the landed nobility and the church were able to undertake an impressive amount of new building, much of it designed by Italians. In the 1680s and 1690s, when the greater sense of security after the defeat of the Turks may have been a further incentive to building, there appeared the first great German architects of the century. Johann Bernhardt Fischer von Erlach, 'Inspector of Royal Buildings' to the Emperor Joseph I, produced the original grandiose plans for the palace of Schönbrunn—which were drastically altered after his death—and a great variety of buildings in Vienna, Prague, and Salzburg. Lukas von Hildebrandt, once an engineer in the Imperial army, built in a rather less ponderous manner than Fischer's many of the huge palaces that were within the means not only of princes but of aristocrats who had reaped the benefits of successful war.

One difficulty about the claim that baroque art expressed the essence of Catholic civilisation in the seventeenth century is that in Spain it was not a distinctively dominant style. The façade of Granada Cathedral, designed by Alonso Cano, was the first really impressive building of this kind, and it would have been completely unfamiliar in the north. Francisco de Herrera and Francisco de Zurbaran were far more restrained and realistic than their Italian contemporaries. Diego de Silva Velasquez, chosen by Philip IV as his principal court portrait-painter, produced naturalistic figures enlivened by a magnificent use of light and colour, but closer in manner to the later Renaissance than to the baroque. There was not much trace of religious passion in him. His *Coronation of the Virgin* treats the theme of heavenly glorification in a way that is comparatively rigid and angular. Indeed the Spanish church did remarkably little to make use of the attractions of great art: it was the court and the confident superiority of royalty and aristocracy that provided Velasquez with his subject-matter.

French art

Harder still to fit into the idea of the all-pervading baroque is the Catholic country that by the end of the century dominated the whole culture of Europe. Though Bernini and Rubens had a prolonged influence in France, characteristics that in any other period would be unhesitatingly called 'classical' were prominent all the time and in the great days of Louis XIV's court clearly had the upper hand. Henry IV had ambitions for Paris comparable to those of the popes for Rome. He also led the way for the higher nobility in the building or expanding of châteaux. But it was not until Richelieu's time that successful state encouragement was given to French art. In 1627 Simon Vouet, who had spent most of his adult life in Rome, was invited to the French court. His painting in the Louvre and the other royal palaces, and his panels and altars in churches, established a style of decoration that was bright and luminous but a good deal more restrained than the Italian fashion. He did not achieve as much success with the Parisian aristocrats as did another French settler in Rome, Nicolas Poussin. Though Richelieu brought him to Paris in 1640, two years of the life of an approved court painter proved as much as he could stand. But when he returned to Italy he continued to work for French patrons. A landscape, a biblical scene, or a piece of ancient mythology by Poussin was a highly fashionable acquisition for any office-holder aspiring to social advancement. He became the recognised model for French artistic taste; and the qualities he imposed were predominantly classical ones. In his wide range of style and subject-matter his interest was always in carefully calculated geometric pattern and unity of theme rather than in excitement or splendour. His greatest source of guidance was antique sculpture. 'Cold' is one of the commonest terms applied to him; but through the various 'periods' into which his work has been analysed there runs a love of smooth, glowing light that may have been more apparent before the pictures became darker with age. More dramatic effects of light appear in many of the landscapes of Claude Lorrain, another Frenchman who lived almost entirely in Italy. He was much more responsive than Poussin to the beauty of country and sea —and less favoured by the best circles in Paris. In complete contrast to the followers of Poussin were the Le Nain brothers, Antoine, Louis, and Mathieu. They worked in the same studio, and often on the same picture, which they signed with the surname alone. Their one characteristic theme, realistic scenes of rural life and peasant faces, acquired something of a vogue of its own. They did not make fun of the peasant, or idealise him. They offered no comment on poverty or injustice. But they used the pictorial qualities of houses, dress, and furniture that had not been designed for ornament or ostentation, and of faces not apparently posed for the painter. They did not hide themselves away in the countryside that provided their material: they sought the same courtly patronage as others, and just before the deaths of Antoine and Louis they were admitted as original members of the *Académie de Peinture et de Sculpture*.

The foundation of the *Académie* in 1648 was a decisive step in the organisation of French art for the glory of the state. But it was not until the energy of Colbert was applied to the integration of the nation's artistic resources that the great era of regulated art began. What remained of baroque freedom was firmly subordinated to an officially approved style for which classical sculpture and Raphael were highly recommended models. There was prolonged hesitation over the eastern façade of the Louvre. Though Bernini was brought from Rome and welcomed with adulation, in the end his plans were rejected in favour of classical severity. The first leaders of the new artistic hierarchy were the men who created Fouquet's great château at Vaux-le-Vicomte and were promptly conscripted by Colbert for Louis' own even more magnificent scheme. Louis le Vau had been employed by Fouquet not simply as an architect but as manager of a great company of painters, sculptors, and craftsmen of all kinds. Charles le Brun, the principal painter throughout Colbert's period in power, was himself an organiser and co-ordinator who would happily turn from his massive pictures such as *Louis XIV adoring the Risen Christ* to sketch out a tapestry, plan the complete decoration of a room, or settle contests for advancement among the artists as bitter as any among politicians. His own supremacy ended with the fall of Colbert. At least as important in the Versailles project and in the aggrandisement of Paris was the landscape-designer André le Nôtre, who brought buildings, lakes, woods, and gardens into designs of calculated symmetry and proportion. When le Vau was succeeded by Jules Hardouin Mansard no doubt remained about the classical emphasis in the immense exterior and even in the interior of Versailles.

The Dutch painters

An impressive piece of evidence for the effect on the arts of religious and social factors is the contrast between the painters of the United Provinces and those of the Spanish Netherlands.[1] Before the revolt the mixture of Italian and native traditions had been much the same in Utrecht as it was in Antwerp. After it the artists of the north lived in a different world from that of Rubens. Though official and individual patronage was not unknown, the Dutch painter normally completed his canvas first and then offered it for sale in his studio or even in a fair. Much of the demand was for the realistic scenes of the household, the tavern, and the street, or for local landscapes, or for group portraits as well as individual ones. Dutch bourgeois art was firmly condemned by the French academies. But the modern assessment of Dutch painting can give a misleading impression. The Italian style was not driven out: men like Cornelis van Poelenburgh had great success with biblical and mythological subjects while some of what are now seen as the greatest pictures were unsold. Rembrandt was in his earlier years a successful portrait-painter in Amsterdam. He had many of the baroque techniques, even if they were applied to townsmen rather than angels. When he became introspective and tragic, painting Christ in tender humanity rather than glory, and landscapes that were more dreamlike than real, he went bankrupt. Jan Vermeer, disregarded and impoverished in his lifetime, achieved his powerful emotional effects by new techniques for the creation of luminosity and depth. Many of this generation of painters—Pieter de Hooch, Salomon and Jacob van Ruisdael, Jan Steen and others—died in the seventies or early eighties.

[1] See the article by W. R. Jeudwine, 'The Golden Age of Holland' in *History Today*, vol. 1 no 6 (June 1951), pp. 39–50.

After them Dutch art as we admire it was almost extinct: the influence of Antwerp and of Paris dominated the market.

It is hard to find in the art of other northern countries a style as distinctive or successful as that of the Dutch. The Stuarts drew their favoured painters from the Netherlands, Rubens' pupil Sir Anthony Van Dyck from Antwerp and Sir Peter Lely from Haarlem. Inigo Jones, whose ideas were formed in his visits to Italy, brought to the service of the Crown and the court nobility the 'Mannerist' style of Palladio, with its rules of symmetry and proportion, its columned façades and its restraint in exterior ornament. Sir Christopher Wren kept away from Italy: it was France that he recognised as a source of ideas, though not of rules. In the work of this state architect who was originally a scientist and mathematician, and who could evade both conventional standards and the views of his patrons, it is easy to find traces of almost every European style. The connection of St Paul's with St Peter's was as recognisable but as restricted as that of Anglicanism with Catholicism. Sir John Vanbrugh produced at Blenheim and Castle Howard massive palaces that can certainly claim to be more baroque than Versailles. But it was not in great houses or in churches that a distinctive English architecture appeared. Perhaps the most successful buildings in combining function with appearance are the more modest gentry houses, often of brick, aping the aristocratic ones in some of their features—notably the long gallery—and adorned with the best portraits, furnishings, and plate the owner could afford to keep. A great deal of gentry wealth found its way to the craftsmen who produced what prestige and taste required.

Music

The painter, the sculptor, and even for most purposes the architect had in 1600 materials that were as good as any available today. This was not true of the musician. There could not have been a musical equivalent of St Peter's because the instruments that existed were incapable of the range and richness of sound it would demand. The lute and viol, the virginals and clavichord, imposed severe limitations on the composer. It was in the course of the seventeenth century that the essentials of the modern orchestra appeared. The violin evolved slowly into the form produced by Nicolo Amati and his apprentice Antonio Stradivari. The oboe now gave more quantity than quality of sound; but the introduction from about 1690 of the clarinet made possible the successful combination of strings and woodwind. The mechanical developments were part of a change in the rôle of music in cultured life. Outside the church it had come mainly from the solo instruments the playing of which was an accomplishment familiar in the middle as well as upper ranks of society, from small professional groups, and of course in song. The innovation that did most to expand its scope was the opera.

Many other art-forms contributed to the conventions of opera. The secular cantata and the oratorio made the telling of a story the framework for large-scale vocal music with alternating 'recitative' and 'aria'; the French *ballet-de-cour* demanded elaborate instrumental accompaniment; the English masque blended music and drama with spectacular costume and scenic effects. But it was in Italy that the popularity of opera was first established. The church accepted without controlling it; the nobility patronised it. As Italian artistic energy seemed to move from painting and sculpture towards music[1] opera provided the perfect combination of skills. *Orfeo*, the most popular work of Claudio Monteverdi, was performed in 1608. In 1637 Venice had its Opera House—an institution that soon became necessary to most self-respecting cities and monarchs. Though Monteverdi was himself a writer of madrigals, his operas made more use of simple melodic solos than of verbally incomprehensible choral polyphony. A large orchestra was as much a part of them as the singers. Despite the fame of Italian opera, it was only under Louis XIV that the French developed an enthusiasm for it. Jean-Baptiste Lully was a court musician ready to turn his hand to whatever form of entertainment the king demanded. The dramatic plot tended to be rather more coherent than in Italy and the music unemotional; but orchestra and chorus, as well as the indispensable ballet, got plenty of prominence.

Protestant Germany was as open as Vienna itself to the influence of Italian music. Hamburg in the 1680s became a centre of opera, despite some religious opposition; in Dresden the Italian-trained Kappellmeister to the Elector of Saxony, Heinrich Schütz, turned from his early operatic work to religious choral music, and made the oratorio an opportunity for vast and unrestrained compositions. But the greatest German initiative was in writing for the organ. This too underwent great technical development during the century. Girolamo Frescobaldi as organist of St Peter's expanded the musical possibilities of the instrument and initiated the demand for improvement. It culminated at the

[1] See the article by H. G. Koenigsberger, 'Decadence or Shift' in *Transactions of the Royal Historical Society*, 5th ser., vol. 10 (1960).

end of the century in the great organ at Lübeck on which Dietrich Buxtehude worked out the organ chorales and toccatas that are seen as leading directly to Bach. Much more than opera, or than the sonata and concerto that were taking shape in the instrumental music performed in great and not so great houses, church music was accessible to everyone. Indeed it was inescapable. Despite the suspicions of some Protestant sects, the churches on the whole helped to give music its importance in the leisure of poor as well as rich. Not that much help was needed: enough has survived of the folk-songs and traditional airs of the period to show that the cultured élite had no monopoly in the creation of melodic beauty.

VIII

Political Ideas

Ideas about the working of the organised community, and about the duties of rulers and ruled, had always been an important part of European philosophy. The *Politics* was one of the most familiar books of Aristotle. Augustine and Aquinas had both regarded questions of

BIBLIOGRAPHY. Commentaries on political theorists, individually or collectively, are seldom as readable or as enlightening as the works themselves, but are often shorter. A compromise can now be found in edited extracts from the major writers. Among these is *The Seventeenth Century*, ed. Andrew Lossky (New York, 1967), which includes Grotius, Hobbes, de la Court, Bossuet, and Locke. *Puritanism and Liberty*, edited and introduced by A. S. P. Woodhouse (London, 1938) prints the Putney Debates and extracts from Roger Williams, Lilburne, Overton, Winstanley, and from many of the constitutional proposals of the Civil War radicals.

For a short account dealing with all the later part of the century, chapter 5 of the *New Cambridge Modern History*, vol. 5 (1961) by S. Skalweit is more helpful than the relevant parts of the most-used textbook, G. H. Sabine, *A History of Political Theory* (London, 1937). F. M. Watkins, *The Political Tradition of the West* (Cambridge, Mass., 1948) is another comprehensive survey. The *Journal of the History of Ideas* has had many articles on the period. Discussions of the writers of particular countries include: W. J. Stankiewicz, *Politics and Religion in Seventeenth-Century France* (Berkeley, 1960); Henri Sée, *Les Idées politiques en France au XVIIe siècle* (Paris, 1923); J. W. Allen, *English Political Thought 1603–1660* (London, 1938), of which only the first of two volumes appeared; E. H. Kossmann, 'The Development of Dutch Political Theory in the Seventeenth Century'—an essay in *Britain and the Netherlands*, vol. 1, ed. J. S. Bromley and E. H. Kossmann (London, 1960); S. K. Utechin, *Russian Political Thought* (London, 1963); J-A. Maravall, *La Philosophie politique espagnole au XVIIe siècle* (Paris, 1955).

On major individual writers there is usually a modern edition of the 'works' with an authoritative introduction and a choice of biographical studies. The literature on Hobbes is enormous; among modern studies are L. Strauss, *The Political Philosophy of Thomas Hobbes* (Oxford, 1936), and H. Warrender, *The Political Philosophy of Hobbes* (Oxford, 1957). Recent controversies about him can be found in *Hobbes Studies*, ed. K. C. Brown (Oxford, 1965). There are justice and government as relevant to their theology. To early seven-teenth-century writers who ranged, more or less selectively, over the whole expanse of human understanding, it was natural to treat political questions in the traditional way. They asked how the state originated; and answered the question with little or no regard to historical evidence. They defined, as Aristotle had, the various possible forms of the state; and the descriptions were usually remote from reality. The men they envisaged as its subjects were remarkably free from poverty, greed, and stupidity. To some extent this was a conventional pose, concealing a strong concern with current conflicts; but it was one that tended to keep the influence of the theorists on events small. While men were dying and destroying through the blunders and follies of the state, those who studied it seemed to devote themselves largely to such notions as the fictitious contract that justified political power and the ill-defined Natural Law that might limit it.

Even so, this was a period in which theories about fundamental political problems were closer than before to what was happening. The conflict between authority and doubt in religion was accompanied by a questioning of the accepted reasons for obeying earthly powers. Most theorists, heavily influenced by Bodin, agreed that there must be a 'sovereign' whose ultimate power no-one could challenge; and sov-ereignty was justified by an uneasy mixture of divine command, meta-phors about the family or tribe, and general conceptions of justice and morality. But, increasingly, sheer expediency was added to these. The gap between theoretical pronouncements and the minister coping with an empty treasury or the crowd cheering a rebel leader, wide though it remained, was not unbridgeable. Within the concept of sovereignty there was room for argument about the ways in which a ruler might normally limit and share his power. It was possible to consider as a practical problem the circumstances in which a subject might resist his

differing views of Locke in J. W. Gough, *John Locke's Political Philosophy* (Oxford, 1950) and W. Kendall, *John Locke and the Doctrine of Majority Rule* (Urbana, 1941).

An outstandingly original approach to Hobbes, the Levellers, Harrington, and Locke is C. B. Macpherson, *The Political Theory of Possessive Individualism* (Oxford, 1962). Other specialised studies include O. von Gierke, *Natural Law and the Theory of Society*, trans. E. Barker, 2 vols. (Cambridge, 1934); L. Roth, *Spinoza* (London, 1954); W. S. M. Knight, *The Life and Works of Hugo Grotius* (London, 1925). The classic work by J. N. Figgis, *The Divine Right of Kings* (Cambridge, 1896) has been reprinted with an introduction by G. R. Elton (New York, 1965).

sovereign. Political theories were becoming less a preserve of the clergy and the intellectuals and closer to the mere craft of statesmanship. Many of the most relevant ideas about the state came from men directly involved in its working. In France Sully, Richelieu, Colbert, even Louis XIV himself, left in one form or another their thoughts on monarchy. England produced a rare assortment of political thinkers who were also practitioners. There was James I, the king who claimed to be a philosopher; Bacon the philosopher who became a Lord Chancellor; Eliot the hero of opposition who wrote in prison his treatise accepting royal sovereignty; Coke and Selden the state lawyers; Lilburne and Rainsborough the leaders of popular rebellion; Milton the poet and official propagandist. Descriptions of the various forms of government in Europe became a necessary part of the cultivated gentleman's library. In the study of states, as of planets, accurate observation was now the first essential—with sometimes a dangerous assumption that both moved in unchanging orbits. The aim of observation was, for many writers, to construct a science of politics, in which principles could be laid down with mathematical certainty. By the end of the century there were the beginnings of political statistics, and investigations of national economies. It was a great advance on Aristotelian theorising; but its confident ambition was liable to produce new unrealities.

To political theorists from the most conservative to the most revolutionary, it still seemed important to ask why the state existed, and why the subject accepted its authority. There were three things that men in general seemed prepared to obey. They obeyed God, or whatever institution they regarded as his mouthpiece. They obeyed the monarch and his deputies—if such a term could be taken to include the manifold local and central wielders of powers that depended directly or indirectly on his. More vaguely, they obeyed the 'law'. The fact that for most men individually none of these had as much practical authority as the landlord did not seem relevant to the theory of politics. It was necessary for the monarch, on whose success in maintaining his power security of life and property depended, to align the other two sources of authority behind him. The churches had now become politically less dangerous. In the west at any rate, medieval disputes between *regnum* and *sacerdotium* were reduced to a comparatively small frontier conflict. Even the Spanish Jesuit Francisco Suarez, though he insisted on the Pope's supremacy over kings in spiritual matters, was more concerned to limit royal authority by a legal than an ecclesiastical system. The law was a 'professional' interest, asserting in many countries a power that might somehow be derived from the monarchy but was independent of the personal command of the King or his ministers. Assemblies of the Estates of the Realm, were still in 1600 able to restrict many actions of the Crown.[1] Judges often made claims no less extensive for an untouchable body of law that only they 'interpreted'. The monarchy needed to assert a theory of its own supremacy.

The king and God

It was not difficult to take over for the king some of the individual's duty to God. James I, 'supreme head' of a Church more closely bound to the Crown than any other in Europe, expounded for his subjects and for his son the notion of Divine Right: kings were established by God, they sit on God's throne, they are responsible to God alone.[2] This was little more than trumpet-blowing that did not greatly affect James's realistic appraisal of his relations with Parliament. But many writers on various levels went further, threatening damnation for resistance to the Lord's Anointed. Roger Manwaring announced in his sermons in the 1620s that to achieve salvation the will of the sovereign must be obeyed unless 'flatly against the law of God'—a larger loophole than he admitted. In France homilies on the Christian duty of obedience to kings were common—some of them in atrocious verse.

> Par moi règnent les rois, dit la bouche suprême;
> Ils tiennent de moi seule, en foi, leur diadème.[3]

Expositions of the unlimited power of monarchs were a favourite type of literature throughout the century. Sir Robert Filmer in England showed absolutism to be in harmony with all the other works of God; Prokopovitch in Russia blended Divine Right with consent by proving that God had commanded the people to confer their power on the Tsar; tracts and sermons almost everywhere made God and kings inseparable. One of the last comprehensive expositions of divine right came from the French theologian and court preacher Jacques Bossuet. With massive biblical quotation he set out in a logical series of 'Propositions' to show that the law of God ordained absolute hereditary monarchy as the best of all forms of government.[4] Some of the reasons for this were practical, not to say cynical: people naturally show envy towards those in power,

---

[1] See pp. 207–14.
[2] *The Political Works of James I*, ed. C. H. McIlwain (Cambridge, Mass., 1918).
[3] By P. de Nancel, quoted in E. Thuau, *Raison d'État et pensée politique à l'époque de Richelieu*, p. 18.
[4] *La politique tirée des propres paroles de l'Écriture Sainte.* (1709.)

but a royal family can arouse their affection instead. The monarch whose kingdom will be passed on to his sons will feel that his own interests are so closely identified with those of the state that he will act entirely for its good. Royal authority was sacred, paternal, and absolute; but it was also subject to reason and to the law. This was the point at which Bossuet startlingly turned Divine Right into Divine Obligation. True the King could never be liable to the penalties of the law, or to coercion by his subjects. But the law to which he must submit was not simply the law of God: it included the law of the land. The monarch should be greatest in virtue as well as in power, and his virtue included setting an example to his subjects of obedience to his own just laws. It was the sacred duty of the monarch to rule in accordance with reason—the implications of which he set out in what was by then the familiar form of a series of rather trite pieces of moral advice. But the relation between the ruler of the state and 'law' had long been a much more pressing field of dispute than his relations with God.

The king and law: Grotius

The term 'law'—or its Latin equivalent '*ius*'—had so many meanings that it was in itself a source of abundant confusion. 'Positive' law included what was ordained by monarchs, legislative assemblies, and those who derived authority from them; but it also included in England the Common Law that had grown out of the decisions of lawyers through the ages and in France and much of southern Europe the Roman Law that was accepted as the basis of the system of justice. 'Natural' law, a much overworked term, was a less definable notion, with both classical and religious origins. As could be expected, seventeenth-century philosophy increasingly separated Natural Law from its religious, and especially its scriptural aspects and put the emphasis on those versions that made it a statement of how men and communities behave and how in their own interests they ought to behave. In this sense Natural Law seemed to be one means of bringing to the study of men in communities the processes both of observation and of deduction from what was certain. The writer who first made this attitude obvious was the Dutch lawyer and states-man Huig van Groot, who Latinised his name as Grotius. To Nether-lands theorists after the Revolt, conventional explanations of the need to obey the state and the monarch were embarrassing. The Dutch were almost bound to stress the importance of law as a safeguard against tyranny. Grotius was anything but remote from political realities or from religious conflict. As a leading theologian of the Remonstrants he was sentenced to life imprisonment when his patron Oldenbarnevelt was executed.[1] After his celebrated escape in a load of books and dirty linen, he lived in Paris with a pension from Louis XIII, and for a time was in the diplomatic service of Sweden. He described the Law of Nature as emanating from God; but he noted that if—which it would of course be sinful to believe—God did not exist, the arguments would still be valid.[2] For his aim was to construct its principles with the precision and certainty of geometrical theorems. God could no more change Natural Law than he could make two and two into something other than four. Grotius was in fact firmly separating the principles on which societies should be founded from the revealed religion in which he continued to believe.

When it came to actual definition there was nothing startling in Grotius' Natural Law. Men should fulfil their promises and contracts, specific or implied; they should respect property; they should obey those whose authority they had accepted, and in groups with no such authority they should conform to the will of the majority; they should punish transgressors according to their deserts. Some of his precepts might seem to owe as much to the needs and habits of the Dutch commercial class as to universal truth. But Grotius claimed to distinguish firmly between principles and the differing positive laws which states could make within them. Unlike most theorists, he was concerned at least as much with international as with national questions. It was in relations between states that the problems of society without a sovereign could be seen. If the principles of Natural Law could be applied there, its benefits would be immediately obvious. *Mare Liberum*, intended as an attack on the trading and colonial monopolies of the Spaniards, used the theories as part of a pamphleteering war. But *De Jure Belli ac Pacis*, written during the early part of the Thirty Years War, set out in massive and dogmatic detail the rules by which the justness of wars could be tested and their inhumanity and inconvenience mitigated. Though the work had little perceptible effect in his own day, it eventually provided a basis for the polite conventions within which eighteenth-century conflicts were conducted, and even for a sketchy 'international law'.

The supremacy of law: Coke

Grotius was using an artificially devised legal code to solve the difficulties that arose from an absence of sovereign power. In England

---

[1] See p. 391. [2] *Prologemena to De Jure Belli ac Pacis*, sec. 8.

another great codifier, Edward Coke, saw in it the way of settling disagreements between those who shared power. It was a familiar argument for absolutism that a division of power produced anarchy. An institution with power to settle differences within the ruling authorities would itself be the sovereign. To take refuge in appeals to Natural Law, or God, was merely to express the pious hope that the quarrel could be settled by argument. But a solution might exist if there were a set of laws so apt and so well defined that, at least among those skilled in such mysteries, there could be no doubt about what they meant. To this status Coke was ready to exalt the English Common Law. 'The Common Law', he reiterated, 'is the absolute perfection of reason'.[1] It was superior to Parliament, and when (not even 'if') an Act of Parliament is unreasonable the Common Law will declare it void.[2] According to his own account he told James I bluntly that 'his Majesty was not learned in the laws of England' and that kings were under the law as well as under God. But statements as uncompromising as these were not developed into any clear explanation of how they were to be applied. Coke is as guilty of muddle and self-contradiction as any of the philosophers. For some purposes law, and the Common Law especially, appeared as unchangeable, needing only to be declared and applied by the professional experts. For others, such as the reform of the legal system itself, he was ready enough to stress that a 'transcendent and absolute power of legislation' was vested in parliament—which he could, by a convenient piece of antiquarianism, call a court. Coke's intention was to attack the arbitrary power he believed the Crown to be acquiring; but the lawyer-dominated state he seemed to envisage was not attractive to the parliamentarians who wanted power for themselves as representatives of a large section of propertied society. It was one thing to attack such specific evils as the encroachment of ecclesiastical and prerogative courts, but quite another to show how law, or law in the light of reason, would always prevail against tyranny. The best he could offer as an unchallengeable source of ultimate authority was Magna Carta, already something of a legend. Its celebrated but ambiguous clauses protecting the 'free' man and the right of property were hardly more specific than the principles laid down by Grotius; and the rest of its massive text had little relevance four centuries later. Even so, his insistence that a body of law, as systematic and comprehensive as possible, should be used to

---

[1] 2 *Institutes*, p. 179, quoted in Christopher Hill, *Intellectual Origins*, where the contradictions are abundantly illustrated. See also J. W. Allen, *Political Thought*, part 2, c. 2. [2] 3 *Institutes*, p. 111.

protect the citizen became part of a professional tradition. Like Grotius, he was among the theorists who had a direct influence on events.

The division of power: Althusius

In one essential the lawyers tended to agree with the absolutists: the greatest evils were those that came from disorder and conflict. Stability and beneficence of institutions mattered more than the individual's part in them. One of the first writers in the century to concern himself with the relations between ruler and ruled was the German Calvinist Johann Althusen—Althusius. Though he has never been highly regarded by political philosophers, his *Politica Methodice Digesta* (Analysis of Political Method)[1] was, in spite of its artificially rigid and elaborate classifications, a realistic investigation of contemporary government. It was, he believed, natural for human beings to associate with each other in groups of different size and purpose. The family was the smallest of these, an entirely natural community into which some of the individual's rights and activities were merged. Similarly small voluntary associations (*collegia*) could offer other benefits of living together and have appropriate powers conceded to them by their members. Above them the various political institutions, local and regional, contributed to the authority of the state itself. The power of the group, including the unique majesty of the state, was derived from smaller groups that had come together to form it, and ultimately from the people themselves. This notion of authority derived from the whole people through intermediaries had the great attraction of justifying the power of assemblies and of such bodies as the cities and principalities of the Empire, without admitting a right of popular rebellion. The tyrannical monarch could be resisted, but only by the officials or institutions to whom the people had delegated their right to do so. Or at least they must be deemed to have delegated it: one of the difficulties Althusius never quite solved was the gap between 'the people' and the institutions with which he identified them. Somehow the men at every level who had been 'entrusted' with the administration of authority could, like the monarch, have their powers removed if they abused them. It all fitted well enough the teaching of Calvin himself.

The contract

There was another essential ingredient in the scheme of Althusius, which he shared with almost every theorist of the century. The power

[1] See the Introduction to the edition by C. J. Friedrich (1932).

of rulers originated in a 'contract'. Only the most naïve or unscrupulous could offer a historical basis for such an idea. Others had either to brush aside as irrelevant the question of whether a contract ever existed or to admit frankly that it was a myth. But in the thought both of the theorists and of their readers history played a much smaller part than law. The notion that obligation must rest on a solemn agreement was a central part of the lawyers' way of thought; and they were too familiar with the idea of a fictitious or implied contract to be put off by quibbles about its unreality. Moreover the notion of a contractual relation between the sovereign and his subjects was linked, vaguely, with that of feudal obligations. It could make obedience a moral duty—and could do so without reference to religious precepts.

The contract theory did not help to settle arguments about the power of the state. It could be asserted with equal plausibility either that the contract imposed obligations on the ruler or that it freed him from them. Part of the confusion came from haziness about who the 'contracting parties' were imagined to be. Althusius demanded a number of contracts, of two distinct kinds: all his groups were brought into being by contracts between the individuals, or between the smaller groups, that formed them. The group then made a second contract with the man, or men, who saw to the working of its organisation. Looked at in this way the state was different from other associations in the extent but not in the origin of its power; and the monarch was only the dominant part of a complex machinery of government. If he broke his side of the contract, power would revert to the bodies that had made it, and ultimately to the people as a whole. The contract in this form was therefore an argument on the side of the 'monarchomachs'—the term applied loosely to those who justified some kind of resistance to the monarch. It could be used at the same time to rule out mere rebellion, by stressing that the contract setting up the community implied a promise to abide by the decisions of the majority—which could be quietly assumed to mean the majority of those who were able to take part in politics. But there was no logical reason why the contract should be assumed to leave ultimate power in the hands of the majority: it could just as well bestow it, more or less irrevocably, on one or more rulers. All that was necessary in using it to support absolutism was to play down the idea of a contract between government and people and think solely of an agreement to set up the state by surrendering the natural rights of individuals into the hands of a sovereign—an agreement which would be binding so long as a sovereign existed.

Hobbes

This was the version of the contract used by the most outspoken and exciting of all philosophers of the time, Thomas Hobbes. Next to Marx, Hobbes may well be the modern political theorist about whom most has been written. Commentators on the whole agree in praising the logical and uncompromising clarity of his argument and go on to differ fundamentally about what he meant.[1] His life was full of contradictions. He was a dependant of the Cavendishes, one of the greatest aristocratic families, and fled to Paris before the outbreak of the Civil War; but the leading royalist political writers, Clarendon and Filmer, went out of their way to denounce him. Three of his principal works, the English translation of *De Cive*, *Leviathan*, and what was later entitled *The Elements of Law*, were published in England during the Rump Parliament and were soon alleged to be justifications of the rule of Cromwell. At the Restoration Charles welcomed him at court, and the presence of so wicked an atheist was one of the popular explanations of God's wrath manifested in the Plague and the Fire—though he had produced long and not grievously unorthodox expositions of Christianity. Perhaps the habit of simultaneously admiring him and either attacking or 're-interpreting' him springs from a feeling that his pessimistic view of human nature and its political consequences can neither be refuted nor accepted. Before Hobbes, both the classical and the Christian strands in political thought had been concerned with morality: starting from such abstract notions as justice, virtue, and wisdom the theorists asked not what did happen in the creation and working of the state but what ought to happen. The answer tended to be, as Leo Strauss put it, 'that the simply best régime is the rule of the wise and the best practicable régime is the rule of gentlemen'.[2] For Hobbes politics was part of an all-embracing study of the material world, to be treated in the same way as mathematics or astronomy. His starting-point was the nature of human beings—a nature very different from anything the moralists or theologians imagined. Men are so nearly equal, in mind and body, that whatever one man has another can hope to acquire. The weakest can, with a little ingenuity, kill the strongest; everyone thinks himself among the wisest; material possessions are always liable to be stolen. Consequently men constantly quarrel with each other.

[1] There are surveys of the conflicting views in *Hobbes Studies*, ed. K. C. Brown. For earlier attacks on him see J. Bowle, *Hobbes and his Critics* (1951).
[2] *Hobbes Studies*, p. 16.

In the nature of man we find three principal causes of quarrel. First, competition; secondly, diffidence; thirdly, glory. The first maketh men invade for gain; the second, for safety; and the third for reputation.[1]

If there is no power to keep them 'in awe', they will be 'in that condition which is called Warre'. In this state, where life is dominated by fear, there can be no material or cultural improvement. 'The notions of right and wrong, justice and injustice have there no place.' It is not so much a condition men *were* in before government existed as a condition they *would* be in if the power of government were removed. It is also the condition that actually exists not between men but between nations.

To escape from the horrors of the 'State of Warre' Hobbesian men were deemed to have made with each other the contract that set up a sovereign government. In practice, states were usually founded by conquest; but it is still expedient to accept the conqueror as sovereign. It is here that Hobbes throws out completely the pious smugness of traditional theories. He does not divide governments into good and bad: they are all bad. The men who rule will be men who seek power—more power than they need for their own protection. That is one reason why a single person is not quite as bad a ruler as an assembly: his wealth and glory will be largely the same as the wealth and glory of the state. The corrupt and ambitious officers of a democracy will often do best for themselves by 'perfidious advice, a treacherous action, or a civil war'.[2] Not that subjects are essentially different from rulers: if they think they can benefit by breaking the laws, they will do so. In this they are mistaken. When the sovereign is there, it is in the ultimate interests of subjects to obey him whatever he may command, since nothing short of death could be worse than the reversion to anarchy that would result from disobedience. There seem to be only two circumstances in which resistance to the sovereign is desirable. One is when he tries to put the subject to death; since (for some reason not made clear) death is the one evil worse than living in anarchy. The other is when the sovereign has ceased to be able to offer protection, and order can be better preserved by transferring allegiance to another. The Civil War, Hobbes suggests in a postscript to *Leviathan*, might have thrown some light on the tricky problem of when the citizen, and the soldier, can lawfully transfer his obligation from the old sovereign to the new.

[1] *Leviathan* c. 13 (Everyman edition p. 64).
[2] *Leviathan* c. 19 (Everyman p. 98). See also *De Cive* c. 5.

At this point Hobbes is introducing into his argument words such as 'lawful' and 'obligation' which seem to belong not to his strictly amoral outlook but to the familiar ideas of politics that involve some absolute ethical standards laid down if not by God at least by a 'law of Nature'. Indeed he often talks in such terms. In accepting the state, a man grants away his natural rights, and is then '*obliged* or *bound*' not to hinder those who now hold them. He '*ought* and it is his *duty* to avoid the *injustice* and *injury*' that would arise from breaking his covenant. (The emphasis is Hobbes's own.[1]) Similarly he discusses at length the duties as well as the rights of the sovereign. Many twentieth-century commentators have insisted that all this amounts to an explanation of political behaviour that is based on morality rather than expediency and is independent of his dismal view of human psychology.[2] Certainly he wrote a great deal, especially in the earlier statements of his ideas, in the familiar language of moral philosophy. But when he faced the question of how obligations came to exist his answer was generally that they depended on the state. In the condition of 'warre'

> ... nothing can be unjust ... Force and fraud are the two cardinal virtues. Justice and injustice ... relate to men in Society, not in Solitude.[3]

Perhaps the greatest difficulty was to explain how totally selfish men would be so enlightened as to make and keep the imaginary covenant with each other to set up the state. There is a good deal of confusion in the argument that it is a law of Nature, that is to say a 'precept or general rule found out by reason ... that a man be willing, when others are so too, ... to lay down this right to all things'. One recent comment is that the descriptions he applied to mankind in general were really derived from the 'market society' of his own time where feudal obligations had disappeared and sovereignty was manifestly necessary for the preservation of property.[4] But property-owners did not usually consider collective rather than individual interests. Hobbes avoids all the errors that arise from assuming that men are virtuous: he cannot always reconcile his ideas with the fact that they are stupid.

Part of the task of the Hobbesian sovereign is to cope with popular

[1] *Leviathan* c. 14 (Everyman p. 67).
[2] H. Warrender, *The Political Philosophy of Hobbes*, puts this view uncompromisingly.
[3] *Leviathan* c. 13 (Everyman edition p. 66).
[4] Macpherson, *Possessive Individualism*, part II, sect. 3.

ignorance. 'Common people are not of capacity enough to be made to understand' the principles of government. They must be constantly taught to conform. It would be a help if times could be set aside from labour when they could 'hear their duties told them', and 'put in mind of the authority that maketh laws'. To this end the Jews had a sabbath, 'in the solemnity whereof they were put in mind that their King was God'. Without specifically relegating the Church to the rôle of a propaganda instrument for the state, Hobbes insists that the interests of the two are identical. Religious teaching, like every other aspect of life, is subject to the orders of the sovereign. If the subject is ordered to believe what in fact he does not, then though the cleric may reasonably suffer martyrdom for his faith, the layman must outwardly conform—and trust that God will hold the sovereign responsible. Hobbes's discussions of Christianity cannot however be written off easily as those of an atheist practising the outward conformity he advised. He compared religion to pills 'which swallowed whole have the virtue to cure, but chewed are for the most part cast up again without effect.'[1] He chewed a great deal himself. Sometimes he devotes all his intellectual power to an effort at reconciling Christianity with a rational theism and incorporates both into his explanation of politics. But his reflections on religion repeatedly turn away from what he insists are unprovable assertions to investigation of its rôle in human society. Delusion and deception have played a very great part in this. For a man to say that God 'hath spoken to him in a dream is no more than to say he dreamed that God spake to him'. Being a man, he 'may err, and (which is more) may lie'. Clergy who pretended to political wisdom and authority were to Hobbes an intolerable menace. 'It is not the Roman clergy only that pretends the Kingdom of God to be of this world, and thereby to have a power therein distinct from that of the Civil State.'[2]

Pufendorf and Spinoza

Two of the century's later philosophers were especially influenced by Hobbes in their efforts to construct a comprehensive system of politics as part of a general philosophy. Samuel Pufendorf was a German scholar in the tradition of encyclopaedic learning. Like Althusius, he was very well aware that the idea of a single sovereign state made no sense in Germany. Few of the philosophers had faced so honestly the need to reconcile theories of the state with historical and contemporary facts.

[1] *Leviathan* c. 32 (Everyman edition p. 199).
[2] *Leviathan* c. 47 (Everyman edition p. 383).

He was perhaps less honest in admitting how hard it was to do so. He accepted the Hobbesian view that the sovereign state was necessary for civilised existence; but it must be a sovereignty that provided for such a relationship as that between the German states and the Empire. Security was no longer the sole purpose of sovereignty: it was the duty of princes and emperor alike to provide for the well-being of their people—in a largely material sense. *De jure Naturae et Gentium*—a title suggesting acceptance of the scholarly conventions—set out in massive and arid detail how Natural Law could be elaborated into a code of conduct for both subject and ruler. Pufendorf was an orthodox, though tolerant, Lutheran. But he was nearly thrown out of Sweden for laying down too precisely the need to separate the sphere of reason from that of religion. Swedish clergy were not taken in by his bland assertions that there need be no conflict between the two.

If Pufendorf shared Hobbes's rationalism, it was a far more profound philosopher who completed his removal of Christian religion and orthodox morality from politics. Benedict (or Baruch) Spinoza was a man detached from all allegiances. His family were Portuguese Jews who had moved to Amsterdam, where he so quickly became a known heretic that at the age of twenty-four he was expelled with solemn curses from the Jewish community. He lived, a consumptive recluse, by making lenses. Even in Holland his *Tractatus Theologico-Politicus* had to be published under a false name, and his main works did not appear at all until after his death. Spinoza's God was the whole substance of the universe, timeless, self-creating, unconcerned with human affairs. The real connection of religion with politics was shown very clearly in Old Testament history: it was exploited by monarchs as a means of strengthening their own rule. Religious authorities had designed their doctrines to 'impress the minds of the masses with devotion'. His theories of the state showed the same mixture of idealism and scepticism. He did not put as much weight as did Hobbes on a rational decision of the subject that government, with all its horrors, was better than anarchy: the state survived by simultaneously making its citizens fear it and persuading them to love it. There are limits to what can be done by sheer terror: consequently the state needs to avoid arousing too much 'indignation' in the majority of its subjects. Even though its sole aim is security, it will be responsive to the will of the majority. In this it is unlikely that monarchy will prove the best form of government, since the monarch will be concerned mainly with preserving his individual power. The *Tractatus* breaks off in the middle of the discussion of the three Aristotelian forms of government without coming to any conclusion about the merits and defects of democracy. But it is evident that Spinoza saw a good deal of virtue in the Netherlands government of de Witt, with effective power in the hands of a narrow but comparatively enlightened section of the community. It was in the Netherlands more than any-where else that those in power were prepared to concede, however hesitantly, some freedom of thought and speech to whoever accepted the authority of the state. 'The true purpose of the state', he said, 'is liberty' —and what now sounds a platitude was then a startling declaration. But Spinoza's view of the practicable functions of the state appeared to change as he became increasingly disillusioned about the behaviour of those involved in its work. The assassination of the de Witts and the French victories have been seen as a cause of his retreat into a less hopeful view. The state, he continued to insist, was as much a part of the divine creation as everything else in the universe. Its purpose was more than merely enabling the individual to remain alive and secure: it should also make his life worth living—which for Spinoza was a spiritual rather than a material achievement. The idea that it could contribute positively to the collective quest for the good life seemed to give way to the admission that the most that could be expected from it was the freedom and peace necessary for a cultured existence.

Parliament in England: Whitelock and Parker

Most of the conventions of philosophical theorising about the state made it convenient to assume that the ruler was an individual. The other possibilities sometimes seemed a rather awkward afterthought. The failure to ask who in fact exercised power in the state was one of the main reasons for the unreality of so much of the argument. It was only in England that the problems of 'mixed monarchy' formed a central part of political debate; and the events of the century did not encourage Europeans to regard it as a desirable topic.

The decades of growing tension between English monarchs and their subjects did not produce any outstanding prophet who could explain either how or why royal power should be restricted. The notion of 'consent' was of course familiar; and parliament was readily deemed to 'represent' the freely expressed will of all citizens. The difficulty was to show why the representative body should share the king's power in some topics and circumstances but not in others. A favourite device for having the best of both worlds was the sovereignty of the king 'in' parliament. James Whitelock told the Commons in 1610 that the king had a twofold power, and that what he did alone could be overruled by what he did in parliament. The most relevant explanation of this was derived from the sanctity of property: it was only with the consent of an assembly representing owners of property that taxes could be justly imposed. But Whitelock extended this argument to apply to any alteration in the law. The Commons were always ready to welcome the idea that they were not merely the temporary representatives of taxpayers but an embodiment of the whole community. M.P.s claimed such privileges as freedom from arrest on the grounds that they were 'not now private men but supplied the room of a multitude'. This was the notion that was developed by Henry Parker in pamphlets that were intended merely as part of the rather arid debate between Charles and the Commons in the months before and after the outbreak of civil war. It was possible by then to say bluntly that all political power remained in the hands of the people, which in practice meant the hands of parliament, 'the people artificially congregated'. The invention of representative assemblies had solved the problem of reconciling order with protection against tyranny. Whatever laws parliament judged necessary the king must pass; his ministers must be approved by parliament and his resources provided by them. What would have seemed in 1610 a fantastic exaggeration of the theory of representation was now only a restatement of claims that the majority in parliament had made. What Parker did not make clear was whether they were an emergency measure—the assertion of parliament's ultimate authority against a tyrant—or a normal procedure that left the king as a mere servant of parliament.

The state and property: Harrington and the Levellers

The English Civil War turned many of the stock ideas of political theory into practical reality. Resistance to the sovereign had actually happened —not as the rebellion of a faction but as an act of policy debated *ad nauseam*. While it went on, and when it was over, there were repeated attempts to draw up a real contract between king and subjects. Mixed monarchy was to be defined by a document and upheld by an agreed form of control over the armed forces. The attempts were monotonously unsuccessful. When it came to the point statesmen, lawyers, and gentlemen fully conversant with the works of political thinkers from Plato to Coke, and desperately anxious to find a workable settlement, could not do it. With the state on the edge of dissolution there appeared the theories that took account of a fact normally evaded: citizens were not alike, but were divided into rich and poor, powerful and powerless.

From the early days of the war, some pamphleteers had seen the conflict as one between different sections of propertied society from which lesser men had nothing to gain. But it was only when the fighting had ended that there occurred, mainly in the army and in the City of London, the astonishing episode of the Levellers. Speeches, pamphlets, and broadsides were filled with the debate about the connection between political rights and ownership of property. In the greatest moment of the controversy, at Putney in 1647 when officers and men of the army met on equal terms, the spokesmen of the soldiers put forward the 'Agreement of the People', a draft for a real social contract. Colonel Rainsborough, in his simple and moving speeches, set out some principles of democracy:

> Truly sir, I think it's clear that every man that is to live under a government ought first by his own consent to put himself under that government: and I do think that the poorest man that is in England is not at all bound in a strict sense to that government he hath not had a voice to put himself under . . .[1]

Rainsborough's most lucid opponent was not a supporter of absolutism, or even of the mixed constitution the Stuarts were alleged to have violated, but the future regicide Henry Ireton, advocate of parliamentary sovereignty and a wide franchise. Ireton's alarm was that any appeal to the natural equality of men led logically to the abolition of private property. Power must be restricted to those with a 'permanent fixed interest' in the country. Rainsborough, firmly denying the allegation that the supporters of the Agreement sought to take away property, stuck to the principle of universal—or perhaps only universal male—suffrage. But the leading trio of Leveller pamphleteers, John Lilburne, Richard Overton, and William Walwyn, were less confident when it came to expanding the first Agreement into detailed constitutional proposals. 'Servants', a conveniently vague term which seemed to apply to the whole body of wage-labourers, were excluded from the franchise on the implausible grounds that they were 'included' in their masters and by accepting dependence had forfeited their 'birthright'. Recipients of alms had lost it too by their subjection to the charity of others. The franchise was in any case not the main part of Leveller demands. Parker had been content to assume that parliament was the voice of the people. The Levellers had seen the triumph of a parliament that then revealed itself as the voice of successive minorities. 'Having by woeful experience found the prevalence of corrupt interests' among men entrusted with

[1] A. S. P. Woodhouse, *Puritanism and Liberty*, p. 53.

authority, they concluded that the power naturally inherent in the people in general could only be protected by an irrevocable written constitution. 'The people', Lilburne proclaimed 'are now dissolved into the original Law of Nature'; and in this unique moment when the state could be created afresh there was available an instrument capable of doing so—the New Model Army. But in the end the army, under Cromwell, was kept loyal to the new privileged minority.

To the Levellers the state should have a constitution that would ensure the separation of power from wealth. To the most original—but hardly the most practical—of the republican philosophers it should redistribute wealth in a way that would produce political stability. James Harrington, former courtier and friend of Charles I, and a passive neutral in the war, was one of the few who recognised immediately the merit of Hobbes. ('He will in future ages be accounted the best writer, at this day, in the world.'[1]) But he loathed Hobbes's opinions, and applied a method no less rational and materialist to the design of a commonwealth in which power would be widely shared. *Oceana*, published—with Cromwell's reluctant consent—in 1656, was both an interpretation of English history and a future constitution based on economic determinism. From a study of history Harrington believed he had discovered an all-important scientific principle—that power depended on the possession of land. English history from the dissolution of the monasteries to the Civil War was a splendid demonstration of this: the growth of a new class of landowners had brought about the collapse of the old rule of monarch and nobility. The victors must now construct a new state in which the accumulation of property in the hands of the few would be prevented by an Agrarian Law limiting landed estates to the annual value of £2,000. The practical details of the constitution of Oceana were hardly a logical triumph. On Harrington's own calculation there could still be a landed minority of 5,000 people. Only by assuming that everyone would work out his own interests with perfect and law-abiding rationality (and by some very odd arithmetic) could he show why the republic should not be overthrown. But he did succeed in breaking away from the fiction of monarchies, aristocracies and democracies to invent a system that recognised what he regarded as the powers of leadership 'peculiar to the Genius of a Gentleman'. Only the Senators, consisting of gentry and nobility, had enough wisdom to debate. The assembly, chosen largely by 'the meaner sort' in a secret

[1] Quoted in P. Zagorin, *Political Thought in the English Revolution*, p. 34 (London, 1954).

ballot, was to vote without discussion. Administration was to be done by elected councils and paid officials. Every position in the state was to be relinquished after a fixed period—for only a system of rotation could prevent the formation of parties. Given this perfect constitution, Oceana would be exempt from all the consequences of human wickedness and folly. It would last for ever, and as an imperial power and leader of a great alliance would spread its blessings over the whole earth. Cromwell, cast for the rôle of its founder, was unconvinced.

None of the theories about the just distribution of political power produced a practical form of government to replace the Stuart monarchy. Among the various radical opinions those of Milton proved more fragile than most. In 1650 he showed how it was justifiable for the people, from whom all political authority is derived, to slay a tyrant. By 1654 he had discovered that 'nothing is more pleasing to God or more agreeable to reason than that the most worthy should possess supreme power.[1] The one writer who seemed to achieve consistency was Gerrard Winstanley, the passionate spokesman of the little Digger community, who believed that only the abolition of property would end the evils of power. Mankind would then put away its covetousness, pride and oppression, and act in accordance with the 'great Creator, Reason' which Winstanley identifies with God. But when he too indulged in the exercise of drafting a constitution, the fruits of the Common Treasury of the earth were to be distributed under the control of 'overseers' with formidable powers of punishment. In 1660, though radicalism in its religious forms struggled on, the revolutionaries seemed to be silenced as well as defeated. In place of the conflict and disintegration that produced Lilburne, Harrington, and the great ferment of ideas and ideals, there came the compromises that produced Locke.

The English compromise: Locke

Though most countries found philosophers able to demonstrate that their current régime was exactly the one required by God or the Law of Nature, few of them made quite such comfortable reading as John Locke. Where writers of the previous generation had inculcated either angry hope or resigned despair, Locke offered to all who accepted the settlement of 1688–9 the assurance that while foreigners might live in the darkness of absolutism, in England justice and freedom had at last been reconciled with security. Locke's men in the state of nature were not the bloodthirsty savages of Hobbes: they recognised that 'no-one

[1] *Defensio secunda.*

ought to harm another in his Life, Health, Liberty or Possessions'.[1]
They agreed to set up government 'for the regulating and preserving of
Property'. The agreement is a conditional one. Men have not consented
to a government that would enslave them, or rule by arbitrary decrees,
or seize their property, or hand over its power to others. What happens
if governments do misbehave is not so clear. Where there lies no appeal
on earth, men 'have just cause to make their appeal to Heaven', and
only if they are confident of their success before 'a Tribunal that cannot
be deceived' will they resort to armed revolt. The difficulty is partly
that, though he asserts the distinction between what men do and what
they have a right or a duty to do, Locke easily assumes that the people, if
not always the politicians, will be both moral and rational. Representative government is the best form because an elected legislature 'is not
nor can possibly be absolutely arbitrary' but 'is bound' to rule justly.
Even so, since human frailty is tempted to grasp at power, the legislative
and executive functions must be separated. The executive is completely
subject to the legislative; but it must have some discretion to act for the
public good 'without the prescription of the Law, and sometimes even
against it'. The implications of this do not seem to worry Locke at all.

To make the England of William and Mary the ideal state, it was
necessary to show that it depended on the free consent of its citizens.
Ignoring the debates and experiments on the franchise forty years
before, Locke was happy to regard the Commons as an assembly of
representatives chosen by the people. Similarly the all-important institution of property was made compatible with equality. Private
property was originally whatever the individual could acquire and use
through his own labour. But the happy invention of money had made
possible the virtuous process of storing property without wasting it.
Yet behind what now sounds like smug self-deception, Locke was upsetting a good many conventional attitudes of his time. Of all the
political philosophers of the century, he was probably the most influential; and his influence was, within its limits, humane and liberalising.

The state and the individual

One thing that separated Locke from the vast majority of earlier
theorists was his view that excessive state authority was immoral whoever wielded it; and he was sometimes inclined to count as excessive
what most politicians considered necessary for the security of the state.
There had long been voices on the outer fringe of the world of political

[1] *Civil Government* II, c. 6.

ideas arguing that freedom of speech was one right with which the state ought not to interfere too much. In 1644 Roger Williams, after being expelled from Massachusetts for his dangerous views, had published the *Bloudy Tenent of Persecution for the Cause of Conscience* in which he suggested that it was outside the proper sphere of the state's activity to disturb the worship even of 'Papists, Jews, Turks, or Indians'. It was almost the only plea for toleration that did not vitiate its principles by making exceptions to them. Milton's *Areopagitica*, which appeared in the same year, reached the heights of poetic prose in defending the right of uncensored printing. From its arguments for free expression, which rested on practical as well as historical and moral grounds, there were exceptions too obvious to need more than the briefest mention: what is 'impious or evil . . . no law can possibly permit that intends not to unlaw itself'. Naturally this included popery. The attack on censorship was one instance of a more general change that had taken place in political thinking during the century. In 1600 people who sought to reduce the powers of the monarch were usually concerned to defend those of some other authority—or to advocate one of the various forms of decentralisation of state functions. By 1700 they were more likely to be concerned with the 'rights' of the individual which authority of every kind ought to uphold.

Even within the absolutist states, the order of society was less rigid; the individual, by his own efforts, skill, or unscrupulousness, could more easily achieve rank and power. Authoritarian religion was attacked on all sides by what amounted to individual judgment. Above all, the production of wealth was increasingly seen to be advanced by individual enterprise. This was the argument in an anti-Orangist pamphlet of the 1670s *The Interest of Holland* which became a popular manifesto of the uncompromising wing of de Witt's party and was sometimes ascribed to the Grand Pensionary himself. Its real author, Pieter de la Court, had already produced works on the problem of reconciling liberty with good government that had been admired by Spinoza. He had now concluded that to attain 'the highest perfection of a political society', in Holland especially, 'there is an absolute necessity that the commonalty be left in as great a natural liberty as possible for seeking the welfare of their souls and bodies, and for the improvement of their estates'. A republic was, in de la Court's view, the only 'free government', in which the liberty of the individual would not conflict with the interest of the state. It was not an assumption that the old theorists of absolute monarchy would accept. Ludwig von Seckendorf was a widely read German Lutheran, whose

Princely State and *Christian State* added to the conventional applauding of absolutism exhortations to the ruler to make the welfare of his subjects, both moral and economic, a main concern. It was the view taken up in Vienna under Leopold I by the economic theorists later known as 'cameralists'. But the title of one of the most popular of their works left no doubts about the purpose: Philip von Hornigk in his *Oesterreich über alles, wann es nur will*—Austria at the top when it shows the will to be—was continuing the teaching of his father-in-law Johan Becher.[1] His nationalism was essentially an economic one, based not on the accumulation of bullion but on increasing the sale and output of goods. To achieve this the state must do everything to advance internal prosperity, enterprise, and education. In the jargon usually applied to the next century, despotism must be, for its own good, benevolent and enlightened. The ruler was ceasing to be a god and becoming a manager.

[1] See p. 74.

IX

Government

Monarchy

Whatever the views of seventeenth-century theorists, there is abundant justification for the common description of the period as an age of royal absolutism. Nearly every country was deeply affected by the history of its royal family, and by the personal characteristics of monarchs and of their wives, heirs, and guardians. The king himself could clearly be anything from an irresistible controller of the state

BIBLIOGRAPHY. Modern writers on constitutional history are generally more interested than their predecessors in the normal working of government at every level, and in the realities of power behind the institutions. Several general surveys are kept up to date, such as F. Hartnung, *Deutsche Verfassungsgeschichte* (6th ed., Stuttgart, 1948). J. P. Kenyon, *The Stuart Constitution* (Cambridge, 1966) is among recent collections of documents with commentary; and there are brief comparative sketches such as M. Beloff, *The Age of Absolutism* (London, 1954). Two topics that have been prominent in recent work are office-holding, with its effects on government and society, and representative assemblies. K. W. Swart, *The Sale of Offices in the Seventeenth Century* (The Hague, 1949) deals with western Europe generally. Much more detailed studies are R. Mousnier, *La vénalité des offices sous Henri IV et Louis XIII* (Rouen, 1945) and G. E. Aylmer, *The King's Servants* (London, 1961). Many results of the investigation of assemblies and their members can be found in the *Études* of the *Commission internationale pour l'histoire des assemblées d'états*. F. L. Carsten in *Princes and Parliaments in Germany* (Oxford, 1953) shows the great differences in the power of Estates between one German state and another.

The nature of 'absolutism' in the period has been debated a good deal. The reports (*Relazioni*) of the Tenth International Congress of Historical Sciences, vol. 4 (Florence, 1950) contain the well-known article by R. Mousnier and F. Hartnung, 'Quelques problèmes concernant la monarchie absolue'. This, and the subsequent controversies, are discussed by J. Vincens Vives in the reports of the eleventh congress, vol. 4 (Stockholm, 1955) under the title *Estructura administrativa estatal en los siglos XVI y XVII*. A later contribution on French monarchical institutions by Mousnier is in *Dix-Septième Siècle*, vols. 58–61 (1963), which also has articles by F. Dumont ('La Royauté française et la monarchie absolue') and by C-J. Nordmann ('La monarchie mixte en Suède').

machine to a child or a half-wit. Almost the only function monarchs had in common was the ability by their mere existence to make the fate of their nations irrational and accidental. Because succession to the throne usually depended on rules of inheritance that were rigid but not entirely beyond argument, the matrimonial and reproductive affairs of royalty were sometimes more important politically than all the country's economic and military efforts. Almost the worst misdeed a monarch could commit was to die without providing an unquestioned adult heir; and the risk that this would happen seemed higher among royal families than others. The shape of English politics for ten years depended on Charles II's lack of a legitimate Protestant successor. The Russians, who were most in need of an effective monarch, suffered more than their share of minorities. It was striking proof of the stability of the French state that it carried off without serious harm two long regencies that became in effect the rule of women and their factions.

Illogically, doubts and disputes about the king's accession had little effect on his eventual status. The wearer of the crown, however he acquired it, became for many a sacred ruler, with such vestigial miraculous powers as the curing of the King's Evil, and with a hazy recollection of pagan and Christian myths preserved in his coronation ceremony. Most of these rituals also contained reminders of his rôle as a popular leader: he was presented to and acclaimed by 'the people' and took oaths which often committed him vaguely to uphold their 'rights'. In an extreme form, the notion of power delegated by the people was occasionally used to defend rebellion and tyrannicide. There were traces of the theory of 'popular' monarchy in the royal elections, real or nominal, that were still common in 1600. The Polish Crown was outstanding in this only because for a time the choice was a genuinely open one.[1] Denmark, Bohemia, Hungary, and Russia all held elections for their monarchs, and though at this stage they seldom went outside the reigning dynasties, they could help to make some sort of bargain possible. But it was not a

Specialised monographs include H. F. Schwarz, *The Imperial Privy Council in the Seventeenth Century* (Cambridge, Mass., 1943); J. H. Shennan, *The Parlement of Paris* (London, 1968); L. Konopczynski, *Le liberum veto* (Paris, 1930); D. H. Willson, *The Privy Councillors in the House of Commons, 1604–1629* (Minneapolis, 1940). G. Ziegler, *The Court at Versailles* (London, 1966) is one of the many accounts of the subject. M. Marion, *Dictionnaire des institutions de la France aux XVII⁰ et XVIII⁰ siècles* (Paris, 1923) is a helpful work of a kind lacking for other countries.

[1] See pp. 177–8.

bargain with the people: the king in another of his aspects was the greatest of the landowners, ruling with their consent and in their interest. The kingdom was still, in part, regarded as a piece of property to be bequeathed and sometimes shared out among the family. Philip II had no difficulty in handing over the Spanish Netherlands to his daughter and her husband the Archduke Albert with provision for their reversion to the King of Spain if they died childless. The tangled claims to the Spanish Succession depended on the wills made by Philip IV and his son Charles, and on the renunciation and transfer of rights under them.[1] But perhaps the most ludicrous application of the notion of the monarch as proprietor was the invention, by a French official, of the claim to an assortment of little territories in the Netherlands on the grounds that local laws of land-inheritance would bring them by 'devolution' to Louis XIV's wife Maria Theresa.[2]

Maria had been chosen by Mazarin as a bride for the reluctant Louis in the hope that France would eventually benefit from her Spanish inheritance, and the marriage was a major part of the peace settlement of 1659. But on the whole foreign matches proved a less important foundation for alliances and territorial unions than diplomats assumed. The earlier marriage alliance between France and Spain, in 1612, made little difference to the long hostility between them. England's relations with these two powers were not decisively affected by the unhappy fiasco of Charles I's journey to Madrid in 1623 or by his subsequent marriage to Henrietta Maria of France. Nor did it prove to matter very much that Gustav Adolf, after a similar incognito expedition to Berlin in 1620, succeeded in marrying the Elector's daughter in face of the rivalry of the Poles. One permanent consequence of diplomatic control over royal marriages was that the monarchs who were figureheads of national sentiment often had little claim to any nationality of their own by birth. Louis XIV's grandparents came from France, Italy, Spain, and Germany, James II's from Scotland, Denmark, France, and Italy. (His marriage to an English subject, Ann Hyde, was much more remarkable in the west than it would have been in Russia, where the Romanovs took their brides from rival court families.) It is open to argument how far the other obvious fact of royal ancestry—the prolonged in-breeding—was responsible for physical and mental defects: they were common enough at every level of society. Considering the horrors of their upbringing and environment, seventeenth-century monarchs were a fairly normal sample of humanity.

[1] See p. 313.   [2] See p. 433.

Most of them worked hard for their living. If none was quite the model of industry that Philip II had been, there were plenty—Maximilian of Bavaria, the Great Elector, and for many years the *roi soleil* himself—who devoted an immense amount of time to the detailed tasks of government. Not only did the monarch combine the work of presiding over councils with a good deal of bureaucratic routine and with his indispensable ceremonial functions: he was often still expected to lead his armies in war. If warfare had been a rational activity it would have been absurd for kings, on whose survival so much depended, to risk the fate of Gustav Adolf and Charles XII. The king on the battlefield was part of the feudal tradition of monarchy, still appropriate in so far as he was directing the state's principal activity, but a serious hindrance both to efficiency and to political stability at home.

The court

However important the accidents of the sovereign's personal life, the real centre of absolute monarchy was not so much the individual ruler as the court. It was here that the monarch encountered the organised pressures, from the political factions, from the priests, confessors, and astrologers, that shaped his inclinations. And it was here that he came into contact with the two kinds of power in his subjects that can be loosely called the 'aristocratic' and the 'bureaucratic'. The character of absolutism depended a great deal on the king's relations with on the one hand the men whose greatness came primarily from their status at the top of the landowning pyramid, and on the other those who owed it to the holding of office. The court was in its ancient form the household of the greatest of landowners, to which the high nobility tended to assume that they could belong if they wished. The Russian court in the Time of Troubles and the Polish court, such as it was, for most of the century were grim examples of how it could be the battleground of fights for control of the Crown, which prevented it from being anyone's established home. In many countries it had only just become permanently fixed in the capital: though kings continued to move frequently about their territories, they could leave many of the functions of their courts behind. Instead of demanding hospitality from the nobles, the king was now assumed to give it. To great men no longer able to live in the style they deemed appropriate on the resources of their estates, the court was a source of wealth. Spanish kings suffered as badly as any. When Philip II established his court firmly at Madrid he kept its size and splendour within bounds: only a minority of the grandees were courtiers. Philip III allowed large numbers of aristocrats great and small to come there and to bring with them their households, on the size of which their prestige was thought to depend. The palace and the whole capital were filled with men seeking favours, sinecures, positions at whatever level was within their reach. It was a vast and for the most part unproductive community living ultimately on the rents and taxes of those outside it, and on growing debts. Efforts to make the nobles go back to their estates had little success, and court expenditure continued to grow under Philip IV and Charles II until it was estimated at a quarter of the whole revenue of Castile.

Louis XIV's Versailles was not quite the ingenious new invention for taming the nobility and keeping them out of politics it is sometimes alleged to have been: only the long process of centralisation and the economic problems of landed families had made it possible. Louis was merely doing more magnificently what almost every monarch accepted as part of his life. The gorgeous costumes, the festivities, the lavish buildings and furnishings, the throngs of servants in strict order of rank formed a world of mingled luxury and squalor proclaiming that every man had his position, and must rise and fall according to the rules[1]. But just as most monarchs were the active heads of government, most courts were the frames within which power was both fought for and exercised. Under Gustav Adolf the 'Chancery Wing' was added to the palace at Stockholm: the bureaucratic function was different from the ceremonial one but closely attached to it. A clear line between household service and political service was almost impossible. The English Secretaries of State dined at court, and the great household officials were members of the Privy Council, even though government offices were recognised as different from purely household ones. At Vienna the court had the advantage, for the emperor, of being attached neither to the Holy Roman Empire nor to the Habsburg hereditary lands. Its principal officer, the *Obersthofmeister*, was often the emperor's chief minister.[2] The Great Elector of Brandenburg made his court almost entirely a working body. But he was no more able than the rulers of greater states to escape one major problem in government—the quest for office as a source of profit and prestige.

[1] See pp. 424–6. Contemporary impressions of the court at Versailles can be found in Jean de la Bruyère, *Les caractères, ou les mœurs de ce siècle.*
[2] See p. 315.

Office

The passion for holding offices, nominally or really in the work of central administration, and for acquiring titles,[1] was an outstanding characteristic of seventeenth-century Europe. It led, since governments were always short of money, to the twin devices of 'venality of office' and 'inflation of honours'. Office and title were alike in the profit their sale brought to the Crown. But while the sale of titles was the most harmless way of raising money, the sale of offices had a profound and generally evil effect on government. A post in the king's service became a piece of property to be acquired, exploited, and handed on to heirs in much the same way as a piece of land. The supply of offices, unlike that of land, had no fixed limits: the Crown could create as many as it chose for the joint profit of itself and the favoured subject. As central government became more active, some new officials were undoubtedly needed. Many worked hard; and usually they were rewarded to a small extent by a fixed payment from the Crown. But their principal sources of income from office were the fees which they were entitled to charge the victim or beneficiary of their work, the proportion they kept of the money collected for the Crown, and the gifts and bribes that in greater or less degree were assumed to be their due. If an office enabled its holder to make in this way profit that depended on his energy and enterprise, it was natural that he should be ready to pay a lump sum for the opportunity; and from this it was an easy step for the Crown to multiply offices not in order to get necessary work of government done but in order to make money. There were many ways in which the man who wanted to work his way up the office-holding ladder might begin.[2] He might buy directly from the Crown a post, or the 'reversion' of a post after its existing holder died or moved up. He might buy from the holder a post that had been granted not just for life but with the right to sell or bequeath it. Or he might pay the man who had acquired not the office but the 'gift' of it. At every stage the process probably involved suitable rewards to those in a position to put in a good word. The first Duke of Buckingham was believed, perhaps with some exaggeration, to have made himself the centre of a huge office-market, and under James I the great majority of posts in central government were probably sold in one way or another. But in England the disease took a mild form: jobs were not created in outrageous numbers, and the court did not

[1] See p. 93.
[2] G. E. Aylmer, *The King's Servants*, chap. 3.

concern itself with most of those in local government. Charles I reduced the sale of at least the higher offices and made an effort to remove some of the worst abuses of fees. Certainly many English landed families found office-holding an important part of their economy. The cleavage between those who were involved and those who were excluded has sometimes been made to appear too rigid; but family connection and patronage were as necessary as cash for progress in the royal service, and the tendency to keep the fruits of office an exclusive benefit helped to restrict their multiplication.

In Spain there was far less restriction. Under Philip IV the Castilian Cortes largely abandoned its opposition to a system that seemed for the Crown one of the few sources of genuine extra revenue and for the subject a way of acquiring some sort of distinction. Under Charles II it was estimated that a fifth of the population of Castile held a government office of some sort. But Spanish 'empleomania' was more a low-level than a high-level affair: most of the offices sold were trivial local ones not producing any opportunities for large profits, though the title of nobility attached to some of them was valued not only for its status but for the exemptions from taxation it carried. The higher offices, and places at court, were obtained more by bribery of individuals than by open sale; their holders grew rich through corruption rather than through recognised fees or allowances.

It was in France that the sale of offices reached its height. Even in proportion to its large population, France probably had more offices than any other country. Creating and selling them brought money to the Crown and was thought to make the purchaser loyal to the state. Buying an office, like lending to the state through the *rentes*, was a form of investment that seemed to most Frenchmen with capital available more attractive than industry or commerce. No-one knows how many offices there were.[1] One estimate is that 50,000 new posts were made under Louis XIII. In Normandy there were more than 4,500 holders in 1638, two and a half times the number in the 1570's. In Dijon it was calculated that almost half the citizens were of families with some title in the great mass of municipal officials, lawyers, and so on. Henry IV's principal contractor for offices, Charles Paulet, devised the edict whereby in return for an annual payment to the Crown of one-sixtieth of the recognised value of the office, the holder could ensure its transfer to his successors. The *paulette* or *droit annuel* together with the sales, even-

[1] The most elaborate calculations are those of R. Mousnier in *La venalité des offices*, pp. 106–33.

tually produced between a quarter and a half of the state's whole revenue. Richelieu in 1625 announced his determination to abolish the sale of offices completely. But when he wrote the *testament politique* in the 1630s he admitted that though in a newly established state it would be a 'crime' to allow venality of office, 'prudence did not permit' the destruction of the institution once it was there.[1] By the time of Louis XIV, even though the creation of new offices had fallen off under Mazarin, administration was a major national industry. From the high legal and governing families of the *grande robe* to the swarm of local collectors and clerks, the office-holders had a common interest in protecting their *charge* and its profitable rights. To improve the efficiency of government and its yield of money to the Crown it was often necessary to create posts outside the old venal system. Richelieu's intendants were meant to cut across the vested interests and corruptions of officials. Their posts were not *charges* but *commissions*, which the Crown could grant and revoke at any time. They were chosen mainly from the *maîtres de requêtes*, local administrators of comparatively lowly origin who did much to extend royal authority in the provinces. Under Colbert the intendants and various *commissaires* gradually extended their functions into jealously guarded areas of local government. When they began to appoint a growing number of '*sub-délégués*' to do work that became permanent instead of temporary, there was something very like a rival bureaucracy imposing itself on top of the old one. The *sub-délégués*, whose existence the Crown had refused to recognise, succeeded in making their own positions marketable in much the same way as the old ones.

The Minister

Neither the most energetic of monarchs nor the most efficient system of departments could function without the two institutions on whose character and relative power the nature of the régime depended—the minister and the royal council. Despite the obvious exceptions, this was in the west more an age of the great minister than of the great king. They had rare opportunities to combine the enormous power derived from effective central institutions with the wealth and half-regal patronage monarchy made possible. Perhaps the ideal ministerial figure of the period is the Swede Axel Oxenstiern, Chancellor to Gustav Adolf in 1612 and still in office at the abdication of Christina in 1654. He was born into the court nobility; he built up a great family connection and

[1] Mousnier, *Venalité*, p. 620.

was succeeded by his son; he lived in considerable splendour. In return he devoted a calm precise mind and an unflagging capacity for work entirely to the service of the state. Under him was the collegiate system of administration in which departmental officials could make and uphold their own policies.[1] Above him was a king with whom he developed a confident, harmonious relationship. Unlike many of his European equals, he did not need to fear dismissal or worse. Though he often disagreed with Gustav's ideas—including military aggression in Germany—he adopted the 'civil service' habit of working out alternative lines of action, urging the one he thought best, but when necessary applying another. On the king's death he quickly became a virtual monarch, so confident of the Regency Council, which was dominated by his brother and cousin, that he spent much of his time in Germany.

Most of Oxenstiern's contemporaries in ministerial power lived with one foot in the world of administration and the other in that of court ceremony and intrigue. Richelieu after his success in the 'Day of Dupes' affair[2] eventually made of Louis XIII a fairly reliable ally. He kept his grip on the royal mind only at the cost of incessant letter-writing and interviews and of intense concern with the activities of his enemies at court. Mazarin owed his power and sometimes his life to the ability and willingness of Anne of Austria to uphold him not only against the normal hazards of ministerial life but against the rare threat of popular revolt. For Frenchmen whose political ambitions were more limited, survival could be easier. Pierre Séguier, whom Richelieu made Chancellor in 1635, held his office until 1672. But this was an almost unique achievement. In Spain Olivares found that neither his huge array of dependants nor his zeal as a reforming minister could save him once it seemed to his master expedient to sacrifice him. No continental minister was quite so tragic a victim of the failure of the royal régime he managed as was Strafford;[3] but Count Griffenfeld, the chief architect of Danish absolutism, spent his last twenty-two years in prison. Under Frederick III, who broke the grip of the old nobility and in 1660 was proclaimed as the first hereditary monarch, Griffenfeld presided over a centralised absolutism that had all the institutional apparatus of strong ministerial rule. But by the time of Frederick's successor Christian V a new court aristocracy had arisen, as hostile to reforming efficiency as the old. Griffenfeld was accused of treason by a faction that preferred military glory to good government. It was one of Louis XIV's great successes that he could cause ministers to rise and fall without every

[1] See pp. 347–8. [2] See p. 248. [3] See pp. 398–9.

change being a matter of triumph or disaster. The dynasties of Colbert and Louvois shared out many, but never all, of the highest offices for most of the reign; yet as Colbert's own fall from favour showed, they were men whose services the King could use or discard without upsetting the steady work of government. In part this was connected with his management of the other instrument of royal absolutism, the council.

The Council

In every state the distribution of power depended a good deal on who attended the various meetings of high political and administrative servants. To be a counsellor of the king was a right traditionally claimed by the greatest nobles; but it had long been a common practice for monarchs to draw their chief advisers from the ranks of the working servants of the Crown. It was equally common for such great men to turn themselves into a new aristocracy with all the characteristics of the old. The Austrian Habsburgs, in their various capacities, had an assortment of councils, whose changing functions were deeply involved in the struggle for power between emperor and princes. The members of the Imperial Privy Council[1] were mainly high nobility—often nobles of the first or second generation whose rank was won by service. In Sweden membership of the council (the Råd) was still a right of the great aristocrats. Most of them in 1600 rarely attended and left its work to the five principal officers of state. Gustav and Oxenstiern, far from driving them out, persuaded them to spend more time in Stockholm or with the king. In the successive minorities and absences of the monarch that Sweden suffered throughout the century the council became the centre of a noble oligarchy so firmly entrenched by the time Charles XI was of age that he had to establish his royal authority by getting the Estates to declare that he had the power to act independently of the council. But it was again Spain that provided the most dismal specimen of conciliar government in excess. Philip II's Council of State (the *Consejo de Estado*), though endless faction quarrels occupied its time, was an instrument of royal authority that effectively resisted challenge from the councils of the various kingdoms. Under his two successors, councils multiplied almost as rapidly as offices. The Council of Finances with its many subdivisions, the Council of War, the Council of Aragon still resisting Castilian domination—these and many others became highly institutionalised bodies with strong vested interests in their hierarchical structure.[2] Against them were set up the juntas, small

---

[1] See pp. 314-15.   [2] See pp. 321-2.

secret, informal committees of ministers which were supposed to cut through the elaborate procedures of the conciliar system but which rapidly became weapons in petty struggles for power. New juntas and old councils alike were composed of nobility, and in the main of the higher nobility—'unintelligent, inexperienced, devoted entirely to their own interests', as the French Ambassador Villars put it. To him as to others the conciliar system of Louis XIV seemed the standard by which others should be tested.

If accounts of the French councils at the height of their importance in the 1670s or 1680s tend to be confused and contradictory, this comes partly from one of their merits: they were not so firmly organised that rights and procedures mattered more than functions. The innermost council had three, four, or five members, who belonged to it if the king summoned them and had no redress if he did not. Its meeting, commonly three times a week, was the moment in the royal routine when reports on any part of the work of government could be received, policy made, power redistributed. It did not even have an official name: it was often called the 'Conseil d'en haut' (because it met upstairs) but also the 'Conseil d'État', a name that in older terminology applied to the whole body of royal councillors. The most impressive title, 'Conseiller du Roi en ses Conseils d'État et Privé', did not give the holder membership of anything at all; 'Conseiller d'État' was used mainly for members of the Conseil Privé, which was also known as the Conseil des Parties. Members of the Conseil d'en haut were simply 'ministres'. It is difficult too to define exactly the work of the lower and larger Councils. The Conseil des finances was the body in which the King and the Controlleur-Général des Finances (Colbert's post) imposed order on the chaos of receipts and payments; and the Conseil des Dépêches handled a great many of the problems arising from the papers of the intendants and from petitions. But the Conseil Privé, a large body meeting usually in the absence of the King, could be involved in almost any dispute or plea. Though most of the work of the councils emerged as directions to the intendants and the lesser local administrators, a good many of their decisions were in effect judicial. They inserted themselves into the spheres of the old courts of justice, sometimes to the benefit of the subject, often by applying a separate administrative justice for the protection and support of officers of the state. As the English opposition to the Stuarts had seen, the mixing of judicial with administrative functions was one of the characteristics of absolutism.

Representative assemblies

In nearly every state there was during the century conflict between royal government and old-established representative assemblies. With a few obvious exceptions, the assemblies had by 1700 either disappeared or become passive instruments of the monarchy. This did not mean that virtuous, democratic, liberty-loving institutions had been crushed by reactionary tyranny. The assemblies represented not subjects as individuals but the 'Estates of the Realm', unchanging entities into which men were naturally divided according to their functions and possessions. It was an increasingly unrealistic concept. It tended to prevent assemblies from reflecting the true distribution of power in the community, and to make it difficult for the Crown to use them as means of getting the support it needed. The English parliament, the only central representative body that flourished in a unified monarchy, was the one in which the notion of 'Estates' meant least. Peers and M.P's were a homogeneous body of landowners, with a minority of townsmen and lawyers big enough to put forward their special interests but not to come into serious conflict with the majority. Ministers of the Crown themselves belonged to it and normally held the initiative in its proceedings. In contrast the French Estates-General was of little use to the deeply divided landed class.[1] Neither the princes nor the great office-holders took much part in it; the Crown had ceased to exercise any control over its proceedings; provincial and local interests of narrow ruling groups were more important to it than national issues. Its difficulties were increased by an elaborate voting system in which each chamber was divided into twelve regional '*gouvernements*' which had each to take a separate poll and then vote as a unanimous unit in a second count. Hardly anyone regretted its extinction much. The great majority of assemblies lay somewhere between these two extremes in their activity and in their ability to survive. The growing need of governments for money and the firm tradition that extraordinary levies were a matter for consent and bargaining meant that it was often easier for monarchs to make use of the assemblies than to abolish them. Internal divisions were as important as government hostility in producing their decline.

In practice the Estates that could usually claim a voice in politics were the clergy, the 'nobility'—usually in the broad sense of landowners—and the towns. The 'assembly of Estates' did not necessarily include all of them—for a variety of reasons. In some German states the nobles

[1] See p. 260.

were glad to avoid the obligations involved in attending the diets by acquiring the status of Imperial Free Knights. Clergy could often claim to hold entirely independent assemblies of their own, which might or might not accord to the temporal ruler a voluntary gift of money. One of the many illogicalities of the English system was that bishops continued to sit in the House of Lords while lower clergy were excluded from the Commons. The 'Convocations' of the church, completely detached from parliament, were a substitute for a clerical House. In Brandenburg[1] the clergy as such had ceased to belong to the Estates at the Reformation; in Saxony, where the bishops—almost invariably of noble family—had an assembly of their own, there was a vestigial clerical Estate with representatives of universities and cathedral chapters. There was endless variety in the representation of lesser landholders, however defined. Sometimes, as in the Cortes of Aragon, they met separately from the higher nobility and formed one of four Estates. In Poland they almost monopolised the lower of the two Houses of the Diet,[2] from which towns had been largely excluded. Though townsmen on the whole remained in control of the 'third Estate', there were many signs of the decline in their power. The English House of Commons had by 1600, seen most of its 'borough' seats taken over by the gentry though townsmen were usually the most numerous voters in the elections. The French *Tiers-État* had become mainly a preserve of lawyers and office-holders. In the Netherlands[3] the one outstanding example of a state where government was more in urban than in rural hands, the delegations from towns were normally drawn from an oligarchy that was becoming less representative of the merchant community and seldom considered the artisans. But ordinary townsmen were usually in a better position than the peasants. The theory that tenants and labourers were 'represented' by their masters provided a thin rationalisation of the exclusion of the poor. There were places where peasants still had a voice. Sweden had a peasant Estate, and though only freeholders and tenants of Crown lands were involved, their number was large and elections reasonably free. The snag was that the Crown often omitted to summon it. In Switzerland the rural cantons had assemblies elected on a much wider franchise than was common in the towns; and there was peasant representation of one sort or another in some of the south German states. Their governments did not show much concern.

The structure and powers of assemblies were in most countries a mixture of tradition and improvisation. England was exceptional again

[1] See p. 210.   [2] See p. 213.   [3] See p. 212.

in having by this time an exactly defined membership of the two Houses and a rigid procedure. The Scottish Parliament was more typical.[1] Though the lesser landholders and representatives of royal burghs had been brought back into it to approve the successive religious changes of the sixteenth century, the Crown and the nobility could each use various devices for preventing any initiative from below. The 'Convention of Estates' was a body not easily distinguished from a parliament but containing only those whom the Crown chose to summon. Its decisions could be ratified by a more formal parliament when it was politically safe to hold one. The 'Lords of the Articles' were a small executive committee chosen from the bishops, nobles, lesser landowners, and townsmen by an elaborate system that made opposition to the Crown almost impossible. But Charles I found that if he could adapt the system of assemblies of Estates to his own ends, others could do the same. In 1637 the opponents of Laud's religious innovations provided a rare instance of representative bodies coming together without the initiative or consent of the Crown. Each of the four Estates chose, by one improvised process or another, 'Commissioners' who in turn elected the 'Tables', the small committees that formed the nucleus of a resistance movement.

The Swedish assembly, the Riksdag, had in 1600 no fixed place of meeting, no recognised electoral system, no regular forms of legislating or petitioning. Which of the Estates attended depended on the immediate circumstances. Groups normally outside them, such as army officers, sometimes successfully claimed representation; many of those named as members failed to attend; sessions often ended in disorder and the drifting away of members rather than in formal dissolution. In the constitutional reforms of 1617 and 1626 Gustav Adolf and Oxenstiern brought more definition to the proceedings. One of their objects was to establish the noble Estate as the essential part of the Riksdag. The status of nobility was for the first time made to depend entirely on royal patent; three classes within the Estate were arranged; and the function of the nobles in leading the other Estates in the direction the king wanted them to go was made abundantly clear. The 'Form of Government' of 1634[2] made the alliance between Crown and nobility closer still; but it kept the Riksdag as a regular part of the governing machinery. It survived because the elements that might have resisted the Crown were too weak to be a serious threat. All the initiative in

---

[1] R. S. Rait, *The Parliaments of Scotland* (Glasgow, 1924).
[2] See p. 348.

legislation and discussion came from the monarch: the Estates were merely invited to discuss what was brought before them. Though their enactments were unquestionably valid, the Crown could if it chose legislate without them. During Christina's reign the Estates did make some progress. Taxation was levied only with their consent; policy, though never controlled, was at least debated. In 1650 they put forward demands that were clearly influenced by events in England.[1] But it was only in the minority of Charles XI that the Riksdag contrived to extend its independence by uniting against the nobles of the Council of Regency. When the king came of age he had no great difficulty in using the Riksdag to punish the regency nobles while at the same time curtailing its own political influence. By 1686 the Estates were content to accept the convention that they no longer offered any comment at all on official expositions of the government's decisions, on the rare occasions when the King was graciously pleased to give them.

In many other countries the fate of Assemblies of Estates was determined by conflicts between Crown and nobility. In Denmark[2] Frederick III's triumph over the nobility was made possible by the support of the clerical and urban Estates, who resented the efforts of the nobles to extend both their exemption from taxation and their claims to Crown land. The Estates then accepted with hardly a murmur the destruction of their own power. German princes were able to use their power as members of the Imperial Diet to force the emperor to uphold them against their own Estates. In Brandenburg the diet most often summoned was now a small body. The nobility, who nearly everywhere else assumed that they could all attend, chose representatives, and the urban Estate was drawn only from a few big towns. The Thirty Years War was as damaging to the diet as to all the institutions of government; but the Great Elector, in the early years after his accession in 1640, was on better terms with the Estates than his predecessor had been. It was only when wars and the army became his main concern that there developed the triangular struggle between Elector, nobility, and towns. In 1652 a large 'General Diet', with all the nobles and wide urban representation, was expected to show how popular the Elector's policies were. Instead it proved determined to drive a hard bargain. Some of the demands were for constitutional rights; but the ones most effectively pressed, far from showing a concern for liberty, were for extensions of the servitude of the peasants. For the moment the Estates got most of what they wanted. But no General Diet met again: the Elector's hope of

[1] See pp. 351–2. [2] See pp. 357–8.

gaining the regular support of the Estates for his wars and the taxation they involved was not fulfilled, and for him the inevitable answer was to collect money on his own authority. The nobles, largely exempt from taxation, did not much mind. Not that the urban representatives put up much resistance: most of them came to accept a system that put the heaviest burdens on the ordinary townsmen. By the time of the Great Elector's death the urban Estate in Brandenburg had been virtually eliminated and the nobility could be relied on as supporters of official policy.

The Brandenburg Diet was not Frederick William's only assembly. He had similar difficulties with the Estates of Prussia (which at one stage tried to appeal to the King of Poland as the Elector's overlord); and the Estates in his western possessions of Cleves and Mark were more resolute and successful in preserving their powers. There was nothing unusual in this situation. The unification and centralisation of states did not mean that assemblies necessarily followed the same pattern. In Spain the Cortes of Castile remained distinct from the Cortes of the Crown of Aragon; and within the territories of the Crown of Aragon there were in addition the three separate Cortes of Catalonia, Aragon, and Valencia. In France those provincial Estates that had a well-established traditional authority proved better able to resist the Crown than did the Estates-General.[1] No other French assembly was as healthy as the Estates of Brittany, which kept under their own supervision a system of taxation quite unlike that of the rest of the country. In Normandy, where in the sixteenth century the Estates had consented to an exceptionally heavy share of national taxation in return for some attention to their own grievances, royal promises became increasingly vague and pleas for reduction a formality. Their meetings came to an end in 1657. In Provence the Estates put up some resistance to royal demands until 1671. Resistance to the consolidation of monarchical power in France was in the long run hindered rather than helped by the existence of a quite different institution through which opposition could be expressed. The Paris Parlement was one of the four 'sovereign courts' of law. Princes of the blood, great nobles, and a few clergy kept the right to sit in the *Grand'Chambre*, along with the principal lawyers. Its *premier président*, appointed directly by the king, had a ceremonial status higher than that of the princes themselves. But the hundred or so ordinary members, who had got there by buying or inheriting their

[1] Vol. 29 of the *Études sur l'histoire des Assemblées d'États* (1964) has a collection of articles on the financial rôle of French Estates.

offices, came mainly from the leading Parisian families and, increasingly, from the *noblesse* too. Like the Parlements that sat in some provincial towns, it was closely linked to municipal government and membership was a jealously guarded mark of privilege that separated the *magistrats* of the Parlement from the urban community. Unlike them it showed some sign of developing into a national body. Its judicial area had extended to cover nearly a third of the country. Its right to register royal decrees had grown into a claim to discuss and even to reject them. This process of inserting itself into the legislative process came to an end in 1641, when it registered without serious protest a decree forbidding it to discuss matters of state except by specific royal command. Richelieu preferred to see it as part of the royal administrative machine, and as the scene of the king's occasional solemn *lit de justice* where his pronouncements acquired unchallengeable authority. A body of which Richelieu could more safely make use was the *assemblée des notables*, which had a brief importance in 1625–6. Convoked entirely on royal authority, and ranging from the princes down to members of the sovereign courts, it accepted its function of granting the war subsidies demanded and approving measures to strengthen government power. Once the taming of the nobility was complete there was no further use for it.

In the Netherlands the States General was in most respects less powerful than the Estates of the separate provinces. It was a committee of mandated delegates from the provincial assemblies, theoretically requiring unanimity for its decisions. Nevertheless its members acquired some of the characteristics of an executive body, exercising day-to-day control over military and diplomatic affairs and raising money to run them. Frederick-Henry in the 1630s got its effective work transferred to the *Secreet Besogne*, a committee largely in his power. By the time of the mid-century conflict, the States General was firmly attached to the Orange party. In retaliation the Estates of Holland tried in 1651 to create a new representative institution, the 'Grand Assembly', to which provincial Estates were invited to send large contingents. It developed all the worst characteristics of an international delegate conference, with ponderous prepared speeches taking the place of argument. There was certainly no sign in all this that the existence of central representative institutions had any unifying influence.

Netherlands assemblies depended on no superior authority for their summoning and dismissal. Most other such bodies accepted the uneasy dual status of representative institutions and advisers to the monarch, and were happy to come and go as he chose. The newest of them all, the Russian Zemsky Sobor,[1] had originated as an assembly convoked by the Tsar with no pretence of election or intention of regular meetings. Yet for the first half of the seventeenth century it appeared to be among the most active of representative institutions in Europe. It never acquired a formal structure: its very name of 'Assembly of the Land' was bestowed on it only after it had ceased to function. Its surviving records are slight. What they seem to show is a body influenced to some extent by western ideas of 'Estates' in a society where such divisions were scarcely recognised. It owed its success largely to the collapse of tsarist government in the 'Troubles', when successive claimants to the throne needed spectacular approbation and when any political body that could unify resistance to the invaders was in a strong position. The assembly that elected Michael Romanov to the throne was exercising in reality a power that in the west had become at most an antiquarian formality. During his reign it met frequently, and debated matters of foreign policy and war which few monarchs allowed their Estates to meddle with. The great Zemsky Sobor of 1648–9 not merely ratified the new code of law but extracted some concessions such as a restriction on tax-exempt lands that was demanded by the townsmen. An element of petitioning against grievances of local communities seems to have crept into its proceedings. But it did not come anywhere near to risking a serious dispute with the Tsar: in the 1650s when its occasional complaints became a nuisance its meetings were brief and infrequent.

The great eastern example of a successful representative assembly was the Polish Diet. English and Dutch advocates of such institutions did not find it expedient to cite this as an example of their ideal form of government. But the comparisons were by no means irrelevant. The Seym, like the English Parliament, was a two-chamber assembly in which landowners were completely dominant over the few townsmen and lawyers. Power in it was not monopolised by the magnates: the lower house, including some quite small freeholders, kept on equal terms with the upper. Perhaps 10 per cent of the population were involved in its election. Under Sigismund III there were signs of an organised opposition party, determined to resist the central authority of a monarch devoted to dynastic wars. But the Seym proved to be a grim example of the weakness that came from particularism: the overriding aim of most of its members was to prevent national authority from

[1] See the article by J. H. L. Keep in *Slavonic and East European Review*, vol. 36 (1957).

trespassing on local. The interests Polish landowners had in common seemed entirely negative ones. In 1652 their disputes culminated in the acceptance of the *liberum veto* whereby meetings of the *Seym* could be, and were, broken by a single dissenting voice. During the next forty years the use of the *liberum veto* was extended with disastrous effects on the raising of revenue especially. It was easy for western constitutional theorists, then and later, to scoff. But the problem of combining representative powers with effective political authority was one that no assembly succeeded in solving.

Taxation

Assemblies, it was wisely and reasonably believed, depended above all for their survival on the need of kings for money. Their decline nevertheless came in a period when governments were spending far more, and raising a growing proportion of what they spent by taxation. It was still felt that the Crown, as a large landowner itself, had resources which ought to enable it, in the familiar English phrase, to 'live of its own' except in times of special expense. But such an assumption was no longer compatible with the realities of government finance. The Crown had either to extract regular and, by earlier standards, huge sums from its subjects or to exhaust its capital and accumulate debts. The days when a national debt was an indispensable part of the economic system were still far ahead. France seemed at the beginning of the century to be closest to them. The *rentes*, loans to the Crown backed by the City of Paris, had since their introduction early in the sixteenth century become a form of investment so profitable that it was a normal upward move in the social scale for a trader to turn himself increasingly into a *rentier*. Unhappily the *rentes*, like offices, came to be sold for the benefit of the subject more than of the Crown, and one of Colbert's main financial aims was to redeem them. Generally the ability of a government to borrow depended on the easily shaken confidence of merchants and bankers in its capacity to repay. The debts a minister bequeathed were regarded as a mark of mismanagement, and his successor often appealed successfully for new taxes to pay them off. Official royal bankruptcies were a risky and discreditable but not uncommon device. Another was to get money by minting it, as cheaply as possible. Debasement of the coinage had been a process familiar in the sixteenth century and was still used at times and places as far apart as Philip III's Spain and Peter the Great's Russia. But such methods could not postpone for long the need to extract more wealth from the vulnerable sections of the community.

The development of regular systems of taxation, imposed with tolerable efficiency, was a slow achievement of western governments that was well on the way by 1700. For most of the century public finance was a matter of improvisation by the ruler and struggles by the subject to escape. The heavier the demands, the greater the incentive for those who could to win exemption for themselves at the expense of the less fortunate. It was not only nobilities who held or acquired such privileges: towns and provinces could often find means of mitigation. Indeed it was seldom assumed, outside England, that a uniform system for a whole country was possible. The sufferings of Frenchmen varied enormously according to where they lived. The *taille* was in some areas a tax on land, in others on personal property, in a few non-existent. The regions of the *grandes gabelles* paid anything up to five times as much tax on their salt as those of the *petites gabelles*. In German states there was intricate conflict between town and country and between one small area and another. The unit with which most governments were concerned in administering taxation was not an individual but a district. Its contribution was fixed by tradition, bargaining, or threats, and local authorities were left to apportion it as their circumstances permitted. The collector was less likely than in earlier centuries to be a direct servant of the Crown: tax-farming had become the normal way of ensuring a quick return from every imposition granted or decreed. Though it was often believed that half or more of the amount paid failed to reach the government, the system at least gave to those who managed the collection an incentive to do the job thoroughly. But it was often necessary to collect taxes by the threat of force. The armies that absorbed most of the money also gave to the Crown a means of extracting it that sometimes avoided the necessity for constitutional formalities.

The need for making subjects pay more led governments to invent new devices. We have seen the wide effects of the sale of office and title; but only in France and Spain, of the larger countries, was their contribution to the revenue of great and lasting importance. New taxes were the only general solution. The simplest was the crude poll-tax or tax on households, which could to some extent be graded according to the apparent wealth of the victim. It was tried, with no great success, in England in 1641; in Russia it provided a large source of revenue, and under Peter a fairly advanced administrative machinery was evolved to assess and collect it. But it was an almost universal experience of governments that indirect taxes were more easily brought under the complete control of the Crown than direct ones. Customs duties, almost the only money-raising method that had also, by discouraging or regulating imports, a wider economic purpose, were constantly being extended. In the second half of the century the excise—the taxation of selected commodities, or even of everything that was sold—came rapidly into favour. The Spanish *alcabala*, in theory a general sales tax, and the *millones*, a tax on essential foods and other commodities, were already well established before 1600, though to some extent their impact was changed by allowing towns to compound for them at a fixed sum. France was only one of many countries that taxed salt, which was so necessary that an increase in price had little effect on demand and in many areas so restricted in its sources that the tax was hard to evade. The Dutch were the first to use the excise widely, and probably raised more money per head than any other country. In England it was the most hated of the Civil War innovations. The Great Elector fought his bitterest political struggle to extend the excise to all the towns.[1] But he never succeeded in imposing it universally. In taxation as in everything else the range within which governments could increase their authority over the rich was very limited.

Despite all their difficulties monarchs in 1700 had, by the standards of their great-grandfathers, enormous financial resources and enough military power to make successful rebellion by their subjects highly unlikely. They had, with few exceptions, destroyed the threat of opposition from representative institutions; they had reduced their dependence on aristocracies, on venal office-holders and on clerical magnates. Government had become far more of a profession, in which monarchs needed to become expert. But it was government with little consistent purpose beyond its own survival. The welfare of the subject certainly mattered no more than it had a century earlier. The burden governments imposed on him was decidedly heavier.

[1] See p. 306.

X

Rebellion

A large part of the history of seventeenth-century Europe is made up of violent resistance to authority. Rebellion was everywhere almost as much a part of life as were famine, plague, and war. There were, as there always had been, rebellions among the aristocracy. There were rebellions in which the initiative came from men of substance below the aristocratic level—from the English gentry, or the French lawyers,

BIBLIOGRAPHY. The first serious attempt to examine the similarities and links between the revolutions of the 1640s is R. B. Merriman, *Six Contemporaneous Revolutions* (Oxford, 1938). H. R. Trevor-Roper's essay on the 'General Crisis of the Seventeenth Century' which first appeared in *Past and Present*, no. 16 (1959) is reprinted both in *Crisis in Europe 1560–1660*, ed. Trevor Aston (London, 1965) and with some amendment in H. R. Trevor-Roper, *Religion, the Reformation, and Social Change* (London, 1967). *Past and Present*, no. 18 (1960) contains a discussion of this essay by some leading writers on the subject. R. Mousnier, *Fureurs paysannes: les paysans dans les révoltes du XVIIme siècle*, compares the risings in France, Russia, and China. The detailed studies organised by Mousnier, and also his controversy with B. Porchnev, have made the French popular revolts a familiar topic. Porchnev's book appeared in a French translation—*Les soulèvements populaires en France de 1623 à 1648* (Paris, 1963); Mousnier's criticisms of it are in his article 'Recherches sur les soulèvements populaires' in the *Revue de l'histoire moderne et contemporaine*, vol. 4 (1958). These and other contributions to the subject are discussed by J. H. M. Salmon in *Past and Present*, no. 37 (1967).

The Irish rebellion has not had as much detailed study. It is examined in T. L. Coonan, *The Irish Catholic Confederacy and the Puritan Revolution* (London, 1954) and Aidan Clarke, *The Old English in Ireland 1625–42* (London, 1966). On the Russian risings there are G. Vernadsky, *Bohdan, Hetman of Ukraine* (New Haven, 1941) and A. Tchapyguine, *L'émeute de Stenka Razin* (Paris, 1930). C. Field, *The Great Cossack* (London, 1947) is a fairly colourful narrative of Razin's career.

N. Cohn, *The Pursuit of the Millennium* (London, 1957) is a very successful attempt to compare movements widely separated in time. E. J. Hobsbawm, *Primitive Rebels* (Manchester, 1959) shows some interesting parallels in the nineteenth century.

or the leading townsmen of Prague. And always there were rebellions of the rural and urban poor. It is with these last, the rebels who were normally far outside political life, that this chapter will be mainly concerned. They were important for their own sake, but still more so because of the way in which they changed the course of attacks on government by those whose object was to seize rather than diminish its power. Efforts to define a distinction between rebellion and 'revolution' do not always help. Between the local riot at one extreme and the nation-wide civil war at the other no rigid categories can be marked out. A common characteristic of the big revolutionary movements of the century was that they involved a great variety of popular risings. Strong, centralised, narrowly-based governments imposing more effective burdens and restrictions everywhere evoked resistance. Revolt by the masses seemed to be part of an explosive conflict between those who held power and those who sought or rejected it.

Rebellion and revolution

The 1640s and 1650s were an age of rebellions. Men said so at the time, and tried to interpret the warning of comets, explain the prophecies of the millennium, or calculate the average lifetime of empires. It is easy to point to the English Civil War,[1] the successful revolt in Portugal against the Spanish monarchy, and the unsuccessful ones in Catalonia, Sicily, and Naples,[2] to the peaceful overthrow of the Orange stadtholderate in the Netherlands[3] and to the Fronde in France,[4] and to insist that the occurrence of all these in the space of ten years cannot be just coincidence. The great rebellion of the Ukraine in 1649—and even the revolts in the same years that led to the overthrow of the Ming dynasty in China—have some comparable features; but they can hardly be claimed as part of the same movement. There are in fact two difficulties in showing the revolts as parts of a single event that formed the watershed between the world of the Renaissance and that of the Enlightenment.[5] One is that, despite some obvious links, they did not decisively affect each other in their outbreak or in their course. The other is the fallacy of assuming that if revolutions were independent they ought to be evenly spaced throughout whatever period is discussed, and of ignoring those outside the 'peak' years. If the Revolt of the

---

[1] See pp. 396–404. [2] See pp. 326–34.
[3] See pp. 404–5. [4] See pp. 274–9.
[5] For a broad survey of the changes see H. R. Trevor-Roper, *Religion, the Reformation, and Social Change*, chap 1.

Netherlands, or the Bohemian rising, or the later troubles in Hungary had occurred in the forties, they too would naturally have been hailed as part of the grand revolutionary upheaval. Nevertheless, after 1660 there were few revolts on anything like the scale of the earlier ones. Governments nearly everywhere had overcome the threats, and were now defended by armies bigger and better controlled than any their subjects could possess. The absolutist state seemed to have survived the challenge.

Rebellions had usually started in either the highest or the lowest levels of society. Landed magnates who revolted against the king had always been the greatest internal threat to order and stability. If royal courts were intended to strengthen the loyalty of the great men who benefited directly from the power and wealth of the monarch, they were also places where conspiracies thrived and challenges to the inner-most circles of privilege developed. Palace conspiracy could still easily turn into wider conflict. The discontented noble could call out his dependants, and could usually find plenty of allies against the estab-lished authority. A danger-signal for the French monarchy was when great men began to leave the court for their provincial homes—where some were virtually monarchs in courts of their own. Throughout the reign of Louis XIII and the minority of his successor, the threat remained that noble insurrection would bring France back to the chaos of the sixteenth-century Wars of Religion. Russia before 1613 suffered similar disasters on a scale nowhere else could match. Among the mani-fold origins of the English Revolution, the Bishops' Wars were at least in part a Scottish baronial revolt; and in the leadership of both the Royalist and the Parliamentary sides there were clear vestiges of the old-style wars of the nobility.[1] But the difference between the Earl of Essex under Charles I and his father under Elizabeth was significant: seventeenth-century noble rebels, much more often and prominently than their predecessors, acted in the name of a larger cause than the power and independence of their own kind. Often their rôle was that of the military leaders in movements for which much of the initiative came from lower down the scale.

Religion was naturally one of the most effective stimulants for revolt; and round it everyone from the duke to the beggar could unite in im-passioned resistance. French Huguenots, Russian Old Believers, Irish

[1] On the aristocratic element in the opposition see the articles by B. S. Manning in *Past and Present*, no. 9 (1956) and V. F. Snow in *Journal of Modern History* (1960).

Catholics, English Puritans, and Bohemian Protestants showed the same capacity for joining the claims of the religious minority with a great variety of aspirations and grievances. Regional loyalties could be as deeply felt as religious ones. It was not only places under alien rule that could rise in assertion of local privileges or separatist aims. From Bordeaux to Novgorod almost every city had its memories of struggles for independence in trade, law-making, and administration, and often of disputes with lords of the surrounding territory. They were memories that any new incentive could revive. But above all it was economic burdens that brought normally peace-loving subjects gradually to the side of the advocates of forcible resistance. One simple fact about the major revolutionary movements is beyond doubt: the great common grievance was taxation. The 'illegal' exactions of Charles I, the fiscal devices of Mazarin, the Neapolitan fruit tax—all were as bitterly hated as had been the burdens the Spaniards had imposed on the Netherlands in the sixteenth century. Taxation did not necessarily distinguish the rich as such from the poor: it distinguished those who paid from those who were exempt and those who benefited. Nothing else could so effectively concentrate resentment against the whole social and economic order into one sharply felt cause for anger.

One interpretation of the deeper causes behind both the popular rebellions and the larger revolutions is that, in their different ways they were part of the class conflict.[1] The revolutionaries were the bourgeoisie; the governments they sought to overthrow were upholders of a changed but still recognisable 'feudal' or 'aristocratic' ruling class. It is largely on the English Civil War that the concept of a seventeenth-century 'bourgeois revolution' is based. Many familiar facts appear to uphold it: the comparatively backward north-west was mainly Royalist; the south-east, the clothing-towns, and the men who had the controlling voice in London and in many cities and ports, were Parliamentarian. Puritanism, the religion of the hard-working, the thrifty, and the self-made, was as firmly associated with Parliament as Catholicism was opposed to it. But on the whole the more closely these identifications are examined the less convincing they appear. The geographical alignment can be seen as the result of Parliament's weakness in places remote from London, and relates more to military control than to popular sympathies. Corporations and merchant communities of towns were deeply divided within

<hr/>

[1] Christopher Hill, *The English Revolution, 1640* (London, 1940); E. J. Hobsbawm, 'The Crisis of the Seventeenth Century' in *Crisis in Europe,* ed. Trevor Aston (London, 1965).

themselves.[1] In the group that clearly mattered most in the war and in national politics, the landed gentry, it is very difficult to show that alignment coincides with any economic or social differences. It would be harder still to show the assorted enemies of Mazarin's government who created the Fronde, or the narrow urban oligarchies who supported de Witt and the dominance of Holland, as representatives of a single capitalist class. Nor is it apparent that where the revolutions were successful, or partly successful, they had more than a marginal effect on the development of a capitalist economy.

A view of the 'general crisis' that has to some extent displaced the Marxist one is that the revolutions were an outcome of the anger of the 'country' against the 'court' in its widest sense.[2] It was the expenditure on royal extravagance, on offices and pensions, on unpopular wars that appeared to its victims the cause of the burden of taxation. The emphasis is not on common characteristics of the revolutionaries but on those of their enemy. The wasteful, inefficient absolutist state could be attacked by almost any section of society excluded from a share in the spoils. Against the king and his officers the lord was the ally of the peasant. It is possible, on this view, to show how the character of the revolutions differed according to the particular sins of the régime, from Spain where monarchy was at its worst to the Netherlands where the Orange dynasty threatened only a mild reversion to the evils that had already been overthrown, though the connection is clearly not a simple one. What is more difficult is to reconcile it with the claim that the 1640s and 1650s were a unique moment of change. The evils and the resistance to them had existed all through the century; and though, in the west at least, the widespread victories of the monarchies made further violence less feasible, the conflict of interests changed only very slowly. Perhaps no explanation of the major revolts can be satisfactory if it is excessively rational. The closer men come to collective violence, the further their reasoned aspirations fall into the background. It is much easier to account for a conflict of interests than it is to say why, at one moment rather than another, it turned into insurrection or war.

[1] Valerie Pearl, *London and the Outbreak of the Puritan Revolution* (Oxford, 1961). Other urban studies that touch on this include Roger Howell, *Newcastle-upon-Tyne and the Puritan Revolution* (Oxford, 1967).
[2] H. R. Trevor-Roper, *Religion, the Reformation, and Social Change* (London, 1966), chap. 2.

Popular revolt

A vital factor in turning hostility into revolution was the crowd. The emotions and actions of the masses in Paris, in Lisbon, Barcelona, and Naples, and not least in London were more important at critical moments than anything the political leaders could do. Revolts in the countryside, common though they were, could when they reached exceptional proportions contribute decisively to the atmosphere of violence and danger. One of the main ingredients of rebellion—but one which England escaped almost entirely—was irrational fear. Whether it was bandits or soldiers, papists or witches or werewolves in the next village might not be certain: they could equally well lead some to bar their doors and others to band together in arms. Governments lived in fear of violent destruction: sporadic revolts against oppression were magnified into nation-wide conspiracies. The presence of armed but undisciplined soldiers—common enough in any country during and after a war—could touch off a riot that rumour would depict as a revolution. Brutal and indiscriminate punishment was the accepted way to reduce the likelihood of more disturbances, even if it meant drawing forces away from a foreign war. Left to themselves, rural disorders usually died out quickly. Harvests had to be gathered; and winter made the life of the rebel less tolerable. But there were occasions when the fears of greater upheaval were well-founded.

The French émeutes

French historians have made in recent years an intensive study of the rural and urban revolts of the seventeenth century. It was to France too that the Russian historian Porchnev turned for an investigation of the same question.[1] It has consequently become a matter of controversy going far beyond the events themselves. Small rebellions were not necessarily more significant in France than elsewhere; but they are probably the best-recorded. There were few if any years, in the first half of the century at least, when there was not a popular rising somewhere in the French countryside. In towns, major violence was liable to occur at almost any time. 1623, 1629, 1633, and 1642 were years of insurrection in Lyons, 1634 and 1639 in Rouen. Bordeaux had two of its worst riots in 1635 and 1675. Most of these risings of the *menu peuple* were apparently unconnected with those of the great men. They were widespread in years of crop-failure, plague, urban unem-

[1] See pp. 11–12, 217.

ployment, and foreign war, but the coincidence in time and place between the worse of these disasters and the most forceful of the rebellions is seldom close. It was in the mid-twenties that the risings of the *croquants*, which had happened sporadically ever since the Wars of Religion, became almost a nation-wide phenomenon. Besides the tax-collectors, the army commanders demanding free quarters, and sometimes lawyers and judges were attacked as manifestations of authority. But the alignments were unpredictable. Parlements, and local office-holders hostile to the intendants, sometimes made use of the rebels. The small landholders were often ready to identify themselves with the cause of the peasants and were sometimes alleged to be arming their rebellious tenants. The clergy, too, could be either victims or allies. Relations between urban and rural rebellion were equally erratic. The appearance in the market-town or outside the city walls of a gathering of peasants armed with scythes and pikes, sometimes with muskets or fowling-pieces too, might touch off a sympathetic assembly of townsmen; or the urban militia might prove reliable defenders of property. The great fear of the government was unity of the many groups opposed to Parisian authority. The fear of property-owners great and small was that any rising was liable to turn into an indiscriminate attack on buildings and crops. The house of the *élu*—the local tax-collector—might be attacked first, and the rebel landowner see to it that his hated neighbour's vines were torn up. But once destruction had started, the distinction between those who crushed the peasant with taxes and those who demanded rents, tithes, or labour-dues could cease to matter. The simple element of poor versus rich was always somewhere in the background.

From 1635, when the war with Spain brought enemy armies into France, and almost doubled the burden of taxation, waves of rural disorder appeared each spring, often dying away of their own accord when the harvest had to be gathered. The central government did not panic at the wild rumours of plunder and massacre. A policy of dividing the rebels, making concessions to townsmen to encourage them in resisting the peasantry, and using troops occasionally but decisively had some success. These were not aimless riots: many of them involved meetings where political and practical aims were decided. In 1636 a great revolt in the country round Angoulême was ended when an assembly of delegates from the towns and villages agreed to stop all rebellious activities in return for concessions on taxation and promises to hear petitions of grievances. In 1637 a rising of the *croquants* in Périgord was organised as a regular military operation under its elected leader, a local *gentilhomme* who was accused of betraying the cause after his forces were defeated. Then, in the summer of 1639, there came the fiercest and most concentrated of the rural revolts—that of the *nu-pieds* in Normandy. Years of plague and bad harvests had brought poverty to towns as well as the countryside. A long succession of new taxes for the war had been proclaimed, of which the most hated was the order tightening up the *gabelle*. Towns such as Rouen, exempt from the *taille*, had their trade ruinously taxed. Soldiers were quartered on the province; Spanish prisoners were taken there and left ill-guarded. Rumours of revolt which seem to have filled the province before there existed much real basis for them quickly turned into reality. Sometimes towns were attacked by armies of peasants; sometimes the townsmen rose first. Offices of tax-collectors were burned, and here and there individuals suspected of being obnoxious officials were killed. Avranches became the alleged headquarters of the mythical Jean Va-nus-pieds in whose name printed orders were distributed calling on men to arm themselves 'for the service of the king'. By the winter the grand army of the *nu-pieds* moving through Normandy was said to be 20,000 strong. It had leadership of a sort—townsmen, a few impoverished nobles, perhaps one or two clergy. Local office-holders, angered by the government's creation of new posts, supported the rebels. The situation was serious enough to bring out an army from Paris, which crushed the rebels fairly easily and indulged in indiscriminate killing of any who could be caught.

It was against this background of almost incessant popular unrest, supported by many groups at every level of society, that the chaotic revolutionary upheaval of the Fronde began.[1] It was only because the political conflict so easily touched off risings in Paris and in the country that the state was brought close to anarchy. How much coherent purpose there was behind the mass movements has been bitterly disputed. There was nothing to compare with the emergence as leaders of the Parliamentary cause in England of people previously below the level of central politics and stirred by radical ideas. One man who became momentarily the most successful popular leader was the arch-aristocrat and turncoat Condé, another the unprincipled Cardinal de Retz, a third the aged *magistrat* Broussel. Certainly the breakdown of government was the occasion for a succession of revolts against urban and provincial authority on a larger scale than ever before. Landlord and tax-collector were permanent villains, Mazarin the personification of tyranny. But

[1] See pp. 274–9.

every popular movement became swamped by the cynical and shapeless quarrels among political leaders great and small. The calamity was that the oppressed had as little sense of purpose and as great a devotion to petty faction-fights as the oppressors.

The restoration of order, and Louis XIV's achievements in winning the loyalty of the provincial *noblesse* and strengthening the authority of the state, changed the character of revolts. It did not end them. In Artois and in the Bourbonnais 1662 was another year of revolts against taxation and high prices; from 1664 to 1666 the outbreaks were mainly in the south. They were punished efficiently and quietly. The Dutch War of the 1670s, like that against Spain in the thirties and forties, produced still more new taxes and military burdens. In 1675 the biggest of the provincial rebellions under Louis XIV broke out in Brittany. It was a province where more judicial power remained in the hands of landlords than elsewhere but where many of the minor *noblesse* led a life not much different from that of the peasants. Impositions like the tax on tobacco and the notorious stamp-duty on paper were the occasion for successive revolts throughout the peninsula. Alarm about possible Dutch invasion had led to the recruiting of an armed peasant militia, which could easily become a nucleus for rebel bands. The movement had a good deal of co-ordination, and was even linked, through coastal shipping, with the simultaneous rising in Bordeaux and its countryside. It produced not only protests against taxation and poverty, but demands for the removal of the barriers of privilege and status that separated the peasant from even the poorest *gentilhomme*. At the end of the summer royal troops could be spared to put down the rebels in both Brittany and Bordeaux, and to remain there in winter quarters to punish and plunder as they thought fit. There were no more risings on such a scale. But at the turn of the century there appeared a form of rebellion that seemed to revert to an earlier generation. The *Camisards* of the Cévennes were a Protestant group led by visionary prophets. It became a big enough movement to attract the interest of the Dutch and English. For a time Catholic bands of the same character fought a local guerilla war against them. But governments no longer felt that religious warfare was to be taken too seriously as a threat to their power.

The Irish rebellion

Sixty years before the *Camisards* one remote corner of Europe had produced a rebellion in which religion was uppermost among the familiar ingredients. The Irish rising of 1641 was the outburst of an oppressed nationality against alien rule. It was also the protest of a religion which the majority accepted and the minority forbade. Its leaders were landlords who had lost their estates, local ruling families who had lost their power, priests and friars whose activities were permanently illegal. It was linked with the whole network of Catholic politics in Europe and with court intrigues in England. And it was one of the immediate origins of a prolonged Civil War. Yet nothing in it happened at high pressure. Most of the oppressed did not rebel at all; and those who did were cautious and discriminating in their vengeance. The plotting by Catholic lords and gentry was a tangle in which it was hard to say who were the rebels and who the rulers—so much so that while some of its threads led to the pope others were connected to the king. Almost certainly the authorities in Dublin Castle, or some of them, could have stopped it but preferred not to do so. The Irish rebellion that had an undoubted effect existed not in reality but in the skilled imagination of Pym and the English Parliamentarians.[1]

For many of those outside it, Ireland seemed more closely connected with Europe than with England. In the Irish seminaries of France, Italy, and Spain, and in Irish companies among the armies in Germany and the Netherlands men talked of heroically rescuing their land and its faith. The active conspirators did nothing heroic at all. Rory O'More and Sir Phelim O'Neill were the descendants of traditionally rebellious clans. Another O'Neill, Owen Roe, was a mercenary officer in the Spanish armies who made extravagant promises of men and money from abroad. The talk of a rising was turned into specific plans by the conflict in England. While the Long Parliament was thought likely at any moment to add to its reforming programme the complete destruction of Irish Catholicism, Charles, in his typically indirect and half-informed way, was involved in schemes to re-establish the Irish army that had been disbanded under Parliamentary pressure and to seize control of Dublin Castle and the central administration. Cautiously, and with neither of them fully understanding the purpose and prospects of the other, the two conspiracies were in touch.

In the summer of 1641 there emerged the scheme for a rising in Ulster at the same moment as a *coup d'état* in Dublin to overthrow the ruling group in the Castle. Some at least of the plans were revealed to the English Lords Justices, Parsons and Borlase. How far they deliberately allowed the rising to come to a head is impossible to say. Since

[1] See p. 399.

the Castle was not taken over, and the leaders of the plot fled or were
arrested, the provincial insurgents were left without the armed support
they had expected. Even so, it was at first largely a military demonstration led by the Catholic gentry who recruited a disciplined army.
The true peasant movement grew more slowly as the news and rumours
of the rising spread. Then the plundering and burning and killing began.
The Dublin government, officially supported by both Charles and the
English Parliament, was able to send an army that attacked the peasant
bands and their homes with enough ferocity to remove any restraint
from the rebels. There were a few pitched battles; but the truth behind
the stories of huge massacres seems to have been a short period of widespread unco-ordinated violence different in scale but not in kind from
the local peasant risings familiar everywhere. From the successive enquiries and depositions and the later manipulation of them there is
not much prospect of arriving at any meaningful figures of the dead.
One well-established fact suggests both some degree of control and a
limitation of the possible number of victims: the Ulster Scots, far
more numerous than the English, were largely left alone—on the
instructions of the leaders who thought them possible allies against the
English Parliament. Another is that many of the rebels had originally
the simple and attainable object of driving English settlers away from
lands and houses they regarded as belonging legally to the Irish, rather
than of attacking landlords, or Protestants, as such. Not many of them
can have been aware of the political demands drawn up in the name of
Sir Phelim O'Neill after the rebellion was more or less over, for the
restoration of Catholicism and the return of confiscated lands. A
document whose existence was probably more widely known was the
alleged royal proclamation giving Irish Catholics permission to seize
the property and persons of English—but not Scottish—Protestants. It
would be interesting to know how far this notion of a king devoted to
Catholic interests was held. There were many at Charles's court who
would have been glad to encourage it. In fact, once the northern rebellion had begun, the need to restore order and security seemed to English
royalists at least as important as scoring points against the Parliament.
To everyone with property to lose, popular rebellion was even in this
situation a dangerous weapon to handle.

Russia

The local discontents of the French and the politically manipulated
rising of the native Irish were events on a scale that could be matched

in many western countries. Switzerland had a long series of peasant revolts against the wealth and power of the towns. In most of the Italian states, quite apart from the rebellions against Spanish rule in 1646–7, bandit attacks and sporadic violence by peasants were common. But all these seem trivial manifestations of forces that appeared in their full horror and splendour only in the east. As we have seen,[1] Russia and Poland had in the Cossacks something like permanent rebellion on a huge scale. They had also, in the forest zones especially, the little bandit groups, supported by some villagers, feared by others, that could always form a nucleus of wider repudiation of authority. The Russian government had its department of banditry that tried to limit their activities. For the peasant the prospects of improvement within the village community, and the incentives to compromise for the sake of peace and stability, were far less remote from reality than the hope of improvement through political action. The whole of the 'Time of Troubles'[2] was in part a succession of rural and urban disorders instigated but never fully controlled by the political and military groups. In 1606 they culminated in the mass rebellion that spread northward and eastward from the Ukraine to affect something like half of European Russia. Partly it was an offshoot of the movement exploiting the 'false Dmitri', partly a response to the belief that a new and even more brutal government of the Boyars had taken, or was about to take, power in Moscow. Its leader, Ivan Bolotnikov, 'the Thief', brought to his banner an astonishing assortment of followers. There were serfs and slaves, free peasants, deserters from the armies, Cossacks and townsmen; but also many of the provincial *dvoriane* who were ready to use any weapon against the Boyars and did not take Bolotnikov's propaganda too seriously. His war-cries were the wildest of revolutionary threats: slay the landlords, seize their houses, land, and women; abolish every kind of restriction and taxation. But he claimed also a loyalty to the 'true tsar' who seems to have been vaguely imagined as ruling over a peasant democracy. Behind the despair of the peasant was a half-legendary belief in a lost freedom that would be restored when the usurpers were overthrown. Bolotnikov's host expanded at fantastic speed. It was supported by more organised forces under one of the politically ambitious nobles, Prince Shakhovskoy, who saw it as a possible source of power for himself. But Bolotnikov soon had his own 'court' with more authority, for the moment, than that of the tsar. He was at the gates of Moscow before he suffered his first setback.

[1] See p. 35.   [2] See pp. 363–7.

Once the illusion of victory was broken, a better disciplined royal army began to break up the host and take its revenge. By the end of the year Bolotnikov was defeated and in hiding.

For the next forty years local risings of the peasants continued, even under the 'good Tsar' Michael. Every landlord ran the risk of a village revolt that might end in the burning of his house and destruction of his crops. Then, in the peak period of political revolution in the west, there came the great rising of the Ukraine that turned agrarian revolt into international war. The Zaporozhian Cossacks who owed a nominal allegiance to the Polish Crown had long been in a state of intermittent warfare against it. Repeatedly the Polish nobility and Crown officials had used the opportunity of a defeated rising to curtail Cossack privileges and exemptions and to confiscate land. 'Registered' Cossacks were taken in large numbers into the Polish forces. In 1637 a new hetman of the independent Cossacks, Pavluk, attempted a mass attack on the Poles and those who accepted their rule. It was a big enough affair to encourage peasants, in the Dnieper region especially, to begin a new wave of manorial revolts; but Pavluk's army, after it had captured a few towns, was destroyed by the Polish cavalry. The Polish government organised a vast campaign of retribution, hanging the men of rebel villages, driving out peasant families, handing over lands to whatever Poles were prepared to buy or lease them. The autonomous status of the Zaporozhie was repudiated and even the loyal Cossack regiments were put under Polish officers. It was the hope of Vladislav IV that eventually he would be able to use the Cossacks as an instrument of his own military power. But in 1648 there appeared the leader who turned their resistance into a united war against the state.

Bogdan Khmelnitsky was among the most successful of all upper-class leaders of popular revolt. He was a small landowner, son of a registered Cossack, and an officer in Polish service who had fought for the French in the Netherlands. It seems to have been largely personal grievances that made him put himself at the head of a few thousand Cossacks and attack the new Polish fortifications. His victories produced a sudden surge of support and the most widespread of all the agrarian risings. He got military help from the Tartars of the Crimea and created out of the Cossack host a modern disciplined army. But the explosion of peasant fury was soon beyond his control. The whole of the Ukraine was filled with crudely armed men, burning, killing, destroying, and vaguely aware that all this was an act of liberation. Despair alone had never sustained rebellions for long; and in this one there was also a religious element that provided a streak of hope. The Catholic Church and its Jesuit missions had worked long and persistently to drive Orthodox Christianity out of the Polish Ukraine. The Cossacks had sometimes been militant supporters of the Orthodox priesthood and had set up a new Metropolitan of Kiev under their protection. The rebel cause could now be held up as that of the accepted religion; and for the few there was the prospect of a share-out of the lands of the Catholic Church. In 1649, the year of the final imposition of serfdom in Russia, Khmelnitsky was able to approach the feeble Polish government almost as a victor making peace with the vanquished. Polish troops were to be withdrawn, Jews and Jesuits expelled, Cossack autonomy restored and the numbers of registered Cossacks increased. Grievances of the peasantry were no longer of much interest to him.

For two years Khmelnitsky ruled the Ukraine in regal splendour—with the help of approved Polish officials. But his military power was slowly being eroded as he expounded his schemes for becoming the hereditary monarch of a vast new state. In 1651 he began to negotiate with the tsar who, after long hesitation, agreed to the incorporation of the Cossacks into the Russian state. The status and possessions of Cossack leaders were to be guaranteed; but politically there was room for a good deal of doubt about how much Cossack autonomy would survive. War with Poland was the main preoccupation. Khmelnitsky remained in power in the Ukraine during the years when in England the leader of a different kind of military rebellion was Lord Protector. Each was succeeded by a less effective son who relinquished his post—though Yuri Khmelnitsky, unlike Richard Cromwell, became a priest.

The Ukrainian revolt produced neither strong government nor relief for the peasants, but the 'years of ruin' in which armies of Poles, Russians, and eventually Turks completed the devastation. It was not the only Russian rising during the 'crisis' decades of the west. In 1648 Moscow had one of its most savage outbreaks of mass violence, in which the rebels occupied the Kremlin before the foreign mercenaries of the palace guard drove them out. In the 1650s the tighter imposition of serfdom made banditry more tempting than ever; and rebels now had the support of the Old Believers. A village priest giving to enemies of the tsar and the patriarch assurance of divine approval was an excellent recruiting agent. Then, in 1667, there appeared the rebel leader who more than any of the others played the part of the messianic saviour rather than the politician or soldier. Stenka Razin, real though he was, belonged to the line of Robin Hood and Jean Va-nus-pieds. Within a few months of his appearance at the head of some Don Cossacks, his symbol of the horsetail was known everywhere from the Ukraine to Persia and was spreading northward into Muscovy. The throngs who joined him included serfs and refugee peasants, soldiers from all the armies, priests, the urban poor, landlords impoverished by taxation or war. Razin became a liberator who could work miracles, fly through the air, rise from the dead. Sometimes he was himself acclaimed as the true tsar who had come to recover his throne from the usurpers; sometimes he insisted that his only aim when the traitors had been defeated was to live among the peasants as a brother, serving God, the Virgin, and the Tsar. Sometimes he was proclaiming an almost anarchic Cossack freedom and equality, sometimes a powerful state that would rescue the poor from the landlords and rule through elected assemblies. But always in Razin's message the idea of social revolution was uppermost. It was partly this, partly a sheer rivalry for power, that produced a split between his followers and the established Cossacks. Whatever Razin's aim, his method was destruction—of houses and crops and cattle, of landlords and tax-collectors, of the whole apparatus of oppression. In 1670 he captured Tsaritsyn (Stalingrad, Volgagrad) and led his throng northwards with the cry 'To Moscow against the Landlords'. Peasants rushed to join him; townsmen overthrew their rulers and welcomed—at first—the 'liberators'; monasteries saw him as the saviour of the Old Believers. But it took only a few victories of government forces to make the legend collapse. Razin himself was handed over to the 'enemy' and publicly executed in Red Square with spectacular tortures. The campaign of vengeance that followed was probably as devastating in its destruction of property and order as the rebellion itself. It did not produce any significant reduction in the number of local risings in town and country: their pattern was still the same when Pugachev, the greatest of all the Russian rebels, began his peasant war a century later.

Central Europe

The Empire and the lands of the Habsburgs were only a little further removed than Russia and Poland from a condition in which rebellion was a constant threat to the rule of law. The Bohemian revolt of 1618 that merged so quickly into more widespread war, and was so successfully and brutally suppressed, might have had very different consequences if its popular and nationalist elements had been less entangled in noble politics. Often during the wars there are glimpses of a truly independent resistance to the depredations of the armies. In 1626 the peasants of Upper Austria, where Maximilian of Bavaria had brutally attacked Protestantism and left his soldiers to make the most of the process of enforcing his edicts, found a leader—Stefan Fadinger—who for a few months had a rebel army big enough to defeat the Imperial forces. There were popular risings against the occupying armies in Silesia and Moravia. In 1633 the peasants of Bavaria succeeded in compelling Maximilian to take his troops away from the areas of worst starvation. But the greatest danger to the Emperor's prospects of achieving stable government in the areas under his sovereignty came from Hungary. After the Peace of Westphalia 'Royal' Hungary looked like becoming a new Bohemia, more dangerous because of the heathen intervention which any disturbance there was liable to bring.

As the 'bulwark of Christianity' against the Turk, the Hungarian nobility from time to time asserted a claim to greater protection by the Emperor than his western subjects. One form they would now like it to take was help in imposing on their peasants the serfdom that profitable cultivation of their lands seemed to require. But the ambiguity of Imperial policy towards Hungary was demonstrated after the victory over the Turks at St Gotthard in 1664 when, far from driving the enemy out of the rich territory of the Danube plain for the benefit of Christian landowners, the Emperor Leopold made the Treaty of Vasvár that gave to the Sultan roughly what he had before. To the Hungarian nobility treatment like this left no good reason for loyalty to the Habsburgs. A conspiracy of nobles in the next few years was so mismanaged and so lacking in any national support that both the French and the Turks decided it was not worth backing. In 1671 the 'three counts' who led it were executed; many of their followers who escaped death went as galley-slaves to Italy; an Austrian army of occupation was quartered on the country; ruthless new taxes were imposed; a campaign against Protestantism began. It was all reminiscent of what had happened after the White Mountain fifty years before. Gradually a wider and deeper movement of revolt developed, helped by the great outbreak of plague in 1678 and the poor harvests of the next year. Exiles who had fled from Austrian vengeance formed on the northern frontiers the partisan army of the *kurucok*, organised first by the Transylvanian Calvinist noble Teleki and then by the young grandson of one of the executed counts, Imre Thököli. In him the Hungarians had what Bohemia had so conspicuously lacked—a successful popular leader. Peasants, landlords, and townsmen joined an army that began to take on some characteristics of a Cossack-like community. Ignoring frontiers, it moved into Slovakia, Silesia, and Moravia. Thököli and the Transylvanian princess he married claimed a half royal status, producing their own coinage, receiving the envoys of Louis XIV and the sultan, establishing a military régime that destroyed the authority of imperial officials. Royal Hungary and many of the regions beyond it came largely under his control. But against the *kurucok* there appeared a similar rival organisation, the *labanc* in support of the monarchy. Between the two fighting was inconclusive. In 1681 Leopold made to the Hungarian Estates far-reaching promises of 'liberties'.[1] It amounted to a surrender, as a matter of political expediency, to the 'gentry' rebellion. A year later Thököli reached agreement with the Turks for a joint attack on Imperial forces in Hungary. The 'popular' rebellion was submerged by foreign invasion.

In Bohemia the succession of plague and famine led to peasant movements that for a moment seemed near to being a general revolt against serfdom. Peasants in the north began to act in unison and with some political awareness. They sent deputations to Leopold to complain of the increased burdens. Alarmed landowners hastened to use their influence at the imperial court to get a decree prohibiting such actions and strengthening the authority of landlords still further. In the spring of 1680, risings of serfs reached a scale large enough to call for a military campaign against them. The familiar bands of crudely armed peasants merged into an 'army' big enough for artillery to be used against it. Within a few weeks the gatherings had ended. While order was being restored with the help of indiscriminate hanging and beheading, Leopold issued a new decree ostensibly fixing the maximum obligation of serfs but in fact giving them no worth-while protection against their lords.

A good many other specimens of rebellion could be added to these. No-one could claim that any popular insurrection suceeded in changing for long the distribution of wealth or power. Few of them consistently advocated any such ideas. The mixture of material and emotional incentives that determined the behaviour of the masses had a great deal in common with the motives of politicians. Groups and strata in the countryside and the streets came together and split apart with as little consistency as palace cliques or alliances of nations. The policies of rebel leaders were twisted by their ambitions and jealousies as much as were

[1] See p. 311.

233

those of ministers. But in the protests there appeared, sometimes hazily, sometimes stated with inspiring clarity, the belief that the organized community need not always be run in the interests of the rich and the privileged. It was better to resist in vain than to acquiesce.

XI

War

In the seventeenth century the state came, more and more, to be an organisation for fighting wars; and wars came, more and more, to be fought by states. The methods and materials of warfare influenced every aspect of history, but their study has too often been neglected by everyone but the military experts. There is no lack of material for it.

BIBLIOGRAPHY. A major study of seventeenth-century war and its influence on the state and society is one of the most important unwritten works on the period. G. N. Clark's lectures, *War and Society in the Seventeenth Century* (Cambridge, 1957) are a short indication of some of the themes it could develop. J. U. Nef, *War and Human Progress* (London, 1950) and his article in the *Economic History Review*, 1st ser., vol. XII, p. 15 have some forthright ideas. On the changes in strategy M. Roberts, *The Military Revolution* (Belfast, 1956), is another short monograph that suggests greater possibilities. C. H. Firth, *Cromwell's Army* (London, 1902) is relevant to the general topic; so are some of the studies of Vauban, such as P. E. Lazard, *Vauban 1633–1707* and the essay by H. Guerlac in *Makers of Modern Strategy*, ed. E. J. Earle (Princeton, 1945).

On France D. G. Léonard, *L'Armée et ses Problèmes au XVIIIme siècle* (Paris, 1958) has a valuable opening chapter turning back to the seventeenth century. G. Zeller, *L'Organisation défensive des frontières du nord et de l'est au XVIIme siècle* (Paris, 1928) and L. André, *Michel le Tellier et Louvois* (Paris, 1942) show something of the disputes on military policy.

On naval history R. G. Albion, *Forests and Sea Power* (Cambridge, Mass., 1926), though primarily on the English navy, is relevant to the timber problem and shipbuilding generally. J. Ehrman, *The Navy in the War of William III 1689–97* (Cambridge, 1953) also has a good deal on France and the Netherlands. The chapter on the Swedish navy in M. Roberts, *Gustavus Adolphus*, vol. 2 (London, 1958) clarifies many technical points. R. Memain, *La Marine de Guerre sous Louis XIV* (Paris, 1937) is one of the good studies of France's naval problems. J. S. Bromley, 'The French Privateering War 1702–13' in *Historical Essays presented to David Ogg*, ed. H. E. Bell and R. L. Ollard (London, 1963) shows the importance of the attack on commerce. *The Mariner's Mirror*—a more academic periodical than its title may suggest—is an abundant source of articles on naval history.

Specimens of weapons and fortifications survive in abundance; so do the despatches, orders, and reminiscences of generals, the muster-rolls and accounts of army units, the complaints and petitions of those who suffered. A battle or siege was obviously an event worth describing, and eye-witness accounts are sometimes only too plentiful. Nevertheless there are many dangers to avoid. Those who live through wars tend to magnify their own achievements and sacrifices and to imply that the most dramatic incidents are the typical ones—hence, for instance, the controversies about the extent of devastation in the Thirty Years War. Innovations, such as the flintlock, the paper cartridge, and the rifle, are sometimes thought of as normal when they were still experimental. Technical terms can easily change their meaning or be mistranslated. Like other scholars, the military historian is often deceived by figures that were written down to deceive someone else. The account that follows must be read with these reservations in mind.

Armies

The changes in warfare that have been called the 'military revolution' of the seventeenth century meant above all an increase in its scale and cost. In 1600 war was within the means of individuals. A large land-owner could have an army virtually his own, without claiming to be a sovereign. It was intended to be used on behalf of the monarch but everyone knew that it was sometimes used against him. The French Wars of Religion, and the Revolt of the Netherlands had shown that wealthy subjects could control forces well able to challenge the Crown. In the Thirty Years War, armies more or less independent of political rule ranged from the mighty force of Wallenstein to the little democratic bands of Landsknechter that wandered in the most depressed areas. On the death of Bernard of Saxe-Weimar Richelieu concluded a treaty with his army, not with his state. Kings who recruited large forces kept them for a single summer's campaign rather than for a prolonged war, and were certainly not expected to maintain them in peacetime. Even when an army was firmly loyal to a state, its management was not necessarily under close state control. Commanders like Spinola provided men and supplies largely on their own initiative. The armies most closely controlled by rulers were perhaps those of the petty German princes who went into the trade themselves and hired out their forces as profitably as they could. But by 1700 almost every state that could claim true independence had, more or less permanently, armed forces far too large and too expensively equipped to be matched by any private enterprise. Their recruitment and management formed a major part of the work of governments, their supplies a means of wealth for industrialists and financiers; and in one way or another the sections of society that held political power continued to regard military command as a natural part of their functions. How much of the available resources of the world was wasted on armies active or inactive is beyond calculation.

Soldiers

The first essential in any armed force was obviously men. In 1600 major battles could still be fought between armies of twenty thousand or so. The main combatants in the Thirty Years War acquired more than this: Wallenstein's high-powered recruiting eventually gave him over 100,000 and Gustav Adolf commanded a total of 175,000—though fewer than a tenth of them were Swedes. But this was for very short periods. The decisive change in the west came when Louis XIV, from the Dutch War onwards, kept almost continuously a force of between 200,000 and 300,000, recruited mainly in the north and east of France. No other country could equal it—except perhaps the Turks who sent 200,000 men into Hungary and kept a large eastern army as well. Even the Russian national forces, after all Peter's efforts, were no bigger than those of Louis. No-one supposed that numbers were everything: a complaint that continued everywhere throughout the century was that only the 'meanest sort of people' served in the infantry, and there were many arguments about how to overcome this. In theory most European males were under some sort of obligation to serve in armed forces. In practice universal service was impossible. It could be modified to produce selective forces like the French *ban* and *arrière-ban* or the English militia, but these were seldom used for more than local defence. Free tenants who had been persuaded by tradition or threats to serve under the command of their lords were not much use in a long foreign campaign. In the east the demand for more, and more obedient, soldiers gave the state a direct interest in extending serfdom. In the west a mixture of forcible conscription, pay, and occasionally appeals to patriotic duty produced the national element in the armies. But until mid-century at least, the fully trained soldier was likely to be a mercenary.[1] The professional fighting-man served where his prospects were best—sometimes for a middleman who hired out troops in bulk, sometimes for a commander whose reputation as an employer was good.

[1] V. G. Kiernan, 'Foreign mercenaries and absolute monarchy' in *Past and Present*, no. 11 (1957). See also pp. 288–9.

The supply of soldiers was a great international business. Switzerland was throughout the century the source of the highest-quality product; but Scotland was not far behind. Even in the Spanish Succession War, both the British and the Dutch armies consisted less of their own nationals than of Germans, supplied in return for subsidies by the rulers of various northern states of the Empire. From every country, and every level of society, men went—for long or short periods—to serve in foreign armies. Since commanders with a vested interest in keeping their men avoided dangerous battles if they could, it was not a particularly risky occupation. To the homeless, war was far better than vagabondage. Religious persecution helped the supply of mercenaries a good deal; so did every economic disaster. Wars, in fact, helped to produce their own human material.

Weapons and battles

Next to man the most important creature, in war as in peace, was the horse. Western cavalry in 1600 normally used the 'great horse', ponderous and slow but capable of carrying the heaviest armour. This was now commoner than the much smaller 'northern horse'. During the century Arab horses became increasingly fashionable for racing and hunting.[1] At first, despite the notorious successes of Turkish cavalry, they were denounced as useless for fighting; but in the wars of Louis XIV lighter and swifter cavalry horses were a vital part of the armies. The distinction between the types of horse used for different purposes was by no means rigid: at a pinch the same animal could be used for transport, ploughing, and fighting. Armies invariably stole them—and the scarcity of horses after prolonged war was a major source of harm to agriculture. Since it takes three years to produce a full-grown horse, output could be expanded only very gradually. Cavalry had often to be recruited from men who could bring their own mounts. Traditionally it had always been superior in status to the infantry, though in the early part of the century its military value was not very great. The lance was falling into disuse, and the main weapons of the horseman were two wheel-lock pistols of such short range that massed pikes were a good defence against them. The fashionable cavalry operation was the 'caracole', an intricate manœuvre which was supposed to enable successive squadrons of horsemen to trot close to the enemy, first from the right and then from the left, and having fired each pistol to leave the way clear

[1] Claud Cockburn, 'The Origins of British Bloodstock' in *History Today*, vol. 2 no. 11, (November 1952).

for the next attempt. It seldom did anyone much harm.[1] Only the Poles, who fought with sabres and charged at a gallop, won decisive cavalry victories in the first part of the century.

The 'caracole' originated as an attempt to break the new formation of foot soldiers introduced by the Spaniards—the 'tercio'. This was based on the two standard infantry weapons, pike and musket. Pikes eighteen feet long (though their bearers usually contrived to reduce this burden by sawing a few feet off) were massed together in a square formation to form a very formidable 'hedge' that could gradually move forward. Muskets were unwieldy objects loaded through the muzzle with powder and ball, and fired by applying the spark burning on the end of a length of 'match'. In the 'tercio' this slow process was achieved by musketeers, about equal in number to the pikemen, forming the outside of the square, marching in front of the pikes to fire and retreating to reload. Eight relays of musketeers were needed to keep up a steady fire. Though less mobile and with a slower rate of fire than the unduly discredited longbow, and so inaccurate that there was little benefit in skilled marksmanship, the musket could penetrate armour, which became increasingly useless. The great advantage of the 'tercio' was that inexperienced and unreliable men could be of some use: anyone big enough could wield a pike, and from the middle of the square it was difficult to run away. But its drawback in wasting manpower and slowing down movement had long been argued by military writers. One of the first achievements of the 'military revolution' was the introduction of more adaptable formations, for which Maurice of Nassau[2] was largely responsible.

Maurice was an intellectual among rulers, a student both of classical writers on strategy, particularly Vegetius, and of contemporary theorists like Justus Lipsius, the great admirer of Roman warfare. He developed ideas of linear rather than square formations, of small units capable of quick tactical manœuvre, and above all of the need for highly trained soldiers. His battalion of pikemen, fifty wide and only five deep, with the musketeers on either side, could hold its ground well. Its training made it less expendable; and Maurice's armies, which set the fashion for Protestant Europe especially, tended to avoid major battles if they could. His other main improvements were also defensive—the devising of better fortifications with greater fire-power against the besieger. So long as commanders found it more profitable to establish garrisons to occupy territory than to seek out and destroy enemy armies,

[1] M. Roberts, *Gustavus Adolphus*, vol. 2, p. 180.   [2] See pp. 390–1.

the siege was one of the most important military operations; and to the contest between artillery and fortifications much of the new technology of the day was applied. Maurice's friend Simon Stevin designed elaborate defences that kept pace with the casting of heavier siege guns and the more accurate calculation of range. The other royal commander who had most to contribute to the reforms was Gustav Adolf, the aggressor fighting beyond reach of quick retreat to his homeland, who put new power into attack. His sudden decisive assaults were delivered by the pike in linear formation and musketeers firing a single simultaneous salvo. His cavalry was armed with sabres and trained to charge at speed. Light field artillery, able to move during battle, replaced the heavy guns drawn by huge teams of horses that had tended to sink irrevocably into mud; and artillery regiments were formed instead of the loosely organised companies of gunners. Indeed the essence of both Dutch and Swedish reforms was close integration of all the weapons under a co-ordinated command; and this meant that orders must be given through a hierarchy of well-trained officers whose numbers and status were related to the way the armies fought rather than to the way they were recruited and paid.

Officers

In feudal society military service had been closely related to economic and social status. The high nobility were the principal recruiters and commanders of armies. Below them the main class distinction was between cavalry and foot. The 'knight' could equip himself with a horse and with increasingly heavy and expensive armour. The 'esquire' went on a smaller horse with lighter protection, and sometimes fought on foot. In the new armies such differences were no longer apparent; and though cavalry remained in general socially superior, there were complaints that 'the very scum of the commons'[1] could now fight on horseback. It was only after the Thirty Years War that it became universally assumed that in any military formation commanders and men were different kinds of being, with the main grades of 'officer' immutably fixed. In such armies as Wallenstein's the difference was more between those who enrolled and paid the units of the army, taking a profit for themselves, and the soldiers who depended on them for such reward and sustenance as they legitimately got. The essential commissions were therefore those of colonels of regiments and captains of troops of horse or companies of foot. In France it was these two ranks

[1] M. Roberts, *The Military Revolution*, p. 24.

alone that could be bought or inherited, even when they no longer involved any particular function; the other officers came to depend on actual duties or even merits.

The status of officer remained of course largely a monopoly of the landed classes. To many sons of gentry and aristocracy, service in war was a welcome opportunity for advancement and adventure; and since victories increasingly required commanders with professional skill, many such people were ready to acquire it. The numerous military textbooks and military academies that were now appearing did something to help. In the independent mercenary armies, so long as they survived, gentlemen from almost any country could serve in conditions suitable to their station in life. It was common for the sons of wealthy English and Scottish families to have such experience almost as part of their education. With the growth of national armies, military offices came to resemble civil ones in being handed on by purchase or inheritance. While some officers were professional soldiers with a zeal for their job, others were more concerned to make what they could out of the handling of provisions and equipment or the collection of pay for fictitious companies. Most of the evils associated with other kinds of power in the state—the accumulation of offices by a single individual while their duties were performed by deputies, the abuse of authority for private or political ends, nepotism and corruption—could flourish even more easily in armies. The class, and at the highest level the individuals, that controlled the army also controlled the governments. War was a part of their way of life.

Pay and plunder

The new methods of managing armies led only very slowly to changes in the life of ordinary soldiers and in their impact on the rest of the population. The almost universal complaint was that they were unpaid, if not unfed. At the beginning of the century the soldier could expect to receive on joining his regiment a sum large enough to prevent him from immediately deserting. With luck he might get some more when he was discharged. During his service he was probably entitled to pay comparable to that of a labourer, out of which he was supposed to feed and clothe himself; but since more often than not it was far in arrears, armies in fact lived mainly at the expense of the countryside they occupied. At best this was done by organised billeting, either as avowed freequarter or for sums which the householder had a poor prospect of getting. At worst it was done by plunder. Between the comparatively mild complaints in England against billeting of soldiers and the devastation wrought by armies in the Palatinate or East Prussia, every degree of hardship to civilians occurred. It was common for towns to be sacked and the countryside destroyed as a matter of military policy: a commander's principal object was often to find territory which he could exploit for supplies, and to deprive the enemy of it. If he ran his army independently for profit, he had even more incentive to leave it to feed itself; and a defeated army quickly disintegrated into the 'bands of soldiers' that were the worst terror to the civilian.

As states gradually took over the task of supplying their forces, first during campaigns and eventually in peacetime too, they found themselves creating much the biggest economic organisations of the time. Resources were now extracted from the countryside partly by the administrative work of clerks and commissaries employed in what became the early forms of a war-office and a general staff, partly by private civilian suppliers who ran the business with great profit to themselves. More and more of the cost to the community took the form of money payments by the government, and consequently of taxation. The soldier became, however unwillingly, a lifelong servant of the state, which had an interest in preserving his loyalty and efficiency. One manifestation of this was in his dress. The ordinary soldier in 1600 was not provided with uniform, and was distinguishable from a labourer, if at all, by the knapsack that held his possessions and the leather coat that protected him against the weather and even against sword-thrusts. Colonels sometimes found it paid to supply their regiments with distinctive colours of cloth, buying it in bulk and deducting the price they fixed themselves from the pay they promised. But for an army as a whole the 'token' worn perhaps as a scarf or in the hat was the only identification. Mercenaries naturally found this conveniently easy to change. The red coats of the New Model Army, adopted under the Protectorate for all English forces, were one of the first 'national' uniforms. Gradually it seems to have been realised that identical dress varied by badges of rank contributed to a change in the whole outlook of the soldier. With strict parade-ground drill, marching in step, and enthusiastic ceremonial it helped to create the warrior who would remain a faithful automaton even in face of death, and a spirit of emotional identification with the success of the state that spread beyond the ranks of the army to the whole community.

The French army

By the end of the century the state and its armed forces could often be seen as a single entity devoted to the contest for power; but the military state could still take many different forms. The development of three of them, France, Brandenburg, and Russia, will show how the characteristics varied. Though Richelieu had made some efforts to restrict the independence of commanders, he had not seriously altered the French army's social character. But it was already a standing army in the sense that ten or fifteen thousand men remained in the guards and provincial regiments during peace, many of them officers paid to keep a skeleton of their units in being. The prospect of war in 1666 was the signal for many of the nobility to seek commissions to which they felt entitled, and to recruit companies more or less by force. Nevertheless, the army was already showing the first benefits of the great achievement of turning war into a huge nationalised industry. Michel le Tellier had held since 1643 the office of Secretary of State for War, and during Louis' minority had produced a series of ordinances bringing order into the previously chaotic methods of recruiting, supplying, and disciplining the army. His bourgeois origins and consequent exclusion from military command did not endear him to the high military officers whose position was soon threatened. Some of the traditional offices, like that of colonel-general of the infantry, were abolished; the title of Marshal of France became an empty honour; the military power of provincial governors was gradually eroded. Absentee colonels lost their regiments and their profits. Louis alone was the head of his armed forces, and under him Le Tellier quietly continued his work. Despite the contempt of the old school of commanders the technicians and administrators came to the forefront. The Marquis de Chamlay as *Maréchal Général des Logis* (a post he had to buy) produced the arrangements for supply and communications, the maps, the calculations, the grand strategies that made victories on the eastern frontier predictable rather than merely possible. From 1662 Le Tellier was less conspicuous, though not in fact less active, than his son the Marquis de Louvois, Secretary of State. Louvois was the great advocate at court of the army's claims, and associated the call for glory with the new militarism. It was Louvois too, moving among the armies in the provinces and the war zones, who became the notorious enemy of corruption and incompetence. Every aspect of the army was investigated ruthlessly by his intendants. The *passe-volant* who paraded in place of non-existent soldiers on the pay roll, the absentee colonel, the idle commissary went in fear of his personal attention. But Louvois was as alert to positive innovations as he was to removing inefficiency. Production of the efficient army was a continuous process. In the 1660s Martinet earned the unlikely reward of making his name a part of the English language by his relentless drilling and marching and firing. In the seventies the main innovations in armament began. The ring bayonet, fitted to a flintlock musket—often with a rifled barrel—which seems to have been common first in the Emperor's armies, gradually became standard equipment in France. The sabre, long familiar in the east, at last became a normal weapon for the French cavalry, whose charges were a feature of the great battles in the Spanish Succession War. Grenadiers and dragoons became an essential part of the foot regiments. Artillery which previously had been a haphazard private enterprise largely independent of the army command, was reorganised into regiments. Industrial development made iron and brass cannons far more reliable than before. Control of the engineers, the men who applied the new techniques of fortification, became involved in the quarrel between the Louvois and Colbert factions, until in 1667 Louvois' expert Vauban was appointed commissary-general in charge of the whole task. The outcome of the wearisome but vital sieges on the eastern frontier depended largely on the technical struggle between the builder of the defences and the master-gunners and mining engineers who attacked them. In practice the siege and eventual capture seem often to have followed an easily predictable pattern and even timetable—to the benefit of everyone involved.

Almost every improvement depended for its application on adequate new supplies. One lesson of the 1660s had been the need for reliable methods of sending arms and provisions to the frontiers in far greater quantities; and again it was Le Tellier and Louvois who established an adaptable system of reserve stores and planned mobility. Behind it were industries and factories, some owned by the state directly and others by privileged entrepreneurs, into which huge funds were poured. The need for competent officers was met by offering a military education to people whose origins would not previously have made them acceptable as commanders. The cadet colleges set up in the 1680s were not altogether welcome to those of the *noblesse* who had spent large sums on buying commissions. As with civilian office, it became possible to attain high rank in the army through hard work and the favour of superiors, and—theoretically after three generations—to attain thereby the status of nobility.

Lists of changes can easily give a false impression of their extent; and it has to be remembered that even in the Spanish Succession War, the French army though vastly bigger and better than in 1660, had not altogether escaped from the basic defects of officers chosen by purchase or birth and soldiers hired abroad or recruited by fair means or foul from the dregs of the people. It was nothing unusual if half the army deserted at the end of a campaign. The main army units still 'belonged' to their aristocratic commanders, for whom war, like hunting, might be more a part of the good life than a full-time profession. At regimental level the state could not produce the great social change that would give it full control over its forces. At the top it was often felt to control them too much. The sole authority even for day-to-day decisions was Louis himself, and he seldom had enough information to take them well. An obedient general found more favour than a victorious one. This was partly Louis' fault; but it was also a characteristic of national war. Fighting was no longer an affair of the individual but the main object of a vast state machine. In it the brilliant independent commander could be a dangerous misfit.

The Brandenburg army

The rise of the military state in the seventeenth century is usually associated above all with Brandenburg. The danger in stressing this obvious example is that too much can be read back from later Prussian militarism: other German states, Bavaria especially, were at this stage developing their forces in comparable ways. But the Great Elector was certainly outstanding in creating almost from nothing an army that was the avowed focus of all state activity.[1] In 1640 he had four or five thousand men, many of them deserters from other German states, or from companies that had turned almost into independent nomadic tribes. By the time of Westphalia the most irresponsible colonels and their regiments had been eliminated, and a useable force of perhaps eight thousand was being paid by the various Estates, whose interest was solely in defending their own territory. After the peace, when they refused to go on paying, the army almost disappeared. The compromise between the Elector and the Estates in 1653 made possible a permanent nucleus of five thousand mercenaries and volunteers. With the Northern War of 1655 there began the process of ruthless conscription that enabled Frederick William in the next thirty years to expand the army to nearly 100,000 in war and 30,000 in peace. To the Junker families military office was an

[1] See p. 305.

economic and social necessity; but they now performed it as servants of the state, not as entrepreneurs. The Great Elector's commander, Otto von Sparr, and the administrative head of the army, Claus Ernst von Platen, achieved a centralised control much more complete than that of the French. Pay, recruiting and commissioning were gradually taken out of the hands of the colonels, and all officers became part of a unified hierarchy. Even the rank-and-file soldier, however harshly disciplined, was a comparatively privileged person, maintained at the cost of the agrarian serf. To turn military service into a way of life rather than a temporary adventure or disaster there arose the scheme for making disbanded officers and soldiers remain in the care and at the call of the state, in civilian government services or on estates taken out of the electoral domain. How far in fact the Junkers underwent a change of outlook, giving up political privilege to become loyal allies of the Elector and his military state is a matter of doubt. Certainly militarism and centralisation developed together; the 'General War Commissariat' was the name not just of an army department but of the principal governing institution of the state.

The Russian army

In Russia the provision of fighting men formed an even larger part of the work of government than it did in the west. Service in the army was one aspect of the service to the state on which the whole structure of society depended. Descriptions of the recruitment and organisation of the tsar's forces are not usually very lucid or consistent, partly because they changed so much from time to time and from place to place, partly because the government itself rarely had more than a rough idea of what units it could command. Total figures can vary enormously according to which of the huge more or less independent forces are included. The most we can attempt here is to arrive at a general impression of the kind of developments that took place during the century.

Ivan the Terrible's first concern had been to bring under his control the armies of the great Boyars and to establish the *streltsi* ('archers') as a loyal garrison force in Moscow. With a regular wage and living-quarters and a well-defined regimental organisation, these garrison soldiers—now mainly musketeers—were intended to form the most reliable part of a full-time standing army. But most of the campaigning troops were brought together when they were needed, and then abandoned. Under Michael Romanov this part-time force was recruited mainly by selective conscription, with villages each providing a specified number of soldiers according to how many houses they had. Training hardly existed, and central organisation was extremely hazy. The great change in the middle decades of the century was the rise of a permanent army on western lines. Professional soldiers from Scotland, Poland, Sweden, and above all Germany became the officers and technicians of new regiments; foreign mercenaries came into the rank and file of what were now called *soldati* (infantry), *reitari* (cavalry), and *draguni*; many were settled in militarised districts where land was allotted to them. With the *streltsi* and some of the 'registered' Cossacks they formed a reasonably well-equipped force. But the fate of the army always depended on internal politics. During the struggles for power in Peter the Great's childhood the old type of force seems to have revived as an instrument of the nobility. By the time he began to rule there was not much left of the 'foreign' army. For his first campaigns troops were brought together haphazardly from the villages. Apart from these there were only two professional regiments and two regiments of *poteshnye* that had developed out of the live toy-soldiers of his boyhood war-games.[1] The defeat at Narva seemed to uphold the familiar complaint that Russian forces were an ignorant rabble.

At first Peter's reforms were concerned only with maintaining a large force in spite of the enormous losses from disease and desertion, and battle. The number of men demanded from the villages was increased and the principle of the 'immortal' soldier firmly established: for every man who disappeared or died a replacement had to be supplied. By the time of the victory at Poltava (1709) the regular forces probably numbered something like 100,000. More important, they were now being trained in centres where 'western' discipline and tactics were taught, and equipped from a military budget that accounted for four-fifths of the tsar's entire revenue. At this point army reform became inseparable from the attempt to reconstruct the Russian nobility as a whole. The series of decrees that began with the measures for registering the *dvoriane* in 1711 and culminated in the 'table of ranks' in 1722 turned the theory that noble status and landholding depended on service into an inescapable reality. Two-thirds at least of the young men in the families of *dvoriane* were to be conscripted for military service, all but the highest ranking families beginning as ordinary soldiers. The rest went to civil offices. Promotion was to be only by merit and commoners who achieved a commission as lieutenant were supposed to

[1] See p. 382.

acquire hereditary nobility. By the end of the reign the permanent army of something like 200,000 gave Russia, for what it was worth, the status of a great power in western eyes.

War at sea

Fighting at sea played in 1600 an entirely different part in the affairs of European states from fighting on land. Obviously the great majority of rulers, if the German Principalities are included, could not be concerned with it at all. Many states that had a coastline nevertheless had nothing that could be called a navy. France was for a long time one of them. Spain, having very quickly made good the losses of 1588, had large numbers of warships both in the Atlantic and in the Mediterranean. Under Philip III more and more of them were left in harbour, eaten away by the worm and dry-rot that were the curse of all the shipping of the day, until Olivares revived the policy of a strong navy. Then, in the Battle of the Downs in 1639 and off the Brazilian coast a year later, the Dutch destroyed almost the whole battle-fleets of Spain and Portugal. Thereafter England and the Netherlands were the only powers with a worldwide naval strength. It is well known that Richelieu founded the French navy. Colbert gets as much credit for exactly the same initiative thirty years later. A good deal of Richelieu's effort it is true produced Mediterranean galleys rather than the Atlantic fleet Colbert demanded; but again the main reason is that two decades of neglect were enough to reduce fighting ships to a state of useless decay.

To look at ships built for war and owned by governments gives little idea of the real resources on which warfare at sea relied. While armies still had in their organisation traces of private enterprise, navies depended overwhelmingly on the ships of merchants and even fishermen. Throughout the first half of the century the armed merchantman, hired or seized by the state, was the commonest fighting ship, and the regular troop-carrier. Any ship on an ocean voyage would necessarily be armed, and its chances of being involved in fighting before it returned were usually high. Even in peace, the rule of law and the sanctity of private property could not be relied on at sea. Attacks on the Spanish treasure fleet were only the most spectacular part of a process that made the distinction between war, piracy, and legitimate commerce extremely hazy. The 'letters of marque' from their governments gave the captains of ships almost a free hand to get involved in hostilities. Sometimes local clashes were encouraged by governments as acts of provocation. For maritime nations formally at war, the destruction of each other's commerce was as always a major activity, which could be indulged in without the risk of total disaster involved in big naval battles.

Privateers

Fighting ships often belonged more to a port than to a state. The French King's fleet did not assert its power as readily as did the privateers of Marseilles, Toulon, St Malo, and above all Dunkirk. For every small island privateering was a major industry. Encounters with the ships of Jersey, Malta, Corsica, and the West Indies were part of the normal hazards of trading. A large share of the slave-trade was run by heavily armed privateers. Most notorious of all, the 'Barbary Corsairs' from Algiers, Tunis, and Tripoli, attacked the shipping of every European maritime state, claiming to be subjects of the sultan or not as the occasion required.[1] Major wars enormously expanded the privateering business without changing its character. The Spanish Succession War saw the century's greatest activities of this kind. The defeat of the French fleet at La Hogue in 1692 put an end to its hope of achieving complete domination of the seas. But it was reasonable to argue that France as the most self-sufficient nation and one with good land communications would suffer less in a destructive commercial war than her enemies England and Holland. The navy became therefore hardly distinguishable in its functions from the ships of the great syndicates that made privateering a profit-making business on a sound financial basis. The ships, cargoes, and ransoms that were seized in this way became the subject of elaborate legal and administrative procedures in the Prize Courts, which ensured that the state got its share of the reward. It was this state-sponsored piracy that made the heroic reputation of Jean Bart, the fisherman from whose home port of Dunkirk a hundred ships were reported to be involved in the warfare. While Bart's Drake-like fame took him eventually into the ranks of the *noblesse*, a good many sons of ancient nobility who had expected to command ships in battle were glad to turn to privateering instead.

Ships

By the time of the Anglo-Dutch wars, most of the fighting ships of the western and Baltic nations were built for the purpose and owned by the state. On their design and effectiveness the character of naval war largely depended. One basic development was now almost complete: outside the Mediterranean and the Baltic, sail had replaced oars as the chief means of propulsion. The Turks, the Swedes, and the Russians

[1] See the article by G. N. Clark in *Cambridge Historical Journal*, vol. 8 (1944).

continued to build the ships that condemned galley-slaves to what must have been one of the worst lives on earth. Richelieu's Mediterranean fleet used them too. But in all but the narrowest and most sheltered waters, it proved better to rely on sail alone. Apart from other advantages canvas did not catch the plague, or run away. The purpose of the 'great ship' was to carry artillery which was fired broadside, sometimes at enemy ships, sometimes at ports. The heavy cannon had to be mounted near the waterline, or their recoil could be disastrous—and this seems in any case to have been the factor that limited the size of naval guns. The main defence was to hold the ship together with massive pillars and stays. It took in fact an enormous amount of shot to sink a large ship: usually the worst that gunfire could do was to break the masts—and it was so inaccurate that this was a matter of luck. In favourable conditions a few old hulks used as fireships could be far more damaging. But once a ship had been put out of action it could do little but await destruction or capture. A lost battle at sea was likely to be more expensive than one on land.

An outstandingly large warship was naturally a great thing to have for prestige. The *Couronne* in Louis XIII's fleet and the *Sovereign of the Seas* in Charles I's were both well over 1,000 tons—though statements like this would be more significant if the method of reckoning the naval 'ton' had not varied.[1] The largest normal ships of the line were said to be 800 or 900 tons, carrying perhaps a hundred guns of which twenty might be the largest cannon. The smallest—the English 'fourth-rate' ships—were not less than half that size. By the end of the century it was sometimes argued that the light swift frigate,[2] low in the water, was a better weapon than the great ship—whose size, an eminent shipwright assured Pepys and Evelyn, was only for the vanity and comfort of Gentleman Commanders.[3] It was always hoped that much larger vessels could be built; but there was no method of joining the heaviest timbers end to end with adequate strength. Size was limited by the extent of the beam that could be constructed on the traditional principles and by the belief that the ship intended to fire broadsides could not be much longer than three times its width. The fate of the *Vasa*—another royal showpiece—was the result of attempts by the Swedes to build big ships four or five times as long as their beam. In 1628 this

---

[1] *Cambridge Economic History of Europe*, vol. 4, pp. 218–19.
[2] The use of the term 'frigate' varied a good deal, but this meaning seems to have been accepted by 1700.
[3] *The Diary of John Evelyn* (ed. E. S. de Beer), vol. 5, p. 10.

pride of Gustav Adolf's fleet sailed into Stockholm harbour for her first trial, rolled over, and went to the bottom. The natural curvature of timbers was another important factor: Protestant winds were believed to have favoured the English not only by dispersing the Armada but by producing the 'gnarled oaks' ready to be cut into just the shapes the shipyards needed. The techniques and theories which Peter the Great picked up from Dutch and English shipbuilders, and which were expounded in works like Renaud's *Architecture Navale* did not differ much from those used a century earlier. But they had become a matter of bitter argument between the practising experts and the scientists. The Royal Society had many discussions on shipbuilding; and in Paris a conference of mathematicians and naval designers in 1681 tried to settle some of the disputes.

Every naval power had, in one way or another, its worries about the supply of materials for building and repairing ships. In England there had already been alarm about timber shortage under Elizabeth. Royal woodland had been sold and exhausted rapidly under the early Stuarts, and the Commonwealth period became notorious for its squandering of timber resources. But only the Baltic countries could now build fleets entirely with their own materials. England, France, and Holland all used firs from Riga for mainmasts. The danger of being cut off from naval supplies was an important factor in diplomacy. By the end of the century American firs were proving a bigger and better substitute for Scandinavian ones. Whatever the sources and the means of obtaining them, navies were by the accepted standards of state expenditure extremely costly. It was a great blow to the States-General to find that in mid-century the fleets it could put to sea were smaller and less well-equipped than those of England. The Dutch had many advantages. Amsterdam supplied not only merchant ships but naval ones too to almost every European country. Dutch contractors controlled much of the supply of hemp and tar from the Baltic. Nowhere else was so high a proportion of the population able to serve as crews of warships. But the division of responsibility among the separate admiralties, which in turn relied on the contributions of individual towns, meant that the money and labour actually diverted to naval building was not enough. It was normal in most countries to make the navy a charge partly on the profits of the trade it protected; English Ship Money, the Danish sound dues, and the tolls imposed on merchants by Gustav Adolf were all examples of this. But in the Netherlands decentralisation proved a serious obstacle to financing as well as organising a national fleet.

'Everywhere', Tromp complained in 1653, 'fine new ships remain ashore only partly finished.[1] By the time of the Spanish Succession War the Dutch navy was only a minor reinforcement for the English.

Sea power

How important did naval warfare in European waters prove to be? The famous battles do not seem in themselves to have produced any vital changes. Perhaps the most significant episode was the absence of a battle: neither the French nor the English fleet was ready to prevent William of Orange from landing in England. The consequences of this were greater than anything that happened as a result of the Anglo-Dutch wars: England could, with luck, inflict defeats on the Dutch fleet; the Dutch, when the luck went their way, could still horrify the English by sailing into the Medway and the Thames. But each of the wars ended without decisive loss to either side. Blockade and bombardment were less exciting than naval battles, but often more effective in achieving a limited purpose. De Witt within two years—1657–8— ended French interference with Dutch trade by a mere threat to blockade the coast, punished the Portuguese for their intervention in Brazil by a blockade of Lisbon, and preserved Dutch interest in the freedom of Baltic trade by rescuing both Danzig and Copenhagen from the Swedes. Naval power was in fact generally more important in the Baltic than in the open seas: Sweden's successes in war depended entirely on the ability to convey troops and supplies safely and to cripple her enemies by blockade. Mediterranean naval war was an activity highly important to western states when their merchant shipping was threatened; but for long periods the little republic of Venice was left to fight largely on its own what the powers occasionally regarded as the Turkish menace to Christendom. When a fleet of eighty Turkish galleys attacked Crete in 1645, the Venetians showed that the government of even a small state could, by putting all its power and resources into the effort, maintain quite a formidable fleet. For nearly twenty-five years they kept up a war that prevented any full Turkish control of the eastern Mediterranean, in the course of which the English, Dutch, and French who benefited from this took over what was left of Venetian trade. When peace was made in 1669 Venice had ceased to be an anti-Habsburg commercial state and turned into a minor ally of the Emperor and the Church. It was one of the many unheeded demonstrations of the real cost of war.

[1] Quoted in Geyl, *The Netherlands in the Seventeenth Century* (London, 1963), vol. 2, p. 33.

XII

France 1598-1660

This was the century of France. By the end of it, French language, culture, manners and dress had permeated the richer levels of the whole European community. French wars and diplomacy dominated western political affairs, and influenced eastern ones too. The French treasury

BIBLIOGRAPHY. For the central political narrative it would be difficult to improve on the old large-scale works, notably the *Histoire de France*, ed. E. Lavisse, vol. 6, part 2, *1598–1643*, by J. H. Mariéjol and vol. 7, part 1, *1643–1685*, by E. Lavisse (Paris, 1905). Another is A. Chéruel, *Histoire de France pendant la minorité de Louis XIV*, 4 vols. (Paris, 1879–80) and *Histoire de France sous la ministère de Mazarin*, 3 vols. (Paris, 1882). A modern history of the whole period is V. L. Tapié, *La France de Louis XIII et de Richelieu* (Paris, 1962), one of the French books that has neither an index nor an adequate list of contents. G. Pagès, *La naissance du grand siècle* (Paris, 1948) is a short commentary. In the *Nouvelle Clio* series R. Mandrou, *La France aux XVII*^e *et XVIII*^e *siècles* (Paris, 1967) is an excellent discussion of the most recent work and outlook. In English J. M. Wallace-Hadrill and J. McManners, *France: Government and Society* (London, 1967) contains a lucid short survey of the period 1559–1683 by Menna Prestwich. A. D. Lublinskaya, *French Absolutism: the Crucial Phase, 1620–1629* (trans. B. Pearce, Cambridge, 1968) is a first-rate book by a Russian historian, critical of 'general crisis' theories. G. R. R. Treasure, *Seventeenth-Century France* (London, 1966) combines familiar topics with more recent approaches to political and economic questions. J. Lough, *An Introduction to Seventeenth-Century France* (London, 1954) is a deservedly popular survey, derived—with abundant quotation—from literary sources.

On the early part of the century a modern study is D. Buisseret, *Sully and the growth of Centralised Government in France* (London, 1968). The massive work on Richelieu by J. Hanotaux, *Histoire du Cardinal de Richelieu* (Paris, 1893–1947!) was eventually completed by its author in collaboration with the Duc de la Force. H. Hauser, *La pensée et l'action économiques du Cardinal de Richelieu* (Paris 1944) is the main authority on this aspect. Accounts with a political emphasis include C. J. Burckhardt, *Richelieu and his age: his rise to power* (English trans., London, 1940), L. Battifol, *Richelieu et le Roi Louis XIII* (Paris, 1934) and J. H. Shennan, *Government and Society in France* (London, 1969). There is an seemed to have inexhaustible supplies of money with which the King and his ministers could buy the dependence of other states and fight wars largely of their own choosing. They spent it too on the splendour of the court and the patronage, direct or indirect, of literature and art. The glory may not have been apparent to the peasant starving in a year of famine, or the beggar in the streets of Paris, or the soldier plundering the ruins of a frontier town. The legend that grew in the great days of Versailles makes it easy to forget both how little there was to show for the victories and how unstable the French state had been before the effective rule of Louis XIV began. The political history of France in the seventeenth century is sharply divided by the chaotic years of the Fronde. Before it royal and ministerial governments struggled continually and with no decisive success to prevent the breakdown of the state. Far from being an example of steady progress towards the absolutist ideal, the France of Richelieu and Mazarin showed how narrow the division was between order and anarchy. It is this long period of uncertainty that we shall examine first.

Henry IV

It was a triumph for Henry IV that he was not murdered until 1610, and that the assassin acted alone. Molten lead, boiling oil, and the four horses that tore Ravaillac asunder could not extract from him any evidence of political motive or employers. The stories of imaginative propagandists about great plots to overthrow the monarchy and start a new civil war did not last long. But Louis XIII was nine years old: the great question was whether stable government could survive without a king. The twelve years since the Huguenots achieved security by the Edict of Nantes and the Peace of Vervins ended the war with Spain were

enjoyable non-academic discussion of Father Joseph: Aldous Huxley, *Grey Eminence* (London, 1941). Among other monographs are O. A. Ranum, *Richelieu and the Councillors of Louis XIII* (Oxford, 1963); L-A. Boiteux, *Richelieu, grand-maître de la navigation et du commerce* (Paris, 1955); and P. de Vaissiere, *L'affaire du Maréchal de Marillac* (Paris, 1924).

Important articles include: G. Pagès, 'Autour du "grand orage"': Richelieu et Marillac' in *Revue Historique* (1937); E. Porchnev, 'The Legend of the Seventeenth Century in French History' in *Past and Present*, no. 8 (1955); R. Mousnier, 'Le conseil du roi' in *Études d'histoire moderne et contemporaine*, vol. 1 (1947).

On the Fronde P. Kossmann, *La Fronde* (Leyden, 1954) is the standard authority; but see also the article by P. Goubert, 'Kossmann et la Fronde' in *Annales*, vol. 13. P. R. Doolin, *The Fronde* (Cambridge, Mass., 1955) analyses the theories of the various factions.

certainly, by comparison with the era of St Bartholomew, a period of stable central government, economic improvement, and assimilation of dissident groups into the state. No-one could assume that this meant the end of internal conflicts or the final establishment of a *politique* monarchy. Sully talked of curing the ills of his '*chère patrie*'; but Elizabethan sentiments of national loyalty were not ingrained in many Frenchmen. Their country remained divided. The Edict of Nantes was not so much an act of enlightened toleration as a peace settlement—or perhaps a truce—that took full account of the realities of power. Huguenots were not treated as second-class citizens, or deprived of access to state offices, or left wholly at the mercy of Catholic justice and administration. The one thing they could not do was extend their area of control. Against the ban on public Protestant worship in Paris and in regions where it had not been established already, they could set the recognition of their assemblies and the *chambres mi-parties* for law-suits in which they were involved. A hundred fortified towns, garrisoned for the Huguenots at the state's expense, were intended as a temporary guarantee, but they hardly fitted the idea of a unified, liberally governed state. It was a religious settlement in some ways not unlike that of the Holy Roman Empire. Though there were no Huguenot princes ruling independent territories, and no towns as self-governing as the Imperial Free Cities, Huguenot rights did depend a good deal on the power of the Protestant nobility in the countryside and on that of the ruling groups in the towns. Gradually it was the urban form of Huguenotism that proved the stronger.

The religious division was not the only one in which France had its resemblances to the Empire. The French provinces in their relation to the central government stood somewhere between the status of a German principality and that of an English county. There was an important difference between those—Languedoc, Brittany, Provence, Dauphiné, and Burgundy—which had their own provincial Estates[1] that voted and administered taxation and those subdivided into '*Élections*' where royal officials organised the collection of taxes. (To complicate matters, Normandy had both—but its Estates for most of Henry's reign successfully reduced the amount they were asked to vote.) One of Henry's greatest but least advertised achievements was that bit by bit, partly through political persuasion and partly through ignoring the protests, he overrode provincial powers and whittled down the liberties of the towns. It was by fairly high-handed as well as efficient methods

[1] See p. 211.

that the government managed to become financially strong. Inevitably there was resistance. Popular local revolts against tax-collectors were easily suppressed. A measure of the government's success was that the most serious aristocratic resistance of the reign, when in 1602 Biron, Governor of Burgundy, and the Huguenot Duc de Bouillon were involved in a conspiracy sponsored by Charles Emmanuel of Savoy, failed to get any general support. Biron was executed after a scrupulously legal trial before the Paris Parlement.

The penetration of the central administration into the whole life of the country was accomplished in a great variety of ways, ranging from the King's carefully planned journeys through the provinces to the work of royal supporters inserted into town governments, in regulating industry through the guilds. It did not add up to any master plan for creating absolute monarchy. But Henry had a forceful group of ministers—the Chancellor Pomponne de Bellièvre and his successor Silléry, Villeroy, the former Catholic Leaguer whose allegiance had been bought at a high price, and the *surintendant des finances* Maximilien de Béthune, Marquis de Rosny, who acquired his final title of Duc de Sully in 1606. Sully was in general the enemy of conciliar government, and tends to get—as he would have wished—credit for the work of his rivals. Their methods for strengthening the national economy were those that became monotonously familiar in seventeenth-century centralised states. Money was spent on better roads, land-drainage, agricultural improvement—though the court cost far more than all these. Sully calculated realistically how the yield of taxation could be increased without dangerous loss of support. Sources of revenue alienated to the great men were bought back; profits of tax-farming were cut, and the most blatant swindles penalised. It was Henry's comparatively enlightened fiscal system that regularised the sale of offices; but this was not yet an essential part of the Crown's income: it was more important in breaking the dependence of office-holders on the nobility and building up a vested interest in the monarchy.[1] Only in Henry's last year were offices sold indiscriminately, and then for the reason that was both the object and the destroyer of so many schemes for financial stability: war. Henry had long been working to build up a block of French allies among the German states. When the ruler of the small but strategically important Rhineland duchies of Jülich and Cleves died without heirs in 1609, and the Emperor, asserting his right to settle the succession, 'sequestered' the duchies, France seemed ready to demonstrate its military power. Assassination saved

[1] See p. 202–3.

Henry from the dismal anti-Habsburg enterprise which might well have diminished considerably the legend of the enlightened and benevolent king.

Marie de Medici

For those in Parisian politics the immediate need in 1610 was to attach themselves to the regency. There was no opposing faction to offer better prospects for the ambitious—yet. Henry had left no firm direction for the trusteeship of his kingdom on his death. Fortunately, since he naturally intended to lead his troops personally to capture Jülich-Cleves (and perhaps to win for himself the beautiful Charlotte de Montmorency), he had provided for the newly crowned Queen Marie de Medici to hold power in his absence. Half Italian, half Austrian, and only remotely related to Catherine de Medici, she had not been much of an acquisition as a second wife when Henry got a papal annulment of his first marriage. But she had given him what the last three kings had lacked—legitimate male heirs. All who believed in the stability of the state ought now to back the authority of hereditary Bourbon monarchy. But the method of Marie's proclamation was nevertheless significant: the gouty President of the Paris Parlement, which was already in session in its various chambers for legal business, was summoned from his bed to hold a *lit de justice*, where princes, peers, cardinals, and all the great officers of the Crown should inaugurate the new reign in an ancient court superior to all the upstart councils created by this or that monarch.[1]

The greatest resistance to Marie's power would certainly come from these men—*les grands*—whose ambitions Henry IV had thwarted. They included Henry of Condé, second cousin of Louis XIII but his nearest adult relative and a possible claimant to the throne if Marie's marriage could be invalidated; Condé's uncles, Soissons and the Prince of Conti; Henry Duc de Longueville; and Henry IV's illegitimate son the Duc de Vendôme. All these were 'Princes of the Blood', claiming as of right a share in the power of the monarchy. Hardly less powerful were the non-royal holders of formerly independent principalities such as the Duc de Nevers and the Duc de Bouillon. These leaders of the great families, who now hurried to Paris with their huge retinues, were from their mere existence and outlook a potential threat of renewed civil war. But the new generation of *grands* saw more hope in dominating the monarchy than in overthrowing it. They still had little less

[1] See p. 212.

than absolute control over their territories and virtual subjects; the competition for power at the king's court was now thrown open again. Henry IV had by no means completely separated the running of central government from court service or noble birth. The king's council still in theory included men who were there by birthright or by the holding of ceremonial office. Like the Paris Parlement it could be regarded as the descendant of the ancient 'Curia Regis'. But it had long been a highly adaptable and sometimes almost unidentifiable body, divided and subdivided in ways that could produce, amid endless disputes, specialised committees of administrators. From Henry's inner circle of ministers, by now usually called the *Conseil d'Affaires* or some such name, the principal survivors in 1610 were Silléry, Sully, Villeroy (in charge of foreign affairs), and Jeannin (the president and virtual minister of justice). They had neither bought nor inherited their offices, though there is a hint of how quickly such a group could solidify itself in the fact that Silléry's son married Villeroy's daughter and acquired a place on the council. On Henry's death the foundation of their power and unity had gone. They agreed with Marie in throwing open meetings of the council to anyone at court who chose to attend, so that no-one could claim to be excluded. Sully, the only one to oppose the policies of the regent from the beginning, was turned out of office in 1611 (with a pension of 24,000 livres); the others remained. But against this power of the *barbons*, the grey-beards of the old régime, there were aligned the noble families and the clerical circles whose influence had already been strong in Henry's court. Neither would have things all their own way.

Marie soon had working a 'court' government centred not on the French magnates but on the *confidante* she had brought with her from Italy, her half-sister Leonora Dori. Leonora was a witch—or so the Parlement later decided. At all events she exercised remarkable power over the regent and the court, into which a throng of Italians penetrated. The two thousand French men and women who made up its competitive hierarchy could not be expected to welcome them. Marie bestowed on them most generous pensions out of the funds accumulated by Sully's careful management. Leonora's husband Concini made himself the greatest figure in court and political affairs, and became, by gift or purchase, Marquis d'Ancre, Marshal of France, Governor or Lieutenant-General of several provinces. He won enough power to be hated, but never became a ruling minister of the type of Richelieu or Buckingham. The great men of Henry IV's court did not come off too badly in this; but however much they were given, it appeared that but for the upstart

Italians they might have had more. Some hard bargains were driven before pensions were renewed: the regent's aims seemed to be to buy their loyalty as cheaply as possible, and to leave scope for acquiring by similar means the support of lesser nobles and office-holders.

The Regency, Spain and the Church

The immediate political question for a new régime was the expedition to Jülich and Cleves which Henry IV had been about to lead. Fighting had begun when Dutch troops had tried to occupy the Duchies and had been driven out by Spinola's Spanish army acting on behalf of the Emperor. Though the affair was not expected to begin a major war it would certainly intensify the alignment of European diplomacy into what would seem to be Catholic and Protestant teams, with France committed to the Protestants. Marie and Concini felt themselves to be on the Catholic side: the Protestant war was hastily called off. The succession dispute was temporarily settled in 1614, when Cleves went to one of the main claimants, the Elector of Brandenburg, and Jülich to the other, Wolfgang William of Neuburg, who had hastily become a Catholic.

France's withdrawal was not entirely a matter of foreign policy. The supporters of Henry's schemes, apart from the Protestants who had naturally rejoiced to see him still a friend of their cause, were the *bons français*, the believers in strong central monarchy and a sovereign state. In turning to Spain and Catholicism, Marie was identifying herself with the *Catholiques zélés*, with the Jesuits, and to some extent with all who preferred a weak state to a strong. Spanish diplomacy did not at this time miss its opportunities. The success of the Spanish Ambassador and of the Papal Nuncio, was decisively proclaimed in the double betrothal of the eleven-year-old king to Philip III's daughter, misleadingly known as Ann of Austria, and of Philip's heir to the king's sister Elizabeth.

Noble rebellion

In 1613 the great men rose in revolt. They were not really rebelling against anything: they were asserting themselves. Marie's court, and fights with each other for precedence, did not provide an adequate outlet for their importance. When they had displayed their power, they expected to be paid, and to return to the court. A feeling of frustration among a few princes and dukes could have drastic effects on France. While they were in Paris, central government—however corrupt and

incompetent—worked. When at the end of 1612 they returned in anger
to their 'own' territories there was a partial disintegration of the kingdom. The lesser *notables* hurried to line up behind their leaders;
denunciation of the regency became the accepted orthodoxy. A manifesto appeared complaining of how ill-used everyone was. The clergy
were being deprived of their power, the nobility 'impoverished and
ruined'; most of all, Condé and his friends purported to sorrow for the
ordinary people whose burdens provided the rewards of the rich.
Nothing much happened. The princes took possession of a few towns;
their armies marched about the western provinces. Marie put herself at
the head of an army, but with no intention of fighting. She met the
rebels, negotiated, and agreed to distribute money and governorships
among them. She also agreed to summon the Estates-General.

The Estates-General

There was already a hint of antiquarian solemnity in calling together,
after twenty years, a body which no-one supposed had now a serious
function in the working of French government.[1] The conflicts and
bargaining that took place were largely between the three Estates themselves. The one demand debated at some length was the article '*de la
sûreté des rois*' asserting that the king held his crown from God alone, and
that no power on earth, spiritual or temporal, had a right over the kingdom to deprive him of it. It was a declaration, supported by the great
majority of the Third Estate, against ultramontane Catholicism in its
political form; but it produced a conflict with the clergy which neither
the Third Estate nor the Crown eventually felt it expedient to push to a
conclusion. In the tedious arguments about this article, a more practical
one demanding regular meetings of the Estates-General was largely forgotten. Discussion of taxation also turned into an internal dispute,
between the nobility and the office-holders who formed a majority of the
Third Estate. This was beyond doubt a fundamental social conflict,
however much administrative technicalities obscured it. The Second
Estate, claiming that commoners were acquiring in perpetuity offices
that should be the preserve of the nobility, demanded that the *paulette*
should be abolished. The *Tiers* suggested that the loss of revenue could
aptly be made up by cutting the pensions paid largely to the nobility.
The council agreed, though the changes did not last long. The dispute

[1] See the article by A. D. Lublinskaya in *Album Helen Maud Cam* (vol. 23 of
the *Études présentées à la Commission Internationale pour l'Histoire des Assemblées des États*) (1960), pp. 229–46.

between the Estates meant that the council neither worried about the demand for a reduction of the *taille* by a quarter nor sought any support for a better-administered system of collection.

The end of the Regency

The Estates-General did nothing to upset the palace clique that monopolised power; but habitual leaders of conspiracies among the *grands* were increasingly keen to get rid of Concini's circle. They had a new incentive when Louis XIII, proclaimed of age in 1614, was about to celebrate his marriage to the Infanta: no-one was so good as the Spaniards at keeping their friends and dependants in power. Henry, Prince of Condé, was one of the men with no cause to support and a large private army that could only be kept in being by occasionally allowing it to fight and plunder somewhere. Another Henry, the Duke of Bouillon, whose frontier lands enabled him to pose, when it suited his purpose, as an independent subject of the Emperor, was Condé's principal ally in trying with only slight success to get Huguenot support for a widespread rebellion. In the chaos of intrigues that followed their feeble rising of 1616, the loyalty of great men was bought by sharing out several millions of livres and the control of provinces. Condé found himself first on the royal council and then in the Bastille. But if Concini could outwit rebellious princes, he was not secure against palace revolutions. The King himself was now inevitably a centre of rivalry to the hangers-on of the Regent.

Louis, a bad-tempered, sickly sixteen-year-old, divided his interest, in normal royal fashion, between the exercise of power through patronage and the management of horses, dogs, and falcons. The master of the royal falcons was Charles d'Albret, later Duke of Luynes, whose outlook seems to have been limited entirely to the life of the court and its opportunities. He had no interest in extending or in opposing the 'Catholic' and 'Spanish' policy of the government—merely in killing off the previous favourites. The 'great men' of the provinces were not likely to object to this, and the law of the land was not an obstacle but one possible instrument. So in 1617, with Louis' approval, Concini was stabbed, Leonora tried and publicly burned alive, Marie virtually banished from Paris. Luynes became the effective head of government. With Marie, as her private chaplain, went one of the men to whom Concini had given high office, Armand Jean du Plessis, later Cardinal and Duke of Richelieu. He contrived to support her without losing his contacts with the king. In 1619 he was largely responsible for bringing about a reconciliation between Marie and her son instead of a civil war.

The Huguenots

With the royal government at so low a point, there were bound to be Huguenot leaders attracted by the opportunity of joining the contest for power. A million supporters, including some of the highest nobility, concentrated in a few strongly defended areas but existing everywhere else as a zealous minority, were something most European leaders of resistance could scarcely dream of. Henry IV's scheme had envisaged that they should have their share of high office in the state—a prospect that now seemed to have gone. The greater their seclusion, the more attractive their cause was bound to appear to all opponents of the government. When Europe seemed to be dividing into religious alliances, the more militant wing of the Huguenots asserted itself. The strength of Catholicism at court, the growing activity of the Jesuits, and the continued existence of private armies of Catholic nobility were undeniable threats to the settlement. Sully's son-in-law Henri de Rohan became a typical noble leader, prepared like all the others to be bought off with a court pension but returning to opposition when it suited him. But Huguenot organisation was not an affair of the nobility. The 'circles' they established in 1610 on the German model had each its assembly that revealed in military as well as civil activity something of a popular character. Within the Huguenot movement there was the same division as outside it between those who wanted to accept the authority of the state and those who were ready for any opportunity to create disorder and see what they could get out of it. The Crown's methods of asserting state power did not do much to encourage the pacific element.

In 1620 Louis proclaimed the restoration of Catholicism in Béarn, Henry IV's little territory north of the Pyrenees which claimed to be still independent. It was the occasion for a splendid demonstration of court unity. Louis set forth with a retinue of princes and dukes, among them the Queen Mother and Condé both back in favour. An indignant Huguenot general assembly prepared for war and for two years there were conflicts round some of their fortresses. The Treaty of Montpellier in 1622 deprived the Huguenots of a good many of their opportunities for militancy: they lost most of their military strongholds, and their general assemblies were forbidden. Those of the right status received suitable pensions and offices. The 'war' had also brought more immediate benefits to Louis: Luynes died of the fever he caught, and Condé departed for Italy. In an atmosphere of comparative harmony at court, Richelieu came back into the Council and by 1624 was its effective leader.

Richelieu and the state

Every great minister of the century reached the top by winning the competition in intrigue, self-assertion, and favouritism that occupied the royal courts. Richelieu's rise was a normal one for his kind. His family of second-rank nobility had already served at court and in the law. Armand had entered the Church to keep the Bishopric of Luçon in the family, and performed his duties well. Theology, like war, was not something to believe or disbelieve in but a part of the life of the French upper classes. It was an episcopal group in the Estate of the Clergy in 1614 that sponsored him for the minor post at court that led to his brief experience of political power under Concini. But he was slow to jump on to the wagon of Louis XIII. When he returned, it was as the favourite of the Catholics against the survivors of the *barbon* group whom Louis had recalled. He was already known as a friend of the aristocratic Capucin François de Tremblay—Father Joseph. Both were in touch with the militant Catholic circle of the Duke of Nevers, and with Bérulle and the Oratory. The man who was to make destruction of Habsburg power the purpose of the French state came to prominence as the great hope of the pro-Spanish *dévots*.

Since Richelieu wrote of his ideas on government more fully and intelligently than any of the other great statesmen, it is tempting to see his ministry as the fulfilment of a clear-cut plan to create the strong state and the absolute monarchy. The 'plan' was apparently set out in his celebrated promise to the king, as he afterwards recalled it in the *Testament politique*, 'to use all my industry and all the authority it has pleased you to give me to ruin the Huguenot party, to humble the pride of the great men, to bring your subjects to their duty and to raise your name abroad to the place that is its due'.[1] The first three are negative aims; they do not mean the creation of a centralised unified state but merely the removal of immediate internal dangers. The fourth is as vague as any peroration on foreign policy could be. Richelieu's one permanent centre of policy, other than keeping himself in office, was to preserve and extend the authority of the government. His means were not tied to any dogmatic political theory. Nevertheless, in 1626, details of a programme for French greatness were presented to the Assembly of

[1] *Testament politique*, ed. L. André (1947), p. 95.

Notables. Richelieu and the other ministers—Marillac speaking on finance, Schonberg on military needs—called upon these governing men, great and small, to help in the reform of commerce and of taxation, to get rid of the ruinous cost of civil disorder, and to make the country strong on sea and land. The fact that the object of all this was war on Spain was scarcely noticed.

Richelieu was well aware that the success of his schemes depended on finance. The government in 1626 was spending over half as much again as in 1607[1]—though there were big year-to-year variations. Almost all the increase was in the cost of the army and of pensions. The extra revenue came from loans and above all from the sales of offices. Richelieu held out hopes that taxes would be reduced and the *paulette* abolished. Freed from some of its burdens, the French economy would catch up with the Dutch and the state would become solvent. Nothing of the kind happened. In the 1630s expenditure was more than doubled. Sales of offices certainly declined, and by 1643 had almost stopped—but more through the fall in demand than through deliberate policy. Payment of office-holders, now greatly exceeding the revenue from sales, fell into arrears. The *taille* in 1643 was two and a half times what it had been under Henry IV. The Crown was being further impoverished by the sale and mortgaging of its lands. It was not entirely the fault of the government. Prices had begun to fall; harvests were bad; there was a general shortage of bullion. Industrial and commercial activity declined, partly because there was little investment in them by the owners of land and profiteers from office. Richelieu's efforts to stimulate trade and production had only minor successes. He was heavily influenced by writers like Montchrétien who tended to see foreign commerce as more of a drain on bullion than a source of wealth. Though he made some efforts to limit state expenditure, and sometimes deferred his policies because of their cost, he never accepted that the cost of major wars was in the long run disastrous. Nor could he keep down the cost of preserving and extending the internal power of the régime.

It still seemed possible that the kingdom might disintegrate. Militant Huguenots talked of setting up federated republics like the Netherlands provinces; the disloyalty of great nobles threatened a fate more like the Empire's—of division into principalities. Government from Paris, where court intrigue, patronage, and venality determined how and by

[1] Figures are given in A. D. Lublinskaya, *French Absolutism: the Crucial Phase*, chaps. 5 and 6, and in the chapter by Menna Prestwich in *French Government and Society*, ed. Wallace-Hadrill and McManners.

whom decisions were taken, was not manifestly preferable to the rule of a princely governor or a municipal oligarchy. Richelieu's efforts to bring administration into the hands of men completely dependent on himself were not a dramatic challenge to the existing system. The intendants[1] were not a sudden innovation: they were appointed and their powers extended where and when opportunity arose. Provincial governors, Parlements, and local office-holders of all kinds resented the supervision and encroachment. Richelieu was not prepared to provoke a major conflict with them. Nor did he seek to destroy all existing authorities: those that did their job would benefit from the strengthening of the Crown. Like Strafford, he resisted by whatever means seemed practical what he regarded as disruptive forces within the state. There is no good reason to see the Cardinal as a resolute upholder of good government and Strafford as a tyrant obstructing the progress of liberty. They were similar too in feeling, as men with no strong religious emotions of their own, that religion ought to be a help to the stability of the state. It could easily prove a hindrance. While Richelieu was keeping under control the hideous complications it produced abroad, at home his first concern was to establish a church loyal to the monarchy. Gallican liberties were not a help to him. The object was simply a higher clergy in his own image—men of property and ability willing to teach their inferiors to conform. The state exercised already far more extensive control over the revenue and the assemblies of the church than in other Catholic countries. But the growing hostility of the Jesuits and the *dévots* as the state became more openly the enemy of Spain led to a strict censorship of religious opinion. Ultramontane and extreme Gallican writings were suppressed by the Parlements more severely than Protestant ones.

Huguenot rebellion

Maintenance of a loyal Catholic Church was one of the defences against Protestantism. Henry IV's belief that the Huguenots would eventually be brought within the accepted religion was never abandoned, and indeed proved to be more than half true. Full-scale war against them, for which the *dévots* worked hard, was no way to achieve it. The remedy of the *bons français* was to make closer involvement in the state more attractive to them. No-one could deny the drawbacks of a hostile half-state in the west of France, allied to the English and controlling commercial and military outlets to the sea. But Richelieu dealt with this

[1] See p. 203.

problem as empirically as he did with most. When in 1627 the Huguenots became part of one of Buckingham's twisted political manœuvres
and English ships sailed to the Île de Rè off La Rochelle, he decided
to mount against the Huguenot capital a showpiece of siege warfare.
The *dévots* could welcome this as a Catholic crusade; but to the government La Rochelle was not simply the headquarters of the Protestants.
It was also a privileged municipal community with the same mixture
of interests as independent cities everywhere. State-sponsored monopolistic trading companies, for which new ports were being developed,
seemed likely to divert commercial profit from La Rochelle in particular,
and also from the merchants generally to the court. There was therefore
something of a three-cornered commercial struggle between the French
government, the town, and the English. When Buckingham's force
appeared the leading Rochelais merchants preferred the security offered
by the French government, while many of the lesser inhabitants welcomed their allies in the worldwide Protestant cause. Rohan in Languedoc tried to build up a great Huguenot force to join in the struggle, but
found less support than he had hoped. Neither Buckingham's expedition nor its successor under Denbigh proved very determined; but the
threat of an English base on French soil supported by the Huguenots
was grave enough for Richelieu to turn all his resources against it. The
year-long siege of La Rochelle was made possible by a great feat of
military engineering—the barrier built across the harbour. An equally
remarkable achievement was that when the starving city eventually
surrendered the soldiers were prevented from destroying it. The *dévots*
naturally claimed the fall of La Rochelle as a victory for their cause, and
bitterly denounced the Peace of Alais in 1629 as a shameful compromise
with rebels. But by removing the political and military rights of the
Huguenots without attacking their religious ones Richelieu turned them
into a reliable part of the French community. Once they had lost their
attraction for the enemies of the régime, their religion ceased to imply
political resistance.

Noble conspiracies

'As a party' the Huguenots had, so Richelieu justly claimed, been ruined.
His second subsequently professed aim, 'to humble the pride of the
great men', had to be undertaken cautiously. He did not regard the
noblesse as enemies of the state: they were its most vital part. The danger
came from those who, if they were excluded from a share of central
power, could revert to territorial independence. Their whole life was a

defiance of sovereign law. The huge escorts of horsemen that blocked the streets of Paris behind Condé or Guise and threatened civil war if they met at a cross-roads were a frequent reminder that the days of the religious wars were not very far away. Men like Vendôme in Brittany, Guise in Provence, or Montmorency in Languedoc could almost ignore the central government in the day-by-day exercise of their hereditary power. Lesser noble families borrowed the customs with which the great displayed their superiority to central law. The duel was an assertion of status with remote memories of the feud and of chivalry. Richelieu's edicts against it were a recognition of the fact that to kill an individual according to the strict rules of aristocratic etiquette was as much a repudiation of the state as was armed rebellion. The notion that fighting was an occupation superior to all others, and the natural rôle of the nobility, appeared in their houses, their pseudo-military retinues, their hunts. The lower down the scale, the feebler the substitutes had to be. It was an attitude attacked in a popular work of the period, Turquet de Mayerne's *De la Monarchie Aristodémocratique* (1611), which denounced the devotion of the nobility to the art of war, an 'iniquitous and destructive disease'. They ought, he said, to occupy themselves productively in commerce or the professions.

Richelieu's technique was to avoid a showdown and always to assess realistically his own strength. He dealt with the major plots against his régime by selective revenge. He would hold an execution as high up the scale as was safe. The arch-plotter by birth and temperament, Louis' younger brother Gaston of Orleans, remained beyond his reach, appeased when necessary with governorships and wealth. The 'Chalais' conspiracy of 1626 was a tangle of court plots around Gaston, the queen, and the most dangerous of the court ladies, the Duchesse de Chevreuse, widow of Luynes. It was meant to involve the assassination of Richelieu, perhaps of the king himself. The Marquis de Chalais, not the chief offender, was a person Gaston could safely denounce and Richelieu safely punish; and as his friends had foolishly locked up the skilled executioner, he had a final painful lesson in the incompetence of amateurs. The 'great storm' of court opposition which Richelieu met and survived between 1629 and 1632 was a far more professional political job. It was a palace conspiracy; but it was also a struggle between two coherent policies. The party of the *dévots* was still the strongest influence on Marie; behind it, as always, was the power of the church and of Spain. Things were harder for them now that an adult king exercised the authority of monarchy. His personal support, if expressed with even a moderate amount of energy, could outweigh all the intrigues of the court ladies and their allies. It was by no means clear on whose side it would be exercised. Marie had new allies whose challenge to Richelieu was far less irresponsible. Michel de Marillac was a lawyer who had acquired the posts of Keeper of the Seals and finance minister. He was also a close associate of the leading members of the Oratory. From his place at the centre of political affairs he saw what seemed to him a growing tendency to identify France with the anti-Habsburg cause; and his objection to this was not the simple one of those committed to the Spanish party but the harm he believed it was doing to the cause of strong government and sound finance. Richelieu's foreign policy was already expensive; in 1629 he had sent armies into Italy which were soon devastated by the plague. There was obvious likelihood of greater wars before long. Foreign commitments were preventing the suppression of internal disorder. With his brother Louis, a military officer who had also won promotion with remarkable ease, and Bassompierre, the Marshal and diplomat, Marillac joined Marie and her palace clique in urging the king to dismiss Richelieu. On 10 November 1630, the 'Day of Dupes', Louis, faced with Marie's passionate fury, accepted the seizure of power by Marillac's party, and left Paris for his hunting-lodge of Versailles. Richelieu followed, and proved himself superior both in political manœuvre and in theatrical professions of devotion to the king. Louis, defying his mother and the triumphant palace *dévots*, restored the Cardinal to power. Marie survived in exile, Michel de Marillac and Bassompierre in prison. Only the lesser Marillac perished. The success was not lost on Louis: thereafter Richelieu managed to hold the king in a complex bond of loyalty, fear, and self-interest. But it was a task to which he had to devote an energy and a vigilance as great as those he put into manipulating the diplomacy of all Europe.

The two remaining great conspiracies of Richelieu's day showed how hazy was the line between noble rebellion and foreign war. To men on the level of Princes of the Blood, such places as France, Languedoc, Spain, Lorraine were alike territorial units, differing in size and in the practical relationship they could have with individual magnates, but able to command equal emotional or legal attachment. In their efforts to prevent the French state from depriving them of the freedom this situation implied, the great men would naturally use whatever other territorial units might be helpful. Gaston now spent his time partly in the Spanish Netherlands, where money from Madrid was usually available to pay an army that might be used in support of the Spanish cause in France, partly in Lorraine where he married the ruling Duke's sister, one of the Queen-Mother's large circle of politically active women. Resentment in Languedoc at the extension of the government's taxation machinery in defiance of the province's rights as a *pays d'états* was an opportunity for its governor Henry de Montmorency to raise, in 1632, a fairly formidable army to which Gaston was willing to add his own. The provincial estates and the towns declared their loyalty to the King and joined in what they regarded as a demonstration against the central government. When the rebel forces were beaten, the Toulouse Parlement was willing enough to be used as the legal instrument for sentencing Montmorency to death. It was thought safer to carry out the sentence in private.

France, as Marillac's supporters had feared, became more deeply involved year by year in anti-Habsburg conflict. After 1635 Gaston, abandoning a brief reconciliation, was eager to rouse and exploit complaints against military failures. The central government, he argued, was defying the rights of towns and provinces in impoverishing them through costly and useless war. He found new allies. The Comte de Soissons, a Prince of the Blood and like Montmorency a feudal magnate in the old tradition, was the centre of one plot that ended in a minor battle, with Imperial troops aiding the conspirators. Soissons was conveniently killed in action. The Marquis de Cinq-Mars was a court favourite in the Buckingham style, pushed forward partly by Richelieu himself but firmly appropriated by the opposition. In 1641 by what amounted to a formal treaty with the enemy power it was agreed that Spain would supply money and troops while the French conspirators organised a scheme to kill the Cardinal and take over power in Paris. Naturally the Spaniards would be repaid in territorial concessions and their French friends in offices and titles. The documents setting out the scheme came smoothly into Richelieu's hands through his network of espionage. Cinq-Mars was executed; Gaston once again went free.

Richelieu and Spain

It is easy to build up a picture of Richelieu as the master-mind behind all the wars of his time, planning from the beginning the defeat of the great Habsburg enemy, manipulating from his position of power and wealth every move on the 'Protestant' side and finally, at the prearranged moment, throwing his own invincible forces into the conflict. Such a version fits in well with the view that the Thirty Years War was a single fight to the death between the powers of the future and those of the past in Europe—and to some extent with Richelieu's own retrospective claims. Certainly Spain was from his early years of power an enemy: internal politics alone would have made it so. But it was only in 1629, after five years of intrigue and uncertainty at home and abroad, that he wrote to Louis of his 'perpetual design to stop the progress of Spain' and of the necessity to make gateways into all the neighbouring states and 'guarantee them against the oppression of the Spaniards'. Open war, he explained, must be avoided 'as far as possible'. The enemy is Spain—not the Habsburgs, still less an alliance of all 'Catholic' powers; and the method was encroachment on the frontiers—Metz, Strassburg, Navarre, and wherever opportunity for progress arose.[1]

The Valtelline had already provided one specimen of the intricate connections between local conflict and large-scale alignments. The valley, which offered difficult but usable military routes from Milan and Lake Como east towards the Tyrol and north towards the Rhine, had a mainly Catholic population ruled by the Swiss canton of the Grey Leagues. After a massacre of Protestants in 1621, Olivares, by exploiting the political disputes of the Swiss, had regained effective control. Papal troops, it was agreed, should occupy the valley. Richelieu's first escapade in foreign affairs, in 1624, was to confirm an existing scheme to invade the valley in alliance with Savoy and Venice. Then, in face of opposition at home, he repudiated the action of the army commanders, and by the Treaty of Monçon in 1626 let Spain resume control.

It was one thing to have a general conviction that Spain was an enemy to be thwarted, another to resolve at any given moment the balance of advantages between hostility and agreement. In 1628 the French Duc de Nevers produced a claim to the Duchies of Mantua and Montferrat in the Lombardy plain which gave another opportunity for a limited campaign. In the spring Richelieu led an expedition to the fortress of Casale, but had to call it off without any decisive success in face of the continued dangers at home. The problem was that while a successful foreign expedition, backed by a dominant party at court and occupying the great men happily in the fighting, was a political asset, failures played into the hands of the pro-Spanish circle round Marie. When a second expedition was prepared for the following spring, Richelieu purported to leave to Louis the choice between war—at the cost, as he warned, of abandoning economy and reform at home—and peace at the cost of abandoning power in Italy. Louis was for the moment reconciled

[1] Avenel, *Lettres du Cardinal de Richelieu*, vol. 3, pp. 179–90.
[2] See also p. 325.

to Gaston, and the two set out in full splendour for the battlefields. French forces occupied a large part of the lands of their former ally Savoy, including the fortress of Pinerolo. Sieges and the feeding of troops brought the familiar miseries to the places overrun. Mantua was devastated by Imperial forces. Then the fighting was almost stopped by the plague that shattered all the armies and sent the king and the great men home in panic. Such was the warfare that could be treated by the *noblesse* as an extended hunting-trip.

Richelieu's success on the 'Day of Dupes' gave him a wider range of freedom in which to display his diplomatic strength. It did not mean that he would become the captain, on or off the field, of a Protestant team united in sportsmanlike solidarity. There was still a gap between the anti-Spanish contest and the anti-Catholic one that was being fought out in Germany. Nor was there any praiseworthy skill in his evasion of its implications. The diplomacy that produced treaties with both Sweden and Bavaria[1] made little sense except as a means of postponing irrevocable commitments. However many allies Father Joseph could twist to his purpose, the triumphs of Swedish armies were capable of reducing it all to a slightly comic process of mutual deceit. When Swedish troops appeared on the Rhine and in southern Germany, it was so manifestly embarrassing to Richelieu that cynics asked who paid the unidentified Croats responsible for Gustav's death at Lützen. The contraction of Swedish power was only one of the developments in Germany that led to the armed intervention of France. Richelieu remained as subtle as ever in his determination to keep open every possible line of action but to avoid or at least postpone full military commitment. He offered troops to the Dutch, who throughout the more spectacular German fighting had, since 1621, been resisting the Spanish armies at great cost. He made new treaties with Savoy; he opened negotiations with the best surviving freelance commander, Bernard of Saxe-Weimar. At any point he was ready, if it became the most expedient course, to send French troops into the war. But it was the defeat of the Protestant alliance at Nordlingen in 1634 that made the decision inescapable. 'It is certain', he told Louis, 'that if the Protestant party is ruined, the power of the House of Austria will turn against France.'[2] Saxony and all the other German states would, unless they soon saw some source of help, each act in its own interests in a way that would leave nothing of the alliance. The alternatives were no longer peace or war, but an immediate

---

[1] See p. 293.
[2] Quoted in Pagès *La Guerre de Trente Ans* (Paris, 1949), p. 181.

271

war in Germany that might, with the help of the Protestant allies, be won quickly or a war alone against Spain and Austria that France could certainly not afford. The memorandum, like all Richelieu's expositions of political problems, was carefully directed against the arguments of his opponents. The idea that it would be a short victorious campaign was not borne out by the strategic plans.

There were for the French two wars. There was the German struggle, which in 1635 Richelieu complained the Princes too readily abandoned in making terms with the Emperor at Prague;[1] and there was the war against Spain. If the great danger was really a Habsburg conspiracy to dominate Europe, the Princes had as much reason as France to defeat Spanish forces, in the Netherlands especially. Not many of them saw it that way. Though Richelieu refrained from any fanciful theories about the 'natural frontiers' of the kingdom, many of his preparations had consisted of strengthening his positions on the German border, a process which the neighbouring states did not view with enthusiasm. But it was from the Spanish Netherlands that the greatest danger came. In 1636 an army under the Bavarian general Johann von Werth and the 'Cardinal-Infant' Ferdinand moved into Picardy. Northern France, if not the capital itself, was threatened with the same fate as so much of Germany. The invasion at least helped to achieve what Richelieu had long attempted: the French armies and the *noblesse* at every level were united in alarm. Condé and Turenne were able to build up forces as powerful as any of the armies that had appeared in the earlier stages of the German wars. Rohan, the Huguenot general, was welcomed back from his exile to join them. One German commander remained who was prepared to sell his services to France. Bernard of Saxe-Weimar, who had turned down Richelieu's earlier offers, had now agreed to provide an army of 18,000 men. In 1638 he fought a successful campaign in the southern Rhineland and captured, after a long siege, the fortress of Breisach. There was a violent quarrel about whether Bernard or the French should hold it: his ambition now was to annex the whole of Alsace. When the dispute was ended by Bernard's death, the French were able to hold his army together in their pay and continue the German war.

Very slowly the French armies, pressing forward on the whole frontier but never committing themselves too far inside enemy territory, proved superior to the Spaniards and their allies. The capture of Arras threatened the whole Spanish defensive system in the Netherlands. The

[1] See pp. 297-8, 301.

Dutch fleet by destroying a Spanish squadron off Dover in 1639 cut their sea-route from Spain. The Catalan revolt made possible the capture of Perpignan, securing the French frontier in the Pyrenees. In 1643 Condé shattered the main Spanish forces at the fortress of Rocroi in the Ardennes. The victory had an effect on the political situation even greater than its military consequences. Spain, with 8,000 of her best troops killed, was now regarded as a defeated power. Bavaria became again the faithful ally of France; Saxony let in the Swedes and pretended to have been on the anti-Imperial side all the time. France would clearly be in a position to have the decisive voice in a German settlement.[1] But neither Richelieu nor Louis XIII lived to see the triumph.

Mazarin

The great test of the policies and systems of government created by any minister or monarch was how far they survived when their originator had gone. It was a grim misfortune for the upholders of centralised administrative power in France that Richelieu's death in December 1642 should be followed by that of Louis in the spring. Again there was an infant king; again the regency fell to a woman, and a Habsburg woman at that. Louis XIII's will naming Anne of Austria as regent had made things no better by directing that she should act on the advice of a Council in which Gaston of Orleans, as Lieutenant-Governor of France, was the most distinguished figure. Richelieu too had long ago designated his successor, the inscrutable Father Joseph. But Joseph died in 1639 and was replaced as unofficial heir by a man far less easily acceptable to Richelieu's admirers. Jules Mazarin, formerly Giulio Mazarini, had first been prominent at the French court as Papal Nuncio. Within a few years after 1639 he became a Frenchman, a Cardinal, and the lover of the Queen. (Whether he ever secretly married her is a question for endless argument on unsure evidence.) The one good fortune was that the change-over did not come until the moment of Spain's military defeats, when devotion to Madrid looked a far less attractive policy for the Queen's circle that it had in the past. Mazarin's management of court intrigue immediately justified Richelieu's confidence in his diplomatic skill. By a process of intricate deception, the Cardinal and the Queen outwitted the leaders of the rival court factions and won the support of the men of the *robe* by putting on a show of legality. The Paris Parlement was made to look like a supreme constitutional authority

[1] See pp. 301-3.

in granting the regency unconditionally to Anne alone. It did not prevent the survival of the *cabale des importants*, a group whose principal members were the survivors, or the sons and widows, of the principal conspirators against Richelieu.

By the time of the Westphalia treaties France appeared to be the one stable and victorious state in Europe. The settlement was not quite dictated by the French; but no-one else had a bargaining-power comparable with theirs. To that extent at least Richelieu had won, posthumously, the contest on which he had so cautiously entered. Inside France, the price was still being paid. In the struggle between efficient central government and the decentralised authority of provincial magnates the centre had achieved a good deal; but it had done so at the cost of building up widespread resentment. Instead of the sectional rebellions and palace opposition with which Richelieu had learned to cope, Mazarin faced in 1648 a revolt against the whole central government that involved the *robe*, in its institution of the Paris Parlement, the urban masses, and eventually all those in the provincial communities who were willing or compelled to participate in a new disorder of the magnates.

The Fronde

It is easy to treat the whole affair of the Fronde as a farcical interlude in the rise of absolute monarchy. That is what it became in the end. Though many of the demands put forward strikingly resembled those of the English Parliamentarians, the Fronde was more like a parody of the English Civil War than a repetition. Its very name, from the slings used by Paris children in the game of throwing stones at the carriages of the rich, suggested that it was not to be taken too seriously. Yet it produced a period of misery for the people in much of France, and on the other hand a spate of political controversy and aspiration. Some of the programmes put forward by the pamphleteers would have made the Parlement almost a sovereign body, with control over ministers and over Crown finance.[1] But the constitutional movement did not last long: there was a vast difference between the nation-wide alliance of propertied Englishmen and the much narrower section of professional and merchant interests who supported the Parlement. Its shifting alliances with the mass movement and the noble factions were not held together by any common beliefs. Only the ruinous cost of the war and of ministerial incompetence and dishonesty made men who normally shared in the spoils of the office-holding system rebel against the faction

[1] See P. R. Doolin, *The Fronde*, chapters 5 and 6.

in power. Anne of Austria and Mazarin were foreigners abusing the authority they derived from the boy king. Revolt against them carried no stigma of disloyalty to him. The reign of a minor provided its own kind of royal myth: everyone could be on the side of the absolute power of the monarchy, saving it from the villainy of the others.

Mazarin had learnt in 1643 what French rebellions were like. The *cabale des importants* failed in a plot to murder him. Its leader the Duc de Beaufort was arrested, the others retreated into the country and continued their more or less public conspiracies among the provincial nobility, with the brothers Condé and Conti, Gaston of Orleans, and Gondi (the future Cardinal de Retz) on the fringes. There was no need to worry: when they looked too active some of them could always be sent away with the armies. But in 1648 things were different. There were no more victories; there was to be no peace with Spain. Every Parisian property-owner had been hit by a succession of manœuvres to raise money for the war which enriched those who owned the best official positions. The revival of a penal tax on housing outside the walls and the manipulation of the *rentes*,[1] in which a surprisingly large number of townsmen and small landowners had invested money, were far more obnoxious devices than Ship Money and Forced Loans could ever have been. In January 1648 a group of new money-raising decrees, mainly concerned with the creation of still more offices at the ultimate expense of the citizens, was presented to the Parlement at a *Lit de Justice*. It was no leader of popular opposition but the king's Advocate-General, Omer Talon, who in formally presenting them challenged the constitutional right of the government to use this ceremony—a normal procedure, he claimed, only since the death of Henry IV—as a means of compelling the Parlement to register edicts without discussion. The wrangle between the Parlement and the monarchy that followed was not an affair in which high principles triumphed on either side. But at least the Parlement was prepared to show solidarity with the three lesser sovereign courts in Paris whose members were faced with an announcement that they would have their offices renewed only for a much increased payment. This threat to the sanctity of hereditary office-holding led to the meeting, in defiance of the Regent, of delegates from the four courts. In July this assembly in the *Chambre de St Louis* seemed to be heading for a peaceful constitutional revolution. It proposed reforms that would demolish much of Richelieu's system of centralised power, eliminate the worst of the financial rackets, and turn the Parlement into something

[1] E. H. Kossmann, *La Fronde*, p. 106.

275

approaching a legislative body with control over taxation. There were concessions by the government, some of them transparently unreal. In August Mazarin chose the occasion of an official celebration of Condé's long-awaited victory at Lens to stage a sadly blundering attack on the opposition leaders. The one prominent figure actually arrested was old Pierre Broussel, a radical whose incorruptible disrespect for the government had won the amused affection of Parisians. No-one could have been less the leader of mass insurrection; but it was his name that touched off the émeute. There was more of the demagogue in Paul Gondi, the unscrupulously ambitious Italian cleric, who having failed to sell his services to the Regent as the man who could put down the rebellion, bought his way into the confidence of the townsmen and appeared on the barricades to convey God's blessing to the rioters. If, he seems to have calculated, he could be the means of linking the mass rising with an adequate alliance of nobles he could well become Mazarin's successor. The support of the parish clergy proved to be one of his means of turning diverse elements of resistance into the 'party' of the Fronde. But he was no hero of revolution. 'We were all,' he wrote later, 'playing a comedy.'

The *frondeurs* faced the same problem that had bedevilled peace negotiations between king and parliament in England: Anne and Mazarin, like Charles I, would be able, once they had an army at their command, to repudiate any agreements made under duress. The Declaration of St Germain in October 1648 granted practically everything the Chambre de St Louis had thought of. The peace treaty signed at Münster at the same moment, though it did not affect the war with Spain, would soon make it rather easier to bring up an army against the Parisian forces that were now on the side of the rebels. While Mazarin kept in the background the royal court solemnly returned to Paris. Matthieu Molé, the President of the Parlement, made patient efforts to make the settlement a reality. Then, in January, with an army under Condé ready to blockade the city, Anne revoked the concessions, ordered the Parlement out of the capital, and returned with the king to St Germain. It was a moment when a revolution on the English pattern could well have swung into radical denunciation of the monarchy and its whole corrupt establishment. But in Paris every protest remained within the cage of faith in a sovereign. There was little support in the Parlement for talk of a representative assembly. The most scurrilous of the *Mazarinades*, the leaflets in verse and prose that had been appearing incessantly, never attacked the system of royal government as a whole. Even when the idea of ministerial responsibility to a court or assembly emerged, it had to be hazily reconciled with royal absolutism. There was more interest in the performance of the group of princely nobles—Conti, Longueville, Beaufort, and others—who proclaimed themselves allies of the rebels and made desultory attacks on Condé's small besieging army. One manœuvre showed how far apart the princes and the Parlement were. To Conti it seemed an obvious move to seek the aid of Spain: Molé and his patriotic friends were horrified.

The revolt of the great nobles of the Sword replaced the Parisian rebellion of the Robe by nation-wide disorder. Some of it was in the form of sporadic urban and agrarian popular risings against the sheer misery that had continued to grow. Mainly it was a return to the days of the Wars of Religion, but with alliances that were far less solid. The 'Treaty of Rueil' in March 1649 renewed the court's concessions to the demands of the Parlement and ended the siege. Whatever was left of constitutional theories disappeared in the chaos. The Parlement was left as one of many warring factions, sometimes under Gondi's guidance, still allied with rebellious nobles but aware that its own privileges depended in the long run on the survival of a centralised state. The divisions within it naturally grew wider as its positive programme ceased to be relevant. The intrigues of the nobles, and of the women who played an outstanding and utterly unscrupulous part in them, were in themselves as insignificant as the most petty episodes of international diplomacy; but they had the same effect of killing, maiming, and starving large numbers of people. Glimpses of the events of the next four years are enough to suggest how the natural rulers of the people were now behaving.

In January 1650 Condé, Conti, and Longueville were reunited—in the prison to which Mazarin with the help of Gondi had been able to send them. There were celebrations in Paris and opposition to Mazarin almost disappeared. Some of Gondi's *frondeurs* accepted places in the government. But armies were being collected by many provincial nobles. Despite all the efforts of the court and the ministers to build up loyalty and continue the war against Spain, the anarchy of private armies spread through the country.

In February 1651 Mazarin was in precipitate flight across the frontier and Anne virtually a prisoner in her palace. His fall had come mainly through an alliance between Gondi and Gaston of Orleans, who persuaded the Parlement to demand the release of the imprisoned princes and the dismissal of the minister. Condé and his allies after a triumphal entry into the capital called together an assembly of the Parlement and the nobility where there was talk of an Estates-General, and even preparations for summoning it. The Parlement disliked the idea. As Mazarin himself predicted, the unity between the two Frondes could not last long. During the summer Anne had some success in winning the support of the Parlement.[1]

In January 1652 Mazarin felt it safe to join Anne at Poitiers and had a small army of German mercenaries at his command. Condé with his regiments of dependants was in the south. He had now become an ally of the invading Spanish forces and a leader of those nobles who proclaimed themselves in revolt against the Regent. It was whispered that he would soon be crowned king. In Paris Gondi had abandoned a brief alliance with Condé and was using all his powers of public and private persuasion on the side of Anne, who had persuaded the Pope to grant his burning ambition of holding the title of Cardinal. Nearly all the men of the Parlement now agreed that Condé was the traitor.

In July 1652 Condé's army captured Paris. Scattered warfare had gone on throughout the year—good fun for the nobles, disaster for the peasants. Support for the royal side had generally increased, though only because no-one else could offer a prospect of peace. Condé was saved from defeat in Paris only by the ludicrous affair of Mademoiselle de Montpensier ordering the guns of the Bastille to fire on the army of the Regent's hired commander Turenne. With at least the passive acquiescence of Condé, a mob attacked the Hôtel de Ville, murdered many of the leaders of the sovereign courts and the municipal government and began another day of plunder and destruction. Condé had established a Paris government of his own: at its head was the man whose arrest had begun the first rising in 1648, Broussel. But the support for any form of resistance had almost disappeared. The judges and lawyers of the Parlement, the tough *frondeurs*, the noble supporters of Condé alike began to disappear from the city. Only in Bordeaux did the '*Ormée*', in which municipal leaders had joined with artisans and apprentices to form a broadly-based popular movement, hold out against the royal army. Some of its members even spoke of alliance with the English Republic. In October Condé himself left to return to his command of the Spanish army. As soon as he had gone the king and the Regent entered their capital. There were the most loyal demonstrations of joy. Mazarin returned in February 1653, with no less enthusiasm from the citizens, to be received at the court of Louis XIV.

Of the movement towards constitutional monarchy nothing remained.

[1] See p. 423 for the proclamation of Louis XIV's majority.

A succession of decrees revoking all the concessions, forbidding the Parlement to interfere in finance or in the 'general affairs of state' and imposing massive new taxation was dutifully welcomed. Gondi, consoled with his title of Cardinal de Retz, was imprisoned. Duretête, leader of the *Ormée*, was broken on the wheel. In many parts of the country parish registers showed that the number of children born and surviving to be baptised had fallen in the years of the Fronde to half the normal number or less.[1] Nearly all the main elements that form the political history of the century had been made to appear ineffective and irresolute—ministerial government, legal and representative institutions, popular and aristocratic revolt. A decade later the absolutist state of Louis XIV had been established unshakeably. We shall leave its triumphs and failures to make the end of the story, and look first at the other states of Europe.

[1] P. Goubert, *Beauvais et les beauvaisais* (Paris, 1960), p. 58.

XIII

The Thirty Years War and the Habsburg Empire

The War Years

In the Empire and most of the lands surrounding it the years between 1618 and 1648 were a period in which warfare was more widespread, more continuous, and more devastating than usual. The life of towns and countryside was dominated by the presence—actual or feared—of

BIBLIOGRAPHY. The two most-used modern accounts of the Thirty Years War as a whole are C. V. Wedgwood, *The Thirty Years War* (London, 1938), which makes full use of the German sources, and G. Pagès, *La Guerre de Trente Ans* (Paris, 1949), which has more emphasis on its European context. The short paperback by S. H. Steinberg, *The 'Thirty Years War' and the Conflict for European Hegemony, 1600–1660* (London, 1966) is both a well-simplified sketch of the events and a powerful argument for the view that the 'War' was not a single event and did not turn the Germans into cannibals. For a fuller narrative of the war there is the old standard work by A. Gindely, *Geschichte des dressig-jährigen Krieges* (2 vols., Prague, 1869–78). The series *Les Cours de Sorbonne* (reproduced from typescript and undated) includes lectures on *La Guerre de Trente Ans*, by V. L. Tapié. Extracts from many of the older and newer writers are in *The Thirty Years War: Problems of Motive, Extent, and Effect*, ed. T. K. Rabb (Boston, Mass., 1964).

The evidence on social and economic effects is discussed in G. Livet, *La Guerre de Trente Ans* (Paris, 1965) in the series *Que sais-je?* The article by H. Kamen, 'The Economic and Social Consequence of the Thirty Years' War' in *Past and Present*, no. 39 (1968), sums up the long controversy on this and lists the earlier contributions to it.

Diplomatic activity is dealt with from two contrasting viewpoints in V. L. Tapié, *La Politique étrangère de la France et le début de la Guerre de Trente Ans* (Paris, 1934) and R. Chudoba, *Spain and the Empire* (Chicago, 1952).

On Bohemia there is no more recent substitute in western languages for E. Denis, *La Fin de l'Indépendance bohème* (2 vols., Paris, 1890) and *La Bohème depuis la Montagne Blanche* (2 vols., Paris, 1903). The internal politics and constitution of Brandenburg are clarified in the later chapters of F. L. Carsten, *The Origins of Prussia* (Oxford, 1953). On a rather less academic level is F. Schevill, *The Great Elector* (Chicago, 1947).

armies. They moved, in summer at least, incessantly; they lived on what they could seize; they spread disease, poverty, disorder. Those who controlled, or at least initiated, their movements had an immense variety of motives; but in one way or another they were concerned with the power of the Habsburg monarchy and the Catholic Church. The Bohemian revolt in 1618 seemed a sudden new challenge to the Emperor brought about by a conspiracy of Protestant leaders. The Peace of Westphalia in 1648 seemed a decisive settlement of territorial disputes and a demarcation of Catholic and Protestant areas of control. Soon afterwards the term 'Thirty Years War' was occasionally used,[1] and it has now become firmly established. But it was not felt by many of the participants that this was a single historical event. To the Netherlands the conflicts were part of the Eighty Years War that began with their own revolt. To the French and Spaniards their struggle with each other was more important than German affairs, and it continued uninterrupted for another decade. When the thirty years are subdivided into 'periods' of Bohemian, Danish, Swedish, and French domination, the impression of coherence becomes more misleading still. The one consistent characteristic of this lifetime of warfare, in which armies became more significant units than states, was its confusion of purpose. At every level there were motives of faith, loyalty, and tradition; many leaders had far-sighted ambitions and fears; but all deep-laid plans were quickly submerged in the task of defeating an immediate enemy or simply of surviving. If to the men who made the wars religion was sometimes a determining influence, it was more often a useful badge that did not interfere with the choice of allies. To the men who fought it could be an incentive to courage and cruelty that would otherwise have been unattainable. For some, emotional loyalty to a state or a city counted too. For most, the only aim was to continue to exist in whatever way of life happened to be theirs.

In this chapter we shall look at the Thirty Years War as a great but not a circumscribed part of the wretched history of the peoples of central Europe. It was of course also a part of the diplomatic game that affected

Wallenstein has been the subject of massive German studies since L. Ranke's *Geschichte Wallensteins* (Berlin, 1869). J. Pekăr, *Wallenstein, Tragödie einer Verschwörung* (2 vols., Berlin, 1937) is translated from the Czech. H. von Sribk, *Wallensteins Ende* (2nd ed., Salzburg, 1952) is not entirely on his death. F. L. Watson, *Soldier under Saturn* (London, 1938) is a good popular biography.

---

[1] F. L. Carsten, 'A note on the term "Thirty Years War" ' in *History*, vol. 43 (1958).

in greater or less degree almost every government. The affairs of the Palatinate were a vital issue in English politics; Poland was as much the victim of Swedish ambitions as was Germany; even Russia claimed an interest as a temporary ally of the Swedes. One crucial question is how far the warfare was initiated and maintained by the French for their own political benefit. It is characteristic of governments powerful enough to acquire satellites and dependants that they regard the world as divided into their supporters and their enemies, and the complexities of its quarrels as fit to be manipulated in accordance with their preconceived pattern. Consequently the pattern becomes increasingly significant to everyone else too. This was how Richelieu saw the central European conflicts. The Habsburg side was the side of his main enemy Spain, and various forces might be aligned against it. For some purposes the Habsburg party could be identified with Catholicism—even though the Papacy was rarely attached to it and Catholic France was its enemy. Protestant sentiment was certainly an important anti-Habsburg factor, but not necessarily more powerful than the particularist interest of German rulers great and small of whatever religion. Unfortunately for Richelieu alignment with France was not necessarily any more attractive to them than support of their Emperor.

Bohemia

The thirty years began with a national revolt that failed completely. It was vitally important to the Habsburgs that they held the Crown of Bohemia, which brought them the electoral vote by which they made themselves Emperors. Its various territories straddled the vague border between Slav and Teuton. In the north the Duchies of Silesia and of Upper and Lower Lusatia were German, and claimed that their only connection with Bohemia was that their duke was its king. Bohemia itself, and the Margravate of Moravia in the east, were mainly Slavonic but with strong German minorities. The German language was spreading, helped by the Lutheran Church. German landowners were steadily acquiring Bohemian lands long before the revolt. Few of the magnates were interested in national unification: the smaller nobility who were being deprived of power and lands were the most likely source of opposition. But the Diet, which had once been a thriving political institution where the 'knights' had a large share of power, was now mainly a tax-voting machine. Moravia was said to be governed by fifteen families, who naturally foresaw little benefit from any independent government in Prague. The lands of the Bohemian Crown were a large source of

Habsburg revenue. For it was, comparatively, a rich kingdom. The peasantry was fairly prosperous, paying rents and dues in money. Towns had been thriving in the sixteenth century, though now industries were becoming stagnant, Dutch and English merchants ousting local ones. The Spaniards were rightly alarmed by apparent similarities between the Bohemian and Netherlands risings, even though they did not grasp that the two countries were run by completely different kinds of people.

Court and opposition

Rudolf II, Emperor from 1576 to 1612, had made Prague his capital, to escape the intrigues and feuds of Vienna, where his hated brother Matthias was contriving bit by bit to take over the Habsburg territories. It was this alien and divided monarchy, with its ponderous court maintained at the expense of the excluded native landowners, that brought the Bohemian nobility to the verge of armed revolt. For a time the Protestant Churches—which claimed the allegiance of nine-tenths of the population—benefited from the court rivalry. Matthias thought it expedient to reach agreement with the political leaders of the various Protestant groups; Rudolf to outbid him produced in 1609 the 'Letter of Majesty' purporting to impose equality and freedom of choice between the Catholic Church and the compromise 'Czech Confession' which had been agreed between the Lutherans and Bohemian Brethren, the sect whose antecedents went back to the Hussite wars of the fifteenth century. The assumption was that there would be separate communities with separate political institutions: an elaborate system of arbitration gave the Protestants elected 'defenders' who could appeal to the Crown. Behind the political compromise, Protestant enthusiasts tried to build up a more united and educated clergy able to resist the Jesuits. But the family quarrels of the Habsburgs could not be relied on as a basis for religious compromise. Matthias, once his succession was secure, saw no reason to keep the good will of Protestants: his chief minister, Khlesl, began to erode the guarantees by censorship, restriction of meetings, and so on. The militant Catholic party at court, with the Spanish Ambassador Zuñiga as its moving spirit, hoped to do better than this. Matthias was old and childless, and was likely to be succeeded by his cousin Ferdinand of Styria, an ideal product of Jesuit education obsessed with the need to save his soul by extirpating heresy from his dominions. A rich and energetic group of office-holders in Prague, of whom Jaroslav Martinitz and William Slavata became the most prominent, provided most of the Deputy Governors. It was they who ran the central government in the absence of the Grand Chancellor Lobkovitz. Careful distribution of patronage was, Lobkovitz believed, a sure way to maintain loyalty.

Against them the outlines of an opposition party developed, hindered by the alarm of many Protestant nobles at any sign of popular insurrection. Count Matthias Thurn, the mildly Calvinist German noble who had become commander of the army of the Bohemian Estates, was almost alone in opposing the vote of the Bohemian Diet in 1617 when, accepting the threats of Lobkovitz and the pleas of the dying Matthias, it elected Ferdinand as the new king. Only when Lobkovitz began a general attack on the concessions to Protestantism, whittling down the provisions in the Letter of Majesty about building new churches, was Thurn able to get enough organised support for a show of resistance.

The Bohemian revolt

In March 1618 the Protestant 'Defenders' summoned, as the Letter of Majesty allowed, an Assembly which petitioned the emperor. It also appealed for support to the free territories outside Bohemia. The Imperial government believed, with good reason, that Thurn's party was now in touch with Protestant forces in Germany and beyond it. Austria, Transylvania, and the Palatinate were known to be possible sources of support. A suspiciously prompt royal reply rejecting the petition and banning further meetings produced in Prague one of those surges of popular anger that can be turned in almost any direction. Thurn became for the moment an acclaimed leader of Protestant Nationalism, Martinitz and Slavata the embodiments of alien tyranny. When the assembly met again its numbers had grown and the streets were filled. In the early morning of 23 May a procession of delegates took a new petition to the Hradčany Palace, surrounded by demonstrators—many of them armed. In the Council Chamber they were met by four of the Deputies of the royal government, and the argument that followed turned into a summary trial, in which those of the crowd who had got into the room were asked whether Martinitz and Slavata were guilty of treason. Thurn himself took the lead in dragging them to the window; and the crowd outside had their historic moment of joy when the representatives of the King and Emperor were tipped firmly over the window-ledge into the moat below, followed at a suitable distance by their secretary Fabricius. But they were not the first obnoxious matter to be defenestrated from the palace. Their descent ended not in martyrdom but in a dung-heap of regal proportions. Martinitz and Fabricius climbed a ladder to a ground-floor window; Slavata who had been damaged in the fall was eventually retrieved by his servants. It was the end of the brief moment when a popular urban movement had taken a hand in the affairs of the rulers.

The comedy of the defenestration was an ominously mismanaged beginning for a rebel state. Thurn commanded a few thousand troops and had the backing of some of the nobles, a few royal officials, and most of the elected delegates of the towns. But neither the Bohemian Diet nor the Protestant Assembly could form the basis of a government able to keep an army supplied and paid. Nothing had been done to organise similar movements in Moravia or the Duchies. There was no attempt to seek popular support in town or country. Thurn did not even put himself at the head of a state: power was to be held 'temporarily' by thirty 'directors' who proclaimed their loyalty to the emperor and the Estates. They ordered the expulsion of the Jesuits, sent ambassadors to the various princes and diets of the Empire, and waited for the Habsburg thunderbolts. They came eventually not from Matthias but from Ferdinand, and from Philip of Spain. It was in Madrid, with the war in the Netherlands about to be resumed, that the danger of another independence movement was seen most clearly, and the troops that marched through Moravia and into Bohemia were Flemish, paid with Spanish money.

Catholic and Protestant alliances

Matthias had reason to move cautiously. Though the Catholic states of the Empire were more inclined than the Protestant to sell their support to the emperor, they felt no moral compulsion to do so. After a moment of violence in 1608 between groups of states aligned by religion, there had been formed two alliances—though by no means all the states were involved. The Protestant Union had as its figurehead the man who was to be the unhappy victim of other people's ambitions. The Elector Palatine Frederick V, grandson of William the Silent and in 1613 bridegroom of James I's daughter Elizabeth, ruled the widely separated territories of the Rhine Palatinate and the Upper Palatinate. He was an unassuming youth with no zeal for leading anything, least of all a rebellion. But he was managed by an able and unscrupulous politician, Christian of Anhalt, in whose care he had been educated with almost as much bigotry as the Jesuits had imparted to Ferdinand. The Catholic League was run by Maximilian of Bavaria, the most ambitious of the major German princes and the least impossible rival to the Habsburgs for the Imperial throne. Both alliances were hostile to Habsburg power: Maximilian, far from yearning to fight his distant cousin Frederick, had suggested a combination of the two groups. The smaller states within them would want good rewards before going to war for the ambitions of other princes.

Christian and Frederick might dream of a Protestant Germany and a Protestant Europe rallying to their cause. In England their agents campaigned vigorously against Gondomar and the 'Spanish' faction; in Denmark and Sweden they were encouraged to hope for help, from someone else. Bohemia and the Palatinate on one side, Spain and (though the Spaniards began to doubt it) Ferdinand on the other were deeply committed to war. Everywhere else there was reluctance and careful calculation of the odds and the profits. The rebels did find offers of support. Charles Emmanuel, Duke of Savoy, who had his own quarrel in Italy with the Habsburgs, and whom Christian of Anhalt had encouraged to hope for the Bohemian Crown, was employing under Ernst von Mansfeld the best mercenary army in Europe. Gabriel Bethlen of Transylvania briefly became a popular leader against the Habsburg menace. Thurn's native troops not only held off the invaders but for a moment threatened Vienna itself. The Protestant Estates of Upper Austria, led by the forceful and intelligent Erasmus von Tschernembl, seemed ready to support them; German bankers began to supply money for the Protestant cause, and the Prague Diet triumphantly proclaimed Ferdinand deposed and Frederick 'elected' King of Bohemia. It was a calamitous choice, making nonsense of the 'national' revolt and giving Spain, for whom Frederick's Palatinate was a military route to the Netherlands, a direct interest in its defeat. Yet when, in June 1620, an army of the Protestant Union came within striking distance of forces of the Catholic League near Ulm, they carefully avoided meeting. A treaty was signed declaring that they would not act against each other in Germany.

The crucial disaster for the Bohemian rebels was the decision of Maximilian of Bavaria to rescue the Emperor. His immediate reward was to be the Upper Palatinate and the title of Elector Palatine. But somewhere in the background of all his actions, and of his complex relations with Ferdinand and his fellow princes, was his dream of an Empire some day ruled by his own Wittelsbach family. He now had a Catholic army of twenty or thirty thousand men. Its commander, the Flemish general Tilly, whom a Jesuit upbringing had impressed as deeply as Ferdinand's own, imposed on his soldiers an almost monastic discipline. The 'Catholic Crusade' story he thrust on them may have made them a little less reluctant to fight than their enemies. His first attack was on the threatened Protestant revolt in Austria itself, where the estates at Linz were on the point of war with their Emperor. Then, in September 1620, he marched into Bohemia, where he quarrelled with Ferdinand's general Bucquoy as angrily as did Thurn with Christian of Anhalt. Nevertheless, the forces on Ferdinand's side were more united than their enemies. On November 8th, when the armies met on the White Mountain, a low chalk hill west of Prague, Bethlen's troops were plundering twenty miles away, and Mansfeld was doing nothing because his contract had expired. Frederick was dining happily in the palace when the first fugitives from his shattered armies reached the city.

The challenge of Czech nobility, gentry of Silesia and Upper Austria, scheming politicians and rioting townsmen had not added up to a serious danger to Habsburg power. Nowhere had a clear alternative to Imperial rule emerged. When the strongest of the Protestant Electors, John George of Saxony, invaded Lusatia he did so on behalf of the Emperor, claiming a few concessions to the Lutherans in return: Germany was much as it had been. Only the firm presence of Spanish forces in Frederick's former Rhineland territories was new. But for Bohemia as a nation with a culture and tolerance of its own the price of defeat was destruction. It was not a sudden planned vengeance. At first only twenty-seven leading Protestants had their lands confiscated and distributed to Imperial officials and Catholic nobles. The process developed over a period of seven years into a scramble for free or cheap lands in which most of the great estates were transferred to adventurers from many parts of Europe, with great profit to the Crown as well. The new Governor in Prague, Liechtenstein, a convert to Catholicism who envisaged Bohemia as a showpiece of the Counter-Reformation, sentenced rebel leaders to death. The Papal Legate, Carafa, organised the final establishment of Jesuit education. Protestant clergy lost their livings or experienced a sudden conversion. At every level of society, security could only be won by acceptance of Catholicism. Continued plunder by armies led to ever-deepening poverty. The greater the misery, the more easily miracles and festivals did their work. Belief in witchcraft grew too, and was persecuted as savagely as heresy. A Protestantism as old and deep-rooted an any in Europe was completely overthrown.

The rise of the armies

The next ten years can provide specimens of most of the factors that provoked seventeenth-century wars. One, usually concealed behind a political façade but now blatantly displayed, was that the professional commanders of armed forces like to use them, to increase them, and to take control of policy. Princes and statesmen shared their influence on events in and around Germany with Mansfeld, Tilly, and above all with Wallenstein, one of the greatest organisers of the war industry in history. Albert de Valdstein was by birth a Bohemian and a Lutheran, from a family of impoverished nobility. After changing his name and religion, he built up an immense fortune by marrying a rich and dying widow, by sharing in the company that produced a new Bohemian currency, and especially by buying up confiscated Protestant lands. Soon he was able to make loans to the emperor on almost the scale of the Fugger a century earlier. He was never primarily a strategist: he entered the emperor's military service by contracting to supply 20,000 armed men, farming out the recruiting with great profit to himself. Food and equipment of every kind were supplied by Wallenstein's own organisation, with his officers as middlemen. Soldiers got their pay or not as the situation required: if they could live entirely by plunder, so much the better, but in emergency Wallenstein's Bohemian wealth could give support. Desertions became fewer than in other armies, and were provided for in his calculated recruiting programmes. The terms he made with Ferdinand gave him stage by stage completely independent control over the use of his forces. But Wallenstein having become a political power identified himself completely with the cause of the Empire. More than Ferdinand himself, he worked for a reunited Imperial and Catholic power, dominating the German princes and the lesser states of Europe. The emperor began to reward him with lands and titles in Germany, the Catholic princes waited for the moment when they could demand his dismissal.

Many German princes were themselves behaving more as military commanders than as rulers. But for them it was the holding and expanding of territory that mattered. From the Emperor himself down to the pettiest count, everyone with control of some sort over a piece of land was faced with the fear of annexation and devastation, and with the possibility through careful choice of alliance or neutrality, that he might in the end benefit from the wars. For the great men like Maximilian, continuing war increased the opportunity to build alliances they could dominate. Since the division of Germany into Catholic and Protestant groups was roughly matched by the division of Europe, the prospect of intervention from the great powers had always to be taken into account. It became much more immediate when in 1621 the war between Spain and the Netherlands was resumed. The Rhine Palatinate was, like the Valtelline,[1] part of Spain's strategic route. Spinola, one of the finest and best-equipped generals in Europe, now had a direct concern with German affairs. So, in consequence, had the Dutch. Neither was anxious to get involved in fighting deep inside Germany; but it was partly the hope of Dutch backing that encouraged the rash enterprise of King Christian of Denmark.

Denmark

Since Christian IV[2] was also Duke of Holstein, he had an interest in the German situation not shared by the Danish aristocracy. In 1624 he made clear his hope of acquiring on behalf of his son one or more of the great bishoprics, in which Maximilian, John George, and Ferdinand himself were also interested. But he was able to win support at home for his intervention because it had wider economic motives. For the state that relied on its control of the Sound Dues to grow rich on other people's Baltic commerce, the conquest of the German coast and the entrance to the Elbe and Weser offered magnificent prospects. Conversely a sweeping Habsburg victory in the north would give Denmark a most undesirable neighbour. The plight of the Protestant states offered him the prospect of becoming a hero of the anti-Catholic cause—in other words a link between the German dog-fights and the more exalted diplomacy of European powers. Not only the Netherlands but England and even his ancient enemy Sweden ought, Christian believed, to follow his leadership. No such alliance materialised. England eventually sent a few conscript soldiers to join the cosmopolitan army of Mansfeld; Dutch bankers raised a small subsidy; Gustav Adolf, with no desire to help Danish ambitions in the Baltic, refused to have anything to do with such schemes. Only the little states of the Lower Saxon Circle, faced with the threat of Tilly's army, agreed to make Christian their president and to let him recruit freely in their territory. With no more encouragement than this, Christian sent in his army. His only reward was to bring into northern Germany and into Denmark itself the full horror of the marching soldiers. The little states were looted repeatedly: the pitiful efforts of George William of Brandenburg to keep forces out of his territory by agreeing with almost anyone only added to the

[1] See p. 270. [2] See p. 345.

complexities of the fighting there. The one state never troubled by the forces was Mecklenburg—which the emperor had conferred on Wallenstein. With the defeat of Mansfeld's army, there seemed to be a prospect of a complete Imperial conquest of the north—which so alarmed Maximilian and the Catholic princes that the League made a vain attempt to arrange a compromise peace. This was Ferdinand's great difficulty: Catholic princes were no less threatened than Protestant ones by any extension of Habsburg power. A prospect of decisive victory for the emperor brought to the surface the neutrality movements that the particularism of the states, great and small, always tended to produce. It was largely Wallenstein's own awareness of the dangers facing Ferdinand that led in 1629 to the reasonably generous Peace of Lübeck which removed the Danes from the war without grievous punishment.

The bishoprics

The ending of the Danish episode speeded up the land-grabbing in Germany. The most tempting morsels had, ever since the Reformation, been the former Catholic bishoprics. Some in Protestant areas had been completely 'secularised' and were now principalities heritable like any other; some kept their theoretically clerical chapters of canons but were controlled by a lay 'administrator' who took the profits. They were often a welcome solution to the problem of providing for the younger sons of great families. While English gentlemen found parochial livings for their dependants, the Emperor acquired for his son the bishoprics of Strassburg and Passau, and the electoral families of Brandenburg and Saxony had half a dozen bishoprics between them. Episcopal possessions could be expanded no less than others: the Bishop of Speier got Ferdinand's authority to recover whatever lands he could claim had once belonged to his diocese. Out of the scramble for bishoprics the successive confiscations, and the general insecurity of territorial possession, there developed among the ministers of both Ferdinand and Maximilian the scheme for giving legal and religious blessing to Catholic acquisitions which emerged in 1629 as the 'Edict of Restitution'. All Church property that had been alienated since 1552 was to be restored to the rightful successors of its former owners—episcopal lands to Catholic bishops, monastic ones to re-established religious houses. Protestant 'administrators' were declared to have no legal rights at all. Only the Lutheran religion was recognised as benefiting by the old principle of '*cuius regio eius religio*'; and Protestants of any kind who now found themselves back under a Catholic ruler could change their faith or get out. It would mean the destruction of many Protestant princes, the imposition of Catholicism on Protestant towns like Augsburg and Dortmund, the re-establishment of many hundreds of monastic foundations. The fact that it was an Imperial Edict, issued without reference to the diet or the princes, was in itself a defiance of the accepted division of power. Ferdinand had acted quickly enough to ensure that he rather than Maximilian and the other Catholic princes got the greatest benefit. It would have been hard to devise a better combination of the war-provoking motives of property, power, and belief.

The Edict was in itself an indication of how possession of land was merged with political power, and religious with secular control. There was room for endless arguments on such questions as its application to the Imperial Free City of Augsburg which was also the Protestant centre of a Catholic bishopric. The Imperial 'Commission' that purported to hear the legal arguments was in practice part of the process of ordering armies to carry out the transfers. When the Augsburg citizens had heard what Wallenstein's army could do to places that resisted the execution of the Edict, they surrendered without a blow. Eight thousand Protestants were later said to have fled from the city. On the whole the spoils were distributed with due regard to the realities of power. Maximilian, who after initiating the idea of the Edict had drawn back when the Emperor seemed strong enough to get more for himself, was pacified with the sees of Verden and Minden for the Wittelsbach family. Magdeburg, Halberstadt, and Bremen had already gone to the Habsburg Archduke Leopold. Believers in the triumph of the Catholic faith could claim it as a great victory over the forces of evil. In fact the scramble for lands brought out more bitterly than before the conflict between the emperor and the Catholic princes, while for Protestant princes withdrawal of the Edict became a major aim.

Emperor, princes, and foreign powers

It was typical of the German situation that in the midst of the forcible seizures of territory and with the armies still the most effective power in a country suffering disastrous impoverishment, the Emperor in 1630 resolved to invite the Electors, Catholic and Protestant alike, to assemble at Regensburg and give formal recognition to his son as successor to the throne. This, he hoped, would be the moment when Germany would reunite against its outside enemies—which meant, as the electors soon saw, the enemies of the Habsburgs. The Electors of Saxony and Brandenburg refused to take part in the meeting at all. The others were determined to use the opportunity to diminish the emperor's military power. Their principal demand was that Wallenstein should be dismissed. For Ferdinand to fling away his great source of armed strength seemed incredible folly. But the emperor like the Electors was suspicious of the growing power of the commander who seemed to be running a foreign policy of his own. The Spanish party at Ferdinand's court, hoping to get Wallenstein's forces put under its own nominee, and hence at the disposal of Spain, was also in favour of his dismissal. At the moment when Germany was invaded by Swedish armies the man most able to resist them was persuaded to 'resign'.

The Regensburg meeting marked a further stage in the development of the wars in Germany into the centre of a single European struggle. But the great powers were still cautious in their commitments. While Ferdinand's Jesuit confessors had growing hopes of a new Catholic Empire in which both German and Spanish Habsburgs would be loyal instruments of the Church, the great aim of the Spaniards was to get German troops to fight against the Dutch. Saving Catholic Germany from Protestant aggression was no concern of theirs: they had already shown a cynical readiness to negotiate with Frederick for the restoration of the Palatinate to his family under Spanish protection. Richelieu, feeling that home affairs now left him a little freer to manœuvre against Spain, had been working to strengthen the German princes, and keep Ferdinand's empire divided. The Capucin secret diplomats Father Hyacinth and Father Alexander had long been involved in intricate chicanery on his behalf; and at Regensburg Father Joseph himself turned up to take charge of it. Franco-Spanish rivalry was now involved in the affair of Mantua.[1] Under Spanish pressure, and despite the hostility of the princes, Ferdinand had asserted his authority over the disputed Duchy and sent Imperial troops against the invading French. They won some surprising military successes, which did a good deal to weaken France's position in Germany.

Richelieu had made clear to the Electors his 'very sincere' wish to deliver Germany from the 'oppression to which the manifest violence and ambition of the House of Austria have reduced it'.[2] He encouraged them in their demand for the dismissal of Wallenstein, and helped to persuade Wallenstein that it might be a way to prove how indispensable he was. At this stage it was no part of French policy to distinguish between Catholic and Protestant among German princes. It was important to let

[1] See p. 270.
[2] Quoted in Pagès, *La Guerre de Trente Ans*, p. 121.

Maximilian of Bavaria especially see the benefits of relying on French support rather than making terms with Ferdinand. (Maximilian for his part felt so strong, with Wallenstein out of the way, that he could accept French help without making any binding commitments.) But Richelieu intended to leave open as long as possible the option of keeping up peaceful relations with the emperor. Father Joseph actually signed an agreement by which France would withdraw all help from the princes in return for a favourable settlement of the Mantuan war. Richelieu indignantly repudiated it; but his intervention at Regensburg had been far from a triumphant success. One satisfaction that remained was that Ferdinand had been even less successful. Another was that in July 1630 Gustav Adolf's well-prepared and well-advertised invasion force had landed at Peenemunde.

Though Richelieu had long been encouraging, cautiously, the schemes for Swedish intervention, it was a complication that made it harder than ever to build up an alliance of German states within a French system. Gustav was no-one's mercenary soldier. It was not until January 1631 that he reached agreement with Richelieu in the Treaty of Barwälde. In return for a subsidy not big enough to be vital to Sweden's plans, Gustav agreed to tolerate Catholicism, to make no separate peace, and to keep out of Bavarian territory if Bavaria remained strictly neutral towards Sweden. Since Gustav was pledged to restore the Elector Palatine to his lands, the prospect of this part of the treaty being effective were not good. In May Maximilian, alarmed not so much by the Swedes as by Spain's apparent threats to the Palatinate, made with France the agreement at Fontainebleau by which each side promised to uphold the other's possessions and give no assistance to their enemies. The difficulty of reconciling the two treaties looked formidable. It was some satisfaction that in April the Peace of Cherasco ended the Mantuan war in favour of the French claimant; but it also released Imperial and Spanish troops for other purposes. At least it indicated that the emperor felt himself in a weaker position than he had at Regensburg.

The Swedish invasion

Gustav's landing was a spectacular achievement. Within a fortnight the Pomeranian capital of Stettin was occupied and the Dukes of Pomerania and Mecklenburg quickly became his first German allies. After that, progress slowed down. The political obstacles to a united campaign against the emperor became apparent. John George of Saxony had his own aspirations to outbid Maximilian for the rôle of defender of German liberties, and tried to align George William of Brandenburg and lesser Protestant rulers behind him. After a meeting at Leipzig in the spring of 1631 they offered Ferdinand the choice of accepting their terms for a united resistance to the Swedes or seeing them in alliance against the Empire. Saxony's behaviour in the Bohemian War did not suggest that this was worth taking too seriously. The principal aim of both Electors was to preserve their own territories. Gustav Adolf's appearance as the Protestant deliverer of Germany did not arouse their enthusiasm. He was able, after a well-timed invasion of Prussia, to persuade his brother-in-law George William to promise Sweden a benevolent neutrality. Saxony on the other hand did for a time become a significant military power. Wallenstein's second-in-command von Arnim found no more difficulty in transferring to the service of Saxony than he had formerly in invading his native Brandenburg. John George, temporarily, was rich enough to pay him.

In May 1631 the rulers and their political servants were still deeply involved in the refinements of professional diplomacy. Swedish troops had occupied much of Pomerania and lived at the expense of its people; then they had moved on to take and plunder Frankfurt on the Oder. But ever since the autumn of 1630 the great Protestant city of Magdeburg, which had rebelled against its 'restitution' to Catholic control, had held an essential place in Gustav's programme. Both in strategy and in propaganda, its possession was immensely valuable. He promised repeatedly to come to its rescue; and he needed to do so in a spectacular way that would establish his rôle as Protestant saviour. Tilly's subordinate Pappenheim was besieging it with an ill-supplied force. It could, Gustav believed, hold out until the Swedish army, depleted by the need to hold down the territory it had occupied, could be reinforced. There were long negotiations to try to get John George of Saxony to help in its relief. Tilly decided that a final assault on the city was the chance for a great blow to Swedish prestige. Its success was not quite what he had hoped.

When the city's resistance ended, soldiers suddenly released from inactivity into a source of wealth and drink robbed and killed indiscriminately; and somehow there began the fires that merged into the total destruction of the city, of the supplies the Catholic commanders had hoped for, and of most of the inhabitants and soldiers alike. Whether Magdeburg experienced the phenomenon of a 'fire-storm' that three centuries later produced the greater horrors of Hamburg and Dresden is impossible to say; but probably the holocaust was exceptionally great only because it was a very windy day. At all events, it became in Germany and in Protestant Europe the basis of a story of Catholic atrocity that provided a new incentive for war. Tilly made amends in his own way: he attended a mass to mark the restoration of the city to the true faith, and urged the surviving soldiers that they ought to marry the women they had seized for themselves. But Magdeburg had not changed his main problem—to find supplies for his army. Maximilian, still hoping to lead an alliance of princes and discouraged by Richelieu from an encounter with Gustav, did not want the Catholic army to attack John George. But for Tilly the needs of the army were an end in themselves: at the end of August 1631 he invaded Saxony. A fortnight later John George signed a military alliance with Gustav, and at Breitenfeld, north of Leipzig, enough of Tilly's army was destroyed for the Swedes to be sure of living successfully for some time off the Catholic states.

Sweden and Germany

In the next year, as Gustav continued to lead his armies through south Germany, his ambitions expanded. Instead of the hastily improvised extraction of wealth from the countryside to support the alien army, he began to consider, with Oxenstiern, reorganising the 'Circles' to provide a new government for conquered territory. Even Richelieu took seriously the awful possibility of a Swedish Empire extending to the Rhine. In Bohemia, though John George's activities often looked more like the familiar plundering than liberation, there was briefly a hope that Protestantism might be restored. For among the countless secret soundings that went on between all the parties in the conflicts Gustav was in touch with Wallenstein. If revenge for his dismissal was a motive, Wallenstein could hardly do better than get troops and money from the Swedes to reconquer for Protestantism his native Bohemia. Gustav evidently decided the risks were not worth while. Ferdinand, now that the Pope, Spain, and Poland were all for their different reasons refusing to give him substantial help, might soon be completely at the mercy of the Swedish army. Only by making what seems, from uncertain accounts of it, to have been a humiliating bargain with Wallenstein, who acquired practically the status of an independent sovereign ally, could the Emperor acquire a new army. Catholic Germany had shown no sign of uniting against the Swedish invader. On the contrary, there was, in the winter of 1631-2, a reasonable chance that one of Richelieu's many alternative schemes might be brought off—an agreement for the Catholic League to remain neutral while Gustav fought the Emperor on Protestant territory. The negotiation failed, less perhaps through any reluctance of Gustav to limit his freedom of action against Catholics than because he needed to let his army live off the produce of Catholic lands. The distinctions between ally and enemy had come to matter less than the contest between all armies for what food was left, and the efforts of rulers to send the soldiers elsewhere. Maximilian tried to hold an awkward balance between preserving his Bavarian lands from destruction by the armies and preventing a Swedish victory that might deprive him of them altogether. In the end he decided to fight as best he could.

There was no more progress towards a united Protestant cause in Germany than there was towards a Catholic one. John George of Saxony was ready to support any move for a general pacification, unless he could see better prospects of becoming the leader of a new alliance. Certainly there were some rulers ready to join in a Swedish triumph. Transylvania had been an intermittent threat to the emperor ever since 1619, when Gabriel Bethlen, the Calvinist magnate who had acquired its more or less independent throne, had proclaimed his support of the Bohemian rebels and got the Protestant Estates of Hungary to give him the title of king. He was not an enemy to be treated lightly. Not only was Transylvania itself a thriving state with an efficient army: Bethlen had also brought in Turkish troops. Twice Ferdinand had bought him off with promises of large additions to his territory, and twice he had renewed hostilities. In 1630, a year after Bethlen's death, a new Transylvanian prince, George Rakoczy, had established himself. He hoped to make an alliance with Gustav Adolf that would guarantee him a large share in the glorious Protestant triumph. Gustav rejected the terms demanded by Rakoczy: he was not an ally worth buying. But the Translyvanian envoys had at least had better treatment than the ludicrous delegation of Crimean Tatars who turned up in Stockholm with an offer of 30,000 men.[1] They were sent off to Germany to see the king if they could find him—which they never did. In 1632, before the diplomatic consequences of his victories had even begun to clarify, Gustav—at the end of the campaigning season—met Wallenstein's army in the battle at Lützen where he was killed. Though the outcome was indecisive and the opportunities of his armies unchanged, the hero-myth had gone from the Swedish cause at a moment when the practical limits in their advance into Germany had probably been reached.[2]

[1] M. Roberts, *Gustavus Adolphus*, vol. 2, pp. 571-2.   [2] See p. 346.

It was ironic that of the two men whose personal successes had most influence on the fighting the king should die on the battlefield and the professional soldier be the victim of politically motivated assassination. There is no great mystery about Wallenstein's conduct in the years after Gustav's death. Since his first agreement with Ferdinand he had remained in part a manager of the business of war, selling his services where he thought best, in part a politician with the same standards of conduct as the rest of them. He had therefore been in frequent touch with many leading figures on whatever at any given moment was the 'other side'. Wallenstein's 'treason' in being prepared to reach agreements with the French, with Protestant Electors, with his fellow-soldiers Bernard of Saxe-Weimar and Arnim, or with the Swedes differed from the normal honourable proceedings of diplomacy only because he was still on the borderline between subject and monarch. Perhaps if he had added a touch of Cromwellian passion to his wealth and ability he might have become a Lord Protector of the Empire. But an essential part of the business was to hold the loyalty of his mercenary soldiers and subordinate commanders; and his prospects were now too uncertain for all of these to follow him unquestioningly against the emperor. Nor had he won popular support in Bohemia: none of his astrologers had revealed to him that Prague might have been worth a Protestant sermon. In 1634 Ferdinand agreed to his dismissal and, it appears, to a secret order that he should be captured or killed. So for his disloyalty to the German Emperor he was murdered by the conspiracies of men with such names as Butler, Gordon, Leslie, and Devereux, officers in the Imperial armies.

The Peace of Prague

The forces that remained in Germany were gradually abandoning such coherence as they had had in the days of the great commanders. Mansfeld in 1626 had lost the support of his army in Silesia and died obscurely in the mountains of Bosnia. Tilly had been fatally wounded in a minor encounter with the Swedes. An alliance of the smaller Protestant states concluded at Heilbronn in 1633 did little more than thwart the schemes of Saxony for making peace. Clearly the French would before long have to decide whether to forsake German politics or intervene directly. It was the extension of French control over German Protestant politics that encouraged a new Catholic commander to bring help to the emperor. Philip IV's brother Ferdinand, the 'Cardinal-Infant', governor of the Spanish Netherlands, was not a man to allow his high sacred office to prevent him from becoming a highly skilled soldier. He was delighted to have the opportunity of taking an army into Germany to practise his theories of war. In September 1634 his force, with the remains of Wallenstein's army, fought the Swedes and the German Protestants organised by Bernard of Saxe-Weimar at Nordlingen. It was a victory for the emperor's cause formidable enough to end the resistance of most of the Princes, and to bring nearly all southern Germany under the control of Imperial commanders. In the spring of 1635 the Elector of Saxony completed his long negotiations and signed with the emperor the Peace of Prague. John George was to have the reward of Lusatia and the bishopric of Magdeburg. The whole principle of the Edict of Restitution was to be quietly abandoned and lands to revert to those who had held them in 1627—but only for a period of forty years, during which, by some conveniently unspecified process, the disputes would be settled. Lutheran worship was to be tolerated in some Imperial cities. In return John George was to assist the Imperial government against such princes as refused to join the settlement. Few of those that mattered did refuse. Bavaria and Brandenburg, the Rhineland bishoprics and the Duchies of Mecklenburg were equally ready to accept. Only Bernard of Saxe-Weimar, still in command of an army but not of any territory, decided that his future lay in a Wallenstein-like existence as a mercenary sovereign with dreams of becoming the saviour of Germany. It was by no means the end of the fighting or the plundering. But the German war as such had petered out. The eighteen years of destruction had settled that Maximilian of Bavaria should rule the Palatinate, that Bohemian Protestants should continue to be persecuted, and that a number of bishoprics should be shared out equitably among the younger sons of the emperor and the princes. Ferdinand, to whose new Imperial army Catholic and Protestant states were expected to contribute, had reason to be moderately pleased. But when he died in 1637 he had few illusions about the struggle with France that faced his son.

Devastation

To incalculable numbers of men, women, and children the warfare in Germany meant the loss of homes, crops, and livestock; their possessions were stolen, their families broken up; they were in constant danger from plague and famine. Many towns suffered in greater or less degree the fate of Magdeburg; many villages were abandoned. None of this can be denied; but round the attempt to put it into more precise and quantita-

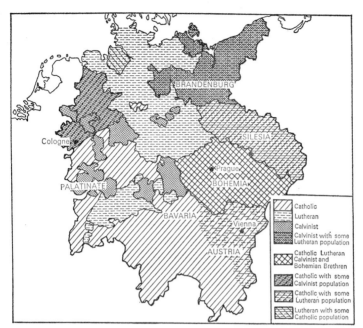

Map 3 (a). Religious divisions of Germany before the Thirty
Years War

Legend:
- Catholic
- Lutheran
- Calvinist
- Calvinist with some Lutheran population
- Catholic Lutheran Calvinist and Bohemian Brethren
- Catholic with some Calvinist population
- Catholic with some Lutheran population
- Lutheran with some Catholic population

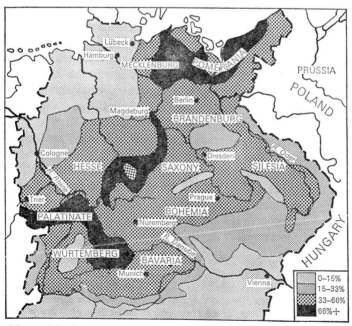

Map 3 (b). Germany: Loss of population in the Thirty Years War

Legend:
- 0–15%
- 15–33%
- 33–66%
- 66%+

tive terms a good deal of controversy has developed. Historians have been guilty of a variety of crimes. One is to accept descriptions of the worst horrors as typical of the whole period and country. Another is to disregard the ulterior motives that may have led to deliberate exaggeration. Samuel Pufendorf, as the Great Elector's official historian, has been held responsible for exaggerating the miseries of the war period in order to glorify the achievements of his master.[1] But the most specific corrections that have been made to the earlier views are in the use of statistical material. The claims that the population was everywhere reduced by anything from a half to two-thirds come either from repeating the guesses of impressionistic writers or from extending to the whole of Germany figures for the worst-hit places. Not all those who disappeared from a town had necessarily died, though to say that they had merely 'migrated' does not make it less important in economic or human terms. There were large areas where the evidence for a reduction of well over a half in the population is strong and consistent. They include Mecklenburg and Pomerania in the north, Würtemberg and the Rhine Palatinate in the west. In other places, such as Oldenburg and Hanover, the losses were comparatively small. Much of Lower Saxony suffered badly at the beginning of the war and then recovered. Bavaria had its worst losses in the 1630s. Some towns—Hamburg for one—had an almost uninterrupted rise in population and commercial activity.[2]

Even when the extent of the demographic and economic changes has been assessed, there remains the problem of how far the war alone was responsible. We have seen that it is now generally accepted that somewhere about 1610 to 1620 the whole of western and central Europe suffered economic depression in one form or another.[3] There were many signs of it in Germany before 1618, and later in areas still untouched by the war. Food prices rose, coinage was debased, commercial activity declined. But whatever the underlying causes of impoverishment, there is no doubt that the war made it worse. Armies consumed food and destroyed the means of producing it. The cost of maintaining them wrecked the economy of states great and small. Though the correlation between the movement of armies and the areas of the worst depression

[1] S. H. Steinberg, 'The Thirty Years War: a new interpretation' in *History*, vol. 32 (1947).
[2] Detailed estimates are given by Günther Franz in *Der dressigjährige Krieg und das deutsche Volk*. See also the map on p. 299. Another map with slightly different zones is on p. 42 of the *Cambridge Economic History of Europe*, vol. 4.
[3] See p. 76.

and depopulation is not complete, it is generally close. The highest mortality nearly everywhere came from disease; and the movement of soldiers was clearly a means by which it spread.

It can of course be pointed out that conditions in the Thirty Years War were not as different from those at other times as is readily assumed. There were few years in the century when somewhere in Europe there was not warfare as destructive as that of 1618–48. Even in peacetime towns of wooden houses were always liable to be burnt, crops and animals were destroyed by inescapable natural misfortune. Plunder, riot, and rebellion were constant threats to the poor as well as the rich. It is true also that recovery from the disasters was in most places quick. It did not take long for a shattered town to be rebuilt; deserted lands were reoccupied and the fertility of the soil was soon back to its normal level. A few years of abnormally high birth-rate and low infant mortality could soon restore the demographic balance. Yet when all allowances have been made for exaggerations of the disaster, there is too much evidence of the deep and long-lasting impoverishment of vast areas of the country and of the impression it left in popular memories for it to be written off as a normal part of seventeenth-century life. 'In our century, and many believe it to be the last...' So Grimmelshausen opened his novel *Simplicius Simplicissimus*; and the descriptions of wartime Germany that follow show that the mood was not one of ordinary millenarianism. Life seemed to have become not merely wretched but hopeless.

The Peace of Westphalia

The Peace of Prague seemed to mean the end of resistance to the emperor inside Germany. Richelieu must now fight his battles himself. In May 1635 he issued a solemn declaration of war against Spain.[1] The war in Germany had become a minor part of the European conflict—a conflict itself almost as lacking in coherence as the German ones. It was round the western frontiers of the Empire, from northern Italy to the Netherlands, that the long struggle for control of territory was fought out. The French were glad to leave German affairs to their Swedish allies and to Bernard of Saxe-Weimar. Bit by bit the Swedish generals Torstensson and Banèr recovered control of the north from the Saxon and Imperial armies. Swedish forces even went through Bohemia with the intention of joining George Rakoczy of Transylvania, whom the sultan had allowed to undertake a sporadic campaign against Imperial forces in Hungary. In the south Bernard won a series of victories over the Bavarian

[1] See p. 272.

and Imperial troops. One by one the new emperor's allies deserted him. Brandenburg and Saxony made separate truces with the Swedes; Bavaria in unavailing efforts to keep armies away made and broke agreements with almost everyone. More and more the armies remained in being only because there was no means of safely getting rid of them. Only a large-scale settlement among the great powers could enforce a general pacification in Germany.

Great treaty-making Congresses are easily overrated as turning-points of history. The various agreements that made up the Peace of Westphalia in 1648 did not put an end to the one major conflict still being fought in the west—between France and Spain; nor did they much affect the strength or interests of the northern and eastern states whose intermittent wars were soon resumed. Sweden achieved part of Gustav's original aim in Germany—Western Pomerania and some smaller territory on the Baltic, and the bishoprics of Bremen and Verden on the North Sea. France established absolute sovereignty over the long-disputed frontier towns of Metz, Toul, and Verdun, and a position in Alsace militarily strong, but so unpopular and legalistically so complicated as to ensure future wrangles. Breisach and Pinerolo were two other desirable fortresses returned to the French. But it was as a settlement of the internal affairs of Germany and the Habsburg Empire that Westphalia mattered, even though the conflicts it officially ended had exhausted themselves years before. The essential point, nowhere put in black and white, was that though the German states were still, in varying degrees, linked by the institutions and traditions of the Empire, the strongest of them could become completely sovereign units. The clause that came nearest to recording this was the one giving the German states control over their relations with each other and with foreign powers—provided that they did not ally against the Empire. There was room still for renewed conflict between state and Imperial power. In general the crimes and the acquisitions of territory since 1618 were obliterated; but in the vital question of the tenure of ecclesiastical lands, though there was no longer any question of reviving the Edict of Restitution, it was possible to bargain about the 'normal year' to which conditions should return. At the Peace of Prague 1627 had been more or less agreed; now it was 1624. Calvinist rulers were to have most of the rights granted in 1555 to Lutherans. There was even some protection for subjects who found themselves under a new sovereign of a different faith. But for any who persisted in rejecting the beliefs prescribed under the territorial settlement, the one concession was that they could flee from their homes and even take their goods with them. For the Bohemian Protestants there was no relief at all. Ambitions of the Churches to extend their dominion no longer interfered much with dynastic and diplomatic aims. The problem of the Palatinate was typical: Maximilian used all his bargaining power to keep the gains that had always cost him the hope of Protestant support, and Frederick's son Charles Louis had no friends among the European powers. The balance was eventually expressed by giving Charles Louis only the shattered Rhine Palatinate, though a new electoral seat was created for him. Maximilian kept the Upper Palatinate and its electorate. Brandenburg, in exchange for the lost Baltic lands, acquired Magdeburg and the Bishoprics of Halberstadt, Minden, and Kamin. Its title to East Pomerania was confirmed—though without the vital port of Stettin.

Germany and the Habsburgs after the War

Post-war Germany: Bavaria, Saxony, and Brandenburg

The history of Germany after 1648 tends to be chapter one of the 'Rise of Prussia'. Even if it is true that we should hear less of the Great Elector had he not been the forerunner of Frederick the Great and Bismarck, there is no doubt that a startlingly successful independent state was created out of material that would have been unpromising even without the war. Brandenburg at this stage seemed less likely to achieve prosperity for its people and its rulers than either Bavaria or Saxony. All three were states where a centralised professionally competent administration was closely linked with a landed nobility and a politically powerful army. The war had not diminished the status of landowners; and it had greatly increased that of military commanders. In Bavaria Maximilian had something of a rehabilitation policy, resettling the land that had gone out of cultivation, importing horses, rapidly disbanding the army. Under his son Ferdinand Maria an efficient absolutism was established on a conciliar system. The Elector evaded pressure to permit regular meetings of the Estates by co-operating with a small self-perpetuating committee of 'deputies' which granted taxes and petitioned for redress of grievances. The chancellor and council took a good deal of paternal interest in the economy, encouraging more productive agriculture, mining, and the export of finished cloth. Slowly, revenue from customs and state monopolies grew; and except in the war years not much of it was spent on a new, well-equipped army. In many areas peasant holdings flourished. Though the church was still enormously rich, the resistance of the nobility prevented it from extending its landholding.

The richest Protestant state was, or had been, Saxony; and John George was the only serious rival to Maximilian in political leadership of the Princes. Neither he nor his son and grandson of the same name could claim much success as monarchs. Perhaps if Saxony had eventually flourished in the diplomatic race their reigns would have appeared as the beginnings of German democracy, since this was the one major state in which representative institutions were able to use the financial difficulties of the Crown to strengthen their own position. To some extent the Electors paid the penalty of following dynastic ambitions: John George was more concerned to divide the material benefits of the territories acquired through his misdeeds in the war among his family than to establish a centralised administration. His successors got involved in the fatal game of becoming King of Poland. In 1697 Frederick Augustus I actually won the prize, at the cost of a conversion to Catholicism that kept alive the hostility of the nobility.[1] The contrast between Saxon failure and Brandenburg success in establishing energetic absolutist government is not easily explained. The Saxon Electors spent money on a standing army—but not as much as Brandenburg; Brandenburg turned the excise into a large independent source of funds—but the Saxons imitated the method. Saxony spent resources on Turkish war, Brandenburg on Baltic ones, both on French. It was just that from the point of view of the state Brandenburg governments did things better—which did not make it, for most people, a pleasanter place to live in.

The Great Elector

Brandenburg-Prussia was the most accidental of all the large units in Germany. In the early seventeenth century dynastic schemes had worked out well: John Sigismund inherited the Duchy of Prussia as a 'fief' of the Polish Crown, divided from the Electorate by West Pomerania, which was a part of Poland itself, and by East Pomerania which was seized by the Swedes before a Brandenburg claim to inherit it could be enforced. In the west the affair of the Duchies of Jülich and Cleves[2] was eventually settled by a division that gave Brandenburg an excellent

[1] See p. 361.   [2] See pp. 256, 259.

base for provocation and bargaining. At the wrangles in 1648, Brandenburg as a French client did undeservedly well. Schwarzenberg, the
brilliant minister of the Elector George William, had used the misfortunes of the war to establish a War Council, predominantly of commoners, as a professional ruling institution. He may well have had
ambitions to be one of the great military-political figures of the war.
When Frederick William succeeded at the age of twenty in 1640, he
was regarded as the enemy of Schwarzenberg and the bright hope of
the landowners, restoring the old Privy Council and negotiating cautiously with the separate Estates in each of his dominions.[1] It involved
dissolving Schwarzenberg's army and starting afresh with a force he
could hope would be loyal to the Elector alone.

The Great Elector's army of the 1640s was one of the lesser forces in
Germany.[2] and his political tergiversations were rapid even by the standards of those years. It was the resumption of war in the north from
1655 to 1660 that enabled Frederick William to establish his military
state. The use he made of his army was on the same lines as before: after
triumphantly entering Warsaw as the ally and military equal of Charles
X of Sweden, he accepted the efforts of Ferdinand III's diplomat Franz
von Lisola—a man with almost French standards of conspiratorial skill
—to get him to switch to the Polish side. There was no point in taking
his soldiers deeper into the east for the benefit of the Swedes. There
were not a mercenary force to be discarded when no longer useful but a
part of the machinery of the state. The General War Commissariat was
a body in which civil government was merged with the administration of
the army. Its officers were outside the hierarchies and patronages of the
separate dominions, and independent of the Estates. They established
themselves so successfully that the Commissariat was able to survive the
peace and become the ideal instrument of the Elector's rule. The war
had been financed at first as German wars had been in the 1640s—by
taking money from those who had it with only perfunctory regard to the
theoretical tax on property voted by the diets. To expand the army and
the central administration in peacetime would involve a permanent
source of revenue. The method that seemed most likely to produce it
was an excise of roughly the type on which the Netherlands government
appeared to flourish.

The long struggle with the Estates that centred round the question of
taxation produced what amounted to a tacit agreement between the
government and the landed nobility. The state would demand no

[1] See p. 210.   [2] See pp. 245-6.

sacrifices from them. It would uphold the extension of their power over the peasants and leave them almost sovereign rights over their lands. In return they would support the army and the civil authority without demanding political control. The men who now dominated the Estates of both Brandenburg and Prussia were the lesser nobility—the Jung-Herrn or Junkers—who had in many places begun to exploit their lands with great success through new agricultural techniques and investment of capital. Unfree labour and tax-exemption seemed to them necessary to their prosperity and to recovery from the wartime devastation that had completed the ruin of many of the towns.

The process in Brandenburg was absurdly tedious: collective privileges of the Diet still meant more to many representatives of towns and to the nobility than immediate economic benefit. The first effort in 1653 to introduce an excise failed completely. Through the years of war and after the peace in 1660 the government continued to put on all the pressure it could to get a permanent source of revenue. It had to do so by making use of the split between townsmen and nobility that arose originally from the fact that total taxation was supposed to be divided in a fixed proportion between the towns and the tenants of the tax-free nobles. A powerful group of the townsmen saw an excise as the only way of shifting some of the burden off themselves. The outcome of the quarrels was a gradual and complicated extension of the excise system, partly by royal decree. The towns soon had cause to regret the support they had given to it: every device that would have lightened their payments was stopped, and the split in the Estates had enabled the Elector almost to eliminate them as a political force.[1] Town and country became separated by a rigid system of customs barriers, and industries had every incentive to move outside the urban boundaries. The state's economic programme largely disregarded old-style urban power.

The nobility correspondingly benefited from the industries attracted to their territory. Fortunes were alleged to be made from the tax-free inns on their estates. Lucrative offices in the government were still their preserve. But above all the landowners, who had regarded the Elector's wars as no concern of theirs unless their own territory was affected, began to accept military service as a matter of social prestige. A unified landed class was coming to feel that its interests were permanently identified with those of the state. The Elector's well-known economic innovations—the trading companies, the artificially stimulated industries, the land improvements[2]—were intended to put Brandenburg on the

[1] See p. 211.   [2] See pp. 69–70.

level of the great powers. To extend serfdom and to welcome refugees from persecution were equally desirable parts of a way of statesmanship that drew no distinction between the well-being of the government and that of the landed class. It is easy to exaggerate the achievement, to stress the 'progress' or the 'Colbertism' in economic life and in 'unification' and forget the hostile and impoverished towns, the tolls and monopolies, the dismal rural poverty. If Frederick William rejoiced that his Prussian territories were now freed from their antiquated status as a 'fief' of Poland, he thought in similar terms himself when he repeatedly amended his elaborate wills to bequeath bits of his supposedly unified state as sovereign principalities for his younger sons. It was only his less celebrated successor Frederick who began to play the part of the Versailles-style monarch.

The Habsburg monarchy

The Peace of Westphalia had for the time being removed both the fears of Habsburg hegemony in the west and the danger that the Empire might be dismembered by predatory states inside and outside it. But it had not put an end to warfare in central Europe. For the next sixty-five years the Empire and the hereditary lands of the Habsburgs were as much as ever the centre of successive wars. The affairs of the Habsburg dynasty were prominent in every diplomatic conspiracy. The unhappy position of Austria as the last defence against Turkish invasion of Europe was more an opportunity for its enemies than a stimulus to its friends.

Leopold I never established himself as one of the epoch-making monarchs. His reign, from 1657 to 1705, is inescapably the 'age' of his cousin and brother-in-law Louis XIV. He was of course poorer than Louis. French bribes were a constant, if sometimes exaggerated, factor in the political difficulties of the Empire, while Habsburg money seldom got further afield than the Electors. The Imperial court at the Hofburg, on a restricted site in a Vienna that was not then regarded as one of the great cities of Europe, was a very inferior imitation of Versailles. Leopold himself—'a clock', said the French envoy Grémonville, 'always needing to be rewound'—was not among the industrious crowned bureaucrats. He hunted, like the rest of them, but he devoted more time to music and less to reading despatches. Nevertheless, he played the diplomatic game as well as his resources allowed. The more forceful rôle of Louis, the great quantity of French writing on the period, and the 'Gallomania' of the time make it easy to forget that in the end it was the Austrian Habsburgs who could show by far the greatest gains of European territory.

Leopold succeeded automatically to the hereditary Austrian dominions of his father Ferdinand III. The nominally elective crowns of Royal Hungary and of Bohemia were his without question. But the Empire was a different matter. Though the possibility of a non-Habsburg emperor was remote, it was just conceivable enough for the Electors, under French influence, to extract unusually onerous conditions (as well as bribes) for accepting Leopold. He was not to support Spain in the still unfinished war against France, and in a variety of ways was to uphold local rulers against their Estates. He also had to accept the existence of the French-sponsored 'League of the Rhine'. It lasted only ten years; it included—even when the Elector of Brandenburg eventually joined it—only a minority of princes; it became more and more openly an instrument of French penetration. But it was also in a small way part of the unhappy story of attempts to create, within a political system based on conflict between states, an organisation designed to keep some sort of order. The Elector of Mainz, Philip von Schönborn, who was its leading German advocate, gave it a permanent headquarters in Frankfurt, an army that was intended to become as large as those of the great powers, and links with Sweden as well as France—in the hope that they would somehow counterbalance each other. To Leopold its purpose seemed beyond question: it was one more alliance between the princes and his foreign enemies.

It was indeed from Sweden rather than France that the first dangers for Leopold came, The ambitions of Charles X were at least as great as those of Gustav Adolf. He was thought to be interested in the prospects of a new revolt in Bohemia that would enable him to win its Crown; he made alliances with the Great Elector and with George Rákóczy II; with their help he carried out the invasions of Poland that seemed about to produce its total disintegration.[1] The next stage might be a vast Swedish-controlled Protestant league, if not an actual Swedish Empire, threatening the Habsburgs from the north and east. Austrian forces showed themselves capable of winning battles not only in Poland but as far away as the Baltic; and Austrian diplomats formed their own circle of supporters in Warsaw; but neither played a very distinguished part in the pacification of the north that was ratified at the Peace of Oliva in 1660. The two great sources of alarm for the emperor were the influence of the French in nearly all the neighbouring states, and the

[1] See p. 354.

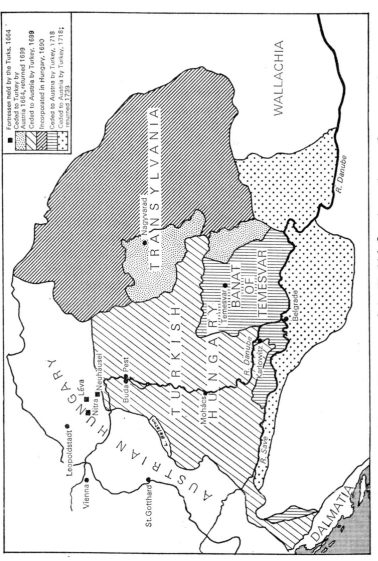

Map 4. Hungary and the Turkish frontiers, 1600–1718

Fortresses held by the Turks, 1664
Ceded to Turkey by
Austria 1664, returned 1699
Ceded to Austria by Turkey, 1699
Incorporated in Hungary, 1690
Ceded to Austria by Turkey, 1718
Ceded to Austria by Turkey, 1718;
returned 1739

WALLACHIA

R. Danube

TRANSYLVANIA

Nagyvarad

BANAT
OF
TEMESVAR

Temesvar

Belgrade

TURKISH

HUNGARY

Mohács

R. Danube

Karlowitz

R. Save

Leopoldstadt

HUNGARY

AUSTRIAN

Léva

Nitra

Neuhäusel

Buda

Pest

Vienna

St. Gotthard

R. Leitha

DALMATIA

appearance as the decisive power in Transylvania and Poland of a revived Ottoman Empire. Repeatedly from this time onward a choice had to be made between the eastern and the western concerns; but except in the most dangerous periods of Turkish attack it was the west that determined Leopold's actions.

For many years Turkish incursions into Royal Hungary had been frequent; and from 1658 George Rákóczy was struggling to hold on to his Transylvanian throne. In 1661, after Rákóczy had been killed in battle, Leopold at last sent an army under his successful general Raimondo Montecuccoli against the invaders. It was too late to save Transylvania from complete Turkish control. In the spring of 1663 the huge forces of Ahmed Kiuprili[1] began to move rapidly towards Vienna. Imperial envoys were sent round the capitals of Europe to plead for help. For a moment the almost inconceivable happened: Louis XIV, Philip IV, the Pope, the Great Elector, and a variety of other German rulers—including those in the League of the Rhine—united in sending men or money or both in the cause of Christianity. Louis XIV, though he gave up the idea of leading the enterprise, sent 6,000 of his best soldiers. In 1664 their victory at St Gotthard, fifty miles from Vienna, ended the immediate danger. Crusading enthusiasm disappeared when the Emperor hastened to make the Peace of Vasvar. By this Transylvania, under Turkish suzerainty, was demilitarised and the Turks kept the vital fortresses on which Imperial defences had previously relied. Hungary was to remain divided between Austrian and Turkish rulers.

The Hungarian nobles who rebelled against their Imperial overlords[2] believed, with some reason, that Leopold had abandoned the war partly because he preferred a divided Hungary to a free and united one, partly because Philip IV of Spain was dying and the succession question already made western diplomacy more important to him than security in the east. Feeble though the revolt was, it provided the occasion for a policy of treating the Hungarians as the Czechs had been treated after 1620. An army of occupation was permanently quartered on the country; confiscated estates went largely to Germans; toleration of Protestant Churches which even Ferdinand II had maintained in some areas, came to an end and many Protestant clergy were expelled. Jesuits were encouraged to extend their familiar process of Catholic education. Administration was increasingly in German hands; and though the ruling council, the *gubernium*, consisted half of Hungarians, it was little

[1] See p. 372.   [2] See p. 232.

more than an instrument of the effective ruler, Johann Ampringen. After ten years of intermittent Hungarian resistance, and in face of the renewed Turkish threat, Leopold in 1681 conceded a good deal. The elected Estates were summoned to meet and a new constitution gave extensive powers to the Hungarian nobility. Some of the liberties of Protestants were restored. Most Hungarians still had no reason to think that the Habsburgs were preferable to the Turks.

The Empire, the west, and the Turks

A constant difficulty for Leopold was the presence in Vienna of foreign diplomats who cultivated their own parties at his court. Louis XIV aimed simultaneously at having a reliable group of client states within the Empire, encouraging the dissension in Hungary, and yet keeping whenever possible the alliance of the Emperor himself. Wenzel Lobkowitz, the Czech prince who was Leopold's principal minister, notoriously supported alliance with France. In 1668 it seemed to be abundantly justified when a very secret agreement with France promised that the possessions of Charles II of Spain would, on his apparently imminent death, be shared between Leopold and Louis.[1] All the treaty in fact brought was constant anxiety that it would be discovered and would wreck the other side of Imperial policy—the precautions against French attacks. Louis' invasion of the Netherlands produced a complete change. From 1672 until the peace of Nymegen in 1678, most of Leopold's resources were devoted to war against France. The Dutch and the Protestant Electors were now Leopold's allies; Lobkowitz and the Francophil party were overthrown. The Spanish and Dutch envoys to Vienna became unlikely allies in building up hostility to France as a permanent Imperial policy.

In 1683 the Turks launched their new attack on the Empire. Until the last possible moment Leopold still regarded the territorial schemes of Louis XIV as more important than the threat to Vienna. He made a truce with Thököli's forces in Hungary and tried unsuccessfully to hold off the Turks by renewing the Treaty of Vasvar which expired in 1682.[2] But it was only when the great invading armies were on their way that he completed the alliance with John Sobiesky of Poland,[3] the one monarch to whom the defence of Christendom against the Turks was a central purpose. For three months Vienna was besieged while the armies of Poland, the Empire, Saxony, and Bavaria came together under Sobiesky's command. In September, thanks largely to the superiority of Polish

[1] See pp. 356–7, 434.   [2] See p. 373.   [3] See p. 360.

cavalry and artillery, the besiegers were put to precipitate flight. Only when the worst danger was over did Innocent XI manage to form his 'Holy League'. The only power he was able to bring into formal alliance with Poland and the Empire was Venice. But the propaganda of the church did not depend on convincing the diplomats. Its own financial resources were poured into the crusade. From all over Europe money and volunteers were contributed. In 1686 Russia joined the League. Only France, England, and the Netherlands firmly resisted the appeals. The League could soon claim that it had ended once and for all the threat of the infidel in central Europe. Leopold's response to the liberation of Hungary from Ottoman power was to re-establish his own authority. In 1687, when the allied armies had recaptured Buda and again heavily defeated the Turks at Nagyharsány, near Mohacs, the Hungarian Estates were made to declare that the throne was now hereditary (Sobiesky was suspected of having an eye on it) and that the medieval notion of a right of resistance to kings who did not observe the liberties of the nobility was repudiated.

Leopold and the Spanish Succession

As it turned out the Turks had not been so decisively crushed that Leopold could concentrate without interruption on the west. In 1690 they recaptured Belgrade, and for the next nine years the Emperor had to keep up his military strength in the Danube region. Frederick Augustus of Saxony, and then Prince Eugene of Savoy, were commanders willing to take charge of the Imperial forces. But in Vienna the two aims of diminishing French power and bringing Spain and its possessions under the Austrian Habsburgs were now all-important. On the whole they were pursued with more energy than skill. By failing to appreciate the power and interests of the Dutch and English enemies of Louis, and by putting forward claims to the whole Spanish inheritance, the Emperor constantly overplayed his hand.

Immediately after the 'twenty-year truce' signed at Regensburg in 1684—which no-one expected to last very long—Leopold's schemes were changed by the birth of his second son, significantly named Charles. Since he would not inherit the Empire, it seemed feasible to make him the candidate for the Spanish succession. To him, it was proclaimed in Vienna, were transferred the rights claimed under the will of Philip IV by Leopold's daughter Maria Antonia, wife of the Elector of Bavaria. In Madrid the efforts to establish an 'Austrian' party to uphold such a view were badly bungled: the official Spanish theory was that Maria Antonia's claim could not be transferred in this way, but passed to the son, Joseph Ferdinand, who was born to her in 1692. Leopold had to combat both this Bavarian pretension and the insistence of Louis XIV (who like Leopold was Philip III's grandson) that the renunciation by his wife Maria Theresa was invalid and that the rightful heir was now her son Louis.[1]

Through all the years of tedious dynastic wrangling, Leopold was building up the Imperial armies and making himself as far as possible the leader of the anti-French coalitions. At Ryswick in 1697 he had the satisfaction of a peace treaty that registered the complete failure of the French to make any serious impact on Imperial defences. But his object was still the whole Spanish inheritance. To all the Protestant powers it seemed as necessary to prevent this new Habsburg menace as it was to thwart Louis XIV's dreams of abolishing the Pyrenees by putting the Bourbon candidate on the Spanish throne. Louis proved more realistic in his greed than Leopold. The Partition Treaty of 1698 between France, Holland, and England would have given Spain, the Spanish Netherlands, and the West Indies to the Bavarian Joseph Ferdinand. Only Sicily and Naples would go to the Dauphin. Leopold's son the Archduke Charles would have Milan. Leopold refused to agree. So did Charles II, who in an attempt to avoid any division of his Empire made the will that left the whole of his possessions to Joseph Ferdinand. All the schemes came to nothing, since Joseph Ferdinand died immediately afterwards. A second partition had to be hastily devised, by which the Archduke Charles was to have the enormous share previously intended for the Bavarian. Incredibly, Leopold refused again. As it turned out, it was not his decision that made certain the arguments would be settled by a major war. When Charles II by a second will left everything to Louis XIV's younger grandson Philip, the prospects of an agreed share-out quickly disappeared.[2] In 1701, a year before the declaration of war, Imperial troops under Prince Eugene of Savoy made a successful attack on the French in northern Italy. But this was not to be a war of limited frontier conflicts. By 1703 Leopold was facing the threat of an attack on Vienna that might well have changed the whole character of the Empire. Francis Rákóczy in Hungary led a revolt almost as menacing as the attacks of the Turks twenty years earlier, at a moment when the French seemed to have opened the way to the capital. It was not until 1711 that Hungarian resistance ended in a negotiated settle-

[1] See pp. 446–7 and the table on pp. 466–7.
[2] For the events of the war see pp. 448–50.

ment, with further promises of constitutional liberties. The new Emperor Charles VI was crowned King of Hungary.

The Holy Roman Empire

The Emperor and his ministers still faced a choice between eastern and western interests. But there was a significant difference in the resources they could draw upon. Though German states came fairly readily to the Emperor's help against the Turks, the affairs of Hungary and Bohemia affected the German Empire only indirectly. In the west the wars demonstrated, increasingly, that despite all the forces of disintegration the Empire was still a working political unit. From 1633 the Imperial Diet at Regensburg was deemed to be in permanent session. Its long and trivial deliberations made it a laughing-stock in Europe. Nevertheless its support mattered a great deal to the Emperor. Of its three houses the first consisted of the seven Electors. (The Emperor as Elector of Bohemia was in theory an eighth, and in 1692 Leopold on his own authority created the Electorate of Hanover as a ninth.) In the second house, ecclesiastical and temporal 'princes' exercised a hundred votes, a few being those of minor prelates and counts grouped together. The third, with very restricted powers, represented the Free Cities. The diet voted money to the Emperor, and provided armed forces; but it claimed no right to enforce its decisions on any state that dissented from them. Yet despite its inefficiency and its devotion to the particularist interests of its members, it did provide men and money for Imperial wars, in increasing amounts. In 1681 it was laid down that an army of 60,000 should be raised. For the Spanish Succession War the number was increased to 120,000. A separate treasury for war expenses was established, though the diet had little control over it. The situation was complicated further by the existence of the ten 'Circles' that were supposed to form administrative units of the Empire. In theory contributions towards the wars were shared out among all the Circles; in practice the Upper and Lower Saxon Circles— the former including Brandenburg—and the Austrian Circle no longer functioned much; it was from the western Circles, and the Bavarian one, that the effective Imperial forces raised through the diet came.

At Leopold's accession there was a chaotic mixture of governing institutions in Vienna. Round them there continued the struggle for power between the Emperor and the German states which Westphalia had left unresolved. The *Reichshofrat* (usually translated as 'Aulic Council') combined in its name the terms *Reich*, which was coming to mean the Empire as distinct from Habsburg authority, and *Hof* meaning the court. The princes claimed that this body, where disputes about powers and privileges within the Empire were supposed to be settled, should be more under their control than the Emperor's. (The rival institution, the *Reichskammergericht*, which had been more closely controlled by the diet, had declined through sheer inefficiency.) The princes were also anxious to exclude from the affairs of the Empire bodies which were concerned with the Habsburg lands outside it and which had Czechs, Hungarians, and Italians in prominent positions. Many of them held that the main governing institution, the *Geheimer Rat* (Privy Council), was one of these. It had become large and cumbersome, allowing many of its powers to be taken over by small committees. Leopold's first effective reform was to make one of these, the 'Privy Conference' of four members, into an almost independent ministry. But after the fall of Lobkowitz its numbers grew and its authority declined, until this in turn began to split up into smaller informal committees. There was conflict too between the two administrative bodies, the Imperial Chancery (*Reichskanzlerei*) and the Chancery of the Habsburg lands (*Hofkanzlerei*). Leopold completed the process begun under Ferdinand III by which the power of the Habsburg body rose at the expense of the Imperial one. The *Hofkriegsrat*, the Court War Council, was also a body dominated by men from the Emperor's non-German lands. The *Hofkammer*, the Court Chamber, was not only the Emperor's central treasury but something of a ministry of commerce too. Both, under Leopold, extended their power and functions. But the Emperor who devoted so much energy to the dim hope of adding the Spanish Empire to his own never solved the problems of his existing dual function.

Before 1618 the Empire and the Austrian hereditary lands contained no unified centralised state. A century later the long era was beginning when Austria and Prussia seemed, to European diplomats, comparable and rival powers each with lesser states in its orbit. It had been a century of almost incessant warfare. The far-ranging armies of the Thirty Years War, the more concentrated sieges and frontier battles in the wars of Louis XIV, the sweeping invasions of the Turks, and the sporadic fighting against the northern powers had been by far the greatest influence on political development. Some sources of conflict disappeared: in the eighteenth century neither the Turks nor religious divisions mattered much. There were new sources to replace them. In 1700 the Elector Frederick of Brandenburg sold his support to Leopold for the price of becoming King Frederick of Prussia—a kingdom geographically disunited and devoted more than ever to the interests of its army. Leopold's son Charles, despite his gains at Utrecht, had no reason to feel that Imperial territories, or his family's hold on them, were more secure. It would be hard to say whether the subjects of the two monarchs came off better or worse from the activities of the state than those of Electors, bishops, or towns.

XIV

The Spanish Empire

Spain under Philip III

In 1598 Philip III succeeded to the throne of Spain, the country that dominated Europe by its military strength, its wealth, and its diplomatic power. Yet its army and navy were outmoded and had repeatedly been defeated, its treasury was empty, its economic life stagnant, its government corrupt, incompetent, and insecure. The paradox was scarcely noticed. It seemed that a long reign of triumphant strife could well be followed by one of stability, and—for those at the top—of

BIBLIOGRAPHY. Though good modern work on Spain and its empire is scarce, especially in the fields of administration and provincial politics, the position for English readers has been greatly improved by the work of J. H. Elliott. His general survey, *Imperial Spain 1469–1716* (London, 1963) is a condensed but readable account, with bibliographies that reveal the gaps frankly. His detailed study of one of the rebellions, *The Revolt of the Catalans* (Cambridge, 1963) also deals with many wider questions. Some of its points appear more briefly in his article (in English) in *Estudias de Historia Moderna*, no. IV (Barcelona, 1954). J. Lynch, *Spain under the Habsburgs*, vol. II (Oxford, 1969), appeared after this chapter was written. On economic questions, the two books by E. J. Hamilton, *American Treasure and the Price Revolution in Spain, 1501–1650* (Cambridge, Mass., 1934) and *War and Prices in Spain, 1651–1800* are still the starting-point of debates on the causes of decline. His main conclusions on this period appear in the article, 'The Decline of Spain', in *Economic History Review*, 1st ser., vol. VIII (1938), reprinted in *Essays in Economic History*, ed. E. M. Carus-Wilson, vol. I (London, 1954). An outstanding modern Spanish historian is J. Vincent Vives whose *Historia Económica de España* (Barcelona, 1959) has some detailed demographic calculations. Henry Kamen, *The Spanish Inquisition* (London, 1965) replaces, for many purposes, H. C. Lea, *A History of the Inquisition in Spain* (4 vols., New York, 1906–7).

Biographies include G. Marañón, *El Conde-Duque de Olivares* (Madrid, 1936, 3rd ed. 1952) and J. Nada, *Carlos the Bewitched* (London, 1962). On foreign affairs A. van der Essen, *Le Cardinal-Enfant et la politique européenne de l'Espagne* (Louvain, 1944) and A. Lemar, *Richelieu et Olivares* (Lille, 1938) are useful;

luxury. The stern old bureaucrat-king whose personal decisions had settled everything was replaced by a young sovereign with little capacity or inclination for work. Philip III's interest turned in time from the luxury of the court to priests and miracle-working relics: at either stage the way was open for the rule of a minister, and it was on the behaviour of ministers that the country's political fate depended.

The first of them, the Duke of Lerma, was one of the aristocratic politicians whose success did not extend much beyond amassing power for himself and his dependants. This involved the familiar encouragement of central institutions at the expense of provincial ones. The King's Council was now a large and subdivided body with both legal and administrative functions, and Lerma began to make use of the small ministerial *Juntas* as the effective ruling bodies. But the state was largely a means of maintaining the court, and of distributing wealth among the place-holders and bribe-takers who spent it on competitive splendour. Lerma's personal fortune was nearly twice the annual revenue of the state. After Philip II's successive repudiations of the Crown's debts, no-one could now suppose that silver and gold imports (which in any case had only produced a quarter of the revenue) were an inexhaustible source of funds. Taxes, particularly the '*alcabala*', the 10 per cent sales-tax, were largely absorbed in tax-farming and corruption. The *millones*, levies on wines and some other goods, were administered more effectively by a central commission, but were evaded by the nobility. The Spanish Crown gave an unhappy lead to the rest of Europe in living by selling things—offices, privileges, and its own lands. Between a peasantry kept down to subsistence level and the great consumers of riches there was hardly any commercial or industrial class making use of the opportunities for profit and investment that the colonial Empire provided.

C. H. Carter, *The Secret Diplomacy of the Habsburgs 1598–1625* (New York, 1964) and B. Chudoba, *Spain and the Empire* (Chicago, 1952) show the methods and extent of Spanish influence on other governments. Among older works still relevant are Martin Hume, *The Court of Philip IV* (London, 1907) and R. Altamira y Crevea, *Historia de España y de la Civilización española* (6 vols., Barcelona, 1900–30), of which there is an English abridgement by C. E. Chapman (New York, 1937).

Material on the other Spanish possessions is not easy to find, except what is included in such wider summaries as L. Salvatorelli, *A Concise History of Italy* (New York, 1940) and H. V. Livermore, *A History of Portugal* (Cambridge, 1947). An article by C. M. Cipolla, 'The Decline of Italy' in *Economic History Review*, 2nd ser., vol. 5 (1952) deals with the collapse of industry. A later version of this is among the essays in *Crisis and Change in the Venetian Economy*, ed. Brian Pullan (London, 1968).

Lerma's most startling action was to expel the people who were the main exception to this. The Moriscoes, Christians of mixed or Moorish descent, had long been accused of secretly adhering to the Moslem faith, avoiding taxation—largely by not drinking—helping the Barbary pirates, and of being too prosperous. They were not allowed to own land, though they often held it on long leases, and by good technique and labour, made it profitable to both landlord and lessee. They were excluded from office, and therefore had an incentive to commercial activity. In 1609 there began the series of decrees that expelled them first from Valencia, where they formed an organised community amounting to perhaps a third of the population, and then from their more scattered centres elsewhere. Most of the quarter of a million who left probably died in North Africa from poverty and persecution. It was a spectacular blunder that may get more than its due share of the blame for the long-term decline;[1] but in Valencia at least the loss of labour and rents was an immediate disaster. The expulsion of the Moriscoes brought almost to perfection the one great source of Spanish unity—the relentless grip of the Church on every activity, individual or communal. The Inquisition now had few serious doctrinal errors to punish: it spent much of its time on eliminating rural witchcraft and illicit contacts with foreign culture such as the import of books. It became not so much a religious body as a political police, imposing in its own courts a totalitarianism as efficient as any Europe has known. The clergy, even though many were poor, were a privileged Estate extracting even more of the country's resources than the court. With the occupants of an enormous number of monasteries and nunneries added to the parish priests, they formed the only occupational group that was thriving and expanding.[2] Education and charity were their monopolies; popular anti-clericalism seemed scarcely to exist. There was much to be said for the life the religious orders could offer to the individual compared with his prospects anywhere outside them, but little for their effect on the economy of the state. They may even have been an appreciable factor in the decline of population.

[1] The weakness of the theory that the expulsion was a major cause of economic disaster is discussed by E. J. Hamilton in *Essays in Economic History*, ed. Carus-Wilson, vol. 1, p. 218.

[2] The Castilian Cortes of 1626 was told that there were 9,000 monastic institutions for men. For this and other estimates see Elliott, *Imperial Spain*, p. 307 and Trevor Davies, *The Golden Century of Spain*, p. 289.

The reforms of Olivares

The one mitigation of the evils of royal courts was that a brilliant politician could usually make his way to the top if he tried. Incompetent favourites tended eventually to be overthrown by competent ones. While Philip III, desperately ill, was calling for the corpses of saints to diminish his prospects of eternal damnation, a palace conspiracy replaced Lerma in 1618 by his son the Duke of Uceda. The immediate difference was imperceptible; but in Uceda's gang was Gaspard de Guzman, Count of Olivares and Duke of Sanlúcar, the ambitious son of one of Philip II's former Viceroys. When the king died in 1621, his sixteen-year-old son Philip IV was firmly under the control of the clever and hard-working statesman who was the real successor of Philip II. The 'Count-Duke' combined with his lust for power a manic-depressive instability of temperament; but he supervised the new monarch constantly, accompanying him throughout his days of work and ceremony and his nights of varied entertainment. The Lerma family and its hangers-on were imprisoned, fined, or exiled. Olivares at once became the hope of the *arbitristas*, the theorisers who for decades had demanded radical reform of court and aristocratic society. Such writers as Gonzáles de Cellorigo were well aware that Spain, and Castile especially, could only be saved from disaster by increasing its agriculture, industry, and commerce and by abandoning the habit, individual and collective, of trying to live at someone else's expense. Olivares was all in favour of enterprise and productive activity, but not of diminishing Spain's imperial glory.

Cautiously, he began to erode the worst of the privileges that made the idleness and pride of Spaniards proverbial. The church was made to pay a bigger share of taxation; its acquisition of land was restricted. The Inquisition felt that its political power was being undermined, and became a dangerous enemy of Olivares. He made no secret of his intention to curtail drastically court extravagance, the multiplication of offices, the whole corrupt and parasitic idleness of the aristocracy. The one celebrated success in his sumptuary laws was in banning the ruff, the ludicrously expensive status-symbol of its day. (An acceptable substitute was produced from cardboard, said to last for a year without washing.) To take away the uniform of a social group does much to destroy its exclusiveness, and the action was at least a symbol that the great days of the grandees were ending. But of the numerous other reforms produced with the help of the long-established *Junta de*

Reformacion, most were soon evaded. A miscellany of royal decrees reduced the numbers of office-holders, restricted their retinues, investigated their more flagrant forms of enrichment, and sent a good many back to their estates. There could not of course be an open attack on the privileges of nobility as such. Perhaps a fifth of the population was included in the well-demarcated ranks that ranged from their Excellencies the Grandees of the court to the provincial hidalgos, and the sale of honours was constantly increasing their number. Yet gradually, and without diminishing the demand for titles, Olivares was able to evade the aristocracy's exemption from taxation. The Cortes of Castile successfully opposed his schemes for a national and a complete reform of the fiscal system that would have replaced the *millones* by new direct taxes. Some of his measures hit the few native merchants so hard that they were blamed for the final collapse of the commercial activities he claimed to be encouraging. Long-term projects, ranging from the improvement of communications to restricting the teaching of Latin in order to limit the number of unproductive careers, had little serious effect. His economic achievement was not to increase the total wealth but to allow more of it to be wasted by the state and less by the individual.

If the country could not be saved from poverty, it might at least be better governed. Olivares' political ideas, set out in his memorandum to the king in 1624, amounted to a practical instead of a bogus centralisation. Though the 'liberties' of other provinces would have to be curtailed and uniform laws imposed, the programme was not to be merely 'Castilianisation'. The whole country must share the benefits of strong government as well as the obligations. Offices should be open more freely to non-Castilians. Intermarriage between families from different provinces should be encouraged. Philip should become more effectively the King of all Spain and of its possessions, with a residence in each part of the peninsula; and in his absence viceroys should be his personal servants unconnected with the region they governed. An essential part of the reform would be the 'Union of Arms': all the King's dominions, including even the Indies, were to contribute to a reserve army, part of which would be immediately available for whatever region was attacked. The most effective reform was the further reduction in the powers of the old councils, efficient instruments of administration under Philip II, but now increasingly in the hands of nobles and hidalgos who bought their places. The Council of State itself lost most of its real powers to the *Junta de Ejecucion*, drawn from the highest court nobility, and for every new administrative task a special Junta was set up, directly responsible to Olivares. These reforms too had only limited success. Few of the men at the top took kindly to the imposition of virtuous ways; Olivares' own group of dependants, though less vicious than Lerma's, became as ridden with patronage and favouritism; the Cortes of Aragon, Catalonia, and Valencia were roused to the defence of their privileges. But as usual the final obstacle to good government was foreign war.

Spain in Europe

The 'Spain' seen by foreign peoples and rulers was not the 'Spain' seen by a Castilian courtier or an Andalusian peasant. Internal poverty was in part the price of external success, and there was no apparent decline in the amount Spanish governments could spend on foreign enterprises. The servants of the Spanish crown outside the peninsula worked in a very different tradition from that of the Madrid court: their reward was the power they built in the country or province allotted to them, and it was this service that attracted most of the gifted politicians. Sometimes European politics still seemed to be managed by the viceroys and ambassadors of Spain. Gondomar in England, Zúñiga and Oñate, successive ambassadors to the emperor in Prague, Bedmar, ambassador in Venice, and Feria, Governor of Milan, were men at the summit of international politics. Spinola and Toledo were among the most respected experts on war. It was not for them to consider very deeply what cause they were serving. In Philip III's view it was more that of the dynasty than of the nation—the scoring of points for the Habsburg side against its enemies. Those who wished could easily equate this with furthering the triumph of the Catholic faith. Neither Philip nor Lerma wanted to assert Spanish power at the cost of further involvement in European war. They were ready enough to abandon the struggle in the Netherlands as soon as it could be done without excessive humiliation. But they lacked both the ability and the effort that would have been needed to maintain a pacific policy within a diplomatic system whose purpose was to win allies for war. Spaniards abroad were preparing for a new age of military glory.

For the time being their schemes had to be developed slowly in face of strong resistance and suspicion. Though the Stuart régime appeared to have ended the Elizabethan tradition of Protestant war, Gondomar never quite succeeded in establishing the secure dominance of a 'Spanish Party' in James I's government. At the French court Spain could encourage and organise opposition to Henry IV; but French pressure during the negotiations for the Netherlands truce made its terms more favourable to the Dutch. Discussions about a marriage alliance between France and Spain were broken off, and only the death of Henry IV in 1610 averted a war. The regency that followed was much more amenable to Spanish influence: in 1612 the double marriage between the children of the two royal houses was agreed.[1] The defensive alliance that accompanied the marriage agreement provided for mutual help against rebels as well as foreign enemies. It was naturally in Prague, for the time being the effective capital of the Empire, that Spanish power was most firmly established. Zúñiga was deeply involved in the formation of the Catholic League. In his view it was to be no mere alliance of German states but the core of a great European system to which the Pope, the Emperor, and the Spanish King would contribute in their different ways. His successor Oñate took the decisive step of offering Spanish support to Ferdinand of Styria as a candidate for the Imperial throne.[2] On Ferdinand's accession, Oñate became his principal adviser, and in alliance with the Emperor's Jesuit confessor filled him with the notion of triumphant war for the Church and the Habsburgs. Philip III was not so sure of its benefits.

The Southern Netherlands

In 1621 the new King and the new minister found themselves committed to a more aggressive policy without having planned it, but equally without any desire to resume what seemed the discredited inactivity of Philip III. The Bohemian revolt had added to the difficulty of renewing the Netherlands truce that expired at the moment of Philip's death. The Orange party in the north was eager to take part in the Protestant war; the Portuguese had long been pressing for revenge on the Dutch for their unscrupulous commercial expansion and piracy during the truce; the large armies maintained in the Southern Netherlands had, not surprisingly, cost almost as much in peace as in war. Spinola was convinced that success in a new war would depend even more than before on the transport of men and money from northern Italy. The route that began in the Valtelline included the fifty miles of the Rhine controlled by the Elector Palatine; and it was a stroke of luck that Frederick involved himself in war with the Emperor. Spain could now invade the Palatinate and contribute to the Imperial cause without sending troops outside her immediate sphere of interest. Their success would still depend heavily on the resources of the Southern Netherlands. There the Archduke

[1] See p. 259. [2] See p. 283.

Albert and his wife Isabella, sister of Philip III, were nominally independent sovereigns of the Netherlands. When Albert died in 1621, Isabella remained as regent, but was expected to be no more than a viceroy of the Spanish King. By Spain's low standards, the Netherlands were well governed. Because of the obvious dangers in provoking a new rebellion the burden of taxation was not outrageous, and the administration became what Pirenne was to call a 'modified absolutism'. The principal offices were held by Spaniards and important matters were referred to a committee in Madrid which usually failed to settle them; but on minor questions a good deal of autonomy was allowed. Under Albert the Spaniards held the support of the rural gentry and nobility, good Catholics and enemies of the suspect townsmen, contented with rising rents and reliable markets. Olivares was as anxious to reduce the powers of the Netherlands Council and of Isabella as he was those of the provinces of the peninsula itself. Between 1629 and 1632 hostility to Spain became widespread: losses caused by the renewed war, and the beginnings of tighter Spanish control, led to attempts at rebellion by groups of nobles with some popular support. They were prevented from growing into a national rising largely by the initiative of Isabella, who ignored instructions from Madrid and summoned a States-General, where arguments and petitions gave time for the revolt to fade away.

Spain against France

At this stage Spanish forces were at least holding their own. Funds had been provided, largely by the minting of twenty million ducats in *vellón*—which now meant pure copper—for a great increase in the armies and the navy. Spinola's capture of Breda in 1625, after nearly a year's siege, and the defeat of a Dutch fleet off Gibraltar in 1626 suggested that Spain was far from collapse. Amid a tangle of diplomatic bickerings with the emperor and Maximilian of Bavaria, Spanish forces remained in occupation of a large part of the Palatinate, and English support for the Protestant cause there ended with a ludicrous attempt to attack Cadiz. Yet there remained a world of difference between the real Spain, staving off a financial and administrative collapse, and the Spain envisaged by Richelieu as a menace to the rest of Europe. Olivares had even better reason than Richelieu to avoid a major war; but neither could back out of the local territorial conflicts. The more dependent the Madrid government became on the money and troops it could raise outside the peninsula, the greater the need to prevent French encroachment on the fortresses and the lines of communication. The episodes of the Valtelline in 1621 and Mantua in 1628 developed without any firm plan either for limiting or for extending them.[1] Spinola from the Netherlands and Córdoba, the Governor of Milan, were left to their own devices in a dreary and unsuccessful campaign that could easily be used as evidence of continued Spanish aggressive designs. By the time the Treaty of Cherasco in 1631 registered the Spanish defeat, both sides were acting on the assumption that a major war was the inevitable next stage. More money had to be found for the forces in Italy; the Empire had to be supported in its worst years of danger from Protestant attack; the struggle in the Netherlands had to go on. It meant making the non-Castilian provinces contribute more than ever before to the cost of wars that seemed to bring them only misery.

In 1634 a new saviour of the Spanish Netherlands was found—Philip IV's brother Ferdinand, the Cardinal-Infant whose influence Olivares was glad to remove from Madrid. It was his army, on its way north, that won the victory at Nordlingen which made possible the restoration of Habsburg control in southern Germany.[2] But the success had disastrous consequences. It confirmed Richelieu's decision that he would soon have to intervene openly in the war; and that the forces of Spain were a greater threat than those of the emperor.[3] He did not plan to attack Spain itself, which might induce the Catalans at least to contribute more readily to the cost of the war, and would be a bad risk with no-one to share it. He preferred to attack the whole strategic line from Italy to the Netherlands. In the first years of the war Spain on balance did well. Rohan in 1635 drove Spanish forces out of the Valtelline, but only at the cost of so alienating the Grey Leagues that eventually they defeated the army of occupation and agreed to give Spain access to the valley in return for guarantees of religious liberty. In the north the Cardinal-Infant, with German reinforcements, occupied territory as far west as the Somme, and made Paris itself expect a siege. But gradually the slightly greater efficiency of Richelieu's France in the organisation of war had its effect. The vital fortresses of Breda, on the Netherlands dividing-line, and Breisach, on the upper Rhine, were lost, and the fleet was all but destroyed by Tromp. By 1639 both the land and the sea-routes to the Netherlands were cut. Once Spanish support seemed to be useless, the Emperor abandoned dynastic solidarity and concentrated on saving his own power in Germany, leaving Olivares to think bitterly of the Spanish funds that had paid Imperial soldiers. The project for an invasion of France from Catalonia, which Olivares hoped

---

[1] See pp. 270–1.   [2] See p. 298.   [3] See p. 272.

would arouse some enthusiasm for the war, led only to the loss of the Spanish frontier fortress of Salses, and the siege that followed increased rather than diminished Catalan hostility to Madrid. 'God', wrote Olivares to the King, 'wants us to make peace; for he is depriving us of all the means of war.'[1]

It was in this condition that the government in Madrid faced those consequences of defeat which Olivares had long feared. The greater the burden imposed on the outlying dependencies of Castile, the nearer the moment came when they would attempt to go the way of the northern Netherlands. The message instilled at every possible point by Richelieu's collaborators was becoming undeniable: Madrid squeezed the provinces dry for a war that was no concern of theirs, failed to defend them against external enemies, held them in poverty while the life of luxury at the court continued. The question was whether and where the inescapable movements of rebellion would turn into revolutions capable of breaking up the Spanish monarchy entirely. Olivares would not let this happen without a heroic struggle.

Revolt in Catalonia

The story of the revolts reveals as much about the behaviour of governments as of subjects. Philip IV might well have been left as King of Castile—a succession that would have been hardly worth fighting for. But only the full collaboration of the French could have brought the rebels such a success; and though statesmen readily fomented discontent against each other as a normal part of the competition, when it came to actual support and exploitation of popular rebellion, they were fumbling and cautious. At the end of it all, Portugal was the only major possession lost.

The rising in Catalonia contained almost all the familiar ingredients of rebellions. Partly it was an agrarian revolt touched off by the latest additions to the oppression of the peasants; partly it arose from the resistance of men of property who wanted not separation from Spain but a larger share in the power and profits of office. There was an element of national sentiment and one of religious fervour; and in the end the resistance was both used and destroyed by the foreign enemy. Under Philip II Catalonia had been a place where bandits who had cut themselves off from organised society formed something like a permanent rebellion. In parts of the countryside their power was notoriously greater than that of the government. The wars and depressions in the

[1] Quoted in J. H. Elliott, *Imperial Spain*, p. 388.

first decades of the century kept them in being. A good many of the rural nobility, for whom the feud was still a normal part of life, were involved in bandit activity, though by now more and more of them were drifting into the towns, as were their tenants. Commerce was increasingly linked with France, and gave Richelieu's agents opportunities they did not overlook. Indeed, the fear of French heresies was a reason for the Inquisition being more active there than in the rest of the country. When French troops crossed the Pyrenees in 1638 the Catalans did not give the support Richelieu had hoped for; but they showed no enthusiasm for raising an army or building fortifications in their own defence. Olivares decided that the opportunity should be taken to crush the recalcitrant province as well as the invaders. Soldiers, both Castiilans and alien mercenaries, were quartered in Catalonia and left there unpaid to live off the country through the winter. There was no surer way to incite rebellion.

The revolt that exploded in the spring of 1640 was both rural and urban. Catalan villages had grown accustomed through the years of brigandage to join in self-defence. When the town of Santa Coloma de Farner refused to billet soldiers and appealed for help against the expedition sent to punish it, church bells called together peasants in the surrounding villages, and within days armed revolt had spread through the province. Such united action was only possible with the help of the clergy. Catalan priests were the most heavily taxed section of the population, and high offices in the Church were as much a preserve of hated Castilian outsiders as those in the state. Castilian as well as French troops were blamed for the destruction of churches and images, and reforms derived from the Council of Trent were regarded as Castilian innovations. Royalist commanders accused the clergy of 'rousing the people and . . . inducing the ignorant to believe that rebellion will win them the kingdom of heaven'.[1] The towns sometimes tried to protect themselves from the plundering peasants; but many, including the city of Barcelona, opened their gates to let the insurgents join with the urban mob of poor and homeless. The climax of the revolt in Barcelona came when the Segadors, the labourers who flocked to the city in the summer to be hired for the harvest, joined in the fighting. Many of the surviving royal officials and judges fled for their lives, and the Viceroy, Santa Coloma, was murdered. In other towns the municipal oligarchies were the first victims of the rioters. More and more the social and political purposes of the rebellion were lost amid the plundering, and the

[1] Quoted in J. H. Elliott, *The Revolt of the Catalans*, p. 487.

rumours of nameless disasters, unknown enemies, miracles and witch-craft. Among it all, since it was a year of drought, incongruous processions of prayer for rain continued to win great support.

Catalonia never produced a real rebel leader—not even a mythical one. At the height of the revolt there appeared letters threatening destruction to towns that resisted the rebels, some of them signed by the 'Captain-General of the Christian Army', who in Madrid was reported to be a galley-slave released from prison. But he failed to emerge as an identifiable hero. The fate of the rebellion depended a great deal on the attitude of those political leaders who had built up their own resistance to Madrid. There had been a prolonged quarrel between the Viceroy and the *Diputació*, the small executive committee which was chosen by lot from the rural, urban, and clerical oligarchies and controlled most of the local patronage. Its president, Pau Claris, was a cleric connected with some of the leading families in the country and in Barcelona. Without being a separatist, still less a believer in social revolution, he saw himself as the defender of Catalan liberties against the misgovernment of Castilian officials. His chief supporter in the *Diputació*, the aristocratic representative Francesco de Tamarit, was arrested in March 1640 for his resistance to the billeting measures, and was released from prison by the insurgent mob in Barcelona. The *Diputació* was in a dilemma familiar to moderate revolutionaries: it was appalled by the threat to propertied society, but at the same time ready to use the situation to win from Madrid concessions for Catalan liberties.

In the capital advocates of stern repression were for a time resisted by those who saw a need to pacify Catalonia with concessions in the interest of unity against France. Olivares at first supported the new Viceroy, the Duke of Cardona, in trying to conciliate Claris and his supporters. But it was doubtful whether Catalonia could now do anything to resist French invasion. Many of the nobility, seeing no move coming from Madrid to save them from revolution, abandoned their estates and left for other parts of Spain. Nevertheless, Olivares delayed the decision to send a punitive expedition until it was known that Claris had begun serious negotiations with the French. For a moment an independent Catalan Republic claimed to exist under French protection; but it then had to accept Richelieu's demand that Louis XIII should be recognised as its sovereign. Allegiance to the new state now meant not the opportunities that the Catalan nobles had hoped for, nor a relaxation of burdens on the lesser men, but a foreign domination in place of a Castilian one. It put an end to the hope that the whole of

Aragon might join in the revolt. Catalan resistance lasted, in theory, until the citizen army of Barcelona was at last defeated in 1652. But the ten years were a period not of successful revolution but of military occupation and intermittent warfare, of economic ruin, and, at the end, of plague and famine. Eventually the surviving rebels received a royal pardon and a vague promise that the traditional privileges of Catalonia would be respected.

Revolt in Portugal

One revolt against Spain was apparently successful—but successful only because the movement of protest was absorbed by a national war of liberation. Portugal, with its own language and traditions, a separate colonial Empire, a large and prosperous merchant class, was the most recent acquisition of the Spanish Crown. The union of 1580 with Spain and hence with its empire, contrived by many of the nobility, had brought some commercial benefits; but they were more than offset by the wars. The Dutch and English were happy to attack Portuguese shipping and colonies when opportunity arose; the Spaniards demanded Portuguese men and money without, it was felt, doing enough to retrieve the American territories lost to the Dutch. Cadiz was driving Lisbon out of the Atlantic trade; and in the general economic decline Castilians kept for themselves an increasing share of what remained. Both Lerma and Olivares incurred the resentment of Portuguese aristocrats by finding profitable offices for Castilians. The king's cousin Margaret of Savoy was sent to Lisbon in 1634 with a body of Castilian counsellors whose task was to build up enough power to make Portugal pay a regular contribution to Spanish war expenses. Two years later there came the real onslaught of Castilianisation. In the years of minor revolts and party rivalries that followed, French agents were hard at work. A more unexpected source of support for resistance was the Archbishop of Lisbon and the leading Portuguese Jesuits. The Catholic institutions of Portugal, including the Inquisition, remained independent and, excluded from the temptations of the Madrid court, took a stern view of Spanish sins. The parish clergy were as willing to support popular revolt as their superiors now were to join in a palace conspiracy. But the union of the two might well have been impossible without the emotional loyalty in both town and country to the old ruling house of Braganza.

For two generations there had existed one of the superstitions, deeply rooted in primitive religion, about the return of a supposedly dead leader who would redeem his people from their sufferings. This was

King Sebastian, who had died in 1578. Several claimants to his identity had already achieved momentary success. The real Braganza heir, Duke John, was now bullied by his wife Luisa de Guzman, despite her Spanish birth, into accepting the rôle of a national leader. She also found an able political organiser, Professor Ribeiro. In the hope of thwarting two revolutions at once, Olivares ordered the Duke of Braganza and many of the Portuguese nobility to command the expedition against Catalonia in November 1640. The planned revolt could only succeed if it began at once. On 1 December, while a French fleet was off the coast, a group of court nobles cut to pieces the chief Spanish representative, Vascollenos, and proclaimed the reign of John of Braganza as King John IV. Simultaneously there was a mass rising in Lisbon, and the Spanish fortifications throughout the kingdom were seized. There were in fact few Spanish troops left in Portugal, and none that could be spared to go there. Opposition to the new régime had to consist of bribery, counter-plots, and propaganda. One device was to make sweeping offers to the Christian-Jewish community for their support: the Grand Inquisitor himself was induced to promise that their persecution would cease. It all made little difference. Portugal had one outstanding asset that made it possible to sustain a struggle against Spain—the Brazilian sugar fleet. Though the war went on until 1668, the Spaniards were fighting against a nation with a sounder economy than their own, and a strong material incentive to defend their independence.

The fall of Olivares

Every European statesman who faced revolt of one sort or another in the provinces or dependencies of his country had also to keep a close eye on the response at the centre. Aristocratic plots against the régime of Olivares had always been one of his minor burdens. He was well aware, from the beginning of the Catalan rising, and especially after the failure of his first attempts to suppress it, of the new threats to his authority in Castile itself. The movement that he discovered in 1641 combined both palace conspiracy and provincial separatism. The Duke of Medina Sidonia, brother of the new Queen Luisa of Portugal, was at the centre of a group of Andalusian grandees who planned a revolt that could lead to the overthrow of Olivares or to an independent Andalusian kingdom, or even to both. This time the plan was betrayed to the Count-Duke and broken before it could take effect. But every failure in the wars and every increase in the economic chaos they were producing added to the

chances that the king would be forced to make a scapegoat of his minister
—and hence to the number of courtiers who thought it expedient to be
on good terms with his enemies. Like Richelieu, Olivares had maintained
his position by never allowing the king to escape from his day-to-day
influence and by keeping careful track of the manœuvres against him
at the palace. It was always a difficulty that from time to time the king
chose to leave his capital. Olivares did his best to dissuade Philip from
undertaking a journey to the armies in Catalonia. Though it was more
of a ceremonial excursion than a serious attempt to intervene in the
organisation of the campaign, it was bound to reveal how dangerous the
situation was and to leave Madrid at the mercy of the enemies of
Olivares. In the spring of 1642 the king insisted on going; Olivares
decided that the lesser evil was to go with him. The queen, the Count
de Castrillo who was left in charge of the administration, and all the
opposition group made the most of their opportunity. When Philip
returned in the winter he was faced with an organised and apparently
universal demand for the dismissal of his minister. The best Philip
could do was to save him from Strafford's fate and send him to die in
exile.

Revolt in Italy

While Mazarin was establishing his position as Richelieu's successor,
no-one in Spain made any open attempt to take over the position left
by Olivares. The king made it known that he intended in future to rule
as Philip II had done, with a large Council of State restored to its old
supremacy. To some extent he does appear to have devoted himself to
administrative tasks, though his political views came increasingly under
the influence of the church, and in particular of the mystical abbess Sor
Maria de Agreda. Luis de Haro, a nephew of Olivares, was able to
emerge from the former opposition group to become an effective minister who, with none of the ostentation of Olivares, made himself almost
as powerful in both home and foreign affairs. It was his realistic assessment of the military situation that led to the agreement with the Netherlands in the Westphalia negotiations recognising, after eighty years of
war, that there was no longer hope of crushing their 'revolt'.[1] The fact
was made a little clearer by the outbreak of rebellion in yet another part
of the European empire.

In the two provinces of southern Italy Spanish government was at
its worst, and local political ambition at its feeblest. The administration

[1] See p. 392.

of both Sicily and Naples had been, even under Philip II, a conflict between attempts at efficient central control and a great variety of local forces. The Inquisition had often proved a better instrument for maintaining loyalty to the Crown than were the Viceroys and their officials. There was a vast difference between the two territories. Sicily was still regarded as one of the richest parts of the Spanish Empire: it exported grain to Spain and to northern Italy, and one of its specific grievances in the 1630s was the attempt to buy the crops at cheap monopolistic rates for the armies. It had a tradition of representative institutions that made possible the startling claim that the only parliaments in Europe that kept their powers were in London and Palermo. But the secular powers that really resisted royal government were those of the great landowners and the towns. The Sicilian nobility were at the stage where the quest for office, with all its opportunities for extortion and corruption, was slowly changing the habits of territorial independence and baronial warfare. The towns, with their governments more or less dominated by the guilds, clung to their control over justice and taxation and their rivalries with each other. Anything begun in Palermo was inevitably opposed in Messina. Viceroys survived—usually not for long —by exploiting disunity and buying support with titles and offices.

The harvest of 1646 was a disastrous failure; and in the following spring there were not only the expected sporadic riots in the countryside but a succession of full-scale urban risings. The pattern was fairly uniform: houses of officials held responsible for the taxes or the hoarding of grain were attacked first; then for two or three days there was indiscriminate plundering and fighting. But behind the hunger-riot there was a good deal of well-informed political motive. In Palermo a goldbeater, Giuseppi Alessio, became the spokesman of demands for the restoration of Sicilian privileges, the abolition of new taxes, and the removal of the Viceroy, the Marquis of Los Velos. After three days of anarchy in Palermo, the Viceroy fled for his life and announced almost unlimited concessions. But although the revolt had a political programme, no-one could produce the means of putting it into effect. There was irreconcilable conflict between the pro-French party in Palermo (carefully fostered but not much helped from Paris) and those rebels who shouted their loyalty to a King of Spain remote enough to be something of a legend himself. The real Philip produced a tougher Viceroy who restored order.[1]

[1] H. G. Koenigsberger, 'The revolt of Palermo in 1647' in *Cambridge Historical Journal*, VIII (1946).

The Kingdom of Naples was a poorer region with none of the remnants of Aragonese liberties. Power was shared between the Viceroys and the small councils of the nobility, the *sediles*, among whom titles and offices were lavishly distributed. The heavy taxation benefited the Genoese tax-farmers and the Spanish armies, but not the Neapolitans. Peasant revolts, brutally suppressed, were a common enough feature of rural life, and the city had a large population of the homeless and starving. It was the revolt of 1647 in Naples that produced the most spectacular of the messianic demagogues in the west. Thomaso Aniello ('Masaniello') was a fisherman with a genius for popular oratory. He first appeared as a mob leader after a normal market scuffle, involving a petty Castilian official, had turned into a riot against the latest piece of war taxation—a levy on fruit which was the only food the poor could get in summer. Within a few days the crowds were spreading palms beneath his feet. At his behest they attacked the palace, the prisons, the tax-collectors, everything that was part of the machinery or display of Spanish government. The pitiful efforts of the Viceroy, the Duke of Arcos, to hold off the rioters with promises and at the same time organise a plot to murder Masaniello turned the agitator into a paranoiac dictator whose alleged enemies were executed in the streets. But the hysteria of the crowd produced conduct as irrational as Masaniello's own. When, in response to a more subtle move on the Viceroy's part, he was invited to negotiate as an equal with the Spanish authorities, there was a sudden movement against him. He was shot and beheaded by a gang of obscure origin; his corpse was dragged through jeering and celebrating crowds; and next day he was venerated as a martyr. Four hundred priests and a hundred thousand spectators were said to have attended his funeral, where the body miraculously pieced itself together to give them a saintly benediction.

The Masaniello episode in the city was only the beginning of a revolt that spread through the whole of southern Italy. Too many of the Neapolitan landowners had a stake of some sort in the Spanish régime for anything like a national resistance to be possible. By the autumn a war of peasants against landlords had merged with the eternal local feuds and rivalries. The man now regarded by the rebels as their leader, Prince Massa, was an eccentric nobleman half in league with the Viceroy but also seeking power for himself as the restorer of order. When a Spanish fleet appeared in the bay, leading some of the revolutionaries to believe that the king across the water had at last come to their rescue, Massa negotiated with the commander, Don Juan; but the Viceroy demanded that the city should be bombarded. The gunfire and the

Spanish troops who landed gave the revolt a new realism and purpose. It was Massa who now became the traitor to be killed, and Naples was proclaimed a republic. Realism also meant that help from a powerful state must be found; the source of it could only be France. In November one faction of the rebels called on Henry Duke of Guise, who had a remote claim to a Neapolitan throne, to come from Rome (where he was arranging his divorce) and lead a war against the remaining Spanish garrisons. The spectacle of a member of the House of Guise heading a rebel republic did not appeal to Mazarin. Any serious attempt to exploit the revolt as a weapon against Spain would have to be organised by the French government. Fear of proletarian revolutionaries made him, as he later admitted, miss 'the finest opportunity' for a triumph in Italy. The fleet he eventually sent to Naples proved almost as hostile to the rebels as the Spanish one. Guise escaped arrest by Mazarin only to be caught by the Spaniards instead. Six months after it began, the revolt disintegrated into aimless recriminations.

Spain after the revolts

The crisis of the 1640s at last made it clear in Europe that the Spain of the Armada no longer existed. Though there is still argument about the basic causes of the decline, and not enough information that would help to settle it, it is clear that both inescapable changes and misgovernment are involved. Despite the efforts of Olivares, it was still Castile that bore the main cost of the court and the wars; and Castile had been, throughout the century, suffering more than most of the other possessions from a diminishing population, a lower output of food and exportable raw materials, a reduction in every form of commercial activity. The power of the wool-producers in the sixteenth century had done much to make Spain depend on imported grain. Now the wool that had helped to pay for the imports was in smaller demand. The less profitable agriculture became, the greater the temptation for both landlord and peasant to abandon it. Often their debts left them no alternative. The lord might try to get a living at court, the tenant in a town. But the towns were if anything in a worse plight than the country. As the colonies became more self-sufficient, their demand for goods exported from Spain shrank. The crushing and unpredictable taxation imposed on native merchants increased the tendency for trade to be run by foreigners. Though the extent to which Spain had lived on imports of silver can be exaggerated, the steady fall in the yield as mines became less profitable to work added to the government's difficulties and hence to the taxpayer's burden. The Atlantic trade of Seville collapsed in the 1640s; and the disaster was completed by the plague of 1649 in which half its people were said to have died or fled. Such epidemics were often blamed for a decay that had more lasting causes.

The floundering attempts of the ministers and bureaucrats to solve difficulties that were partly of their own making produced one of the most startling symptoms of economic disease: more than any other country, Spain, and Castile especially, suffered from a succession of violent inflations and deflations. Ever since 1617, when the Cortes of Castile released the king from a promise to use only silver coinage, *vellón* was repeatedly minted to pay government debts. A period of rising prices in the 1620s was brought to a sudden end by Olivares when he stopped payment of the government's debts to Italian bankers, tried in vain to fix prices by decree, and then, in 1628, halved the value of all existing copper coins. (The government's profits from this were lost in the Mantuan war and the subsidies to Imperial forces.) By the 1640s, Castilian coins were being repeatedly restamped to raise or lower their value, bringing momentary relief to the Crown and disaster to almost everyone involved in commerce or finance. Since silver seemed a safer form of wealth than copper, its disappearance was completed by hoarding. In 1660, when the war with France was over, there was another effort to stop the inflation by introducing a completely new copper coinage with greater intrinsic value; but within a few years the price of silver and of commodities generally was higher than ever. Eventually, in 1680, the desperate measure of 1628 was repeated: the value of the new coins was halved. This time the collapse of the economy in Castile seemed complete. After an outburst of rioting and robbery, the choice for most people lay between leaving Castile altogether and living on what they could produce or acquire by barter.

Bad as it was, the economic failure was not unrelieved. For the lucky or enterprising few there were ways of prospering. Fortunes could be made as well as lost by smuggling and hoarding foreign coin, silver, and scarce commodities. Lucrative offices could still be bought. The Church offered riches on earth for its higher clergy as well as holy poverty for the majority of priests. But it was only the holders of large landed estates who, by avoiding economic enterprise and living on the misery of their peasants, could achieve secure luxury. Such property became concentrated in the hands of fewer and fewer families as the hidalgos increasingly shared in the general decline. Outside Castile the misfortunes were more varied. Though taxation was grievous everywhere, it was Castile that suffered most from the follies of the central government it housed. With their own coinage and a smaller proportion of unproductive population to maintain, the other provinces were able to preserve some links with the economy of the rest of Europe. For Catalonia especially, peace with France and recovery from the effects of the rebellion brought a real revival of prosperity. Barcelona, abandoning the old Mediterranean trade, began to export textiles to America and northern Europe. A good deal of the commercial activity was under foreign control: native merchants protested against the concessions first to the Portuguese and then to the Dutch and English. But any stimulus to the economy was better than none; and foreign immigration was as beneficial to Spain as it was to Russia or Brandenburg. Astonishingly, even Protestants were not excluded: provided they kept their religion to themselves, foreigners were not subject to religious persecution. To the French, land in Spain was cheap, and opportunities for skilled artisans attractive. While European statesmen were interested in Spain only as the kingdom without an heir, there was in many parts of it by the end of the century a slow return of economic stability.

When Philip IV died in 1665, there was not much left of the legend of Spanish power. At the Peace of the Pyrenees in 1659, Artois and the outlying defences of the Spanish Netherlands had been surrendered to France. So had the Catalan province of Roussillon, and a large part of Cerdagne. The marriage of the Infanta Maria Theresa to Louis XIV instead of to an Austrian prince, though it was in the well-established tradition of Franco-Spanish royal matches, looked like a further recognition that the Habsburg axis was broken. Ironically, Spain remained at the centre of Europe's diplomacy, but as the victim to be dismembered rather than the feared leader. The question was how far the centralised monarchy would disintegrate of its own accord before the succession question brought the great powers to fight over its fate. As the diplomats were soon to be reminded, it was still accepted in Spain that the will of a deceased king could determine in some detail the management of his possessions. Philip IV showed an unusual amount of perception and initiative in the schemes he laid down for the long minority of the four-year-old Charles II. Philip's illegitimate son, whose name of Don Juan was his chief qualification for the rôle of saviour of the country, was excluded from the power he had assiduously prepared for. The regent, contrary to custom, was to be the queen, Philip's second wife Maria Anna. Effectively, the authority of the Crown would be exercised by a Junta of Regency. Though it included two leading figures from the old government, the Counts of Castrillo and Peñaranda, its other members came from outside Castile. There seemed a possibility that it would constitute a deliberately inactive central power representing the interests of the provinces.

One obstacle to any happy solution on federal lines was that a queen-regent, however ineffective herself, was bound to be exploited by the power-seekers of the court. Maria soon came under the control of her Austrian Jesuit confessor, Father Nithard, who was able to reduce the Junta to the level of a powerless advisory body. Against him Don Juan mounted in 1669 a short-lived but spectacular rebellion. The support he had built up in Aragon enabled him to stage a triumphant march on Madrid where he was received as a popular hero. Nithard hastily departed for Rome, and if—as was already believed to be likely—Charles II had died, Don Juan could well have become the new king. He was not the man to lead an armed rebellion; and when the king made the first of his many unexpected recoveries the queen was able to end the episode by making Don Juan Viceroy of Aragon. In Nithard's place she adopted as favourite an upstart courtier from Andalusia, Fernando de Valenzuela, who in his turn became a hero of the Madrid populace. If Don Juan had been something of a False Dmitri, Fernando behaved like one of the less reputable Roman Emperors, entertaining the plebeians of the city with circuses and the court with lavish and amorous banquets. The grandees were scandalised: he was not even of noble birth. When Charles attained his official majority—the age of fourteen—Don Juan had the support of a solid party of courtiers for a second descent on the capital, this time at the head of an army. For two years he held power—the years in which Franche-Comté and a few more Netherlands fortresses were finally lost to the French. When he died in 1679, the enthusiasm of the court and the capital had turned into ridicule. The Council of Sate was left to preside, with no perceptible policy or leadership, over the worst years of economic chaos.

Charles II himself has always been known only as the moribund half-wit whose lack of an heir produced the 'Spanish Succession Question'. There is no doubt that this offspring of a series of marriages between cousins, which made him the descendant of Charles V by six or seven tangled lines, was not a paragon of health or intellect. But the fact that he reigned for thirty-five years in spite of the incessant torment inflicted on him by his doctors suggests that he was tougher than those in Spain and abroad who were preparing for the moment of his death liked to believe. It may well have been a beneficial change when the doctors were largely replaced by exorcists. His deep suspicion of everyone around him, which was reported as a sign of madness, seems in the circumstances entirely reasonable. As the succession loomed larger in European politics, palace rivalries in Madrid took on the character of a struggle between French and Austrian parties. In 1689 Charles's second marriage, to the Emperor's sister-in-law Maria Anna of Neuburg, brought a strong 'Austrian' contingent to the court, led by the new queen's confessor Father Gabriel. For the moment Charles had found in the Count of Oropesa a minister who was showing some ability and determination in trying to sort out the economic calamities and establish a workable system of government finance. In 1691 the pressure of courtiers whose interests he threatened to override was enough to remove him. Nevertheless it was Oropesa's favoured candidate for the throne, the Bavarian Joseph Ferdinand,[1] whom Charles decided to name as his heir. The French and Austrians, though they were fighting against each other a desperate battle of court conspiracy, agreed that this was another proof of royal insanity. In fact it was the best hope of avoiding surrender to one or other of the great powers whose rivalries now seemed likely to end in the invasion and break-up of the Spanish possessions. Everything Charles could do in his last wretched years to preserve his Empire he carried out, however slowly, in face of merciless diplomatic and palace intrigue. When the Bavarian candidate died, nearly all the favoured advisers of the king agreed with the French that Philip of Anjou was now the most desirable successor. Despite all the efforts of the queen and her clerical allies, Charles kept firmly to his decision to make a new will leaving all his territories to Anjou. If the French refused, the Austrian Archduke was to succeed instead. The only important condition was that the new king was not to become the sovereign of any other power as well. In November 1700, a month after the signing of the will, the news was proclaimed that the last of the Spanish Habsburgs really was dead.

[1] See p. 313.

XV

The Baltic

The lands that surrounded the Baltic Sea brought together some of the most thickly tangled threads of seventeenth-century history. It was through the Baltic that eastern Europe had its economic links with the west. The exchange of the surplus grain from the great estates of Poland for manufactures and for southern produce[1] made Baltic ports the most

BIBLIOGRAPHY. The supply of modern works on the Baltic in western languages is uneven: Sweden has for this period naturally had a good deal more attention than the other countries, and there is not much in the way of collective or comparative study. One article that treats the whole subject perceptively is Wladyslaw Czaplinski, 'Le problème baltique aux XVIᵉ et XVIIᵉ siècles' in the *Reports (rapports)* of the *Eleventh International Congress of Historical Sciences*, vol. IV (Stockholm, 1960). The same volume contains an article by B. F. Porchnev, 'Les rapports politiques de l'Europe occidentale et de l'Europe orientale à l'époque de la Guerre de Trente Ans'. Of the general histories of the three countries mainly considered here, the *Cambridge History of Poland*, vol. I, *From the origins to 1694*, ed. W. F. Reddaway and others (Cambridge, 1950) is a solidly reliable survey; O. Halecki, *A History of Poland* (London, 1942) is patriotic, with no claims to subtlety; G. E. Slocombe, *A History of Poland* (2nd ed., London, 1939) is a little more detailed. On Sweden C. Hallendorf and A. Schück, *History of Sweden* (Stockholm, 1929) is still the standard short work, though I. Andersson, *History of Sweden*, trans. C. Hanney (London, 1955) has some newer ideas. On the Danish kingdom there are L. Krabbe, *Histoire de Danemark* (Copenhagen, 1950); K. Larsen, *A History of Norway* (New York, 1948); K. Gjerset, *A History of the Norwegian People* (New York, 1932). The *Nouvelle Clio* series includes P. Jeannin, *L'Europe du Nord-Ouest et du Nord aux XVIIᵉ et XVIIIᵉ siècles* (Paris, 1969).

Much the best recent writer in English on Sweden is Michael Roberts, whose most important articles are now collected in his *Essays in Swedish History* (London, 1967). His *Gustavus Adolphus: a History of Sweden 1611–1632*, 2 vols. (London, 1953–58) is masterly on every aspect of the reign. The later part of the period is less well covered. F. G. Bengtsson, *The Life of Charles XII, King of Sweden* (London, 1960) and O. Laskowski, *Sobieski, King of Poland*, trans. F. C.

[1] See p. 52.

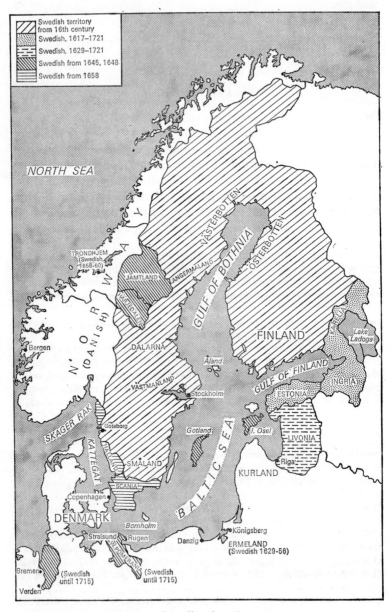

Map 5. Scandinavia, 1600–1721

desirable of territorial prizes and gave to the Dutch and the English a special interest in Baltic politics. As forest products began to rise in importance at the expense of the grain, and Russian markets became more accessible, the tsars were increasingly concerned too. The Empire had nearly four hundred miles of Baltic shore; and the Habsburgs soon found to their cost that Scandinavian politics were anything but remote from theirs. Poland as a Catholic power brought the religious alignment into Baltic affairs, and even linked them with the Danube and the ebb and flow of Turkish pressure.

In 1600 frontiers and political predominance in the whole region were a matter of dispute principally between the three kingdoms with which we shall be concerned in this chapter, Denmark, Sweden, and Poland. This was in itself something fairly new. A century earlier the Hanseatic League, and even the Teutonic Knights whom the Poles had defeated, were still in their different ways at least as great as the kings. The Danish Oldenburg dynasty reigned over the whole Scandinavian peninsula, the Polish Jagiello kings over Lithuania, much of the Ukraine, and—less directly—Prussia. The estates of the great nobles, spreading through all these territories, had often been more effective units than the kingdoms. But the conflict of dynasties was now more decisive than the interests or passions of any of their subjects. When the Swedish Vasas, helped by the merchants of Lübeck, were finally able in 1523 to break the 1396 Union of Kalmar with Denmark, there remained two kingdoms eager to expand, and divided from each other by fears and ambitions beside which the new bond of Lutheranism counted for very little. Sweden had very strong material incentives to acquire the rich provinces on her own side of the sound still held by the Danes, to gain a more secure outlet to the Atlantic, and to win control of Baltic commerce. Danish kings still hoped to regain their hegemony over all Scandinavia. For both an immediate aim was to annex the lands round the Gulf of Finland and especially Livonia, a largely German region which contained the rich port of Riga.

It was partly the contradictory promises about these duchies on the eastern Baltic that had led to the quarrels between Swedish nobles and

Anstruther (Glasgow, 1944) are readable biographies. One good work available in French on a constitutional and political topic is L. Konopczynski, *Liberum Veto* (Paris, 1930). C. E. Hill, *The Danish Sound Dues and the Command of the Baltic* (Durham, N. Carolina, 1926) is concerned more with the conflicts than with technical detail. E. Ekman, 'The Danish Royal Law of 1665', in *Journal of Modern History*, vol. 29 (1957), is one of the few articles in English on Danish politics.

Sigismund III who in 1587 had been elected King of Poland. Five years later he succeeded his father on the Swedish throne. But Sigismund was also a Catholic, a Jesuit-inspired crusader for the Counter-Reformation, the husband of a Habsburg princess. In 1599 a Riksdag in Stockholm voted to dethrone him. His schemes to reconquer Sweden could lead not only to Polish pre-eminence in the whole Baltic area but to a victory for Catholicism in northern Europe that would rouse Protestant fears of the complete collapse of their cause. Since Sigismund soon came within reach of overthrowing the disorganised Russian state and securing the tsar's throne for himself or one of the Polish-sponsored pretenders, he seemed on the verge of creating the greatest empire in Europe. In spite of the success of Polish armies and of their allies among the Russian nobility—who to Sigismund's disgust preferred his son Vladislav as tsar—there was no easy conquest. In 1612 the Polish garrison that had occupied Moscow was driven out. To Sigismund it was less important to defeat Russia than to recover his 'own' Swedish kingdom; but the wars on Russia, with huge fronts in both north and south, had occupied most of his resources. To reduce his commitments he had to abandon control of East Prussia to the Hohenzollerns, leaving them with the hope of consolidating their possessions on the southern Baltic shore. Meanwhile, his uncle Charles IX became firmly established on the Swedish throne, with a guarantee from the Estates of hereditary succession.

The Danish monarchy

Of all these rivals for expansion in the Baltic area, the one that by any material tests looked most likely to achieve it was Denmark. She had a comparatively large population, productive soil, and easy access to the European mainland without a long southern frontier to defend. The Sound Dues were a source of revenue large enough to be envied by most states, and provided valuable bargaining power. If Norway was an almost colonial area too poor to be beneficial, at least there was no need to fear its hostility. By the standards of the time Christian IV was a prosperous monarch able, for instance, to offer subsidies to James I. He also had private resources in his large German estates, and had long been eager to acquire full sovereignty over Schleswig and Holstein, duchies which in the sixteenth century were partitioned between the King of Denmark and his brothers. German was still the language of government and of the court. Though Christian, like Sigismund, regarded war on Sweden as the reconquest of his own kingdom and the means to complete control of the Baltic, expansion in northern Germany was for him a great personal ambition. He was one of the monarchs who tried to be a strong, centralising reformer, but never quite escaped the position and outlook of a landed magnate.

The Danish Crown was elective. The Oldenburgs retained it only by granting at each election a 'capitulation' confirming a system of government in which the monarch shared his power with the nobility and its council the Raad. The Assembly of Estates had become completely ineffective, with the peasant estate no longer meeting at all. Of the other three the clergy were helpless dependants of the nobles, and the burgesses tended to represent family cliques in towns that had retained their medieval constitutions but not their privileges. Political power was in the hands of the nobility alone, and indeed was hardly distinguishable from land ownership. With an expansion of the great estates many peasants had become labourers not far removed from serfdom, and the Crown was in the same position as other great landowners in being able to tax the peasants on its own estates and no others. Christian and his group of court supporters were involved throughout his reign in a half-hearted and largely unsuccessful conflict with a nobility that resisted every measure of reform. Eventually he did, in spite of the opposition, set up trading companies, build roads and harbours, strengthen municipal governments. Both Christiana (Oslo) and Copenhagen were largely his creation. But for the first decade of the century the Raad in resisting royal policy could complain rightly that Christian's purpose was a war of reconquest. In 1611 the nobles refused to support an attack on Sweden—a country they believed was too poor to support an invading army. Christian threatened to make war himself as Duke of Holstein; but before he did so Swedish activities made the Raad more bellicose.

The War of Kalmar

If Poland won a decisive victory in Russia, Sigismund would certainly resume his efforts to reconquer Sweden. It was therefore expedient for Charles to join in the free-for-all of the Russian 'Troubles'. His forces too entered Moscow. One of the most revealing specimens of seventeenth-century war took place at Klutsjino in 1610, when in the depths of Russia a Swedish army consisting largely of Frenchmen, Englishmen, and Scots with their Russian allies was heavily beaten by a Polish army, also with Russian allies. It did not prevent Charles from keeping up with Sigismund by getting his son too invited to be tsar—though only by the city of Novgorod. At the same time Charles was continuing to fight the Poles in Livonia and sending forces to the far north to assert his right to tax more of the Lapps and to control the White Sea trade-routes and fishing grounds. It was these opportunities that helped Christian of Denmark to manœuvre his council into agreeing that an invasion of Sweden might be worth trying.

Sweden's hero-king, Gustav Adolf, thus began his reign in 1611 with a prospect of being dethroned by the Poles or the Danes, or conceivably of becoming Tsar of Russia. The War of Kalmar can hardly have encouraged either Sweden or Denmark in immediate hopes of aggrandisement. Armies headed by their respective kings devastated a fair amount of the Swedish countryside without much harming each other, until the Danes captured the fortress of Älvsborg on the tiny Swedish outlet to the North Sea, where Charles had founded the port of Göteborg. The war was ended (by the Peace of Knäred, in 1613) with the help of Britain and Holland, who were feeling the commercial effects of the conflict. Sweden agreed to pay an enormous ransom for the return of Älvsborg. But fighting in the east continued until 1617, when—with Dutch help—Gustav made peace. In the Treaty of Stolbova the tsar agreed to Swedish acquisitions of territory that gave her control over all the outlets to the Gulf of Finland. By their common hostility to Poland, Gustav and Michael Romanov became reluctant allies.

The Protestant Cause

In 1621, when the Poles were deeply involved with their Turkish enemies, Gustav won a decisive success against them: the port of Riga surrendered after a short siege. This was startling news in the Europe that had just seen the collapse of the Bohemian revolt. Riga was one of the great international trading cities, created largely by German merchants and second only to Danzig in handling exports from Poland and eastern Europe. More important still, the wars between Swedes and Poles were now a matter of crucial importance to believers in a general conflict of faith. Sweden would evidently be a major force in a 'Protestant Alliance'. Protestantism was now responding, however hesitantly, to the dangers that followed the defeat in Bohemia. There was nothing new in the religious aspect of Baltic warfare: Sweden and Poland had each advertised itself as the champion of true religion. The notion of great European conspiracies, with Jesuits and Huguenots as their respective agents, was believed in the Baltic as elsewhere on very slight evidence. To Gustav war in Poland had the advantage of being a good Protestant enterprise that ought to win the support of the Dutch and the north German states. It was also an opportunity, without involving his own forces directly in Germany, to outdo Denmark as a champion of Protestantism. Sigismund, once the danger from the Turks was diminished, believed that he could not only regain Riga but at last win back his Swedish throne too. A new army and a new fleet would be needed; but there was good hope of subsidies from the Pope and, more important, from Spain. It seemed possible that Catholicism, now triumphant in Bohemia, might be restored throughout northern Europe. But the great Polish invasion of Sweden never came. Opposition at home, the insecurity of the other frontiers, and the formidable strength of the Swedes led Sigismund to postpone it repeatedly. In 1624 the two Protestant kings, after new threats of war against each other, concluded a formal peace pact in which the Danes made all the concessions. Two years later Christian, proclaiming his duty to defend Protestantism and Danish interests, embarked on his ill-fated German adventure.[1]

The Danish war in Saxony was not a conflict between nations: Christian headed a mercenary army, bought in Germany, and his equals were not so much the Emperor or the Electors of Brandenburg and Saxony, but Mansfeld and Tilly. When his campaign ended not in Protestant triumph but in the invasion and plundering of Jutland by Wallenstein's army, which many of Christian's troops hastened to join, the Raad, with better reason than usual, complained bitterly against royal policy, and demanded peace. The war had all the time, they now remembered, been fought by Christian as Duke of Holstein. His forces and those of his enemies must alike be kept away from noble estates. At Lübeck in 1629 Christian signed the treaty which restored his Danish territory.

To Gustav Adolf the humiliation of Denmark was one of the disasters to Protestantism that he found it easy to bear bravely, even though, in 1628, he made promises of limited assistance against the Imperial forces. With the German war in this situation, Sweden needed to leave open the chance either to intervene directly, as the one and only Protestant Champion, or to exploit the mutual destruction of other states for the benefit of her own Baltic aims. The invasion of Polish territories on the German shore of the Baltic would meet the need very well. The logical step in economic warfare against Poland after the capture of Riga would be to take, or at least cut off, Danzig. If the Habsburgs did prove triumphant in Germany, it was essential for Sweden to have strong Baltic defences. If not, there was now, somewhere in the optimistic background, the notion of the 'Swedish Lake'. So in 1626 and 1627, while

[1] See pp. 289–90.

Tilly and Wallenstein were disposing of the Danish invasion, Gustav's new fleet carried his army of native soldiers to Prussia. But his attack on the Polish forces there made no decisive progress. Denmark and all north Germany were now dominated by Catholic armies; and Spain was taking an alarming interest in Baltic affairs. A secret committee of the Riksdag agreed that if necessary Sweden should undertake the invasion of Imperial Germany. When Gustav in 1628 went to the rescue of the Pomeranian port of Stralsund from Wallenstein's army, he demanded a pledge that it could be used as a base for a larger German campaign. 'All the wars that are waged in Europe', he wrote to Oxenstiern, 'are mingled together and become one.'[1]

The decision to devote Sweden's whole energy to an invasion of Germany was taken only after solemn debates in the Råd and even some hesitation on Gustav's part. The rational argument was that a Catholic victory in Germany would be as great a threat to Sweden as any from Denmark or Poland, and that it would be safer and cheaper to fight on enemy territory rather than wait to be attacked. Less rationally, Gustav was beginning to adopt his pose as 'lion of the north' which Protestant Europe gladly applauded. In his brief moment of glory he began to see Sweden as the dominant state in an anti-Habsburg alliance. Other commitments had to be dropped. In 1629, with French help, he negotiated the Truce of Altmark with Sigismund of Poland, to whom Wallenstein had unexpectedly sent help. A year later the victorious progress through Germany began. It was made as clear as possible that the Swedes were no-one's agents. In 1631, at the Treaty of Bärwalde, he accepted French subsidies he had previously refused, but only on terms that left him, in effect, free to campaign as he wished. His victory over Tilly at Breitenfeld and his rapid march towards the Rhine created the legend of invincible Swedish armies holding all Germany at their mercy. Yet by the time he was killed at Lützen he had already drawn back to defend the north.[2] His army had now become, like those he fought against, mainly a force of German mercenaries paying their way by plunder. They could not be held together by such means for ever; and the Baltic still mattered more to Sweden than Protestant Europe. Oxenstiern and the Råd began to work for a peace settlement on realistic and orthodox diplomatic lines: to annex Pomerania, and acquire some allies in north Germany, was as much as they could hope. Though Swedish expeditions, and even victories, continued, the dreary peace negotiations

[1] Quoted in M. Roberts, *Gustavus Adolphus*, vol. 2, p. 363.
[2] See pp. 293–7.

offered no prospect of the 'Swedish Lake'. The gains of Western Pomerania, the Bishoprics of Bremen and Verden, and the town of Wismar, were commercially valuable; but the southern provinces of the peninsula, Skane and Halland, remained in Danish hands. Baltic conflicts would obviously continue.

Sweden, the Great Power

Why did Sweden in the seventeenth century become a great power? It is one of the most familiar and nevertheless difficult and significant questions about the period. By any European standards she was, in 1611, a poor country. There were a few wheat-growing areas, increased by the conquests, and some fairly good pasture. But most of the country was forest. In the north a semi-migrant population could be deemed to belong to whatever state succeeded for the time being in collecting taxes from it. Elsewhere the Swedish Crown seemed to be even less competent than most in the task of diverting a steady share of what resources there were into its own hands. The great asset was minerals. The Crown, in its eagerness to get quick funds for itself, allowed the celebrated Falun copper-mine to be worked in ways that diminished the long-term benefits. The Swedish currency had been repeatedly debased. A great deal of internal trade in the sixteenth century was by barter, and many taxes were collected in kind. In 1625 Gustav Adolf decreed that marks should be minted only in copper worth their face value. Thus the amount available for export would fall, and since Sweden had virtually a monopoly, the price on the Dutch market (which had been sinking disastrously) would rise while the Crown would still draw profits from the increasing output. The silver for which it was exchanged abroad would be kept for the government's foreign expenses, including repayment of loans raised in Holland to pay the ransom for Älvsborg. The most visible effect of this was that Swedes found themselves, when they had anything to pay for, pushing around carts loaded with ludicrous coins nine inches in diameter, as well as suffering all the usual effects of inflation. In the end Gustav began the process, familiar in the west, of keeping the Crown solvent by selling its lands. It was soon clear that the Swedish nobility—again like many of their western counterparts—were the real beneficiaries.

The system of government seemed no better fitted than the economy for a century of foreign wars.[1] The effective powers of the Crown still depended on the state of its perpetual conflict with the ancient nobility.

[1] See pp. 205, 209-10.

Charles IX had begun his reign by executing four of the leading members of the Råd who had supported Sigismund too long. He had also made some attempt to restrict noble influence by creating a secretariat from men without landed property. This was not the line suggested to the young Gustav Adolf by Axel Oxenstiern.[1] Stable monarchy, the new Chancellor believed, would depend on a nobility actually serving the state. The 'Charter' which the king and minister persuaded both Råd and Riksdag to accept in 1617 was the first stage in their plan for a monarchy run by the landowners and upheld by every section of the community. The old aristocracy and new office-holding families were to join with lesser landowners in a 'first estate' that would fill the posts needed by an expanded central government. In 1626 their gradations and precedence were firmly laid down: nobility, a status hitherto acquired or asserted as a recognition of military obligations, was made to depend wholly on royal patent. There was a rapid expansion of numbers; and generous grants of royal land to the newcomers did not endear them to the old noble families. Symbolically the centre of life for the nobles was to be not the court but the newly built 'Riddarhus', which was primarily the meeting-place of the First Estate. Equally symbolically the building was not completed until 1660.

The 'Form of Government' of 1634,[2] framed by Oxenstiern after Gustav's death, purported to complete the King's work. By a system of administrative 'colleges' the departments of state were organised under the Råd whose members became 'working statesmen' in Stockholm rather than provincial magnates. Oxenstiern may have gone beyond Gustav's intentions in relegating the Riksdag, whose powers the 1617 Charter had in theory upheld, to a minor rôle. The aristocratic politicians used the opportunity of the regency to impose permanent restrictions on the monarch. They had not much success. The royal prerogative remained the ultimate authority and both Råd and Riksdag were more important in winning acceptance for decisions than in making them. If the Riksdag had none of the theories of the English Parliamentarians, Gustav had none of those of the Stuart monarchs. His way was to avoid prescribed forms of government where it suited him, and deal directly with those able to expedite or resist his projects. This was part of the answer to the problem of Sweden's victories. A king who was one of the military entrepreneurs as well as one of the unhampered sover-

---

[1] See pp. 203–4.

[2] Printed in *Sweden as a Great Power*, ed. M. Roberts (London, 1968), pp. 18–28.

eigns could create an army as formidable as any of its rivals without needing the population and materials of a large state. Once it was involved in the wars, it had the chance to 'live of its own'. Moreover Swedish power is measured by Baltic and north German rather than by western standards. Had they been enemies rather than clients of the French, or faced greater risks of invasion, their triumphs could hardly have lasted so long.

Poland

Polish kings were notoriously the creatures of their mighty subjects. The manœuvres involved in their election, and the *Pacta Conventa* by which each of them on his accession accepted legal restrictions on his power, made them the least 'absolute' of all European monarchs. The diet[1] that restricted the Crown's authority without exercising much of its own represented a thriving body of landlords. Polish agriculture was probably, in 1600, the richest in Europe, in the sense of producing the greatest surplus over the amounts consumed locally. The grain market in the sixteenth century had been an incentive both to the great nobles and to the lesser gentry, the *szchlachta*, who consolidated their lands and made increasing use of servile labour. There was a considerable urban population, but no politically significant Polish bourgeoisie. Though Warsaw was a growing industrial city, Cracow and Lwow flourishing centres of overland transit trade, their commerce was largely run by immigrant German and Jewish communities, often refugees from the harsher persecution of western rulers. The church was, after the firm re-establishment of Catholicism, a thriving institution: there were extensive monastic lands. It was largely with Jesuit help that Sigismund was able to build up a 'royal' party in the Seym. The remarkable thing was that a monarchy so weak in its internal position, in a state surrounded by enemies on the long and indefensible land frontiers that are usually held to account for its subsequent partition, was able to fight simultaneously wars against two or three of its neighbours with apparently as good a chance of victory as anyone else. They were possible only because the nobles thought it in their own interests to put their resources into warfare. Poland was a popular source of mercenary soldiers. Foreign rulers and generals who recruited them needed the goodwill of the nobles from whose estates they came, or of the King. The line between supplying troops for a war and fighting in it was not a rigid one. Sigismund's campaigns in Russia began when the False Dmitri acquired

[1] See p. 213.

a Polish army and with it the backing of many Polish nobles opposed to the Crown.[1] A practical reason for the King's assertion of his own claims to the Tsardom was that it might at least bring him some territory on his eastern borders. When his expedition collapsed in 1612 the army retreated in disorder and recompensed itself by plundering Polish estates and coercing the Seym into voting its arrears of pay. Five years later the Russian career of Sigismund's son Vladislav was ended partly by the mutiny of his mercenaries against the prospect of a winter with little food or pay.

The wars of Polish kings that were intended to serve their own ambitions or the Habsburg cause in the west were a different matter. The Seym successfully resisted an attempt by Sigismund to join as an ally of the Emperor in war against Gabriel Bethlen of Transylvania who in 1619 thought the Bohemian war would give him the chance of conquests in Hungary. Ferdinand had to buy his Polish soldiers for himself. It was hardly to be expected that the Emperor would then respond to Polish requests for help against the infidel: he was happy to see Turks and Poles destroy each other. But the great Turkish victory at Cecora in 1620 aroused the fears of the magnates and some national enthusiasm for revenge. In 1621 the Poles defeated a huge Turkish army to recapture the fortress of Khocim, and the sultan had to abandon his hopes of conquests on the Danube. The two sovereigns agreed to discourage their subjects from further fighting: neither was able to promise more. Sigismund's efforts to recover his Swedish throne were naturally no more popular in Poland. They had touched off one of the few rebellions against the monarchy, when in 1606 the Palatine of Cracow, Zebrydovski, formed an alliance with the Protestants against Sigismund and his Catholic court. It was an indication of how carefully the king would have to move in his war policies. The attitude of the nobles to the Swedish conflicts had to be sweetened by lavish grants of land and lucrative office in such territories as were conquered. Few of them remained in Polish hands for long. On the whole the nobles were glad to accept the Truce of Altmark in 1629 and hoped for a period of peace. But the general outlook remained the same: Sigismund would happily make agreements with the Danes, the Russians, or anyone else who might offer good prospects.

The mid-century conflicts: Sweden

The Baltic countries did not—apart from Poland's involvement in the Ukrainian rising—experience in the 1640s any internal conflicts as out-

[1] See pp. 365–6.

wardly dramatic as those that in the west have been invoked to support the idea of a mid-century 'crisis'. Even so, they all underwent, in different ways, social tensions and political changes that had a good deal in common with the more violent upheavals and led eventually to a strengthening of monarchy. Any full study of the revolutions would have to look at places where they did not happen in the same terms as at those where they did.

Sweden after the death of Gustav Adolf seemed to demonstrate the astonishing success of his internal policy. Few misfortunes could be worse for monarchical power than a long and unexpected minority with a woman as eventual sovereign. The six-year-old Queen Christina would, as her father had said when he considered the possibility that he might die in battle, be 'in great danger'. It was Oxenstiern's now closely united ministry—formed from his relations and dependants—that kept the well-defined constitutional machinery working and the armies fighting, on a more modest scale, in Germany. It did not prevent the nobility from exploiting the financial difficulties that a slow war entailed. The 'frälseköp' in 1638, by which the Crown made large grants of lands from royal estates and of the status of nobility, marked a speeding-up of a process that strengthened the division between those who benefited from the activities of the state and those who suffered. At first the Crown's finances were improved by exchanging lands for lump sums in money, and the support it bought enabled it to impose heavy indirect taxation. When Christina took a hand in government herself, and handed out huge indiscriminate rewards to the returning commanders, the situation got worse. In ten years the number of counts and barons was multiplied by six. The revenue of the Crown fell by 40 per cent.[1]

In 1650, after the harvest had proved to be the worst for half a century, the peasants seemed on the verge of a major revolt. The Estates of townsmen and clergy joined them in denouncing the nobility and attacking alienation of lands, sale of offices, and private jurisdiction. The peasants were afraid—afraid not merely of poverty but of serfdom, or something near to it. Nobles, to whom the Crown alienated the right of taxing freeholders, were easily able to confiscate their land for arrears, reducing them to the status of landlords' peasants and thereby depriving them of most of their legal rights. The view was aired that only nobles were direct subjects of the Crown. Against this threat to the constitutional settlement and to the Riksdag, ideas familiar in the English

[1] M. Roberts, 'Queen Christina and the General Crisis' in *Past and Present*, no. 22 (1962), p. 39.

parliaments of the 1620s were put forward in combined resolutions of the three non-noble estates. Far more than in England the reformers saw the nobility as the enemy. The Råd, though it had become a narrow oligarchy of office-holding families, was supported by the upper Estate; while the lower Estates claimed to uphold the power and independence of the monarch.

Queen Christina was not prepared seriously to support peasants against nobles: though she regarded the social order like everything else as open to intellectual questioning, the culture to which she was devoted was that of a rich leisured class and an extravagant court. The queen who gathered round herself many of the leading scholars of Europe, and claimed to debate on equal terms with Grotius and Descartes, showed no great interest in wider aspects of government. She gave some harmless promises of sympathy for peasant grievances, and welcomed the discomfiture of the nobility as a chance to insist on the recognition of her cousin Charles as her hereditary successor—since she had long since decided not to marry. She was ready enough to see the non-noble Estates resist any extension of noble power, but also to help the nobility in avoiding any really dangerous attack on the system. A few more privileges for the clergy, a few offices for leaders of the urban oligarchies, and death for the leaders of a faction that got as far as trying to involve the heir in treasonable conspiracies—actions like these proved enough to make sure that the rebellious atmosphere cooled. The popular demand for a *reduktion*—resumption by the Crown of the estates it had alienated to the nobility—was firmly put aside. So was the pressure for an extension of office-holding outside the ranks of the nobility.

The mid-century conflicts: Poland

For Poland the middle of the century was beyond doubt the time of 'the deluge'. Though Sigismund's son Vladislav IV had got himself elected to the throne easily enough, he did nothing to re-establish hereditary monarchy. Ineffectively, he tried to be a European figure: he would have preferred the Swedish Crown to the Polish, and was not averse to the idea of another attempt to become tsar. But unlike his father he was no crusader: if the Catholic religion was an obstacle he was prepared to be tolerant. The Polish landowners, as suspicious as ever of royal diplomatic schemes, forbade him to claim Estonia or Livonia from Sweden as hereditary possessions. The Treaty of Viasna that ended another Polish invasion of Russia in 1634, and the Treaty of Stummdorf a year later accepting a long truce with Sweden, brought only minor material gains. An alternative path of glory might be found by becoming a mediator on the Thirty Years War. At one time or another Polish diplomats approached almost every ruler, from Charles I to Wallenstein, and were snubbed so effectively that in the end they were not even present at the Westphalia negotiations. Vladislav's final hope of triumph, a war against the Turks, was again opposed by the Seym. Paradoxically, the reign of a king who sometimes seemed to regard Poland as merely a base and recruiting-ground for his armies was one of comparative peace. Yet Vladislav was not merely a warrior: he had plans for a unified and enlightened kingdom. The Orthodox Church was to be re-established beside the Catholic Uniats, and even Protestantism tolerated in the hope of reunion. Sometimes he made efforts to introduce western culture to the capital—a Rubens painting, a theatre, Italian operas. Galileo and Grotius were favoured with his correspondence. Such things were no more attractive to the Seym than dynastic wars. They not only objected to paying money, but obstructed all efforts to raise it by customs dues. Poland remained too much a federation of the half-independent estates of magnates and gentry to be ruled effectively by its kings. It now became more of a battle-ground even than Germany in the worst of the Thirty Years War. But if elected monarchs could not rule it, neither could conquering ones. The conditions that let invaders in did something to ensure that they drove each other out.

Sigismund III's second son John Casimir, formerly a Jesuit and a Cardinal, took over from his brother both the throne and the Queen, Marie Louise de Nevers. It was at the moment of his election, in 1648, that Poland became involved in the most catastrophic of all the mid-century revolts.[1] There were many allies in Poland whose help the Cossack leader Khmelnitsky could seek against the Warsaw government—the peasants who saw him as a saviour from serfdom, the Orthodox Church to whom he offered domination over Catholicism, the Lutheran nobility. The quarrels of the magnates about relations with the Cossacks were the occasion for the first completely unscrupulous use of the *liberum veto* to dissolve the Seym.[2] But the constitutional procedure was simply the reflection of the political situation. The outlines of a Polish state survived less through any strength of its own than because its enemies failed for the time being to agree on partition. Before long it became the centre of the first general 'northern war.'

[1] See pp. 229–30.   [2] See p. 214.

The Northern War, 1655–60

When Charles X of Sweden attacked Poland in 1655, a year after his accession, he seems to have had no other motive than undefined hopes of aggrandisement or at least of escaping his internal problems and employing his armies. It was not difficult for him to capture Warsaw, drive John Casimir into exile, and win hasty assurances of loyalty from Polish gentry and Polish generals. The success did not last long. Charles's commitment in Poland offered to both Russia and Denmark the chance to redeem some of their Baltic territories. He could find only one active ally—the Elector of Brandenburg, who for the first time had to be reckoned as one of the powers in the Baltic contest. As Duke of Prussia he held the rather absurd status of a vassal of whatever Polish king there happened to be, and was ready to fight for complete sovereignty over his territories. A Poland invaded by the armies of Sweden, Russia, the Tartars, and the Cossacks and with central government shattered might well have seemed beyond survival. Land was going out of cultivation, serfdom on the demesnes of the nobility increasing, industry disappearing. But faintly, out of the total misery of the occupation, a Polish nationalism, Catholic and predominantly western in outlook, began to emerge. There was a brief attempt, initiated partly by the queen, to reform the constitution and set up hereditary monarchy. Townsmen plundered by the armies, and peasants disillusioned by Charles's indifference to serfdom, began to harass the Swedes in guerilla fighting. And for John Casimir an elective throne, however feeble, was something to bargain with: he was ready at one time or another to promise it to almost anyone. By offering to support the tsar's own candidate he won a truce with Russia in 1656. A year later the prospect of a Habsburg succession brought an Austrian army to rescue him from the Swedes. Nevertheless it was the French influence of the queen's circle that dominated court policy; and a French candidate seemed the most likely successor to the childless John Casimir. Consequently the movement for a strengthened monarchy, and an election to the throne before the king's death, could not claim to be a nationalist one. Nobles, gentry, and army officers saw their 'liberties' threatened by a foreign absolutism; and when in 1663 the Grand Marshal of Poland, George Lubomirsky, led a rebellion against the king (with Russian armies still occupying much of the country) his actions seemed no more treasonable than the plans of John Casimir himself.

It was easier for armies to devastate and occupy large areas of land than for governments to destroy each other completely. The tendency for diplomats to hand back what generals seized was shown repeatedly in the northern wars. When Swedish troops withdrew from Poland in 1657 Charles X was already involved in war with Denmark. It was in this campaign that the nobility of Zealand, who thought themselves and their estates safe from the dangers of the war they had demanded, and rejoiced that the hard winter had cut off the invading Swedes from their bases, were punished by the dramatic spectacle of Charles's armies marching over the frozen sea of the Great Belt to occupy the island and besiege Copenhagen itself. Instead of hoping to rule the Baltic, Denmark was soon faced with appalling losses. By the Treaty of Roskilde she handed over her remaining possessions on the Swedish side of the Sound, together with the Norwegian province and port of Trondheim and the Baltic island of Bornholm. Within a few months Charles invaded Denmark again—an act for which it is again difficult to find any better reason than his personal craving to have another war somewhere. His apparent intention of destroying Denmark completely was not likely to be tolerated by the diplomats of western Europe, and he was soon faced by a formidable alliance of Dutch, Austrian, and Polish forces. Since at this moment he died, to the general relief, the powers were able to conclude in 1660 the treaties of Oliva and Copenhagen which confirmed Denmark's surrender of the Swedish provinces (but not of Bornholm and Trondheim). The Elector of Brandenburg, who changed sides at the right moment, won his sovereignty over East Prussia.

Crown and nobility in Sweden, 1654–97

In 1654 Christina had dramatically announced her decision to abdicate. Her conversion to Catholicism made her by law ineligible for the throne, and the cultured life of Europe attracted her more than the problems of Swedish finance. Oxenstiern died soon afterwards, and though his office-holding dynasty had seemed as well established as the Vasas themselves, the nephew who succeeded him could not aspire to the same dominant position. Charles X owed nothing to the goodwill of the old nobility: he was even prepared to attempt again the formidable task of recovering some of the Crown lands so rashly handed out to them. The *reduktion* of 1655, in which a quarter of each new estate was handed back to the Crown in return for security of tenure for the rest, was not so severe a blow as to alienate the nobility from a government that still protected their status. But it touched off a conflict between the great aristocracy, who were the principal sufferers, and the lesser and newer nobles. Many of the latter, as office-holders, had an interest in Crown prosperity: gradually, the division between a bureaucratic and a territorial nobility was becoming deeper and firmer.

It took another twenty-five years of intermittent war, and the rule of an increasingly corrupt Council of Regency after Charles X's death in 1660, to bring about the decisive attack on the great ruling families and their cliques. During Charles XI's minority, opposition in the Estates grew. When the king came of age in 1672 he quickly broke away from the inner group of high nobles led by Magnus de la Gardie. The alliance with England and the Netherlands, made in 1668, was abandoned and Sweden became Louis XIV's ally in his Dutch war.[1] In 1675 Charles left Stockholm to lead his armies in the field. Inspired by his new minister Johan Gyllenstiern he saw bright prospects for monarchical absolutism with popular support. Both king and minister determined to put an end to court extravagance, to the power of the great families, and eventually to the expense of fighting Louis XIV's wars. In the Riksdag of 1680 the former regents and the great landowners were bitterly attacked by the 'service-nobility' and by the free peasants. They demanded further 'reductions' of noble estates and the return of money supposed to have been squandered or filched under the Regency. The old nobility having consented to a *reduktion*, in the hope of winning Crown support for their privileges, found the security of their property and offices completely destroyed. Their power was not replaced by a constitutional one. Without much political manœuvring on his own part, Charles got an assurance from the Estates that he was not obliged to consult them at all.[2] Throughout his reign more specific extensions of royal power were recorded as occasion arose, until in 1693 he and his heirs were declared 'absolute, sovereign kings, responsible for their actions to no man on earth'.[3] But Swedish despotism rested less on political developments than on financial security. By the end of Charles XI's reign the Crown could, in peacetime, 'live of its own' without calling on the Estates for supply, and could raise properly secured loans when it needed them. Much of the land recovered from the old nobility was occupied by the servants of the Crown. The peasants who worked it paid rent directly to the Crown which used it to pay the office-holders—the system of *indelningswerk*. In one way or another the peasants still bore a heavy burden for the state. But compared with most of their counterparts in other countries they were for-

[1] See pp. 358–9, 436.   [2] See p. 210.
[3] *Sweden as a Great Power*, ed. M. Roberts, p. 89.

tunate: their complaints were heard and their status protected by a Crown that valued their support.

Crown and nobility in Denmark, 1648–99

The Danish nobility had lost none of its political power through the disasters of the German wars. Frederick III signed at his accession a 'capitulation' virtually handing over to the magnates in the Raad all the powers of the Crown. Denmark like Sweden went through a period of alienation of Crown land to the nobility. It was supposed to increase revenue but in fact benefited almost entirely the purchasers. A decade of corrupt and inefficient government and defeat in war produced by 1660 the complete collapse of government finances. The cession to Sweden of the provinces on the further side of the Sound, which meant that dues could now only be collected with the consent of Denmark's main enemy, was a final blow to the system of aristocratic rule. A meeting of the Estates in 1660 achieved something like a bloodless revolution. The Copenhagen townsmen, in alliance with the clergy and with one of the rival groups at the court, repudiated the policies of the Raad. An excise, with no full exemption for nobles' estates, was introduced; the powers of provincial governors were restricted; Frederick, in defiance of the nobility, solemnly accepted Denmark from representatives of its people as a hereditary kingdom. In 1665 a new and absolutist constitution was proclaimed, asserting the theory that royal power was derived from this contract with the Estates as the equivalent of the whole body of subjects. Most subjects were not even allowed to know in detail what the constitution said.

The Danish peasantry, most of whom were already in a state of dependence not far from serfdom, gained nothing from the constitutional changes. Though the nobility could not escape taxation entirely, it remained a privileged class, active in administration and justice, and economically thriving. While the Swedish Crown was recovering its lands, in Denmark Frederick's reforming minister Sehested handed over most of the remaining Crown possessions to pay off debts accumulated in the wars. But it was not the old-established aristocrats who benefited most. A new nobility of civil and military office-holders, many of them German by origin, slowly supplanted the old families. Lacking resources of its own, the Crown now depended on a well-administered general land-tax, levied on the king's sole authority. The Rigsraad disappeared entirely. Under Christian V a centralised administration was developed, with civil divisions replacing the old fiefs as the local units, and a Privy Council closely controlled by the King. The real creator of the system was Peter Schumacher, later Count Griffenfeld,[1] the merchant's son who at Christian's accession in 1670 became his all-powerful chancellor. Besides his reform of government, he did his best to be a Danish Colbert, but without the resources for a successful commercial power. Beginning as an advocate of peace and neutrality, he was soon committed to the anti-French alliance, and to the attempt to exploit the military misfortunes of Sweden.

One region which escaped the worst effects of Baltic wars was Norway. It was not a possession the Danes could afford to lose. The timber trade through its many little ports was more significant to the free peasants than to big commercial concerns; but there were iron, copper, and silver mines. Gustav Adolf did not regard it as territory worth conquering, or even bargaining for. To the Danish nobility estates and offices in Norway offered opportunities for exploitation well away from the control of the central government. Though there was a Norwegian Diet, administration was almost entirely kept by the Danes in their own hands. It was in the war of 1657 that they came nearest to losing Norway altogether, when the Swedes briefly occupied Trondheim as well as a good deal of territory in the south. Since the Dutch disliked the presence of what was now beyond doubt the stronger Baltic power on the route to the White Sea, most of the Norwegians in 1660 found that they were back under Danish rule and in theory 'consenting' to the new hereditary monarchy. In fact they had some reason to welcome it. The reformed administration, even though it still treated Norway more or less as a backward area, destroyed the power of the Danish nobility over its estates there. A rigid alien government and taxation system was probably for most of the peasants a lesser evil than total subjection to landlords.

The Baltic Powers, 1660–1700

Charles XI of Sweden was much less consistent and resolute in trying to reduce the amount of resources devoted to war than in achieving monarchial absolutism. To say that the need for French subsidies compelled him, in 1674–5, to make war on Brandenburg and Denmark is no explanation: the war cost more than the French ever paid. After Brandenburg had defeated the Swedes at Fehrbellin in 1675, German forces occupied the Swedish lands in Pomerania. When Denmark joined

[1] See p. 204.

in the war there was for a time a risk that the provinces of southern Sweden annexed by Charles X would be lost again. In 1679 it was made clear that Baltic wars were now a subsidiary part of the European contest: peace was made almost entirely by the French, who permitted only small territorial changes. There was for the Baltic states one possible way out of this rôle of pawns to be sacrificed or preserved by the western powers. If Denmark and Sweden made a firm alliance, the French and Dutch would have to fight without them. Behind the Treaty of Lund in 1679 which publicly settled the frontiers were secret articles that did envisage some such long-term agreement. Both in fact still based their military and diplomatic activities on the assumption that war between them would be renewed. The Swedes were anxious to control Holstein–Gottorp (a Baltic equivalent of the little duchies on the French frontiers), which would be a base for attacking Denmark from the south. In 1681, at the cost of abandoning attempts to drive the Dutch out of Baltic trade, Charles made at The Hague an alliance with the United Provinces which inevitably led Louis XIV to make Denmark his Scandinavian assistant instead of Sweden. A long and insecure semi-peace in the Baltic was maintained only because none of the major powers felt it worth while to extend their wars there.

To the Poles, Baltic affairs after the Peace of Oliva were as always, only one of many dangers and ambitions. For the great Polish-Lithuanian state, the 1660s were a period of territorial as well as economic disaster. The war against Russia, resumed in 1658, continued until, by the armistice at Andrusovo nine years later, Kiev, all the Ukraine east of the Dnieper, and large areas in the Smolensk region were handed over to Russia. The Polish state lost something like a fifth of its land—an area larger than England and Wales. Not much of it was inhabited by Poles. The losses did not mean the Polish Crown could now be written off as a major factor in European diplomacy. When John Casimir decided in 1668 to abandon the unrewarding office of Polish King, at least five foreign countries were involved in electoral intrigues. The younger Condé was one subject who thought that a throne, even of Poland, was worth having. For once the majority of the *szlachta* felt a native candidate was less likely to involve them in further calamitous adventures. Michael Wisnowiecki was chosen as a king vaguely committed to the Habsburg cause.

The settlement with Russia did nothing to preserve Poland from the other eastern invaders. In 1672 a new Cossack attack provided the opportunity for the intervention by the Turks that was a prelude to their last big advance in Europe. In the decade of war that followed, Poland was hardly less of an army-state than the Turks themselves, but with a king who, on the strength of his success against them, became briefly a major participant in European diplomacy. John III—John Sobieski—was in some ways an ideal specimen of the seventeenth-century monarch. Though he came from one of the great families, he was a professional soldier. The elective throne enabled him in 1674 to win the ultimate reward for military power that was denied to Wallenstein and to Condé —who was again among the rivals at the election. He proved also to be well able to hold his own in the diplomatic game, though he was certainly not a politician in the Richelieu class. It was no part of his ambition to undertake a drastic reform of Polish internal politics: the international conflicts interested him more than the national ones. Turkish aggression ought, he claimed, to be met by a coalition that would override existing alignments. His status as a national hero and Christian idealist had been established by an almost treasonable defiance of the monarchy. King Michael had signed the Peace of Buczacz with the Turks at the cost of recognising their suzerainty over the Ukraine and promising a large annual tribute. Sobieski ignored the treaty, made appeals to national loyalty, and while the Seym was doing nothing to re-create the shattered forces raised a new army at his own cost. By a stroke of political luck he not only won a brilliant victory over the outraged Turks, but did so at Khocim (Chotin), famous as the scene of the heroic siege in 1621,[1] and on the day following the death of the king in November 1673.

Even so, his election as John III was not unanimously welcomed. He was the candidate of the 'French' party against the 'Austrians'; and his actions as king mingled with crusading passions plenty of the familiar diplomatic behaviour. Secret treaties with the French and Swedes held out a hope of an alliance against Brandenburg that would lead to the recovery of some of the territory lost in the Baltic area. The price of French support was an agreement with the sultan that left in Turkish hands almost all the territory Michael had signed away. It was not until 1678, when the schemes for invading Prussia had fallen through, that the Holy League against the infidel again became Sobieski's dominant idea. Gradually he abandoned his ties with Louis XIV in favour of the alliance with the emperor that made possible his dramatic appearance as the saviour of Vienna in 1683.[2] The exploit that momentarily made Poland look like a European power again did not in fact bring much

[1] See p. 350.   [2] See p. 311.

benefit to the country or its king. Wars against Turkey dragged on until Sobieski's death, shaped more and more not by devotion to Christianity but by his zeal to conquer Moldavia as a sovereign principality for his son. It would be an excellent base from which to work for the establishment of a hereditary Sobieski dynasty in Poland.

The hope did not materialise. At the election in 1697, the year after Sobieski's death, the successful candidate, in spite of French opposition, was Frederick Augustus the Lutheran Elector of Saxony. He had been supported by one of the most energetic enemies of the Swedes, John Reinhold Patkul, leader of the resistance by the Livonian nobility to the alleged oppression by the Swedish government. Like Henry IV of France a century earlier, Augustus decided that a crown was worth a mass, and as soon as he was established in his joint capitals of Warsaw and Cracow, began the soundings for an anti-Swedish alliance. It was a great help that in 1699 he was able to join in the Treaty of Karlowitz between the emperor and the sultan[1] and regain some of the lost Ukrainian territory. It was in 1697 too that Charles XII inherited the Swedish throne and succeeded, at the age of fifteen, in disposing of the regents appointed by his father and taking power himself. His boyhood had been devoted entirely to his training as a military sovereign. A great new conflict in the north was obviously at hand.[2]

[1] See p. 374.
[2] The Northern War is described in the next volume in this series, M. S. Anderson, *Europe in the Eighteenth Century* (London, 1961).

XVI

Russia and Turkey

The habit is only slowly disappearing of treating the history of Russia at any time before Peter the Great, as a brief appendix to the more significant affairs of Jülich-Cleves or Pinerolo. As for the Turks, though they are well known as a 'menace' to Europe, their internal régime tends to be regarded as an Asiatic monstrosity unrelated to the political development of civilised countries. Yet the affairs of tsars and sultans

BIBLIOGRAPHY. G. Vernadsky, *The Tsardom of Moscow, 1547–1682*, 2 vols. (New Haven, 1969) could not be used here, but will now be the standard authority in English. General histories of Russia that make use of modern work include M. T. Florinsky, *Russia: a History and Interpretation*, 2 vols. (2nd ed., New York, 1953) and J. D. Clarkson, *A History of Russia from the Ninth Century* (London, 1962)—both fairly substantial on this period. There is still much of value in V. O. Kluchevsky, *A History of Russia*, trans. C. J. Hogarth (London, 1913). Volumes 3 and 4 cover the seventeenth century; but most of volume 4 is now available in a better translation by L. Archibald as V. Klyuchevsky, *Peter the Great* (London, 1958). B. H. Sumner, *Survey of Russian History* (London, 1944) seems designed to frustrate those who use it for a single period; but his very short work *Peter the Great and the Ottoman Empire* (Oxford, 1949) packs in many of his ideas. P. Milioukov, C. Seignobos, and L. Eisenmann, *Histoire de Russie*, vol. 1 (Paris, 1932) is a good source of information. The *Slavonic and East European Review* has several helpful articles, such as L. R. Lewitter, 'Poland, the Ukraine, and Russia in the Seventeenth Century' in vol. 27 (1948–9), and J. H. L. Keep, 'The Regime of Filaret' in vol. 38 (1960–1). *Readings in Russian Civilisation*, ed. Thomas Riha, 2 vols. (Chicago and London, 1964) prints some very useful extracts from both primary and secondary authorities.

The complexities of land tenure and its essential place in political development are made comprehensible in J. Blum, *Lord and Peasant in Russia* (New York, 1964), which has a good glossary and bibliography. M. Cherniavsky, *Tsar and People* (New Haven and London, 1961) is an effort to interpret the changing concept of Tsardom. A monograph that throws light on administration in Russia as well as on colonisation is G. V. Lantzeff, *Siberia in the Seventeenth Century* (Berkeley and Los Angeles, 1943). W. E. D. Allen, *The Ukraine* (Cambridge, 1940) deals with both Russian and Turkish aspects of the question.

are highly relevant, not so much because—wherever the meaningless boundary of the continents is drawn—they ruled between them something like half Europe, as because in each of the eastern empires there were played out on a far larger scale than in the west the same struggles to establish the unified and centralised state. Russia by the end of the century was beyond doubt a monarchy in the western style and a part of the diplomatic entanglement. The Ottoman Empire was in one of its periods of retreat; but there was no reason to assume that it would not recover as it had before, or that a 'westernising' movement would not arise to change its political character. The rulers of both countries had achieved more successfully than any of their western counterparts the almost universal aim of applying their resources to military power. There are many difficulties in the way of making the comparisons as enlightening as they ought to be. Barriers of language and accessibility still make even the work of current Russian historians slow to penetrate to the west; and in both countries the nature of society and government in the period limits the range of surviving sources. Too many questions will have to go unasked.

Russia in the Time of Troubles

The 'Time of Troubles' is a term applied aptly enough to the whole generation between the death of Ivan IV in 1584 and the reign of Michael Romanov. But it was in the decade before Michael's accession in 1613 that central authority was at its lowest. It was not merely a matter of rivalry for the throne among noble families. They were able to exploit, on a Russian scale, the forces that in their smaller way such rebels as the magnates of the French religious wars had used. It was easy for Russians to find a claimant to the throne. The story which now circulated that Dmitry, the murdered son of Ivan IV, had survived, or miraculously resurrected, was an ordinary part of the mythology

The Ottoman Empire is a less accessible topic. The chapters in Lavisse and Rambaud, *Histoire Générale*, vol. v (Paris, 1905), chap. 20 and vol. vi, chap. 22, and in the *New Cambridge Modern History*, vol. 5, chap. 21 (by A. N. Kurat) are helpful. For fuller details on the whole subject it is still necessary to approach the old and ponderous German works, J. W. Zinkeisen, *Geschichte des Osmanischen Reiches in Europa*, vol. v (Hamburg, 1840–63) and N. Jorga, *Geschichte des Osmanischen Reiches*, vol. iv (Gotha, 1908). H. A. R. Gibb and H. Bowen, *Islamic Society and the West* (London, 1950), though covering a wider period has a good summary of the institutions. D. M. Vaughan, *Europe and the Turk* (Liverpool, 1954) deals with the 'crusade' movement as well as the more hardheaded diplomatic and military affairs. P. Coles, *The Ottoman Impact on Europe* (London, 1968), is a well-written illustrated survey.

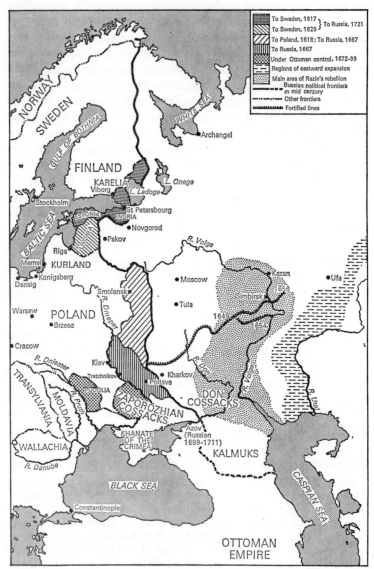

Map 6. Russia and Poland, 1617–1721

surrounding tsardom. Nor was there any difficulty for the boyars excluded from the court in finding allies among men of their own kind whose estates happened to be under the Polish instead of the Russian Crown. Surrounded by his Russian and Polish sponsors and backed by the forces they could raise as easily as could monarchs, the 'False Dmitry' enjoyed a triumphal entry into Moscow and a brief reign in which he retained some of the popularity of the rebel hero. Who he really was remains a matter of speculation. The Poles proclaimed that he had become a Catholic, and there were hopes among the Jesuits of a movement for the reunion of the two churches. For the moment no-one seemed to expect any policy or promises from him: merely to be the enemy of the existing régime was enough to win the support of many great families, of peasants, of smaller landholders, and of the Moscow townsmen. But the pseudo-tsar was no mere Perkin Warbeck: he showed signs of an almost progressive outlook, complaining of boyar ignorance and isolation, rejecting both the brutality and the ceremonial of palace custom. It was not a situation that could last for long. Like later occupants of the Kremlin, 'Dmitry' became more and more afraid of treason among his supporters. His Polish allies were not in a position to defend him with adequate force, and rivals of those boyars he favoured could easily denounce him as an instrument of the foreigners. In 1606 a new mass rising in Moscow was organised—ostensibly to defend the tsar from the Poles—and 'Dmitry' was murdered. The head of one of the greatest boyar families, Vasily Shuisky, was proclaimed as the true tsar who would restore the traditional forms of Russian paternal rule.

Shuisky appears to have made some effort to play the part of an up-holder of law rather than a wholly irresponsible boyar-sponsored despot. Whatever constitutional ideas could be read into his promises did not matter much. Nor did it really improve his security when he arranged that the church should prove the fraudulence of the False Dmitry by bringing the remains of the Real Dmitry to Moscow and showing them working miracles. Shuisky's fumbling efforts to win the support of the church included what later proved an important move: he repudiated the appointment as Patriarch of Filaret, the head of the boyar family of Romanov. Outside Moscow none of these palace manœuvres seemed to matter much; for it was at this moment that the rising of the Cossacks[1] threatened to destroy the entire apparatus of the state. Shuisky, once the rebels had been turned back from Moscow, put

[1] See p. 228.

all the armed force he could raise at the disposal of his supporters in the provinces to punish their enemies.

No consecutive account of the events between 1606 and 1610 can make much sense. There was in 1607 a second Polish-sponsored False Dmitry, and a blockade of Moscow which led Shuisky to make an agreement with Sigismund of Poland. It did not last long; and the tsar was soon seeking support of the Swedes instead. At the rebel capital at Tushino Russian opponents of Shuisky gathered whatever forces they could get, including Poles acting independently of their king. The more ingenious or widely connected nobles, as well as ambitious lesser men, contrived to play off one source of authority against another and demand rewards from both. Marina, the Polish wife of the first False Dmitry, turned up at Tushino with the claim that the new one must obviously be her husband too. In 1610, when Sigismund had established a headquarters at Smolensk, the Tushino leaders rallied round his son Vladislav as tsar. Shuisky was overthrown by a military defeat and by another Moscow urban rising; and slowly power seemed to be passing into Polish hands everywhere except in the Swedish-dominated areas of the north.

There was still a strong 'Cossack' element in the peasant population that aimed not to take over the state but to dissolve it or simply escape from it. But there were also many among the rebels of various allegiances who retained their hope of a stable propertied society in which they would share. The increase of Polish and Swedish power produced, in towns and among the *dvoriane*, an element of national resistance. The church, though rightly regarded as one of the most merciless landowners, was an influence on the side of order. In 1611, with the Poles occupying the Kremlin, the Swedish army in Novgorod, and hordes under Cossack inspiration imposing a military rule of terror on much of the countryside, there developed a movement in favour of some kind of collective national stability. It came chiefly from what can reasonably be described as the middle classes—the propertied townsmen and the provincial *dvoriane*. Some of Sigismund's supporters had already attempted to get the Poles to commit themselves to a document that would guarantee a stable form of administration and in particular give a better legal and social status to landowners below the boyar level—a move which the boyars had then tried to frustrate. One of the military leaders responsible for Shuisky's fall, Prokopy Liapunov, went some way towards becoming a national leader of the *dvoriane*, with a strongly conservative religious element in his appeal and a vague promise to get rid of foreigners. His movement became such a tangle of incompatible aims and alliances that it easily fell to pieces when he was murdered by disillusioned Cossack supporters. But in 1612 a new armed force appeared, recruited partly by an urban leader, Kuzma Minin—a butcher, in the literal sense, from Nizhny-Novgorod. Its commander was a boyar general, Prince Dmitry Pozharsky, who had kept well away from the murders and executions of Moscow. Their range of support was meant to extend from the peasants to the great landowners; Cossacks, and the palace nobility, were as much the enemy as were foreigners. The appeal to all seekers of order and peace was strengthened by calling, at Yaroslavl, a Zemsky Sobor.[1] The 'assembly of the land', however uncertain its power, was a means of reconstituting out of the local communities a Russian state separated from the foreign invaders and their discredited princely allies. It had surprising success in collecting men and money for an attack on Moscow and the Poles. The leaders of the assembly were by no means high-minded patriots rejecting the sordid world of alliances and compromises. Pozharsky was quite prepared to reach an agreement with the Swedes, or to become a candidate for the throne himself. Eventually he became the ally of the Cossacks in forming an army under Prince Trubetskoy which decisively beat the Poles. The army was soon the one effective political power; at its headquarters a new Zemsky Sobor assembled in 1613. Besides the Cossacks and soldiers all sections of the landholders down to the free peasantry had a voice, as well as the towns and the church. It was this body that proclaimed as tsar Filaret's sixteen-year-old son Michael, the first of the Romanov dynasty. Though the Romanovs were not much different from any other great family, there was just enough of the *politique* and the nationalist in the régime of Minin and Pozharsky to establish a feeling that the boyars and the foreigners had been more decisively beaten than before and that the disbanding of armies could begin. No-one took very seriously the talk of written constitutions or guarantees against unacceptable royal power.

The troubles of the Turks

If the Russian conflicts can appear to western eyes as one caricature of the affairs of powers that thought themselves politically more advanced, the Ottoman Empire provided another—but by an artist with an even more extravagant imagination. To the Turks Europe was still a region for military expansion, a source of slaves, and a place that supplied a growing variety of manufactures with no effort on the part of the con-

[1] See p. 213.

sumer. It also provided some useful military technicians; but nothing in the cultural, political, or economic life of the unbelievers seemed likely to have any effect on the centre of universal civilisation or on its non-European dependencies. No-one could deny that Turkish power had been badly shaken in the later part of the sixteenth century. Though there was no serious danger to the North African possessions—of which Egypt as a source of grain was the most important—the naval defeats and the decline in effectiveness of central control meant a loss of bargaining-power. The allegiance of the Danube lands was insecure. The treaty of Zitva-Torok in 1606 was remarkable mainly because it was a document in western form, signed outside Constantinople, which involved recognising the infidel Habsburg Emperor as in some sense an equal of the sultan. On the whole these matters were of less concern than the long and at first unsuccessful wars against Persia.

The dangers must not be exaggerated. Constantinople was unlikely to undergo humiliations comparable with the occupation of Moscow by foreigners. But it was an unhappy period for the monarchy. Ahmed I, who became sultan in 1603, was a boy with some zeal for maintaining a reign of terror in the palace and costly but unproductive military campaigns on the frontiers. His younger brother Mustafa was regarded as so helpless an idiot that there was no need to insist on the custom whereby he would have been strangled as a potential pretender to the throne. He became the instrument of one of the rival groups round the palace—the *ulemas*, the great officers of the Muslim Institution, whose learning extended equally to the Koran and to the civil administration and who had some prospect of bestowing on an imbecile sultan the rôle of saintly sovereign. With them the rival military élites, the Janissaries and the Spahis, fought a struggle for power made more chaotic by occasional urban risings. A major part in the palace intrigues was played by women—mainly European women, since the subject peoples, and the Greeks in particular, provided the royal wives. The mother of the reigning sultan, the *valida*, was a figure who usually had a good chance to become something of a Catherine de Medici. Mustafa was soon deposed, but reappeared in 1622 after his rival, Ahmed's son Osman,[1] had been murdered. There was even, in these years of instability, a pretender—but one who had to confine his activities to the European fringes of the Empire. Jachia ben Mehemet claimed to be a son of Mohammed III, hidden away to escape the strangling, and educated in the Greek Church. Throughout the Thirty Years War he and his little

[1] For the war with Poland under Osman, see p. 350.

group of associates wandered round the courts of Catholic Europe with schemes for the liberation of Balkan Christians and a great Crusade against Constantinople. Father Joseph and Wallenstein at different times showed some interest in the idea. The prospect of a Christian sultan and caliph was not one to be taken seriously; but a union of European powers against the Turk had its attractions as one of the moves in diplomatic trickery. The Jesuits always kept it in their store of possible weapons.

Even Islam had its religious divisions; and the Moslem Institution was no longer a means of maintaining the purity of political life or its separation from hereditary wealth. The Janissaries had ceased to be recruited mainly by the *devshirme*, the system of seizing selected boys from Christian families. They could grow rich, marry, introduce their sons and favoured dependants into the corps, and devote themselves when they chose more to political action than to the defence of the Empire. The central administration, from the Grand Vizir downwards had also become corrupted by nepotism and patronage. In theory the world was still divided into the Domain of Islam, where the believers had unchallenged control, and the Domain of War where there lived the tolerated unbelievers, principally Christians and Jews, and the idolaters who should be made to accept Islam. In practice the political condition of provinces varied according to the military situation and the type of inhabitants. Only a Muslim population was supposed to do military service in return for their holding of land; the rest paid tribute in money or in kind. The *byelerbeys* who ruled provinces and the *sandjakbeys* in charge of the districts into which, on the basis of the number of troops raised, provinces were divided, were originally military commanders first and administrative rulers only as a part of their recruiting and taxing duties. But where frontiers were stable and armies inactive they had become the greatest landowners. In most of the European territories they were still dependent for their appointment on central patronage; but in the principalities of Wallachia and Moldavia, the most autonomous of the European possessions, the rulers were virtually chosen by the rest of the native nobility. The Barbary states and the Khanate of the Crimea were more independent still, acknowledging the suzerainty of the sultan largely as a matter of practical convenience that cost them nothing.

Murad IV was a successful sultan. When he came of age, after taking the throne as a minor in 1623, he beheaded, strangled, or drowned everyone who caused him even trivial irritation, and did so with enough speed and confidence to prevent conspiracies against him. More important for his success, he was able to reconquer most of the territories lost to the Persians in the war of 1602–18 and to distribute lands that won him supporters and revenue. Fiefs that had ceased to supply funds were confiscated. The Janissaries and Spahis were denounced for their rebellious conduct and purged of their political leaders. Not only vizirs but a Grand Mufti and a Greek Patriarch lost their heads on suspicion of disloyalty. He was also a puritan in the colloquial sense of the word: smoking was prohibited on pain of death, idleness treated as evidence of criminal intent.

Ibrahim I was an unsuccessful sultan. Though he executed the Grand Vizir and planned a general massacre of Christians, he was regarded as weak, effeminate, and interested more in ostentatious luxury than government as the function of the palace. He also had the bad luck to be in power at the time of the alarming success of the Venetians in the Balkans and the Mediterranean that enabled them to blockade the Dardanelles. Cossack invasions in the north were producing repeated losses of territory; governors and armies in the frontier provinces were mutinous. So in 1648 the Turks too held their revolution—a palace conspiracy that led to the murder of Ibrahim and the accession of his seven-year-old son Mohammed IV.

The Turkish revival

The decline of central government in the worst periods of both Russian and Turkish misrule was helped by the fact that neither system now enabled a strong ministerial government to supply the deficiencies of hereditary monarchs and warring nobilities. The Tsars had never had an official like the Grand Vizir who had sometimes, in the sixteenth century, been a man with the immense industry and skill needed for central government on such a scale. The Grand Vizir had been head of the 'slave' system of government. But his power had declined, through venality, the strength of the military cliques, and the dominance of the harem. Nevertheless, it was still possible for a strong Vizir to emerge from the palace intrigues. It happened briefly in 1652, when Tarkhan, the sultan's Russian mother, secured the appointment of Tarhondju Ahmed—a highly efficient administrator who unfortunately quarrelled with the corrupt Grand Mufti and was beheaded after only a year in office. It was Tarkhan too who in 1656 won the office for Mohammed Kiuprili.[1] Seventy years old, unworried by the prospects

[1] Köprülü, Koeprili, and Kuprili are among the other versions. The transliterations used here aim to be familiar rather than scholarly.

of dismissal or death and—though hardly literate—immensely experienced in both central and provincial office, Kiuprili made his own terms for accepting the post. In a manœuvre with the sultan and his mother reminiscent of Richelieu, Kiuprili won what amounted to guarantees of absolute power. In his remaining five years of life he carried out a merciless purge of the governing establishment in the capital and the provinces. For any office-holder guilty of corruption or disloyalty the doubt was not whether he would keep his place or lose it but whether he would be strangled or beheaded. The nearest to the position of a Gaston of Orleans[1] too powerful to be a victim was the Chief Eunuch, who escaped with exile. Every execution meant an estate that could be used for the benefit of the central Treasury. Whether the totals quoted for the number of victims, which range from 30,000 to 60,000, are exaggerated or not, Kiuprili certainly brought about a startling change in the sultan's effective power. There were rebellions, organised by frightened office-holders, but with an element of popular resistance to the more efficient taxation. They were crushed because the armies were loyal; and the loyalty was maintained by victories. In the Mediterranean the Venetian advanced bases were recaptured: in Hungary and Transylvania there was the beginning of the new expansion that threatened the Habsburgs.[2] Armies, Kiuprili impressed on the sultan, must be kept on the move; and he added that the same applied to the sultan himself. Kiuprili's vision was in fact a return to the old days of the military empire. Stability, rich estates, and corrupt palace politics had been the cause of disaster—all of them characteristics of the western monarchies. It was the mobile, aggressive power, based on a well-regulated financial system, that avoided rebellion and rewarded its loyal subjects.

Kiuprili's reign of terror is one side of Turkish government. The other, far less conspicuous, is the beginning in the same period of the slow extension of western influence and western administrative methods. Most of the Ottoman Empire's commerce was in the hands of Greeks—so far as it was not run by the Dutch, French, and English companies; and they naturally had a strong interest in competent administration. The post of Interpreter became the centre of a circle of Greek bureaucrats. Keeping well clear of the political struggles, they were able not only to preserve their lives but to build up a system of patronage and hereditary office-holding of their own. A few became, in spite of their origin, powerful landed aristocrats in the western provinces.

[1] See p. 267. [2] See p. 310.

Hereditary power was not one of the forms of decadence that alarmed old Kiuprili: he was succeeded in office by his son Ahmed Kiuprili. The second of what became almost a dynasty of Grand Vizirs could hardly have been more unlike his father. Ahmed represented the old cultural traditions of the empire rather than the military. Poets, historians, and astrologers were as conspicuous in his entourage as executioners in that of his father. He was also a professional politician who defeated the palace intrigues so successfully that he kept his office until his death in 1676. His concern for central administration did not mean that he, any more than his equals in the west, absented himself from military campaigns. He kept the armies in Europe under his direct command. Neither the Hungarian campaigns that ended in 1664 nor the invasion of Poland in the 1670s produced any lasting success, though Kiuprili had no difficulty in posing as a victorious hero for the benefit of the sultan and the people of Constantinople. In the Mediterranean success was more decisive: the surrender of Crete by the Venetians re-established the security of the Empire's homeland from western attack. Kiuprili was naturally well aware of the repercussions his activities were having on the wars among Christian monarchs. Most of them now had their regular diplomatic representatives in Constantinople. But in making western alliances and exploiting other people's conflicts the Turks were still backward. They did not join in the custom of sub-sidising supporters to exercise political pressure in foreign courts. It was not even possible to exploit the competition for Mediterranean commerce except as a source of minor economic advantage. Privileges in Constantinople went to the representatives of whichever power seemed for the moment to be strongest. The French victories over the Dutch in the 1670s won them the sultan's permission to trade in the Red Sea—which may well have been in the end more valuable than any European frontier gains. But the Turks did not in return see any increased prospect of a second front against their European enemies. On the contary, the growth of Mediterranean trade to the east led to talk in Paris of an attack on Egypt and development of the Suez route to the east.

Turkish attacks in Europe

Ahmed Kiuprili was a statesman able to recognise the limits to his reasonable ambitions. To expand the area of warfare too much was to risk defeats that could not be concealed. His successor Kara Mustafa, son-in-law both of the elder Kiuprili and of the sultan, set no bounds at all to his schemes to extend Ottoman power and his own. He had already made an immense fortune before he acquired the highest office: a household of 2,000 slaves and 1,500 concubines was enough to make life at Versailles look frugal. 'Red Apple', the project for an attack on Vienna, was not his invention. The memory of 1529 was still strong in Turkish military tradition, and hopes had risen again during the campaigns of the sixties in Hungary. The Turks had accepted western diplomatic customs to the extent of regarding the Treaty of Vasvar,[1] made with the Emperor in 1664 and timed to remain in force for eighteen years, as at least a strong deterrent to outright attack on Austria. Consequently 1682 had become a date to which advocates of the western invasion looked forward. Mustafa virtually committed himself to a great new advance somewhere when he made with Russia the humiliating Treaty of Radzin (1681) by which Turkey practically withdrew from the Ukraine. The cautious support given to Thököli did not mean that the Hungarian rebel ruler was to play any major part in Turkish plans; but it provided one useful occasion for war. Envoys sent by Leopold to negotiate a renewal of the Treaty of Vasvar mysteriously died. (The Turks saw it as Allah's condemnation of the Christian Emperor; the Austrians could think of other possible reasons.) In the spring of 1683 the march that was to subordinate Christendom to the rule of the sultan began. By July Vienna was summoned to surrender and to accept the true faith of Islam.[2]

It is easy to find reasons on the Turkish side for the failure of the last of all the invasions of Europe from the east. Though Louis XIV gave a firm promise of neutrality, the sultan's only allies were the Crimean Tartars, who were afterwards blamed for failing to hold the relieving army on the Danube. Turkish artillery was not up to the standard against which western defences were now designed to survive. Discipline was not good enough to maintain the long siege while the surrounding countryside was there to be plundered. Fortresses that threatened the Turkish supply-lines were not captured. Nevertheless, it is perfectly conceivable that, at any rate if help had not been forthcoming from John Sobieski, Vienna might have fallen. As it turned out, the victory of the allied force in September began an unprecedented disaster for Turkish power. The army, apart from the Janissary corps, disintegrated. Mustafa was strangled; but his death did not prevent the development of a movement against the sultan himself. When the Holy League of European powers opened in 1684 its unco-ordinated but widely successful attacks on all the western frontiers of his empire, Mohammed IV still showed

[1] See p. 310.   [2] See pp. 311–12.

no great interest in its defence. The Grand Mufti and many of the army commanders joined in the palace revolution of 1687 that finally overthrew him. His brother Suleiman II, who had been kept a virtual prisoner to prevent conspiracies to put him on the throne, was coerced into accepting the succession of which he was very reasonably afraid.

A year later Belgrade fell to the armies under Maximilian of Bavaria. The Venetians, steadily destroying what was left of Turkish Mediterranean power, had occupied most of Greece. A final attack on Constantinople itself seemed possible. But if Islam was in a grievous condition of internal conflict, Christendom was even worse. It was clearly in Louis XIV's interest to keep Turkish forces in the field against the Habsburgs. The French ambassador in Constantinople was able, with plausible assurances that the sultan's principal enemies in Europe were in a desperate plight, to prevent a peace treaty with the Emperor. Under the third Kiuprili Grand Vizir new armies were conscripted and much of the lost territory retaken. The basic military situation was unchanged: whenever a first-rate western force was available it could now defeat any that the Turks could put into the field. European technology in firearms and in defences was better than Turkish; European capacity to devote resources to war hardly less. While in the west the machinery of government could operate tolerably well with no outstanding leadership, accidents of personality still determined the strength or weakness of the sultans. In 1697, when the Emperor was for the moment free to send his best forces against the Turks, the victory of Eugene of Savoy at Zenta left the sultan no escape from a peace settlement that would involve a heavy loss of territory. The Treaty of Karlowitz in 1699 secured the whole of Hungary for the Emperor and the Dalmatian coast for Venice. Otherwise most of the sultan's losses in the Balkans were restored.

The Russian 'Service State'

However important the duties and rewards of service to the state in the Ottoman Empire, its social system was based primarily on the distinctions between believer and unbeliever, bond and free, and within them on the rigid divisions imposed by religious law. In Russia the solution to the Troubles was bound up with the establishment of the 'service state' in which subjects should be put into rigid categories according to the type of service they owed. Social and economic status was in theory a subsidiary matter, and was itself derived from the individual's relationship to the state. A great deal of the effort of Michael Romanov's government went into reconstructing an administrative system extensive enough to ensure in one way or another that obligations to the state were not evaded. A surprising amount of bureaucratic work was in fact achieved. An elaborate census, completed in 1628, though obviously not capable of listing and classifying the entire population, did something to make legal resistance to the flight of the peasants easier. The Treasury in 1631, pressing for an increase in taxation, produced a survey of the armed forces it maintained and the money spent on them—which revealed that in spite of the state's devotion to military service the available *dvorianin* force only amounted to about 40,000 men. Trivial grievances and problems of the provincial officials found their way to Moscow in enormous quantities, and slowly the gulf between the theory of the centralised state and the real life of the peasants, the landlords, and the multiplicity of officials began to narrow.

Conditions in Moscow as Michael's government gradually became established did not make efficient administration easy. For his first six years the tsar shared with the weak sultans of his time the fate of being dominated by his mother. This was 'Martha the Nun', whose connection with church was, like that of her husband, more the result of the Troubles than of religious zeal. Round her a typical palace group of relations and dependants collected. When Filaret himself escaped from Polish captivity by the truce made in 1619, and took up his office as Patriarch, he became even in name an equal ruler with the tsar and in practice the sole head of the state.[1] The church had not much success in trying to use his regal status as a means of introducing a clerical element into the political structure. What did matter to Filaret was that he could add to his power in the state direct control over the huge domains of the church. He sent his wife back to her nunnery, carried out the normal purge of her dependants, and established a carefully restricted princely circle of his own in the highest court offices. The Council of Boyars— the *Duma*—and the Holy Synod of the church became more or less equal political powers.

Below them, Russian office-holding was a matter in which the most intricate problems of family status and right were involved. The *mestnichestvo* was an institution, or legalised custom, of the boyars which depended on a strict order of prestige among officers. Though the office itself was not hereditary, the status it conferred was—and extended to the whole family of the holder. The element of heredity inevitably became far more important in any reckoning of one man's rank against another's than the individual career; but it was an intoler-

[1] See pp. 102–6.

able derogation to have anyone inferior in the rating appointed to a higher post than one's own. The relevant lists of offices had become frozen; so that the introduction of 'new men' to the bureaucracy and of new positions within it was a matter of immense complexity. The whole of Michael's reign was a period in which the '*mestnichestvo* feuds' made the development of a competent central administration difficult. Departmental organisation expanded, more through the 'empire-building' efforts of those who had acquired high office than on any rational system. The *prikazy*—the departments of central government—multiplied. Their size, function, and survival depended mainly on the personal rivalries that surrounded them. The armed forces came in theory under the same system: there were *prikazy* for the cavalry, the artillery, even the Cossacks. Locally the *voevoda*, originally military commanders, organised every aspect of government in the districts they controlled, and were generally undermining the power of older institutions less dependent on the Crown. Two or three hundred of them shared out all but the most sparsely populated areas. Some were almost completely independent rulers, others intermediaries between central and local authority. The almost unanimous view expressed in complaints from the provinces was that they were more corrupt and oppressive than any former authority. But as outsiders they were inevitably open to such accusations. In theory they held office for only a few years and had no opportunity of profitably controlling taxation. To the peasant the Moscow-appointed official was merely one more creator of poverty to add to the landlord, the moneylender, and the priest.

By the time of Michael's death in 1645 the stability of Russian government had certainly improved. The wars against Sweden and Poland were comparatively inexpensive, and had been settled at the cost of abandoning the Baltic lands and the Smolensk region. The conflicts against the Turks had been left to the Cossacks. When they captured the fortress of Azov and offered to cede it to the tsar, Michael refused—on the advice of a Zemsky Sobor. It did not mean that Russia was turning into a peaceful constitutional monarchy. Alexis I, who came to the throne as a youthful tsar surrounded by the familiar palace gangs, was faced during the first years after his accession with urban risings in Moscow and Novgorod, and then with the great Ukrainian revolt.[1] In the midst of it, in 1649, the Moscow government undertook the production of a comprehensive legal Code, the *Ulozhenie*, which was supposed to incorporate the pleas for reform that had been brought

[1] See pp. 229–30.

before it. It was an attempt to assert in a solemn documentary form the total power of the state over the Russian people, and to give to those who administered it a practical new instrument. There had been such Codes before; but the latest was a century old and had little relevance left. In nearly a thousand articles, the *Ulozhenie* brought together a mixture of legal practices and principles, assembled hastily from a great variety of sources. Some of them were familiar parts of Russian tradition, some originated in the requests of the Zemsky Sobor. But the essential articles were those that froze the existing social structure and completed the legal imposition of serfdom.[1] Nothing could be done that would deprive the state of a taxpayer; the Church could no longer expand its estates; townsmen could not leave their towns, nor outsiders compete in town trade; no-one outside the ranks of the *dvoriane* could come into them; no-one could use slavery as an escape from obligations. Existing landholdings were generally confirmed, and the hereditary rights of the boyar families were strengthened. In spite of its size and complexity, the Code did not really define the legal relationship between lord and peasant closely. There were rules about circumstances in which the lord could move his peasants from the land—designed not to protect the peasant but to prevent tax-evasion. What legal rights remained to the serf, in such matters as ownership of his household goods, depended on incomplete rules rather than any comprehensive principles. Where there were doubts, it was clear that the landlord and the knout would normally settle them.

With the defeat of the Ukrainian rebellion and the imposition of the Code, the state seemed to be on the verge of an unprecedented efficiency. It was achieved not by brutal treatment of its subjects—except of course that vast majority of them who lived at the lowest levels of society—but under the reputedly gentle and cultured Alexis. There remained outside the state the Orthodox Church, with its capacity to intervene in political affairs hardly impaired. The Patriarch Nikon, elected in 1652, was one of the great ministers who rose to power by capturing the devotion of the sovereign. His proclaimed purpose was to restore the church to its ancient purity of observance and efficiency of organisation;[2] his political ambition was to re-establish its dominant rôle in the state of which he alleged the 'satanic law' of 1649 was meant to deprive it. Before long he had achieved the same status as Filaret—the equal in majesty of the tsar. It was a position that a conservative church politician of his skill

[1] Extracts from the Code are translated in *Readings in Russian History*, ed. T. Riha, pp. 173–9. See pp. 82–3 above. [2] See pp. 105–6.

could easily have kept; but not one compatible with his leadership of the religious schism. The great reforms of the church created an opposition not only among the clergy and the Russian people, but among the courtiers who were always ready to line up against a royal favourite. By 1658 the great quarrel between Alexis and Nikon had begun. In one sense it demonstrated the strength of the royal government, since it was conducted with no alarming violence and no outside intervention. The reforms had their attractions for the tsar. A united Orthodox Church under the leadership of Moscow would be a great asset in extending Russian power and influence southward. But the settlement by which Nikon was dismissed and his reforms retained was a victory for the state won at the cost of establishing a faith round which opposition could collect. In the resistance of the Old Believers and the use made of them by rebels of every kind, the Russian government for the first time experienced the inconvenience for the state of religious minorities. It was not backward in taking revenge.

Peter the Great

Alexis married twice. His first wife, from the great Miloslavsky family, produced a daughter Sophia and the two defective sons who became the Tsars Fedor III and Ivan V. The second wife of Alexis, Natalia Naryshkin, was a very different character. The daughter of a provincial noble, she was related, through the foreign service of another of her family, to the Scottish Hamiltons and had been educated in a household corrupted—as all good Russians saw it—by western culture. Her son Peter was born in 1672. There was nothing that an older generation of Muscovites would have thought unusual in the events that followed the death of Fedor ten years later. The Miloslavsky and the Naryshkin families were naturally the centre of a palace feud, involving accusations of witchcraft, poisoning, and treason. The Naryshkins had Peter 'elected' tsar at a mass meeting in Red Square. But by superior bribes and promises the Miloslavsky had won over the rank and file of the *streltsi*, the large part-time army of Moscow guards. They now invaded the Kremlin, murdering all the Naryshkins they could find. With the help of a city mob they attacked the houses of boyars, rich merchants, and—in the name of the Old Belief—clergy. Peter, who had watched the proceedings, was allowed to remain 'joint tsar' with Ivan; Sophia was to be regent. For five years the rival parties continued to use torture, public flogging, and execution as their normal weapons. Sophia and Peter, on different occasions, fled for their lives to the Trinity Sergius monastery. Eventually she was defeated and spent the rest of her days under guard in a nunnery; many of the *streltsi* ended theirs on the block. By 1689 Peter's family were in fairly secure control, though the tsar himself was in no hurry to devote himself to politics.

Peter's reign was a translation into Russian terms of the absolute monarchy of the west. In the imagination of the peasants he kept some of the mystery of Tsardom. To those who knew him he was the 'sovereign emperor', and the man in disguise at the dockyards or at the riotous parodies of court and church ceremonial. To the Old Believers he was either a simple usurper or another manifestation of Antichrist. Peter's elaborate week-long orgies of blasphemy and promiscuity with the Most Drunken Synod were no more incompatible with efficient monarchy than was the ceremonial life of Versailles. Western kings went hunting three times a week and had their enemies killed in moderate numbers by professional experts. Peter occasionally wielded the axe himself, and the executions were counted in hundreds. Russian tortures were not more blood-curdling than those applied, for instance, to Henry IV's assassin Ravaillac—they were merely more numerous. Alexander Menshikov, who despite his illiteracy and his obscure origins acquired the highest offices in state and army under Peter, became the owner of 90,000 serfs; but French and English chief ministers seldom died in poverty. Monarchs in their different ways amused themselves extravagantly, rewarded their faithful servants, destroyed those who threatened them: in Peter's Russia the scale was bigger and the manner more candid. All the same, nothing in the west could quite compare with the range of his activities, or his defiance of tradition.

The Great Embassy to the west in 1697 was certainly unique. Though its immediate purpose was less a great vision of westernising Russia than to seek help in defeating the Turks, Peter's acquaintance with the isolated German community in Moscow had made him see how remote in culture and economy Russia had become, by the standards of a nation that was not itself in the forefront of western civilisation. As the half-incognito Peter Mihailov, he contrived to give western court society something of a lesson in not taking itself too seriously. He met the Elector of Brandenburg, the Emperor Leopold, the King of Poland, and William III; he took a gunnery course in Berlin, worked in Dutch shipyards, studied architectural and engineering drawing. There was time for the happier activities that disillusioned Burnet, who had thought him a 'holy man' and made John Evelyn send for Wren to estimate the cost of repairs after the royal party had borrowed his house. Peter returned to deal with a great new revolt of the *streltsi*. As soon as he arrived in Moscow he organised the punishment of the already defeated rebels, with a bloodbath of tortures and executions in which he took a personal share. It was not entirely incongruous that he combined this with the notorious cutting-off of the beards of courtiers. The revolt, partly just the work of the court opposition, was also directed against foreigners, the new mercenary forces, the new church; and the beards, held by Old Believers to be essential for salvation, were a cherished symbol of the old patriarchal authority. God, as everyone knew, had a beard, and man was made in his image. Attempts to make the Russians enjoy themselves in the image of Peter, with tobacco and women to help, were seen rightly as an attack on the church's crushing of thought and enterprise. More seriously, Peter encouraged an expansion of lay printing and publishing. Textbooks on geometry, engineering, and geography, translations of western literature, and even a newspaper appeared—all in a simplified Slavonic alphabet.

Peter's reforms of Russian government did not spring from any sudden inspiration to 'westernise' a 'backward' country. They fluctuated in immediate aim and method; but the consistent purpose was to win military victories. In them his ruthless energy impinged on the old conflict between central and local, territorial and bureaucratic powers. The greatest need was of course money. One of the first features of western economy to be introduced was repeated debasement of the currency followed by a rise in prices. With no merchant and banking community able to lend large sums, the Crown lived on the direct income from lands, and on taxes, a large part of which got lost in the central administrative machine. In 1699 a new central institution, the *Ratusha* run by the merchants of Moscow, was put in charge of the taxation of all the towns. Indirect taxes on almost every purchase and a poll-tax on every individual, though it was claimed that they trebled the revenue, were a new cause of flight and revolt. The assessment of these was closely supervised from the centre. But Peter's policy in the first decade of the new century was to run down the old Moscow administration and rely on the eight provinces into which the whole country was now divided, each responsible for its own unit of the army. Only when the new capital at St Petersburg was usable—at first, like other reforms, it was in constant danger of sinking into a swamp—did a more effective central government appear. The Senate, originally a small body picked by Peter to exercise some of the tsar's authority in his frequent absences at the wars, took advantage of the decline of the old departments. With the help of its vague judicial powers, it became something like a ruling council. But it had to fight for its authority against the *oberfiscal*, who by rooting out corruption was supposed to augment the revenue. In fact, he became the head of a secret service that acquired power by denunciation. 'We all steal,' said Yaguzhinsky, procurator-general and the tsar's chief link with the Senate, 'some on a bigger scale than others.'[1]

Beside the Senate there began to flourish the new-style departments, the Kollegii, modelled on the theories of Leibnitz and on Swedish practice and to some extent staffed by Swedes and Germans. The notion of territorial division had gone: the 'colleges' exercised their departmental function over the whole country. Commerce, industry, and mining had their 'colleges'; one dealt with taxation, another with state expenditure. They were supposed to combine the virtues of committee decisions with professional expertise. But they were also one more addition to the complexities of the competition for central power. The presidents of the 'colleges' became bureaucrats engaged in contests for supremacy which, despite the great personal authority of the Procurator-General and Peter's occasional violent interventions, tended to make government as heavy and almost as inefficient as before.

The effect of the 'Petrine reforms' has ever since been an inexhaustible subject for historical dispute. In the west they have often been imagined far too vividly as a moment when Russia was suddenly translated from barbaric isolation to second-class membership of the community of civilised states. To contemporaries what mattered was the burden of service that the tsar's government could impose; and in this Peter was merely a little more relentless and thorough than most. Much of the 'westernising' was certainly a façade that collapsed. Though there was some increase in textile and metal production, and even some improvement in agriculture, too few of the people were far enough above a bare subsistence level for enterprises maintained by monopoly and urban serfdom to develop into a thriving native capitalism. Cities did become safer and, for the fortunate, freer places to live in. The worst religious taboos were less easily enforced; begging, brigandage, and the oppression of women diminished. The apparently preposterous 'Table of Ranks' of 1721 marked a real success in replacing the intricacies of status and privilege that were the essence of Russian upper society by distinctions that the state could control and exploit more effectively. In the great monarchical task of taming the nobility, Peter must be rated highly among his contemporaries.

[1] Quoted in Klyuchevsky, *Peter the Great* (1958 trans.), p. 244.

Russia and Turkey at war

Peter as a child had liked to play at soldiers. His first regiments were his boy-companions; then young men of the court volunteered to serve in them; real horses, artillery, specially built fortresses were provided for him to play with. For his make-believe wars German officers and technicians were recruited to teach methods of fighting unknown to the old Russian armies. His commander-in-chief, Patrick Gordon, was a Catholic Scot. The two 'regiments of boy-soldiers' became a part of the Russian forces. It was hard to say where the game ended and reality began. (Western kings and western generals thought themselves different from Peter.) Of the thirty-five years of the reign, Russia was at peace for about two. The wars were not unproductive frontier clashes or dynastic quarrels of the kind that kept western soldiers occupied: they involved great territorial hopes and fears on fronts a thousand miles apart. The three great enemies—Poland, Sweden, and Turkey—were still capable of inflicting almost unlimited destruction; and the Turks, in spite of their retreat after 1688, still seemed to Russia the greatest menace.

The last great manœuvres of Peter's make-believe armies led in 1695 and 1696, to attacks on the Turkish fortress of Azov, with Peter as a bombardier and then as a captain in his newly built fleet. The capture of the strongpoint that Russia had previously refused as a gift from the Cossacks was in itself no great triumph for Peter, and a minor addition to the disasters that were threatening the Turks; but it was a demonstration of the success of the technical advances in both land and naval armaments for which Peter had begun to employ western engineers. Except as an oratorical convention, the Christian crusade against the infidel was not at this stage more important to Peter than it was to his allies in the 'Holy League'. But the prospect of a great drive against the Turks became much more attractive to Peter after the capture of Azov: it was an enterprise in which he could win and exploit the close support of the western powers. The Great Embassy was intended to make Russia for the first time a leading partner in European warfare. Unluckily it came at the moment when the western powers, involved in the profundities of the Spanish Succession, were anxious to take their gains from the successes in the east and establish peace. The Treaty of Karlowitz[1] was from the Russian point of view a misfortune, which destroyed the prospect of consolidating their power on the Black Sea.

[1] See pp. 361, 374.

The splendid new fleet could not be used without risking a war on too wide a front.

In 1700, with vague hopes of support from the Poles and the Danes, Peter switched his military activity to the north. The 'window on the west' was even less of a deep-laid policy than the 'crusade': the object was victory for its own sake wherever it could be won—though Peter was well aware of the possibilities that Baltic conquests could involve. His defeat at Narva, by a far smaller Swedish force than the 40,000 soldiers the vast Russian recruiting system was able to supply did not for a moment suggest to him that the resources of the state might be better used for other ends. He began immediately on the schemes that were to produce an army to fight the Swedes on equal terms. Numbers were still the principal aim. But modernisation of arms and equipment, with the help of a renewed supply of western technicians, was an essential part of the plan. It was just as important to build up a diplomatic 'presence' in the courts of Europe. While the sultan remained a remote and alien potentate, whose envoys to Europe were unthinkable as members of the ambassadorial 'club', Peter's lavishly spending embassies and well-informed political intriguers were becoming an accepted part of the scene. In 1709 the Battle of Poltava, which destroyed the army Charles XII had taken into the Ukraine, established Russia unshakeably as an ally or enemy that no-one could ignore. With Russian forces securely in possession of a Baltic coastline, Peter could at last become the mighty liberator of Christians from the Turk. Ten thousand Moldavian soldiers and twenty thousand Serbs were, their secret envoys were said to have promised, ready to rise in support of their champion. 'Peter, Emperor of the Russo-Greeks', as his portrait, circulated in the Turkish possessions, was inscribed, could dominate the Black Sea and the eastern Mediterranean, with limitless lines of expansion open to him. It was a dream that he managed to reconcile with anxious diplomatic negotiations in Constantinople designed to prevent the Turks from assisting their embarrassing guest Charles XII. The anxieties soon proved more realistic. In 1711, on the banks of the Pruth, Peter's modern army found itself at the mercy of the horde, 200,000 strong, that the decadent empire of the sultan could still assemble. Only negotiation on the spot saved him from the final irony of being taken prisoner by the forces of the east.

XVII

Britain and the Netherlands

Kings and their dependants were nearly everywhere the triumphant rulers of nations and makers of wars. But in two of the great states of the west, government by a monarch and a court was in the end successfully resisted. By an oddly appropriate combination of design and accident, William of Orange, who had brought the Netherlands[1] closer than ever before to dynastic rule, arrived in 1688 on the throne from which English political leaders had, for the second time in half a century, in effect

BIBLIOGRAPHY.   There is no modern substitute for the large-scale account of British history in the seventeenth century begun by S. R. Gardiner in his *History of England 1603–42* (10 vols., London, 1883–4), *History of the Great Civil War* (2nd ed., 4 vols., London, 1893), and *History of the Commonwealth and Protectorate* (2nd ed., 4 vols., London, 1903). The last of these was continued by C. H. Firth, *The Last Years of the Protectorate* (2 vols., London, 1910), which in turn was finished by Godfrey Davies, *The Restoration of Charles II* (Oxford, 1955). David Ogg, *England in the Reign of Charles II* (2 vols., Oxford, 1934) and *England in the Reigns of James II and William III* (Oxford, 1955) cover a wide range of topics in the later period. G. M. Trevelyan, *England under Queen Anne* (3 vols., London, 1930–4) is an account closer to the Macaulay tradition. One-volume surveys incorporating recent research and interpretation are Christopher Hill, *The Century of Revolution* (London, 1961), Perez Zagorin, *The Court and the Country* (London, 1969), and Ivan Roots, *The Great Rebellion, 1642–1660* (London, 1966).

Among the many specialised studies of the English Revolution and its aftermath are M. A. Judson, *The Crisis of the Constitution* (New Brunswick, 1949); D. Mathew, *The Jacobean Age* (London, 1938); J. H. Hexter, *The Reign of King Pym* (Cambridge, Mass., 1941); H. F. Kearney, *Strafford in Ireland* (Manchester, 1959); C. H. Firth, *Cromwell's Army* (London, 1902); P. H. Hardacre, *The Royalists in the Puritan Revolution* (The Hague, 1956); J. R. Jones, *The First Whigs* (Oxford, 1961); J. H. Plumb, *The Growth of Political Stability in England, 1675–1723* (London, 1967); Keith Feiling, *A History of the Tory Party, 1640–1714* (Oxford, 1924) and *British Foreign Policy 1660–1672* (London, 1930); C. Wilson, *Profit and Power* (London, 1957); G. S. Holmes, *British Politics in the Age of Anne* (London, 1967).

---

[1] The term 'Netherlands' is used here for the United Provinces of the north, as distinct from the Spanish Netherlands.

deposed their king. Throughout their internal conflicts, the affairs of the two countries had been interwoven by rivalries, alliances, and similarities of theory and practice. Each had been bitterly divided between centralising and decentralising forces, between rival economic interests, between versions of Protestant Christianity that served to rouse emotion and belligerence. Each had a single great city so rich that governments could not easily resist its political demands. After repeated commercial and military struggles against each other, they now seemed firmly united in the exhausting wars against France. They were agreed in offering a limited toleration in religion and in political ideas, combined with intense suspicion of their Catholic minorities. They were agreed too in accepting as a permanent part of their governing machinery a central representative body. A large share of power was held, in Holland and England more than in the countries joined to them, by men whose wealth came from the accumulation and use of capital rather than simply from land; though to label the Regents and the Parliamentary leaders alike as 'bourgeois' does not take us far. If the two stories are set side by side they may throw some light on each other.

Not all the major figures have good biographies. Of the immense number on Cromwell that by C. H. Firth (London, 1900) remains one of the best straightforward accounts. H. R. Trevor-Roper, *Archbishop Laud* (London, 1940); D. H. Willson, *James VI and I* (London, 1956); Andrew Browning, *Thomas Osborne, Earl of Danby* (3 vols., Glasgow, 1951); J. P. Kenyon, *Robert Spencer, Earl of Sunderland* (London, 1958); C. V. Wedgwood, *Thomas Wentworth, First Earl of Strafford* (rev. ed., London, 1961); and Menna Prestwich, *Lionel Cranfield: Politics and Profits under the Early Stuarts* (Oxford, 1966) are a few that attempt very different tasks successfully.

On the Netherlands the indispensable work in English is by Pieter Geyl: *The Revolt of the Netherlands, 1555–1609* (2nd ed., London, 1958), and *The Netherlands in the Seventeenth Century*, part one, *1609–1648* (London, 1961— first published in 1936 as *The Netherlands Divided*), part two, *1648–1715* (London, 1964). Earlier general histories are P. J. Blok, *History of the People of the Netherlands*, trans. O. A. Bierstadt and R. Putnam (vols. 3 and 4, London, 1898–1912) and G. Edmundson, *History of Holland* (Cambridge, 1912). Much the best short account is C. Wilson, *The Dutch Republic and the Civilisation of the Seventeenth Century* (London, 1968.) There is a useful survey of the period in B. H. M. Vlekke, *The Evolution of the Dutch Nation* (New York, 1945). C. R. Boxer, *The Dutch Seaborne Empire 1600–1800* (London, 1965) has a good deal of material on conditions at home. There are several articles on seventeenth-century topics in *Britain and the Netherlands*, ed. J. S. Bromley and E. H. Kossmann, 3 vols. (London, 1960, Groningen, 1964, and London, 1968). A brilliant essay on social, economic and cultural aspects is now available in English: J. H. Huizinga, *Dutch Civilisation in the Seventeenth Century* (London, 1968).

The accession of James I in 1603 and the truce in the Netherlands six years later each produced a political agglomeration in which one state was dominant over the others. But to most Englishmen their Irish colonial territory and their monarch's separate realm of Scotland were far less important than were the lesser Netherlands provinces to the inhabitants of Holland. In both countries it became clear how different was the central power of the court and the dynasty from that of the economic capital. Charles I and the House of Orange both drew their support more from the outlying regions than from the centre of wealth. In England this was less obvious because the long-established monarchy had collected round itself a large number of allies and beneficiaries—officeholders, monopolists, higher clergy, and all whose aspirations, traditions, or connections drew them towards the court. The Netherlands, much to its economic benefit, had no court, and no established royalty. But the members of the Orange family soon came to represent no less than the Stuarts the hereditary principle, the power of the rural nobility, and foreign policies based on dynastic ambitions and alliances. Ironically they attempted to gain prestige by the marriage of Maurice's nephew William to Charles's daughter Mary at the moment when royal power in England was about to collapse.

Political power in Britain

James I came to the stable, broadly supported English monarchy from a land where heads of great clans could still fight for control of the Crown. English courtiers and ministers indicated respectfully that they would not tolerate a preponderance of barbarous Scots in the English court or council. Not all Elizabeth's kingdom was a model of advanced civilisation. At the moment of her death Ireland had just been brought back under military control; but despite Tudor efforts to impose an English system of landownership and government on the Irish chiefs, only the Pale of Dublin with its English gentry and official class was reliably administered on the queen's behalf. Outside it the process of turning Ireland into an area of new colonisation was still far from complete. Direct government from London was out of the question. Even in England itself local loyalties and, faintly, the possibility of local rebellion survived. An M.P. who spoke of his 'country' usually meant by it his county. The county was the principal unit of justice, within which the J.P.s, the Sheriff, and the Deputy Lieutenants formed a ruling community that meant more in the lives of most inhabitants than the central government. The Council in the North and the Council in the Marches of Wales were instruments of royal power that were liable to fall under the control of the great men of the region.

Nevertheless, by contemporary standards, England was now the most centralised of states. There were no significant internal customs barriers; the privileges of towns were limited to administrative matters; regional representative assemblies were unheard of. The king's Privy Council was a governing body whose powers, through proclamations, directions to local authorities, and influence on the 'prerogative' courts of justice, seemed to be growing continually. But the efforts of the representative assembly to extend its political influence were already a very familiar problem. In their dealings with the monarch, Elizabeth's parliaments had learnt how to combine toughness on specific points with fulsome assurances of loyalty. The range within which dispute and bargaining about spheres of authority and financial pressure could operate seemed to be fairly well defined. There was no reason to think that relations with James would be much different.

Behind his pompous verbiage about Divine Right, the new king accepted, as had Elizabeth, that the most decisive way of making or declaring a law was by statute.[1] He accepted that for any abnormal revenue the Crown was dependent on parliament; and in resisting any tendency for direct taxation to become a main source of regular revenue, all politicans were agreed. Peers and M.P.s accepted that the king was entitled to call and dissolve parliament when he saw fit, and that in emergency he could exercise virtually unlimited powers of government. The notion of collective resistance to a monarch, to which the United Provinces owed their very existence, had scarcely arisen in England. Rebellion was an act of local defiance, certain, since the successes of the Tudors against it, to meet with due retribution. If evil ministers of the Crown were opposed by parliament, this was in principle the same thing as resistance to rebels—the upholding of the state against those who would harm it for their private ends. Nowhere else did the possibility of civil war seem so remote.

Political power in the Netherlands

Stuart England inherited the stability of a century of Tudor administration. The United Provinces were still uncertain of survival after their thirty years of war against Spain. In their outward forms of government

[1] But see the articles by R. W. K. Hinton in *Cambridge Historical Journal*, vol. 11 (1955) and vol 13 (1957), and the criticism of his ideas by J. P. Cooper in *Britain and the Netherlands*, vol. 1, pp. 63–8.

the two nations could hardly have been more different. The revolt had never produced agreement either on military strategy or on the kind of state that was to be established when the military Union of Utrecht was succeeded by a permanent peacetime system. Both William the Silent and his son Maurice had come close to establishing a monarchy, and had drawn back in face of widespread opposition. There had been an attempt to set up an ecclesiastical Synod with political powers. Mistrust within and between the various provinces led to a requirement of unanimity not only in the Estates General but for many purposes in provincial assemblies too: it has been reckoned that a decision could depend on the assent of 1,200 individuals.[1] The Council of State, itself composed of provincial representatives, was pushed into comparative insignificance. To foreign governments willing to incur the displeasure of Spain by establishing relations with the new state there were many diplomatic problems. Their Noble High Mightinesses the States General were not an easily acceptable substitute for a king. It seemed natural to regard Maurice as an effective head of state. But it was Johan van Oldenbarnevelt who, from his position as leader of the Holland delegation, established himself as a virtual chief minister. He and his immediate circle of dependants initiated policy, conducted internal and external negotiations, and formed increasingly a governing political party. His office of Grand Pensionary and Advocate of Holland did not exist in the other provinces, and easily came to be regarded by his supporters as making him the civil head of the Union.

The hostility between Oldenbarnevelt and Maurice, Count of Nassau and from 1618 Prince of Orange, gradually aligned the many different strands of dispute during the twelve-year truce. It was Oldenbarnevelt himself who had urged the Estates of Utrecht, Overyssel, and Gelderland to elect Maurice to the office of Stadholder, primarily but not entirely a military position, which he already occupied in Holland and Zeeland. (His cousin William Louis was Stadholder of Friesland and Groningen.) Though the immediate aim was to avoid further danger of monarchy, it was also a move towards a real federation. By the time of the truce the prospect of unity seemed to the Regents of Holland to depend on their own hegemony over the rest of the provinces. So long as each state ran its own army and fleet, raised its own taxes, and pursued its own interests in foreign affairs and war, the one whose economic strength was overwhelmingly the greatest could not easily be resisted. National forces were almost entirely mercenaries. Maurice had good

[1] R. Mousnier, *Histoire générale des civilisations*, vol. 4 (Paris, 1956), p. 168.

reason to oppose the growth of the power of Holland. It meant in effect rule by a narrow and closed group of rich Amsterdam families, interested primarily in destroying the economy of Antwerp and monopolising European and overseas commerce. As administrative offices grew in number, they became the virtual property of the Regents—and it was doubtful whether this was much better in its effects than the system of venality in royal courts. Amsterdam was by no means united in support of the rulers of Holland. The majority of its burgomasters and merchants resented the power of the East India Company, a preserve of the Advocate and his circle who refused permission for a new West India Company.[1] Whatever the constitutional theory, the little group of active politicians seemed to be depriving the city of its power. No part of the United Provinces, except possibly Friesland, could be said to have a widely representative political system. But as the Regents of Holland gradually lost their direct connection with commerce and became pure financiers and exploiters of office, the Netherlands developed some of the worst characteristics of aristocratic government. On paper it all seemed to add up to a state as bad as Poland. In practice it achieved a prosperity and a culture unrivalled in Europe. Even in its worst moments of defeat, the Dutch state remained solvent.

Disputes in the Netherlands

In England and in the Netherlands the political quarrels of the first half of the century showed that, even within the Protestant faith, religious differences could be highly effective in turning a complex assortment of rivalries into a clash between two impassioned causes. In both countries the basis of the doctrinal conflict was the debate between strict Calvinism and the more relaxed Protestantism of the Arminians.[2] It was felt to be annoying but not astonishing that James I in 1611 formally conveyed to Oldenbarnevelt and the Estates General detailed arguments on predestination and denunciations of the heretical doctrines being taught at Leiden. The offending professor, Vorstius, was dismissed. Oldenbarnevelt and the majority of the Regents of Holland saw in the church's claims to enforce its dictates a threat both from within Holland and from the Union as a whole to their own political power. Dutch Arminianism was therefore unlike the later English movement that borrowed its name in that it represented, as its 'Remonstrance' showed, a generally tolerant and erastian attitude. In 1614 the Holland Estates carried Oldenbarnevelt's resolution condemning the imposition of ex-

[1] See pp. 64–5, 67.　　　　　　[2] See p. 115.

tremist doctrines. They could not enforce their policy in towns whose burgomasters disliked it. Those in Amsterdam who had wanted to continue the war with Spain that brought them great commercial benefits backed the Counter-Remonstrants[1]—despite a brilliant lecture from Grotius on the virtues of secular state government. As the quarrel spread from clergy to congregations there was a good deal of popular resistance to whichever side was in power: at the Hague Counter-Remonstrants were driven to worship outside the town; in Amsterdam it was the Remonstrants who had to hold their services in warehouses.

The real threat of civil war came when Maurice of Nassau, not normally a religious zealot of any kind, decided to use the occasion for a showdown with Oldenbarnevelt. As the accepted leader in war, Maurice had disappointed the opponents of the truce with Spain by agreeing to Oldenbarnevelt's negotiation. Since then he had on various political issues moved nearer to the Calvinist side. While Oldenbarnevelt was trying to maintain good relations with the French government, Maurice became involved in intrigues with the Huguenot nobility. Instead of France he saw a possible ally in England—a prospect unwelcome to some of his supporters in Amsterdam. Though Maurice stood for the supremacy of the Union in war and diplomacy, there was never a simple division between central and local power. The Remonstrant party worked to establish the authority both of the Estates of Holland and of those town magistracies that supported them. In 1617 the Estates after long debate carried the 'sharp resolution', asserting their supremacy in religion, authorising the recruitment of local mercenary forces—the *waardgelders*—and demanding oaths of obedience from the national armies. Maurice and William Louis as Stadholders, and Reinier Pauw the leading Burgomaster of Amsterdam, were ready to act as decisively as they could against this threat to the very existence of the Union. If either side had found solid support it might well have resorted to armed attack; but in fact every assembly and every town and province was divided. Though in most places the Counter-Remonstrant cause was the popular one, it had little connection with ideas of resistance. The only consistent theme in the flood of propaganda was that the Remonstrant party was secretly in league with Spain and Rome—a notion the Catholics themselves did hardly anything to justify. In face of the hostility of the majority in every provincial government except Holland and Utrecht, the Remonstrants gradually abandoned what had never been a wholehearted struggle. Maurice was able one by one to turn out the Remon-

[1] See p. 116.

strant magistracies in towns outside Holland and disband the *waard-gelders*. When he had eliminated serious opposition elsewhere he staged what amounted to an invasion of Holland with a national army, purging the town magistracies and so creating a Counter-Remonstrant majority in the Estates. In May 1619 a specially created court sentenced Olden-barnevelt to death and Grotius to the life imprisonment from which he soon escaped to exile.[1]

Maurice's success against Oldenbarnevelt and Holland, and the demonstration of unity at the Synod of Dort, did not noticeably strengthen the authority of the Union. It showed the lack of any central political or judicial institutions through which his personal supremacy could work. His brother Frederick Henry, who in 1625 succeeded him in the five Stadholderates and the office of Captain-General, had—for what it was worth—the advantage of appearing as the next war leader. The end of the truce in 1621 brought a new and exhausting war with Spain. Though there was no serious hope of reconquering the south, Frederick Henry's victories at 's Hertogenbosch in 1629 and Maastricht in 1632, and the capture of Breda in 1637, gave him popular glory. On the other hand he was blamed for the troubles of the navy, largely through his reluctance to appoint professional admirals. The tendency to give such offices to men of noble family was part of his one consistent aim—to turn the Netherlands into a monarchy under the House of Orange. His court, in various newly built palaces, gave to the nobility a fresh unity and ambition. It was corrupt, French in speech and culture, isolated from provincial politics. Gradually court influence was inserted into the government of the smaller provinces and poorer towns by securing the appointment of its nominees to local offices and hence to the Estates. But Frederick Henry had no coherent plan for creating a central government: his concern was with the European status of a future Orange dynasty. The one institution he developed was the '*Secreet Besogne*', a foreign-affairs committee of the Estates General, now effectively dependent on the Stadholder. Through it he was able to establish his policy of alliance first with France and then, in 1641, with the tottering Stuart monarchy. The first could be justified as part of the struggle against the Habsburgs; but the support of English royalism looked like an attempt to buy dynastic status in defiance both of Calvinist principles and of commercial interests. When it became clear that Frederick Henry was trying to bring the Netherlands gradually to the point of intervention against the Parliament, the Estates of Holland gave instructions to their

[1] See p. 179.

representatives at the Hague that amounted to repudiation of the authority of the *Secreet Besogne*. Worse still, Frederick Henry just before his death in 1647 was found to be involved in a Spanish proposal to hand over the Southern Netherlands to France in exchange for Catalonia, giving Antwerp to the Stadholder as a reward for his assent. (The return of Antwerp to the Union was the last thing Amsterdam merchants would welcome.) The prospect of final peace with Spain found the provinces as disunited as had the truce negotiations forty years earlier. Before the peace treaty was signed at Münster a good deal of Spanish gold was alleged to have been distributed. It meant abandoning the alliance with France, and the hope of new conquests in the south. But the success of William the Silent's rebellion was at last, after eighty years, accepted by the King of Spain.

The Stuarts and Parliament

The nature of English government in 1603 is as much debated by historians today as it was by contemporaries. Some, then and now, have described it as an absolute monarchy;[1] most, in the past century at least, have stressed the powers of parliament that seemed incompatible with the accepted definition of royal sovereignty. A few have emphasised the practical rôle of the Law in limiting the actions of the king. The activity of parliament can certainly be exaggerated. In the thirty-seven years from the death of Elizabeth to the crisis of 1640, the weeks when parliament sat totalled three and a half years. After the widely separated sessions of 1604 to 1611, the brief Addled Parliament of 1614 was the only one until 1621. In 1629 the eleven years of non-parliamentary royal government began. Peers and M.P.s were surprisingly slow to claim outright the most essential privilege of parliaments—the right to exist. They asserted, at tedious length and with eventual success, their personal freedom from arrest, their right to settle disputes about elections, their freedom of speech—first on limited topics that did not encroach on royal prerogative and then, in 1621, on anything they chose. But they accepted that their survival depended in theory on the will of the monarch, and in practice on his uncertain need for taxation. Since taxes were still supposed to be granted only on special occasions, a parliament could be regarded as an unusual event. In 1610 the Commons spent many months debating a possible solution to the financial prob-

[1] F. Hartnung and R. Mousnier in the *Reports (Relazioni) of the Tenth International Congress of Historical Sciences*, vol. 4 (Florence, 1955).

lems which might have greatly reduced the necessity for summoning parliaments. The 'Great Contract' would have abolished wardship, purveyance, and other 'feudal revenues', and in return guaranteed a permanent income from taxes that was supposed to enable the Crown to live comfortably. When it came to details, it was evident how many people were linked to the Crown by the profits involved in these matters. The Commons demanded more concessions by the court; the ministers became alarmed at the widening split between royal and parliamentary interests. The idea was abandoned. Its failure marked the end of a period of generally successful financial administration by Robert Cecil, the originator of the 'Contract' scheme, who had, within the limits of the system, made royal government more efficient and less extravagant. After him there began the period of outrageous court spending, grants to favourites, venality and corruption.

Even at its most lavish, James's government was not hopelessly insolvent. The loss of revenue through the sale of Crown lands, and the failure of many sources to keep up with the inflation of the past century, were partly offset by the increase of customs duties through expansion of trade. Since the Commons, as was customary, had voted 'tunnage and poundage' to the new monarch for life, this was a source that lay on the frontier between the king's own revenue and parliamentary assistance. James, by attempting to increase and extend the levies on trade angered both the Commons and the merchants. (Sir John Eliot claimed that the Dutch got more revenue by encouraging trade through a low rate of duty.) Indeed nearly all the Crown's expedients for solving its financial difficulties took forms that deepened the hostility between the majority of gentry and merchants represented in the Commons and the group of royal dependants and beneficiaries from which they felt excluded. The feudal right of the king to the 'wardship' of heirs who were minors was a frequent disaster to landed families, the benefit of which was shared by the exchequer and those to whom the Court of Wards handed on its profitable tasks. 'Purveyance', the compulsory purchase of supplies for the court at low prices, gave obvious opportunities for profit. 'Monopolies' was a term that covered a great variety of economic privileges, some with a large element of genuine state regulation and support, some amounting simply to the right to an unearned rake-off. The grant of a monopoly was not always clearly distinguishable either from farming-out tax-collection or from the sale of an office: the harmfulness of all of them depended on how far the Crown's gain was subordinated to private profit.

State intervention in English industry, designed more for the benefit of the privileged few than for economic improvement, did a great deal to prevent successful rivalry with the Netherlands. The scheme of Alderman Cokayne in 1614 showed the difference in spectacular fashion. The Dutch had for many years combined the carrying trade with local industry by importing unfinished English cloth which was dyed and re-exported to Baltic and German ports. The English Crown now used its power of granting and withdrawing monopolies to stop the export of any but finished cloth: the monopolists controlling alum and dyestuffs were expected to benefit, and Cokayne's company claimed to be confident of such success in exports that it could pay the Crown £300,000 a year and make even more in profits for itself. The scheme was a disaster—though it may have borne more than its due share of the blame for the slump in the English cloth industry. The Dutch were adaptable enough to retaliate by banning all imports of English cloth and supplying the market themselves; the English could neither finish all the cloth they produced nor find the ships to carry it to the Baltic.

Apart from the uncertain threat of making 'supply' dependent on 'redress of grievances', there were two processes by which parliament could make its claims to authority effective. One was the gradual encroachment, mainly through the activity of committees, on the day-to-day work of government. The other was the ancient device of impeachment—putting the king's ministers on trial for legal offences with the Commons as accusers and the Lords as judges. On the whole the introduction of 'the law' as an element in the dispute about sovereignty was not a help to the parliamentary cause.[1] Sir Edward Coke's efforts to exalt the Common Law meant in effect giving political power to a small group of successful lawyers. After his dismissal in 1616 the Crown was able, though never with certainty, to keep the judges on its side. But impeachment offered a means of attacking the actions of ministers without raising theoretical arguments about royal prerogative, and without appearing to undermine the authority of the state itself and hence the security of the propertied establishment. A man shown to be a criminal could not be regarded as rightfully representative of the Crown. The use of impeachment against Francis Bacon, perhaps the greatest intellectual figure of his day, and Lionel Cranfield, the merchant turned statesman who was the only minister after Robert Cecil to have some success in putting the government's finances in order, was hardly an auspicious beginning. But it was the threat to impeach the Duke of Buckingham

[1] See p. 180.

that brought to a head the opposition to the whole conduct of royal government.

George Villiers, Earl, Marquis, and finally—in 1623—Duke of Buckingham, personified everything that opponents of the Stuart system of government believed was wrong. Having exploited James's homosexual propensities to make himself the king's inseparable counsellor, he remained, even after the accession of Charles I in 1625, the unrivalled head of the patronage system and the maker of foreign and military policy. Foreign affairs had always been a matter on which parliament felt passionately but acted hesitantly. To all who saw these as a conflict between a Protestant God and the Devil in the shape of Spain, the power of the 'Spanish party' at court was the obvious source of all the other evils. The reality was less simple. The chief villain in the trade depression that was a constant subject of complaint was manifestly not Spain but the Netherlands. To James the Bohemian war gave a personal interest in recovering the Palatinate for his daughter Elizabeth and her husband, which the parliamentarians could only encourage. When Buckingham's visit with Prince Charles to Madrid to arrange a marriage alliance proved a humiliating fiasco, parliament rejoiced; but though he then adopted their policy of war against Spain, his support of the French monarchy against the Huguenots was almost as bad as the Spanish alliance. When this policy in turn was reversed and France became the enemy he had to carry the blame for the failure of the expedition to relieve La Rochelle. His assassination in 1628 probably deprived parliament of a demonstration of its power of impeachment that would have left the real disputes unaffected.

The parliaments of the 1620s were by no means confined to sterile disputes with the king. In 1624 there was a spate of legislation that carried out some of the specific opposition policies such as the reform—up to a point—of industrial monopolies. But the great question of the power of the Crown was never far in the background. On Charles's accession in 1625 the Commons offered to grant tunnage and poundage not for life but for one year. He collected them without parliamentary authority and raised more money—necessary, it could be argued, for foreign policies parliament itself demanded—by forced loans. In 1628 the Commons achieved the unconvincing success of the Petition of Right. The typically antiquarian title was given to a document—the ancestor of many longer ones—that denounced, in good Magna Carta style, unparliamentary taxation and arbitrary imprisonment. Its other two clauses, directed against martial law and the billeting of soldiers, concealed behind these immediate grievances of southern England anxiety at the possibility that the king would use his control of armed forces for political ends. After trying to delay and qualify his acceptance, Charles eventually assented to the Petition in the form the Commons demanded. In theory it was a statement of unchanged law. In practice there was a growing demand for a shift in the distribution of power. Under the energetic leadership of Sir John Eliot, the Commons were now prepared, despite their devotion to royal sovereignty as a symbol of order, to challenge ministerial power much more decisively. In each of the great issues—taxation, religion, foreign policy, and the privileges that upheld the status of parliament—M.P.s were demanding a degree of control that was manifestly new. The line between supporters and opponents of the parliamentary demands was rapidly hardening. Sir Thomas Wentworth, until now a prominent opposition spokesman, entered the king's service. In the second session of the Parliament, in 1629, Charles despaired of conciliation and was about to announce the dissolution. There then occurred the dramatic episode in which the Speaker was held in his chair while another—though not very novel—set of resolutions was read. That done, members obeyed the royal command to go home. Their demonstrations had not done much to secure the permanence of parliament.

The personal rule of Charles I

The eleven-year 'personal' rule of Charles is frequently seen as an 'interlude' of unprecedented tyranny. But James had, for most practical purposes, escaped parliaments for almost as long. England, it could reasonably be thought, was following the general tendency of representative assemblies to decline. Precariously, the government continued for seven or eight years to avoid both financial disaster and massive resistance. The administrative and financial reforms of Richard Weston Earl of Portland did something towards enabling the Crown, in peacetime, to survive without parliamentary subsidies. The old sources of royal revenue, and a few new ones such as the fines for failing to take knighthoods, yielded enough—in a period of comparative prosperity—to persuade London merchants that they could profitably continue their loans to the Crown. Royal government was in some ways moderately good government. Though it is absurd to praise the personal rule as a 'welfare state', the Crown could not by any stretch of the imagination have been said to use its instruments of prerogative rule—the Council in the North, the Court of Star Chamber, and the rest—exclusively for tyrannical purposes. They removed some power from the hands both of local gentry and of central legal institutions into those of court nominees. But the government in some of its activities showed an element of paternal interest in the poor and a vague notion of equal rights for subjects that had not been upheld enthusiastically by those to whom protection of property was the principal function of the law. Charles had the advantage, in his attempt to create an enlightened monarchical state, of ministers nearer in their quality to those of Elizabeth than to James I's unsavoury court. The friends and allies Laud and Wentworth between them established the doctrine and practice of 'thorough'. Allegiance to the state was to be as much the concern of a church that instilled the habit of respect for authority as of a government that imposed order and obedience to the law. The state and the social order, the administrative institutions, the church, and the law were all parts of that 'arch of order and government' that was held together in its 'strength and beauty' by the keystone of the monarchy.[1] Devotion to such ideals did not prevent Wentworth from making a fortune out of his offices in the north and then in Ireland.

The dissolution of parliament in 1629 was a blow to an opposition that had become more coherent in the years when they had met regularly at Westminster. But as the government continued to offend the interests and ideas of a large section of the parliamentary classes, new centres of political organisation appeared. Puritan congregations provided a ready-made network for opposition ideas—as Laud was well aware. The colonising ventures that combined commercial enterprise with religious zeal were a centre of leadership. Family connection was more important still. The original generation of parliamentary leaders had now gone. Sir John Eliot died in prison in 1632, Sir Edward Coke in quiescent retirement in 1634. They were succeeded by a new inner group of peers, ex-M.P.s, and lawyers, many of whom were connected with one or more of the Puritan trading ventures, the Massachusetts Bay, Saybrooke, and Providence Island Companies.[2] John Pym, the formerly obscure Somerset gentleman patronised by the Earl of Bedford, was one. John Hampden, the rich, respectable, and far from fiery Buckinghamshire landowner, another. But the rôle of the peers was no less important than that of the commercially and legally active gentry. Elements of aristocratic faction, political management, and religious idealism merged with the resistance of ordinary men of property.

In 1637 there came the opportunity to create a nation-wide movement

---

[1] Wentworth's speech to the Council in the North, quoted in I. Roots, *The Great Rebellion*, pp. 14-15.   [2] See p. 68.

of defiance. Many of the financial expedients by which the Crown had maintained its solvency—the forced loans, the compulsory knighthoods or fines in default, the extension of antiquated feudal revenues—had aroused complaints and occasional legal cases. When 'ship-money' was extended from the ports, which were accustomed to finding ships for defence or paying money instead, to inland areas where it amounted to widespread new taxation, there came the deliberately contrived *cause célèbre*, in which Hampden was an ideal figurehead. No-one could have been less of a fanatic or a natural rebel. When the legal argument produced a division of opinion among the judges there began a widespread campaign of respectable disobedience. There was popular disobedience too. Prynne, Burton and Bastwick, sentenced in Star Chamber for their opposition to Laud, became the martyr-heroes of mass demonstrations.[1] Economic depression stimulated the demands for a new parliament.

Predictably, it was the need to pay for a war that eventually made a parliament inescapable. But the war itself was another act of resistance by Charles's own subjects, in Scotland. Since the days of Knox the Scottish church had been closer to continental Calvinism than was the English, and its quarrels between the strict and the less strict had been complicated by the imposition of a half-hearted episcopacy, as well as by the traditional clan and regional loyalties. Opposition to Laudian religion in Scotland was a more popular movement than in England. In 1638 most of the landowners, clergy, lawyers, leading townsmen, and eventually many ordinary men signed the Covenant, the long document upholding the existing religion. It marked a startling unity of the whole people in all but the Catholic areas. When Scottish forces invaded the north of England in the 'Bishops Wars' of 1639 and 1640 they demonstrated not only the disunity of Charles's kingdoms but the incapacity of his English armies. To the English opposition the Scots proved in the next decade highly embarrassing allies—plundering barbarians in popular opinion, treacherous in the eyes of statesmen and soldiers. To Charles the failure of the first war was a disaster, from which he hoped that Wentworth, summoned from his rule in Ireland and encouraged with the Earldom of Strafford, could somehow rescue him.

The English Civil War

The 'Short Parliament' in the spring of 1640 showed Strafford how wrong he was in expecting to manage an English assembly as he had the Irish. Putting aside the government's demand for an immediate vote

[1] For the Puritan movement generally, see pp. 116–20.

of money, the Commons made the whole history of the personal rule a matter for debate. In the three weeks before Charles angrily dissolved the parliament, Pym's mastery of Westminster tactics was established. For the new parliament that met in November a much more intensive election campaign was organised. A spate of supposedly spontaneous petitions from freeholders of many different counties demonstrated the solidarity of opposition among the gentry. The next twelve months saw the first phase of the revolution: by legislation which a large majority of the Commons actively supported and the Lords accepted, the institutions of prerogative rule were demolished one by one. When the plan to impeach Strafford failed for lack of any 'crimes' plausible enough to win the hesitant peers, he was executed by the legislative process of an Act of Attainder. Fewer than one-eighth of the M.P.s voted in his favour. No less important than the abolition of High Commission, Star Chamber, and other prerogative courts, of unparliamentary taxation and of the political power of the bishops, was the rapid increase in parliament's participation in the actual work of government. Having at last secured control over its own dissolution and reassembly, it began, by the work of committees whose number multiplied incessantly, to insert itself into the running of finance, of the armies, and of countless minor administrative affairs. When the royal government in the capital broke down completely, there was already a sketchy substitute for it.

It was a godsend to Pym that in the autumn of 1641 rebellion broke out in Ireland.[1] Stories of Catholic atrocities in the land Strafford was supposed to have pacified seemed to confirm the great legend of the popish menace. The Armada, the Gunpowder Plot, the wars on the continent had all been used to demonstrate that a vast conspiracy existed to overthrow Protestantism and its adherents. Strafford was alleged, on shaky verbal evidence, to have hinted at using an Irish Catholic army in England. The armies that fought the Scots were said to have been dominated by Catholic officers. Could Charles and his suspect councillors be trusted to fight the Irish rebellion? It was this doubt that led Pym to draw up the 'additional instruction' to parliament's envoys to the king, now in Scotland, threatening that unless he appointed ministers they approved of they would take control of the army themselves. On the constitutional level, this was real revolution.

But even while the king's power to govern was apparently being taken from him stage by stage, a Royalist party was coming into being in parliament. Though, in the Lords especially, there were consistent supporters

[1] See p. 226.

of the royal government, war against the opposition was only made possible by the 'moderate royalists', the men, roughly speaking, who had condemned Strafford in May 1641 but who refused in November to support the Grand Remonstrance. This was the vast rambling document in which Pym's party set out their view of the history of Stuart government and, vaguely, their demand for a truly parliamentary monarchy. Pym had contrived to put on the shelf one great source, or symptom, of division among his own followers—the demand of the extremists for the 'root and branch' abolition of episcopacy. But it proved impossible to find on detailed matters like the Prayer Book a compromise that would keep his original majority together. The Remonstrance was passed by eleven votes. It was a division between those who were ready to risk the overthrow of church and state in their existing form and those who believed that they could hold what had been gained without going further. When the Remonstrance had been carried, its opponents were alarmed still more by the proposal to publish it, to 'remonstrate downwards' and stir up resistance in the country as a whole. Fortunately for Pym, Charles came to his rescue, in January 1642, with the fiasco of his personal appearance in the Commons to arrest five opposition leaders. Nothing could have demonstrated more dramatically both his ill-intentions and his incompetence. In August the fighting began.

Parliament won the war by gradually acquiring better resources of men, money, and materials. At first its military effort was financed almost entirely from London and a few nearby counties. Then, in his last great feat of political management before his death in 1643 Pym produced the series of financial measures that enabled all the areas under Parliament's control to be exploited mercilessly for war. Taxes on land and goods were collected on a scale that made all the impositions of the past thirty years insignificant. Huge forced loans were demanded. An excise, the most hated of all forms of taxation, was imposed for the first time. All the estates of Royalists were liable to be 'sequestered' for the use of Parliament. Committees of Parliament, with their executive body the Committee of Both Kingdoms which brought the Scots their share of power, took complete charge of the work of government. Committees in every county brought together in the vastly increased work of local administration the parliamentarian gentry and others below their level. The victory was made certain in 1645 with the creation of the New Model Army to replace the fumbling decentralised forces of rival generals and county authorities. From the beginning two kinds of warfare had gone on side by side—the rapid movements of the main armies, with their occasional mostly indecisive battles, and the war of garrisons and leaguers on which control of territory depended. Royalist power was largely destroyed at Naseby in 1645, both because Parliament now had the better soldiers and because it had more territorial resources. A year later Charles sought refuge, ironically, with those of his subjects who had been the first to fight against him, the Scots.

Social revolution in England

In 1647, when the Scots had handed over the king as a prisoner to Parliament, he had not lost hope of recovering his authority. His great source of comfort was the divisions among the victors. Once the fighting ended, hostility became more open between the peacemakers, now misleadingly referred to as 'Presbyterians', and the 'Independents', a word applied in its loose political sense to those supporters of the army who now demanded a settlement that would give a good deal of power to men below the level of the county gentry. The Independents were not, as a whole, democrats or egalitarians. They were the spokesmen of an assortment of lesser property-owners—principally of those to whom the war had brought unaccustomed power. Ireton and Cromwell, as leaders of the army officers, assumed that, since government was concerned primarily with property, only those with a 'permanent fixed interest' in the nation, however small, should have a voice. They now encountered new and frightening doctrines. The army, idle, angry about its arrears, steeped in puritan preaching, created a representative system of its own; and in the Council of Officers and Soldiers Rainsborough and Wildman argued passionately the democratic ideas that Lilburne, Overton, and Walwyn were expounding in a torrent of popular pamphlets.[1]

It was not the extreme left that vehemently demanded the execution of the king though few of them opposed it. His trial was brought about by the army leaders and the small group of active 'Independents' in the Commons. In 1648 some of his new supporters—English 'Presbyterians' and Scottish adherents of the secret 'Engagement' to bring an army to his aid—made possible the scattered battles known as the Second Civil War. It demonstrated again that whatever Charles might say or sign, once he was back in his capital and the army disbanded nothing could prevent him from restoring a great deal of the old form of government, recompensing the plundered Royalists at the expense of the victors, and punishing the leaders of the rebellion. In December, with a nominal show of force at Westminster, the army removed from Parlia-

[1] See pp. 190–1.

ment those members who refused to renounce further negotiation. On 30 January 1649 Charles showed more strength of character at his death than at any time in his life, and helped to establish the legend of the martyr-king. The Leveller movement, easily defeated by the renewed imprisonment of its leaders, perished less gloriously, though its ideas achieved in the end a greater immortality.

The English Republic

For ten years the English tried in vain to find what seemed easy enough to the Dutch—a stable form of republican government. In more realistic terms, the conflicts in the Netherlands were about the distribution of powers within an accepted ruling section of society; in England many, as Royalists, had lost their powers completely and many newly risen in the army and in the counties would forfeit their status, lands, and perhaps lives in any broad reconciliation. The 'Rump' of the Long Parliament (or rather, since the House of Lords was abolished along with the monarchy, of its House of Commons) survived until 1653, a core of twenty or thirty active politicians with perhaps another hundred who turned up at one time or another[1] Its executive 'Council of State' was dominated by the army officers. And in the army the power of Oliver Cromwell was now unchallenged. When his campaigns against the remains of royalism in Scotland and Ireland were over, Oliver became the one decisive force in English government. Like so many successful statesmen, he combined ruthless and skilful playing of the political game with persuasive idealism. He dragged his decisions slowly out of a tangle of doubts and quest for support; but he had the gift of convincing himself and others that they were right—which often was enough to make them work. He had the energy of puritanism without its pigheadedness, and the rare quality among despots of wanting others to share his power—if only they would agree with him. The period of his political dominance was a ceaseless search for the institutions that would make 'healing and settling' possible. As he tentatively admitted, there was much to be said for a government with 'somewhat of monarchical in it'. Having won the fight for the power of parliament, he now found himself dismissing one parliament after another more brutally than James or Charles had ever done. In April 1653 the Rump surrendered tamely to his soldiers and his angry denunciations. The

[1] For the controversies about the political and religious groups in and outside the Rump see the articles by David Underdown and George Yule in *Journal of British Studies*, vol. 3 (1964), vol. 7 (1968), and vol. 8 (1968).

'Parliament of Saints', nominated to some extent by the Puritan congregations, but largely in effect by the army officers, produced impressive proposals for reforms, but no machinery for carrying them out or defending its power. In December 1653 the 'Instrument of Government', the only written constitution England had known, made Oliver a half-monarch, changing the title at his insistence from 'King' to 'Lord Protector'. Meetings of parliament (to be elected every three years on a franchise that brought in more of the lesser gentry, but hardly anyone below that level) were to last at least five months. Lunar months, Oliver decided—when he could not wait another few days to drive out a body that had insisted on debating the constitution itself. In 1656–7 the second Protectorate Parliament was no less critical, and a new constitution moved closer still to the old order, with a nameless 'other house' and an installation for the Protector that was a coronation with everything but the crown. At his death in 1658 'healing and settling' were not much nearer. Part of the blame for the failure of the Protectorate certainly rested on the constitutions. The semi-official propagandist Marchamont Needham praised them because the legislative and executive powers were separate—a notion that has been a curse of written constitutions ever since. The Council of State was the permanent centre of authority that attracted the power-seekers, and the occasional Parliaments, despite the exclusion or expulsion of undesirables, were inevitably centres of opposition. There was no plan for a return to purely civilian rule, and nothing to re-establish an accepted system of government in the counties. The 'Major Generals', appointed by the Protector in 1655 as virtual military governors of the eleven regions into which they divided the country, aimed to impose a more rigid state control than Strafford or Laud had dreamed of.

The great unsolved problem was that of the Royalists. So long as a large section of propertied society was excluded from power and subject to fierce penalities and restrictions, and so long as many who did hold power were believed to have grown rich on plundered estates, normal political stability was hardly possible. The constant obstacle to the tolerance and conciliation Cromwell wanted was the existence of Charles II and of a large and probably increasing opinion in favour of his restoration.

Any attempt to follow the chaotic events of the eighteen months after Oliver's death in 1658 requires more space than it is worth here. The story is aptly symbolised in the slow inexorable march from Scotland to London of the army under General Monck, a professional soldier who at some indefinable time resolved to 'restore' the king. An opposing force under Cromwell's former associate Lambert melted away without a battle. The quarrels between the various military and civilian groups in central politics were becoming ludicrous. The decisive power favouring restoration was that of the City of London, on whose financial support any successful government was bound to depend. Every opinion had its adherents in London; but the government of the City since 1641 had been firmly of the right wing of the Parliamentarian side—which meant now that it was Royalist. At Westminster the Parliament of Richard Cromwell, as ineffectual as the second Protector himself, had been replaced by the restored Rump, to which under the aegis of Monck the survivors of the members driven away in 1648 now returned. In March 1660 they made way for the newly elected 'Convention' Parliament that invited King Charles to his throne.

The Netherlands Republic

Republican rule in England lasted for eleven years of turmoil, in which not only a king but a whole governing section of society had been ousted from power. Yet a restoration was accepted easily and smoothly. In the Netherlands the House of Orange was out of action from 1650 to 1672; but its return seemed a greater change than its fall. William II in his few years as Stadholder had brought the quarrel between the Orange and Holland parties to a new crisis, in part a reflection of the English one. The Hollanders, in defiance of the States General's control over foreign relations, welcomed ambassadors from Parliament. William dreamed of the benefits to his family of intervening in the cause of monarchy. He opposed, without effect, peace-negotiations with Spain which the Estates of Holland had controlled. When he formally 'visited' the towns of Holland, appealing over the heads of provincial estates for support, Amsterdam refused to receive him. Only after his cousin the Stadholder of Friesland had brought an army to the gates of the city did the burgomasters agree to a political compromise. And then, in 1650, William died—leaving a posthumous son whose birth inflicted on the House of Orange the longest possible minority. Amid the quarrels of William III's guardians, the Regents of Holland were able to impose the 'System of True Liberty'. This pompous slogan denoted the federated anti-royal and anti-clerical government through which from 1653 the new Grand Pensionary, John de Witt, ruled the Netherlands more securely than Cromwell ever ruled England. While English constitutions were succeeding each other more and more rapidly, the Netherlands remained without one. In 1651 the Estates of Holland had held a sort of constituent assembly of the provinces, which produced a great many words but agreed only on dividing up control of the armed forces to prevent a revival of the office of Captain-General—a process that hastened the decline of Dutch power on land. In 1654, as part of Cromwell's price for peace, de Witt persuaded the Estates of Holland to pledge themselves in great secrecy never to accept a member of the Orange dynasty as their Stadholder or agree to his appointment as Captain-General. By an elaborate piece of deception, the States General were made to accept this. The 'Act of Seclusion', though it was repealed—also in the interests of good relations with England—after Charles II's restoration, was a demonstration of de Witt's success in reducing the power of the Orange party, which had, when he was first appointed, commanded overwhelming popular support; but it also showed how complete the supremacy of Holland's ruling families had become. For many municipal and provincial councillors, office was now a full-time occupation and a matter for competition, rival patronage, and venality. More rigidly than ever, the governing families cut themselves off from outsiders, even from leading merchants. Prosperous though these were, commerce expanded less in the period of unchallenged rule by the oligarchy of Holland than in that of Orange power. Though Amsterdam was still the pre-eminent centre of banking and bullion exchange, the carrying trade suffered from the decline in Baltic grain exports and possibly from English competition. Unemployment and high food prices in the towns helped to produce in the fifties an active popular opposition with which both the Calvinist Church and the Orange party identified themselves. Another check to prosperity was the failure to maintain the generally neutral foreign policy that financial interest needed. In seeking security for the state, its prosperity, and its régime, de Witt was drawn inexorably into the European power game.

England and the Netherlands at war

The war between the United Provinces and England from 1652 to 1654 was not sought by de Witt, or by Cromwell. The two new governments had almost everything in common. Both were Protestant and Republican; both had emerged from long and exhausting warfare; both were threatened by former ruling dynasties and upheld by merchants who had the whole world to exploit and the retreating commercial empires of Spain and Portugal to overthrow. Cromwell, on his idealist tack, repeatedly sought alliance and even union with Holland as the other great

Protestant power. In 1651 a commercial clique in London and in the Rump Parliament, seeking protection against a more successful competitor, succeeded in pushing through the Navigation Act. It was designed primarily to exclude the Dutch from their carrying trade with English colonies; but it also represented a general strengthening of the commercial motive in British politics that proved more lasting than the republican constitutions. The Dutch demand for a war of reprisal came from popular as well as mercantile resentment, fostered by the pro-Stuart Orange party. Since Blake's fleet was now on the whole a match for Tromp's, there was no prospect of a decisive Dutch victory. In the peace treaty Cromwell was able to appease his commercial supporters by insisting that the Dutch should concede almost every substantial demand made by the English merchants. In 1660—when every action of the Interregnum ought, politically, to have been anathema, the Navigation Act was renewed and made more workable. But England's rôle in Dutch politics was reversed. Downing, Cromwell's ambassador to The Hague, returned under Charles to become a leading advocate of the Orange cause. Fighting between the two powers was renewed overseas in 1664, with little regard to diplomatic manœuvres. In 1665 it became official. It was a merchants' war; and the Peace of Breda in 1667, without settling much of the quarrel, marked the stage at which they more or less agreed to cultivate their own patches of trade. It also marked, for both England and Holland, the beginning of a new era of diplomats' wars—an era in which the constantly shifting alliances were determined by personal persuasion and corruption. The expansive power of France was the one constant factor: for the Dutch and the English, as for most other states, it was arguable whether they would do better by alliance with or against the French.

De Witt, in spite of Colbert's tariffs and in spite of actual French annexations on the frontier of the Spanish Netherlands, on the whole preferred alliance with France. It was essential, as the moment when William of Orange would be of age approached, to build up the strongest possible support for the republic. In 1668, with many misgivings, de Witt accepted the Triple Alliance with Sweden and England. The Dutch did not mind much that Sweden, against whom they had briefly intervened in the Baltic wars, was soon back to her normal alliance with France: all the Netherlands needed was moderate hostility between Sweden and Denmark.[2] The real disaster, of which de Witt was only dimly aware, was that Louis XIV now determined that the Nether-

[1] See p. 73.   [2] See pp. 358-9.

lands should be the victim of his quest for land and glory. The full terms of the Treaty of Dover between England and France in 1670 remained unknown. Its mere existence was alarming enough. The Triple Alliance had enraged Louis against the Dutch at a time when Colbert was also happy to make a commercial agreement with England against them. So there emerged the vague fear of a plan for England and France to take their pick of Dutch territories, and to impose an Orange monarchy on what was left. There was little prospect that any other European power would promise aid to the Netherlands.

The House of Orange restored

The war with England and France in 1672[1] made certain what already seemed likely, that de Witt's republic would not long survive the coming-of-age of William of Orange. De Witt had tried to prepare for it by a fierce attack on the Orange politicians, by putting William's education under the supervision of the Estates of Holland, and by the 'Eternal Edict' of 1667 which abolished the office of Stadholder of Holland altogether. Though provincial Estates eventually accepted the theory that William might be a Captain-General without other office, it would, even in peace, be impossible to ignore his political influence. Inescapably he was drawn into the affairs of the inland provinces, and everywhere the Orange movement revived to unify all the hostility to the oligarchy. Faced with war and invasion, the Netherlands rallied to William with at least as much enthusiasm as, twelve years before, England had shown for Charles. Provincial nobility, urban oppositions, and rioting crowds backed by the preachers demanded William's appointment to all the offices of his ancestors. De Witt despite his resignation was the victim of a savage mob murder. But the crowds did not get, and apart from a little pamphlet literature did not demand, a popular government. The monopoly of the old urban oligarchies was broken to the extent of letting in some Orange supporters hitherto outside the charmed circle. Otherwise the Stadholder—to whom royal titles were still refused— found the distribution of power and the disunity much as before.

The very fact of his lack of a crown may well have strengthened William's determination to demonstrate his full membership of the dynastic war-and-peace-making club. Since the triumphs of his great-grandfather, the dynasty had always been most successful as leaders in war. Now, at the moment of his arrival in power, he was presented with the opportunity to appear as another saviour of his country from the

[1] See pp. 435–7.

foreign and popish enemy. More than Louis himself—perhaps more than any other ruler—William was devoted to war. The peace with France in 1678 was made by the States General against his wishes. His marriage to Mary Stuart a year earlier had naturally increased suspicion that his dynastic ambitions were unlimited and unrelated to the interests of Amsterdam especially. Yet gradually in the ten years before the crucial moment of 1688 he built up his pseudo-royal power. More and more offices came under his control; more and more allies were bought or won in the states of the Union. The journey to England, when it came, involved no fears of resistance at home.

The Stuarts restored

The English Restoration had been a vastly greater change—almost, it seemed, a complete return to Stuart absolutism. The king's reign was dated from 1649 and the legislation of the Interregnum annulled; but judicial proceedings, on which innumerable property transactions depended, were in general confirmed—as indeed they had been through all the changes of régime. For the parliament of 1661 the old system of elections was resumed. Even at the beginning it was not entirely a 'Cavalier Parliament', and at the many by-elections in its seventeen-year course former Parliamentarians came quietly back. By a variety of expedients a great many Royalist estates confiscated or sold since 1642 found their way to the former owners or their heirs. Generalisations about the ultimate effect of the land settlement are still uncertain; but it is clear that, though some Royalist families suffered, very few of the 'upstarts' were able to keep their status. Perhaps the most surprising phenomenon was the disappearance of Presbyterianism. Charles had promised toleration, and a synod to settle official doctrine. But at the Savoy Conference in 1661 between bishops and Presbyterian leaders the Puritans won no concessions. Parliament and the Convocations of the Church established an Anglicanism that avoided everything firmly Calvinist, but fell short of Laudianism. Ejected ministers came back and usurpers were put out in their turn, though a good many former Presbyterians found their way into livings. In Presbyterian London, solid resistance by those who controlled the supply of funds would have been very hard to resist; but after some argument the aldermen dutifully went to St Paul's to welcome their Bishop. The 'Clarendon Code' meant that 'dissenters' escaped the worst forms of persecution at the cost of exclusion from politics and from the chance to propagate their ideas. Though Quakers and the other sects continued to resist the state and to suffer for doing so, it was a sad end to the mighty victories of the saints. But it was also a sign that, despite all the appearances to the contrary in the conflict that lay ahead, religion was not quite as closely or as universally linked with political loyalties and hostilities as it had been.

The old symbols of royal 'tyranny' had gone for good. There were no prerogative courts or 'feudal' exactions; traffic in offices no longer dominated the working of government, and in the seventies tax-farming was quietly ended; M.P.s were no longer imprisoned for their speeches; the new Habeas Corpus Act of 1679 protected the ordinary citizen too from 'arbitrary' imprisonment, leaving him to the mercies of the lawyers. Parliament's survival seemed secure: no-one worried much that the Triennial Act of 1664, unlike that of 1641 which it repealed, contained no precautions against defiance by the Crown. The great failure was to establish any effective parliamentary control over the choice and policy of the king's ministers. Opposition to Clarendon in 1667 and to the Earl of Danby in 1679 had to take the old form of impeachment. There was a great difference between the two cases. Clarendon had managed without any firm support in Parliament; his fall came when the disappointments of the Dutch war were added to a multiplicity of minor grievances, and his unpopularity at court made him the obvious scapegoat. Danby had seen the need for a parliamentary following—though he built it up more by bribery and patronage than by policy. He too was a victim of hostility at court. But he was blamed for two things— the alleged concealment of the imaginary Popish Plot that threw the nation into hysterical panic in 1678, and the secret negotiations with France. The latter he had certainly supported, however reluctantly. To save him, Charles dissolved the Parliament that had lasted since 1661. The election, with the 'Plot' still raging, was a startling failure for government management. Danby was lucky to get away with five years in the Tower.

Very slowly, the question of Catholicism had once more come to be all-important. It was made inescapable by accidents of personality and genealogy. Like Elizabeth, though for different reasons, Charles failed to produce a legitimate son. His brother James, unless his Catholicism could be made a legal ground for excluding him, was the undoubted heir; and when James made a second marriage in 1673 it was likely that a son would be born to continue the Catholic line. Meanwhile the next in succession was Mary, James's Protestant daughter by his first wife Anne Hyde. Danby had arranged her marriage in 1677 to William of Orange.

Advocates of a Protestant monarchy were now faced with a Dutch connection that not everyone saw as preferable to the Stuart links with France. The course of the conflict was set partly by Charles's views on religious policy. Protestantism, or so he had cause to believe, contained a latent threat to monarchy. Repeatedly he attempted without success to win enough support for such measures as the Declaration of Indulgence that would have removed the disabilities of both Catholics and Protestant nonconformists. In return for Louis XIV's promises of support he added the secret clauses to the Treaty of Dover in 1670 promising in due course to declare himself a Catholic. He recognised that it would be difficult to convince a large enough proportion of the aristocratic and gentry families that Catholicism was the best form of religion for defending the Restoration monarchy that upheld their power—difficult, but not impossible.

The prospect was made much more hopeful by the Crown becoming once again less dependent on parliament for its revenue. The greatest weapon of the old parliamentary cause seemed to have been allowed to rust. The customs, and the hated excise, had been settled on Charles for life, together with other revenues such as the 'hearth tax' invented in 1662. (None of these fell directly on land.) At first the revenue they produced was less than the rather arbitrary estimate made in 1660, and the Crown depended heavily on loans from the City and on more closely controlled and non-recurrent parliamentary grants. The rapidly rising cost of gifts and bribes, under various names, helped to produce the shortage of money that culminated in the disastrous 'Stop of the Exchequer' in 1672. But then the Crown's position improved. Indirect taxes, taken out of the hands of farmers, increased automatically with the expansion of trade, until—just at the time when parliamentary control of finance would have been decisive—the Crown could almost 'live of its own' again. The notorious subsidies from France, though they rescued Charles in some difficult moments, were too small a proportion of the total to have a major effect on the outcome of a long conflict.

Charles was right in thinking that a substantial part of landed and political society would accept Catholicism—not in the sense of being ready converts themselves, but to the extent that, if faced with a choice between resistance to the Crown and loyalty to a Catholic king who would bring about equality of status between Catholic and Protestant subjects, they would not risk another rebellion. Men had to choose between the fear of popery and absolutism and the fear of civil war, with the threat to property which this would involve. The 'Exclusion Crisis' produced three Parliaments between 1679 and 1681. They were not only concerned with fears for the future but, like the parliaments of the 1620s, with current grievances which only a constitutional change would remedy. Charles, despite the Triennial Act, resolved to rule without Parliaments. Louis promised his support. It was in these years that the old 'Court' and 'Country' groupings became recognisable as the two 'parties' of the next century, under the nicknames that compared them to the Whiggamores of Scotland and the Tories of Ireland. (There was no greater insult than association with popular rebels, and Celtic rebels at that.) To exclude James from the throne by legislation would greatly alter the division of power between parliament and the monarchy. Shaftesbury's Exclusionist party, the immediate ancestor of the Whigs, had an unmistakable if pale resemblance to the party of Pym. It included a group of political leaders, peers among them, in whom William of Orange began to take an interest; gentry outside rather than inside the established ruling circle in the counties; many merchants and their associates; and many dissenters who contrived to evade the restrictions enough to take some part in political life. It was associated too with movements well below the level of parliamentary politics—a fact its enemies were quick to exploit. Anglicans who, whether from a connection with royal government or simply from a belief in non-resistance, supported the Crown convinced themselves that James (who still lacked a son) would not seriously interrupt the power of the Protestant ruling classes. By using royal authority to revoke the charters of many boroughs and eventually of London itself, the Tory ministers were able to remove the main electoral strongholds of the opposition. There was no serious doubt that Charles had won.

James II and the 'Glorious Revolution'

The peaceful accession of James II in 1685 was an astonishing success for those who sought a strong monarchy at almost any price. At the decisive moment, many who had believed in the Popish Plot, who had voted for exclusion, and who had regarded themselves as unshakable supporters of Parliament and Protestantism, preferred acquiescence to rebellion. When a new parliament met, it seemed to have been tamed at last—as Strafford had long before believed it could be—by efficient manipulation of franchises and elections. Two members out of five held some sort of Crown office; four our of five were new. It voted a generous revenue, which James was able to supplement by the willing assistance of Louis XIV. When Charles II's most energetic bastard, the Duke of Monmouth, made his theatrical attempt to claim the throne, the extent of acquiescence was demonstrated still more clearly. It became not a revolution but a local popular rebellion reminiscent more of Tudor risings than of the Civil War. Yeomen, clothiers, and miners in the south-west were no substitute for the support of peers and gentry which Monmouth sought in vain. John Wildman, veteran of the democratic movement of 1647, failed to get any substantial following for the Duke in London.

One effect of the rebellion on James was to increase his determination to have a loyal army, commanded as far as possible by Catholics. Another was his decision to punish the rebels with a ruthless demonstration of the authority of law. The 'Bloody Assizes' of Judge Jeffreys were by any standard a brutal affair, which the Whig politicians who had kept well away from the rebellion afterwards exploited as propaganda, James, like Charles I, had a great capacity for making blunders. Step by step it lost him the support of those who at first were eager to seize any opportunity of reaching a compromise with the Crown that would leave them a share of power. Anglican Tories were not likely to be reassured by the insistence that concessions were being sought for all dissenters, Protestant and Catholic alike. If anything was worse than outright popery, it was tolerance that would enable Puritans to resume their attack on the monopoly of office held by established families. But it was significant that some of the Quakers and other nonconformists were willing to take the king at his word and accept the liberty and the ending of their legal disabilities that he offered. It was no longer universally agreed that religious doctrines were inseparable from political. It seemed to most people strange, if not sinister, that William Penn, the Quaker coloniser, should be a confidant of James. A generation earlier it would have been inconceivable. The *Letter to a Dissenter* from one of the most skilful of practical politicians, the Marquis of Halifax, did a great deal to convince the most cautious nonconformists that any favours offered from Rome would prove to be traps for the unwary.

James's pose as the benevolent devotee of tolerance was not made more convincing when he established an army, under Catholic officers, on Hounslow Heath just outside London. If fears were diminished by the reports that the English soldiers were more likely to mutiny than to terrorise the citizens, the army that was being created in Ireland seemed to prove that there was a real threat of popery being imposed by force. Less obviously, James was time after time going a little further in the direction of prerogative rule than those who in general were ready to support him would accept. His 'High Commission' for the exercise of the Crown's ecclesiastical powers, not being a court of law, was not strictly illegal under the terms of the Act of 1641—but it was made to look like a defiance of the opposition to such bodies. His use of the 'dispensing power' to insert his nominees into Universities was seen, with good reason, as an effort to undermine the future strength of Anglicanism. The judges, when those less amenable had been removed from office, were used as the most authoritative upholders of the doctrine that the king could dispense individuals from the operation of the law. More and more the actions of the king grew horribly reminiscent of Charles I; but no second Pym appeared. There was no second Strafford either. Robert Spencer, second Earl of Sunderland, was like Wentworth in being a former opponent of the Crown who became its chief minister; but he had no heroic devotion to the principle of monarchical rule. He despaired of the Catholic policy sooner and more decisively than did James, and at the last moment departed for Holland and tried to persuade the future king that he had long been working in favour of the revolution. The theory that he deliberately led James into more extravagant policies in order to destroy him has no convincing proof. But he certainly did nothing to prevent the follies that in 1687–8 drove believers in stable monarchy to the conclusion that James must go.

James had not allowed parliament to meet since November 1685; but sooner or later he would need to call another. Success in this, as in everything else, would ultimately depend on the acquiescence of a sufficient number of the politically active landed proprietors. Charles had got away with an attack on borough charters that enabled him to increase the influence of the government. James attacked them a second time with the intention of replacing respected county families by unheard-of landless dissenters, in accordance with his policy of merging concessions to Catholics with those to Protestant nonconformists. The scheme was such a failure that the proposed new parliament had, for the moment, to be abandoned. Faced with this first sign of mass opposition, James demanded a new demonstration of his control over the church, which he believed, more and more justifiably, was ceasing to preach the doctrine of unquestioning obedience and even giving positive encouragement to resistance. The first Declaration of Indulgence in 1687, suspending all religious discrimination, was an extension of his questionable use of royal authority, but not a deliberate defiance. There was a soothing promise that the declaration would be submitted to a future parliament. When it was reissued in the spring of 1688 with the instruction that it was to be read in every cathedral and church, James seemed to be openly challenging the Anglican clergy to resist. Nine-tenths of them did so. Sancroft, the Archbishop of Canterbury, and six of the bishops, drew up the petition against it. Between the presentation of the petition and the trial of the seven prelates, deliberately designed by the government to give maximum publicity to the expected confirmation of royal authority, James's son was born and the prospect of a Protestant succession ended. On 30 June the bishops were acquitted after a trial in which their fate had been linked with the question of the king's power to dispense with the law. The people of London saw it as a great victory. Sancroft, far from becoming a rebel hero, resumed his efforts to persuade James to compromise with his Church. On the day of the acquittal another group of seven—some of the most prominent English peers—sent off their invitation to William of Orange.

William had controlled his ambitions with unexpected skill. A single prematurely overt move might have identified opposition to James with support of a foreign invader. Soundings among the English aristocrats had been carried out cautiously; careful assessments were made of the possible extent of James's support. One obvious risk was that James's patron Louis XIV might come to his rescue. Another—which Louis himself, fortunately for William, thought would benefit the French more —was that there might be a civil war. If that happened, William insisted, he would refuse to come. As part of his elaborate preparations, he had copies of his soothing Declaration ready for immediate distribution all over England.

The States General had to be handled tactfully too: use of the national fleet and army depended on their consent. So had the Burgomasters of Amsterdam, whose opposition to the scheme would have produced an intolerable political division for William to leave behind. As it turned out there was enough public enthusiasm to suppress the doubts of some of the commercial interests. James, still in the best Stuart tradition, tried, when it was far too late, to reverse his entire policy. It was impossible now to alter the unformulated but clear decision of the 'political nation'. Loyalty to the monarch was still the creed of the ruling section of society. But the loyalty must be transferred, with as little fuss as possible, to a different monarch. There were to be no cries of 'King in Parliament', no armies to develop dangerous democratic ideas, no elaborate paper constitution. The problem of what, in constitutional theory, had happened could be solved with no very painful stretching of the truth. The throne was 'vacant': William and Mary, with the unconditional invitation and assent of the nation, subsequently ratified in parliament, occupied it. God, the Church proclaimed, had upheld divine right by sending a deliverer. There was no need to dwell on such awkward details as the fact that James had fled (at the second attempt) only after William had landed and made him a virtual prisoner.

English government after 1688.

When the embarrassing episode of James's departure was over, it was not difficult to contrive the performances which would avoid admitting that a monarch had been overthrown or that another had been appointed after bargaining with his prospective subjects. The 'Convention'—not yet, for want of a royal summons, a parliament—produced the 'Declaration of Rights' which was read out immediately before William and Mary accepted the ceremonial offer of the Crown. By the end of 1689 the Declaration had been turned into a Bill which could receive the royal assent in the normal way. It was not the kind of document to be recited on patriotic occasions, or to settle legal disputes, but a mixture of specific and hazy assertions. Catholics were barred from the throne. The king's power to suspend laws, and the dispensing power 'as exercised of late' were illegal.[1] So were levying money, and raising an army in peacetime, without parliamentary consent. There was to be freedom of parliamentary speech and elections; there were to be no 'cruel and unusual punishments'; parliaments were to be 'frequent'. There was no hint of parliamentary control of the king's ministers, or of foreign policy, or of religion. The promise of the monarchs to maintain the 'Protestant Reformed Religion established by law' appeared in the Coronation Oath, and was by no means unambiguous. There were later clarifications: the Triennial Act of 1694 insisted that there must be, at least every three years, not only a meeting of parliament but a new election. The Act of Settlement of 1701 added to its arrangement of the succession in favour of the descendants of the Electress Sophia of Hanover[2] a variety of provisions intended to protect the independence of judges and—absurdly—to prevent the discussion of major matters of state in informal bodies instead of in the Privy Council. More significant

---

[1] A later clause adds that a statute must not be subject to royal dispensation unless it contained a statement to that effect. See W. C. Costin and J. S. Watson, *The Law and Working of the Constitution* (London, 1952), vol. 1, p. 74.
[2] See genealogical table on p. 466.

than all this was that the Crown was now entirely dependent on parliamentary votes of money. The lifetime grant to William of £700,000 a year was enough in time of peace for the cost of a fairly modest court and the payment of existing office-holders, but not much more. Customs and other taxes were voted for short periods. Against this could be set the fact that the Crown could continue unimpeded its management of parliamentary elections and its methods of persuading members to give it their support. Even the narrowing of borough franchises carried out by Charles and James was in general retained. Almost a third of the M.P.s represented boroughs with fewer than a hundred voters. The cost of controlling a seat was rising, and contested elections were becoming less common.

There was plenty of scope for the creation of a powerful ministerial government and a docile and united parliament. Nothing of the kind appeared. Ministerial changes throughout the rest of the century were frequent. Parliaments were the scene of incessant disputes and manœuvres between factions. How far it was a period of two-party politics is a matter of controversy.[1] Contests for seats and offices were now fought in terms of Whig versus Tory. It did not mean either that ministries were formed exclusively of one party or that Lords and Commons were divided into two unchanging sides. Least of all did it mean that Tories were the party of strong monarchical government and Whigs that of radical nonconformity, parliamentary independence, and hostility to the court. In the first six or seven years of his reign William had to be taught by Sunderland that a change, almost a reversal, was taking place in the character of the two parties. 'Whenever the government has leaned to the Whigs, it has been strong; when the other has prevailed it had been despised.'[2] The Whigs moved away from their dangerously democratic allies in town and country to become the defenders of the constitution eager to build within it a strong and efficient executive machinery. The Tories increasingly drew their support from the less politically active county families. They liked to appear as defenders of the church against the insidious spread of dissent, and of an economy soundly based on landed property against the risky and unscrupulous financial dealings of the Whig bankers and war profiteers in the City. As before, at every level, in every district and every occupation local and

---

[1] See R. Walcott, *English Politics in the Early Eighteenth Century* (Cambridge, Mass., 1956) and the criticism of it in J. H. Plumb, *The Growth of Political Stability in England*, especially chaps 2 and 5 (London, 1967).
[2] Quoted in Plumb, *The Growth of Political Stability*, p. 135.

personal rivalries could be aligned, often irrationally, by party loyalty. But the alignment was growing weaker rather than stronger. The 'independent country gentlemen' were a group in the Commons larger than any other—sometimes as many as two hundred. Their decisions, on both great questions and small, could be influenced not only by the pressure of party and government organisers but by arguments in the House and by the views of their electors. It was a situation inconceivable in twentieth-century democracy.

The wars with France

One question on which parliamentary opinion could be decisive and on which it emerged from a great variety of pressures was that of war or peace—a matter still in theory left entirely to the Crown. In 1689 there was no doubt that in welcoming William England was committing herself to war with France. The Netherlands declared war in 1689 at the moment when William made his formal acceptance of the Crown; and his odd dual status was demonstrated when, as King of England, he made a treaty with the States General for the joint use of his two navies against French forces. The early stages of the war seemed to threaten the overthrow of William's rule. With Louis at last giving James his full support, a simultaneous invasion from France and Ireland looked possible. William's victory in the Battle of the Boyne brought the Irish back under the unrelenting rule of Protestant Englishmen; but it was not until 1692 that the allied fleet was able to avenge the defeat it had suffered off Beachy Head. Land warfare was a fruitless use of men and money. Once the invasion scare was over, complaints in the Commons against the war grew. It was hinted that William was proving himself a foreign King employing in his continental wars the armies that were meant for the defence of England. His occasional use of the royal veto did not help his popularity. Only because enough M.P.s were involved in the forces or in the supply of war materials was the risk averted that the Commons might refuse outright to vote further supplies.

The war cost at least three times as much as Charles II's war against the Dutch, seven times as much as the regular revenue voted to William. It was paid for partly by a land tax, which in 1692 rose to four shillings in every pound of rental, partly by the excise. Regular government borrowing was essential to the financing of the war, and indeed to the whole economy of the country. The creation of the Bank of England in 1694 was only the most conspicuous single event in a long process of establishing a financial system in which bullion became a far less important form of wealth and government debts produced stability rather than weakness. The more the government borrowed, the larger the number of subjects who had a heavy vested interest in its survival. The costlier wars became, the greater the incentive to invest in the concerns that supplied their material. Nevertheless, financial exhaustion, in England as in the other states involved, was one major cause of the temporary peace settlement at Ryswick in 1697.[1]

William, in the two years before his death in 1702, had to fight against a strong anti-war feeling among the gentry in the Commons. The successive schemes, open or secret, for the partition of the Spanish possessions were not an obvious reason for England to prepare for the renewed war against France which was the centre of William's whole policy. When the 'Junto' of Whig ministers was found to have agreed in the absence of a parliament to the second partition treaty[2]—though William had negotiated it without consulting them—the newly elected Commons set in motion the clumsy impeachment procedure. Whig peers were in a strong enough majority to defeat it. The question of war or peace became the main difference between the two parties. Those eager to resume the fight with France were saved by pressure from outside parliament. Daniel Defoe took over the leadership of a campaign of public propaganda and petitioning, smearing the Tory advocates of peace as hirelings of the French and stressing the threats implied in Louis XIV's recognition of James III as King of England. In the Netherlands too William did not find it easy to keep up enthusiasm for war. Before Ryswick, while London had on the whole supported the continuance of the fighting, Amsterdam had been the centre of the peace movement. News of Charles II's will in 1700 was received there with general relief on the assumption that the powers would accept it. William relied on his close ally Heinsius, the Grand Pensionary, to bring the City round to support of war, while he himself took on the harder task of defeating the peacemakers in England. 'I hope to conduct myself', he wrote, 'with such circumspection as will carry them along gradually without their noticing it.'[3]

Before his death, William had appointed John Churchill as commander of the forces of both nations. Under Anne, who in her first year as queen created him Duke of Marlborough and made his Duchess the most powerful figure at court, he and the Treasurer Godolphin had little difficulty in keeping support for the campaigns. They had the

---

[1] See p. 445. [2] See p. 313.
[3] P. Geyl, *The Netherlands in the Seventeenth Century*, part 2, p. 275.

advantage not only of a well-managed and generally enthusiastic parliament, but of an administrative system which had slowly, since the
days of Charles II, become a complex but tolerably efficient professional
service. Though places were still regarded as rewards, the old venal
hierarchies had gradually been replaced by a system of departments
completely detached from the court, with the Treasury as the recognised superior body. The number of court places had fallen, that of
departmental jobs rose continually. The process of government by committee, which parliament in the Civil War had improvised from within
itself, was now developing rapidly outside it—though many of the
Boards remained under close parliamentary scrutiny. While Anne
continued to attend, without much influence, formal meetings of the
Privy Council and of smaller groups of ministers, the growth of a
recognised Cabinet was beginning. It remained unsure of parliamentary
support.

In the first years of the war the ministry was predominantly Tory.
The most extreme of its members, Nottingham, resigned in 1704 when
his efforts to take a tougher line against dissenters were unsuccessful.
Robert Harley and Henry St John, Tories less dogmatic and more
devoted to political manœuvre, came into the government. But the
general trend was for Tory supporters of the war to work in alliance
with the moderate Whigs. After the election of 1705, when the Whigs
increased their strength in the Commons, the ministry became a coalition within which the Whigs were able gradually to establish themselves
in complete power. By 1708 Marlborough and Godolphin were the only
Tories left. Harley and St John worked both at court, where they
exploited Anne's reliance on her confidante Mrs Masham, and in the
country to bring about a decisive rejection of the Whigs and of Marlborough. In the distance there lay the prospect of another succession problem. But the Tories did not make the blunder of appearing to
be Jacobites. Their great rallying-cry was the one raised by Henry
Sacheverell in his much-publicised sermon at St Paul's in 1709—'the
Church in danger'. To the Whigs his authoritarian line appeared as a
denial not only of even the most limited toleration, but of the whole
principle of the 1688 settlement. Their attempt to impeach Sacheverell
played into the hands of the Tories, who made him a hero of the reactionary country gentry and clergy, and of an emotional London mob.
A more rational motive for opposing the ministry was that the war, and
the taxation it involved, now seemed to be prolonged quite unnecessarily.
In 1710 Harley became the leader of a new government, and had no

difficulty in getting a reliable Commons majority in his favour at the election that followed. The ruthless political intrigues of the next year brought about the fall of Marlborough. However thin the evidence on which he was charged with dishonest financial dealings, he had certainly been reluctant to complete the long negotiations for peace. So were many of his fellow peers: it was only when they were faced with the creation of new titles to produce a majority in the Lords that they agreed to the Utrecht terms. The contrast between England's triumphant status in the world of diplomacy and the squalid political scene at home could hardly have been greater.

The Netherlands after 1688

While William III[1] was concerned mainly with his English kingdom and his European wars, he had little cause to worry about the affairs of the Netherlands. Before 1688 he had faced constant opposition from the Amsterdam regents, who claimed that his government was run for the benefit of a court nobility and of the Orange dynasty. But as King of England he was in an unchallengeable position. There was no question about the need to resist the French in the Spanish Netherlands as well as to protect the territory of the Union itself, and the danger would have been immeasurably greater without the English alliance. Fortunately for the republicans, the chances of a permanent union of the English throne and the Dutch stadholderate receded. William remained childless, and announced that his heir in the Netherlands was the Stadholder of Friesland, John William Friso, who was fifteen when William died in 1702. The only possible rival was the new King of Prussia. It was therefore easy for the republicans in Holland and William's other provinces to seize control. The movements in many towns by which the Orange party was swiftly removed from its offices were victorious demonstrations rather than acts of rebellion—though in Nymegen the ex-Burgomaster who attempted a counter-coup was executed. The rival parties continued to fight a bitter political struggle throughout the Spanish Succession War. No new stadholder was elected; and the misfortunes of the Orange supporters were completed when John William died leaving another minor as heir.

In many ways the effective successor of William III was the Duke of Marlborough. In 1702 the States General agreed to his appointment as 'Lieutenant-Captain-General' of the Netherlands forces; but every

[1] Conveniently, he was the third William to be Stadholder of Holland as well as the third to be King of England.

effort was made to restrict his authority by attaching to him the 'Deputies' whose approval had to be given to all plans for the use of the army. These were the men whom Marlborough blamed for frustrating his bold strategic concepts by their belief in old-fashioned garrison warfare. After the Blenheim campaign he was in a strong position to argue that with better Dutch support the war might have been won outright. The States General became more ready to accept Marlborough's direction of the war, and concentrated on winning from the English government the 'barrier' agreements that promised a strong defensive line extending into the Southern Netherlands.

It was not only military considerations that they had in mind. If Austria was to replace Spain as ruler of the southern provinces, at least the Dutch could prevent a revival of the commercial rivalry of Antwerp or any of the other towns. Moreover they could extract from England a share in the commercial benefits that were expected to accrue from the victory over France and the break-up of the Spanish European Empire. On the face of it the Netherlands economy survived the war well. Despite the enormous burden of taxation and the general depression of the years around 1710, there was no major financial crisis and no spectacular industrial or commercial collapse. In 1715 Dutch shipping was as prosperous as ever.[1] But it gradually became apparent that the relative position of Britain and the Netherlands, both economic and diplomatic, had changed. While Britain's commercial and industrial activity expanded, and the cost of the great colonial and European wars seemed to be absorbed without greatly hindering the rising investment in all kinds of economic development, the Dutch lost their pre-eminence in the carrying trade. They were not in a position to replace it by new industrial activity. Yet helped by their neutrality in most of the wars of the next seventy years they remained the masters of international finance. Nor was there any evidence that the people of the Netherlands were worse off than the British for lack of glory.

[1] C. H. Wilson, 'The Economic Decline of the Netherlands' in *Essays in Economic History*, vol. 1, ed. E. M. Carus-Wilson.

XVIII

Louis XIV's France

The King

French history from 1661 to 1715 contains almost the whole story of royal absolutism seventeenth-century. It is a story, like so many others, of mitigated disaster. To give to its tragic elements the firm dramatic form approved at his court, Louis ought to have destroyed himself amid the ruin of his state. Instead he lived to see slow deterioration and indecisive defeat. It was never apparent to him that the cost of the state and its wars impoverished his country, still less that in the long run a state identified with too narrow a privileged minority would collapse. But he

BIBLIOGRAPHY. In addition to the works covering the whole century mentioned on p. 253, there are plenty of surveys of the reign. The biography by J. B. Wolf, *Louis XIV* (London, 1968)—which appeared too late to be used here—puts the emphasis on the king's work in civil and military administration. On a smaller scale P. Goubert, *Louis XIV et vingt millions de français* (Paris, 1966) summarises much of the recent French writing, with the social interest its title suggests. For the central narrative the account by P. Gaxotte, *La France de Louis XIV* (Paris, 1946) is sound. Two short introductions are M. P. Ashley, *Louis XIV and the Greatness of France* (London, 1946) and David Ogg, *Louis XIV* (London, 1933). *The Greatness of Louis XIV*, ed. W. F. Church (Boston, Mass., 1959) is a collection of opinions on the king himself. *XVIIe Siècle* has published many articles on political as well as cultural aspects of the reign. They include F. Dumont, 'La royauté française et la monarchie absolue' in no. 58 (1963) and V-L. Tapié, 'Quelques aspects généraux de la politique étrangère de Louis XIV' in no. 46 (1960), which also contains articles on French relations with Germany, England, and Italy. The standard general account of foreign policy is L. André, *Louis XIV et l'Europe* (Paris, 1950). See also C. G. Picavet, *La diplomatie française au temps de Louis XIV* (Paris, 1939), and H. Kamen, *The War of the Spanish Succession* (London, 1969).

On religious policy there are two books by J. Orcibal, *Louis XIV et les protestants* (Paris, 1951) and *Louis XIV contre Innocent XI* (Paris, 1949). W. S. Scoville, *The persecution of the Huguenots and French Economic Development* (Berkeley, 1960) is a massive work giving a new version of the consequences of the revocation of the Edict of Nantes. See also the articles by J. H. M. Salmon, could hardly fail to see that the glory he so assiduously manufactured lost its magic. At the beginning of his reign the eulogies were unanimous. Ten years before its end Fénelon wrote:

> Even the people . . . who have so much loved you, and have placed such trust in you, begin to lose their love, their trust, and even their respect. They no longer rejoice in your victories and conquests: they are full of bitterness and despair. They believe you have no pity for their sorrows, that you are devoted only to your power and your glory.[1]

Louis had grown up as a king who was both an object of adulation and, from time to time, a refugee. His memories were of hazardous journeys into and out of a half-rebellious capital and through a kingdom where his mother, to whom he was devoted, was clearly not treated by her important subjects as a ruling sovereign. Amid the treachery and intrigue he received the approved education in the classics and the arts, with a large dose of carefully selected history. Mazarin took a personal interest in the political training of, as he saw it, his own successor. Louis' first great experience of public life was significant. In September 1651, the day after his thirteenth birthday, there was held in the Paris Parlement the *lit de justice* at which his majority was proclaimed. Paris was still the centre of chaotic warfare and unconcealed treason. But now the streets that could at any moment be the scene of mob violence were lined with the most orderly and loyal of crowds. Through them passed the vast procession of the king's cavalry, the heralds, the court nobility, the great clergy, the provincial governors, the warring princes of the blood. Only Condé humbly excused himself on the grounds of the danger he would be in. The English diarist Evelyn, watching the ceremony with his friend Hobbes, was deeply impressed by the appearance and manner of the King his people 'idolised'. When it was all over the desultory civil war was resumed. In June 1654 there was a very different

---

'The King and his Conscience' in *History Today*, vol. 15 (1965), pp. 240 and 336. The political power of military leaders is shown in L. André, *Michel le Tellier et Louvois* (Paris, 1943). J. Saint-Germain, *Les financiers sous Louis XIV* (Paris, 1950) reveals the villainies of Bourvalais and his kind. Two aspects of political ideas are discussed in J. E. King, *Science and Rationalism in the Government of Louis XIV* (New York, 1949) and L. Rothkrug, *Opposition to Louis XIV: the political and social origins of the French Enlightenment* (Princeton, 1965).

---

[1] Fénelon, *Ecrits et lettres politiques*, ed. C. Urbain (Paris, 1920). There have been doubts about the authorship of the letter.

ceremony—the coronation at Rheims. Few of the great men of the kingdom bothered to attend. It was no longer of any benefit to Mazarin or the court that attention should be drawn to a king who was already making some effort to assert his powers. But in August 1660 he had again a central part to play. The celebration of his marriage to the Infanta was to mark the peace with Spain which formed the climax of Mazarin's achievement. It was also a sign of the restored harmony between Paris and the government that had at last achieved peace. The ceremony had been planned in lavish detail: one part of it was the homage to the king by representatives of every section of his rich and respectable Parisian subjects, another the great procession through streets decorated with the utmost baroque extravagance. This time Condé, undeterred by the fact that he had been fighting for the enemy, took his place with the other princes.

These were the beginning of the splendours that for the next twenty years were to be not a relaxation from the business of the state but a vital part of it. In 1662 the birth of the Dauphin was celebrated with the '*caroussel*', a gorgeous mixture of procession, ballet, and charade to which the royalty and nobility of all Europe were invited. Louis appeared as an improbably bejewelled Roman Emperor, Orleans and Condé as Persian and Turkish generals, Guise as commander of the Red Indians. Royal dignity was certainly not equated with stuffiness. Splendour now became a permanent and brilliantly administered form of public service. At first it had to be adapted to a mobile court. Louis progressed from place to place, though seldom far from Paris, taking with him a mass of servants and equipment that included much of the apparatus of government. His entertainment varied according to the surroundings and the season: usually a lavish amount of scenery, fireworks, or fountains had to be added to the first essential, costume. Sometimes a military parade was the main performance; and the line between participation by the army in festivities and a visit of the king to a frontier campaign was not always clear.

But outdoor spectacles and cardboard castles were not an entirely satisfactory representation of French glory. From the beginning Louis was much concerned with fine architecture. All the royal palaces were repaired, extended, ornamented. Paris got public buildings and monumental archways. An enormous park was constructed round the hunting-lodge of Versailles, where in 1664 was held the nine-day festival of the '*Plaisirs de l'Île enchantée*'. In 1671 the decision was taken to make this the site of the château that was to provide splendour as a truly national institution. It was more than a decade before the full court was permanently established there; and building was still in progress until a few years before the king's death. Tens of thousands of workers had been employed on it, of whom a good many died from the fevers they caught there. When it was occupied, seven or eight thousand of the King's dependants lived amid discomfort and dirt that must have been worse than the grim conditions any moderately prosperous Parisian accepted. One of Louis' most remarkable qualities was the physical toughness that kept him alive while most of those around him, from the royal children to the workers on the fever-stricken canals, were dying prematurely. At frequent intervals, when the smell of the palace became intolerable even to seventeenth-century noses, the court went on its travels while the gorgeous rooms were cleaned up. But very few of the court ever fled permanently from Versailles. Apart from the pleasures of food and drink and promiscuity, and the best products of all the artists and craftsmen of Europe, there was the irresistible attraction of the great court game, whose essence closely resembled that of the game of war. Success depended on a mixture of patient skill in building up alliances and displaying power with the unpredictable luck that could produce triumph or disaster in a moment. It was a war in which Louis played his favourite rôle of Mars. For most of those involved, the ultimate result was likely to be slow impoverishment as neglected estates were burdened with the debts incurred in keeping up a competitive retinue and wardrobe. But to abandon the game was to lose the prospect of salvation by winning court office, a royal pension, or even the estates of the disgraced.

Why Versailles should be regarded as the outstanding achievement of absolute monarchy is not obvious. It was more the product than the cause of the acceptance by the magnates of their exclusion from a hereditary right to political power. To the Parisians, and still more to most provincials, it meant that the monarchy had become more remote. There was not much left of Louis' boast that French subjects had free and equal access to the king. The earlier Louis, playing the part of the young Apollo with great success—despite his lack of height—had been seen as the long-awaited saviour of his people. Now, as his glory grew more costly, it was made less easy for the poor to imagine that they shared it. The image of Louis, however carefully it might be presented, changed with his mistresses. Louise de la Vallière, the 'little violet', detached from the normal palace intrigues, was a link with the lesser nobility and the Robe. Her replacement by the gorgeous and ill-tempered Mme de Montespan (whose husband successfully publicised his misfortune) seems to symbolise all the capriciousness and the contempt for outsiders of the Versailles circle. Intrigues to remove Mme de Montespan became a major court preoccupation. When at last Louis permanently shifted his affections, it was to the daughter of a minor noble who by a normal piece of good fortune in exploiting connections had become governess to Mme de Montespan's bastards. Mme de Maintenon, secret wife of the king from about 1683, acquired an almost unchallengeable influence. Though the original splendour of Versailles was to a great extent under her management, she seems to have become the principal instrument through which Louis was captured by the *dévots*. Even in the first years of Versailles, religious observances had been strictly enforced. Now compulsory gaiety turned gradually into compulsory respectability and holiness. Whether or not the story is true that the Duke of Orleans had the complete works of Rabelais between the covers of his book of devotions, there must have been many who found the change difficult.

King and ministers

Splendour was one part of what Louis regarded as the proper function of a king; but it was not the main one. The *métier du roi* to which he justly claimed to devote himself was that of managing the state. It was the death of Mazarin in March 1661 that marked the real beginning of his reign. Both the Cardinal and the young king had intended that from that moment there should be no more ministerial despotism: Louis would do the whole work of sovereignty. He was one of the rare and enviable men who appear to pack into a day activities that for most people would fill two or three. In spite of the ritual, and the mistresses, and the hunting, his rigorous timetable was so arranged that, according to Colbert, he spent six or eight hours a day at his desk. From it, within a few years, he reconstructed the central machinery of the state. In England Charles II's accession after a revolution that had appeared completely victorious marked only a return to the régime accepted in 1641. Ten months later Louis' assumption of power after the pseudo-revolution of the Fronde was a decisive moment in the shifting of power in the state. The king's council at the centre had become a body where high birth and the possession of great hereditary office ensured political power. All but three of its members Louis peremptorily expelled. The new *conseil d'état*,[1] or *conseil d'en haut*, consisted first of three survivors from

[1] See p. 206.

the government of Mazarin who were unconnected with the great families and free from any suspicion of conspiracy. Hugues de Lionne had been involved in diplomacy from his earliest youth through being the nephew of one of Richelieu's secretaries of state. Under Mazarin he was already virtually a foreign minister. Michel Le Tellier, lawyer and former intendant, had been secretary for war for nearly twenty years. Nicholas Fouquet, *surintendant des finances*, had also come from a *Robe* family, and held among his minor offices that of *procureur-général* to the Parlement of Paris. But unlike the others he had not limited his ambition to administrative power. He had become, by the obvious means open to him, immensely rich. In Paris he was a lavish patron of the arts and the centre of a large circle of dependants. He built for himself one of the most ostentatious of all private châteaux in France,[1] and made the mistake of entertaining the king in a week of wildly expensive festivity. Louis decided that this was a man of too much eminence to belong to his innermost circle. Fouquet was tried for treason and eventually imprisoned for life. His fall may have owed something to the skill of the man who replaced him, Jean-Baptiste Colbert. The bourgeois origin of the great minister, which he later made ludicrous efforts to conceal, merely demonstrated that access to the centre of power could, for the fortunate, be wide open. His father was an unsuccessful member of a fairly prominent merchant family. His cousin was a brother-in-law of Le Tellier, through whom Colbert came to the notice of Mazarin. The process of building up an impregnable court connection that led eventually to the Colbert dynasty among the king's greatest servants began long before Louis came to power. Jean-Baptiste seems soon to have seen himself as Fouquet's successor at the head of the financial administration—though he collected his offices one by one. By 1669 he had formally acquired control of every department of state except those of war and foreign affairs.

Central and local powers

Of the other holders of high office in the period of peace and internal reform down to 1672, only Le Tellier's son Louvois, already assured of the succession to his father's post, could compare in status with the three great men over whose deliberations the King presided two or three times a week. The rest—the *conseillers d'état*, the *maîtres de requêtes*, and the thirty provincial intendants—formed a small and close-knit administra-

[1] See p. 169.

tion, outside which the mass of office-holders exercised little power. One recent estimate is that in the whole work of central government not more than a thousand men were employed. Against the possible dissentients a slow process of attrition was begun. The 'great men', from Condé and Séguier downwards, found their most important administrative functions gently removed. The 'sovereign courts' were told that all decisions taken in the Council must be accepted, and had their title reduced to *cours supérieures*. The local office-holders, who had been regarded as initiators of revolt during the Fronde, were rendered harmless, sometimes by buying back their offices, sometimes by drastically diminishing their powers. Far more thoroughly than Richelieu, Louis and his ministers were able to replace the authority of the *officier* by that of men wholly dependent on the continuing goodwill of the central power. Colbert selected for special attack the *trésoriers de France*—the finance officials who, with their clerks, did more to defraud than increase the revenue. Even provincial governors were limited to three years' tenure of office—renewable on good behaviour—and prevented from residing permanently in their provinces. Provincial nobility had still to be handled with care. Visitations, of which the *Grands jours d'Auvergne* in 1665 was the most drastic, revealed that local tyrannies upheld by private armies were still common. They were not eliminated; but sometimes titles could be found invalid, high-sounding rewards for good behaviour agreed on, loyal families raised above the unreliable ones. It was all a matter for skilled manœuvre; and money shared between the state and its servants was still a means of moderating the rigour of most official policies.

There was a steady campaign against the surviving 'liberties' of provinces and towns. The Fronde had not shown that the Estates of Brittany and Languedoc were capable of offering any deeply entrenched resistance to the Crown, and the other *pays d'états* had been even less dangerous. Even so, there were the remains of a process by which they had struck a bargain about their own taxation and linked it with the presentation of 'grievances'. Without stirring up any issues of principle, the government now contrived to reduce these to a complete formality. Municipal liberties were treated in the same way. Town governments could often be persuaded, by the mixture of threats and corruption that was the key to success in all these matters, that exemptions from free-quarter, or privileges in taxation, or free election of municipal officials should be voluntarily renounced while any local customs of a purely decorative kind could rely on the blessing of the Crown. Paris was a different problem. However much the Parlement and the municipal governments were reduced to obedience, the capital was still the centre, to which there came the growing numbers of starving poor from the countryside, disbanded soldiers, hopeful fortune-seekers. Retainers of the great men were still a major source of disorder. It was here that the state really needed to show its strength. Nicolas la Reynie, carefully chosen for the new post of '*lieutenant-général pour la police*', imposed on Paris a régime that authorities in every other European city could envy. One side of it was the cavalry that paraded the streets, the spies who watched every threat of the formation of gangs, the censorship that put an end to the presses that had produced the *mazarinades*. The other was the improvement of the town itself: six thousand street lanterns, the rudiments of a drainage system, the feeding of the beggars even in the grim conditions of the *hôpital général* all helped to make a dangerous *émeute* less likely. Amid endless rural insurrections, the capital was outstandingly peaceful. Yet Louis seems never to have lost completely his fear of Paris.

State finance

The gradual erosion of sources of independent power—even of those that had grown up as part of the centralised administration in the previous reign—was one side of the new absolutism. The other was the building of a state more efficient, and above all economically sounder. This was the task to which Colbert devoted a personal energy that made even the king's life look leisurely by comparison. The process of government by paper that had occupied the cardinals for a large part of their time, and in which Louis himself was closely involved, was almost the whole of Colbert's life. His attitude to the job was that of every twentieth century civil service. The raw material of the work of governing is information—detailed, precise, and capable of being distilled into manageable brevity. The danger that between the original reporting and the drawing of conclusions the picture can become grievously distorted was as readily pushed aside then as now. The essence of his method appeared in the financial reports he presented to the king. The three 'registers', the receipts, the expenses, and the 'journal', were used to produce a monthly summary and a final yearly balance-sheet. Each October the financial commitments for the year ahead were laid down in something very like a modern British budget. It was Colbert's boast that every item of finance came before the king six times from the first order to the *état au vrai* that showed the final reckoning. A bad activity properly accounted for, he asserted, was better than a good one with no accounts[1]. Le Pelletier, the *contrôleur-général*, soon found that the money in the treasury did not in fact tally with the elaborate balances. But the reports Colbert accumulated on the state of the country's industries, trade, communications, justice, and public order were no doubt capable of giving under his skilled scrutiny a clearer picture than had existed before. The second stage, the evolving of a line of action, or of a number of alternatives, lay largely in the minister's own hands; and though every important decision was officially taken by the King from the reports presented to him, Colbert seems to have been a master of the art of 'overwhelming the King with paper'.[2]

When all allowances have been made for falsification, the record of Colbert's reform of national finances is impressive. No-one could have come to power with better justification for blaming economic difficulties on his predecessor and on circumstances beyond his control. The famine of 1660–1 came at a time when the yield of taxation was already declining. Mazarin, it was claimed, had committed the whole expected revenues for the next two and a half years to the financiers from whom he had borrowed. But one great cause of the state's comparative poverty was that more than in other countries its revenues were absorbed by the tax-farmers and the office-holders at every level and more of them lost in the tangle of exemptions and irrational assessments.[3] If the evil was worse than ever, it was also a moment at which it could be attacked without dangerous resistance. As early as 1661 there was established under Séguier and Omer Talon the fiscal *Chambre de Justice* which began to investigate malpractices of farmers and officials. By backing negotiation with menaces and inflicting exemplary sentences on those least able to offer opposition, the court eventually recovered more than a year's normal revenue. Once there was some money in hand it was possible to begin the buying back of offices and of the *rentes* so that the total of such charges was halved. The reforms of the royal forests deprived many people of a regular income they had derived from defrauding the king of his revenues; and gradually all the royal lands were subject to the process of minute investigation that brought profits back to the Crown.

Colbert's efforts to improve the return from taxation without any revolutionary change in the system relied on the same methods of minute investigation into individual peculation. The tax-farmers who had taken fantastic amounts for themselves were faced with the alternative of mak-

[1] Quoted in E. Lavisse, *Histoire de France*, vol. 7, part 2, p. 185.
[2] P. Goubert, *Louis XIV*, p. 89.　　　　　　　　[3] See p. 215.

ing a reasonable bargain or losing their position. The exemptions illegally bought from or conferred by local nobles were eliminated. The
privileged position of the *pays d'états* was diminished. Unless the official statistics are more consistently misleading than seems likely, the
result was, for the time being, a real diminution in the burden on the
worst victims among the peasantry and at the same time a large increase
in revenue. The net total was supposed to have doubled in the ten years
after 1661. But such reforms never lasted long enough to have any decisive social effect. Their failure was part of the price of glory.

War and diplomacy: the 'War of Devolutions'

The history of Louis' reign is inescapably punctuated by wars on which
convenient names are bestowed and by treaties called after the irrelevant
places where they were signed. But the distinction between war and
peace was not a rigid one. To the nobility, high and low, the army was
a more important part of the ways of life open to them as the range of
other functions narrowed. At the few times when Louis was not providing military activity they could seek it elsewhere. (In 1685 Turenne
and a succession of military men about the court asked the king's permission to go and fight in Poland.) To the administrators the army was a
sphere of control like any other, to be made the subject of competition
among themselves, purged of the more outrageous forms of corruption,
transformed from a mainly private enterprise into a mainly state one.
It all meant that a military campaign was an inescapable part of the
routine of court and political life. Royal diplomacy proceeded on this
assumption.

The Peace of the Pyrenees[1] had marked at least a major pause in the
conflict with Spain. It had not removed the habit of regarding the Spaniards as the 'other side' to be outmanoeuvred at every opportunity. The
king's Spanish marriage was the occasion for establishing a convenient
source of future conflicts when France's renunciation of the right of
succession to the always dying Charles was linked, not too clearly, with
an unpayable dowry. In the first few months of Louis' effective power,
demonstrative anti-Spanish diplomacy became a major preoccupation.
There was the celebrated 'incident' in London when the French ambassador refused to continue an unofficial arrangement by which he and
the Spanish ambassador had avoided a public scramble for precedence.
Two processions, reinforced for the occasion, met, and the Spaniard
won. It was vital that France should extract from Spain, with the maxi-

[1] See p. 336.

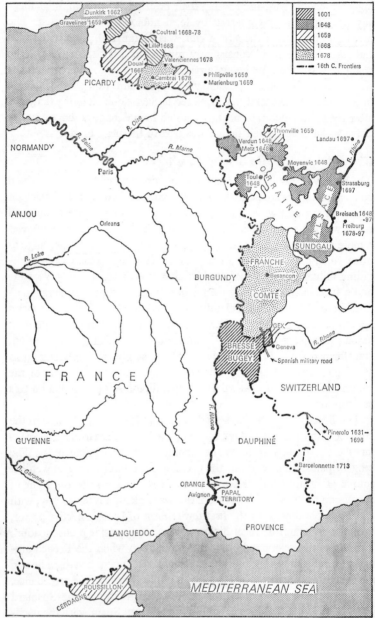

	1601
	1648
	1659
	1668
	1678
— · — · —	16th C. Frontiers

Dunkirk 1662
Gravelines 1659
Coultrai 1668-78
Lille 1668
Douai 1668
Valenciennes 1678
Cambrai 1678
Philipville 1659
Marienburg 1659
PICARDY

NORMANDY

R. Seine
R. Oise
R. Marne
Paris

Thionville 1659
Verdun 1648
Metz 1648
Landau 1697
Moyenvic 1648
L O R R A I N E
Toul 1648
A L S A C E
R. Rhine
Strassburg 1697
Breisach 1648-97
Freiburg 1678-97
SUNDGAU

ANJOU

Orleans

FRANCHE
Besancon
COMTÉ

BURGUNDY

R. Loire

GEX
BRESSE
BUGEY
Geneva
Spanish military road
R. Rhone

F R A N C E

SWITZERLAND

GUYENNE

R. Garonne

DAUPHINÉ

R. Rhone

Pinerolo 1631–1696

Barcelonnette 1713

ORANGE
Avignon PAPAL TERRITORY

LANGUEDOC

PROVENCE

ROUSSILLON
CERDAGNE

MEDITERRANEAN SEA

Map 7. French acquisitions during the seventeenth century

mum publicity, an admission that precedence was due to the French. The Ambassador to Rome, by getting involved in quarrels about the extension of the area of his embassy's privileges, was involved in another infantile brawl. French troops avenged the insult by occupying Avignon and threatening to march on Rome itself. The Pope made an abject surrender. It was in this atmosphere that Louis involved himself in the preposterous legalistic tangle of the 'devolutions'.

The French attitude to the chaotic dependent and independent territories on the eastern frontier was much less cautious now than it had been in Richelieu's day. It was assumed that France ought to acquire whatever lands she could, just as she needed to acquire bullion and markets. The simplest method was the one used with Dunkirk. In 1662 Louis bought it from Charles II of England as any peasant proprietor might buy a field from his neighbour. Vauban, as chief engineer in Turenne's army, used it as his first showpiece of design in fortifications. The Duchy of Lorraine, where France already had some complicated rights of passage, was nearly acquired by paying its Duke Charles and making his whole family 'Princes of the Blood' of France in return for a promise that Louis would be successor. There were loud objections; a small French army was sent to keep the Duke to his bargain; for many years there was argument about whether a valid agreement existed or not. With the same merging of the concepts of sovereignty and property, a list of territories was presented to the Spaniards as a bill for the first instalment of the Infanta's dowry. Franche-Comté, Luxemburg, Hainault, and Cambrai would do to begin with. It was not, of course, expected that they would be handed over; and at this point there was devised, apparently by one of Turenne's secretaries, the claim that in some of the desirable areas property descended to the children, even females, of a first wife in preference to those of a second. Louis therefore, in his anxiety to prevent injustice, required that lands—not restricted to those where such a custom did apply—should be handed over to his wife Maria Theresa as heiress to her father. On this argument the will made by Philip IV, who died in 1665, was invalid. By it he excluded Maria and her descendants from all inheritance.[1] The 'devolutions' theory was more in the realm of war propaganda than of practical diplomacy. It could hardly be expected to satisfy believers in divine right or dynastic solidarity; but it sounded sensible to lawyers and bureaucrats. While the reasons for a quarrel with Spain were being worked out, Turenne and Louvois were building up the forces they intended for the occupation

[1] See pp. 312–13.

of Spanish towns in Flanders. In 1666 the entire court was invited to see the reorganised armies, and to accept the fact that they were there to be used.

In the summer the parades turned into genuine war. With no great difficulty town after town was besieged and occupied. If nothing but military success had mattered, the whole Spanish Netherlands could have been annexed. But there was also the diplomatic score to be reckoned. Ever since the Peace of the Pyrenees, Louis and Lionne had continued the policy of the two Cardinals in collecting as many allies as possible without worrying too much about conflicting obligations. Portugal, Sweden, and Denmark all got their share of French money. The Swiss cantons, for once, united in a grand embassy to establish their alliance with France and collect the rewards. The agreement made in 1662 with the United Provinces proved momentarily embarrassing. It was an advantage to get the Dutch to accept the prospect of the Spanish Netherlands being conquered by France rather than the notion that was being canvassed of some sort of independent federation or 'cantonment'. But Louis was committed to support the Dutch at the moment when they were involved in war with another desirable French ally, England. The solution was not difficult: in 1666 France, fulfilling her treaties, declared war on England and attacked the very small Caribbean island of St Christopher. It was made clear to Charles how grateful he should be to Louis that no more serious harm was done.

The Empire was another problem and opportunity. It had become normal French practice to make, and where necessary pay for, alliances with whatever German states were amenable, vaguely directed against the Emperor. Hence the support of Brandenburg and Bavaria, and the separate treaties with Rhineland States that kept alive the general idea of a 'League of the Rhine'. How much more in accordance with French grandeur it would be to arrange with the Emperor himself a future division of the possessions of the Spanish monarchy. In January 1668 the agreement was signed in Vienna in which lands ranging from Spain and the West Indies to the towns of St Omer and Douai were dealt out and exchanged like cards from a pack. France's eventual collection, on the death of Charles II of Spain, was to include the Netherlands, Naples and Sicily, North Africa and the eastern Philippines. Spain, Milan, the West Indies, and Sardinia were to go to the Emperor. Lionne and Louis were delighted with their ambassador's triumph, which unfortunately could not be made public. The one practical effect of the agreement with the Emperor was that within a few days Condé marched his small army into Franche-Comté. It was a most unconventional time of year for an invasion; but with no risk of serious resistance the troops and inhabitants could be relied on to accept it passively.

The shape of the conflicts emerged not from any master plan but from a succession of minor frustrations and successes in which the military leaders were constantly at odds with the diplomats. To Turenne, Condé, and Louvois the easy victories in Flanders were an obvious opportunity to crush the United Provinces. To Lionne it seemed certain that any further military advance would wreck the system of alliances. Almost at the same moment as Louis' partition treaty with the Emperor, England and Holland had made the alliance which French diplomacy at once sought to break by the secret approaches to Charles II.[1] Sweden by joining it had become the first renegade from Louis' party. Since the fighting had no particular objectives in the first place, there was no loss of face in making the 'magnanimous' peace of Aix-la-Chapelle in May 1668 at which Franche-Comté, with its defences destroyed, was returned to Spain and only an illogical assortment of fortifiable towns in the Spanish Netherlands retained. To the diplomats, with their eye on the Spanish succession, the major war against Holland only gradually became accepted as the next move. But the party of the army that was working for it gained in the four years of inactivity the decisive support of Colbert. France was losing the commercial struggle with the Dutch: it must become a miltary one.

The Dutch War

We have seen something of Colbert's efforts to apply the power of the state to industrial and commercial expansion.[2] As they developed, he became, more than the military or diplomatic policy-makers, obsessed with the need to defeat the Netherlands. It was humiliating that French goods should be carried in Dutch ships; that France should still find it necessary to import both luxuries and war materials from Dutch merchants; that Dutch overseas companies should treat their French imitators with unworried disdain. In a trade war with the Netherlands, all the natural advantages ought to have been on the French side: France was larger, able to supply almost all the raw materials she needed, ruled by an ideal monarchy instead of a heretical, unstable, and decentralised bourgeois oligarchy. To defeat the Dutch at their own game seemed not just economically advantageous but morally necessary. England was as much affected by the tariff war as Holland; but the two were, in Col-

[1] See p. 406. [2] pp. 70–3.

bert's eyes as in those of Louis and Lionne, by no means the same. Though Colbert may not have known all about the prospects held out by the Treaty of Dover in 1670, by which Charles II agreed to join in an attack on the Netherlands and to become—someday—an avowed Catholic, England was clearly less dangerous as a centre from which the material rewards of Protestantism and revolution could be shown to the French. Nor could she claim any superiority so offensive to the notion of a proper hierarchy of nations as the 16,000 ships that Colbert's information showed, wrongly, the petty state of Holland to possess. With England there were long and unsuccessful negotiations for a tariff agreement. The Dutch did not wish to negotiate: they retaliated, with measures that amounted to a complete ban on French imports. 'It is impossible', Colbert announced in 1670, 'that his Majesty should tolerate any longer the insolence and arrogance of that nation.'[1] The alternatives he offered to Louis for his decision were to abolish the United Provinces altogether, taking over for the benefit of his French subjects the most profitable parts of the trade and industry of his new Dutch ones, or to leave them their sovereignty on condition that they handed over their colonies and trade. It was a choice the king was unlikely to have to make.

In April 1672 Louis set forth in person on his most glorious excursion so far. Every preparation had been made: the alliances had been reconstructed, and England—most necessary to the success of an attack on the greatest naval power—had declared war already. The army of 120,000 was probably the biggest western Europe had seen. The king, so the Parisians were officially informed, was about to punish the Dutch for the ill satisfaction he had received from their Estates-General. There were more sieges, more surrenders. In June there was the great occasion of the crossing of the Rhine, which opened the road to Amsterdam. Condé would have risked everything to take the city without which the survival of the Netherlands state was inconceivable. Louvois and Turenne wanted further sieges; Louis wanted the ceremonial restoration of Catholicism in the Cathedral of Utrecht. So the Dutch army survived; the dykes were opened; the fleet still had secure bases from which it was beating the English. A month after the first invasion the party of de Witt, in favour of a compromise peace, had offered to Louis all the territory he had occupied and more, together with a large payment in cash. Louis suggested more territory, more money, more commercial concessions. But above all the Dutch must agree to an annual mission

[1] See pp. 406–7.

to Paris to present to him a formal token of their submission. The Dutch envoys went home. Louis returned to France to receive the triumphant welcome of a hero whose conquests were not yet quite complete.

The conduct of the Dutch war was not simply a series of follies in which vanity overcame military and diplomatic good sense. But it was nevertheless the point at which unbounded French ambitions for territory and for glory made European countries that had previously been within the orbit of Louis' alliance-building see the defeat of France as a common necessity. The once glorious invading armies spent the next year burning villages, living off a countryside that gradually fell into desolation, here and there falling back into French territory. In 1674 the English, despite all Charles's secret commitments, made peace. William of Orange built his coalition, with Spain and the Empire fighting as the principal allies of the Protestant power. The lesser states began to follow the example of Brandenburg in being prepared to desert and rejoin the French as expediency required. A frontier war and a display of military glory for the French court turned within a couple of years into a struggle for the survival of French prestige and long-term hopes. It was a war of many different aspects. In the Mediterranean the French fleet won a succession of improbable victories. In Franche-Comté there was another conquering military parade, with the festivities seldom interrupted by any resistance. In the north there were long and hard-fought sieges. In Alsace and deep into the German Rhineland the war became a succession of marches and battles in which the object was to obstruct the enemy's movements by destroying the country off which he tried to live. Even among the French commanders there were a few who protested against the brutality. Imperceptibly, the dreary negotiations that continued for most of the last two years of war became more realistic as every state involved suffered heavier costs. In 1678 the separate treaties known as the Peace of Nymegen[1] distributed the frontier towns in a manner that reduced a little the intermingling of fortifications without humiliating either side. But the French had to abandon the fiercest of the tariffs against Holland. Their only serious gain was the territory of Franche-Comté which the Spaniards had written off long before. Their loss was the end of Colbert's economic expansion.

[1] Many different spellings remain in use for the town whose modern Dutch name is Nijmegen. The treaty between France and the Empire was not signed until February 1679, that with Denmark in September 1679.

437

War and the nation

The costs of the wars in 1667–8 had been borne without much difficulty: the Treasury had ceased for a couple of years to show a credit balance, but the activities of the state had not been restricted nor the burden of taxes increased. From 1672 the change in government finance was unmistakable. Month by month the precisely summarised accounts showed a growing deficit: by 1676 the normal revenue was meeting only two-thirds of the expenses. Solvency had once more to depend on the *affaires extraordinaires*. Offices that had been bought back by the Crown were sold again; new rights of inspection and monopoly were created to be sold; exemptions from the *taille* could be bought for a lump sum; royal lands were put on the market, new direct taxes imposed and the rate of old ones raised. State borrowing in the form of *rentes* at the equivalent of 7 per cent interest, loans from bankers at even higher rates—every device short of debasement of the currency had to be used. This was merely the inescapable condition of a state of war, and far better controlled than usual. France, with the help of the financiers, proved that the cost of a big war could be met. But it could only be done by reducing the state's support of the economy. The overseas companies, carefully fostered as a part of the effort against Dutch supremacy, failed when the government's support was withdrawn. The royal manufactures, sustained by subsidies and state purchases, became as indebted as the Treasury itself.

To judge the immediate effect of the wars on the French economy is still, in spite of the intensive studies of economic historians, difficult. Against the complaints of growing debts and falling profits must be set the evidence that France in the 1680s was, even by Dutch standards, a land of booming commerce and high standards for all but the poorest. St Malo rose from comparative obscurity to be one of the great ports of Europe; Marseilles and Toulon had a huge trade with eastern markets. Some of the expenses of the wars found their way from the armament-makers, the suppliers of the armies, and the financiers into capital investment. On the other hand the peasant and his landlord had often good reason to feel that the good days were over and the familiar succession of disasters beginning again. From 1677 there were several years of poor harvests. Coming after the neglect and depredations of the war they led to frightening local shortages of food. Epidemics became more frequent. One piece of evidence for a return to misery was that rebellions, which had been less common than at any other time in the century, were now resumed. When the summer campaign of 1675 was over, the armies instead of being quartered in the frontier areas they had occupied were sent to western France to show what could be done to rebels.

Religion in the service of the state

Brutal repression of revolt was easy as long as a large and loyal army could from time to time be spared for the purpose. It was not, as the king and his ministers knew, a substitute for the ideal of a harmonious state in which the order of society was not brought into question. To this ideal it was more and more assumed that religion must contribute. The pompously named 'Peace of the Church' in 1669 whereby the terminological concessions on behalf of the nuns of Port Royal had put an end to what was regarded as a dangerous controversy did not remove Jansenism from the social and political scene.[1] It had for many of the intellectuals and the ladies of fashion the attraction of a minority circle that conferred a sense of moral superiority without the stigma of heresy or disloyalty. But its success among the clergy had made it a nation-wide movement too. It was a pair of southern Jansenist bishops who brought the controversy back into political prominence by protesting against what began as a comparatively minor manifestation of royal supremacy and administrative tidiness—the extension in 1673 of the régale. Appointments to offices in the church were a matter of agree-ment between the Papacy and the Crown, largely settled by the Con-cordat of Bologna in 1516. It seemed reasonable to claim that the arrange-ment should be extended to territories to which it had not orginally applied or which had bought exemptions. The issue affected not only noble and clerical society, but Crown revenues: by the régale spirituelle benefices in a vacant diocese were filled by the king; and by the régale temporelle he had the right to the episcopal revenues. It was bad luck that three years after the decree the amenable Pope Clement X was succeeded by Innocent XI, supposedly a pro-French candidate but as it turned out a pape de combat who was not prepared to take any snubs from Louis. The régale turned into a burning issue of ecclesiastical and national politics reviving all the ancient emotions about Gallican Liber-ties. The Jansenists became almost accidentally the defenders of clerical interests against the Crown. Louis had no difficulty in finding other clergy to support him in a struggle against the Pope; and there were many ready to follow the lead of Bossuet in devising formulae that would satisfy both sides. An Assembly of the Clergy, convened under a certain

[1] See pp. 121–2.

amount of royal manipulation, produced in 1682 the 'Four Gallican Articles'. Apart from the first, which simply reaffirmed the king's sole authority in temporal matters, their precise meaning was comprehensible only to the ecclesiastical mind. The second favoured, with some circumlocution, the supremacy of General Councils; the fourth, more obscure still, indicated that the Pope was not infallible. The crucial article was the third, which upheld Gallican liberties without defining them. The Assembly then expressed its unlimited obedience to and admiration for the Pope. The Pope denounced the Assembly so forcibly that a French breach with Rome began to seem possible at the moment when England was awaiting the accession of a Catholic king. As neither Pope nor King would accept bishops appointed by the other, the number of vacant sees was rapidly increasing. Louis, and Madame de Maintenon, had the task of reconciling their religious duty with political necessity. It was in these circumstances that the rights of the Huguenots became a question of renewed political significance.

In 1609 Philip III of Spain had expelled the Moriscoes, an action commonly believed to have added substantially to his economic difficulties. In 1685 Louis XIV signed the Edict of Fontainebleau which put an end to the rights of co-existence which the Huguenots had enjoyed—decreasingly—for nearly a century. Louis has been bitterly denounced for his bigotry and stupidity. The insatiable territorial ambitions, the indiscriminate hanging of possibly rebellious peasants, the savage devastation of enemy territory have often been excused as the normal behaviour of the time, by writers who nevertheless found the revocation unpardonable. In the light of history it was certainly ill-advised: the economic consequences—even though they have sometimes been exaggerated—obviously outweighed any advantages in national and international politics. But Louis' decision arose from an accumulation of immediate incentives with much the same mixture of petty self-assertion and administrative tidiness as most of his others. The principal difference was that the existence of the Huguenot problem was itself so astonishing.

At the beginning of the reign there were probably well over a million Huguenots, with six or seven hundred churches, still—in spite of Richelieu's erosion of their privileges—more secure and less penalised legally or socially than almost any religious minority in Europe. As their total inactivity in the Fronde had shown, Huguenotism was no longer the weapon of a section of the nobility and had no political cohesion of its own. Huguenots survived as village communities loyal to their traditional faith, or as individual townsmen, or as families often of noble or prosperous mercantile status. Louis in 1661 believed—as had Henry IV—that they would come to 'consider from time to time whether there was any good reason to deprive themselves of the advantages that they could have in common with the rest of my subjects'.[1] They were therefore to receive no royal benefits, but no persecution. There were obvious reasons for refraining from any open attack on them: the 'Protestant' foreign policy which had in the past always been an obstacle to any religious activity that would arouse the wrath of France's allies was not destroyed by the peace with Spain. Colbert could provide a list of Huguenot bankers, merchants, arms manufacturers whose loss would be calamitous, quite apart from the large numbers of prosperous artisans. It was however possible to hold out greater incentives to conversion. Once the 'converti' became a familiar figure, it would be clear how readily he acquired state favours. Sometimes he was exempted from taxation that his 'old Catholic' neighbours continued to pay.

The drive to convert the Huguenots originated however less from the state than from private enterprise. Paul Pélisson, himself a convert, became in 1676 the controller of the caisse de conversions: Huguenots who renounced their faith were 'compensated' from the revenues of vacant abbeys for pecuniary losses that were not always too closely scrutinised. The complementary process, to which many of the dévots, the judges, and the clergy applied themselves zealously, was the stringent enforcement of every penalty and disability that a careful scrutiny of the wording of the Edict of Nantes could extract from it, and the banning of every activity not specifically and unambiguously authorised. Visitations of the Huguenot areas arranged by the Assembly of Clergy were able to demonstrate that the Huguenots had gradually extended their teaching and worship beyond what had originally been permitted. By steady pressure normal life for the Huguenot communities could then be made impossible. The saving of Huguenot souls did not contribute to unanimity among Catholics: while Jansenists were energetically instructing those ex-Huguenots for whom six livres a head—the minimum payment from the caisse —was felt to have been only the means towards divine grace, Jesuits resented Pélisson's success and claimed that his converts were becoming a heretical sect within the church with Huguenot pastors still dominating it. All the political influence of the Jesuits was used to get a dramatic royal move that would destroy French Protestantism and identify the majesty of the king with that of the church. In 1685 an assortment

[1] Quoted in Gaxotte, La France de Louis XIV, p. 241.

of circumstances gave them their way. One of them, paradoxically, was the success since 1681 of greatly increased state persecution. In Poitou the 'dragonnades' organised by the intendant René de Marillac, in which soldiers were encouraged to treat Huguenots with unlimited brutality, aroused such protests that Louis intervened to stop them. Elsewhere they were successfully imitated. They had produced tens of thousands of conversions; but they were bad for discipline and for the unity of the state. The European situation too, with James on the English throne, the Turks in retreat, and the Truce of Ratisbon registering a new set of territorial gains for France, seemed to have set a scene for Louis to appear as the leader of triumphant Catholicism. Revoking the Edict would make it difficult for anyone to question the king's staunchness as an ally of the Church. Besides, it would now be cheaper to throw the remaining Huguenots out than to pay the cost of further conversions.

The devout and the loyal in France celebrated the 1685 revocation enthusiastically. European Catholics—even the pope—offered rather tepid approbation. To Protestant statesmen the misfortune of their co-religionaries was a godsend. Louis had proclaimed himself the brutal persecutor of Protestantism, and had done so in a way that brought material as well as moral strength to his enemies. Something like a quarter of a million refugees took their skill and their capital to the states that were aligning themselves more firmly against the French. In England the demonstration of what Catholic rule might mean to Protestants could hardly fail to damage the prospects of James II. The effects inside France were not merely to remove a small section of the population that was on balance an economic asset. Huguenotism itself was turned from a declining and passive form of dissent into a militant faith of permanent resistance. In the Cévennes and here and there throughout the old Huguenot regions, secret Protestant congregations and occasional open revolt were met with an unpredictable mixture of ferocity and disregard. But gradually the sacred duty of extirpating heresy ceased to enthuse even the devout. By 1715 it no longer seemed to matter very much whether Huguenots survived or not.

France and Europe in the 1680s

The peace treaties and truces marked changes in the activity of armies but not, for any length of time, in the habit of hand-to-mouth acquisitions on the frontier and vast schemes for European hegemony, to mature at the happy moment when Charles of Spain would die. The years from 1679 to 1688 were a period of 'peace'. In it Louis scored quiet victories over the Emperor by buying the Poles away from him, backing the Hungarian rebels, encouraging the advance of the Turks. 'Peace' also meant that the armies of 200,000 well-equipped men which Louvois kept constantly available were used less in major warfare than as the threat that made it possible to get away with a succession of piecemeal pseudo-legal annexations. The idea of the *'réunions'* was on much the same level as that of the devolutions; but it depended not on juggling with the laws of private property but on research into the fantastic tangle of dependencies and fiefs that had arisen during centuries of warfare and robbery in Alsace and Franche-Comté. The Treaties of Münster and Nymegen had—in some cases no doubt intentionally —failed to specify precisely all the 'dependencies' of territories that changed hands. Colbert de Croissy, who as one of his brother's 'dynasty' of ministers was now Secretary for Foreign Affairs, carried through the Parlements and municipal Councils the supposedly judicial decisions that 'reunited' to French territories villages and fiefs that had been assumed to belong to Spain or to one or other of the states of the Empire. Louvois was ready with occupying forces. Sometimes the only effect was that the nobles who held the lands involved were expected to do homage to Louis. But two acquisitions were of strategic importance and hence scored immediate points against the other side. Casale, the Milanese fortress, was only included in the process by elaborate bribery and diplomatic trickery. Strassburg was one of the few towns that in the Thirty Years War had got its neutrality respected. Now, after an army thirty thousand strong had surrounded it, its reunion with France was celebrated by the entry of Louis in person.

French diplomacy was soon faced with a new opportunity that needed careful management. The emperor was temporarily unable to fight in the west because of the advance of the Turks; and in 1683 the folly of the Spaniards in declaring war was an occasion for Louvois to move his armies forward in the Netherlands. But there were still some limits to the public cynicism of western sovereigns and aristocrats. It would be inexpedient for the prospective master of Christendom to take advantage too openly, for his immediate gains, of the coalition formed by the Emperor to defend its eastern frontiers. It was better to assure the Turks privately that France, despite the pope's threats of hell, would as usual do nothing against them, and make a settlement with Leopold that would not appear too outrageous. Some day Louis might still be able to emerge as a valiant champion of the cross against the crescent. The Truce of Ratisbon, or Regensburg, in 1684—which was supposed to last for twenty years—accepted most of the *réunions* and the French seizure of Strassburg and Luxemburg. As it turned out, this was the height of French power. Helped by the Protestant indignation at the Revocation of the Edict of Nantes, the movement in Europe for an anti-French coalition began to grow. At home, some of the old 'Colbert Party' now hoped that territorial claims might really be ended and the cost of 'the enterprises of M. Louvois armies' diminished. But the militants were firmly convinced that further triumphs were to come.

The only result of the truce was that for a short time French power was asserted against the smaller states outside the Empire: Venice, Genoa, Algiers, and the Papacy continued in their different ways to serve as victims for the advertisement of French authority. When the marriage of the Emperor's daughter Maria Antonia to the Elector of Bavaria raised the hideous complexities of the Spanish Succession affair again, a large French army appeared on the Pyrenees as a warning. A quarrel about the choice of a new Archbishop of Cologne was added to the dispute with the Papacy. In September 1688 the armies were brought into action again. The Habsburgs, Louis proclaimed, had spurned the generosity shown at Ratisbon, had created, in the 'League of Augsburg', an aggressive coalition against France, had thwarted his just policies in Cologne and his claims to lands in the Palatinate. The Emperor would be given three months in which to accept the French proposals and convert the Truce into a formal Treaty. Meanwhile a few more frontier towns would have to be temporarily occupied. Three days later the massive attack along the whole eastern frontier began. In the winter, under Louvois' direction, there was carried out the destruction of the Rhine Palatinate and its population which became the most notorious atrocity of its kind in the century. The party of war had taken decisive charge of French policy at the moment when William of Orange was at last in a position to bring an even greater force against it.

War, depression, and recovery in the 1690s

The alliance against France was probably the strongest any power had yet faced. Louis failed to prevent in 1688 a success for William of Orange that made his own schemes for acquiring territory either by inheritance or by conquest look clumsy and futile. Under William England and the Netherlands together became allies of the already formidable league of the Emperor, Sweden, Spain, Savoy, and several German states. The war was fiercer and more costly in lives and material than any of the frontier struggles. For the first time the Anglo-Dutch navies effectively cut off French commerce. Colonial governors, commanders, and traders seized the chance to step up their hostilities. The French armies won victory after victory on the frontiers with little to show for it. Then, as every government found itself unable to keep up the supply of men and materials, the pace slackened and talk of peace became more serious. Yet the treaties made in 1696 and 1697 were due less to exhaustion than to firm reports from Spain that at last the helpless invalid king was clearly on the point of death. Since William III was on the whole in favour of ending the fighting and Louis was prepared to pay a good territorial price, Leopold was the main obstacle. His position was greatly weakened in 1696 when Savoy was bought out of the war by the secret Treaty of Turin. France abandoned Casale and Pinerolo and restored the occupied territories of Duke Victor Amadeus, who was happy to bring his army over to the French side. At Ryswick in 1697 the French sacrificed most of their gains since Nymegen. The fortresses of Trier, Phillipsburg, Breisach, and Freiburg were handed back. Only Strassburg remained as an addition to French defences. Almost all Lorraine was restored to its duke. The French forces that had invaded Catalonia were withdrawn; Luxemburg, Charleroi, Ath, Mons, and Courtrai became Spanish Netherlands strongpoints again. Louis at last accepted that William III was a king and not a rebel against James II.

Once again Charles II did not die. Once again the carefully calculated improvements in French national finance and the commercial and industrial progress had been sacrificed in vain to the demands of war. Le Pelletier, who had been quietly reducing the government's debt, took the astonishing step during the war of resigning his post rather than resort to the financial evil for which he held Louvois' lust for power responsible. But the war had not been a complete financial disaster. So long as harvests remained good, the yield of the *taille* was increased. The *gabelle*, the *aides*, and the Crown's other resources had risen for a year or two and then fallen back. When the war was at its height it was costing almost double the revenue from taxes and from the various *dons gratuits* of the clergy and of those other nominally exempt classes who could be pressed to pay. Consequently the familiar 'extraordinary' devices were used again. Pontchartrain, *contrôleur-général* from 1689 to 1699, manipulated the currency, anticipated future revenue by the sale of exemptions, collected royal and noble plate to be melted down, pushed the venality of honours further than ever by supplying to intendants blank patents of nobility that could be sold to the highest bidder. Up to a point, the cry of the nation's honour and glory had its effect. Estates and municipal councils did vote higher sums than before—though less willingly as the demands were repeated. Most remarkable of all was the scheme, first publicly advocated by Vauban, for a capitation tax that would override all exemptions except that of the clergy. In 1695 it was introduced as an addition to older levies. Despite a crude grading by social class rather than wealth, men who had never paid anything to the state before, unless for their own profit, did for two or three years contribute to the cost of the war. If victory depended on resources and the means of diverting them, Louis would not be easy to defeat.

France had not only the capacity to pay for wars—however grim the impoverishment for most of the people. She was also able to make quicker recovery than the central, let alone the eastern, nations from a whole succession of calamities. In 1694 it was shown once again that small changes in barometric pressure could determine how much the lives of the great majority of the population were affected by the follies of statesmen. From 1691 to 1693 there was a succession of bad harvests. Probably the natural failure was no worse than the normal fluctuations. What mattered was that the fall in supply coincided with the greatest demand of the armies, the loss of manpower, the insecurity aroused by fears of invasion, and the maximum burden of taxation. All these contributed to the spiral of famine: rising prices were an incentive to hoarding which led to further rises; impoverishment of employers produced shortage of work, which increased the starvation of the labourer. The extent of the depression of course varied very much even within quite small areas; but the reports and statistics that were produced in increasing quantity and complexity give, when all allowance has been made for motives that might tempt their compilers to exaggerate, a consistent picture of decline. The yield of taxes never returned to the amounts reached in Colbert's day; the numbers of beggars rose, the value of land fell. It is easy to imagine that the entire economy of the country was collapsing. Yet eighteenth-century France could hardly be regarded as one of the poor or materially backward states of Europe. The peasants, on the whole, did not go desperately short of food for long, but did not achieve for themselves any general increase in prosperity. They provided a surplus which the state and the landlords and the merchants absorbed in rapidly changing ways.

The peace of 1697 happened to follow a few years of improved harvests. Taxation fell; industrial activity revived; exports rose at unprecedented speed. The efforts in overseas trade of the Colbert period and the steady growth of ports and shipping could now show their real value.

For the first time French goods became a main part of European exports to America, both north and south—making possession of the Spanish Empire more tempting than ever. Amsterdam and Cadiz were no longer needed as entrepôts. The harvest of 1698 was not good—but the increased price seems to have been accepted with no great suffering. (One suggestion from the demographic studies is that the deaths of so many old and unproductive people four years before had made life easier for the survivors.) The burdens imposed by the state were to some extent diminished without any weakening of the central authority. The intendants and their *subdélégués* were now a permanent feature of life in every part of the country. The naval war was an occasion for establishing them for the first time in Brittany. Only the privileges of towns and of the nobility restricted the scope of the intendants' powers. But once the war was over there were even ways in which the state could appear as a beneficent paternal authority. The horror of the *milice*—selective conscription at the expense of the parish—ended. The *lieutenant de police*, an office extended from Paris to towns everywhere, was of course an instrument for enforcing conformity and obedience; but he could also offer some protection against the worst oppressions of the petty officials and tax-gatherers. An enlightened despotism—even the glimmerings of a state concerned with the well-being of its people—seemed on the point of emerging from the gloom whenever war ceased to be the one essential purpose.

France and the Spanish Succession

The end of the war in 1697 had brought France little benefit either in territory or in prestige. To give up so many of the frontier fortresses when they were firmly held by French armies was a remarkable assertion of diplomatic over military attitudes. Vauban, and Madame de Maintenon, were enraged. But the 'diplomatic' party could claim that by leaving open the possibility of agreement with almost any of their former enemies except the Emperor they were playing for the prize of a share in the imminent carving-up of Spanish territories either without war at all or with a war in which it would be France's turn to have a large coalition on her side. The diplomats could well have proved right. In the two Partition Treaties French demands were not those of an insatiable aggressor: they were intended to win the support that the Emperor by his more blatant hopes of expansion was losing.[1] France would be content with Naples and Sicily, plus—in the second version—

[1] See p. 313.

Lorraine or perhaps Savoy. When the Spanish King made his second will leaving all his possessions to Louis' second grandson Philip of Anjou, there was some doubt about whether so dazzling an offer should be accepted. Colbert de Torcy, the latest French foreign minister, recognised that there was in any case a risk of war against the Emperor, who had refused to agree to the Partition Treaty. If France stuck to the treaties, there was hope that England and the United Provinces would be her allies; if she accepted the will instead almost any alignment of the powers would be possible. The optimists believed that the Dutch and English would be at least as hostile to a Habsburg seizure of Spain as to a Bourbon one, and that the Spaniards themselves would be on the side of France. To reject the will meant a risk that the old nightmare of France being surrounded by a solid Habsburg barrier would come true; to accept it gave hope of a commercial as well as military alliance that would solve the economic troubles of the nation. It was not simply dynastic ambition that led Louis to accept the inheritance. The question was hotly debated in the Council and the court. The weight of opinion clearly favoured the will; even heredity of this kind was felt to uphold divine right.

It took a year and a half from the death of Charles II to the outbreak of war between France and a new 'Grand Alliance', in the spring of 1702. Once the possibility of war was obvious, the pressure to begin it appeared irresistible. An ambiguous pronouncement on the French attitude to the succession left a way open for breaking the agreement that Philip V of Spain should not also become King of France. French troops occupied the Netherlands frontier fortresses—in the name of the Spanish King. A French company acquired from Spain the immensely valuable 'asiento' for the supply of negro slaves to the Spanish colonies, formerly held by the Dutch. When the former James II died a few days after the formation of the alliance of The Hague, Louis, in spite of his promises at Ryswick, greeted the pretender as James III. To each major pressure-group—the military, the commercial, and the Catholic—Louis had conceded a measure that played into the hands of those in Holland and England who were avidly seeking popular reasons for war.

The French appeared to have a reasonable prospect of defeating the new coalition. Their agreements with Spain, Bavaria, and—for the time being—Savoy gave them excellent bases for moving forward against the Empire. They spent money lavishly on the armies and on buying support. There seemed every hope that the Emperor, interested mainly in the Spanish throne, could be divided from the English and Dutch who sought to beat the French and get what spoils they could. France's defensive fortifications in the east were strong and almost continuous. In the first year of fighting on the eastern frontier and in Italy the advantage, such as it was, went their way. But this proved to be a war in which long sieges, cautious occupation of territory, and evasive marches took second place. On both sides improvements in weapons[1] gave to armies larger than ever before the power of rapid destruction. Marlborough, appointed in 1702 captain-general of the Anglo-Dutch forces, and the Emperor's general Eugene of Savoy both believed in swift movement and ruthless, decisive battles. Both held at this stage enough political influence at home to keep full control of the fighting, while Villeroi, Vendôme, Villars, and the other French commanders suffered constant interference and supervision from Versailles.

The first serious misfortunes for France were diplomatic: in 1703 Savoy went over to the Emperor's side, and Portugal in the Methuen Treaties became a military ally and economic dependant of England. Part of the price was that all the members of the coalition recognised the claim of Archduke Charles to the Spanish throne.[2] Against this France could set the chance of a great victory over the Emperor. French and Bavarian armies joined in an advance towards Vienna. At the same time a new rising in Hungary under Francis, grandson of George Rakoczy,[3] had produced with French help a large force able to threaten the city from the east. In August 1704 Marlborough, Eugene, and Louis of Baden shattered the French armies at Blenheim, with heavy losses to themselves. Germany was brought almost completely under allied control. In the same month the English and Dutch navies captured Gibraltar. With the allies in command of the Mediterranean, 'Charles III' was soon able to land in Catalonia and win popular support as an enemy of Castile.

Not all the allied efforts were as forceful as the Blenheim campaign: there was pressure, notably from the Dutch, to move carefully and even to have some regard for the cost in lives. In 1706 Villeroi, with a new but inferior French army, was ordered to take the offensive in the Netherlands and suffered at Ramillies a defeat on almost the scale of Blenheim. From northern Italy too the French were driven out. There remained one unexpected source of hope: Charles XII of Sweden was winning decisive victories in Saxony. If France could buy him as an ally the Empire would again be in danger. But neither side could make the Swedes involve themselves in western quarrels: Russia was more

[1] See p. 244.   [2] See p. 313.   [3] See p. 310.

important to them. In 1708 another effort by Vendôme's army to recover the Spanish Netherlands ended with his defeat at Oudenarde. Lille, one of the key points in Vauban's line of defences, was occupied. With the enemy on French soil, Louis began to consider terms for a settlement. There was now a well-defined peace-party, with the Duc de Beauvillier as its spokesman in the Council. Its great source of strength was the misery of France, and the poverty of the Crown.

Defeat and depression

The war had soon increased government expenses to three times the ordinary revenue. Many devices, old and new, were used to supplement it. The issue of receipts for loans developed into the printing of paper money, which circulated at far below its face value. There were repeated efforts to make profits for the government by devaluing the *livre*, the ordinary circulating currency, in terms of the *Louis d'or* and the *écu*. In 1709 a general recoinage was announced, so that loans would be repaid in coins worth three-quarters of their former value. A capitation tax on those exempt from normal taxation was tried again. Revolts in the Cévennes in 1704, which diverted large forces from the war, were an indication of the dangers if things got worse. As before, it was when bad weather was added to the burden of war that the worst suffering came. There was a grim winter in 1709: the cold that was killing off the armies of Charles XII in Russia extended far enough to freeze the Rhone. Both grain and vines were destroyed almost everywhere. In face of the English blockade, such corn as could be imported had to be used to keep the armies alive while the poor died. The intendants reported with growing panic the gathering of armies of rebels, against which they had not the means to act.

A great difference from earlier wartime crises was that now the court and the government and literate society were full of critics of the war and its management. Madame de Maintenon was convinced that the frosts were an indication of God's disapproval of the war. Chamillart, the latest finance minister, announced as early as 1707 that France could not afford to go on fighting. His successor Desmarets was soon of the same opinion. In broader terms their views were upheld by successful writers. Pierre de Boisguillebert, *lieutenant de police* at Rouen, had written before the war his *Détail de France* expounding the follies of the economic system and demanding a real tax on the rich. The *taille*, he said, was 'the ruin of goods, of bodies, and of souls'. His sustained campaign on these lines was now backed by Vauban, old and respected, who just before his death in 1707 published an attack on the crushing of the *menu peuple* by taxation. Fénelon and Saint-Simon were blaming not merely administrative defects but royal absolutism itself. Round the Dauphin and his son the Duc de Bourgogne there gathered shifting groups of nobles interested in the movements for reform and their probable effects on the distribution of power. The Dauphin died in 1711, the Duc de Bourgogne and his elder son in 1712. If, as seemed likely in the epidemics that were sweeping the court, the Duc de Bourgogne's younger son and the Duc de Berry also died, Philip V of Spain would be the sole survivor of the Bourbon line. There was talk of legitimising some of the royal bastards, and hasty realignments among the court factions.

There were of course important Frenchmen who neither suffered from nor opposed the war. The lower the credit of the state sank, the greater the opportunity of profit for the financiers. The bigger the scale on which wars were fought, the bigger profits there were in supplying the material for them. Samuel Bernard, the greatest of the financiers, was involved in the hoarding of grain, in manipulating the exchanges, in shipping and munitions and the *asiento*. His bankruptcy in 1709, from which the government had to rescue him, was a mere incident in the accumulation of his millions; though it was also part of a general financial upheaval that brought some of his kind on to the side of peace. From time to time, the most unscrupulous of the profiteers were made to repay some of their gains. But on a less spectacular scale there were opportunities at every level for taking a share of the money that was flowing into and out of the Treasury. The sale of office and of patents of nobility remained a source of benefit to both government and subject to which there seemed no limit. Those who had capital to lend continued to regard the *rentes* as a safe investment. In the last years of the war, government borrowing increased at an unprecedented rate. There was no longer any question of paying for the war out of revenue in a foreseeable time. While the state itself was accumulating a vast debt, its subjects were divided sharply into those who suffered and those who gained.

The Utrecht settlement

In investigating the possibilities of peace, the French hoped that the enemy alliance would as usual be divided by the prospect of territorial gains. At first this seemed unlikely. Marlborough's victories produced powerful groups in England and in the Netherlands determined to

Map 8. Europe, 1721

Boundary of the Empire
Austrian possessions
Kingdom of Prussia

St Petersburg
INGRIA
ESTONIA
LIVONIA
HLAND
Swedish)
Moscow ●
LITHUANIA
SEA
EAST
PRUSSIA
R U S S I A
POLAND
CASPIAN
SEA
JEDISAN
UNGARY
MOLDAVIA
TRANSYLVANIA
ONIA
WALLACHIA
IA
BLACK SEA
BULGARIA
ARMENIA
TREBIZOND
T T O
Ragusa
M
Constantinople
ALBANIA
A N
E M P I R E
KURDISTAN
MOREA
CRETE
CYPRUS

achieve a total defeat of France. By demanding that Louis should abandon Philip completely, and even fight against him, and by talking of the
occupation of French territory, the allies momentarily evoked in France
an indignant enthusiasm for the war, even among the former peacemakers. The fall of the English Whig ministry in 1710, followed by the
dismissal of Marlborough, changed the situation completely. In 1711
there came the last of the changes in the tangle of the Spanish Succession: the Emperor Joseph I died of smallpox and was succeeded by his
brother Charles, the allies' claimant to the Spanish throne. In keeping
the succession away from the French, England and the Netherlands
suddenly found themselves faced with a revival of the vast Habsburg
Empire of Charles V. The objections to Philip V immediately became
far less serious. Ignoring their commitments to their allies, the English
ministers Harley and St John began negotiations with the French and
ordered the new military commander, Ormonde, to avoid further
fighting. The Dutch and Austrians were not even to be informed.
French armies were naturally able to win some victories that improved
their position appreciably.

The new Emperor at first refused to have any part in the negotiations
with the French which were initiated by what he reasonably denounced
as English treachery. The Dutch abandoned their militancy and decided
to get what they could out of the conference. Portugal, Savoy, and
Prussia also joined in the meetings at Utrecht. In the negotiations and
the separate treaties that emerged from them it made little difference
which nations had been allies and which enemies. The proclaimed intention was 'to establish the peace and tranquillity of Christendom by a
just balance of power (*équilibre de puissance*), which is the best and most
solid basis of mutual friendship . . .'[1] In practice it meant that the
Spanish possessions would be shared out and other adjustments of territory made in accordance with a more or less recognised order of precedence among the powers and with regard to both strategic and economic
interests. The agreement between France and Britain was signed first in
April 1713; the other powers continued to bargain within its general
assumptions. It was only in March 1714 that the emperor made peace
with France at Rastatt. Portugal, getting little gratitude from Britain
for her help, did not submit to Spanish demands until 1715.

From the terms of the settlement it might be supposed that the Emperor was the one triumphant victor. The Spanish Netherlands, Milan,
Naples, and Sardinia were handed over to him, and French conquests

[1] See C. Dupuis, *Le principe de l'équilibre et le concert européen* (Paris, 1909).

on the right bank of the Rhine restored. (Sardinia was then exchanged for Sicily which had been the main reward given to Savoy.) The diplomats, seeking an arrangement that would not provoke immediate further wars, had produced a far bigger change than any military conquests.

Britain collected some colonial territories from France—Newfoundland, Hudson Bay, Acadia (the eastern part of modern New Brunswick), and St Christopher (St Kitts)—and Gibraltar and Minorca from Spain. The French accepted the Hanoverian succession in Britain, at the expense of the Jacobites. There was an elaborate commercial treaty between Britain and France; and Spain conceded to Britain for thirty years a monopoly in the shipping of 4,800 negro slaves a year to America.

For Louis XIV the outcome was far better than had seemed likely in the black days of 1709–10. He kept Alsace, Franche-Comté, and a frontier with the new Austrian Netherlands much the same as in 1679. His ally the Elector of Bavaria got his former territories back. Philip V, having confirmed his renunciation of any claims to the French succession, not only retained Spain—including Catalonia which tried hard to escape—but the South American possessions too.

The Dutch, who now ranked fairly low in the diplomatic hierarchy, eventually gained most of the barrier fortifications they wanted, and were enabled to thwart any commercial rivalry from Antwerp by closing the Scheldt. The King of Prussia, with his new title formally recognised, acquired Guelderland, the outlying bit of the former Spanish Netherlands adjoining his Rhineland possessions.

Utrecht, like any settlement of its kind, contributed at least as much to future conflicts as to the 'tranquillity of Christendom'. The Empire was if anything an even more irrational agglomeration than before; France still held isolated scraps of territory amid the Duchy of Lorraine; the boundaries of the Netherlands had no other justification than the military one. The monarchs and ministers had devoted themselves to making their states into mechanisms of enormous power and complexity, concerned with nearly every aspect of the lives of their subjects. Yet when they came to settle the vital question of what lands and people they ruled, they behaved like children or like brigands. What the diplomats spoke of pompously as a 'system' and an 'equilibrium' meant in practice that territories and their inhabitants were disposed of by their sovereigns in whatever way the bargaining permitted. It sprang not from villainy or stupidity but from the fact that political authority was held by men who had acquired, at first or second hand, the outlook of a landed nobility, and treated sovereignty as the equivalent of ownership. They assumed equally that war, which for many of them was a major interest in life, should be one of the prime purposes of the state. There were of course other considerations as well. Religious allegiances, which had been crucial in earlier peace settlements, no longer caused much difficulty. Instead the commercial treaties that were coupled with the territorial ones gave the settlement some connection with the material interests of subjects. It was true also that acquisitions of territory, especially colonial, could bring economic benefits. But on the whole if Utrecht ushered in a new era it was not one in which 'enlightenment' had much place in international affairs.

Chronological List of Political Events

1598 The Edict of Nantes establishes the rights of the Huguenots. Philip III of Spain succeeds Philip II. Peace of Vervins between Spain and France.

Boris Godunov succeeds Fedor I as Tsar.

1599 Swedish Riksdag deposes Sigismund III.

1600 Henry IV of France invades Savoy.

1601 The Earl of Essex executed for rebellion.

1602 Attack on Geneva by Charles Emmanuel of Savoy repelled.

1603 James VI of Scotland succeeds Elizabeth on English throne.

1604 Peace between England and Spain.
Charles IX recognised as King of Sweden.

1605 Death of Boris Godunov and murder of his son Fedor. The first 'False Dmitry' crowned as Tsar.

1606 The 'False Dmitry' murdered: Vasily Shuisky proclaimed Tsar.
Treaty of Zitva-Torok between the Empire and Turkey.

1608 The Protestant Union formed in Germany. The Emperor Rudolf II cedes Austria, Hungary, and Moravia to his brother Matthias.
Second 'False Dmitry' in Russia.

1609 Twelve-year truce in the Netherlands.
Catholic League formed in Germany. Rudolf II grants the 'Letter of Majesty' promising religious liberty in Bohemia.
Sigismund III of Poland invades Russia.

1610 Henry IV of France murdered: Louis XIII succeeds him, with Marie de Medici as regent.
Vasily Shuisky overthrown: Vladislav proclaimed Tsar.

1611 War between Sweden and Denmark. Gustav Adolf succeeds Charles IX of Sweden.

1612 Matthias succeeds Rudolf II as Emperor.
Polish invaders defeated in Russia.

1613 Michael Romanov elected as Tsar by a *zemsky sobor*.
Gabriel Bethlen becomes Prince of Transylvania.
Peace of Knaeroed between Sweden and Denmark.

1614 Meeting of the Estates-General in France.

1615 Rebellion of princes in France.

1616 Richelieu's brief term as Secretary of State.

1617 Treaty of Stolbova between Russia and Sweden.

1618 Revolt of Bohemia; the 'Defenestration of Prague'.

1619 Ferdinand of Styria succeeds Matthias as Emperor; Bohemians
elect Frederick, Elector Palatine, as their King in place of Ferdinand.
Oldenbarnevelt executed.

1620 Agreement at Ulm between Protestant Union and Catholic
League.
Frederick of Bohemia defeated at Battle of the White Mountain.
Turks defeat Poles at Cecora.

1621 Philip IV succeeds Philip III of Spain; Olivares chief minister.
War between Spain and the Netherlands renewed.
Religious war in France.
Sweden invades Livonia.

1622 Peace of Montpellier between Huguenots and French Crown.
Tilly wins victories in Germany.

1623 Urban VIII succeeds Gregory XV as Pope.
Maximilian of Bavaria made Elector Palatine.
Murad IV succeeds Osman II as Sultan.

1624 French invade the Valtelline
Richelieu becomes Chief Minister.

1625 Charles I of England succeeds James I.
England at war with Spain.
Frederick Henry succeeds Maurice of Nassau as Stadholder in the
Netherlands.
Huguenot revolt in France.
Danes enter the war in Germany.

1626 Christian IV of Denmark defeated at Lutter.

1627 Huguenot revolt: siege of La Rochelle.

1628 The Petition of Right in England; Buckingham assassinated.
The Mantuan War.

1629 Huguenot wars ended by Peace of Alais.
Edict of Restitution and Treaty of Lübeck in Germany.
Truce of Altmark between Sweden and Poland.

1630 'Day of Dupes' in France.
Swedes invade Pomerania; Wallenstein dismissed.
Victor Amadeus succeeds Charles Emmanuel as Duke of Savoy.

1631 Treaty of Barwälde between France and Sweden.
Mantuan War ended by Treaty of Cherasco.
Sack of Magdeburg.

1632 Rebellion of Gaston of Orleans defeated.
Gustav Adolf killed at Lützen; Christina Queen of Sweden.
Vladislav IV succeeds Sigismund III of Poland.

1633 League of Heilbronn in Germany.
Laud becomes Archbishop of Canterbury.

1634 Wallenstein murdered; Swedes defeated at Nördlingen.
Treaty of Polianov between Poland and Russia.

1635 Peace of Prague between Emperor and Protestant states.
France declares war on Spain.

1637 Ferdinand III succeeds Ferdinand II as Emperor.
Charles Emmanuel II succeeds Victor Amadeus as Duke of Savoy.

1638 'Ship Money' trial in England; National Covenant in Scotland.

1639 First Bishops' War in Scotland.
French invade Alsace.
Tromp defeats Spanish fleet in the Downs.

1640 Short Parliament and opening of Long Parliament in England;
Second Bishops' War in Scotland.
Revolts in Catalonia and Portugal.
Frederick William succeeds George William as Elector of Brandenburg.

1641 Execution of Strafford in England; the Irish Rebellion; the Grand
Remonstrance.

1642 Civil War in England; John Pym Parliamentary leader.
Conspiracy of Cinq-Mars in France; death of Richelieu; Mazarin
chief minister.
Imperial army defeated by Swedes at Breitenfeld.

1643 Louis XIV succeeds Louis XIII; Anne of Austria Regent.
Fall of Olivares; Spain defeated by France at Rocroi.
Solemn League and Covenant; Westminster Assembly; death
of Pym.

1644 Parliamentary victory at Marston Moor.
Innocent X succeeds Urban VIII as Pope.
Sweden makes war on Denmark.

1645 Execution of Laud; Self-Denying Ordinance; formation of New
Model Army; Parliamentary victory at Naseby.
Treaty of Brömsebro: Sweden gains territory from Denmark.
Beginning of peace negotiations in Germany.

1646 Charles I surrenders to the Scots.

1647 Charles I handed over to the English Parliament; the Putney
Debates.
William II succeeds Frederick Henry as Stadholder.
Rebellion in Naples.

1648 The Peace of Westphalia.
Beginning of the *Fronde* of the *Parlement*.
Second Civil War in England; Pride's Purge.
Frederick III succeeds Christian IV of Denmark; John Casimir
King of Poland.

1649 Charles I executed; monarchy and House of Lords abolished;
sack of Drogheda and Wexford.
Legal Code establishing serfdom in Russia; revolt in the Ukraine.

1650 Cromwell defeats the Scots at Dunbar.
Condé imprisoned.
Death of William II: republican government in the Netherlands.

1651 Charles II crowned in Scotland, defeated by Cromwell at Worces-
ter; the Navigation Act.
Mazarin leaves France; Condé enters Paris, becomes ally of Spain.

1652 War between England and the Netherlands.

1653 Barebone's Parliament; Cromwell becomes Lord Protector.
De Witt becomes Grand Pensionary of Holland.
End of the Fronde; Mazarin back in Paris.

1654 Coronation of Louis XIV.
Peace of Westminster ends Anglo-Dutch war.
War between Russia and Poland.
Queen Christina abdicates: Charles X King of Sweden.

1655 Swedes declare war on Poland.

1656 Mohammed Kiuprili becomes Grand Vizir.
Alliance of England and France against Spain.

1657 'Humble Petition and Advice' creates new upper house in Cromwellian Parliament.

1658 Death of Oliver Cromwell; Richard Cromwell Protector.
Leopold I succeeds Ferdinand III as Emperor.
Peace of Roskilde between Sweden and Denmark followed by renewed war.

1659 Peace of the Pyrenees between France and Spain.
Richard Cromwell abdicates; Long Parliament restored.

1660 Charles II restored to English throne.
Charles XI of Sweden succeeds Charles X; Peace of Oliva ends Northern War.

1661 Death of Mazarin; effective rule of Louis XIV begins.
Ahmed Kiuprili becomes Grand Vizir.
Cavalier Parliament meets; first measures of the 'Clarendon Code'.

1662 England sells Dunkirk to France; Colbert becomes finance minister.

1663 Turks declare war on Austria.

1664 Turks defeated at St Gotthard: peace agreed.

1665 Charles II of Spain succeeds Philip IV.
Second Anglo-Dutch war.

1666 Schism in the Russian Church begins.

1667 War of Devolution between France and Spain.
Peace of Breda between England and Netherlands.
Peace of Andrusovo between Russia and Poland.

1668 Triple Alliance of England, Sweden, and Netherlands.
Treaty of Aix-la-Chapelle ends War of Devolution.
John Casimir of Poland abdicates.

1669 Michael Wisniowiecki elected King of Poland.

1670 Treaty of Dover between Charles II of England and Louis XIV.
Stenka Razin's revolt in Russia.
Christian V succeeds Frederick III of Denmark; Griffenfeld chief minister.

1671 John Sobieski elected King of Poland.

1672 De Witt murdered; William III becomes Stadholder.
England and France at war with the Netherlands.
War between Turkey and Poland.

1673 Test Act in England excluding Catholics from office.

1674 Peace between England and the Netherlands; Spain and the
Empire join in war against France.

1675 Swedes attack Brandenburg; defeated at Fehrbellin.

1676 Fedor III succeeds Alexis as Tsar.
Innocent XI becomes Pope.
Kara Mustafa succeeds Ahmed as Grand Vizir; peace between
Turkey and Poland.

1677 War between Turkey and Russia.

1678 Treaties of Nymegen between France and the Netherlands,
France and Spain.
Popish plot in England.
Thököli becomes national leader in Hungary.

1679 Cavalier Parliament dissolved; first 'Exclusion Parliament' meets.
Further treaties at Nymegen; Treaty of St Germain between
Brandenburg and Sweden.

1680 *Chambres de Réunion* on French frontier.

1681 Peace of Radzin between Russia and Turkey.

1682 The Gallican Articles.
Turks make war on Austria and Poland.
Ivan V and Peter I joint Tsars; Sophia as Regent.

1683 Vienna besieged by the Turks.
French invade Spanish Netherlands.

1684 Twenty-year Truce of Ratisbon between France and the Empire.
'Holy League' against the Turks.

1685 James II succeeds Charles II of England; Monmouth's rebellion.
Revocation of the Edict of Nantes.

1686 League of Augsburg against France.
Buda recaptured from the Turks.

1687 Turks defeated at Mohacs; Mohammed IV deposed and succeeded by Suleiman III; Venetians bombard Athens.

1688 War of the League of Augsburg begins; devastation of the Palatinate.

William of Orange lands at Torbay; James II flees.
Frederick III succeeds the Great Elector of Brandenburg.

1689 Convention Parliament declares William III and Mary joint sovereigns; the Bill of Rights.

1690 James II defeated at the Battle of the Boyne; Anglo-Dutch fleet defeated by the French off Beachy Head.
Turks recapture Belgrade.

1691 Innocent XII succeeds Alexander VIII as Pope.
Turks defeated by Imperial armies at Salem Kemen; Mustafa Kiuprili killed.

1692 Massacre of Glencoe.
Anglo-Dutch fleet defeats the French off La Hogue.

1693 French victory over William III at Neerwinden.

1694 Augustus the Strong becomes Elector of Saxony.

1695 Mustafa II succeeds Ahmed II as Sultan.

1696 Peter the Great captures Azoff.

1697 Treaty of Ryswick between France and the allies.
Peter the Great's visit to western Europe.
Charles XII succeeds Charles XI of Sweden.
Augustus II succeeds John Sobieski of Poland.
Eugene of Savoy defeats the Turks at Zenta.

1698 First partition treaty to settle Spanish Succession.
Revolt of the *streltsi* in Moscow.

1699 Peace of Karlowitz between Turkey and Venice, Poland, Austria.
Peter the Great's reforms of Russian government.

1700 Second treaty for partition of Spanish possessions; death of Charles II.
Northern War begins; Charles XII defeats Russians at Narva.
Peace of Traventhal between Sweden and Denmark.

1701 Fighting between French and Spaniards in Italy; alliance of England, Netherlands, and Empire against France.
Frederick III of Brandenburg crowned King of Prussia.

1702 Anne succeeds William III in England; Heinsius and the States-General take control in the Netherlands.
War of the Spanish Succession begins.

1703 Portugal and Savoy join the alliance against France.
Foundation of St Petersburg.

1704 The French defeated at Blenheim.
Stanislas Lesczynski elected King of Poland.

1705 Josef I succeeds Leopold as Emperor.

1706 The French defeated at Ramillies; Marlborough's troops occupy the Spanish Netherlands; French driven out of Piedmont.

1707 Union of England and Scotland.

1708 The French defeated at Oudenarde.

1709 Russian victory over the Swedes at Pultava; Charles XII takes refuge in Turkey.
Peace negotiations with France; Marlborough and Eugene take Tournai, defeat French at Malplaquet.

1710 Tory ministry in England; peace negotiations break down; indecisive fighting in Spain and Netherlands.

1711 'Charles III of Spain' succeeds Josef I as Emperor.
Peace between Russia and Turkey.

1712 Negotiations at Utrecht; deaths of Louis XIV's son and grandson; Philip V renounces claim to French throne.

1713 Peace of Utrecht: France makes treaties with Britain, Prussia, Netherlands, Savoy, Portugal; England makes treaty with Spain.

1714 Treaty between Spain and Netherlands; Peace of Rastatt between France and the Emperor.
George I succeeds Anne in England.

1715 Death of Louis XIV.
Jacobite rising in Scotland.

1718 Death of Charles XII of Sweden.

1721 Peace of Nystad between Sweden and Russia ends Northern War.

1725 Death of Peter the Great.

Bibliographical Note

There is no satisfactory recent bibliography in English of works on European history. *A Bibliography of Modern History*, ed. John Roach (Cambridge, 1968), suffers from being partly tied to the arrangement of chapters in the *New Cambridge Modern History*, and from the lack of an index of authors. The big standard bibliographies on particular countries include those by E. Bourgeois and L. André on France, Godfrey Davies on Stuart England (soon to be replaced by a new version), M. Nijhoff on the Netherlands, and B. S. Alonso on Spain. A new edition of the Dahlmann-Waitz bibliography of German history is appearing progressively. P. A. Crowther, *A Bibliography of Works in English on Early Russian History* (Oxford, 1969), will be helpful for one of the most difficult areas. An excellent source of information on recent books and articles is the *Nouvelle Clio* series, each volume of which devotes a substantial chapter to bibliography. Some of them are listed in the relevant chapters above; others are due to appear shortly. The *Revue Historique* regularly prints specialised bibliographical articles.

Only one of the three volumes in the *New Cambridge Modern History* that will cover the seventeenth century has so far appeared—*The Ascendancy of France*, ed. F. L. Carsten (1961). The older *Cambridge Modern History*, vol. 4, *The Thirty Years War*, and vol. 5, *The Age of Louis XIV*, are good sources of factual detail. On a slightly smaller scale the *Rise of Modern Europe* series, ed. W. L. Langer, has three volumes on the period: C. J. Friedrich, *The Age of the Baroque, 1610–1660* (1952); F. L. Nussbaum, *The Triumph of Science and Reason, 1660–1685* (1953); and J. B. Wolf, *The Emergence of the Great Powers, 1685–1715* (1951). All have been reprinted in paperback. In the comparable French series, *Peuples et Civilisations*, the seventeenth-century volumes are H. Hauser, *La prépondérance espagnole, 1559–1660* (new edition, 1948) and A. Saint-Léger and P. Sagnac, *Louis XIV, 1661–1715* (1949). A single-volume history of the century, with a very modern approach and lavish illustration, is P. Chaunu, *La civilisation de l'Europe classique* (1966).

The old *Cambridge Modern History* included two very useful volumes for reference, the *Cambridge Modern History Atlas* and the *Tables and General Index*. For exact dates of political events *An Encyclopaedia of World History*, ed. W. L. Langer, is a reliable and well-arranged source.

THE RULERS OF ENGLAND, FRANCE, SPAIN,
AND THE EMPIRE

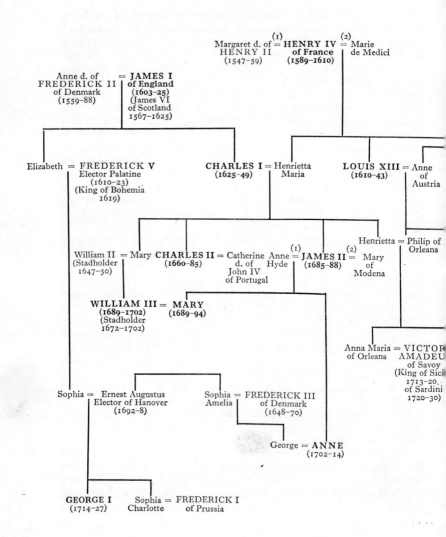

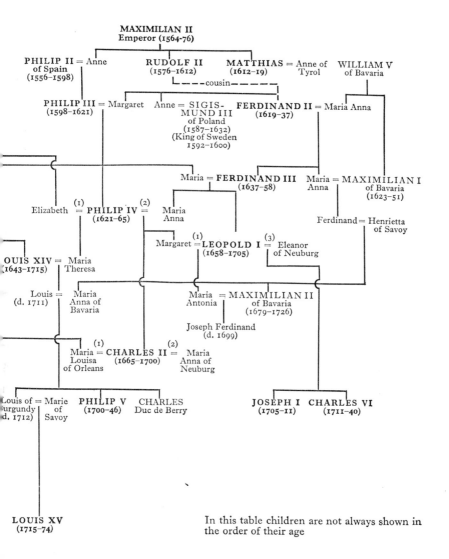

MAXIMILIAN II
Emperor (1564-76)

PHILIP II = Anne   **RUDOLF II**   **MATTHIAS** = Anne of   **WILLIAM V**
of Spain   (1576-1612)   (1612-19)   Tyrol   of Bavaria
(1556-1598)
                  └ — — cousin — — — ┘

PHILIP III = Margaret   Anne = **SIGIS-**   **FERDINAND II** = Maria Anna
(1598-1621)   **MUND III**   (1619-37)
                  of Poland
                  (1587-1632)
                 (King of Sweden
                 1592-1600)

                     Maria = **FERDINAND III**   Maria = **MAXIMILIAN I**
                           (1637-58)   Anna   of Bavaria
                                              (1623-51)

              (1)   (2)   Ferdinand = Henrietta
Elizabeth = **PHILIP IV** =   Maria   of Savoy
        (1621-65)   Anna

                     (1)   (3)
              Margaret = **LEOPOLD I** =   Eleanor
OUIS XIV = Maria   (1658-1705)   of Neuburg
(1643-1715)   Theresa

     Louis =   Maria   Maria = **MAXIMILIAN II**
   (d. 1711)   Anna of   Antonia   of Bavaria
           Bavaria   (1679-1726)

                      Joseph Ferdinand
                       (d. 1699)

              (1)   (2)
            Maria = **CHARLES II** =   Maria
           Louisa   (1665-1700)   Anna of
          of Orleans   Neuburg

Louis of = Marie   **PHILIP V**   **CHARLES**   **JOSEPH I**   **CHARLES VI**
urgundy   of   (1700-46)   Duc de Berry   (1705-11)   (1711-40)
d. 1712)   Savoy

LOUIS XV
(1715-74)

In this table children are not always shown in
the order of their age

RULERS OF POLAND

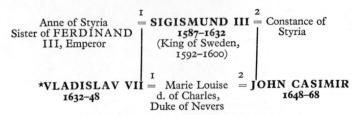

Anne of Styria
Sister of FERDINAND
III, Emperor

SIGISMUND III
1587–1632
(King of Sweden,
1592–1600)

Constance of
Styria

★VLADISLAV VII = Marie Louise
1632–48   d. of Charles,
           Duke of Nevers

= **JOHN CASIMIR**
1648–68

**MICHAEL
WISNOWIECKI** = Eleanora Maria
1669–73   Sister of Leopold I
           Emperor

JOHN SOBIESKI = Marie d'Arquien
1674–96

AUGUSTUS II
1697–1704, and 1709–33

STANISLAS LESZCZYNSKI
1704–9

★ Also known, by counting only Jagellon kings, as Vladislav IV.

TSARS OF RUSSIA

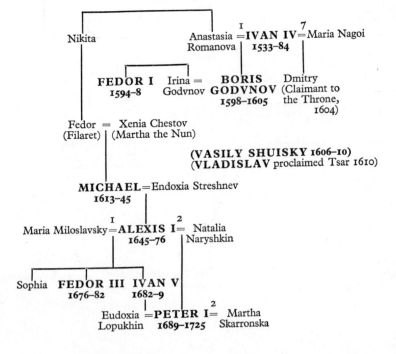

Nikita

Anastasia = **IVAN IV** = Maria Nagoi
Romanova   1533–84

FEDOR I Irina = **BORIS
1594–8** Godvnov **GODVNOV**
              1598–1605

Dmitry
(Claimant to
the Throne,
1604)

Fedor = Xenia Chestov
(Filaret) (Martha the Nun)

(VASILY SHUISKY 1606–10)
(VLADISLAV proclaimed Tsar 1610)

MICHAEL = Endoxia Streshnev
1613–45

Maria Miloslavsky = **ALEXIS I** = Natalia
           1645–76   Naryshkin

Sophia **FEDOR III IVAN V**
   1676–82 1682–9

Eudoxia = **PETER I** = Martha
Lopukhin 1689–1725 Skarronska

RULERS OF SWEDEN

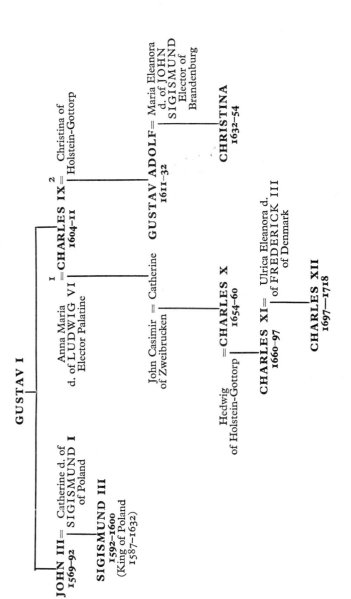

GUSTAV I

JOHN III = Catherine d. of SIGISMUND I
1569–92   of Poland

SIGISMUND III
1592–1600
(King of Poland
1587–1632)

Anna Maria
d. of LUDWIG VI
Elector Palatine

¹
= CHARLES IX ² = Christina of
1604–11   Holstein-Gottorp

GUSTAV ADOLF = Maria Eleanora
1611–32   d. of JOHN
                 SIGISMUND
                 Elector of
                 Brandenburg

CHRISTINA
1632–54

John Casimir = Catherine
of Zweibrucken

Hedwig
of Holstein-Gottorp

= CHARLES X
1654–60

CHARLES XI = Ulrica Eleanora d.
1660–97   of FREDERICK III
               of Denmark

CHARLES XII
1697–1718

OTTOMAN SULTANS

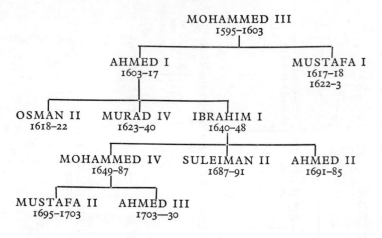

THE POPES (1592–1721)

Clement VIII 1592–1605
Leo XI 1605
Paul V 1605–21
Gregory XV 1621–23
Urban VIII 1623—44
Innocent X 1644–55
Alexander VII 1655–67
Clement IX 1667–69
Clement X 1670–76
Innocent XI 1676–89
Alexander VIII 1689–91
Innocent XII 1699–1700
Clement XI 1700–21

Index

Abbeville, 57

Abelin, Jean Philippe (died c. 1635), 9

Absolutism, 196–7, 203–6; in Denmark, 357–8; in France, 263–74, 422–31, 439–42; in Germany, 304–7; in Russia, 378–82; in Spain, 317–22, 334–8; in Sweden, 356–7

Académie de peinture et de sculpture, 169

Académie française, 143

Académie royale des Sciences, 15, 71, 138, 144

Academy of Sciences (Berlin), 2, 144

Accademia del Cimento, 143

Accademia dei Lincei, 143

Africa, 65–8

Agrarian Law, 191

Agreda, Maria Fernandez, Abbess of (1602–65), 15, 331

Agriculture, 50–4

Ahmed I (b. 1589, Sultan 1603–17), 368

Aiguillon, Marie Madeleine, Duchesse de (1604–75), 10

Aix-la-Chapelle, treaty of, 435

Alais, peace of, 113, 266

Albania, 103

Albert of Austria, Archduke (b. 1559, Prince of the Netherlands 1598–1621), 39, 107, 166, 198, 323–4

Alcabala, 216, 318

Alchemy, 146

Alexander VII, Fabio Chigi (b. 1599, Pope 1655–67), 165

Alexander, Father (Alessandro da Ales), 292

Alexis I (b. 1629, Tsar 1645–76), 54, 107, 376–8

Algiers, 444

Alsace, 44, 272, 437, 443, 455

Althusius (Johannes Althusen 1557–1638), 181–2

Altmark, truce, 346, 350

Älvsborg, 42, 344, 347

Amati, Nicolo (1596–1684), 171

America, 64–8

Ampringen, Johann (1619–84), 311

Amsterdam, 25, 60–2, 116, 405, 418, 447

Anabaptism, 118–19

Anatomy, 139

Andrusovo, truce, 359

Anhalt, Christian of (1568–1630), 286–7

Animalculism, 141

Anne of Austria (1601–66, French Queen 1615–43, Regent 1643–51), 204, 259, 273, 275, 278

Anne (b. 1665, Queen of England 1702–14), 418–20

Antwerp, 47, 60, 166, 170, 389, 392

Aquinas, Thomas (c. 1227–74), 154

Arabian Nights, 158

Aragon, 39, 208, 211, 322

Arbitristas, 320

Architecture, 164–6, 424–5

Archives, 7–13

Aristocracy, *see* Nobility

Aristotle (384–322 B.C.), 131, 134, 139–141, 154, 174

Armenians, 103

Armies, 236–48; conscription, 237, 247; English, 189–91, 400–2; French, 288–9, 305; pay, 241; German, 431, 438, 445, 449; Russian, 80, 375, 382–3; Spanish, 325; Turkish, 373–4; uniforms, 242

Arminianism, 115–16

Arminius (Jacob Harmensz 1560–1609), 115

Arnauld, Angélique (1591–1661), Antoine the elder (1560–1619), Antoine the younger (1612–94), 121

Arnim, Hans Georg von (1581–1641), 297

Arras, 272

Artillery, 239–41

Asia, trade with, 63–7

Asiento, 448, 451

Assemblies, *see* Representative assemblies

Astrology, 132, 134

Astronomy, 131–5, 144

Ath, 445

Atoms, 145

Aubrey, John (1626–97), 158

Augsburg, 291; League of, 444

Augustinus, 121–2

Aulic Council, *see* Reichshofrat